Nicene Christianity

Old Western Culture Reader

Volume 8

NICENE CHRISTIANITY

OLD WESTERN CULTURE READER

VOLUME 8

ROMAN ROADS PRESS

Nicene Christianity: Old Western Culture Reader, Vol. 8

Published by Roman Roads Press
Moscow, Idaho, USA
romanroadspress.com
info@romanroadsmedia.com

General Editor: Daniel Foucachon
Interior Layout: Carissa Hale
Illustrations: Cooper Salmon
Cover Design, Valerie Anne Bost, Daniel Foucachon, and Rachel Rosales

Early Christianity: Old Western Culture Reader, Volume 8
Roman Roads Press, an imprint of Roman Roads Media, LLC.
ISBN: 978-1-944482-01-5

Version 2.0.0 May 2021

NICENE CHRISTIANITY

OLD WESTERN CULTURE READER

VOLUME 8

ROMAN ROADS PRESS

Nicene Christianity: Old Western Culture Reader, Vol. 8

Published by Roman Roads Press
Moscow, Idaho, USA
romanroadspress.com
info@romanroadsmedia.com

General Editor: Daniel Foucachon
Interior Layout: Carissa Hale
Illustrations: Cooper Salmon
Cover Design, Valerie Anne Bost, Daniel Foucachon, and Rachel Rosales

Early Christianity: Old Western Culture Reader, Volume 8
Roman Roads Press, an imprint of Roman Roads Media, LLC.
ISBN: 978-1-944482-01-5

Version 2.0.0 May 2021

This is a companion reader for the *Old Western Culture* curriculum by Roman Roads Press. To find out more about this course, visit www.romanroadspress.com.

OLD WESTERN CULTURE

Great Books Reader Series

THE GREEKS

VOLUME 1	*The Epics*
VOLUME 2	*Drama & Lyric*
VOLUME 3	*The Histories*
VOLUME 4	*The Philosophies*

THE ROMANS

VOLUME	*The Aeneid*
VOLUME 6	*The Historians*
VOLUME 7	*Early Christianity*
VOLUME 8	*Nicene Christianity*

CHRISTENDOM

VOLUME 9	*Early Medievals*
VOLUME 10	*Defense of the Faith*
VOLUME 11	*The Medieval Mind*
VOLUME 12	*The Reformation*

EARLY MODERNS

VOLUME 13	*Rise of England*
VOLUME 14	*Politics and Poetry*
VOLUME 15	*The Enlightenment*
VOLUME 16	*The Novels*

Contents

On the Incarnation by Athanasius 1

- Introduction by C. S. Lewis 1
- Chapter I: Creation and Fall 7
- Chapter II: The Divine Dilemma and its Solution in the Incarnation 12
- Chapter III: The Divine Dilemma and its Solution in the Incarnation—continued 16
- Chapter IV: The Death of Christ 24
- Chapter V: The Resurrection 30
- Chapter VI: Refutation of the Jews 36
- Chapter VII: Refutation of the Gentiles 44
- Chapter VIII: Refutation of the Gentiles—continued 50
- Chapter IX: Conclusion 59

The Life of St. Anthony by Athanasius 61

Paschal Homily by John Chrysostom 119

Baptismal Instructions by John Chrysostom 123

- First Instruction 123
- Second Instruction 134

On the Holy Spirit by Basil the Great 149

Funeral Oration on the Great St. Basil by Gregory Nazienzen 181

Confessions by Saint Augustine 187

- Book One 187

Book Two 203
Book Three 212
Book Four 224
Book Five 240
Book Six 256
Book Seven 273
Book Eight 292
Book Nine 310

City of God by Saint Augustine 331
Book One 331
Book Five 353
Book Eight 372
Book Ten 389
Book Eleven 414
Book Fourteen 438
Book Fifteen 460
Book Eighteen 474
Book Nineteen 495
Book Twenty 524
Book Twenty-One 554
Book Twenty-Two 590

The Consolation of Philosophy by Boethius 647
Book One: The Sorrows of Boethius 647
Book Two: The Vanity of Fortune's Gifts 664
Book Three: True Happiness and False 684
Book Four: Good and Ill Fortune 719
Book Five: Free Will and God's Foreknowledge 748

ATHANASIUS

On the Incarnation

Athanasius

Translated by Sister Penelope

Introduction
by C. S. Lewis

There is a strange idea abroad that in every subject the ancient books should be read only by the professionals, and that the amateur should content himself with the modern books. Thus I have found as a tutor in English Literature that if the average student wants to find out something about Platonism, the very last thing he thinks of doing is to take a translation of Plato off the library shelf and read the Symposium. He would rather read some dreary modern book ten times as long, all about "isms" and influences and only once in twelve pages telling him what Plato actually said. The error is rather an amiable one, for it springs from humility. The student is half afraid to meet one of the great philosophers face to face. He feels himself inadequate and thinks he will not understand him. But if he only knew, the great man, just because of his greatness, is much more intelligible than his modern commentator. The simplest student will be able to understand, if not all, yet a very great deal of what Plato said; but hardly anyone can understand some modern books on Platonism. It has always therefore been one of my main endeavours as a teacher to persuade the young that first-hand knowledge, but is usually much easier and more delightful to acquire

This mistaken preference for the modern books and this shyness of the old ones is nowhere more rampant than in theology. Wherever you find a little study circle of Christian laity you can be almost certain that they are studying not St. Luke or St. Paul or St. Augustine or Thomas Aquinas or Hooker or Butler, but M. Berdyaev or M. Maritain or M. Niebuhr or Miss Sayers or even myself.

Now this seems to me topsy-turvy. Naturally, since I myself am a writer, I do not wish the ordinary reader to read no modern books. Bur if he must read only the new or only the old, I would advise him to read the old. And I would give him this advice precisely because he is an amateur and therefore much less protected than the expert against the dangers of an exclusive contemporary diet. A new book is still on its trial and the amateur is not in a position to judge it. It has to be tested against the great body of Christian thought down the ages, and all its hidden implications (often unsuspected by the author himself) have to be brought to life. Often it cannot by fully understood without the knowledge of a good many other modern books. If you join at eleven o'clock a conversation which began at eight you will often not see the real bearing of what is said. Remarks which seem to you very ordinary will produce laughter or irritation and you will not see why—the reason, of course, being that the earlier stages of the conversation have given them a special point. In the same way sentences in a modern book which look quite ordinary may be directed "at" some other book; in this way you may be led to accept what you would have indignantly rejected if you knew its real significance. The only safety is to have a standard of plain, central Christianity ("mere Christianity" as Baxter called it) which puts the controversies of the moment in their proper perspective. Such a standard can be acquired only from the old books. It is a good rule, after reading a new book, never to allow yourself another new one till you have read an old one in between. If that is too much for you, you should at least read on old one to every three new ones.

Every age has its own outlook. It is specially good at seeing certain truths and specially liable to make certain mistakes. We all, therefore, need the books that will correct the characteristic mistakes of our own period. And that means the old books. All contemporary writers share to some extent the contemporary outlook—even those, like myself, who seem most opposed to it. Nothing strikes me more when I read the controversies of past ages than the fact that both sides were usually

assuming without question a good deal which we should now absolutely deny. They thought that they were as completely opposed as two sides could be, but in fact they were all the time secretly united—united with each other and against earlier and later ages—by a great mass of common assumptions. We may be sure that the characteristic blindness of the twentieth century—the blindness about which posterity will ask, "But how could they have thought that?"—lies where we have never suspected it, and concerns something about which there is untroubled agreement between Hitler and President Roosevelt or between Mr. H. G. Wells and Karl Barth. None of us can fully escape this blindness, but we shall certainly increase it, and weaken our guard against it, if we read only modern books. Where they are true they will give us truths which we half knew already. Where they are false they will aggravate the error with which we are already dangerously ill. The only palliative is to keep the clean sea breeze of the centuries blowing through our minds, and this can be done only be reading old books. Not, of course, that there is any magic about the past. People were no cleverer then than they are now; they made as many mistakes as we. But not the same mistakes. They will not flatter us in the errors we are already committing; and their own errors, being now open and palpable, will not endanger us. Two heads are better than one, not because either is infallible, but because they are unlikely to go wrong in the same direction. To be sure, the books of the future would be just as good a corrective as the books of the past, but unfortunately we cannot get at them.

I myself was first led into reading the Christian classics, almost accidentally, as a result of my English studies. Some, such as Hooker, Herbert, Traherne, Taylor, and Bunyan, I read because they are themselves great English writers; others, such as Boethius, St. Augustine, Thomas Aquinas, and Dante, because they were "influences". George Macdonald I had found for myself at the age of sixteen and never wavered in my allegiance, though I tried for a long time to ignore his Christianity. They are, you will note, a mixed bag, representative of many Churches, climates and ages. And that brings me to yet another reason for reading them. The divisions of Christendom are undeniable and are by some of these writers most fiercely expressed. But if any man is tempted to think—as one might be tempted who read only contemporaries—that "Christianity" is a word of so many meanings that it means nothing at all, he can learn beyond all doubt, bu stepping out of his own century, that this is not so. Measured against the ages "mere Christianity" turns out to be no insipid interdenominational transparency, but something positive, self-consistent, and inexhaustible. I know it, indeed, to my cost. In the days when I still hated Christianity, I learned to recognise, like some all to familiar smell, that almost unvarying something which met me, now in Puritan Bunyan, now in Anglican Hooker, now in Thomist Dante. It was there (honeyed and floral) in Francois de Sales; it was there (grave and homely) in Spenser and Walton; it was there (grim but manful) in Pascal and Johnson; there again, with a mild, frightening, Paradisial flavour, in Vaughan and Boehme and Traherne. In the urban sobriety of the eighteenth century one was not safe—Law and Butler were two lions in the path. The supposed "Paganism" of the Elizabethans could not keep it out; it lay in wait where a man might have supposed himself safest, in the very centre of The Faerie Queene and the Arcadia. It was, of course, varied; and yet—after all—so unmistakably the same; recognisable, not to be evaded, the odour which is death to us until we allow it to become life

> ...an air that kills
> From yon far country blows.

We are all rightly distressed, and ashamed also, at the divisions of Christendom. But those who have always lived within the Christian fold may be too easily dispirited by them. They are bad, but such people do not know what it looks like from without. Seen from there, what is left intact despite all the divisions, still appears (as it truly is) an immensely formidable unity. I know, for I saw it; and well our enemies know it. That unity any of us can find by going out of his own age. It is not enough, but it is more than you had thought till then. Once you are well soaked in it, if you then venture to speak, you will have an amusing experience. You will be thought a Papist when you are actually reproducing Bunyan, a Pantheist when you are quoting Aquinas, and so forth. For you have now got on to the great level viaduct which crosses the ages and which looks so high from the valleys, so low from the mountains, so narrow compared with the swamps, and so broad compared with the sheep-tracks.

The present book is something of an experiment. The translation is intended for the world at large, not only for theological students. If it succeeds, other translations of other great Christian books will presumably follow. In one sense, of course, it is not the first in the field. Translations of the Theologia Germanica, the Imitation, the Scale of Perfection, and the Revelations of Lady Julian of Norwich, are already on the market, and are very valuable, though some of them are not very scholarly. But it will be noticed that these are all books of devotion rather than of doctrine. Now the layman or amateur needs to be instructed as well as to be exhorted. In this age his need for knowledge is particularly pressing. Nor would I admit any sharp division between the two kinds of books. For my own part I tend to find the doctrinal books often more helpful in devotion than the devotional books, and I rather suspect that the same experience may await many others. I believe that many who find that "nothing happens" when they sit down, or kneel down, to a book of devotion, would find that the heart sings unbidden while they are working their way through a tough bit of theology with a pipe in their teeth and a pencil in their hand.

This is a good translation of a very great book. St. Athanasius has suffered in popular estimation from a certain sentence in the "Athanasian Creed". I will not labour the point that that work is not exactly a creed and was not by St. Athanasius, for I think it is a very fine piece of writing. The words "Which Faith except every one do keep whole and undefiled, without doubt he shall perish everlastingly" are the offence. They are commonly misunderstood. The operative word is keep; not acquire, or even believe, but keep. The author, in fact, is not talking about unbelievers, but about deserters, not about those who have never heard of Christ, nor even those who have misunderstood and refused to accept Him, but of those who having really understood and really believed, then allow themselves, under the sway of sloth or of fashion or any other invited confusion to be drawn away into sub-Christian modes of thought. They are a warning against the curious modern assumption that all changes of belief, however brought about, are necessarily exempt from blame. But this is not my immediate concern. I mention "the creed (commonly called) of St. Athanaius" only to get out of the reader's way what may have been a bogey and to put the true Athanasius in its place. His epitaph is *Athanasius contra mundum.* "Athanasius against the world". We are proud that our own country has more than once stood against the world. Athanasius did the same. He stood for the Trinitarian doctrine, "whole and undefiled", when it looked as if all the civilised world was slipping back from Christianity into the religion of Arius—into one of those "sensible" synthetic religions which are so strongly recommended today and which, then as now, included among their devotees many highly cultivated clergymen. It is his glory that he did not move with the times; it is his reward that he now remains when those times, as all times do, have moved away.

When I first opened his *De Incarnatione* I soon discovered by a very simple test that I was reading a masterpiece. I knew very little Christian Greek except that of the New Testament and I had expected difficulties. To my astonishment I found it almost as easy as Xenophon; and only a master mind could, in the fourth century, have written so deeply on such a subject with such classical simplicity. Every page I read confirmed this impression. His approach to the Miracles is badly needed today, for it is the final answer to those who object to them as "arbitrary and meaningless violations of the laws of Nature". They are here shown to be rather the re-telling in capital letters of the same message which Nature writes in her crabbed cursive hand; the very operations one would expect of Him who was so full of life that when He wished to die He had to "borrow death from others". The whole book, indeed, is a picture of the Tree of Life—a sappy and golden book, full of buoyancy and confidence. We cannot, I admit, appropriate all its confidence today. We cannot point to the high virtue of Christian living and the gay, almost mocking courage of Christian martyrdom, as a proof of our doctrines with quite that assurance which Athanasius takes as a matter of course. But whoever may be to blame for that it is not Athanasius.

The translator knows so much more Christian Greek than I that it would be out of place for me to praise her version. But it seems to me to be in the right tradition of English translation. I do not think the reader will find here any of that sawdusty quality which is so common in modern renderings from the ancient languages. That is as much as the English reader will notice; those who compare the version with the original will be able to estimate how much wit and talent is presupposed in such a choice, for example, as "these wiseacres" on the very first page.

C. S. LEWIS

Chapter I: *Creation and the Fall*

1. In our former book (The Contra Gentes) we dealt fully enough with a few of the chief points about the heathen worship of idols, and how those false fears originally arose. We also, by God's grace, briefly indicated that the Word of the Father is Himself divine, that all things that are owe their being to His will and power, and that it is through Him that the Father gives order to creation, by Him that all things are moved, and through Him that they receive their being. Now, Macarius, true lover of Christ, we must take a step further in the faith of our holy religion, and consider also the Word's becoming Man and His divine Appearing in our midst. That mystery the Jews traduce, the Greeks deride, but we adore; and your own love and devotion to the Word also will be the greater, because in His Manhood He seems so little worth. For it is a fact that the more unbelievers pour scorn on Him, so much the more does He make His Godhead evident. The things which they, as men, rule out as impossible, He plainly shows to be possible; that which they deride as unfitting, His goodness makes most fit; and things which these wiseacres laugh at as "human", He by His inherent might declares divine. Thus, by what seems His utter poverty and weakness on the cross, He overturns the pomp and parade of idols, and quietly and hiddenly wins over the mockers and unbelievers to recognise Him as God.

Now in dealing with these matters it is necessary first to recall what has already been said. You must understand why it is that the Word of the Father, so great and so high, has been made manifest in bodily form. He has not assumed a body as proper to His own nature, far from it, for as the Word He is without body. He has been manifested in a human body for this reason only, out of the love and goodness of His Father, for the salvation of us men. We will begin, then, with the creation of the world and with God its Maker, for the first fact that you must grasp is this: the renewal of creation has been wrought by the Self-same Word Who made it in the beginning. There is thus no inconsistency between creation and salvation; for the One Father has employed the same Agent for both works, effecting the salvation of the world through the same Word Who made it in the beginning.

2. In regard to the making of the universe and the creation of all things there have been various opinions, and each person has propounded the theory that suited his own taste. For instance, some say that all things are self-originated and, so to speak, haphazard. The Epicureans are among these; they deny that there is any Mind behind the universe at all. This view is contrary to all the facts of experience, their own existence included. For if all things had come into being in this automatic fashion, instead of being the outcome of Mind, though they existed, they would all be uniform and without distinction. In the universe everything would be sun or moon or whatever it was, and in the human body the whole would be hand or eye or foot. But in point of fact the sun and the moon and the earth are all different things, and even within the human body there are different members, such as foot and hand and head. This distinctness of things argues not a spontaneous generation but a prevenient Cause; and from that Cause we can apprehend God, the Designer and Maker of all.

Others take the view expressed by Plato, that giant among the Greeks. He said that God had made all things out of pre-existent and uncreated matter, just as the carpenter makes things only out of wood that already exists. But those who hold this view to not realise that to deny that God is Himself the Cause of matter is to impute limitation to Him, just as it is undoubtedly a limitation on the part of the carpenter that he can make nothing unless he has the wood. How could God be called Maker and Artificer if His ability to make depended on some other cause, namely on matter itself? If He only worked up existing matter and did not Himself bring matter into being, He would be not the Creator but only a craftsman.

Then again, there is the theory of the Gnostics who have invented for themselves an Artificer of all things other than the Father of our Lord Jesus Christ. These simply shut their eyes to the obvious meaning of Scripture. For instance, the Lord, having reminded the Jews of the statement in Genesis, "He Who created them in the beginning made them male and female...", and having shown that for that reason a man should leave his parents and cleave to his wife, goes on to say with reference to the Creator "What therefore God has joined together, let no man put asunder" (Matt. 19.4-6). How can they get a creation independent of the Father out of that? And again, St. John, speaking all inclusively, says "All things became by Him and without Him came nothing into being" (John 1.3). How then could the Artificer be someone different, other than the Father of Christ?

3. Such are the notions which men put forward. But the impiety of their foolish talk is plainly declared by the divine teaching of the Christian faith. From it we know that, because there is Mind behind the universe, it did not originate itself; because God is infinite, not finite, it was not made from pre-existent matter, but out of nothing; and out of non-existence, absolute and utter, God brought it into being through the Word. He says as much in Genesis: "In the beginning God created the heavens and the earth" (Gen. 1.1); and again through that most helpful book of The Shepherd, "Believe though first and foremost that there is One God Who created and arranged all things and brought them out of non-existence into being" (The Shepherd of Hermas, Book II). Paul also indicates the same thing when he says "By faith we understand that the worlds were framed by the Word of God, so that the things which we see now did not come into being out of things which had previously appeared" (Heb. 11.3). For God is good—or rather, of all goodness He is Fountainhead—and it is impossible for one who is good to be mean or grudging about anything. Grudging existence to none therefore, He made all things out of nothing through His own Word, our Lord Jesus Christ; and of all these His earthly creatures He reserved especial mercy for the race of men. Upon them, therefore, upon men who, as animals, were essentially impermanent, He bestowed a grace which other creatures lacked—namely, the impress of His own Image, a share in the reasonable being of the very Word Himself, so that, reflecting Him and themselves becoming reasonable and expressing the Mind of God even as He does, though in a limited degree they might continue forever in the blessed and only true life of the saints in paradise. But since the will of man could turn either way, God secured this grace that He had given by making it conditional from the first upon two things—namely, a law and a place. He set them in His own paradise, and laid upon them a single prohibition. If they guarded the grace and retained the loveliness of their original

innocence, then the life of paradise would be theirs, without sorrow, pain, or care, and after it the assurance of immortality in heaven. But if they went astray and became vile, throwing away their birthright of beauty, then they would come under the natural law of death and live no longer in paradise, but, dying outside of it, continue in death and in corruption. This is what Holy Scripture tells us, proclaiming the command of God, "Of every tree that is in the garden thou shalt surely eat, but of the tree of the knowledge of good and evil ye shall not eat, but in the day that ye do eat, ye shall surely die" (Gen. 2.16ff). "Ye shall surely die"—not just die only, but remain in the state of death and of corruption.

4. You may be wondering why we are discussing the origin of men when we set out to talk about the Word's becoming Man. The former subject is relevant to the latter of this reason: it was our sorry case that caused the Word to come down, our transgression that called out His love for us, so that He made haste to help us and to appear among us. It is we who were the cause of His taking human form, and for out salvation that in His great love He was both born and manifested in a human body. For God had made man thus (that is, as an embodied spirit), and had willed that he should remain in incorruption. But men, having turned from the contemplation of God to evil of their own devising, had come inevitably under the law of death. Instead of remaining in the state in which God had created them, they were in process of becoming corrupted entirely, and death had them completely under its dominion. For the transgression of the commandment was making them turn back again according to their nature; and as they had t the beginning come into being out of non-existence, so were they now on the way to returning, through corruption, to non-existence again. The presence and love of the Word had called them into being; inevitably, therefore, when they lost the knowledge of God, they lost existence with it; for it is God alone Who exists, evil is non-being, the negation and antithesis of good. Bu nature, of course, man is mortal, since he was made from nothing; but he bears also the Likeness of Him Who is, and if he preserves that Likeness through constant contemplation, then his nature is deprived of its power and he remains incorrupt. So is it affirmed in Wisdom: "The keeping of His laws is the assurance

of incorruption" (Wisdom 6.18). And being incorrupt, he would be henceforth as God, as Holy Scripture says, "I have said, Ye are gods and sons of the Highest all of you but ye die as men and fall as one of the princes" (Psalm 82.6ff).

5. This, then, was the plight of men. God had not only made them out of nothing, but had also graciously bestowed on them His own life by the grace of the Word. Then, turning from eternal things to things corruptible, by counsel of the devil, they had become the cause of their own corruption in death; for, as I said before, though they were by nature subject to corruption, the grace of their union with the Word made them capable of escaping from the natural law, provided that they retained the beauty of the innocence with which they were created. That is to say, the presence of the Word with them shielded them even from natural corruption, as also Wisdom says "God created man for incorruption and as an image of His won eternity; but by envy of the devil death entered into the world" (Wisdom 2.23ff). When this happened, men began to die, and corruption ran riot among them and held sway over them to an even more than natural degree, because it was the penalty of which God had forewarned them for transgressing the commandment. Indeed, they had in their sinning surpassed all limits; for, having invented wickedness in the beginning and so involved themselves in death and corruption, they had gone on gradually from bad to worse, not stopping at any one kind of evil, but continually, as with insatiable appetite, devising new kinds of sins. Adulteries and thefts were everywhere, murder and rapine filled the earth, law was disregarded in corruption and injustice, all kinds of iniquities were perpetrated by all, both singly and in common. Cities were warring with cities, nations were rising against nations, and the whole earth was rent with factions and battles, while each strove to outdo the other in wickedness. Even crimes contrary to nature were not unknown, but as the martyr-apostle of Christ says "Their women changed the natural use into that which is against nature; and the men also, leaving the natural use of the woman, flamed out in lust towards each other, perpetuating shameless acts with their own sex, and receiving in their own persons the due recompense of their pervertedness" (Rom. 1.26ff).

Chapter II: *The Divine Dilemma and its Solution in the Incarnation*

6. We saw in the last chapter that, because death and corruption were gaining ever firmer hold on them, the human race was in process of destruction. Man, who was created in God's image and in his possession of reason reflected the very Word Himself, was disappearing, and the work of God was being undone. The law of death, which followed from the Transgression, prevailed upon us, and from it there was no escape. The thing that was happening was in truth both monstrous and unfitting. It would, of course, have been unthinkable that God should go back upon His word and that man, having transgressed, should not die; but it was equally monstrous that beings which once had shared the nature of the Word should perish and turn back again into non-existence through corruption. It was unworthy of the goodness of God that creatures made by Him should be brought to nothing through the deceit wrought upon man by the devil; and it was supremely unfitting that the work of God in mankind should disappear, either through their own negligence or through the deceit of evil spirits. As, then, the creatures whom He had created reasonable, like the Word, were in fact perishing, and such noble works were on the road to ruin, what then was God, being Good, to do? Was He to let corruption and death have their way with them? In that case, what was the use of having made them in the beginning? Surely it would have been better never to have been created at all than, having been created, to be neglected and perish; and, besides that, such indifference to the ruin of His won work before His very eyes would argue not goodness in God but limitation, and that far more than if He had never created men at all. It was impossible, therefore, that God should leave man to be carried off by corruption, because it would be unfitting and unworthy of Himself.

7. Yet, true though this is, it is not the whole matter. As we have already noted, it was unthinkable that God, the Father of Truth, should go back upon His word regarding death in order to ensure our continued existence. He could not falsify Himself; what, then, was God to do? Was He to demand repentance from men for their transgression? You might say that that was worthy of God, and argue further that, as through the Transgression they became subject to

corruption, so through repentance they might return to incorruption again. But repentance would not guard the Divine consistency, for, if death did not hold dominion over men, God would still remain untrue. Nor does repentance recall men from what is according to their nature; all that it does is to make them cease from sinning. Had it been a case of a trespass only, and not of a subsequent corruption, repentance would have been well enough; but when once transgression had begun men came under the power of the corruption proper to their nature and were bereft of the grace which belonged to as creatures in the Image of God. No, repentance could not meet the case. What, or rather Who, was it that was needed for such grace and such recall as we required? Who, save the Word of God Himself, Who also in the beginning had made all things out of nothing? His part it was, and His alone, both to bring again the corruptible to incorruption and to maintain for the Father His consistency of character with all. For He alone, being Word of the Father and above all, was in consequence both able to recreate all, and worthy to suffer on behalf of all and to be an ambassador for all with the Father.

8. For this purpose, then, the incorporeal and incorruptible and immaterial Word of God entered our world. In one sense, indeed, He was not far from it before, for no part of creation had ever been without Him Who, while ever abiding in union with the Father, yet fills all things that are. But now He entered the world in a new way, stooping to our level in His love and Self-revealing to us. He saw the reasonable race, the race of men that, like Himself, expressed the Father's Mind, wasting out of existence, and death reigning over all in corruption. He saw that corruption held us all the closer, because it was the penalty for the Transgression; He saw, too, how unthinkable it would be for the law to be repealed before it was fulfilled. He saw how unseemly it was that the very things of which He Himself was the Artificer should be disappearing. He saw how the surpassing wickedness of men was mounting up against them; He saw also their universal liability to death. All this He saw and, pitying our race, moved with compassion for our limitation, unable to endure that death should have the mastery, rather than that His creatures should perish and the work of His Father for us men come to naught, He took to Himself a body, a human body even as

our own. Nor did He will merely to become embodied or merely to appear; had that been so, He could have revealed His divine majesty in some other and better way. No, He took our body, and not only so, but He took it directly from a spotless, stainless virgin, without the agency of human father—a pure body, untainted by intercourse with man. He, the Mighty One, the Artificer of all, Himself prepared this body in the virgin as a temple for Himself, and took it for His very own, as the instrument through which He was known and which He dwelt. Thus, taking a body like our own, because all our bodies were liable to the corruption of death, He surrendered His body to death instead of all, and offered it to the Father. This He did out of sheer love for us, so that in His death all might die, and the law of death thereby be abolished because, having fulfilled in His body that for which it was appointed, it was thereafter voided of its power for men. This He did that He might turn again to incorruption men who had turned back to corruption, and make them alive through death by the appropriation of His body and by the grace of His resurrection. Thus He would make death to disappear from them as utterly as straw from fire.

9. The Word perceived that corruption could not be got rid of otherwise than through death; yet He Himself, as the Word, being immortal and the Father's Son, was such as could not die. For this reason, therefore, He assumed a body capable of death, in order that it, through belonging to the Word Who is above all, might become in dying a sufficient exchange for all, and, itself remaining incorruptible through His indwelling, might thereafter put an end to corruption for all others as well, by the grace of the resurrection. It was by surrendering to death the body which He had taken, as an offering and sacrifice free from every stain, that He forthwith abolished death for His human brethren by the offering of the equivalent. For naturally, since the Word of God was above all, when He offered His own temple and bodily instrument as a substitute for the life of all, He fulfilled in death all that was required. Naturally also, through this union of the immortal Son of God with our human nature, all men were clothed with incorruption in the promise of the resurrection. For the solidarity of mankind is such that, bu virtue of the Word's indwelling in a single human body, the corruption which goes with

death has lost is power over all. You know how it is when some great king enters a large city and dwells in one of its houses; because of his dwelling in that single house, the whole city is honoured, and enemies and robbers cease to molest it. Even so is it with the King of all; He has come into our country and dwelt in one body amidst the many, and in consequence the designs of the enemy against mankind have been foiled, and the corruption of death, which formerly held them in its power, has simply ceased to be. For the human race would have perished utterly had not the Lord and Saviour of all, the Son of God, come among us to put an end to death.

10. This great work was, indeed, supremely worthy of the goodness of God. A king who has founded a city, so far from neglecting it when through the carelessness of the inhabitants it is attacked by robbers, avenges it and saves it from destruction, having regard rather to his own honour than to the people's neglect. Much more, then, the Word of the All-good Father was not unmindful of the human race that He had called to be; but rather, by the offering of His own body He abolished the death which they had incurred, and corrected their neglect by His own teaching. Thus by His own power He restored the whole nature of man. The Saviour's own inspired disciples assure us of this. We read in one place "For the love of Christ constraineth us, because we thus judge that, if One died on behalf of all, then all died, and He died for all that we should no longer live unto ourselves, but unto Him who died and rose again from the dead, even our Lord Jesus Christ" (2 Cor. 5.14ff). And again another says "But we behold Him Who hath been made a little lower than the angels, even Jesus, because of the suffering of death crowned with glory and honour, that by the grace of God He should taste of death on behalf of every man." The same writer goes on to point out why it was necessary for God the Word and none other to become Man: "For it became Him, for Whom are all tings and through Whom all things, in bringing many sons unto glory, to make the Author of their salvation perfect through suffering" (Heb. 2.9ff). He means that the rescue of mankind from corruption was the proper part only of Him Who made them in the beginning. He points out also that the Word assumed a human body, expressly in order that He might offer it in sacrifice for other like bodies: "Since then the children are sharers in

flesh and blood, He also Himself assumed the same, in order that through death He might bring to naught him that hath the power of death, that is to say, the Devil, and might rescue those who all their lives were enslaved by the fear of death" (Heb. 2.14ff). For by the sacrifice of His own body He did two things: He put an end to the law of death which barred our way; and He made a new beginning of life for us, by giving us the hope of resurrection. By man death has gained its power over men; by the Word made Man death has been destroyed and life raised up anew. That is what Paul says, that true servant of Christ, "For since by man came death, by man came also the resurrection of the dead. Just as in Adam all die, even so in Christ shall all be made alive" (1 Cor. 15.21ff) and so forth. Now, therefore, when we die we no longer do so as men condemned to death; but, as those who are even now in process of rising, we await the general resurrection of all "which in its own times He shall show" (1 Tim. 6.15), even God Who wrought it and bestowed it on us.

This, then, is the first cause of the Saviour's becoming Man. There are, however, other things which show how wholly fitting is His blessed presence in our midst; and these we must now go on to consider.

Chapter III: *The Divine Dilemma and it's Solution in the Incarnation—continued*

11. When God the Almighty was making mankind through His own Word, He perceived that they, owing to the limitation of their nature, could not of themselves have any knowledge of their Artificer, the Incorporeal and Uncreated. He took pity on them, therefore, and did not leave them destitute of the knowledge of Himself, lest their very existence should prove purposeless. For of what use is existence to the creature if it cannot know its Maker? How could men be reasonable beings if they had no knowledge of the Word and Reason of the Father, through Whom they had received their being? They would be no better then the beasts, had they no knowledge save of earthly things; and why should God have made them at all, if He had not intended them to know Him? But, in fact, the good

God has given them a share in His own Image, that is, in our Lord Jesus Christ, and has made even themselves after the same Image and Likeness. Why? Simply in order that through this gift of Godlikeness in themselves they may be able to perceive the Image Absolute, that is the Word Himself, and through Him to apprehend the Father; which knowledge of their Maker is for men the only really happy and blessed life.

But, as we have already seen, men, foolish as they are, thought little of the grace they had received, and turned away from God. They defiled their own soul so completely that they not only lost their apprehension of God, but invented for themselves other gods of various kinds. They fashioned idols for themselves in place of the truth and reverenced things that are not, rather than God Who is as St. Paul says "worshiping the creature rather than the Creator" (Rom. 1.25). Moreover, and much worse, they transferred the honour which is due to God to material objects such as wood and stone, and also to man; and further even than that they went, as we said in our former book. Indeed, so impious were they that they worshiped evil spirits as gods in satisfaction of their lusts. They sacrificed brute beasts and immolated men, as the just due of these deities, thereby bringing themselves more and more under their insane control. Magic arts also were taught among them, oracles in sundry places led men astray, and the cause of everything in human life was traced to the stars, as though nothing existed but that which could be seen. In a word, impiety and lawlessness were everywhere, and neither God nor His Word was known. Yet He had not hidden Himself from the sight of men nor given the knowledge of Himself in one way only; but rather He had unfolded it in many forms and by many ways.

12. God knew the limitation of mankind, you see; and though the grace of being made in His Image was sufficient to give them knowledge of the Word and through Him of the Father, as a safeguard against their neglect of this grace, He provided the works of creation also as means by which the Maker might be known. Nor was this all. Man's neglect of the indwelling grace tends ever to increase; and against this further frailty also God made provision by giving them a law and by sending prophets, men whom they knew.

Thus, if they were tardy in looking up to heaven, they might still gain knowledge of their Maker form those close at hand; for men can learn directly about higher things from other men. Three ways thus lay open to them by which they might obtain the knowledge of God. They could look up into the immensity of heaven, and by pondering the harmony of creation come to know its Ruler, the Word of the Father, Whose all-ruling providence makes known the Father to all. Or, if this was beyond them, they could converse with holy men, and through them learn to know God, the Artificer of all things, the Father of Christ, and to recognise the worship of idols as the negation of the truth and full of all impiety. Or else, in the third place, they could cease form lukewarmness and lead a good life merely by knowing the law. For the law was not given only for the Jews, nor was it solely for their sake that God sent the prophets, thought it was to the Jews that they were sent and by the Jews that they were persecuted. The law and the prophets were a sacred school of the knowledge of God and the conduct of the spiritual life for the whole world.

So great, indeed, were the goodness and the love of God. Yet men, bowed down by the pleasures of the moment and by the frauds and illusions of the evil spirits, did not lift up their heads towards the truth. So burdened were they with their wickednesses that they seemed rather to be brute beasts than reasonable men, reflecting the very Likeness of the Word.

13. What was God to do in face of this dehumanising of mankind, this universal hiding of the knowledge of Himself by the wiles of evil spirits? Was He to keep silence before so great a wrong and let men go on being thus deceived and kept in ignorance of Himself? If so, what was the use of having made them in His own Image originally? It would surely have been better for them always to have been brutes, rather than to revert to that condition when once they had shared the nature of the Word. Again, things being as they were, what was the use of their ever having had the knowledge of God? Surely it would have been better for God never to have bestowed it, than that men should subsequently be found unworthy to receive it. Similarly, what possible profit could it be to God Himself, Who made men, if when made the did not worship Him, but regarded others as

their makers? This would be tantamount to His having made them for others and not for Himself. Even an earthly king, though is is only a man, does not allow lands that he has colonised to pass into other hands or to desert to other rulers, but sends letters and friends and even visits them himself to recall them to their allegiance, rather than allow His work to be undone. How much more, then, will God be patient and painstaking with His creatures, that they be not led astray from Him to the service of those that are not, and that all the more because such error means for them sheer ruin, and because it is not right that those who had once shared His Image should be destroyed.

What, then, was God to do? What else could He possible do, being God, but renew His Image in mankind, so that through it men might once more come to know Him? And how could this be done save by the coming of the very Image Himself, our Saviour Jesus Christ? Men could not have done it, for they are only made after the Image; nor could angels have done it, for they are not the images of God. The Word of God came in His own Person, because it was He alone, the Image of the Father, Who could recreate man made after the Image. In order to effect this re-creation, however, He had first to do away with death and corruption. Therefore He assumed a human body, in order that in it death might once for all be destroyed, and that men might be renewed according to the Image. The Image of the Father only was sufficient of this need. Here is an illustration to prove it.

14. You know what happens when a portrait that has been painted on a panel becomes obliterated through external stains. The artist does not throw away the panel, but the subject of the portrait has to come and sit for it again, and then the likeness is re-drawn on the same material. Even so was it with the All-holy Son of God. He, the Image of the Father, came and dwelt in our midst, in order that He might renew mankind made after Himself, and seek out His lost sheep, even as He says in the Gospel "I came to seek and to save that which was lost" (Luke 19.10). This also explains His saying to the Jews "Except a man be born anew..." (John 3.3). He was not referring to a man's natural birth from his mother, as they thought, but to the re-birth and re-creation of the soul in the Image of God. Nor was this the only thing which only the Word could do. When the mad-

ness of idolatry and irreligion filled the world and the knowledge of God was hidden, whose part was it to teach the world about the Father? Man's, would you say? But men cannot run everywhere over the world, nor would their words carry sufficient weight if they did, nor would they be, unaided, a match for the evil spirits. Moreover, since even the best of men were confused and blinded by evil, how could they convert the souls and minds of others? You cannot put straight in others what is warped in yourself. Perhaps you will say, then, that creation was enough to teach men about the Father. But if that had been so, such great evils would never have occurred. Creation was there all the time, but it did not prevent men from wallowing in error. Once more, then it was the Word of God, Who sees all that is in man and moves all tings in creation, Who alone could meet the needs of the situation. It was His part and His alone, Whose ordering of the universe reveals the Father, to renew the same teaching. But how was He to do it? By the same means as before, perhaps you will say, that is, through the works of creation. But this was proven insufficient. Men had neglected to consider the heavens before, and now they were looking in the opposite direction. Wherefore, in all naturalness and fitness, desiring to do good to men, as Man He dwells, taking to Himself a body like the rest; and through His actions done in that body, as it were on their own level, He teaches those who would not learn by other means to know Himself, the Word of God, and through Him the Father.

15. He deals with them as a good teacher with his pupils, coming down to their level and using simple means. St. Paul says as much: "Because in the wisdom of God the world in its wisdom knew now God, God thought fit through the simplicity of the News proclaimed to save those who believe" (1 Cor. 1.21). Men had turned from the contemplation of God above, and were looking for Him in the opposite direction, down among created things and things of sense. The Saviour of us all, the Word of God, in His great love took to Himself a body and moved as Man among men, meeting their senses, so to speak, half way. He became Himself an object for the senses, so that those who were seeking God in sensible things might apprehend the Father through the works which He, the Word of God, did in the body. Human and human-minded as men were, therefore, to

whichever side they looked in the sensible world they found themselves taught the truth. Were they awe-stricken by creation? They beheld it confessing Christ as Lord. Did their minds tend to regard men as Gods? The uniqueness of the Saviour's works marked Him, alone of men, as Son of God. Were they drawn to evil spirits? They saw them driven out by the Lord and learned that the Word of God alone was God and that the evil spirits were not gods at all. Were they inclined to hero-worship and the cult of the dead? Then the fact that the Saviour had risen from the dead showed them how false these other deities were, and that the Word of the Father is the one true Lord, the Lord even of death. For this reason was He both born and manifested as Man, for this He died and rose, in order that, eclipsing by His works all other human deeds, He might recall men from all the paths of error to know the Father. As He says Himself, "I came to seek and to save that which was lost" (Luke 19.10).

16. When, then, the minds of men had fallen finally to the level of sensible things, the Word submitted to appear in a body, in order that He, as Man, might centre their senses on Himself, and convince them through His human acts that He Himself is not man only bu also God, the Word and Wisdom of the true God. This is what Paul wants to tell us when he says "That ye, being rooted and grounded in love, may be strong to apprehend with all the saints what is the length and breadth and height and depth, and to know the love of God that surpasses knowledge, so that ye may be filled unto all the fullness of God" (Eph. 3.27ff). The Self-revealing of the Word is in every dimension—above, in creation; below, in the Incarnation; in the depth, in Hades; in the breadth, throughout the world. All things have been filled with the knowledge of God. For this reason He did not offer the sacrifice on behalf of all immediately He came, for if He had surrendered His body to death and then raised it again at once He would have ceased to be an object of ours senses. Instead of that, He stayed in His body and let Himself be seen in it, doing acts and giving signs which showed Him to be not only man, but also God the Word. There were thus two things which the Saviour did for us by becoming Man. He banished death from us and made us anew; and, invisible and imperceptible as in Himself He is, He became visible through His works and revealed Himself as the Word of the Father,

the Ruler and King of the whole creation.

17. There is a paradox in this last statement which we must now examine. The Word was not hedged in by His body, nor did His presence in the body prevent His being present elsewhere as well. When He moved His body He did not cease also to direct the universe by His mind and might. No. The marvelous truth is, that being the Word, so far from being Himself contained by anything, He actually contained all things Himself. In creation He is present everywhere, yet is distinct in being from it; ordering, directing, giving life to all, containing all, yet is He Himself the Uncontained, existing solely in His Father. As with the whole, so also is it with the part. Existing in a human body, to which He Himself gives life, He is still Source of life to all the universe, present in every part of it, yet outside the whole; and He is revealed both through the works of His body and through His activity in the world. It is, indeed, the function of soul to behold things that are outside the body, but it cannot energise or move them. A man cannot transport things from one place to another, for instance, merely by thinking about them; nor can you or I move the sun and the stars just by sitting at home and looking at them. With the Word of God in His human nature, however, it was otherwise. His body was for Him not a limitation, but an instrument, so that He was both in it and in all tings, and outside all things, resting in the Father alone. At one and the same time—this is the wonder—as Man He was living a human life, and as Word He was sustaining the life of the universe, and as Son He was in constant union with the Father. Not even His birth from a virgin, therefore, changed Him in any way, nor was He defiled by being in the body. Rather, He sanctified the body by being in it. For His being in everything does not mean that He shares the nature of everything, only that He gives all things their being and sustains them in it. Just as the sun is not defiled by the contact of its rays with earthly objects, but rather enlightens and purifies them, so He Who made the sun is not defiled by being made known in a body, but rather the body is cleansed and quickened by His indwelling, "Who did no sin, neither was guile found in His mouth" (1 Peter 2.22).

18. You must understand, therefore, that when writers on this

sacred theme speak of Him as eating and drinking and being born, they mean that the body, as a body, was born and sustained with the food proper to its nature; while God the Word, Who was united with it, was at the same time ordering the universe and revealing Himself through His bodily acts as not man only but God. Those acts are rightly said to be His acts, because the body which did them did indeed belong to Him and none other; moreover, it was right that they should be thus attributed to Him as Man, in order to show that His body was a real one and not merely an appearance. From such ordinary acts as being born and taking food, He was recognised as being actually present in the body; but by the extraordinary acts which He did through the body He proved Himself to be the Son of God. That is the meaning of His words to the unbelieving Jews: "If I do not the works of My Father, believe Me not; but if I do, even if ye believe not Me, believe My works, that ye may know that the Father is in Me and I in the Father." Invisible in Himself, He is known from the works of creation; so also, when His Godhead is veiled in human nature, His bodily acts still declare Him to be not man only, but the Power and Word of God. To speak authoritatively to evil spirits, for instance, and to drive them out, is not human but divine; and who could see Him curing all the diseased to which mankind is prone, and still deem Him mere man and not also God? He cleansed lepers, He made the lame to walk, He opened the ears of the deaf and the eyes of the blind, there was no sickness or weakness that He did not drive away. Even the most casual observer can see that these were acts of God. The healing of the man born blind, for instance, who but the Father and Artificer of man, the Controller of his whole being, could thus have restored the faculty denied at birth? He Who did thus must surely be Himself the Lord of birth. This is proved also at the outset of His becoming Man. He formed His own body from the virgin; and that is no small proof of His Godhead, since He Who made that was the Maker of all else. And would not anyone infer from the fact of that body being begotten of a virgin only, without human father, that He Who appeared in it was also the Maker and Lord of all beside? Again, consider the miracle at Cana. Would not anyone who saw the substance of water transmuted into wine understand that He Who did it was the Lord and Maker of the water that He changed? It was for the same reason that He walked on the sea as on dry land to prove to the onlookers that He had mastery over all. And the feeding of the multitude, when He made little into much, so that from five loaves five thousand mouths were filled—did not that prove Him none other than the very Lord Whose Mind is over all?

Chapter IV: *The Death of Christ*

19. All these things the Saviour thought fit to do, so that, recognising His bodily acts as works of God, men who were blind to His presence in creation might regain knowledge of the Father. For, as I said before, who that saw His authority over evil spirits and their response to it could doubt that He was, indeed, the Son, the Wisdom and the Power of God? Even the very creation broke silence at His behest and, marvelous to relate, confessed with one voice before the cross, that monument of victory, that He Who suffered thereon in the body was not man only, but Son of God and Saviour of all. The sun veiled his face, the earth quaked, the mountains were rent asunder, all men were stricken with awe. These things showed that Christ on the cross was God, and that all creation was His slave and was bearing witness by its fear to the presence of its Master. Thus, then, God the Word revealed Himself to men through His works. We must next consider the end of His earthly life and the nature of His bodily death. This is, indeed, the very centre of our faith, and everywhere you hear men speak of it; bu it, too, no less than by His other acts, Christ is revealed as God and Son of God.

20. We have dealt as far as circumstances and our own understanding permit with the reason for His bodily manifestation. We have seen that to change the corruptible to incorruption was proper to none other than the Saviour Himself, Who in the beginning made all things out of nothing; that only the Image of the Father could re-create the likeness of the Image in men, that none save our Lord Jesus Christ could give to mortals immortality, and that only the Word Who orders all things and is alone the Father's true and sole-begotten Son could teach men about Him and abolish the worship of idols. But beyond all this, there was a debt owing which must needs be paid; for, as I sad before, all men were due to die. Here,

then, is the second reason why the Word dwelt among us, namely that having proved His Godhead by His works, He might offer the sacrifice on behalf of all, surrendering His own temple to death in place of all, to settle man's account with death and free him from the primal transgression. In the same act also He showed Himself mightier than death, displaying His won body incorruptible as the first-fruits of the resurrection. You must not be surprised if we repeat ourselves in dealing with this subject. We are speaking of the good pleasure of God and of the things which He in His loving wisdom thought fit to do, and it is better to put the same things in several ways than to run the risk of leaving something out. The body of the Word, then, being a real human body, in spite of its having been uniquely formed from a virgin, was of itself mortal and, like other bodies, liable to death. But the indwelling of the Word loosed it from this natural liability, so that corruption could not touch it. Thus it happened that two opposite marvels took place at once: the death of all was consummated in the Lord's body; yet, because the Word was in it, death and corruption were in the same act utterly abolished. Death there had to be, and death for all, so that the due of all might be paid. Wherefore, the Word, as I sad, being Himself incapable of death, assumed a mortal body, that He might offer it as His own in place of all, and suffering for the sake of all through His union with it, "might bring to naught Him that had the power of death, that is, the devil, and might deliver them who all their lifetime were enslaved by the fear of death" (Heb. 2.14ff).

21. Have no rear, then. Now that the common Saviour of all has died on our behalf, we who believe in Christ no longer die, as men died aforetime, in fulfillment of the threat of the law. That condemnation has come to an end; and now that, by the grace of the resurrection, corruption has been banished and done away, we are loosed from our mortal bodies in God's good time for each, so that we may obtain thereby a better resurrection. Like seeds cast into the earth, we do not perish in our dissolution, but like them shall rise again, death having been brought to naught by the grace of the Saviour. That is why blessed Paul, through whom we all have surety of the resurrection, says: "This corruptible must put on incorruption and this mortal must put on immortality; but when this corruptible

shall have put on incorruption and this mortal shall have put on immortality, then shall be brought to pass the saying that is written, 'Death is swallowed up in victory. O Death, where is thy sting? O Grave, where is thy victory?'" (1 Cor. 15.53f)

"Well then," some people may say, "if the essential thing was that He should surrender His body to death in place of all, why did He not do so as Man privately, without going to the length of public crucifixion? Surely it would have been more suitable for Him to have aid aside His body with honour than to endure so shameful a death." But look at this argument closely, and see how merely human it is, whereas what the Saviour did was truly divine and worthy of His Godhead for several reasons. The first is this. The death of men under ordinary circumstances is the result of their natural weakness. They are essentially impermanent, so after a time they fall ill and when worn out they die. But the Lord is not like that. He is not weak, He is the Power of God and Word of God and Very Life Itself If He had died quietly in His bed like other men it would have looked as if He did so in accordance with His nature, and as though He was indeed no more than other men. But because He was Himself Word and Life and Power His body was made strong, and because the death had to be accomplished, He took the occasion of perfecting His sacrifice not from Himself, but from others. How could He fall sick, Who had healed others? Or how could that body weaken and fail by means of which others are made strong? Here, again, you may say "Why did He not prevent death as He did sickness?" Because it was precisely in order to be able to die that He had taken a body, and to prevent the death would have been to impede the resurrection. And as to the unsuitability of sickness for His body, as arguing weakness, you may say "Did He then not hunger?" Yes, He hungered, because that was the property of His body, but He did not die of hunger, because He Whose body hungered was the Lord. Similarly, though He died to ransom all, He did not see corruption. His body rose in perfect soundness, for it was the body of none other than the Life Himself.

22. Someone else might say, perhaps, that it would have been better for the Lord to have avoided the designs of the Jews against

Him, and so to have guarded His body from death altogether. But see how unfitting this also would have been for Him. Just as it would not have been fitting for Him to give His body to death by His own hand, being Word and being Life, so also it was not consonant with Himself that He should avoid the death inflicted by others. Rather, He pursued it to the uttermost, and in pursuance of His nature neither laid aside His body of His own accord nor escaped the plotting Jews. And this action showed no limitation or weakness in the Word; for He both waited for death in order to make an end of it, and hastened to accomplish it as an offering on behalf of all. Moreover, as it was His own, He did not lay aside His body by an individual act of dying, for to Him, as Life, this simply did not belong; but He accepted death at the hands of men, thereby completely to destroy it in His own body.

There are some further considerations which enable one to understand why the Lord's body had such an end. The supreme object of His coming was to bring about the resurrection of the body. This was to be the monument to His victory over death, the assurance to all that He had Himself conquered corruption and that their own bodies also would eventually be incorrupt; and it was in token of that and as a pledge of the future resurrection that He kept His body incorrupt. But there again, if His body had fallen sick and the Word had left it in that condition, how unfitting it would have been! Should He Who healed the bodies of others neglect to keep His own in health? How would His miracles of healing be believed, if this were so? Surely people would either laugh at Him as unable to dispel disease or else consider Hum lacking in proper human feeling because He could do so, but did not.

23. Then, again, suppose without any illness He had just concealed His body somewhere, and then suddenly reappeared and said that He had risen from the dead. He would have been regarded merely as a teller of tales, and because there was no witness of His death, nobody would believe His resurrection. Death had to precede resurrection, for there could be no resurrection without it. A secret and unwitnessed death would have left the resurrection without any proof or evidence to support it. Again, why should He die a se-

cret death, when He proclaimed the fact of His rising openly? Why should He drive our evil spirits and heal the man blind from birth and change water into wine, all publicly, in order to convince men that He was the Word, and not also declare publicly that incorruptibility of His mortal body, so that He might Himself be believed to be the Life? And how could His disciples have had boldness in speaking of the resurrection unless they could state it as a fact that He had first died? Or how could their hearers be expected to believe their assertion, unless they themselves also had witnessed His death? For if the Pharisees at the time refused to believe and forced others to deny also, t many excuses for unbelief would they have contrived, if it had taken place secretly? Or how could the end of death and the victory over it have been declared, had not the Lord thus challenged it before the sight of all, and by the incorruption of His body proved that henceforward it was annulled and void?

24. There are some other possible objections that must be answered. Some might urge that, even granting the necessity of a public death for subsequent belief in the resurrection, it would surely have been better for Him to have arranged an honourable death for Himself, and so to have avoided the ignominy of the cross. But even this would have given ground for suspicion that His power over death was limited to the particular kind of death which He chose for Himself; and that again would furnish excuse for disbelieving the resurrection. Death came to His body, therefore, not from Himself but from enemy action, in order that the Saviour might utterly abolish death in whatever from they offered it to Him. A generous wrestler, virile and strong, does not himself choose his antagonists, lest it should be thought that of some of them his is afraid. Rather, he lets the spectators choose them, and that all the more if these are hostile, so that he may overthrow whomsoever they match against him and thus vindicate his superior strength. Even so was it with Christ. He, the Life of all, our Lord and Saviour, did not arrange the manner of His own death lest He should seem to be afraid of some other kind. No. He accepted and bore upon the cross a death inflicted by others, and those others His special enemies, a death which to them was supremely terrible and by no means to be faced; and He did this in order that, by destroying even this death, He might Himself

be believed to be the Life, and the power of death be recognised as finally annulled. A marvelous and mighty paradox has thus occurred, for the death which they thought to inflict on Him as dishonour and disgrace has become the glorious monument to death's defeat. Therefore it is also, that He neither endured the death of John, who was beheaded nor was He sawn asunder, like Isaiah; even in death He preserved His body whole and undivided, so that there should be no excuse hereafter for those who would divide the Church.

25. So much for the objections of those outside the Church. But if any honest Christian wants to know why He suffered death on the cross and not in some other way, we answer thus: in no other way was it expedient for us, indeed the Lord offered for our sakes the one death that was supremely good. He had come to bear the curse that lay on us; and how could He "become a curse" (Gal. 3.13) otherwise than by accepting the accursed death? And that death is the cross, for it is written "Cursed is every one that hangeth on a tree" (Gal. 3.13). Again, the death of the Lord is the ransom of all, and by it "the middle wall of partition" (Eph. 2.14) is broken down and the call of the Gentiles comes about. How could He have called us if He had not been crucified, for it is only on the cross that a man dies with arms outstretched? Here, again, we see the fitness of His death and of those outstretched arms: it was that He might draw His ancient people with the one and the Gentiles with the other, and join both together in Himself. Even so, He foretold the manner of His redeeming death, "I, if I be lifted up, will draw all men unto Myself" (John 7.32). Again, the air is the sphere of the devil, the enemy of our race, who, having fallen from heaven, endeavours with the other evil spirits who shared in his disobedience both to keep souls from the truth and to hinder the progress of those who are trying to follow it. The apostle refers to this when he says "According to the prince of the power of the air, of the spirit that now worketh in the sons of disobedience" (Eph. 2.2). But the Lord came to overthrow the devil and to purify the air and to make "a way" for us up to heaven, as the apostle says "through the veil, that is to say, His flesh" (Heb. 10.20). This had to be done through death, and by what other kind of death could it be done, save by a death in the air, that is, on the cross? Here, again, you see how right and natural it was that the

Lord should suffer thus; for being thus "lifted up?, He cleansed the air from all the evil influences of the enemy. "I beheld Satan as lightning falling" (Luke 10.18), He says; and thus He re-opened the road to heaven, saying again "Lift up your gates, O ye princes, and be ye life up, ye everlasting doors" (Psalm 24.7). For it was not the Word Himself Who needed an opening of the gates, He being the Lord of all, nor was any of His works closed to their Maker. No, it was we who need it, we whom He Himself upbore in His own body—that body which He first offered to death on behalf of all, and then made through it a path to heaven.

Chapter V: *The Resurrection*

26. Fitting indeed, then, and wholly consonant was the death on the cross for us; and we can see how reasonable it was, and why it is that the salvation of the world could be accomplished in no other way. Even on the cross He did not hide Himself from sight; rather, He made all creation witness to the presence of its Maker. Then, having once let it be seen that it was truly dead, He did not allow that temple of His body to linger long, but forthwith on the third day raised it up, impassible and incorruptible, the pledge and token of His victory.

It was, of course, within His power thus to have raised His body and displayed it as alive directly after His death. But the all-wise Saviour did not do this, lest some should deny that it had really or completely died. Besides this, had the interval between His death and resurrection been but two days, the glory of His incorruption might not have appeared. He waited one whole day to show that His body was really dead, and then on the third day showed it incorruptible to all. The interval was no longer, lest people should have forgotten about it and grown doubtful whether it were in truth the same body. No, while the affair was still ringing in their ears and their eyes were still straining and their minds in turmoil, and while those who had put Him to death were still on the spot and themselves witnessing to the fact of it, the Son of God after three days showed His once dead body immortal and incorruptible; and it was evident to all that it was from no natural weakness that the body which the Word indwelt had died, but in order that in it by the Saviour's power death might be done away.

27. A very strong proof of this destruction of death and its conquest by the cross is supplied by a present fact, namely this. All the disciples of Christ despise death; they take the offensive against it and, instead of fearing it, by the sign of the cross and by faith in Christ trample on it as on something dead. Before the divine sojourn of the Saviour, even the holiest of men were afraid of death, and mourned the dead as those who perish. But now that the Saviour has raised His body, death is not longer terrible, but all those who believe in Christ tread it underfoot as nothing, and prefer to die rather than to deny their faith in Christ, knowing full well that when they die they do not perish, but live indeed, and become incorruptible through the resurrection. But that devil who of old wickedly exulted in death, now that the pains of death are loosed, he alone it is who remains truly dead. There is proof of this too for men who, before they believe in Christ, think death horrible and are afraid of it, one they are converted despise it so completely that they go eagerly to meet it, and themselves become witnesses of the Saviour's resurrection from it. Even children hasten thus to die, and not men only, but women train themselves by bodily discipline to meet it. So weak has death become that even women, who used to be taken in by it, mock at it now as a dead thing robbed of all its strength. Death has become like a tyrant who has been completely conquered by the legitimate monarch; bound hand and foot, the passers-by jeer at him, hitting him and abusing him, no longer afraid of his cruelty and rage, because of the king who has conquered him. So has death been conquered and branded for what it is by the Saviour on the cross. It is bound hand and foot, all who are in Christ trample it as they pass, and as witnesses to Him deride it, scoffing and saying "O Death, where is thy victory? O Grave, where is thy sting?" (1 Cor. 15.55)

28. Is this a slender proof of the impotence of death, do you think? Or is it a slight indication of the Saviour's victory over it, when boys and young girls who are in Christ look beyond this present life and train themselves to die? Every one is by nature afraid of

death and of bodily dissolution; the marvel of marvels is that he who is enfolded in the faith of the cross despises this natural fear and for the sake of the cross is no longer cowardly in face of it. The natural property of fire is to burn. Suppose, then, that there was a substance such as the Indian asbestos is said to be, which had no fear of being burnt, but rather displayed the impotence of the fire by proving itself unburnable. If anyone doubted the truth of this, all he need do would be to wrap himself up in the substance in question and then touch the fire. Or, again, to revert to our former figure, if anyone wanted to see the tyrant bound and helpless, who used to be such a terror to others, he could do so simply by going into the country of the tyrant's conqueror. Even so, if anyone still doubts the conquest of death, after so many proofs and so many martyrdoms in Christ and such daily scorn of death by His truest servants, he certainly does well to marvel at so great a thing, but he must not be obstinate in unbelief and disregard of plain facts. No, he must be like the man who wants to prove the property of the asbestos, and like him who enters the conqueror's dominions to see the tyrant bound. He must embrace the faith of Christ, this disbeliever in the conquest of death, and come to His teaching. Then he will see how impotent death is and how completely conquered. Indeed, there have been many former unbelievers and deriders who, after they became believers, so scorned death as even themselves to become martyrs for Christ's sake.

29. If, then, it is by the sign of the cross and by faith in Christ that death is trampled underfoot, it is clear that it is Christ Himself and none other Who is the Arch-victor over death and has robbed it of its power. Death used to be strong and terrible, but now, since the sojourn of the Saviour and the death and resurrection of His body, it is despised; and obviously it is by the very Christ Who mounted on the cross that it has been destroyed and vanquished finally. When the sun rises after the night and the whole world is lit up by it, nobody doubts that it is the sun which has thus shed its light everywhere and driven away the dark. Equally clear is it, since this utter scorning and trampling down of death has ensued upon the Saviour's manifestation in the body and His death on the cross, that it is He Himself Who brought death to naught and daily raises monuments to His victory in His own disciples. How can you think otherwise, when you

see men naturally weak hastening to death, unafraid at the prospect of corruption, fearless of the descent into Hades, even indeed with eager soul provoking it, not shrinking from tortures, but preferring thus to rush on death for Christ's sake, rather than to remain in this present life? If you see with your own eyes men and women and children, even, thus welcoming death for the sake of Christ's religion, how can you be so utterly silly and incredulous and maimed in your mind as not to realise that Christ, to .Whom these all bear witness, Himself gives the victory to each, making death completely powerless for those who hold His faith and bear the sign of the cross? No one in his senses doubts that a snake is dead when he sees it trampled underfoot, especially when he knows how savage it used to be; nor, if he sees boys making fun of a lion, does he doubt that the brute is either dead or completely bereft of strength. These things can be seen with our own eyes, and it is the same with. the conquest of death. Doubt no longer, then, when you see death mocked and scorned by those who believe in Christ, that by Christ death was destroyed, and the corruption that goes with it resolved and brought to end.

30. What we have said is, indeed, no small proof of the destruction of death and of the fact that the cross of the Lord is the monument to His victory. But the resurrection of the body to immortality, which results' henceforward from the work of Christ, the common Saviour and true Life of all, is more effectively proved by facts than by words to those whose mental vision is sound. For, if, as we have shown, death was destroyed and everybody tramples on it because of Christ, how much more did He Himself first trample and destroy it in His own body! Death having been slain by Him, then, what other issue could there be than the resurrection of His body and its open demonstration as the monument of His victory? How could the destruction of death have been manifested at all, had not the Lord's body been raised? But if anyone finds even this insufficient, let him find proof of what has been said in present facts. Dead men cannot take effective action; their power of influence on others lasts only till the grave. Deeds and actions that energise others belong only to the living. Well, then, look at the facts in this case. The Saviour is working mightily among men, every day He is invisibly persuading numbers of people all over the world, both within and beyond the

Greek-speaking world, to accept His faith and be obedient to His teaching. Can anyone, in face of this, still doubt that He has risen and lives, or rather that He is Himself the Life? Does a dead man prick the consciences of men, so that they throw all the traditions of their fathers to the winds and bow down before the teaching of Christ? If He is no longer active in the world, as He must needs be if He is dead, how is it that He makes the living to cease from their activities, the adulterer from his adultery, the murderer from murdering, the unjust from avarice, while the profane and godless man becomes religious? If He did not rise, but is still dead, how is it that He routs and persecutes and overthrows the false gods, whom unbelievers think to be alive, and the evil spirits whom they worship? For where Christ is named, idolatry is destroyed and the fraud of evil spirits is exposed; indeed, no such spirit can endure that Name, but takes to flight on sound of it. This is the work of One Who lives, not of one dead; and, more than that, it is the work of God. It would be absurd to say that the evil spirits whom He drives out and the idols which He destroys are alive, but that He Who drives out and destroys, and Whom they themselves acknowledge to be Son of God, is dead.

31. In a word, then, those who disbelieve in the resurrection have no support in facts, if their gods and evil spirits do not drive away the supposedly dead Christ. Rather, it is He Who convicts them of being dead. We are agreed that a dead person can do nothing yet the Saviour works mightily every day, drawing men to religion, persuading them to virtue, teaching them about immortality, quickening their thirst for heavenly things, revealing the knowledge of the Father, inspiring strength in face of death, manifesting Himself to each, and displacing the irreligion of idols; while the gods and evil spirits of the unbelievers can do none of these things, but rather become dead at Christ's presence, all their ostentation barren and void. By the sign of the cross, on the contrary, all magic is stayed, all sorcery confounded, all the idols are abandoned and deserted, and all senseless pleasure ceases, as the eye of faith looks up from earth to heaven. Whom, then, are we to call dead? Shall we call Christ dead, Who effects all this? But the dead have not the faculty to effect anything. Or shall we call death dead, which effects nothing whatever, but lies as lifeless and ineffective as are the evil spirits and the idols?

The Son of God, "living and effective" (Heb. 4.12), is active every day and effects the salvation of all; but death is daily proved to be stripped of all its strength, and it is the idols and the evil spirits who are dead, not He. No room for doubt remains, therefore, concerning the resurrection of His body. Indeed, it would seem that he who disbelieves this bodily rising of the Lord is ignorant of the power of the Word and Wisdom of God. If He took a body to Himself at all, and made it His own in pursuance of His purpose, as we have shown that He did, what was the Lord to do with it, and what was ultimately to become of that body upon which the Word had descended? Mortal and offered to death on behalf of all as it was, it could not but die; indeed, it was for that very purpose that the Saviour had prepared it for Himself. But on the other hand it could not remain dead, because it had become the very temple of Life. It therefore died, as mortal, but lived again because of the Life within it; and its resurrection is made known through its works.

32. It is, indeed, in accordance with the nature of the invisible God that He should be thus known through His works; and those who doubt the Lord's resurrection because they do not now behold Him with their eyes, might as well deny the very laws of nature. They have ground for disbelief when works are lacking; but when the works cry out and prove the fact so clearly, why do they deliberately deny the risen life so manifestly shown? Even if their mental faculties are defective, surely their eyes can give them irrefutable proof of the power and Godhead of Christ. A blind man cannot see the sun, but he knows that it is above the earth from the warmth which it affords; similarly, let those who are still in the blindness of unbelief recognise the Godhead of Christ and the resurrection which He has brought about through His manifested power in others. Obviously He would not be expelling evil spirits and despoiling idols, if He were dead, for the evil spirits would not obey one who was dead. If, on the other hand, the very naming of Him drives them forth, He clearly is not dead; and the more so that the spirits, who perceive things unseen by men, would know if He were so and would refuse to obey Him. But, as a matter of fact, what profane persons doubt, the evil spirits know namely that He is God; and for that reason they flee from Him and fall at His feet, crying out even as they cried when

He was in the body, "We know Thee Who Thou art, the Holy One of God," and, "Ah, what have I in common with Thee, Thou Son of God? I implore Thee, torment me not" (Luke 4.34 & Mark 5.7).

Both from the confession of the evil spirits and from the daily witness of His works, it is manifest, then, and let none presume to doubt it, that the Saviour has raised His own body, and that He is very Son of God, having His being from God as from a Father, Whose Word and Wisdom and Whose Power He is. He it is Who in these latter days assumed a body for the salvation of us all, and taught the world concerning the Father. He it is Who has destroyed death and freely graced us all with incorruption through the promise of the resurrection, having raised His own body as its first-fruits, and displayed it by the sign of the cross as the monument to His victory over death and its corruption.

Chapter VI: *Refutation of the Jews*

33. We have dealt thus far with the Incarnation of our Saviour, and have found clear proof of the resurrection of His Body and His victory over death. Let us now go further and investigate the unbelief and the ridicule with which Jews and Gentiles respectively regard these same facts. It seems that in both cases the points at issue are the same, namely the unfittingness or incongruity (as it seems to them) alike of the cross and of the Word's becoming man at all. But we have no hesitation in taking up the argument against these objectors, for the proofs on our side are extremely clear.

First, then, we will consider the Jews. Their unbelief has its refutation in the Scriptures which even themselves read; for from cover to cover the inspired Book clearly teaches these things both in its entirety and in its actual words. Prophets foretold the marvel of the Virgin and of the Birth from her, saying "Behold, a virgin shall conceive and bear a son, and they shall call his name Emmanuel, which means God is with us" (Isaiah 7.14)". And Moses, that truly great one in whose word the Jews trust so implicitly, he also recognised the importance and truth of the matter. He put it thus: "There shall arise a star from Jacob and a man from Israel, and he shall break in pieces the rulers of Moab" (Numbers 24.17)". And again, "How lovely are they dwellings, O Jacob, they tents, O Israel! Like woodland valleys they give shade, and like parks by rivers, like tents which the Lord has pitched, like cedar-trees by streams. There shall come forth a Man from among his seed, and he shall rule over mane peoples" (Numbers 24.5-6). And, again, Isaiah says "Before the Babe shall be old enough to call father or mother, he shall take the power of Damascus and the spoils of Samaria from under the eyes of the king of Assyria" (Isaiah 8.4). These words, then, foretell that a Man shall appear. And Scripture proclaims further that He that is to come is Lord of all. These are the words: "Behold, the Lord sitteth on an airy cloud and shall come into Egypt, and the man-made images of Egypt shall be shaken" (Isaiah 19.1). And it is from Egypt also that the Father calls him back, saying "Out of Egypt have I called My Son" (Hosea 11.1).

34. Moreover, the Scriptures are not silent even about His death. On the contrary, they refer to it with the utmost clearness. They have not feared to speak also of the cause of it. He endures it, they say, not for His own sake, bur for the sake of bringing immortality and salvation to all, and they record also the plotting of the Jews against Him and who reads the Scriptures can plead ignorance of the facts as an excuse for error! There is this passage, for instance: "A man that is afflicted and knows how to bear weakness, for His face is turned away. He was dishonoured and not considered, He bears our sins and suffers for our sakes. And we for our part thought Him distressed and afflicted and ill-used; but it was for our sins that He was wounded and for our lawlessness that He was made weak. Chastisement for our peace was upon Him, and b His bruising we are healed" (Isaiah 53.3-5). O marvel at the love of the Word for men, for it is on our account that He is dishonoured, so that we may be brought to honour. "For all we," it goes on, "have strayed like sheep, man has strayed from his path, and the Lord has given Him up for our sins; and He Himself did not open His mouth at the ill-treatment. Like a sheep He was led to slaughter, and as a lamb is dumb before its shearer, so He opened not His mouth; in His humiliation His judgment was taken away" (Isaiah 53.6-8). And then Scripture anticipates

the surmises of any who might think from His suffering thus that He was just an ordinary man, and shows what power worked in His behalf. "Who shall declare of what lineage He comes?" it says, "for His life is exalted from the earth. Bu the lawlessness of the people was He brought to death, and I will give the wicked in return for His burial and the rich in return for His death. For He did no lawlessness, neither was deceit found in His mouth. And the Lord wills to heal Him of His affliction" (Isaiah 53.8-10).

35. You have heard the prophecy of His death, and now, perhaps, you want to know what indications there are about the cross. Even this is not passed over in silence on the contrary, the sacred writers proclaim it with the utmost plainness. Moses foretells it first, and that right loudly, when he says, "You shall see your Life hanging before your eyes, and shall not believe" (Deut. 28.66). After him the prophets also give their witness, saying, " But I as an innocent lamb brought to be offered was yet ignorant of it. They plotted evil against Me, saying, `Come, let us cast wood into His bread, and wipe Him out from the land of the living" (Jer. 11.19). And, again, "They pierced My hands and My feet, they counted all My bones, they divided My garments for themselves and cast lots for My clothing" (Psalm 22.16-18). Now a death lifted up and that takes place on wood can be none other than the death of the cross; moreover, it is only in that death that the hands and feet are pierced. Besides this, since the Saviour dwelt among men, all nations everywhere have begun to know God; and this too Holy Writ expressly mentions. "There shall be the Root of Jesse," it says, "and he who rises up to rule the nations, on Him nations shall set their hope" (Isaiah 11.10). These are just a few things in proof of what has taken place; but indeed all Scripture teems with disproof of Jewish unbelief. For example, which of the righteous men and holy prophets and patriarchs of whom the Divine Scriptures tell ever had his bodily birth from a virgin only? Was not Abel born of Adam, Enoch of Jared, Noah of Lamech, Abraham of Terah, Isaac of Abraham, and Jacob of Isaac? Was not Judah begotten by Jacob and Moses and Aaron by Ameram? Was not Samuel the son of Elkanah, David of Jesse, Solomon of David, Hezekiah of Ahaz, Josiah of Amon, Isaiah of Amos, Jeremiah of Hilkiah and Ezekiel of Buzi? Had not each of these a father as author of his being? So who

is He that is born of a virgin only, that sign of which the prophet makes so much? Again, which of all those people had his birth announced to the world by a star in the heavens? When Moses was born his parents hid him. David was unknown even in his own neighbourhood, so that mighty Samuel himself was ignorant of his existence and asked whether Jesse had yet another son. Abraham again became known to his neighbours as a great man only after his birth. But with Christ it was otherwise. The witness to His birth was not man, but a star shining in the heavens whence He was coming down.

36. Then, again, what king that ever was reigned and took trophies from his enemies before he had strength to call father or mother? Was not David thirty years old when he came to the throne and Solomon a grown young man? Did not Joash enter on his reign at the age of seven, and Josiah, some time after him, at about the same age, both of them fully able by that time to call father or mother? Who is there, then, that was reigning and despoiling his enemies almost before he was born? Let the Jews, who have investigated the matter, tell us if there was ever such a king in Israel or Judah-a king upon whom all the nations set their hopes and had peace, instead of being at enmity with him on every side! As long as Jerusalem stood there was constant war between them, and they all fought against Israel. The Assyrians oppressed Israel, the Egyptians persecuted them, the Babylonians fell upon them, and, strange to relate, even the Syrians their neighbours were at war with them. And did not David fight with Moab and smite the Syrians, and Hezekiah quail at the boasting of Sennacherib ? Did not Amalek make war on Moses and the Amorites oppose him, and did not the inhabitants of Jericho array themselves against Joshua the son of Nun? Did not the nations always regard Israel with implacable hostility? Then it is worth inquiring who it is, on whom the nations are to set their hopes. Obviously there must be someone, for the prophet could not have told a lie. But did any of the holy prophets or of the early patriarchs die on the cross for the salvation of all? Was any of them wounded and killed for the healing of all? Did the idols of Egypt fall down before any righteous man or king that came there? Abraham came there certainly, but idolatry prevailed just the same; and Moses was born there, but the mistaken worship was unchanged.

37. Again, does Scripture tell of anyone who was pierced in hands and feet or hung upon a tree at all, and by means of a cross perfected his sacrifice. for the salvation of all? It was not Abraham, for he died in his bed, as did also Isaac and Jacob. Moses and Aaron died in the mountain, and David ended his days in his house, without anybody having plotted against him. Certainly he had been sought by Saul, but he was preserved unharmed. Again Isaiah was sawn asunder, but he was not hung on a tree. Jeremiah was shamefully used, but he did not die under condemnation. Ezekiel suffered, but he did so, not on behalf of the people, but only to signify to them what was going to happen. Moreover, all these even when they suffered were but men, like other men; but He Whom the Scriptures declare to suffer on behalf of all is called not merely man but Life of all, although in point of fact He did share our human nature. " You shall see your Life hanging before your eyes," they say, and "Who shall declare of what lineage He comes?" With all the saints we can trace their descent from the beginning, and see exactly how each came to be; but the Divine Word maintains that we cannot declare the lineage of Him Who is the Life. Who is it, then, of Whom Holy Writ thus speaks? Who is there so great that even the prophets foretell of Him such mighty things? There is indeed no one in the Scriptures at all, save the common Saviour of all, the Word of God, our Lord Jesus Christ. He it is that proceeded from a virgin, and appeared as man on earth, He it is Whose earthly lineage cannot be declared, because He alone derives His body from no human father, but from a virgin alone. We can trace the paternal descent of David and Moses and of all the patriarchs. But with the Saviour we cannot do so, for it was He Himself Who caused the star to announce His bodily birth, and it was fitting that the Word, when He came down from heaven, should have His sign in heaven too, and fitting that the King of creation on His coming forth should be visibly recognised by all the world. He was actually born in Judaea, yet men from Persia came to worship Him. He it is Who won victory from His daemon foes and trophies from the idolaters even before His bodily appearing-namely, all the heathen who from every region have abjured the tradition of their fathers and the false worship of idols and are now placing their hope in Christ and transferring their allegiance to Him. The thing is happening before our very eyes, here in Egypt; and thereby another prophecy is

fulfilled, for at no other time have the Egyptians ceased from their false worship save when the Lord of all, riding as on a cloud, came down here in the body and brought the error of idols to nothing and won over everybody to Himself and through Himself to the Father. He it is Who was crucified with the sun and moon as witnesses; and by His death salvation has come to all men, and all creation has been redeemed. He is the Life of all, and He it is Who like a sheep gave up His own body to death, His life for ours and our salvation.

38. Yet the Jews disbelieve this. This argument does not satisfy them. Well, then, let them be persuaded by other things in their own oracles. Of whom, for instance, do the prophets say " I was made manifest to those who did not seek Me, I was found by those who had not asked for Me? I said, `See, here am I,' to the nation that had not called upon My Name. I stretched out My hands to a disobedient and gainsaying people." (Isaiah 65. 1 ,2) Who is this person that was made manifest, one might ask the Jews? If the prophet is speaking of himself, then they must tell us how he was first hidden, in order to be manifested afterwards. And, again, what kind of man is this prophet, who was not only revealed after being hidden, but also stretched out his hands upon the cross? Those things happened to none of those righteous men : they happened only to the Word of God Who, being by nature without body, on our account appeared in a body and suffered for us all. And if even this is not enough for them, there is other overwhelming evidence by which they may be silenced. The Scripture says, "Be strong, hands that hang down and feeble knees, take courage, you of little faith, be strong and do not fear. See, our God will recompense judgment, He Himself will come and save us. Then the eyes of blind men shall be opened and the ears of deaf men shall hear, and stammerers shall speak distinctly" (Isaiah 35.3-6). What can they say to this, or how can they look it in the face at all? For the prophecy does not only declare that God will dwell here, it also makes known the signs and the time of His coming. When God comes, it says, the blind will see, the lame will walk, the deaf will hear and the stammerers will speak distinctly. Can the Jews tell us when such signs occurred in Israel, or when anything of the kind took place at all in Jewry? The leper Naaman was cleansed, it is true, but no deaf man heard nor did any lame man walk. Elijah raised a dead

person and so did Elisha; but no one blind from birth received his sight. To raise a dead person is a great thing indeed, but it is not such as the Saviour did. And surely, since the Scriptures have not kept silence about the f leper and the dead son of the widow, if a lame man had walked and a blind man had received his sight, they would have mentioned these as well. Their silence on these points proves that the events never took place. When therefore did these things happen, unless when the Word of God Himself came in the body? Was it not when He came that lame men walked and stammerers spoke clearly and men blind from birth were given sight? And the Jews who saw it themselves testified to the fact that such things had never before occurred. " Since the world began," they said, "it has never been heard of that anyone should open the eyes of a man born blind. If this Man were not from God, He could do nothing" (John 9.32-33).

39. But surely they cannot fight against plain facts. So it may be that, without denying what is written, they will maintain that they are still waiting for these things to happen, and that the Word of God is yet to come, for that is a theme on which they are always harping most brazenly, in spite of all the evidence against them. But they shall be refuted on this supreme point more clearly than on any, and that not by ourselves but by the most wise Daniel, for he signifies the actual date of the Saviour's coming as well as His Divine sojourn in our midst. "Seventy weeks," he says, "are cut short upon thy people and upon the holy city, to make a complete end of sin and for sins to be sealed up and iniquities blotted out, and to make reconciliation for iniquity and to seal vision and prophet, and to anoint a Holy One of holies. And thou shalt know and understand from the going forth of the Word to answer, ("Answer" is LXX misreading for Hebrew "restore") and to build Jerusalem, until Christ the Prince" (Daniel 9.24-25). In regard to the other prophecies, they may possibly be able to find excuses for deferring their reference to a future time, but what can they say to this one? How can they face it at all? Not only does it expressly mention the Anointed One, that is the Christ, it even declares that He Who is to be anointed is not man only, but the Holy One of holies ! And it says that Jerusalem is to stand till His coming, and that after it prophet and vision shall cease in Israel! David was anointed of old, and Solomon, and Hezekiah; but then Jerusalem

and the place stood, and prophets were prophesying, Gad and Asaph and Nathan, and later Isaiah and Hosea and Amos and others. Moreover, those men who were anointed were called holy certainly, but none of them was called the Holy of holies. Nor is it any use for the Jews to take refuge in the Captivity, and say that Jerusalem did not exist then, for what about the prophets? It is a fact that at the outset of the Exile Daniel and Jeremiah were there, and Ezekiel and Haggai and Zechariah also prophesied.

40. So the Jews are indulging in fiction, and transferring present time to future. When did prophet and vision cease from Israel? Was it not when Christ came, the Holy One of holies? It is, in fact, a sign and notable proof of the coming of the Word that Jerusalem no longer stands, neither is prophet raised up nor vision revealed among them. And it is natural that it should be so, for when He that was signified had come, what need was there any longer of any to signify Him? And when the Truth had come, what further need was there of the shadow? On His account only they prophesied continually, until such time as Essential Righteousness has come, Who was made the Ransom for the sins of all. For the same reason Jerusalem stood until the same time, in order that there men might premeditate the types before the Truth was known. So, of course, once the Holy One of holies had come, both vision and prophecy were sealed. And the kingdom of Jerusalem ceased at the same time, because kings were to be anointed among them only until the Holy of holies had been anointed. Moses also prophesies that the kingdom of the Jews shall stand until His time, saying, "A ruler shall not fail from Judah nor a prince from his loins, until the things laid up for him shall come and the Expectation of the nations Himself" (Gen. 49.10). And that is why the Saviour Himself was always proclaiming "The law and the prophets prophesied until John" (Matt. 11.13). So if there is still king or prophet or vision among the Jews, they do well to deny that Christ is come ; but if there is neither king nor vision, and since that time all prophecy has been sealed and city and temple taken, how can they be so irreligious, how can they so flaunt the facts, as to deny Christ Who has brought it all about? Again, they see the heathen forsaking idols and setting their, hopes through Christ on the God of Israel; why do they yet deny Christ Who after the flesh was born of the root of

Jesse and reigns henceforward? Of course, if the heathen were worshiping some other god, and not confessing the God of Abraham and Isaac and Jacob and Moses, then they would do well to argue that God had not come. But if the heathen are honouring the same God Who gave the law to Moses and the promises to Abraham-the God Whose word too the Jews dishonoured, why do they not recognise or rather why do they deliberately refuse to see that the Lord of Whom the Scriptures prophesied has shone forth to the world and appeared to it in a bodily form? Scripture declares it repeatedly. "The Lord God has appeared to us" (Psalm 118.27), and again, "He sent forth His Word and healed them" (Psalm 107.20). And again, "It was no ambassador, no angel who saved us, but the Lord Himself" (Isaiah 63.9). The Jews are afflicted like some demented person who sees the earth lit up by the sun, but denies the sun that lights it up! What more is there for their Expected One to do when he comes? To call the heathen? But they are called already. To put an end to prophet and king and vision? But this too has already happened. To expose the God-denyingness of idols? It is already exposed and condemned. Or to destroy death? It is already destroyed. What then has not come to pass that the Christ must do? What is there left out or unfulfilled that the Jews should disbelieve so light-heartedly? The plain fact is, as I say, that there is no longer any, king or prophet nor Jerusalem nor sacrifice nor vision among them; yet the whole earth is filled with the knowledge of God, and the Gentiles, forsaking atheism, are now taking refuge with the God of Abraham through the Word, our Lord Jesus Christ. Surely, then, it must be plain even to the most shameless that the Christ has come, and that He has enlightened all men everywhere, and given them the true and divine teaching about His Father. Thus the Jews may be refuted by these and other arguments from the Divine teaching.

Chapter VII: *Refutation of the Gentiles*

41. We come now to the unbelief of the Gentiles; and this is indeed a matter for complete astonishment, for They laugh at that which is no fit subject for mockery, yet fail to see the shame and ridiculousness of their own idols. But the arguments on our side do

not lack weight, so we will confute them too on reasonable grounds, chiefly from what we ourselves also see. First of all, what is there in our belief that is unfitting or ridiculous? Is it only that we say that the Word has been manifested in a body? Well, if they themselves really love the truth, they will agree with us that this involved no unfittingness at all. If they deny that there is a Word of God at all, that will be extraordinary, for then they will be ridiculing what they do not know. But suppose they confess that there is a Word of God, that He is the Governor of all things, that in Him the Father wrought the creation, that by His providence the whole receives light and life and being, and that He is King over all, so that He is known by means of the works of His providence, and through Him the Father. Suppose they confess all this, what then? Are they not unknowingly turning the ridicule against themselves? The Greek philosophers say that the universe is a great body, and they say truly, for we perceive the universe and its parts with our senses. But if the Word of God is in the universe, which is a body, and has entered into it in its every part, what is there surprising or unfitting in our saying that He has entered also into human nature? If it were unfitting for Him to have embodied Himself at all, then it would be unfitting for Him to have entered into the universe, and to be giving light and movement by His providence to all things in it, because the universe, as we have seen, is itself a body. But if it is right and fitting for Him to enter into the universe and to reveal Himself through it, then, because humanity is part of the universe along with the rest, it is no less fitting for Him to appear in a human body, and to enlighten and to work through that. And surely if it were wrong for a part of the universe to have been used to reveal His Divinity to men, it would be much more wrong that He should be so revealed by the whole!

42. Take a parallel case. A man's personality actuates and quickens his whole body. If anyone said it was unsuitable for the man's power to be in the toe, he would bethought silly, because, while granting that a man penetrates and actuates the whole of his body, he denied his presence in the part. Similarly, no one who admits the presence of the Word of God in the universe as a whole should think it unsuitable for a single human body to be by Him actuated and enlightened. But is it, perhaps, because humanity is a thing cre-

ated and brought into being out of non-existence that they regard as unfitting the manifestation of the Saviour in our nature? If so, it is high time that they spurned Him from creation too; for it, too, has been brought out of non-being into being by the Word. But if, on the other hand, although creation is a thing that has been made, it is not unsuitable for the Word to be present in it, then neither is it unsuitable for Him to be in man. Man is a part of the creation, as I said before; and the reasoning which applies to one applies to the other. All things derive from the Word their light and movement and life, as the Gentile authors themselves say, "In Him we live and move and have our being" (see Acts 17.28). Very well then. That being so, it is by no means unbecoming that the Word should dwell in man. So if, as we say, the Word has used that in which He is as the means of His self-manifestation, what is there ridiculous in that? He could not have used it had He not been present in it; but we have already admitted that He is present both in the whole and in the parts. What, then, is there incredible in His manifesting Himself through that in which He is? By His own power He enters completely into each and all, and orders them throughout ungrudgingly; and, had He so willed, He could have revealed Himself and His Father by means of sun or moon or sky or earth or fire or water. Had He done so, no one could rightly have accused Him of acting unbecomingly, for He sustains in one whole all things at once, being present and invisibly revealed not only in the whole, but also in each particular part. This being so, and since, moreover, He has willed to reveal Himself through men, who are part of the whole, there can be nothing ridiculous in His using a human body to manifest the truth and knowledge of the Father. Does not the mind of man pervade his entire being, and yet find expression through one part only, namely the tongue? Does anybody say on that account that Mind has degraded itself? Of course not. Very well, then, no more is it degrading for the Word, Who pervades all things, to have appeared in a human body. For, as I said before, if it were unfitting for Him thus to indwell the part, it would be equally so for Him to exist within the whole.

43. Some may then ask, why did He not manifest Himself by means of other and nobler parts of creation, and use some nobler instrument, such as sun or moon or stars or fire or air, instead of

mere man? The answer is this. The Lord did not come to make a display. He came to heal and to teach suffering men. For one who wanted to make a display the thing would have been just to appear and dazzle the beholders. But for Him Who came to heal and to teach the way was not merely to dwell here, but to put Himself at the disposal of those who needed Him, and to be manifested according as they could bear it, not vitiating the value of the Divine appearing by exceeding their capacity to receive it. Moreover, nothing in creation had erred from the path of God's purpose for it, save only man. Sun, moon, heaven, stars, water, air—none of these had swerved from their order, but, knowing the Word as their Maker and their King, remained as they were made. Men alone having rejected what is good, have invented nothings instead of the truth, and have ascribed the honour due to God and the knowledge concerning Him to daemons and men in the form of stones. Obviously the Divine goodness could not overlook so grave a matter as this. But men could not recognise Him as ordering and ruling creation as a whole. So what does He do? He takes to Himself for instrument a part of the whole, namely a human body, and enters into that. Thus He ensured that men should recognise Him in the part who could not do so in the whole, and that those who could not lift their eyes to His unseen power might recognise and behold Him in the likeness of themselves. For, being men, they would naturally learn to know His Father more quickly and directly by means of a body that corresponded to their own and by the Divine works done through it; for by comparing His works with their own they would judge His to be not human but Divine. And if, as they say, it were unsuitable for the Word to reveal Himself through bodily acts, it would be equally so for Him to do so through the works of the universe. His being in creation does not mean that He shares its nature; on the contrary, all created things partake of His power. Similarly, though He used the body as His instrument, He shared nothing of its defect (literally, "He shared nothing of the things of the body"), but rather sanctified it by His indwelling. Does not even Plato, of whom the Greeks think so much, say that the Author of the Universe, seeing it storm-tossed and in danger of sinking into the state of dissolution, takes his seat at the helm of the Life-force of the universe, and comes to the rescue and puts everything right? What, then, is there incredible in our saying that, mankind having gone astray, the Word descended upon it and was manifest as man, so that by His ,intrinsic goodness and His steersmanship He might save it from the storm?

44. It may be, however, that, though shamed into agreeing that this objection is void, the Greeks will want to raise another. They will say that, if God wanted to instruct and save mankind, He might have done so, not by His Word's assumption of a body, but, even as He at first created them, by the mere signification of His will. The reasonable reply to that is that the circumstances in the two cases are quite different. In the beginning, nothing as yet existed at all; all that was needed, therefore, in order to bring all things into being, was that His will to do so should be signified. But once man was in existence, and things that were, not things that were not, demanded to be healed, it followed as a matter of course that the Healer and Saviour should align Himself with those things that existed already, in order to heal the existing evil. For that reason, therefore, He was made man, and used the body as His human instrument. If this were not the fitting way, and He willed to use an instrument at all, how otherwise was the Word to come? And whence could He take His instrument, save from among those already in existence and needing His Godhead through One like themselves? It was not things nonexistent that needed salvation, for which a bare creative word might have sufficed, but man-man already in existence and already in process of corruption and ruin. It was natural and right, therefore, for the Word to use a human instrument and by that means unfold Himself to all. You must know, moreover, that the corruption which had set in was not external to the body but established within it. The need, therefore, was that life should cleave to it in corruption's place, so that, just as death was brought into being in the body, life also might be engendered in it. If death had been exterior to the body, life might fittingly have been the same. But if death was within the body, woven into its very substance and dominating it as though completely one with it, the need was for Life to be woven into it instead, so that the body by thus enduing itself with life might cast corruption off. Suppose the Word had come outside the body instead of in it, He would, of course, have defeated death, because death is powerless against the Life. But the corruption inherent in the body would have remained

in it none the less. Naturally, therefore, the Saviour assumed a body for Himself, in order that the body, being interwoven as it were with life, should no longer remain a mortal thing, in thrall to death, but as endued with immortality and risen from death, should thenceforth remain immortal. For once having put on corruption, it could not rise, unless it put on life instead; and besides this, death of its very nature could not appear otherwise than in a body. Therefore He put on a body, so that in the body He might find death and blot it out. And, indeed, how could the Lord have been proved to be the Life at all, had He not endued with life that which was subject to death? Take an illustration. Stubble is a substance naturally destructible by fire; and it still remains stubble, fearing the menace of fire which has the natural property of consuming it, even if fire is kept away from it, so that it is not actually burnt. But suppose that, instead of merely keeping the fire from it somebody soaks the stubble with a quantity of asbestos, the substance which is said to be the antidote to fire. Then the stubble no longer fears the fire, because it has put on that which fire cannot touch, and therefore it is safe. It is just the same with regard to the body and death. Had death been kept from it by a mere command, it would still have remained mortal and corruptible, according to its nature. To prevent this, it put on the incorporeal Word of God, and therefore fears neither death nor corruption any more, for it is clad with Life as with a garment and in it corruption is clean done away.

45. The Word of God thus; acted consistently in assuming a body and using a human instrument to vitalise the body. He was consistent in working through man to reveal Himself everywhere, as well as through the other parts of His creation, so that nothing was left void of His Divinity and knowledge. For I take up now the point I made before, namely that the Saviour did this in order that He might fill all things everywhere with the knowledge of Himself, just as they are already filled with His presence, even as the Divine Scripture says, "The whole universe was filled with the knowledge of the Lord" (Isaiah 11.9). If a man looks up to heaven he sees there His ordering; but if he cannot look so high as heaven, but only so far as men, through His works he sees His power, incomparable with human might, and learns from them that He alone among men is

God the Word. Or, if a man has gone astray among daemons and is in fear of them, he may see this Man drive them out and judge therefrom that He is indeed their Master. Again, if a man has been immersed in the element of water and thinks that it is God-as indeed the Egyptians do worship water-he may see its very nature changed by Him and learn that the Lord is Creator of all. And if a man has gone down even to Hades, and stands awestruck before the heroes who have descended thither, regarding them as gods, still he may see the fact of Christ's resurrection and His victory over death, and reason from it that, of all these, He alone is very Lord and God. For the Lord touched all parts of creation, and freed and undeceived them all from every deceit. As St. Paul says, "Having put off from Himself the principalities and the powers, He triumphed on the cross"(Col. 2.15), so that no one could possibly be any longer deceived, but everywhere might find the very Word of God. For thus man, enclosed on every side by the works of creation and everywhere-in heaven, in Hades, in men and on the earth, beholding the unfolded Godhead of the Word, is no longer deceived concerning God, but worships Christ alone, and through Him rightly knows the Father. On these grounds, then, of reason and of principle, we will fairly silence the Gentiles in their turn. But if they think these arguments insufficient to confute them, we will go on in the next chapter to prove our point from facts.

Chapter VIII: *Refutation of the Gentiles—continued*

46. When did people begin to abandon the worship of idols, unless it were since the very Word of God came among men? When have oracles ceased and become void of meaning, among the Greeks and everywhere, except since the Saviour has revealed Himself on earth? When did those whom the poets call gods and heroes begin to be adjudged as mere mortals, except when the Lord took the spoils of death and preserved incorruptible the body He had taken, raising it from among the dead? Or when did the deceitfulness and madness of daemons fall under contempt, save when the Word, the Power of God, the Master of all these as well, condescended on account of the weakness of mankind and appeared on earth? When did the practice and theory of magic begin to be spurned under foot, if not

at the manifestation of the Divine Word to men? In a word, when did the wisdom of the Greeks become foolish, save when the true Wisdom of God revealed Himself on earth? In old times the whole world and every place in it was led astray by the worship of idols, and men thought the idols were the only gods that were. But now all over the world men are forsaking the fear of idols and taking refuge with Christ; and by worshiping Him as God they come through Him to know the Father also, Whom formerly they did not know. The amazing thing, moreover, is this. The objects of worship formerly were varied and countless; each place had its own idol and the so-called god of one place could not pass over to another in order to persuade the people there to worship him, but was barely reverenced even by his own. Indeed no! Nobody worshiped his neighbour's god, but every man had his own idol and thought that it was lord of all. But now Christ alone is worshiped, as One and the Same among all peoples everywhere; and what the feebleness of idols could not do, namely, convince even those dwelling close at hand, He has effected. He has persuaded not only those close at hand, but literally the entire world to worship one and the same Lord and through Him the Father.

47. Again, in former times every place was full of the fraud of the oracles, and the utterances of those at Delphi and Dordona and in Boeotia and Lycia and Libya and Egypt and those of the Kabiri and the Pythoness were considered marvelous by the minds of men. But now, since Christ has been proclaimed everywhere, their madness too has ceased, and there is no one left among them to give oracles at all. Then, too, daemons used to deceive men's minds by taking up their abode in springs or rivers or trees or stones and imposing upon simple people by their frauds. But now, since the Divine appearing of the Word, all this fantasy has ceased, for by the sign of the cross, if a man will but use it, he drives out their deceits. Again, people used to regard as gods those who are mentioned in the poets—Zeus and Kronos and Apollo and the heroes—and in worshiping them they went astray. But now that the Saviour has appeared among men, those others have been exposed as mortal men, and Christ alone is recognised as true God, Word of God, God Himself. And what is one to say about the magic that they think so marvelous? Before the sojourn of the Word, it was strong and active among Egyptians

and Chaldaeans and Indians and filled all who saw it with terror and astonishment. But by the coming of the Truth and the manifestation of the Word it too has been confuted and entirely destroyed. As to Greek wisdom, however, and the philosophers' noisy talk, I really think no one requires argument from us; for the amazing fact is patent to all that, for all that they had written so much, the Greeks failed to convince even a few from their own neighbourhood in regard to immortality and the virtuous ordering of life. Christ alone, using common speech and through the agency of men not clever with their tongues, has convinced whole assemblies of people all the world over to despise death, and to take heed to the things that do not die, to look past the things of time and gaze on things eternal, to think nothing of earthly glory and to aspire only to immortality.

48. These things which we have said are no mere words they are attested by actual experience. Anyone who likes may see the proof of glory in the virgins of Christ, and in the young men who practise chastity as part of their religion, and in the assurance of immortality in so great and glad a company of martyrs (literally, "so great a chorus," *xopos*; being properly a band of dancers and singers.) Anyone, too, may put what we have said to the proof of experience in another way. In the very presence of the fraud of daemons and the imposture of the oracles and the wonders of magic, let him use the sign of the cross which they all mock at, and but speak the Name of Christ, and he shall see how through Him daemons are routed, oracles cease, and all magic and witchcraft is confounded. Who, then, is this Christ and how great is He, Who by His Name and presence overshadows and confounds all things on every side, Who alone is strong against all and has filled the whole world with His teaching? Let the Greeks tell us, who mock at Him without stint or shame. If He is a man, how is it that one man has proved stronger than all those whom they themselves regard as gods, and by His own power has shown them to be nothing? If they call Him a magician, how is it that by a magician all magic is destroyed, instead of being rendered strong? Had He conquered certain magicians or proved Himself superior to one of them only, they might reasonably think that He excelled the rest only by His greater skill. But the fact is that His cross has vanquished all magic entirely and has conquered the very name of it. Obviously,

therefore, the Saviour is no magician, for the very daemons whom the magicians invoke flee from Him as from their Master. Who is He, then? Let the Greeks tell us, whose only serious pursuit is mockery! Perhaps they will say that He, too, is a daemon, and that is why He prevailed. But even so the laugh is still on our side, for we can confute them by the same proofs as before. How could He be a daemon, Who drives daemons out? If it were only certain ones that He drove out, then they might reasonably think that He prevailed against them through the power of their Chief, as the Jews, wishing to insult Him, actually said. But since the fact is, here again, that at the mere naming of His Name all madness of the daemons is rooted out and put to flight, obviously the Greeks are wrong here, too, and our Lord and Saviour Christ is not, as they maintain, some daemonic power. If, then, the Saviour is neither a mere man nor a magician, nor one of the daemons, but has by His Godhead confounded and overshadowed the opinions of the poets and the delusion of the daemons and the wisdom of the Greeks, it must be manifest and will be owned by all that He is in truth Son of God, Existent Word and Wisdom and Power of the Father. This is the reason why His works are no mere human works, but, both intrinsically and by comparison with those of men, are recognised as being superhuman and truly the works of God.

49. What man that ever was, for instance, formed a body for himself from a virgin only? Or what man ever healed so many diseases as the common Lord of all? Who restored that which was lacking in man's nature or made one blind from birth to see? Aesculapius was deified by the Greeks because he practised the art of healing and discovered herbs as remedies for bodily diseases, not, of course, forming them himself out of the earth, but finding them out by the study of nature. But what is that in comparison with what the Saviour did when, instead of just healing a wound, He both fashioned essential being and restored to health the thing that He had formed? Hercules, too, is worshiped as a god by the Greeks because he fought against other men and destroyed wild animals by craft. But what is that to what the Word did, in driving away from men diseases and daemons and even death itself? Dionysus is worshiped among them, because he taught men drunkenness; yet they ridicule the true Saviour and Lord of all, Who taught men temperance. That, however,

is enough on this point. What will they say to the other marvels of His Godhead? At what man's death was the sun darkened and the earth shaken? Why, even to this day men are dying, and they did so also before that time. When did any such marvels happen in their case? Now shall we pass over the deeds done in His earthly body and mention those after His resurrection? Has any man's teaching, in any place or at any time, ever prevailed everywhere as one and the same, from one end of the earth to the other, so that his worship has fairly flown through every land? Again, if, as they say, Christ is man only and not God the Word, why do not the gods of the Greeks prevent His entering their domains? Or why, on the other hand, does the Word Himself dwelling in our midst make an end of their worship by His teaching and put their fraud to shame?

50. Many before Him have been kings and tyrants of the earth, history tells also of many among the Chaldaeans and Egyptians and Indians who were wise men and magicians. But which of those, I do not say after his death, but while yet in this life, was ever able so far to prevail as to fill the whole world with his teaching and retrieve so great a multitude from the craven fear of idols, as our Saviour has won over from idols to Himself? The Greek philosophers have compiled many works with persuasiveness and much skill in words; but what fruit have they to show for this such as has the cross of Christ? Their wise thoughts were persuasive enough until they died; yet even in their life-time their seeming influence was counterbalanced by their rivalry with one another, for they were a jealous company and declaimed against each other. But the Word of God, by strangest paradox, teaching in meaner language, has put the choicest sophists in the shade, and by confounding their teachings and drawing all men to Himself He has filled His own assemblies. Moreover, and this is the marvelous thing, by going down as Man to death He has confounded all the sounding Utterances of the wise men about the idols. For whose death ever drove out daemons, or whose death did ever daemons fear, save that of Christ? For where the Saviour is named, there every daemon is driven out. Again, who has ever so rid men of their natural passions that fornicators become chaste and murderers no longer wield the sword and those who formerly were craven cowards boldly play the man? In a word, what persuaded the barbarians

and heathen folk in every place to drop their madness and give heed to peace, save the faith of Christ and the sign of the cross? What other things have given men such certain faith in immortality as have the cross of Christ and the resurrection of His body? The Greeks told all sorts of false tales, but they could never pretend that their idols rose again from death : indeed it never entered their heads that a body could exist again after death at all. And one would be particularly ready to listen to them on this point, because by these opinions they have exposed the weakness of their own idolatry, at the same time yielding to Christ the possibility of bodily resurrection, so that by that means He might be recognised by all as Son of God.

51. Again, who among men, either after his death or while yet living, taught about virginity and did not account this virtue impossible for human beings? But Christ our Saviour and King of all has so prevailed with His teaching on this subject that even children not yet of lawful age promise that virginity which transcends the law. And who among men has ever been able to penetrate even to Scythians and Ethiopians, or Parthians or Armenians or those who are said to live beyond Hyrcania, or even the Egyptians and Chaldaeans, people who give heed to magic and are more than naturally enslaved by the fear of daemons and savage in their habits, and to preach at all, about virtue and self-control and against the worshiping of idols, as has the Lord of all, the Power of God, our Lord Jesus Christ? Yet He not only preached through His own disciples, but also wrought so persuasively on men's understanding that, laying aside their savage habits and forsaking the worship of their ancestral gods, they learnt to know Him and through Him to worship the Father. While they were yet idolaters, the Greeks and Barbarians were always at war with each other, and were even cruel to their own kith and kin. Nobody could travel by land or sea at all unless he was armed with swords, because of their irreconcilable quarrels with each other. Indeed, the whole course of their life was carried on with the weapons, and the sword with them replaced the staff and was the mainstay of all aid. All this time, as I said before, they were serving idols and offering sacrifices to daemons, and for all the superstitious awe that accompanied this idol worship, nothing could wean them from that warlike spirit. But, strange to relate, since they came over to the school of Christ, as

men moved with real compunction they have laid aside their murderous cruelty and are war-minded no more. On the contrary, all is peace among them and nothing remains save desire for friendship.

52. Who, then, is He Who has done these things and has united in peace those who hated each other, save the beloved Son of the Father, the common Saviour of all, Jesus Christ, Who by His own love underwent all things for our salvation? Even from the beginning, moreover, this peace that He was to administer was foretold, for Scripture says, "They shall beat their swords into ploughshares and their spears into sickles, and nation shall not take sword against nation, neither shall they learn any more to wage war" (Isaiah 2.4). Nor is this by any means incredible. The barbarians of the present day are naturally savage in their habits, and as long, as they sacrifice to their idols they rage furiously against each other and cannot bear to be a single hour without weapons. But when they hear the teaching of Christ, forthwith they turn from fighting to farming, and instead of arming themselves with swords extend their hands in prayer. In a word, instead of fighting each other, they take up arms against the devil and the daemons, and overcome them by their self-command and integrity of soul. These facts are proof of the Godhead of the Saviour, for He has taught men what they could never learn among the idols. It is also no small exposure of the weakness and nothingness of daemons and idols, for it was because they knew their own weakness that the daemons were always setting men to fight each other, fearing lest, if they ceased from mutual strife, they would turn to attack the daemons themselves. For in truth the disciples of Christ, instead of fighting each other, stand arrayed against daemons by their habits and virtuous actions, and chase them away and mock at their captain the devil. Even in youth they are chaste, they endure in times of testing and persevere ins toils. When they are insulted, they are patient, when robbed they make light of it, and, marvelous to relate, they make light even of death itself, and become martyrs of Christ.

53. And here is another proof of the Godhead of the Saviour, which is indeed utterly amazing. What mere man or magician or tyrant or king was ever able by himself to do so much? Did anyone ever fight against the whole system of idol-worship and the whole

host of daemons and all magic and all the wisdom of the Greeks, at a time when all of these were strong and flourishing and taking everybody in, as did our Lord, the very Word of God? Yet He is even now invisibly exposing every man's error, and single-handed is carrying off all men from them all, so that those who used to worship idols now tread them under foot, reputed magicians burn their books and the wise prefer to all studies the interpretation of the gospels. They are deserting those whom formerly they worshiped, they worship and confess as Christ and God Him Whom they used to ridicule as crucified. Their so-called gods are routed by the sign of the cross, and the crucified Saviour is proclaimed in all the world as God and Son of God. Moreover, the gods worshiped among the Greeks are now falling into disrepute among them on account of the disgraceful things they did, for those who receive the teaching of Christ are more chaste in life than they. If these, and the like of them, are human works, let anyone who will show us similar ones done by men in former time, and so convince us. But if they are shown to be, and are the works not of men but of God, why are the unbelievers so irreligious as not to recognise the Master Who did them? They are afflicted as a man would be who failed to recognise God the Artificer through the works of creation. For surely if they had recognised His Godhead through His power over the universe, they would recognise also that the bodily works of Christ are not human, but are those of the Saviour of all, the Word of God. And had they recognised this, as Paul says, "They would not have crucified the Lord of glory." (1 Cor. 2.8).

54. As, then, he who desires to see God Who by nature is invisible and not to be beheld, may yet perceive and know Him through His works, so too let him who does not see Christ with his understanding at least consider Him in His bodily works and test whether they be of man or God. If they be of man, then let him scoff; but if they be of God, let him not mock at things which are no fit subject for scorn, but rather let him recognise the fact and marvel that things divine have been revealed to us by such humble means, that through death deathlessness has been made known to us, and through the Incarnation of the Word the Mind whence all things proceed has been declared, and its Agent and Ordainer, the Word of God Himself. He, indeed, assumed humanity that we might become God. He manifest-

ed Himself by means of a body in order that we might perceive the Mind of the unseen Father. He endured shame from men that we might inherit immortality. He Himself was unhurt by this, for He is impassible and incorruptible; but by His own impassibility He kept and healed the suffering men on whose account He thus endured. In short, such and so many are the Saviour's achievements that follow from His Incarnation, that to try to number them is like gazing at the open sea and trying to count the waves. One cannot see all the waves with one's eyes, for when one tries to do so those that are following on baffle one's senses. Even so, when one wants to take in all the achievements of Christ in the body, one cannot do so, even by reckoning them up, for the things that transcend one's thought are always more than those one thinks that one has grasped. As we cannot speak adequately about even a part of His work, therefore, it will be better for us not to speak about it as a whole. So we will mention but one thing more, and then leave the whole for you to marvel at. For, indeed, everything about it is marvelous, and wherever a man turns his gaze he sees the Godhead of the Word and is smitten with awe.

55. The substance of what we have said so far may be summarised as follows. Since the Saviour came to dwell among us, not only does idolatry no longer increase, but it is getting less and gradually ceasing to be. Similarly,not only does the wisdom of the Greeks no longer make any progress, but that which used to be is disappearing. And daemons, so far from continuing to impose on people by their deceits and oracle-givings and sorceries, are routed by the sign of the cross if they so much as try. On the other hand, while idolatry and everything else that opposes the faith of Christ is daily dwindling and weakening and falling, see, the Saviour's teaching is increasing everywhere! Worship, then, the Saviour "Who is above all" and mighty, even God the Word, and condemn those who are being defeated and made to disappear by Him. When the sun has come, darkness prevails no longer; any of it that may be left anywhere is driven away. So also, now that the Divine epiphany of the Word of God has taken place, the darkness of idols prevails no more, and all parts of the world in every direction are enlightened by His teaching. Similarly, if a king be reigning somewhere, but stays in his own house and does not let himself be seen, it often happens that some insub-

ordinate fellows, taking advantage of his retirement, will have themselves proclaimed in his stead ; and each of them, being invested with the semblance of kingship, misleads the simple who, because they cannot enter the palace and see the real king, are led astray by just hearing a king named. When the real king emerges, however, and appears to view, things stand differently. The insubordinate impostors are shown up by his presence, and men, seeing the real king, forsake those who previously misled them. In the same way the daemons used formerly to impose on men, investing themselves with the honour due to God. But since the Word of God has been manifested in a body, and has made known to us His own Father, the fraud of the daemons is stopped and made to disappear and men, turning their eyes to the true God, Word of the Father, forsake the idols and come to know the true God. Now this is proof that Christ is God, the Word and Power of God. For whereas human things cease and the fact of Christ remains, it is clear to all that the things which cease are temporary, but that He Who remains is God and very Son of God, the sole-begotten Word.

Chapter IX: *Conclusion*

56. Here, then, Macarius, is our offering to you who love Christ, a brief statement of the faith of Christ and of the manifestation of His Godhead to us. This will give you a beginning, and you must go on to prove its truth by the study of the Scriptures. They were written and inspired by God; and we, who have learned from inspired teachers who read the Scriptures and became martyrs for the Godhead of Christ, make further contribution to your eagerness to learn. From the Scriptures you will learn also of His second manifestation to us, glorious and divine indeed, when He shall come not in lowliness but in His proper glory, no longer in humiliation but in majesty, no longer to suffer but to bestow on us all the fruit of His cross—the resurrection and incorruptibility. No longer will He then be judged, but rather will Himself be judge, judging each and all according to their deeds done in the body, whether good or ill. Then for the good is laid up the heavenly kingdom, but for those that practise evil outer darkness and the eternal fire. So also the Lord

Himself says, "I say unto you, hereafter ye shall see the Son of Man seated on the right hand of power, coming on the clouds of heaven in the glory of the Father" (Matt. 26.64). For that Day we have one of His own sayings to prepare us, "Get ready and watch, for ye know not the hour in which He cometh" (Matt. 24.42). And blessed Paul says, "We must all stand before the judgment seat of Christ, that each one may receive according as he practised in the body, whether good or ill" (2 Cor. 5.10).

57. But for the searching and right understanding of the Scriptures there is need of a good life and a pure soul, and for Christian virtue to guide the mind to grasp, so far as human nature can, the truth concerning God the Word. One cannot possibly understand the teaching of the saints unless one has a pure mind and is trying to imitate their life. Anyone who wants to look at sunlight naturally wipes his eye clear first, in order to make, at any rate, some approximation to the purity of that on which he looks; and a person wishing to see a city or country goes to the place in order to do so. Similarly, anyone who wishes to understand the mind of the sacred writers must first cleanse his own life, and approach the saints by copying their deeds. Thus united to them in the fellowship of life, he will both understand the things revealed to them by God and, thenceforth escaping the peril that threatens sinners in the judgment, will receive that which is laid up for the saints in the kingdom of heaven. Of that reward it is written: "Eye hath not seen nor ear heard, neither hath entered into the heart of man the things that God has prepared" (1 Cor. 2.9) for them that live a godly life and love the God and Father in Christ Jesus our Lord, through Whom and with Whom be to the Father Himself, with the Son Himself, in the Holy Spirit, honour and might and glory to ages of ages. Amen.

ATHANASIUS

The Life of St. Anthony

Athanasius

Translated by H. Ellershaw

Athanasius the bishop to the brethren in foreign parts

Prologue

You have entered upon a noble rivalry with the monks of Egypt by your determination either to equal or surpass them in your training in the way of virtue. For by this time there are monasteries among you, and the name of monk receives public recognition. With reason, therefore, all men will approve this determination, and in answer to your prayers God will give its fulfillment. Now since you asked me to give you an account of the blessed Antony's way of life, and are wishful to learn how he began the discipline, who and what manner of man he was previous to this, how he closed his life, and whether the things told of him are true, that you also may bring yourselves to imitate him, I very readily accepted your behest, for to me also the bare recollection of Antony is a great accession of help. And I know that you, when you have heard, apart from your admiration of the man, will be wishful to emulate his determination; seeing that for monks the life of Antony is a sufficient pattern of discipline. Wherefore do not refuse credence to what you have heard from those who brought tidings of him; but think rather that they have told you only a few things, for at all events they scarcely can have given circumstances of so great import in any detail. And because I at your request have called to mind a few circumstances about him, and shall send as much as I can tell in a letter, do not neglect to question those who sail from here: for possibly when all have told their tale, the account will hardly be in proportion to his merits. On account of this I was desirous, when I received your letter, to send for certain of the monks, those especially who were wont to be more frequently with him, that if I could learn any fresh details I might send them to you. But since the season for sailing was coming to an end and the letter carrier urgent, I hastened to write to your piety what I myself know, having seen him many times, and what I was able to learn from him, for I was his attendant for a long time, and poured water on his hands; in all points being mindful of the truth, that no one should disbelieve through hearing too much, nor on the other hand by hearing too little should despise the man.

Birth and beginnings of Antony.

1. Antony you must know was by descent an Egyptian: his parents were of good family and possessed considerable wealth, and as they were Christians he also was reared in the same Faith. In infancy he was brought up with his parents, knowing naught else but them and his home. But when he was grown and arrived at boyhood, and was advancing in years, he could not endure to learn letters, not caring to associate with other boys; but all his desire was, as it is written of Jacob, to live a plain man at home (Genesis 25:27). With his parents he used to attend the Lord's House, and neither as a child was he idle nor when older did he despise them; but was both obedient to his father and mother and attentive to what was read, keeping in his heart what was profitable in what he heard. And though as a child brought up in moderate affluence, he did not trouble his parents for varied or luxurious fare, nor was this a source of pleasure to him; but was content simply with what he found nor sought anything further.

2. After the death of his father and mother he was left alone with one little sister: his age was about eighteen or twenty, and on him the care both of home and sister rested. Now it was not six months after the death of his parents, and going according to custom into the Lord's House, he communed with himself and reflected as he

walked how the Apostles left all and followed the Saviour (Matthew 4:20); and how they in the Acts sold their possessions and brought and laid them at the Apostles' feet for distribution to the needy (Acts 4:35), and what and how great a hope was laid up for them in heaven. Pondering over these things he entered the church, and it happened the Gospel was being read, and he heard the Lord saying to the rich man, "If you would be perfect, go and sell that you have and give to the poor; and come follow Me and you shall have treasure in heaven" (Matthew 19:21). Antony, as though God had put him in mind of the Saints, and the passage had been read on his account, went out immediately from the church, and gave the possessions of his forefathers to the villagers—they were three hundred acres, productive and very fair—that they should be no more a clog upon himself and his sister. And all the rest that was movable he sold, and having got together much money he gave it to the poor, reserving a little however for his sister's sake.

His early ascetic life.

3. And again as he went into the church, hearing the Lord say in the Gospel "be not anxious for the morrow" (Matthew 6:34), he could stay no longer, but went out and gave those things also to the poor. Having committed his sister to known and faithful virgins, and put her into a convent to be brought up, he henceforth devoted himself outside his house to discipline, taking heed to himself and training himself with patience. For there were not yet so many monasteries in Egypt, and no monk at all knew of the distant desert; but all who wished to give heed to themselves practised the discipline in solitude near their own village. Now there was then in the next village an old man who had lived the life of a hermit from his youth up. Antony, after he had seen this man, imitated him in piety. And at first he began to abide in places outside the village: then if he heard of a good man anywhere, like the prudent bee, he went forth and sought him, nor turned back to his own palace until he had seen him; and he returned, having got from the good man as it were supplies for his journey in the way of virtue. So dwelling there at first, he confirmed his purpose not to return to the abode of his fathers nor to the remembrance of his kinsfolk; but to keep all his desire and energy

for perfecting his discipline. He worked, however, with his hands, having heard, "he who is idle let him not eat" (2 Thessalonians 3:10), and part he spent on bread and part he gave to the needy. And he was constant in prayer, knowing that a man ought to pray in secret unceasingly. For he had given such heed to what was read that none of the things that were written fell from him to the ground, but he remembered all, and afterwards his memory served him for books.

4. Thus conducting himself, Antony was beloved by all. He subjected himself in sincerity to the good men whom he visited, and learned thoroughly where each surpassed him in zeal and discipline. He observed the graciousness of one; the unceasing prayer of another; he took knowledge of another's freedom from anger and another's loving-kindness; he gave heed to one as he watched, to another as he studied; one he admired for his endurance, another for his fasting and sleeping on the ground; the meekness of one and the long-suffering of another he watched with care, while he took note of the piety towards Christ and the mutual love which animated all. Thus filled, he returned to his own place of discipline, and henceforth would strive to unite the qualities of each, and was eager to show in himself the virtues of all. With others of the same age he had no rivalry; save this only, that he should not be second to them in higher things. And this he did so as to hurt the feelings of nobody, but made them rejoice over him. So all they of that village and the good men in whose intimacy he was, when they saw that he was a man of this sort, used to call him God-beloved. And some welcomed him as a son, others as a brother.

Early conflicts with the devil.

5. But the devil, who hates and envies what is good, could not endure to see such a resolution in a youth, but endeavoured to carry out against him what he had been wont to effect against others. First of all he tried to lead him away from the discipline, whispering to him the remembrance of his wealth, care for his sister, claims of kindred, love of money, love of glory, the various pleasures of the table and the other relaxations of life, and at last the difficulty of virtue and the labour of it; he suggested also the infirmity of the body and

the length of the time. In a word he raised in his mind a great dust of debate, wishing to debar him from his settled purpose. But when the enemy saw himself to be too weak for Antony's determination, and that he rather was conquered by the other's firmness, overthrown by his great faith and falling through his constant prayers, then at length putting his trust in the weapons which are 'in the navel of his belly' and boasting in them—for they are his first snare for the young—he attacked the young man, disturbing him by night and harassing him by day, so that even the onlookers saw the struggle which was going on between them. The one would suggest foul thoughts and the other counter them with prayers: the one fire him with lust, the other, as one who seemed to blush, fortify his body with faith, prayers, and fasting. And the devil, unhappy wight, one night even took upon him the shape of a woman and imitated all her acts simply to beguile Antony. But he, his mind filled with Christ and the nobility inspired by Him, and considering the spirituality of the soul, quenched the coal of the other's deceit. Again the enemy suggested the ease of pleasure. But he like a man filled with rage and grief turned his thoughts to the threatened fire and the gnawing worm, and setting these in array against his adversary, passed through the temptation unscathed. All this was a source of shame to his foe. For he, deeming himself like God, was now mocked by a young man; and he who boasted himself against flesh and blood was being put to flight by a man in the flesh. For the Lord was working with Antony—the Lord who for our sake took flesh and gave the body victory over the devil, so that all who truly fight can say "not I but the grace of God which was with me" (1 Corinthians 15:10).

6. At last when the dragon could not even thus overthrow Antony, but saw himself thrust out of his heart, gnashing his teeth as it is written, and as it were beside himself, he appeared to Antony like a black boy, taking a visible shape in accordance with the colour of his mind. And cringing to him, as it were, he plied him with thoughts no longer, for guileful as he was, he had been worsted, but at last spoke in human voice and said, 'Many I deceived, many I cast down; but now attacking you and your labours as I had many others, I proved weak.' When Antony asked, Who are you who speakest thus with me? He answered with a lamentable voice, 'I am the friend

of whoredom, and have taken upon me incitements which lead to it against the young. I am called the spirit of lust. How many have I deceived who wished to live soberly, how many are the chaste whom by my incitements I have over-persuaded! I am he on account of whom also the prophet reproves those who have fallen, saying Hosea 4:12, You have been caused to err by the spirit of whoredom. For by me they have been tripped up. I am he who have so often troubled you and have so often been overthrown by you.' But Antony having given thanks to the Lord, with good courage said to him, 'You are very despicable then, for you are black-hearted and weak as a child. Henceforth I shall have no trouble from you , for the Lord is my helper, and I shall look down on mine enemies.' Having heard this, the black one straightway fled, shuddering at the words and dreading any longer even to come near the man.

Details of his life at this time (271-285?)

7. This was Antony's first struggle against the devil, or rather this victory was the Saviour's work in Antony, 'Who condemned sin in the flesh that the ordinance of the law might be fulfilled in us who walk not after the flesh but after the spirit.' But neither did Antony, although the evil one had fallen, henceforth relax his care and despise him; nor did the enemy as though conquered cease to lay snares for him. For again he went round as a lion seeking some occasion against him. But Antony having learned from the Scriptures that the devices of the devil are many (Ephesians 6:11), zealously continued the discipline, reckoning that though the devil had not been able to deceive his heart by bodily pleasure, he would endeavour to ensnare him by other means. For the demon loves sin. Wherefore more and more he repressed the body and kept it in subjection , lest haply having conquered on one side, he should be dragged down on the other. He therefore planned to accustom himself to a severer mode of life. And many marveled, but he himself used to bear the labour easily; for the eagerness of soul, through the length of time it had abode in him, had wrought a good habit in him, so that taking but little initiation from others he showed great zeal in this matter. He kept vigil to such an extent that he often continued the whole night

without sleep; and this not once but often, to the marvel of others. He ate once a day, after sunset, sometimes once in two days, and often even in four. His food was bread and salt, his drink, water only. Of flesh and wine it is superfluous even to speak, since no such thing was found with the other earnest men. A rush mat served him to sleep upon, but for the most part he lay upon the bare ground. He would not anoint himself with oil, saying it behooved young men to be earnest in training and not to seek what would enervate the body; but they must accustom it to labour, mindful of the Apostle's words, 'when I am weak, then am I strong (2 Corinthians 12:10).' 'For,' said he, 'the fibre of the soul is then sound when the pleasures of the body are diminished.' And he had come to this truly wonderful conclusion, 'that progress in virtue, and retirement from the world for the sake of it, ought not to be measured by time, but by desire and fixity of purpose.' He at least gave no thought to the past, but day by day, as if he were at the beginning of his discipline, applied greater pains for advancement, often repeating to himself the saying of Paul: 'Forgetting the things which are behind and stretching forward to the things which are before' (Philippians 3:14). He was also mindful of the words spoken by the prophet Elias, 'the Lord lives before whose presence I stand today' (1 Kings 18:15). For he observed that in saying 'today' the prophet did not compute the time that had gone by: but daily as though ever commencing he eagerly endeavoured to make himself fit to appear before God, being pure in heart and ever ready to submit to His counsel, and to Him alone. And he used to say to himself that from the life of the great Elias the hermit ought to see his own as in a mirror.

His life in the tombs, and combats with demons there.

8. Thus tightening his hold upon himself, Antony departed to the tombs, which happened to be at a distance from the village; and having bid one of his acquaintances to bring him bread at intervals of many days, he entered one of the tombs, and the other having shut the door on him, he remained within alone. And when the enemy could not endure it, but was even fearful that in a short time Antony would fill the desert with the discipline, coming one night

with a multitude of demons, he so cut him with stripes that he lay on the ground speechless from the excessive pain. For he affirmed that the torture had been so excessive that no blows inflicted by man could ever have caused him such torment. But by the Providence of God—for the Lord never overlooks them that hope in Him—the next day his acquaintance came bringing him the loaves. And having opened the door and seeing him lying on the ground as though dead, he lifted him up and carried him to the church in the village, and laid him upon the ground. And many of his kinsfolk and the villagers sat around Antony as round a corpse. But about midnight he came to himself and arose, and when he saw them all asleep and his comrade alone watching, he motioned with his head for him to approach, and asked him to carry him again to the tombs without waking anybody.

9. He was carried therefore by the man, and as he was wont, when the door was shut he was within alone. And he could not stand up on account of the blows, but he prayed as he lay. And after he had prayed, he said with a shout, Here am I, Antony; I flee not from your stripes, for even if you inflict more nothing shall separate me from the love of Christ (Romans 8:35). And then he sang, 'though a camp be set against me, my heart shall not be afraid. ' These were the thoughts and words of this ascetic. But the enemy, who hates good, marveling that after the blows he dared to return, called together his hounds and burst forth, 'You see,' said he, 'that neither by the spirit of lust nor by blows did we stay the man, but that he braves us, let us attack him in another fashion.' But changes of form for evil are easy for the devil, so in the night they made such a din that the whole of that place seemed to be shaken by an earthquake, and the demons as if breaking the four walls of the dwelling seemed to enter through them, coming in the likeness of beasts and creeping things. And the place was on a sudden filled with the forms of lions, bears, leopards, bulls, serpents, asps, scorpions, and wolves, and each of them was moving according to his nature. The lion was roaring, wishing to attack, the bull seeming to toss with its horns, the serpent writhing but unable to approach, and the wolf as it rushed on was restrained; altogether the noises of the apparitions, with their angry ragings, were dreadful. But Antony, stricken and goaded by them, felt bodily pains severer still. He lay watching, however, with unshaken soul, groan-

ing from bodily anguish; but his mind was clear, and as in mockery he said, 'If there had been any power in you, it would have sufficed had one of you come, but since the Lord has made you weak, you attempt to terrify me by numbers: and a proof of your weakness is that you take the shapes of brute beasts.' And again with boldness he said, 'If you are able, and have received power against me, delay not to attack; but if you are unable, why trouble me in vain? For faith in our Lord is a seal and a wall of safety to us.' So after many attempts they gnashed their teeth upon him, because they were mocking themselves rather than him.

10. Nor was the Lord then forgetful of Antony's wrestling, but was at hand to help him. So looking up he saw the roof as it were opened, and a ray of light descending to him. The demons suddenly vanished, the pain of his body straightway ceased, and the building was again whole. But Antony feeling the help, and getting his breath again, and being freed from pain, besought the vision which had appeared to him, saying, 'Where were thou? Why did you not appear at the beginning to make my pains to cease?' And a voice came to him, 'Antony, I was here, but I waited to see your fight; wherefore since you have endured, and hast not been worsted, I will ever be a succour to you, and will make your name known everywhere.' Having heard this, Antony arose and prayed, and received such strength that he perceived that he had more power in his body than formerly. And he was then about thirty-five years old.

He goes to the desert and overcomes temptations on the way.

11. And on the day following he went forth still more eagerly bent on the service of God and having fallen in with the old man he had met previously, he asked him to dwell with him in the desert. But when the other declined on account of his great age, and because as yet there was no such custom, Antony himself set off immediately to the mountain. And yet again the enemy seeing his zeal and wishing to hinder it, cast in his way what seemed to be a great silver dish. But Antony, seeing the guile of the Evil One, stood, and having looked on the dish, he put the devil in it to shame, saying, 'Whence comes a dish in the desert? This road is not well-worn, nor is there here a

trace of any wayfarer; it could not have fallen without being missed on account of its size; and he who had lost it having turned back, to seek it, would have found it, for it is a desert place. This is some wile of the devil. O thou Evil One, not with this shall you hinder my purpose; let it go with you to destruction (Acts 8:20)'. And when Antony had said this it vanished like smoke from the face of fire.

How Antony took up his abode in a ruined fort across the Nile, and how he defeated the demons. His twenty years' sojourn there.

12. Then again as he went on he saw what was this time not visionary, but real gold scattered in the way. But whether the devil showed it, or some better power to try the athlete and show the Evil One that Antony truly cared naught for money, neither he told nor do we know. But it is certain that that which appeared was gold. And Antony marveled at the quantity, but passed it by as though he were going over fire; so he did not even turn, but hurried on at a run to lose sight of the place. More and more confirmed in his purpose, he hurried to the mountain, and having found a fort, so long deserted that it was full of creeping things, on the other side of the river; he crossed over to it and dwelt there. The reptiles, as though some one were chasing them, immediately left the place. But he built up the entrance completely, having stored up loaves for six months—this is a custom of the Thebans, and the loaves often remain fresh a whole year—and as he found water within, he descended as into a shrine, and abode within by himself, never going forth nor looking at any one who came. Thus he employed a long time training himself, and received loaves, let down from above, twice in the year.

13. But those of his acquaintances who came, since he did not permit them to enter, often used to spend days and nights outside, and heard as it were crowds within clamouring, dinning, sending forth piteous voices and crying, 'Go from what is ours. What do you even in the desert? You can not abide our attack.' So at first those outside thought there were some men fighting with him, and that they had entered by ladders; but when stooping down they saw through a hole there was nobody, they were afraid, accounting them to be demons, and they called on Antony. Them he quickly heard, though he had

not given a thought to the demons, and coming to the door he besought them to depart and not to be afraid, 'for thus,' said he, 'the demons make their seeming onslaughts against those who are cowardly. Sign yourselves therefore with the cross , and depart boldly, and let these make sport for themselves.' So they departed fortified with the sign of the Cross. But he remained in no wise harmed by the evil spirits, nor was he wearied with the contest, for there came to his aid visions from above, and the weakness of the foe relieved him of much trouble and armed him with greater zeal. For his acquaintances used often to come expecting to find him dead, and would hear him singing , 'Let God arise and let His enemies be scattered, let them also that hate Him flee before His face. As smoke vanishes, let them vanish; as wax melts before the face of fire, so let the sinners perish from the face of God;' and again, 'All nations compassed me about, and in the name of the Lord I requited them.'

How he left the fort, and how monasticism began to flourish in Egypt. Antony its leader.

14. And so for nearly twenty years he continued training himself in solitude, never going forth, and but seldom seen by any. After this, when many were eager and wishful to imitate his discipline, and his acquaintances came and began to cast down and wrench off the door by force, Antony, as from a shrine, came forth initiated in the mysteries and filled with the Spirit of God. Then for the first time he was seen outside the fort by those who came to see him. And they, when they saw him, wondered at the sight, for he had the same habit of body as before, and was neither fat, like a man without exercise, nor lean from fasting and striving with the demons, but he was just the same as they had known him before his retirement. And again his soul was free from blemish, for it was neither contracted as if by grief, nor relaxed by pleasure, nor possessed by laughter or dejection, for he was not troubled when he beheld the crowd, nor overjoyed at being saluted by so many. But he was altogether even as being guided by reason, and abiding in a natural state. Through him the Lord healed the bodily ailments of many present, and cleansed others from evil spirits. And He gave grace to Antony in speaking, so

that he consoled many that were sorrowful, and set those at variance at one, exhorting all to prefer the love of Christ before all that is in the world. And while he exhorted and advised them to remember the good things to come, and the loving-kindness of God towards us, 'Who spared not His own Son, but delivered Him up for us all' (Romans 8:32), he persuaded many to embrace the solitary life. And thus it happened in the end that cells arose even in the mountains, and the desert was colonised by monks, who came forth from their own people, and enrolled themselves for the citizenship in the heavens.

15. But when he was obliged to cross the Arsenoitic Canal—and the occasion of it was the visitation of the brethren—the canal was full of crocodiles. And by simply praying, he entered it, and all they with him, and passed over in safety. And having returned to his cell, he applied himself to the same noble and valiant exercises; and by frequent conversation he increased the eagerness of those already monks, stirred up in most of the rest the love of the discipline, and speedily by the attraction of his words cells multiplied, and he directed them all as a father.

His address to monks, rendered from Coptic, exhorting them to perseverance, and encouraging them against the wiles of Satan.

16. One day when he had gone forth because all the monks had assembled to him and asked to hear words from him, he spoke to them in the Egyptian tongue as follows: 'The Scriptures are enough for instruction , but it is a good thing to encourage one another in the faith, and to stir up with words. Wherefore you, as children, carry that which you know to your father; and I as the elder share my knowledge and what experience has taught me with you. Let this especially be the common aim of all, neither to give way having once begun, nor to faint in trouble, nor to say: We have lived in the discipline a long time: but rather as though making a beginning daily let us increase our earnestness. For the whole life of man is very short, measured by the ages to come, wherefore all our time is nothing compared with eternal life. And in the world everything is sold at its price, and a man exchanges one equivalent for another; but the promise of eternal life is bought for a trifle. For it is written, The

days of our life in them are threescore years and ten, but if they are in strength, fourscore years, and what is more than these is labour and sorrow. Whenever, therefore, we live full fourscore years, or even a hundred in the discipline, not for a hundred years only shall we reign, but instead of a hundred we shall reign for ever and ever. And though we fought on earth, we shall not receive our inheritance on earth, but we have the promises in heaven; and having put off the body which is corrupt, we shall receive it incorrupt.

17. 'Wherefore, children, let us not faint nor deem that the time is long, or that we are doing something great, for the sufferings of this present time are not worthy to be compared with the glory which shall be revealed to us-ward (Romans 8:18). Nor let us think, as we look at the world, that we have renounced anything of much consequence, for the whole earth is very small compared with all the heaven. Wherefore if it even chanced that we were lords of all the earth and gave it all up, it would be naught worthy of comparison with the kingdom of heaven. For as if a man should despise a copper drachma to gain a hundred drachmas of gold; so if a man were lord of all the earth and were to renounce it, that which he gives up is little, and he receives a hundredfold. But if not even the whole earth is equal in value to the heavens, then he who has given up a few acres leaves as it were nothing; and even if he have given up a house or much gold he ought not to boast nor be low-spirited. Further, we should consider that even if we do not relinquish them for virtue's sake, still afterwards when we die we shall leave them behind—very often, as the Preacher says , to those to whom we do not wish. Why then should we not give them up for virtue's sake, that we may inherit even a kingdom? Therefore let the desire of possession take hold of no one, for what gain is it to acquire these things which we cannot take with us? Why not rather get those things which we can take away with us—to wit, prudence, justice, temperance, courage, understanding, love, kindness to the poor, faith in Christ, freedom from wrath, hospitality? If we possess these, we shall find them of themselves preparing for us a welcome there in the land of the meek-hearted.

18. 'And so from such things let a man persuade himself not to make light of it, especially if he considers that he himself is the servant of the Lord, and ought to serve his Master. Wherefore as a

servant would not dare to say, because I worked yesterday, I will not work today; and considering the past will do no work in the future; but, as it is written in the Gospel, daily shows the same readiness to please his master, and to avoid risk: so let us daily abide firm in our discipline, knowing that if we are careless for a single day the Lord will not pardon us, for the sake of the past, but will be wrath against us for our neglect. As also we have heard in Ezekiel (Ezekiel 18:26); and as Judas because of one night destroyed his previous labour.

19. 'Wherefore, children, let us hold fast our discipline, and let us not be careless. For in it the Lord is our fellow-worker, as it is written, to all that choose the good, God works with them for good. But to avoid being heedless, it is good to consider the word of the Apostle, I die daily (1 Corinthians 15:31). For if we too live as though dying daily, we shall not sin. And the meaning of that saying is, that as we rise day by day we should think that we shall not abide till evening; and again, when about to lie down to sleep, we should think that we shall not rise up. For our life is naturally uncertain, and Providence allots it to us daily. But thus ordering our daily life, we shall neither fall into sin, nor have a lust for anything, nor cherish wrath against any, nor shall we heap up treasure upon earth. But, as though under the daily expectation of death, we shall be without wealth, and shall forgive all things to all men, nor shall we retain at all the desire of women or of any other foul pleasure. But we shall turn from it as past and gone, ever striving and looking forward to the day of Judgment. For the greater dread and danger of torment ever destroys the ease of pleasure, and sets up the soul if it is like to fall.

20. 'Wherefore having already begun and set out in the way of virtue, let us strive the more that we may attain those things that are before. And let no one turn to the things behind, like Lot's wife, all the more so that the Lord has said, No man, having put his hand to the plough, and turning back, is fit for the kingdom of heaven. And this turning back is naught else but to feel regret, and to be once more worldly-minded. But fear not to hear of virtue, nor be astonished at the name. For it is not far from us, nor is it without ourselves, but it is within us, and is easy if only we are willing. That they may get knowledge, the Greeks live abroad and cross the sea, but we have no need

to depart from home for the sake of the kingdom of heaven, nor to cross the sea for the sake of virtue. For the Lord aforetime has said, The kingdom of heaven is within you. Wherefore virtue has need at our hands of willingness alone, since it is in us and is formed from us. For when the soul has its spiritual faculty in a natural state virtue is formed. And it is in a natural state when it remains as it came into existence. And when it came into existence it was fair and exceeding honest. For this cause Joshua, the son of Nun, in his exhortation said to the people, Make straight your heart unto the Lord God of Israel (Joshua 24:23), and John, Make your paths straight (Matthew 3:3). For rectitude of soul consists in its having its spiritual part in its natural state as created. But on the other hand, when it swerves and turns away from its natural state, that is called vice of the soul. Thus the matter is not difficult. If we abide as we have been made, we are in a state of virtue, but if we think of ignoble things we shall be accounted evil. If, therefore, this thing had to be acquired from without, it would be difficult in reality; but if it is in us, let us keep ourselves from foul thoughts. And as we have received the soul as a deposit, let us preserve it for the Lord, that He may recognise His work as being the same as He made it.

21. 'And let us strive that wrath rule us not nor lust overcome us, for it is written, The wrath of man works not the righteousness of God. And lust, when it has conceived, bears sin, and the sin when it is full grown brings forth death. Thus living, let us keep guard carefully, and as it is written, keep our hearts with all watchfulness (Proverbs 4:23). For we have terrible and crafty foes—the evil spirits—and against them we wrestle, as the Apostle said, Not against flesh and blood, but against the principalities and against the powers, against the world rulers of this darkness, against the spiritual hosts of wickedness in the heavenly places (Ephesians 6:12). Great is their number in the air around us , and they are not far from us. Now there are great distinctions among them; and concerning their nature and distinctions much could be said, but such a description is for others of greater powers than we possess. But at this time it is pressing and necessary for us only to know their wiles against ourselves.

22. 'First, therefore, we must know this: that the demons have

not been created like what we mean when we call them by that name; for God made nothing evil, but even they have been made good. Having fallen, however, from the heavenly wisdom, since then they have been groveling on earth. On the one hand they deceived the Greeks with their displays, while out of envy of us Christians they move all things in their desire to hinder us from entry into the heavens; in order that we should not ascend up there from whence they fell. Thus there is need of much prayer and of discipline, that when a man has received through the Spirit the gift of discerning spirits, he may have power to recognise their characteristics: which of them are less and which more evil; of what nature is the special pursuit of each, and how each of them is overthrown and cast out. For their villainies and the changes in their plots are many. The blessed Apostle and his followers knew such things when they said, for we are not ignorant of his devices (2 Corinthians 2:11); and we, from the temptations we have suffered at their hands, ought to correct one another under them. Wherefore I, having had proof of them, speak as to children.

23. 'The demons, therefore, if they see all Christians, and monks especially, labouring cheerfully and advancing, first make an attack by temptation and place hindrances to hamper our way, to wit, evil thoughts. But we need not fear their suggestions, for by prayer, fasting, and faith in the Lord their attack immediately fails. But even when it does they cease not, but knavishly by subtlety come on again. For when they cannot deceive the heart openly with foul pleasures they approach in different guise, and thenceforth shaping displays they attempt to strike fear, changing their shapes, taking the forms of women, wild beasts, creeping things, gigantic bodies, and troops of soldiers. But not even then need you fear their deceitful displays. For they are nothing and quickly disappear, especially if a man fortify himself beforehand with faith and the sign of the cross. Yet are they bold and very shameless, for if thus they are worsted they make an onslaught in another manner, and pretend to prophesy and foretell the future, and to show themselves of a height reaching to the roof and of great breadth; that they may stealthily catch by such displays those who could not be deceived by their arguments. If here also they find the soul strengthened by faith and a hopeful mind, then they bring their leader to their aid.

24. 'And he said they often appeared as the Lord revealed the devil to Job, saying, His eyes are as the morning star. From his mouth proceed burning lamps and hearths of fire are cast forth. The smoke of a furnace blazing with the fire of coals proceeds from his nostrils. His breath is coals and from his mouth issues flame. When the prince of the demons appears in this wise, the crafty one, as I said before, strikes terror by speaking great things, as again the Lord convicted him saying to Job, for he counts iron as straw, and brass as rotten wood, yea he counts the sea as a pot of ointment, and the depth of the abyss as a captive, and the abyss as a covered walk. And by the prophet, the enemy said, I will pursue and overtake (Exodus 15:9), and again by another, I will grasp the whole world in my hand as a nest, and take it up as eggs that have been left. Such, in a word, are their boasts and professions that they may deceive the godly. But not even then ought we, the faithful, to fear his appearance or give heed to his words. For he is a liar and speaks of truth never a word. And though speaking words so many and so great in his boldness, without doubt, like a dragon he was drawn with a hook by the Saviour (Job 41:1), and as a beast of burden he received the halter round his nostrils, and as a runaway his nostrils were bound with a ring, and his lips bored with an armlet. And he was bound by the Lord as a sparrow, that we should mock him. And with him are placed the demons his fellows, like serpents and scorpions to be trodden underfoot by us Christians. And the proof of this is that we now live opposed to him. For he who threatened to dry the sea and seize upon the world, behold now cannot stay our discipline, nor even me speaking against him. Let us then heed not his words, for he is a liar: and let us not fear his visions, seeing that they themselves are deceptive. For that which appears in them is no true light, but they are rather the preludes and likenesses of the fire prepared for the demons who attempt to terrify men with those flames in which they themselves will be burned. Doubtless they appear; but in a moment disappear again, hurting none of the faithful, but bringing with them the likeness of that fire which is about to receive themselves. Wherefore it is unfitting that we should fear them on account of these things; for through the grace of Christ all their practices are in vain.

25. 'Again they are treacherous, and are ready to change them-

selves into all forms and assume all appearances. Very often also without appearing they imitate the music of harp and voice, and recall the words of Scripture. Sometimes, too, while we are reading they immediately repeat many times, like an echo, what is read. They arouse us from our sleep to prayers; and this constantly, hardly allowing us to sleep at all. At another time they assume the appearance of monks and feign the speech of holy men, that by their similarity they may deceive and thus drag their victims where they will. But no heed must be paid them even if they arouse to prayer, even if they counsel us not to eat at all, even though they seem to accuse and cast shame upon us for those things which once they allowed. For they do this not for the sake of piety or truth, but that they may carry off the simple to despair; and that they may say the discipline is useless, and make men loathe the solitary life as a trouble and burden, and hinder those who in spite of them walk in it.

26. 'Wherefore the prophet sent by the Lord declared them to be wretched, saying: Woe is he who gives his neighbours to drink muddy destruction. For such practices and devices are subversive of the way which leads to virtue. And the Lord Himself, even if the demons spoke the truth—for they said truly You are the Son of God (Luke 4:41)—still bridled their mouths and suffered them not to speak; lest haply they should sow their evil along with the truth, and that He might accustom us never to give heed to them even though they appear to speak what is true. For it is unseemly that we, having the holy Scriptures and freedom from the Saviour, should be taught by the devil who has not kept his own order but has gone from one mind to another. Wherefore even when he uses the language of Scripture He forbids him, saying: But to the sinner said God, Wherefore do you declare My ordinances and takest My covenant in your mouth ? For the demons do all things—they prate, they confuse, they dissemble, they confound—to deceive the simple. They din, laugh madly, and whistle; but if no heed is paid to them immediately they weep and lament as though vanquished.'

27. 'The Lord therefore, as God, stayed the mouths of the demons: and it is fitting that we, taught by the saints, should do like them and imitate their courage. For they when they saw these things

used to say: When the sinner rose against me, I was dumb and humble, and kept silence from good words. And again: But I was as a deaf man and heard not, and as a dumb man who opens not his mouth, and I became as a man who hears not. So let us neither hear them as being strangers to us, nor give heed to them even though they arouse us to prayer and speak concerning fasting. But let us rather apply ourselves to our resolve of discipline, and let us not be deceived by them who do all things in deceit, even though they threaten death. For they are weak and can do naught but threaten.

28. 'Already in passing I have spoken on these things, and now I must not shrink from speaking on them at greater length, for to put you in remembrance will be a source of safety. Since the Lord visited earth, the enemy is fallen and his powers weakened. Wherefore although he could do nothing, still like a tyrant, he did not bear his fall quietly, but threatened, though his threats were words only. And let each one of you consider this, and he will be able to despise the demons. Now if they were hampered with such bodies as we are, it would be possible for them to say, Men when they are hidden we cannot find, but whenever we do find them we do them hurt. And we also by lying in concealment could escape them, shutting the doors against them. But if they are not of such a nature as this, but are able to enter in, though the doors be shut, and haunt all the air, both they and their leader the devil, and are wishful for evil and ready to injure; and, as the Saviour said, From the beginning the devil is a manslayer and a father of vice (John 8:44); while we, though this is so, are alive, and spend our lives all the more in opposing him; it is plain they are powerless. For place is no hindrance to their plots, nor do they look on us as friends that they should spare us; nor are they lovers of good that they should amend. But on the contrary they are evil, and nothing is so much sought after by them as wounding them that love virtue and fear God. But since they have no power to effect anything, they do naught but threaten. But if they could, they would not hesitate, but immediately work evil (for all their desire is set on this), and especially against us. Behold now we are gathered together and speak against them, and they know when we advance they grow weak. If therefore they had power they would permit none of us Christians to live, for godliness is an abomination to a sinner (Sirach 1:25). But

since they can do nothing they inflict the greater wounds on themselves; for they can fulfill none of their threats. Next this ought to be considered, that we may be in no fear of them: that if they had the power they would not come in crowds, nor fashion displays, nor with change of form would they frame deceits. But it would suffice that one only should come and accomplish that which he was both able and willing to do: especially as every one who has the power neither slays with display nor strikes fear with tumult, but immediately makes full use of his authority as he wishes. But the demons as they have no power are like actors on the stage changing their shape and frightening children with tumultuous apparition and various forms: from which they ought rather to be despised as showing their weakness. At least the true angel of the Lord sent against the Assyrian had no need for tumults nor displays from without, nor noises nor rattlings, but in quiet he used his power and immediately destroyed a hundred and eighty-five thousand. But demons like these, who have no power, try to terrify at least by their displays (2 Kings 19:35).

29. 'But if any one having in mind the history of Job should say, Why then has the devil gone forth and accomplished all things against him; and stripped him of all his possessions, and slew his children, and smote him with evil ulcers? Let such a one, on the other hand, recognise that the devil was not the strong man, but God who delivered Job to him to be tried. Certainly he had no power to do anything, but he asked, and having received it, he has wrought what he did. So also from this the enemy is the more to be condemned, for although willing he could not prevail against one just man. For if he could have, he would not have asked permission. But having asked not once but also a second time, he shows his weakness and want of power. And it is no wonder if he could do nothing against Job, when destruction would not have come even on his cattle had not God allowed it. And he has not the power over swine, for as it is written in the Gospel, they besought the Lord, saying, Let us enter the swine (Matthew 8:31). But if they had power not even against swine, much less have they any over men formed in the image of God.

30. 'So then we ought to fear God only, and despise the demons, and be in no fear of them. But the more they do these things

the more let us intensify our discipline against them, for a good life and faith in God is a great weapon. At any rate they fear the fasting, the sleeplessness, the prayers, the meekness, the quietness, the contempt of money and vainglory, the humility, the love of the poor, the alms, the freedom from anger of the ascetics, and, chief of all, their piety towards Christ. Wherefore they do all things that they may not have any that trample on them, knowing the grace given to the faithful against them by the Saviour, when He says, Behold I have given to you power to tread upon serpents and scorpions, and upon all the power of the enemy (Luke 10:19).

31. 'Wherefore if they pretend to foretell the future, let no one give heed, for often they announce beforehand that the brethren are coming days after. And they do come. The demons, however, do this not from any care for the hearers, but to gain their trust, and that then at length, having got them in their power, they may destroy them. Whence we must give no heed to them, but ought rather to confute them when speaking, since we do not need them. For what wonder is it, if with more subtle bodies than men have, when they have seen them start on their journey, they surpass them in speed, and announce their coming? Just as a horseman getting a start of a man on foot announces the arrival of the latter beforehand, so in this there is no need for us to wonder at them. For they know none of those things which are not yet in existence; but God only is He who knows all things before their birth. But these, like thieves, running off first with what they see, proclaim it: to how many already have they announced our business—that we are assembled together, and discuss measures against them, before any one of us could go and tell these things. This in good truth a fleet-footed boy could do, getting far ahead of one less swift. But what I mean is this. If any one begins to walk from the Thebaid, or from any other district, before he begins to walk, they do not know whether he will walk. But when they have seen him walking they run on, and before he comes up report his approach. And so it falls out that after a few days the travelers arrive. But often the walkers turn back, and the demons prove false.'

32. 'So, too, with respect to the water of the river, they sometimes make foolish statements. For having seen that there has been

much rain in the regions of Ethiopia, and knowing that they are the cause of the flood of the river before the water has come to Egypt they run on and announce it. And this men could have told, if they had as great power of running as the demons. And as David's spy (2 Samuel 18:24) going up to a lofty place saw the man approaching better than one who stayed down below, and the forerunner himself announced, before the others came up, not those things which had not taken place, but those things which were already on the way and were being accomplished, so these also prefer to labour, and declare what is happening to others simply for the sake of deceiving them. If, however, Providence meantime plans anything different for the waters or wayfarers—for Providence can do this—the demons are deceived, and those who gave heed to them cheated.'

33. 'Thus in days gone by arose the oracles of the Greeks, and thus they were led astray by the demons. But thus also thenceforth their deception was brought to an end by the coming of the Lord , who brought to naught the demons and their devices. For they know nothing of themselves, but, like thieves, what they get to know from others they pass on, and guess at rather than foretell things. Therefore if sometimes they speak the truth, let no one marvel at them for this. For experienced physicians also, since they see the same malady in different people, often foretell what it is, making it out by their acquaintance with it. Pilots, too, and farmers, from their familiarity with the weather, tell at a glance the state of the atmosphere, and forecast whether it will be stormy or fine. And no one would say that they do this by inspiration, but from experience and practice. So if the demons sometimes do the same by guesswork, let no one wonder at it or heed them. For what use to the hearers is it to know from them what is going to happen before the time? Or what concern have we to know such things, even if the knowledge be true? For it is not productive of virtue, nor is it any token of goodness. For none of us is judged for what he knows not, and no one is called blessed because he has learning and knowledge. But each one will be called to judgment in these points—whether he have kept the faith and truly observed the commandments.'

34. 'Wherefore there is no need to set much value on these

things, nor for the sake of them to practise a life of discipline and labour; but that living well we may please God. And we neither ought to pray to know the future, nor to ask for it as the reward of our discipline; but our prayer should be that the Lord may be our fellow-helper for victory over the devil. And if even once we have a desire to know the future, let us be pure in mind, for I believe that if a soul is perfectly pure and in its natural state, it is able, being clear-sighted, to see more and further than the demons—for it has the Lord who reveals to it—like the soul of Elisha, which saw what was done by Gehazi (2 Kings 5:26), and beheld the hosts standing on its side' (2 Kings 6:17).

35. 'When, therefore, they come by night to you and wish to tell the future, or say, we are the angels, give no heed, for they lie. Yea even if they praise your discipline and call you blessed, hear them not, and have no dealings with them; but rather sign yourselves and your houses, and pray, and you shall see them vanish. For they are cowards, and greatly fear the sign of the Lord's Cross, since of a truth in it the Saviour stripped them, and made an example of them (Colossians 2:15). But if they shamelessly stand their ground, capering and changing their forms of appearance, fear them not, nor shrink, nor heed them as though they were good spirits. For the presence either of the good or evil by the help of God can easily be distinguished. The vision of the holy ones is not fraught with distraction: For they will not strive, nor cry, nor shall any one hear their voice. But it comes so quietly and gently that immediately joy, gladness and courage arise in the soul. For the Lord who is our joy is with them, and the power of God the Father. And the thoughts of the soul remain unruffled and undisturbed, so that it, enlightened as it were with rays, beholds by itself those who appear. For the love of what is divine and of the things to come possesses it, and willingly it would be wholly joined with them if it could depart along with them. But if, being men, some fear the vision of the good, those who appear immediately take fear away; as did in the case of Zacharias (Gabriel Luke 1:13), and as the angel did who appeared to the women at the holy sepulchre (Matthew 28:5), and as He did who said to the shepherds in the Gospel, Fear not. For their fear arose not from timidity, but from the recognition of the presence of superior beings. Such then is the nature of the visions of the holy ones.'

36. 'But the inroad and the display of the evil spirits is fraught with confusion, with din, with sounds and cryings such as the disturbance of boorish youths or robbers would occasion. From which arise fear in the heart, tumult and confusion of thought, dejection, hatred towards them who live a life of discipline, indifference, grief, remembrance of kinsfolk and fear of death, and finally desire of evil things, disregard of virtue and unsettled habits. Whenever, therefore, you have seen ought and are afraid, if your fear is immediately taken away and in place of it comes joy unspeakable, cheerfulness, courage, renewed strength, calmness of thought and all those I named before, boldness and love toward God—take courage and pray. For joy and a settled state of soul show the holiness of him who is present. Thus Abraham beholding the Lord rejoiced (John 8:56); so also John at the voice of Mary, the God-bearer, leaped for gladness (Luke 1:41). But if at the appearance of any there is confusion, knocking without, worldly display, threats of death and the other things which I have already mentioned, know that it is an onslaught of evil spirits.'

37. 'And let this also be a token for you: whenever the soul remains fearful there is a presence of the enemies. For the demons do not take away the fear of their presence as the great archangel Gabriel did for Mary and Zacharias, and as he did who appeared to the women at the tomb; but rather whenever they see men afraid they increase their delusions that men may be terrified the more; and at last attacking they mock them, saying, fall down and worship. Thus they deceived the Greeks, and thus by them they were considered gods, falsely so called. But the Lord did not suffer us to be deceived by the devil, for He rebuked him whenever he framed such delusions against Him, saying: Get behind me, Satan: for it is written, You shall worship the Lord your God, and Him only shall you serve (Matthew 4:10). More and more, therefore, let the deceiver be despised by us; for what the Lord has said, this for our sakes He has done: that the demons hearing like words from us may be put to flight through the Lord who rebuked them in those words.'

38. 'And it is not fitting to boast at the casting forth of the demons, nor to be uplifted by the healing of diseases: nor is it fitting that he who casts out devils should alone be highly esteemed, while

he who casts them not out should be considered naught. But let a man learn the discipline of each one and either imitate, rival, or correct it. For the working of signs is not ours but the Saviour's work: and so He said to His disciples: Rejoice not that the demons are subject to you, but that your names are written in the heavens (Luke 10:20). For the fact that our names are written in heaven is a proof of our virtuous life, but to cast out demons is a favour of the Saviour who granted it. Wherefore to those who boasted in signs but not in virtue, and said: Lord, in Your name did we not cast out demons, and in Your name did many mighty works (Matthew 7:22)? He answered, Verily I say unto you, I know you not; for the Lord knows not the ways of the wicked. But we ought always to pray, as I said above, that we may receive the gift of discerning spirits; that, as it is written (1 John 4:1), we may not believe every spirit.'

39. 'I should have liked to speak no further and to say nothing from my own promptings, satisfied with what I have said: but lest you should think that I speak at random and believe that I detail these things without experience or truth; for this cause even though I should become as a fool, yet the Lord who hears knows the clearness of my conscience, and that it is not for my own sake, but on account of your affection towards me and at your petition that I again tell what I saw of the practices of evil spirits. How often have they called me blessed and I have cursed them in the name of the Lord! How often have they predicted the rising of the river, and I answered them, What have you to do with it? Once they came threatening and surrounded me like soldiers in full armour. At another time they filled the house with horses, wild beasts and creeping things, and I sang: Some in chariots and some in horses, but we will boast in the name of the Lord our God ; and at the prayers they were turned to flight by the Lord. Once they came in darkness, bearing the appearance of a light, and said, We have come to give you a light, Antony. But I closed my eyes and prayed, and immediately the light of the wicked ones was quenched. And a few months after they came as though singing psalms and babbling the words of Scripture, But I like a deaf man, heard not. Once they shook the cell with an earthquake, but I continued praying with unshaken heart. And after this they came again making noises, whistling and dancing. But as I prayed and lay singing

psalms to myself they immediately began to lament and weep, as if their strength had failed them. But I gave glory to the Lord who had brought down and made an example of their daring and madness.'

40. 'Once a demon exceeding high appeared with pomp, and dared to say, I am the power of God and I am Providence, what do you wish that I shall give you? But I then so much the more breathed upon him, and spoke the name of Christ, and set about to smite him. And I seemed to have smitten him, and immediately he, big as he was, together with all his demons, disappeared at the name of Christ. At another time, while I was fasting, he came full of craft, under the semblance of a monk, with what seemed to be loaves, and gave me counsel, saying, Eat and cease from your many labours. Thou also art a man and art like to fall sick. But I, perceiving his device, rose up to pray; and he endured it not, for he departed, and through the door there seemed to go out as it were smoke. How often in the desert has he displayed what resembled gold, that I should only touch it and look on it. But I sang psalms against him, and he vanished away. Often they would beat me with stripes, and I repeated again and again, Nothing shall separate me from the love of Christ (Romans 8:35), and at this they rather fell to beating one another. Nor was it I that stayed them and destroyed their power, but it was the Lord, who said, I beheld Satan as lightning fall from Heaven (Luke 10:18); but I, children, mindful of the Apostle's words (1 Corinthians 4:6), transferred this to myself, that you might learn not to faint in discipline, nor to fear the devil nor the delusions of the demons.'

41. 'And since I have become a fool in detailing these things, receive this also as an aid to your safety and fearlessness; and believe me for I do not lie. Once some one knocked at the door of my cell, and going forth I saw one who seemed of great size and tall. Then when I inquired, Who are you? he said, I am Satan. Then when I said, Why are you here? he answered, Why do the monks and all other Christians blame me undeservedly? Why do they curse me hourly? Then I answered, Wherefore do you trouble them? He said, I am not he who troubles them, but they trouble themselves, for I have become weak. Have they not read , The swords of the enemy have come to an end, and you have destroyed the cities? I have no longer a place, a weapon,

a city. The Christians are spread everywhere, and at length even the desert is filled with monks. Let them take heed to themselves, and let them not curse me undeservedly. Then I marveled at the grace of the Lord, and said to him: You who art ever a liar and never speakest the truth, this at length, even against your will, you have truly spoken. For the coming of Christ has made you weak, and He has cast you down and stripped you. But he having heard the Saviour's name, and not being able to bear the burning from it, vanished.'

42. 'If, therefore, the devil himself confesses that his power is gone, we ought utterly to despise both him and his demons; and since the enemy with his hounds has but devices of this sort, we, having got to know their weakness, are able to despise them. Wherefore let us not despond after this fashion, nor let us have a thought of cowardice in our heart, nor frame fears for ourselves, saying, I am afraid lest a demon should come and overthrow me; lest he should lift me up and cast me down; or lest rising against me on a sudden he confound me. Such thoughts let us not have in mind at all, nor let us be sorrowful as though we were perishing; but rather let us be courageous and rejoice always, believing that we are safe. Let us consider in our soul that the Lord is with us, who put the evil spirits to flight and broke their power. Let us consider and lay to heart that while the Lord is with us, our foes can do us no hurt. For when they come they approach us in a form corresponding to the state in which they discover us , and adapt their delusions to the condition of mind in which they find us. If, therefore, they find us timid and confused, they immediately beset the place, like robbers, having found it unguarded; and what we of ourselves are thinking, they do, and more also. For if they find us faint-hearted and cowardly, they mightily increase our terror, by their delusions and threats; and with these the unhappy soul is thenceforth tormented. But if they see us rejoicing in the Lord, contemplating the bliss of the future, mindful of the Lord, deeming all things in His hand, and that no evil spirit has any strength against the Christian, nor any power at all over any one—when they behold the soul fortified with these thoughts—they are discomfited and turned backwards. Thus the enemy, seeing Job fenced round with them, withdrew from him; but finding Judas unguarded, him he took captive. Thus if we are wishful to despise the

enemy, let us ever ponder over the things of the Lord, and let the soul ever rejoice in hope. And we shall see the snares of the demon are like smoke, and the evil ones themselves flee rather than pursue. For they are, as I said before, exceeding fearful, ever looking forward to the fire prepared for them.'

43. 'And for your fearlessness against them hold this sure sign—whenever there is any apparition, be not prostrate with fear, but whatsoever it be, first boldly ask, Who are you? And from whence do you come? And if it should be a vision of holy ones they will assure you, and change your fear into joy. But if the vision should be from the devil, immediately it becomes feeble, beholding your firm purpose of mind. For merely to ask, Who are you? And whence do you come? Is a proof of coolness. By thus asking, the son of Nun learned who his helper was (Joshua 5:13); nor did the enemy escape the questioning of Daniel.'

The growth of the monastic life at this time (about A.D. 305).

44. While Antony was thus speaking all rejoiced; in some the love of virtue increased, in others carelessness was thrown aside, the self-conceit of others was stopped; and all were persuaded to despise the assaults of the Evil One, and marveled at the grace given to Antony from the Lord for the discerning of spirits. So their cells were in the mountains, like filled with holy bands of men who sang psalms, loved reading, fasted, prayed, rejoiced in the hope of things to come, laboured in alms-giving, and preserved love and harmony one with another. And truly it was possible, as it were, to behold a land set by itself, filled with piety and justice. For then there was neither the evildoer, nor the injured, nor the reproaches of the tax-gatherer: but instead a multitude of ascetics; and the one purpose of them all was to aim at virtue. So that any one beholding the cells again, and seeing such good order among the monks, would lift up his voice and say, 'How goodly are your dwellings, O Jacob, and your tents, O Israel; as shady glens and as a garden by a river; as tents which the Lord has pitched, and like cedars near waters' (Numbers 24:5-6).

How Antony renewed his ascetic endeavors at this time.

45. Antony, however, according to his custom, returned alone to his own cell, increased his discipline, and sighed daily as he thought of the mansions in Heaven, having his desire fixed on them, and pondering over the shortness of man's life. And he used to eat and sleep, and go about all other bodily necessities with shame when he thought of the spiritual faculties of the soul. So often, when about to eat with any other hermits, recollecting the spiritual food, he begged to be excused, and departed far off from them, deeming it a matter for shame if he should be seen eating by others. He used, however, when by himself, to eat through bodily necessity, but often also with the brethren; covered with shame on these occasions, yet speaking boldly words of help. And he used to say that it behooved a man to give all his time to his soul rather than his body, yet to grant a short space to the body through its necessities; but all the more earnestly to give up the whole remainder to the soul and seek its profit, that it might not be dragged down by the pleasures of the body, but, on the contrary, the body might be in subjection to the soul. For this is that which was spoken by the Saviour: 'Be not anxious for your life what you shall eat, nor for your body what you shall put on. And do you seek not what you shall eat, or what you shall drink, and be not of a doubtful mind. For all these things the nations of the world seek after. But your Father knows that you have need of all these things. Howbeit do you seek first His Kingdom, and all these things shall be added unto you' (Matthew 6:31; Luke 12:29).

How he sought martyrdom at Alexandria during the Persecution (311).

46. After this the Church was seized by the persecution which then took place under Maximinus, and when the holy martyrs were led to Alexandria, Antony also followed, leaving his cell, and saying, Let us go too, that if called, we may contend or behold them that are contending. And he longed to suffer martyrdom, but not being willing to give himself up, he ministered to the confessors in the mines and in the prisons. And he was very zealous in the judgment hall to stir up to readiness those who were summoned when in their contest, while those who were being martyred he received and brought on

their way until they were perfected. The judge, therefore, beholding the fearlessness of Antony and his companions, and their zeal in this matter, commanded that no monk should appear in the judgment hall, nor remain at all in the city. So all the rest thought it good to hide themselves that day, but Antony gave so little heed to the command that he washed his garment, and stood all next day on a raised place before them, and appeared in his best before the governor. Therefore when all the rest wondered at this, and the governor saw and passed by with his array, he stood fearlessly, showing the readiness of us Christians. For, as I said before, he prayed himself to be a martyr, wherefore he seemed as one grieved that he had not borne his witness. But the Lord was keeping him for our profit and that of others, that he should become a teacher to many of the discipline which he had learned from the Scriptures. For many only beholding his manner of life were eager to be imitators of his ways. So he again ministered as usual to the confessors, and as though he were their fellow captive he laboured in his ministry.

How he lived at this time.

47. And when at last the persecution ceased, and the blessed Bishop Peter had borne his testimony, Antony departed, and again withdrew to his cell, and was there daily a martyr to his conscience, and contending in the conflicts of faith. And his discipline was much severer, for he was ever fasting, and he had a garment of hair on the inside, while the outside was skin, which he kept until his end. And he neither bathed his body with water to free himself from filth, nor did he ever wash his feet, nor even endure so much as to put them into water, unless compelled by necessity. Nor did any one even see him unclothed, nor his body naked at all, except after his death, when he was buried.

How he delivered a woman from an evil spirit.

48. When therefore he had retired and determined to fix a time, after which neither to go forth himself nor admit anybody, Martinian, a military officer, came and disturbed Antony. For he had a daughter

afflicted with an evil spirit. But when he continued for a long while knocking at the door, and asking him to come out and pray to God for his child, Antony, not bearing to open, looked out from above and said, 'Man, why do you call on me? I also am a man even as you. But if you believe in Christ whom I serve, go, and according as you believe, pray to God, and it shall come to pass.' Straightway, therefore, he departed, believing and calling upon Christ, and he received his daughter cleansed from the devil. Many other things also through Antony the Lord did, who says, 'Seek and it shall be given unto you' (Luke 11:9). For many of the sufferers, when he would not open his door, slept outside his cell, and by their faith and sincere prayers were healed.

How at this time he betook himself to his 'inner mountain.'

49. But when he saw himself beset by many, and not suffered to withdraw himself according to his intent as he wished, fearing because of the signs which the Lord wrought by him, that either he should be puffed up, or that some other should think of him above what he ought to think, he considered and set off to go into the upper Thebaid, among those to whom he was unknown. And having received loaves from the brethren, he sat down by the bank of the river, looking whether a boat would go by, that, having embarked thereon, he might go up the river with them. While he was considering these things, a voice came to him from above, 'Antony, where are you going and why?' But he no way disturbed, but as he had been accustomed to be called often thus, giving ear to it, answered, saying, 'Since the multitude permit me not to be still, I wish to go into the upper Thebaid on account of the many hindrances that come upon me here, and especially because they demand of me things beyond my power.' But the voice said unto him, 'Even though you should go into the Thebaid, or even though, as you have in mind, you should go down to the Bucolia , you will have to endure more, aye, double the amount of toil. But if you wish really to be in quiet, depart now into the inner desert.' And when Antony said, 'Who will show me the way for I know it not?' immediately the voice pointed out to him Saracens about to go that way. So Antony approached, and drew near them, and asked that he might go with them into the desert. And they, as though they had been commanded by Providence, received him will-

ingly. And having journeyed with them three days and three nights, he came to a very lofty mountain, and at the foot of the mountain ran a clear spring, whose waters were sweet and very cold; outside there was a plain and a few uncared-for palm trees.

50. Antony then, as it were, moved by God, loved the place, for this was the spot which he who had spoken with him by the banks of the river had pointed out. So having first received loaves from his fellow travelers, he abode in the mountain alone, no one else being with him. And recognising it as his own home, he remained in that place for the future. But the Saracens, having seen the earnestness of Antony, purposely used to journey that way, and joyfully brought him loaves, while now and then the palm trees also afforded him a poor and frugal relish. But after this, the brethren learning of the place, like children mindful of their father, took care to send to him. But when Antony saw that the bread was the cause of trouble and hardships to some of them, to spare the monks this, he resolved to ask some of those who came to bring him a spade, an axe, and a little grain. And when these were brought, he went over the land round the mountain, and having found a small plot of suitable ground, tilled it; and having a plentiful supply of water for watering, he sowed. This doing year by year, he got his bread from thence, rejoicing that thus he would be troublesome to no one, and because he kept himself from being a burden to anybody. But after this, seeing again that people came, he cultivated a few pot-herbs, that he who came to him might have some slight solace after the labour of that hard journey. At first, however, the wild beasts in the desert, coming because of the water, often injured his seeds and husbandry. But he, gently laying hold of one of them, said to them all, 'Why do you hurt me, when I hurt none of you? Depart, and in the name of the Lord come not near this spot.' And from that time forward, as though fearful of his command, they no more came near the place.

How he there combated the demons.

51. So he was alone in the inner mountain, spending his time in prayer and discipline. And the brethren who served him asked that they might come every month and bring him olives, pulse and

oil, for by now he was an old man. There then he passed his life, and endured such great wrestlings, 'Not against flesh and blood,' as it is written (Ephesians 6:12), but against opposing demons, as we learned from those who visited him. For there they heard tumults, many voices, and, as it were, the clash of arms. At night they saw the mountain become full of wild beasts, and him also fighting as though against visible beings, and praying against them. And those who came to him he encouraged, while kneeling he contended and prayed to the Lord. Surely it was a marvelous thing that a man, alone in such a desert, feared neither the demons who rose up against him, nor the fierceness of the four-footed beasts and creeping things, for all they were so many. But in truth, as it is written, 'He trusted in the Lord as Mount Sion,' with a mind unshaken and undisturbed; so that the demons rather fled from him, and the wild beasts, as it is written, 'kept peace with him' (Job 5:23).

52. The devil, therefore, as David says in the Psalms , observed Antony and gnashed his teeth against him. But Antony was consoled by the Saviour and continued unhurt by his wiles and varied devices. As he was watching in the night the devil sent wild beasts against him. And almost all the hyenas in that desert came forth from their dens and surrounded him; and he was in the midst, while each one threatened to bite. Seeing that it was a trick of the enemy he said to them all: 'If you have received power against me I am ready to be devoured by you; but if you were sent against me by demons, stay not, but depart, for I am a servant of Christ.' When Antony said this they fled, driven by that word as with a whip.

53. A few days after, as he was working (for he was careful to work hard), some one stood at the door and pulled the plait which he was working, for he used to weave baskets, which he gave to those who came in return for what they brought him. And rising up he saw a beast like a man to the thighs but having legs and feet like those of an ass. And Antony only signed himself and said, 'I am a servant of Christ. If you are sent against me, behold I am here.' But the beast together with his evil spirits fled, so that, through his speed, he fell and died. And the death of the beast was the fall of the demons. For they strove in all manner of ways to lead Antony from the desert and were not able.

Of the miraculous spring, and how he edified the monks of the 'outer' mountain, and of Antony's sister.

54. And once being asked by the monks to come down and visit them and their abodes after a time, he journeyed with those who came to him. And a camel carried the loaves and the water for them. For all that desert is dry, and there is no water at all that is fit to drink, save in that mountain from whence they drew the water, and in which Antony's cell was. So when the water failed them on their way, and the heat was very great, they all were in danger. For having gone round the neighbourhood and finding no water, they could walk no further, but lay on the ground and despairing of themselves, let the camel go. But the old man seeing that they were all in jeopardy, groaning in deep grief, departed a little way from them, and kneeling down he stretched forth his hands and prayed. And immediately the Lord made water to well forth where he had stood praying, and so all drank and were revived. And having filled their bottles they sought the camel and found her, for the rope happened to have caught in a stone and so was held fast. Having led it and watered it they placed the bottles on its back and finished their journey in safety. And when he came to the outer cells all saluted him, looking on him as a father. And he too, as though bringing supplies from the mountain, entertained them with his words and gave them a share of help. And again there was joy in the mountains, zeal for improvement and consolation through their mutual faith. Antony also rejoiced when he beheld the earnestness of the monks, and his sister grown old in virginity, and that she herself also was the leader of other virgins.

How humanely he counseled those who resorted to him.

55. So after certain days he went in again to the mountain. And henceforth many resorted to him, and others who were suffering ventured to go in. To all the monks therefore who came to him, he continually gave this precept: 'Believe in the Lord and love Him; keep yourselves from filthy thoughts and fleshly pleasures, and as it is written in the Proverbs, be not deceived by the fullness of the belly. Pray continually; avoid vainglory; sing psalms before sleep and

on awaking; hold in your heart the commandments of Scripture; be mindful of the works of the saints that your souls being put in remembrance of the commandments may be brought into harmony with the zeal of the saints.' And especially he counseled them to meditate continually on the apostle's word, 'Let not the sun go down upon your wrath' (Ephesians 4:26). And he considered this was spoken of all commandments in common, and that not on wrath alone, but not on any other sin of ours, ought the sun to go down. For it was good and needful that neither the sun should condemn us for an evil by day nor the moon for a sin by night, or even for an evil thought. That this state may be preserved in us it is good to hear the apostle and keep his words, for he says, 'Try your own selves and prove your own selves' (2 Corinthians 13:5). Daily, therefore, let each one take from himself the tale of his actions both by day and night; and if he have sinned, let him cease from it; while if he have not, let him not be boastful. But let him abide in that which is good, without being negligent, nor condemning his neighbours, nor justifying himself, 'until the Lord come who searches out hidden things', as says the blessed apostle Paul. For often unawares we do things that we know not of; but the Lord sees all things. Wherefore committing the judgment to Him, let us have sympathy one with another. Let us bear each other's burdens (Galatians 6:6): but let us examine our own selves and hasten to fill up that in which we are lacking. And as a safeguard against sin let the following be observed. Let us each one note and write down our actions and the impulses of our soul as though we were going to relate them to each other. And be assured that if we should be utterly ashamed to have them known, we shall abstain from sin and harbour no base thoughts in our mind. For who wishes to be seen while sinning? Or who will not rather lie after the commission of a sin, through the wish to escape notice? As then while we are looking at one another, we would not commit carnal sin, so if we record our thoughts as though about to tell them to one another, we shall the more easily keep ourselves free from vile thoughts through shame lest they should be known. Wherefore let that which is written be to us in place of the eyes of our fellow hermits, that blushing as much to write as if we had been caught, we may never think of what is unseemly. Thus fashioning ourselves we shall be able to keep the body in subjection, to please the Lord, and to trample on the devices of the enemy.

56. This was the advice he gave to those who came to him. And with those who suffered he sympathised and prayed. And oft-times the Lord heard him on behalf of many: yet he boasted not because he was heard, nor did he murmur if he were not. But always he gave the Lord thanks and besought the sufferer to be patient, and to know that healing belonged neither to him nor to man at all, but only to the Lord, who does good when and to whom He will. The sufferers therefore used to receive the words of the old man as though they were a cure, learning not to be downhearted but rather to be long-suffering. And those who were healed were taught not to give thanks to Antony but to God alone.

Of the case of Fronto, healed by faith and prayer.

57. Wherefore a man, Fronto by name, who was an officer of the Court and had a terrible disease, for he used to bite his own tongue and was in danger of injury to his eyes, having come to the mountain, asked Antony to pray for him. But Antony said to him, 'Depart and you shall be healed.' But when he was violent and remained within some days, Antony waited and said, 'If you stay here, you can not be healed. Go, and having come into Egypt you shall see the sign wrought in you.' And he believed and went. And as soon as he set eyes on Egypt his sufferings ceased, and the man became whole according to the word of Antony, which the Saviour had revealed to him in prayer.

Of a certain virgin, and of Paphnutius the confessor.

58. There was also a maiden from Busiris Tripolitana, who had a terrible and very hideous disorder. For the runnings of her eyes, nose, and ears fell to the ground and immediately became worms. She was paralysed also and squinted. Her parents having heard of monks going to Antony, and believing on the Lord who healed the woman with the issue of blood (Matthew 9:20), asked to be allowed, together with their daughter, to journey with them. And when they suffered them, the parents together with the girl, remained outside the mountain with Paphnutius, the confessor and monk; but the monks went

in to Antony. And when they only wished to tell about the damsel, he anticipated them, and detailed both the sufferings of the child and how she journeyed with them. Then when they asked that she should be admitted, Antony did not allow it, but said, 'Go, and if she be not dead, you will find her healed: for the accomplishment of this is not mine, that she should come to me, wretched man that I am, but her healing is the work of the Saviour, who in every place shows His pity to them that call upon Him. Wherefore the Lord has inclined to her as she prayed, and His loving-kindness has declared to me that He will heal the child where she now is.' So the wonder took place; and going out they found the parents rejoicing and the girl whole.

Of the two brethren, and how one perished of thirst.

59. But when two brethren were coming to him, the water failed on the way, and one died and the other was at the point of death, for he had no strength to go on, but lay upon the ground expecting to die. But Antony sitting in the mountain called two monks, who chanced to be there, and urged them saying, 'Take a pitcher of water and run on the road towards Egypt. For of two men who were coming, one is already dead and the other will die unless you hasten. For this has been revealed to me as I was praying.' The monks therefore went, and found one lying dead, whom they buried, and the other they restored with water and led him to the old man. For it was a day's journey. But if any one asks, why he did not speak before the other died, the question ought not to be asked. For the punishment of death was not Antony's but God's, who also judged the one and revealed the condition of the other. But the marvel here was only in the case of Antony: that he sitting in the mountain had his heart watchful, and had the Lord to show him things afar off.

Of the death of Amun, and Antony's vision thereof.

60. And this is so, for once again he was sitting on the mountain, and looking up saw in the air some one being borne upwards, and there was much joy among those who met him. Then wondering and deeming a company of that kind to be blessed, he prayed to

learn what this might be. And immediately a voice came to him: 'This is the soul of Amun, the monk at Nitria.' Now Amun had persevered in the discipline up to old age; and the distance from Nitria to the mountain where Antony was, was thirteen days' journey. The companions of Antony therefore, seeing the old man amazed, asked to learn, and heard that Amun was just dead. And he was well known, for he had stayed there very often, and many signs had been wrought by his means. And this is one of them. Once when he had need to cross the river called Lycus (now it was the season of the flood), he asked his comrade Theodorus to remain at a distance, that they should not see one another naked as they swam the water. Then when Theodorus was departed he again felt ashamed even to see himself naked. While, therefore, he was pondering filled with shame, on a sudden he was borne over to the other side. Theodorus, therefore, himself being a good man, approached, and seeing Amun across first without a drop of water falling from him, inquired how he had got over. And when he saw that Amun was unwilling to tell him, he held him by the feet and declared that he would not let him go before he had learned it from him. So Amun seeing the determination of Theodorus especially from what he had said, and having asked him to tell no man before his death, told him that he had been carried and placed on the further side. And that he had not even set foot on the water, nor was that possible for man, but for the Lord alone and those whom He permits, as He did for the great apostle Peter (Matthew 14:28). Theodorus therefore told this after the death of Amun. And the monks to whom Antony spoke concerning Amun's death marked the day; and when the brethren came up from Nitria thirty days after, they inquired of them and learned that Amun had fallen asleep at that day and hour in which the old man had seen his soul borne upwards. And both these and the others marveled at the purity of Antony's soul, how he had immediately learned that which was taking place at a distance of thirteen days' journey, and had seen the soul as it was taken up.

Of Count Archelaus and the virgin Polycration.

61. And Archelaus too, the Count, on a time having found him in the outer mountain, asked him merely to pray for Polycratia of

Laodicea, an excellent and Christian maiden, for she suffered terribly in the stomach and side through over much discipline, and was altogether weakly of body. Antony prayed therefore, and the Count noted the day in which the prayer was made, and having departed to Laodicea he found the maiden whole. And having inquired when and on what day she was relieved of her infirmity, he produced the paper on which he had written the time of the prayer, and having read it he immediately showed the writing on the paper. And all wondered when they knew that the Lord had relieved her of pain at the time when Antony was praying and invoking the goodness of the Saviour on her behalf.

62. And concerning those who came to him, he often foretold some days or sometimes a month beforehand what was the cause of their coming. For some came only for the sake of seeing him, others through sickness, and others suffering from evil spirits. And all thought the labour of the journey neither trouble nor loss. For each one returned aware that he had received benefit. But though saying such things and beholding such sights, he used to ask that no one should wonder at him for this; but should rather marvel at the Lord for having granted to us men to know Him as far as our powers extended.

Strange tales of the casting out of demons.

63. Afterwards, on another occasion, having descended to the outer cells, he was asked to enter a vessel and pray with the monks, and he alone perceived an exceedingly unpleasant smell. But those on board said that the stench arose from the fish and salt meat in the ship. He replied however, the smell was different from that; and while he was speaking, a youth with an evil spirit, who had come and hidden himself in the ship, cried out. But the demon being rebuked in the name of the Lord Jesus Christ departed from him, and the man became whole. And all knew that the evil smell arose from the demon.

64. And another, a person of rank, came to him, possessed by a demon; and the demon was so terrible that the man possessed did not know that he was coming to Antony. But he even ate the excreta

from his body. So those who brought him besought Antony to pray for him. And Antony pitying the young man prayed and kept watch with him all the night. And about dawn the young man suddenly attacked Antony and gave him a push. But when those who came with him were angry, Antony said, 'Be not angry with the young man, for it is not he, but the demon which is in him. And being rebuked and commanded to go into dry places, the demon became raging mad, and he has done this. Wherefore give thanks to the Lord, for his attack on me thus is a sign of the departure of the evil spirit.' When Antony had said this, straightway the young man had become whole, and having come at last to his right mind, knew where he was, and saluted the old man and gave thanks to God.

Of Antony's vision concerning the forgiveness of his sins.

65. And many monks have related with the greatest agreement and unanimity that many other such like things were done by him. But still these do not seem as marvelous as certain other things appear to be. For once, when about to eat, having risen up to pray about the ninth hour, he perceived that he was caught up in the spirit, and, wonderful to tell, he stood and saw himself, as it were, from outside himself, and that he was led in the air by certain ones. Next certain bitter and terrible beings stood in the air and wished to hinder him from passing through. But when his conductors opposed them, they demanded whether he was not accountable to them. And when they wished to sum up the account from his birth, Antony's conductors stopped them, saying, 'The Lord has wiped out the sins from his birth, but from the time he became a monk, and devoted himself to God, it is permitted you to make a reckoning.' Then when they accused him and could not convict him, his way was free and unhindered. And immediately he saw himself, as it were, coming and standing by himself, and again he was Antony as before. Then forgetful of eating, he remained the rest of the day and through the whole of the night groaning and praying. For he was astonished when he saw against what mighty opponents our wrestling is, and by what labours we have to pass through the air. And he remembered that this is what the Apostle said, 'according to the prince of the

power of the air' (Ephesians 2:2). For in it the enemy has power to fight and to attempt to hinder those who pass through. Wherefore most earnestly he exhorted, 'Take up the whole armour of God, that you may be able to withstand in the evil day' (Ephesians 6:13), that the enemy, 'having no evil thing to say against us, may be ashamed' (Titus 2:8). And we who have learned this, let us be mindful of the Apostle when he says, 'whether in the body I know not, or whether out of the body I know not; God knows' (2 Corinthians 12:2). But Paul was caught up unto the third heaven, and having heard things unspeakable he came down; while Antony saw that he had come to the air, and contended until he was free.

Of the passage of souls, and how some were hindered of Satan.

66. And he had also this favour granted him. For as he was sitting alone on the mountain, if ever he was in perplexity in his meditations, this was revealed to him by Providence in prayer. And the happy man, as it is written, was taught of God. After this, when he once had a discussion with certain men who had come to him concerning the state of the soul and of what nature its place will be after this life, the following night one from above called him, saying, 'Antony, rise, go out and look.' Having gone out therefore (for he knew whom he ought to obey) looking up, he beheld one standing and reaching to the clouds, tall, hideous, and fearful, and others ascending as though they were winged. And the figure stretched forth his hands, and some of those who were ascending were stayed by him, while others flew above, and having escaped heaven-ward, were borne aloft free from care. At such, therefore, the giant gnashed his teeth, but rejoiced over those who fell back. And immediately a voice came to Antony, 'Do you understand what you see?' And his understanding was opened, and he understood that it was the passing of souls, and that the tall being who stood was the enemy who envies the faithful. And those whom he caught and stopped from passing through are accountable to him, while those whom he was unable to hold as they passed upwards had not been subservient to him. So having seen this, and as it were being reminded, he struggled the more daily to advance towards those things which were before. And

these visions he was unwilling to tell, but as he spent much time in prayer, and was amazed, when those who were with him pressed him with questions and forced him, he was compelled to speak, as a father who cannot withhold ought from his children. And he thought that as his conscience was clear, the account would be beneficial for them, that they might learn that discipline bore good fruit, and that visions were oftentimes the solace of their labours.

How Antony reverenced all ordained persons.

67. Added to this he was tolerant in disposition and humble in spirit. For though he was such a man, he observed the rule of the Church most rigidly, and was willing that all the clergy should be honoured above himself. For he was not ashamed to bow his head to bishops and presbyters, and if ever a deacon came to him for help he discoursed with him on what was profitable, but gave place to him in prayer, not being ashamed to learn himself. For often he would ask questions, and desired to listen to those who were present, and if any one said anything that was useful he confessed that he was profited. And besides, his countenance had a great and wonderful grace. This gift also he had from the Saviour. For if he were present in a great company of monks, and any one who did not know him previously, wished to see him, immediately coming forward he passed by the rest, and hurried to Antony, as though attracted by his appearance. Yet neither in height nor breadth was he conspicuous above others, but in the serenity of his manner and the purity of his soul. For as his soul was free from disturbances, his outward appearance was calm; so from the joy of his soul he possessed a cheerful countenance, and from his bodily movements could be perceived the condition of his soul, as it is written, 'When the heart is merry the countenance is cheerful, but when it is sorrowful it is cast down' (Proverbs 15:13). Thus Jacob recognised the counsel Laban had in his heart, and said to his wives, 'The countenance of your father is not as it was yesterday and the day before.' Thus Samuel recognised David, for he had mirthful eyes, and teeth white as milk. Thus Antony was recognised, for he was never disturbed, for his soul was at peace; he was never downcast, for his mind was joyous.

How he rejected the schism of Meletius and the heresies of Manes and Arius.

68. And he was altogether wonderful in faith and religious, for he never held communion with the Meletian schismatics, knowing their wickedness and apostasy from the beginning; nor had he friendly dealings with the Manichæans or any other heretics; or, if he had, only as far as advice that they should change to piety. For he thought and asserted that intercourse with these was harmful and destructive to the soul. In the same manner also he loathed the heresy of the Arians, and exhorted all neither to approach them nor to hold their erroneous belief. And once when certain Arian madmen came to him, when he had questioned them and learned their impiety, he drove them from the mountain, saying that their words were worse than the poison of serpents.

How he confuted the Arians.

69. And once also the Arians having lyingly asserted that Antony's opinions were the same as theirs, he was displeased and angry against them. Then being summoned by the bishops and all the brethren, he descended from the mountain, and having entered Alexandria, he denounced the Arians, saying that their heresy was the last of all and a forerunner of Antichrist. And he taught the people that the Son of God was not a created being, neither had He come into being from non-existence, but that He was the Eternal Word and Wisdom of the Essence of the Father. And therefore it was impious to say, 'there was a time when He was not,' for the Word was always co-existent with the Father. Wherefore have no fellowship with the most impious Arians. For there is no communion between light and darkness (2 Corinthians 6:14). For you are good Christians, but they, when they say that the Son of the Father, the Word of God, is a created being, differ in naught from the heathen, since they worship that which is created, rather than God the creator. But believe that the Creation itself is angry with them because they number the Creator, the Lord of all, by whom all things came into being, with those things which were originated.

How he visited Alexandria, and healed and converted many, and how Athanasius escorted him from the city.

70. All the people, therefore, rejoiced when they heard the anti-Christian heresy anathematised by such a man. And all the people in the city ran together to see Antony; and the Greeks and those who are called their Priests, came into the church, saying, 'We ask to see the man of God,' for so they all called him. For in that place also the Lord cleansed many of demons, and healed those who were mad. And many Greeks asked that they might even but touch the old man, believing that they should be profited. Assuredly as many became Christians in those few days as one would have seen made in a year. Then when some thought that he was troubled by the crowds, and on this account turned them all away from him, he said, undisturbedly, that there were not more of them than of the demons with whom he wrestled in the mountain.

71. But when he was departing, and we were setting him forth on his way, as we arrived at the gate a woman from behind cried out, 'Stay, thou man of God, my daughter is grievously vexed by a devil. Stay, I beseech you, lest I too harm myself with running.' And the old man when he heard her, and was asked by us, willingly stayed. And when the woman drew near, the child was cast on the ground. But when Antony had prayed and called upon the name of Christ, the child was raised whole, for the unclean spirit had gone forth. And the mother blessed God, and all gave thanks. And Antony himself also rejoiced, departing to the mountain as though it were to his own home.

How he reasoned with divers Greeks and philosophers at the 'outer' mountain.

72. And Antony also was exceeding prudent, and the wonder was that although he had not learned letters, he was a ready-witted and sagacious man. At all events two Greek philosophers once came, thinking they could try their skill on Antony; and he was in the outer mountain, and having recognised who they were from their appearance, he came to them and said to them by means of an interpreter, 'Why, philosophers, did ye trouble yourselves so much to come to a

foolish man?' And when they said that he was not a foolish man, but exceedingly prudent, he said to them, 'If you came to a foolish man, your labour is superfluous; but if you think me prudent become as I am, for we ought to imitate what is good. And if I had come to you I should have imitated you; but if you to me, become as I am, for I am a Christian.' But they departed with wonder, for they saw that even demons feared Antony.

73. And again others such as these met him in the outer mountain and thought to mock him because he had not learned letters. And Antony said to them, 'What do you say? Which is first, mind or letters? And which is the cause of which—mind of letters or letters of mind.' And when they answered mind is first and the inventor of letters, Antony said, 'Whoever, therefore, has a sound mind has not need of letters.' This answer amazed both the bystanders and the philosophers, and they departed marveling that they had seen so much understanding in an ignorant man. For his manners were not rough as though he had been reared in the mountain and there grown old, but graceful and polite, and his speech was seasoned with the divine salt, so that no one was envious, but rather all rejoiced over him who visited him.

74. After this again certain others came; and these were men who were deemed wise among the Greeks, and they asked him a reason for our faith in Christ. But when they attempted to dispute concerning the preaching of the divine Cross and meant to mock, Antony stopped for a little, and first pitying their ignorance, said, through an interpreter, who could skilfully interpret his words, 'Which is more beautiful, to confess the Cross or to attribute to those whom you call gods adultery and the seduction of boys? For that which is chosen by us is a sign of courage and a sure token of the contempt of death, while yours are the passions of licentiousness. Next, which is better, to say that the Word of God was not changed, but, being the same, He took a human body for the salvation and well-being of man, that having shared in human birth He might make man partake in the divine and spiritual nature; or to liken the divine to senseless animals and consequently to worship four-footed beasts, creeping things and the likenesses of men? For these things, are the objects of

reverence of you wise men. But how do you dare to mock us, who say that Christ has appeared as man, seeing that you, bringing the soul from heaven, assert that it has strayed and fallen from the vault of the sky into body? And would that you had said that it had fallen into human body alone, and not asserted that it passes and changes into four-footed beasts and creeping things. For our faith declares that the coming of Christ was for the salvation of men. But you err because you speak of soul as not generated. And we, considering the power and loving-kindness of Providence, think that the coming of Christ in the flesh was not impossible with God. But you, although calling the soul the likeness of Mind, connect it with falls and feign in your myths that it is changeable, and consequently introduce the idea that Mind itself is changeable by reason of the soul. For whatever is the nature of a likeness, such necessarily is the nature of that of which it is a likeness. But whenever you think such a thought concerning Mind, remember that you blaspheme even the Father of Mind Himself.

75. But concerning the Cross, which would you say to be the better, to bear it, when a plot is brought about by wicked men, nor to be in fear of death brought about under any form whatever ; or to prate about the wanderings of Osiris and Isis, the plots of Typhon, the flight of Cronos, his eating his children and the slaughter of his father. For this is your wisdom. But how, if you mock the Cross, do you not marvel at the resurrection? For the same men who told us of the latter wrote the former. Or why when you make mention of the Cross are you silent about the dead who were raised, the blind who received their sight, the paralytics who were healed, the lepers who were cleansed, the walking upon the sea, and the rest of the signs and wonders, which show that Christ is no longer a man but God? To me you seem to do yourselves much injustice and not to have carefully read our Scriptures. But read and see that the deeds of Christ prove Him to be God come upon earth for the salvation of men.

76. But do you tell us your religious beliefs. What can you say of senseless creatures except senselessness and ferocity? But if, as I hear, you wish to say that these things are spoken of by you as legends, and you allegorize the rape of the maiden Persephone of the

earth; the lameness of Hephæstus of fire; and allegorize the air as Hera, the sun as Apollo, the moon as Artemis, and the sea as Poseidon; none the less, you do not worship God Himself, but serve the creature rather than God who created all things. For if because creation is beautiful you composed such legends, still it was fitting that you should stop short at admiration and not make gods of the things created; so that you should not give the honour of the Creator to that which is created. Since, if you do, it is time for you to divert the honour of the master builder to the house built by him; and of the general to the soldier. What then can you reply to these things, that we may know whether the Cross has anything worthy of mockery?'

77. But when they were at a loss, turning hither and there, Antony smiled and said—again through an interpreter—'Sight itself carries the conviction of these things. But as you prefer to lean upon demonstrative arguments, and as you, having this art, wish us also not to worship God, until after such proof, do you tell first how things in general and specially the recognition of God are accurately known. Is it through demonstrative argument or the working of faith? And which is better, faith which comes through the inworking (of God) or demonstration by arguments?' And when they answered that faith which comes through the inworking was better and was accurate knowledge, Antony said, 'You have answered well, for faith arises from disposition of soul, but dialectic from the skill of its inventors. Wherefore to those who have the inworking through faith, demonstrative argument is needless, or even superfluous. For what we know through faith this you attempt to prove through words, and often you are not even able to express what we understand. So the inworking through faith is better and stronger than your professional arguments.'

78. 'We Christians therefore hold the mystery not in the wisdom of Greek arguments, but in the power of faith richly supplied to us by God through Jesus Christ. And to show that this statement is true, behold now, without having learned letters, we believe in God, knowing through His works His providence over all things. And to show that our faith is effective, so now we are supported by faith in Christ, but you by professional logomachies. The portents of the

idols among you are being done away, but our faith is extending everywhere. You by your arguments and quibbles have converted none from Christianity to Paganism. We, teaching the faith on Christ, expose your superstition, since all recognise that Christ is God and the Son of God. You by your eloquence do not hinder the teaching of Christ. But we by the mention of Christ crucified put all demons to flight, whom you fear as if they were gods. Where the sign of the Cross is, magic is weak and witchcraft has no strength.

79. 'Tell us therefore where your oracles are now? Where are the charms of the Egyptians? Where the delusions of the magicians? When did all these things cease and grow weak except when the Cross of Christ arose? Is It then a fit subject for mockery, and not rather the things brought to naught by it, and convicted of weakness? For this is a marvelous thing, that your religion was never persecuted, but even was honoured by men in every city, while the followers of Christ are persecuted, and still our side flourishes and multiplies over yours. What is yours, though praised and honoured, perishes, while the faith and teaching of Christ, though mocked by you and often persecuted by kings, has filled the world. For when has the knowledge of God so shone forth? Or when has self-control and the excellence of virginity appeared as now? Or when has death been so despised except when the Cross of Christ has appeared? And this no one doubts when he sees the martyr despising death for the sake of Christ, when he sees for Christ's sake the virgins of the Church keeping themselves pure and undefiled.

How he confuted the philosophers by healing certain vexed with demons.

80. 'And these signs are sufficient to prove that the faith of Christ alone is the true religion. But see! You still do not believe and are seeking for arguments. We however make our proof not in the persuasive words of Greek wisdom (1 Corinthians 2:4) as our teacher has it, but we persuade by the faith which manifestly precedes argumentative proof. Behold there are here some vexed with demons'—now there were certain who had come to him very disquieted by demons, and bringing them into the midst he said—'Do you cleanse them either by arguments and by whatever art or magic you choose,

calling upon your idols, or if you are unable, put away your strife with us and you shall see the power of the Cross of Christ.' And having said this he called upon Christ, and signed the sufferers two or three times with the sign of the Cross. And immediately the men stood up whole, and in their right mind, and immediately gave thanks unto the Lord. And the philosophers, as they are called, wondered, and were astonished exceedingly at the understanding of the man and at the sign which had been wrought. But Antony said, 'Why marvel ye at this? We are not the doers of these things, but it is Christ who works them by means of those who believe in Him. Believe, therefore, also yourselves, and you shall see that with us there is no trick of words, but faith through love which is wrought in us towards Christ; which if you yourselves should obtain you will no longer seek demonstrative arguments, but will consider faith in Christ sufficient.' These are the words of Antony. And they marveling at this also, saluted him and departed, confessing the benefit they had received from him.

How the Emperors wrote to Antony, and of his answer.

81. And the fame of Antony came even unto kings. For Constantine Augustus, and his sons Constantius and Constans the Augusti wrote letters to him, as to a father, and begged an answer from him. But he made nothing very much of the letters, nor did he rejoice at the messages, but was the same as he had been before the Emperors wrote to him. But when they brought him the letters he called the monks and said, 'Do not be astonished if an emperor writes to us, for he is a man; but rather wonder that God wrote the Law for men and has spoken to us through His own Son (Hebrews 1:2)'. And so he was unwilling to receive the letters, saying that he did not know how to write an answer to such things. But being urged by the monks because the emperors were Christians, and lest they should take offense on the ground that they had been spurned, he consented that they should be read, and wrote an answer approving them because they worshiped Christ, and giving them counsel on things pertaining to salvation: 'not to think much of the present, but rather to remember the judgment that is coming, and to know that Christ alone was the true and Eternal King.' He begged them to be merciful and to give heed to justice and the poor. And they having received the

answer rejoiced. Thus he was dear to all, and all desired to consider him as a father.

How he saw in a vision the present doings of the Arians.

82. Being known to be so great a man, therefore, and having thus given answers to those who visited him, he returned again to the inner mountain, and maintained his wonted discipline. And often when people came to him, as he was sitting or walking, as it is written in Daniel, he became dumb, and after a season he resumed the thread of what he had been saying before to the brethren who were with him. And his companions perceived that he was seeing a vision. For often when he was on the mountains he saw what was happening in Egypt, and told it to Serapion the bishop, who was indoors with him, and who saw that Antony was wrapped in a vision. Once as he was sitting and working, he fell, as it were, into a trance, and groaned much at what he saw. Then after a time, having turned to the bystanders with groans and trembling, he prayed, and falling on his knees remained so a long time. And having arisen the old man wept. His companions, therefore, trembling and terrified, desired to learn from him what it was. And they troubled him much, until he was forced to speak. And with many groans he spoke as follows: 'O, my children, it were better to die before what has appeared in the vision come to pass.' And when again they asked him, having burst into tears, he said, 'Wrath is about to seize the Church, and it is on the point of being given up to men who are like senseless beasts. For I saw the table of the Lord's House, and mules standing around it on all sides in a ring, and kicking the things therein, just like a herd kicks when it leaps in confusion. And you saw,' said he, 'how I groaned, for I heard a voice saying, My altar shall be defiled.' These things the old man saw, and after two years the present inroad of the Arians and the plunder of the churches took place, when they violently carried off the vessels, and made the heathen carry them; and when they forced the heathen from the prisons to join in their services, and in their presence did upon the Table as they would. Then we all understood that these kicks of the mules signified to Antony what the Arians, senselessly like beasts, are now doing. But when he saw this

vision, he comforted those with him, saying, 'Be not downcast, my children; for as the Lord has been angry, so again will He heal us, and the Church shall soon again receive her own order, and shall shine forth as she is wont. And you shall behold the persecuted restored, and wickedness again withdrawn to its own hiding-place, and pious faith speaking boldly in every place with all freedom. Only defile not yourselves with the Arians, for their teaching is not that of the Apostles, but that of demons and their father the devil; yea, rather, it is barren and senseless, and without light understanding, like the senselessness of these mules.'

That his healings were done by Christ alone, through prayer.

83. Such are the words of Antony, and we ought not to doubt whether such marvels were wrought by the hand of a man. For it is the promise of the Saviour, when He says, 'If you have faith as a grain of mustard seed, you shall say to this mountain, remove hence and it shall remove; and nothing shall be impossible unto you' (Matthew 17:20). And again, 'Verily, verily, I say unto you, if you shall ask the father in My name He will give it you. Ask and you shall receive' (John 16:23). And He himself it is who says to His disciples and to all who believe in Him, 'Heal the sick, cast out demons; freely you have received, freely give' (Matthew 10:8).

84. Antony, at any rate, healed not by commanding, but by prayer and speaking the name of Christ. So that it was clear to all that it was not he himself who worked, but the Lord who showed mercy by his means and healed the sufferers. But Antony's part was only prayer and discipline, for the sake of which he stayed in the mountain, rejoicing in the contemplation of divine things, but grieving when troubled by much people, and dragged to the outer mountain. For all judges used to ask him to come down, because it was impossible for them to enter on account of their following of litigants. But nevertheless they asked him to come that they might but see him. When therefore he avoided it and refused to go to them, they remained firm, and sent to him all the more the prisoners under charge of soldiers, that on account of these he might come down.

Being forced by necessity, and seeing them lamenting, he came into the outer mountain, and again his labour was not unprofitable. For his coming was advantageous and serviceable to many; and he was of profit to the judges, counseling them to prefer justice to all things; to fear God, and to know, 'that with what judgment they judged, they should be judged' (Matthew 7:2). But he loved more than all things his sojourn in the mountain.

How wisely he answered a certain duke.

85. At another time, suffering the same compulsion at the hands of them who had need, and after many entreaties from the commander of the soldiers, he came down, and when he had come he spoke to them shortly of the things which make for salvation, and concerning those who wanted him, and was hastening away. But when the duke, as he is called, entreated him to stay, he replied that he could not linger among them, and persuaded him by a pretty simile, saying, 'Fishes, if they remain long on dry land, die. And so monks lose their strength if they loiter among you and spend their time with you. Wherefore as fish must hurry to the sea, so must we hasten to the mountain. Lest haply if we delay we forget the things within us.' And the general having heard this and many other things from him, was amazed and said, 'Of a truth this man is the servant of God. For, unless he were beloved of God, whence could an ignorant man have such great understanding?'

Of the Duke Balacius, and how, warned by Antony, he met with a miserable end.

86. And a certain general, Balacius by name, persecuted us Christians bitterly on account of his regard for the Arians—that name of ill omen. And as his ruthlessness was so great that he beat virgins, and stripped and scourged monks, Antony at this time wrote a letter as follows, and sent it to him. 'I see wrath coming upon you, wherefore cease to persecute the Christians, lest haply wrath catch hold of you, for even now it is on the point of coming upon you.' But Balacius laughed and threw the letter on the ground, and spit on

it, and insulted the bearers, bidding them tell this to Antony: 'Since you take thought for the monks, soon I will come after you also.' And five days had not passed before wrath came upon him. For Balacius and Nestorius, the Prefect of Egypt , went forth to the first halting-place from Alexandria, which is called Chæreu, and both were on horseback, and the horses belonged to Balacius, and were the quietest of all his stable. But they had not gone far towards the place when the horses began to frisk with one another as they are wont to do; and suddenly the quieter, on which Nestorius sat , with a bite dismounted Balacius, and attacked him, and tore his thigh so badly with its teeth that he was borne straight back to the city, and in three days died. And all wondered because what Antony had foretold had been so speedily fulfilled.

How he bore the infirmities of the weak, and of his great benefits to all Egypt.

87. Thus, therefore, he warned the cruel. But the rest who came to him he so instructed that they straightway forgot their lawsuits, and felicitated those who were in retirement from the world. And he championed those who were wronged in such a way that you would imagine that he, and not the others, was the sufferer. Further, he was able to be of such use to all, that many soldiers and men who had great possessions laid aside the burdens of life, and became monks for the rest of their days. And it was as if a physician had been given by God to Egypt. For who in grief met Antony and did not return rejoicing? Who came mourning for his dead and did not immediately put off his sorrow? Who came in anger and was not converted to friendship? What poor and low-spirited man met him who, hearing him and looking upon him, did not despise wealth and console himself in his poverty? What monk, having being neglectful, came to him and became not all the stronger? What young man having come to the mountain and seen Antony, did not immediately deny himself pleasure and love temperance? Who when tempted by a demon, came to him and did not find rest? And who came troubled with doubts and did not get quietness of mind?

Of his discernment, and how he was a counselor to all.

88. For this was the wonderful thing in Antony's discipline, that, as I said before, having the gift of discerning spirits, he recognised their movements, and was not ignorant whither any one of them turned his energy and made his attack. And not only was he not deceived by them himself, but cheering those who were troubled with doubts, he taught them how to defeat their plans, telling them of the weakness and craft of those who possessed them. Thus each one, as though prepared by him for battle, came down from the mountain, braving the designs of the devil and his demons. How many maidens who had suitors, having but seen Antony from afar, remained maidens for Christ's sake. And people came also from foreign parts to him, and like all others, having got some benefit, returned, as though set forward by a father. And certainly when he died, all as having been bereft of a father, consoled themselves solely by their remembrances of him, preserving at the same time his counsel and advice.

How, when now 105 years old, he counseled the monks, and gave advice concerning burial.

89. It is worth while that I should relate, and that you, as you wish it, should hear what his death was like. For this end of his is worthy of imitation. According to his custom he visited the monks in the outer mountain, and having learned from Providence that his own end was at hand, he said to the brethren, 'This is my last visit to you which I shall make. And I shall be surprised if we see each other again in this life. At length the time of my departure is at hand, for I am near a hundred and five years old.' And when they heard it they wept, and embraced, and kissed the old man. But he, as though sailing from a foreign city to his own, spoke joyously, and exhorted them 'Not to grow idle in their labours, nor to become faint in their training, but to live as though dying daily. And as he had said before, zealously to guard the soul from foul thoughts, eagerly to imitate the Saints, and to have naught to do with the Meletian schismatics, for you know their wicked and profane character. Nor have any fellowship with the Arians, for their impiety is clear to all. Nor be disturbed if you see the judges protect them, for it shall cease, and their pomp

is mortal and of short duration. Wherefore keep yourselves all the more untainted by them, and observe the traditions of the fathers, and chiefly the holy faith in our Lord Jesus Christ, which you have learned from the Scripture, and of which you have often been put in mind by me.'

90. But when the brethren were urging him to abide with them and there to die, he suffered it not for many other reasons, as he showed by keeping silence, and especially for this: The Egyptians are wont to honour with funeral rites, and to wrap in linen cloths at death the bodies of good men, and especially of the holy martyrs; and not to bury them underground, but to place them on couches, and to keep them in their houses, thinking in this to honour the departed. And Antony often urged the bishops to give commandment to the people on this matter. In like manner he taught the laity and reproved the women, saying, 'that this thing was neither lawful nor holy at all. For the bodies of the patriarchs and prophets are until now preserved in tombs, and the very body of the Lord was laid in a tomb, and a stone was laid upon it, and hid it until He rose on the third day. ' And thus saying, he showed that he who did not bury the bodies of the dead after death transgressed the law, even though they were sacred. For what is greater or more sacred than the body of the Lord? Many therefore having heard, henceforth buried the dead underground, and gave thanks to the Lord that they had been taught rightly.

Of his sickness and his last will.

91. But he, knowing the custom, and fearing that his body would be treated this way, hastened, and having bidden farewell to the monks in the outer mountain entered the inner mountain, where he was accustomed to abide. And after a few months he fell sick. Having summoned those who were there—they were two in number who had remained in the mountain fifteen years, practising the discipline and attending on Antony on account of his age—he said to them, 'I, as it is written Joshua 23:14, go the way of the fathers, for I perceive that I am called by the Lord. And do you be watchful and destroy not your long discipline, but as though now making a beginning, zealously preserve your determination. For you know the

treachery of the demons, how fierce they are, but how little power they have. Wherefore fear them not, but rather ever breathe Christ, and trust Him. Live as though dying daily. Give heed to yourselves, and remember the admonition you have heard from me. Have no fellowship with the schismatics, nor any dealings at all with the heretical Arians. For you know how I shunned them on account of their hostility to Christ, and the strange doctrines of their heresy. Therefore be the more earnest always to be followers first of God and then of the Saints; that after death they also may receive you as well-known friends into the eternal habitations. Ponder over these things and think of them, and if you have any care for me and are mindful of me as of a father, suffer no one to take my body into Egypt, lest haply they place me in the houses , for to avoid this I entered into the mountain and came here. Moreover you know how I always put to rebuke those who had this custom, and exhorted them to cease from it. Bury my body, therefore, and hide it underground yourselves, and let my words be observed by you that no one may know the place but you alone. For at the resurrection of the dead I shall receive it incorruptible from the Saviour. And divide my garments. To Athanasius the bishop give one sheepskin and the garment whereon I am laid, which he himself gave me new, but which with me has grown old. To Serapion the bishop give the other sheepskin, and keep the hair garment yourselves. For the rest fare ye well, my children, for Antony is departing, and is with you no more.'

Of Antony's death.

92. Having said this, when they had kissed him, he lifted up his feet, and as though he saw friends coming to him and was glad because of them—for as he lay his countenance appeared joyful—he died and was gathered to the fathers. And they afterward, according to his commandment, wrapped him up and buried him, hiding his body underground. And no one knows to this day where it was buried, save those two only. But each of those who received the sheepskin of the blessed Antony and the garment worn by him guards it as a precious treasure. For even to look on them is as it were to behold Antony; and he who is clothed in them seems with joy to bear his admonitions.

How Antony remained hale until his death, and how the fame of him filled all the world.

93. This is the end of Antony's life in the body and the above was the beginning of the discipline. Even if this account is small compared with his merit, still from this reflect how great Antony, the man of God, was. Who from his youth to so great an age preserved a uniform zeal for the discipline, and neither through old age was subdued by the desire of costly food, nor through the infirmity of his body changed the fashion of his clothing, nor washed even his feet with water, and yet remained entirely free from harm. For his eyes were undimmed and quite sound and he saw clearly; of his teeth he had not lost one, but they had become worn to the gums through the great age of the old man. He remained strong both in hands and feet; and while all men were using various foods, and washings and various garments, he appeared more cheerful and of greater strength. And the fact that his fame has been blazoned everywhere; that all regard him with wonder, and that those who have never seen him long for him, is clear proof of his virtue and God's love of his soul. For not from writings, nor from worldly wisdom, nor through any art, was Antony renowned, but solely from his piety towards God. That this was the gift of God no one will deny. For from whence into Spain and into Gaul, how into Rome and Africa, was the man heard of who abode hidden in a mountain, unless it was God who makes His own known everywhere, who also promised this to Antony at the beginning? For even if they work secretly, even if they wish to remain in obscurity, yet the Lord shows them as lamps to lighten all, that those who hear may thus know that the precepts of God are able to make men prosper and thus be zealous in the path of virtue.

The end

94. Read these words, therefore, to the rest of the brethren that they may learn what the life of monks ought to be; and may believe that our Lord and Saviour Jesus Christ glorifies those who glorify Him: and leads those who serve Him unto the end, not only to the kingdom of heaven, but here also—even though they hide

themselves and are desirous of withdrawing from the world—makes them illustrious and well known everywhere on account of their virtue and the help they render others. And if need be, read this among the heathen, that even in this way they may learn that our Lord Jesus Christ is not only God and the Son of God, but also that the Christians who truly serve Him and religiously believe in Him, prove, not only that the demons, whom the Greeks themselves think to be gods, are no gods, but also tread them under foot and put them to flight, as deceivers and corrupters of mankind, through Jesus Christ our Lord, to whom be glory for ever and ever. Amen.

JOHN CHRYSOSTOM

Paschal Homily

John Chrysostom

Unknown Translator

If any man be devout and loveth God,
let him enjoy this fair and radiant triumphal feast!
If any man be a wise servant,
let him rejoicing enter into the joy of his Lord.
If any have laboured long in fasting,
let him how receive his recompense.
If any have wrought from the first hour,
let him today receive his just reward.
If any have come at the third hour,
let him with thankfulness keep the feast.
If any have arrived at the sixth hour,
let him have no misgivings; because he shall in nowise be deprived therefore.
If any have delayed until the ninth hour,
let him draw near, fearing nothing.
And if any have tarried even until the eleventh hour,
let him, also, be not alarmed at his tardiness.

For the Lord, who is jealous of His honour,
will accept the last even as the first.
He giveth rest unto him who cometh at the eleventh hour,
even as unto him who hath wrought from the first hour.

And He showeth mercy upon the last,
  and careth for the first;
And to the one He giveth,
  and upon the other He bestoweth gifts.
And He both accepteth the deeds,
  and welcometh the intention,
  and honoureth the acts and praises the offering.

Wherefore, enter ye all into the joy of your Lord.
Receive your reward, both the first,
  and likewise the second.
You rich and poor together, hold high festival!
You sober and you heedless, honour the day!
Rejoice today, both you who have fasted
  and you who have disregarded the fast.
The table is full-laden; feast ye all sumptuously.
The calf is fatted; let no one go hungry away.
Enjoy ye all the feast of faith:
  receive ye all the riches of lovingkindness.

Let no one bewail his poverty,
  for the universal Kingdom has been revealed.
Let no one weep for his iniquities,
  for pardon has shown forth from the grave.
Let no one fear death,
  for the Saviour's death has set us free.

He that was held prisoner of it has annihilated it.
By descending into Hell, He made Hell captive.
He embittered it when it tasted of His flesh.
And Isaiah, foretelling this, did cry:

Hell, said he, was embittered when it encountered Thee in the lower regions.
  It was embittered, for it was abolished.
  It was embittered, for it was mocked.
  It was embittered, for it was slain.
  It was embittered, for it was overthrown.

It was embittered, for it was fettered in chains.
It took a body, and met God face to face.
It took earth, and encountered Heaven.
It took that which it saw, and fell upon that which cannot be seen.

O Death, where is thy sting?
O Hell, where is thy victory?

Christ is risen, and thou art overthrown!
Christ is risen, and the demons are fallen!
Christ is risen, and the angels rejoice!
Christ is risen, and life reigns!
Christ is risen, and not one dead remains in the grave.

For Christ, being risen from the dead, is become the first-fruits of those who have fallen asleep.

To Him be glory and dominion unto ages of ages.
Amen.

JOHN CHRYSOSTOM

Baptismal Instructions

John Chrysostom

Translated by T. P. Brandram

First Instruction

To those about to be illuminated; and for what reason the laver is said to be of regeneration and not of remission of sins; and that it is a dangerous thing not only to forswear oneself, but also to take an oath, even though we swear truly.

1. How delightful and loveable is our band of young brethren! For brethren I call you, even now before you have been brought forth, and before your birth I welcome this relationship with you: For I know, I know clearly, to how great an honour you are about to be led, and to how great a dignity; and those who are about to receive dignity, all are wont to honour, even before the dignity is conferred, laying up for themselves beforehand by their attention good will for the future. And this also I myself now do. For you are not about to be led to an empty dignity, but to an actual kingdom: and not simply to a kingdom, but to the kingdom of the Heavens itself. Wherefore I beseech and entreat you that you remember me when you come into that kingdom, and as Joseph said to the chief butler *"Remember me when it shall be well with you"* (Genesis 40:14). This also I say now to you, do ye remember me when it is well with you. I do not ask this in return for interpreting your dreams, as he; for I have not come to

interpret dreams for you, but to discourse of matters celestial, and to convey to you glad tidings of such good things as *"eye has not seen, and ear has not heard and which have entered not into the heart of man, such are the things which God has prepared for them that love Him"* (1 Corinthians 2:9-10). Now Joseph indeed said to that chief butler, *"yet three days and Pharaoh will restore you to your chief butlership"*. But I do not say, yet three days and you shall be set to pour out the wine of a tyrant, but yet thirty days, and not Pharaoh but the king of Heaven shall restore you to the country which is on high, Jerusalem, which is free—to the city which is in the Heavens; and he said indeed *"You shall give the cup into the hands of Pharaoh"*. But I say not that you shall give the cup into the hands of the king, but that the king shall give the cup into your hand—that dread cup, full of much power, and more precious than any created thing. The initiated know the virtue of this cup, and you yourselves shall know it a little while hence. Remember me, therefore, when you come into that kingdom, when you receive the royal robe, when you are girt with the purple dipped in the master's blood, when you will be crowned with the diadem, which has lustre leaping forth from it on all sides, more brilliant than the rays of the sun. Such are the gifts of the Bridegroom, greater indeed than your worth, but worthy of his lovingkindness.

Wherefore, I count you blessed already before those sacred nuptials, and I do not only count you blessed, but I praise your prudence in that you have not come to your illumination as the most slothful among men, at your last breath, but already, like prudent servants, prepared with much goodwill to obey your master, have brought the neck of your soul with much meekness and readiness beneath the bands of Christ, and have received His easy yoke, and have taken His light burden. For if the grace bestowed be the same both for you and for those who are initiated at their last hour, yet the matter of the intention is not the same, nor yet the matter of the preparation for the rite. For they indeed receive it on their bed, but you in the bosom of the Church, which is the common mother of us all; they indeed with lamentation and weeping, but you rejoicing, and exceeding glad; they sighing, you giving thanks; they indeed lethargic with much fever, you filled with much spiritual pleasure; wherefore in your case all things are in harmony with the gift, but in theirs all are adverse to it. For there is wailing and much lamentation on the part of the initiated, and children stand around crying, wife tearing her cheeks, and dejected friends and tearful servants; the whole aspect of the house resembles some wintry and gloomy day. And if you shall open the heart of him who is lying there, you will find it more downcast than are these. For as winds meeting one another with many a contrary blast, break up the sea into many parts, so too the thought of the terrors preying upon him assail the soul of the sick man, and distract his mind with many anxieties. Whenever he sees his children, he thinks of their fatherless condition; whenever he looks from them to his wife, he considers her widowhood; when he sees the servants, he beholds the desolation of the whole house; when he comes back to himself, he calls to mind his own present life, and being about to be torn from it, experiences a great cloud of despondency. Of such a kind is the soul of him who is about to be initiated. Then in the midst of its tumult and confusion, the Priest enters, more formidable than the fever itself, and more distressing than death to the relatives of the sick man. For the entrance of the Presbyter is thought to be a greater reason for despair than the voice of the physician despairing of his life, and that which suggests eternal life seems to be a symbol of death. But I have not yet put the finishing stroke to these ills. For in the midst of relatives raising a tumult and making preparations, the soul has often taken its flight, leaving the body desolate; and in many cases, while it was present it was useless, for when it neither recognizes those who are present, nor hears their voice, nor is able to answer those words by which it will make that blessed covenant with the common master of us all, but is as a useless log, or a stone, and he who is about to be illuminated lies there differing nothing from a corpse, what is the profit of initiation in a case of such insensibility?

2. For he who is about to approach these holy and dread mysteries must be awake and alert, must be clean from all cares of this life, full of much self-restraint, much readiness; he must banish from his mind every thought foreign to the mysteries, and on all sides cleanse and prepare his home, as if about to receive the kind himself. Such is the preparation of your mind; such are your thoughts; such the purpose of your soul. Await therefore a return worthy of this most excellent decision from God, Who overpowers with His

recompense those who show forth obedience to Him. But since it is necessary for his fellow servants to contribute of their own, then we will contribute of our own; yea rather not even are these things our own, but these too are our Masters's. *"For what have you,"* says He, *that thou did not receive? But if you received it, why do you glory, as if you had not received it?"* (1 Corinthians 4:7) I wished to say this first of all, why in the world our fathers, passing by the whole year, settled that the children of the Church should be initiated at this season; and for what reason, after the instruction from us, removing your shoes and raiment, unclad and unshod, with but one garment on, they conduct you to hear the words of the exorcisers. For it is not thoughtlessly and rashly that they have planned this dress and this season for us. But both these things have a certain mystic and secret reason. And I wish to say this to you. But I see that our discourse now constrains us to something more necessary to say what baptism is, and for what reason it enters into our life, and what good things it conveys to us.

But, if you will, let us discourse about the name which this mystic cleansing bears; for its name is not one, but very many and various. For this purification is called the laver of regeneration. *"He save us,"* he says, *"through the laver of regeneration, and renewing of the Holy Ghost"* (Titus 3:5). It is called also illumination, and this St. Paul again has called it: *"For call to remembrance the former days in which after you were illuminated ye endured a great conflict of sufferings"* (Hebrews 10:32); and again, *"For it is impossible for those who were once illuminated, and have tasted of the heavenly gift, and then fell away, to renew them again unto repentance"* (Hebrews 6:4-6). It is called also baptism: *"For as many of you as were baptized into Christ did put on Christ"* (Galatians 3:27). It is called also burial: *"For we were buried,"* says he, *"with Him, through baptism, into death"* (Romans 6:4). It is called circumcision: *"In whom you were also circumcised with a circumcision not made with hands, in the putting off of the body of the sins of the flesh"* (Galatians 2:11). It is called a cross: *"Our old man was crucified with Him that the body of sin might be done away"* (Romans 6:6). It is also possible to speak of other names besides these, but in order that we should not spend our whole time over the names of this free gift, come, return to the first name, and let us finish our discourse by declaring its meaning; but in the meantime, let us extend our teaching a little further. There is that laver by means of the baths, common to all men, which is wort to wipe off bodily uncleanness; and there is the Jewish laver, more honorable than the other, but far inferior to that of grace; and it too wipes off bodily uncleanness but not simple uncleanness of body, since it even reaches to the weak conscience. For there are many matters, which by nature indeed are not unclean, but which become unclean from the weakness of the conscience. And as in the case of little children, masks, and other bugbears are not in themselves alarming, but seem to little children to be alarming, by reason of the weakness of their nature, so it is in the case of those things of which I was speaking; just as to touch dead bodies is not naturally unclean, but when this comes into contact with a weak conscience, it makes him who touches them unclean. For that the thing in question is not unclean naturally, Moses himself who ordained this law showed, when he bore off the entire corpse of Joseph, and yet remained clean. On this account Paul also, discoursing to us about this uncleanness which does not come naturally but by reason of the weakness of the conscience, speaks somewhat in this way: *"Nothing is common of itself save to him who accounts anything to be common"* (Romans 14:14). Do you not see that uncleanness does not arise form the nature of the thing, but from the weakness of the reasoning about it? And again: *"All things indeed are clean, howbeit it is evil to that man who eats with offense"* (Romans 14:20). Do you see that it is not to eat, but to eat with offense, that is the cause of uncleanness?

3. Such is the defilement from which the laver of the Jews cleansed. But the laver of grace, not such, but the real uncleanness which has introduced defilement into the soul as well as into the body. For it does not make those who have touched dead bodies clean, but those who have set their hand to dead works; and if any man be effeminate, or a fornicator, or an idolater, or a doer of whatever ill you please, or if he be full of all the wickedness there is among men; should he fall into this pool of waters, he comes up again from the divine fountain purer than the sun's rays. And in order that you may not think that what is said is mere vain boasting, here Paul speaking of the power of the laver: *"Be not deceived: neither idolaters, nor fornicators, nor adulterers, nor effeminate, nor abusers of themselves with men, nor covetous, nor drunkards, nor revilers, nor extortioners shall inherit the kingdom of God"* (1 Corinthians 6:9-10). And what has this to do with what has been

spoken? Says one, *"for prove the question whether the power of the laver thoroughly cleanses all these things."* Here therefore what follows: *"And such were some of you, but you were washed, but you were sanctified, but you were justified in the name of the Lord Jesus Christ, and in the spirit of our God."* We promise to show you that they who approach the laver become clean from all fornication; but the word has shown more, that they have become not only clean, but both holy and just, for it does not say only *"you were washed"*, but also *"you were sanctified and were justified."* What could be more strange than this, when without toil, and exertion, and good works, righteousness is produced? For such is the lovingkindness of the Divine gift that it makes men just without this exertion. For if a letter of the Emperor, a few words being added, sets free those who are liable to countless accusations, and brings others to the highest honors; much rather will the Holy Spirit of God, Who is able to do all things, free us from all evil and grant us much righteousness, and fill us with much assurance; and as a spark falling into the wide sea would straightway be quenched, or would become invisible, being overwhelmed by the multitude of the waters, so also all human wickedness, when it falls into the pool of the divine fountain, is more swiftly and easily overwhelmed, and made invisible, than that spark. And for what reason, says one, if the laver take away all our sins, is it called, not a laver of remission of sins, nor a laver of cleansing, but a laver of regeneration? Because it does not simply take away our sins, nor simply cleanse us from our faults, but so as if we were born again. For it creates and fashions us anew not forming us again out of earth, but creating us out of another element, namely, of the nature of water. For it does not simply wipe the vessel clean, but entirely remoulds it again. For that which is wiped clean, even if it be cleaned with care, has traces of its former condition, and bears the remains of its defilement; but that which falls into the new mould, and is renewed by means of the flames, laying aside all uncleanness, comes forth from the furnace, and sends forth the same brilliancy with things newly formed. As therefore any one who takes and recasts a golden statue which has been tarnished by time, smoke, dust, and rust, restores it to us thoroughly cleansed and glistening; so too this nature of ours, rusted with the rust of sin, and having gathered much smoke from our faults, and having lost its beauty, which He had from the beginning bestowed upon it from Himself, God has taken and cast anew, and throwing it into the waters as into a mould, and instead of fire sending forth the grace of the Spirit, then brings us forth with much brightness, renewed, and made afresh, to rival the beams o th sun, having crushed the old man, and having fashioned a new man, more brilliant than the former.

4. And speaking darkly of this crushing, and this mystic cleansing, the prophet of old said, "*You shall dash them in pieces like a potter's vessel.*" For that the word is in reference to the faithful, what goes before sufficiently shows us, "*For you are my Son,*" he says, "*today have I begotten you, ask of me and I will give the heathen thy inheritance, the utmost parts of the earth for your possession.*" Do you see how he has made mention of the church of the Gentiles, and has spoken of the kingdom of Christ extended on all sides? Then he says again, "*You shall rule them with a rod of iron;*" not grievous, but strong: "*you shall break them in pieces like a potter's vessel.*" Behold then, the laver is more mystically brought forward. For he does not say earthen vessels, but vessels of the potter. But, give heed: For earthen vessels when crushed would not admit of refashioning, on account of the hardness which was gained by them from the fire. But the fact is that the vessels of the potter are not earthen, but of clay; wherefore, also, when they have been distorted, they can easily, by the skill of the artificer, be brought again to a second shape. When, therefore, God speaks of an irremediable calamity, He does not say vessels of the potter, but an earthen vessel; when, for instance, He wished to teach the prophet and the Jews that He delivered up the city to an irremediable calamity, He bade him take an earthen wine-vessel and crush it before all the people and say, "*Thus shall this city be destroyed, be broken in pieces*" (Jeremiah 19:11). But when He wishes to hold out good hopes to them, He brings the prophet to a pottery, and does not show him an earthen vessel, but shows him a vessel of clay, which was in the hands of the potter, falling to the ground, and brings him to it saying, "*If this potter has taken up and remodeled his vessel which has fallen, shall I not much rather be able to restore you when you have fallen?*" (Jeremiah 18:6) It is possible therefore for God not only to restore those who are made of clay through the laver of regeneration, but to bring back again to their original state, on their careful repentance, those who have received the power of the Spirit, and have lapsed. But this is not the time for

you to hear words about repentance, rather may the time never come for you to fall into the need of these remedies, but may you always remain in preservation of the beauty and the brightness which you are now about to receive, unsullied. In order, then, that you may ever remain thus, come and let us discourse to you a little about your manner of life. For in the wrestling schools, falls of the athletes are devoid of danger. For the wrestling is with friends, and they practice all their exercises on the persons of their teachers. But when the time of the contest has come, when the lists are open, when the spectators are seated above, when the president has arrived, it necessarily follows that the combatants, if they become careless, fall and retire in great disgrace, or if they are in earnest, win the crowns and the prizes. So then, in your case these thirty days are like some wrestling school, both for exercise and practice; let us learn from thence already to get the better of that evil demon. For it is to contend with him that we have to strip ourselves, with him after baptism are we to box and fight. Let us learn from thence already his grip, on what side he is aggressive, on what side he can easily threaten us, in order that, when the contest comes on, we may not feel strange, nor become confused, as seeing new forms of wrestling; but having already practiced them among ourselves, and having learned all his methods, may engage in these forms of wrestling against him with courage. In all ways, therefore, is he accustomed to threaten us, but especially by means of the tongue, and the mouth. For there is no organ so convenient for him for our deception and our destruction as an unchastened tongue and an unchecked utterance. Hence come many slips on our part, hence many serious accusations against us. And the ease of these falls through the tongue a certain one showed when he said *"Many fell by the sword, but not so many as by the tongue"* (Sirach 28:22). Now the gravity of the fall the same person shows us again when he says *"To slip upon a pavement is better than to slip with the tongue"* (Sirach 29:18). And what he speaks of is of this kind. Better it is, says he, that the body should fall and be crushed, than that such a word should go forth as destroys the soul; and he does not speak of falls merely; he also admonishes us that much forethought should be exercised, so that we should not be tripped up, thus saying *"Make a door and bars for your mouth"* (Sirach 20:25), not that we should prepare doors and bars, but that with much security, we should shut the tongue off from outrageous words; and again in another place, after showing that we need influence from above, both as accompanying and preceding our own effort so as to keep this wild beast within; stretching forth his hands to God, the prophet said *"Let the lifting up of my hands be an evening sacrifice, set a watch, O Lord, before my mouth, keep the door of my lips;"* and he who before admonished, himself too says again *"Who shall set a watch before my mouth, and a seal of wisdom upon my lips?"* (Sirach 22:27) Do you not see, each one fearing these falls and bewailing them, both giving advice, and praying that the tongue may have the benefit of much watchfulness? And for what reason, says one, if this organ brings us such ruin, did God originally place it within us? Because indeed, it is of great use, and if we are careful, it is of use only, and brings no ruin. Hear, for example, what he says who spoke the former words, *"Death and life are in the power of the tongue"* (Proverbs 18:21). And Christ points to the same thing when He says *"By your words you shall be condemned, and by your words you shall be justified"* (Mark 12:27). For the tongue stands in the midst ready for use on either hand. You are its master. Thus indeed a sword lies in the midst, and if you use it against your enemies, this organ becomes a means of safety for you. But if you thrust its stroke against yourself, not the nature of the iron, but your own transgression becomes the cause of your slaughter. Let us then take this view of the tongue. It is a sword lying in the midst; sharpen it for the purpose of accusing your own sins. Thrust not the stroke against your brother. For this reason God surrounded it with a double fortification—with the fence of the teeth and the barrier of the lips—that it may not rashly and without circumspection utter words which are not convenient. Well, do you say it will not endure this? Bridle it therefore within. Restrain it by means of the teeth, as though giving over its body to these executioners and making them bite it. For it is better that when it sins now it should be bitten by the teeth, than one day when it seeks a drop of water and is parched with heat, to be unable to obtain this consolation. In many other ways indeed it is wont to sin, by raillery and blasphemy, by uttering foul words, by slander, swearing, and perjury.

5. But in order that we may not by saying everything at once today, confuse your minds, we put before you one custom, namely, about the avoidance of oaths, saying this much by way or preface,

and speaking plainly—that if you do not avoid oaths, I say not perjury merely, but those too which happen in the cause of justice, we shall not further discourse upon any other subject. For it is monstrous that teachers of letters should not give a second lesson to their children until they see the former one fixed well in their memory, but that we, without being able to express our first lessons clearly, should inculcate others before the first are completed. For this is nothing else than to pour into a perforated jar. Give great care, then, that you silence not our mouth. For this error is grace, and it is exceedingly grave because it does not seem to be grave, and on this account I fear it, because no one fears it. On this account the disease is incurable, because it does not seem to be a disease; but just as simple speech is not a crime, so neither does this seem to be a crime, but with much boldness this transgression is committed; and if any one call it in question, straightway laughter follows, and much ridicule, not of those who are called in question for their oaths, but of those who wish to rectify the disease. On this account I largely extend my discourse about these matters. For I wish to pull up a deep root, and to wipe out a long-standing evil: I speak not of perjury alone, but even of oaths in good faith. But so and so, says one, a forbearing man, consecrated to the priesthood, living in much self-control and piety, takes an oath. Do not speak to me of this forbearing person, this self-controlled, pious man who is consecrated to the priesthood; but if you will, add that this man is Peter, or Paul, or even an angel descended out of heaven. For not even in such a case do I regard the dignity of their persons. For the law which I read upon oaths, is not that of the servant, but of the King; and when the edicts of a king are read, let every claim of the servants be silent. But if you are able to say that Christ bade us use oaths, or that Christ did not punish the doing of this, show me, and I am persuaded. But if He forbade it with so much care, and takes so much thought about the matter as to class him who takes an oath with the evil one—for whatsoever is more than these, namely, than yea and nay, says He, is of the devil (Matthew 5:35)—why do you bring this person and that person forward? For not because of the carelessness of your fellow servants, but from the injunctions of His own laws, will God record His vote against you. I have commanded, He says, you ought to obey, not to shelter yourself behind such and such a person and concern yourself with other persons' evil. Since the great David sinned a grievous sin, is it then safe for us to sin? Tell me: on this account then we ought to make sure of this point, and only to emulate the good works of the saints; and if there is carelessness, and transgression of the law anywhere, we ought to flee from it with great care. For our reckoning is not with our fellow-servants, but with our Master, and to Him we shall give account for all done in our life. Let us prepare ourselves therefore for this tribunal. For even if he who transgresses this law be beyond everything revered and great, he shall certainly pay the penalty attaching to the transgression. For God is not respecter of persons. How then and what way is it possible to flee from this sin? For one ought to show not only that the crime is grievous, but to give counsel how we may escape from it. Have you a wife, have you a servant, children, friends, acquaintance, neighbors? To all these enjoin caution on these matters. Custom is a grievous things, terrible to supplant, and hard to guard against, and it often attacks us unwilling and unknowing; therefore in so far as you know the power of custom, to such an extent study to be freed from any evil customer, and transfer yourself to any other most useful one. For as that custom is often able to trip you up, though you are careful, and guardest yourself, and takest thought, and consideration, so if you transfer yourself to the good customer of abstaining from oaths, you will not be able, either involuntarily or carelessly, to fall into the fault of oaths. For custom is really great and has the power of nature. In order then that we do not continually distress ourselves let us transfer ourselves to another customer, and ask thou each one of your kindred and acquaintance this favor, that he advise you and exhort you to flee from oaths, and reprove you when detected in them. For the watch over you which takes place on their part, is to them too counsel and a suggestion to what is right. For he who reproves another for oaths, will not himself easily fall into this pit. For much swearing is no ordinary pit, not only when it is about little matters but about the greatest. And we, whether buying vegetables, or quarreling over two farthings, or in a rage with our servants and threatening them, always call upon God as our witness. But a freeman, possessed of some barren dignity, you would not dare to call upon as witness in the market to such things; but even if you attempted it, you will pay the penalty of your insolence. But the King of Heaven, the Lord of Angels, when disputing both about purchases and money, and what not, you drag in for a testimony. And how can these things be borne? Whence then should we escape from this evil custom? After setting those guards of which I spoke round us, let us fix on a specified time to ourselves for amendment, and adding thereto condemnation if, when the time has passed, we have not amended this. How long a time will suffice for the purpose? I do not think that they who are very wary, and on the alert, and watchful about their own salvation, should need more than ten days, so as to be altogether free from the evil custom of oaths. But if after ten days we be detected swearing, let us add a penalty due to ourselves, and let us fix upon the greatest punishment and condemnation of the transgression; what then is this condemnation? This I do not fix upon, but will suffer you yourselves to determine the sentence. So we arrange matters in our own case, not only in respect of oaths but in respect of other defects, and fixing a time for ourselves, with most grievous punishments, if at any time we have fallen into them, shall come clean to our Master, and shall escape the fire of hell, and shall stand before the judgment seat of Christ with boldness, to which may we all attain, by the grace and lovingkindness of out Lord Jesus Christ, with Whom be glory to the Father together with the Holy Spirit for ever and ever. Amen.

Second Instruction

To those about to be illuminated; and concerning women who adorn themselves wit plaiting of hair and gold, and concerning those who have used omens and amulets and incantations, all which are foreign to Christianity.

1. I have come to ask first of all for some fruit in return for the words lately said out of brotherly love to you. For we do not speak in order that you should hear simply, but in order that you should remember what has been said, and may afford us evidence of this, by your works. Yea, rather, not us, but God, Who knows the secrets of the heart. On this account indeed instruction is so called, in order that even when we are absent, our discourse may instruct your hearts. And be not surprised if, after an interval of ten days

only, we have come asking for fruit from the seed sown. For in one day it is possible at once to let the seed fall, and to accomplish the harvest. For strengthened not by our own power alone, but by the influence which comes from God, we are summoned to the conflict. Let as many therefore as have received what has been spoken, and have fulfilled it by their works, remain reaching forth to the things which are before. But let as many as have not yet arrived at this good achievement arrive at it straightway, that they may dispel of condemnation which arises out of their sloth by their diligence for the future. For it is possible, it is indeed possible for him who has been very slothful, by using diligence for the future to recover the whole loss of the time that is past. Wherefore He says *"Today if you will his voice, harden not your hearts, as in the day of provocation."* And this He says, exhorting and counseling us, that we should never despair, but so long as we are here, should have good hopes, and should lay hold on what is before us, and hasten towards the prize of our high calling of God. This then let us do, and let us inquire into the names of this great gift. For as ignorance of the greatness of this dignity makes those who are honored with it more slothful, so when it is known it renders them thankful, and makes them more earnest; and anyhow, it would be disgraceful and ridiculous that they who enjoy such glory and honors from God, should not even know what the names of it are intended to show forth. And why do I speak about this gift, for if you will consider the common name of our race, you will receive the greatest instruction and incentive to virtue. For this name *Man* we do not define according as they who are without define it, but as the Divine Scripture has bidden us. For a man is not merely whosoever has hands and feet of a man, not whosoever is rational only, but whosoever practices piety and virtue with boldness. Hear, at least, what he says concerning Job. For in saying that *"there was a man in the land of Ausis,"* he does not describe him in those terms in which they who are without describe him, nor does he say this because he had two fee and broad nails, but he added the evidences of his piety and said *"just, true, fearing God, eschewing every evil deed"* (Job 1:1), showing that this is a man; even as therefore another says, *"Fear God, and keep His commandments, because this is the whole man"* (Ecclesiastes 12:13). But if the name *man* affords such a great incentive to virtue, much rather the term faithful. For you are called faithful on this account, because you have faith in God, and yourself are entrusted from Him with righteousness, sanctification, cleansing of soul, adoption, the kingdom of heaven. He entrusted you with these, and handed them over to you. Thou in turn hast entrusted and handed over other things to Him—alms-giving, prayers, self-control, and every other virtue. And why do I saw alms-giving? If you give Him even a cup of cold water, you shall not indeed lose this, but even this He keeps with care against that day, and will restore it with overflowing abundance. For this truly is wonderful, that He does not keep only that which has been entrusted to Him, but in recompensing it increases it.

This too He has bidden you do according to your power, with what has been entrusted to you, to extend the holiness which you have received, and to make the righteousness which comes from the laver brighter, and the gift of grace more radiant; even as therefore Paul did, increasing all the good things which he received by his subsequent labors, and his zeal, and his diligence. And look at the carefulness of God; neither did He give the whole to you then, nor withhold the whole, but gave part, and promised part. And for what reason did He not give the whole then? In order that you might show your faith about Him, believing on His promise alone, in what was not yet given. And for what reason again did He not there dispense the whole, but did give the grace of the Spirit and righteousness and sanctification? In order that he might lighten your labors for you, and by what has been already given may also put you in good hope for that which is to come. On this account, too, you are about to be called newly-enlightened, because your light is ever new, if you will, and is never quenched. For this light of day, whether we will or no, the night succeeds, but darkness knows not that light's ray. *"For the light shines in the darkness, and the darkness apprehended it not."* Not so bright at least is the world, when the sunbeams come forth, as th soul shines and becomes brighter when it has received grace from the Spirit and learns more exactly the nature of the case. For when night prevails, and there is darkness, often a man has seen a coil of rope and has thought it was a serpent, and has fled from an approaching friend as from an enemy, and being aware of some noise, has become very much alarmed; but when the day has come, nothing of this sort could happen, but all appears just as it really is; which thing also occurs in the case of our soul. For when grace has come, and driven away the darkness of the understanding, we learn the exact nature of tings, and what was before dreadful to us becomes contemptible. For we no longer fear death after learning exactly, from this sacred initiation, that death is not death, but a sleep and a seasonable slumber; nor poverty nor disease, nor any other such thing, knowing that we are on our way to a better life, undefiled and incorruptible, and free from all such vicissitudes.

2. Let us not therefore remain craving after the things of this life, neither after the luxury of the table, or costliness of raiment. For you have the most excellent of raiment, you have a spiritual table, you have the glory from on high, and Christ has become to you all things—your table, your raiment, your home, your head, your stem. *"For as many of you as were baptized into Christ, did put on Christ"* (Galatians 3:27). See how He has become raiment for you. Do you wish to learn how He becomes a table for you? *"He who eats Me,"* says He, *"as I live because of the Father, he also shall live because of Me;"* and that He becomes a home for you, *"he that eats My flesh abides in me, and I in him"* (John 6:56); and that He is stem, He says again *"I am the vine, you the branches"* (John 15:5); and that He is brother, and friend, and bride-groom, *"I no longer call you servants, for you are My friends"* (John 15:15); and Paul again *"I espoused you to one husband, that I might present you as a pure virgin to Christ"* (2 Corinthians 11:2), and again *"That He might be the first-born among many brethren"* (Romans 8:29); and we become not His brethren only, but also His children, *"For behold,"* he says, *"I and the children which God has given me"* (Isaiah 8:18); and not this only, but His members, and His body. For as if what has been said were not enough to show forth the love and the good will which He has shown forth towards us, He has added another thing greater and nearer still, calling Himself besides, our head. Knowing all these matters, beloved, requite your benefactor by the best conversation, and considering the greatness of the sacrifice, adorn the members of your body; consider what you receive in your hand, and never suffer it to strike any one, nor shame what has been honored with so great a gift by the sin of a blow. Consider what you receive in your hand, and keep it clean from all covetousness and extortion; think that thou does not receive this in hour hand, but also puttest it to your mouth,

and guard your tongue in purity from base and insolent words, blasphemy, perjury, and all other such things. For it is disastrous that what is ministered to by such most dread mysteries, and has been dyed red with such blood, and has become a golden sword, should be perverted to purposes of raillery, and insult, and buffoonery. Reverence the honour with which God has honoured it, and bring it not down to the vileness of sin, but having reflected again that after the hand and the tongue, the heart receives this dread mystery, do not ever weave a plot against your neighbor, but keep your thoughts pure from all evil. Thus you shall be able to keep your eyes too, and your hearing safe. For is it not monstrous, after this mystic voice is borne from heaven—I mean the voice of the Cherubim—to defile your hearing with lewd songs, and dissolute melodies? And does it not deserve the utmost punishment if, with the same eyes with which you look upon the unspeakable and dread mysteries, you look upon harlots, and does commit adultery in your heart. You are called to a marriage, beloved: enter not in clad in sordid raiment, but take a robe suitable to the marriage. For if when men are called to a material marriage, though they be poorer than all others, they often possess themselves of or buy clean raiment, and so go to meet those who called them. Do thou too who hast been called to a spiritual marriage, and to a royal banquet, consider what kind of raiment it would be right for you to buy, but rather there is not even need to purchase, yea He Himself Who calls you give it you *gratis*, in order that you may not be able to plead poverty in excuse. Keep, therefore, the raiment which you received. For if you lose it, you will not be able to use it henceforth, or to buy it. For this kind of raiment is nowhere sold. Have you heard how those who were initiated, in old time, groaned, and beat their breasts, their conscience thereupon exciting them? Beware then, beloved, that you do not at any time suffer like this. But how will you not suffer, if you dost no cast off the wicked habit of evil men? For this reason I said before and speak now and will not cease speaking, if any has not rectified the defects in his morals, nor furnished himself with easily acquired virtue, let him not be baptized. For the laver is able to remit the former sins, but there is no little fear, and no ordinary danger lest we return to them, and our remedy becomes a wound. For by how much greater the grace is, by so much is the punishment more for those who sin after these things.

3. In order, therefore, that we return not to our former vomit, let us henceforward discipline ourselves. For that we must repent beforehand, and desist from our former evil, and so come forward for grace, hear what John says, and what the leader of the apostles says to those who are about to be baptized. For the one says, *"Bring forth forth worthy of repentance, and begin not to say within yourselves, we have Abraham to our Father"* (Luke 3:8); and the other says again to those who question him, *"Repent ye and be baptized every one of you in the name of the Lord Jesus Christ"* (Acts 2:38). Now he who repents, non longer touches the same matters of which he repented. On this account, also, we are bidden to say, *"I renounce you, Satan,"* in order that we may never more return to him. As therefore happens in the case of painters from life, so let it happen in your case. For they, arranging their boards, and tracing white lines upon them, and sketching the royal likeness in outline, before they apply the actual colors, rub out some lines, and change some for others, rectifying mistakes, and altering what is amiss with all freedom. But when they put on the coloring for good, it is not longer in their power to rub out again, and to change one ting for another, since they injure the beauty of the portrait, and the result becomes an eyesore. Consider that your soul is the portrait; before therefore the true coloring of the spirit comes, wipe out habits which have wrongly been implanted in you, whether swearing, or falsehood, or insolence, or base talking, or jesting, or whatever else you have a habit of doing of things unlawful. Away with the habit, in order that you may not return to it, after baptism. The laver causes the sins to disappear. Correct your habits, so that when the colors are applied, and the royal likeness is brought out, you may no more wipe them out in the future; and add damage and scars to the beauty which has been given you by God. Restrain therefore anger, extinguish passion. Be not thou vexed, be sympathizing, be not exasperated, nor say *"I have been injured in regard to my soul."* No one is injured in regard to the soul if we do not inure ourselves in regard to th soul; and how is this, I now say. Has any one taken away your substance? He has not injured you in regard to your soul, but your money. But if you cherish ill-will against him, you have injured yourself in regard to your soul. For the money taken away has wrought you no damage, nay has even been profitable, but thou by not dismissing your anger will give account in the other world for this

cherishing of ill-will. Has any one reviled you and insulted you. He has in no way injured your soul, and not even your body. Have you reviled in return and insulted? You have injured yourself in regard to your soul, for the words which you have said you are about to render account for there; and this I wish you to know chiefly of all, that the Christian, and faithful man, no one is able to injure in regard to the soul, not even the devil himself; and not only is this wonderful, that God has made us inaccessible to all his designs, but that he has constituted us fit for the practice of virtue, and there is no hindrance, if we will, even though we be poor, weak in body, outcast, nameless, bondservants. For neither poverty, nor infirmity, nor deformity of body, nor servitude, nor any other if such things could ever become a hindrance to virtue; and why do I say, poor, ad a bondservant, and nameless? Even if you are a prisoner, not even this would be ever any hindrance to you as regards virtue. And how this is I proceed to say. Has any of your household grieved you and provoked you? Dismiss your wrath against him. Have bonds, and poverty, and obscurity been any hindrance to you in this respect? And why do I say hindrance? They have both helped and contributed to restrain pride. Have you seen another prospering? Do not envy him. For not even in this case is poverty a bar. Again, whenever you need to pray, do so with a sober and watchful mind, and nothing shall be a bar even in that case. Show all meekness, forbearance, self-restraint, gravity. For these things need no external helps. And this especially us the chief point about virtue, that it has no necessity for wealth, power, glory, not anything of that kind, but of a sanctified soul alone, and it seeks for nothing more. And behold, also, the same thing happening in respect of grace. For if any one be lame, if he has had his eyes put out, if he be maimed in body, if he has fallen into the last extremity of weakness, grace is not hindered from coming by any of these things. For it only seeks a soul receiving it with readiness, and all these external things it passes over. For in the case of worldly soldiers, those who are about to enlist them for the army seek for stature of body, and healthy condition, and it is not only necessary that he who is about to become a solider should have these along, but he must also be free. For if anybody be a slave, he is rejected. But the King of Heaven seeks for nothing of this kind, but receives slaves into his army, and aged people, and the languid in limb, and is not ashamed. What is more merciful than this? What could be more kind? For he seeks for what is in our own power, but they seek for what is not in our power. For to be a slave or free is not our doing. To be tall, again, or short is not in our own power, or to be aged, or well grown, and such like. But to be forbearing and kind, and so forth, are matters of our own choice; and God demands of us only those things of which we have control. And quite reasonably. For He does not call us to grace because of His own need, but because of doing us kindness; but kings, because of services required by them; and they carry men off to an outward and material warfare, but He to a spiritual combat; and it is not only in the case of heathen wars, but in the case of he games also that one may see the same analogy. For they who are about to be brought into the theatre, do not descend to the contest until the herald himself takes them beneath the gaze of all and leads them round, shouting out and saying, *"Has any one a charge against this person?"* although in that case the struggle is not concerned with the soul, but with the body. Wherefore then do you demand proofs of nobleness? But in this case there is nothing of the kind, but all is different, out contest not consisting of hand locked in hand, but in philosophy of soul, and excellence of mind. The president of our conflicts does the opposite. For he does not take us, and lead us around and say, *"Has any one a charge against this sinner?"* but cries out, *"Though all men, though demons, stand up with the devil and accuse him of extreme and unspeakable crimes, I reject him not, not abhor him, but removing him from his accusers, and freeing him from his wickedness, thus I bring him to the contest."* And this is very reasonable. For there indeed the president contributes nothing towards the victory, in the case of the combatants, but stands still in the midst. But here, the President of the contests for holiness becomes a fellow-combatant and helper, sharing with them the conflict against the devil.

4. And not only is this the wonderful thing that He remits our sins, but that He not even reveals them nor makes them manifest and patent, nor compels us to come forward into the midst, and to tel out our errors, but bids us make our defense to Him alone, and to confess ourselves to Him. And yet among secular judges, if any tell any of the robbers or grave-riflers, when they are arrested, to tell their errors and be quit of their punishment they would accede to this with

all readiness, despising the shame through desire of safety. But in this case there is nothing of this kind, but He both remits the sins, nor compels us to marshal them in array before any spectators. But one thing alone He seeks, that he who enjoys this remission should learn the greatness of the gift. How is it not, therefore, absurd that i case where He does us service, He should be content with our testimony only, but in those where we serve Him we seek for others as witnesses, and do a thing for ostentation's sake? While we wonder then at His kindliness, let us show forth our doings, and before all others let us curb the vehemence of our tongue, and not always be giving utterance. *"For in the multitude of words there wants not transgression"* (Proverbs 10:19). If indeed then you have anything useful to say, open your lips. But if there be nothing necessary for you to say, be silent, for it is better. Are you a handicraftsman? As you sit at work, since psalms. Do you not wish to sing with your mouth? Do this in your heart; a psalm is a great companion. In this case you shall undergo nothing serious, but shall be able to sit in your workshop as in a monastery. For not suitableness of place, but strictness of morals will afford us quiet. Paul, at least pursuing his trade in a workshop suffered no injury to his own virtue (Acts 18:3). Do not thou therefore say, How can I, being a handicraftsman and a poor man, be a philosopher? This is indeed the very reason why you may be a philosopher. For poverty is far more conducive to piety for us than wealth, and work than idleness; since wealth is even a hindrance to those who do not take heed. For when it is needful to dismiss anger, to extinguish envy, to curb passion, to offer prayer, to exhibit forbearance and meekness, kindliness and charity, when would poverty be a bar? For is it not possible by spending money to accomplish these things, but by exhibiting a right disposition; alms-giving especially needs money, but even it shines forth in greater degree through poverty. For she who spent the two mites was poorer than all men, and yet surpassed all (Luke 21:2-4). Let us not then consider wealth to be anything great, nor gold to be better than clay. For the value of material things is not owing to their nature, but to our estimate of them. For if any one would inquire carefully, iron is much more necessary than gold. For the one contributes to no need of our life, but the other has furnished us with the greater part of our needs, ministering to countless arts; and why do I speak of a comparison between gold and iron? For these stones are more necessary than precious stones. For of those nothing serviceable could be made, but out of these, houses and walls and cities are erected. But do thou show me what gain could be derived from these pearls, rather what harm would not happen? For in order that you may wear one pearl drop, countless poor people are pinched with hunger. What excuse will you hit upon? What pardon?

Do you wish to adorn your face? Do so not with pearls, but with modesty and dignity. So your countenance will be more full of grace in the eyes of your husband. For the other kind of adorning is wont to plunge him into a suspicious of jealousy, and into enmity, quarrelsomeness, and strife, for nothing is more annoying than a face which is suspected. But the ornament of compassion and modesty casts out all evil suspicion, and will draw your partner to you more strongly than any bond. For natural beauty does not impart such comeliness to the face as does the disposition of him who beholds it, and nothing is so wont to produce that disposition as modesty and dignity; so that if any woman be comely, and her husband be ill affected towards her, she appears to him the most worthless of all women; and if she do not happen to be fair of face, but her husband be well affected towards her, she appears more comely than all. For sentence is given not according to the nature of what is beheld, but according to the disposition of the beholders. Adorn your face then with modesty, dignity, pity, lovingkindess, charity, affection for your husband, forbearance, meekness, endurance of ill. These are the tints of virtue. By means of these you will attract angels not human beings to be your lovers. By means of these you have God to commend you, and when God receives you, He will certainly win over your husband for you. For if the wisdom of a man illuminates his countenance (Ecclesiastes 8:1) much more does the virtue of a woman illuminate her face; and if you consider this to be a great ornament, tell me what will be the advantage of the pearls in that day? But why is it necessary to speak of that day, since it is possible to show all this from what happens now. When, then, they who thought fit to revile the emperor were dragged to the judgment hall, and were in danger of extreme measures being taken, then the mothers and the wives, laying aside their necklaces and their golden ornaments and pearls and all adornment and golden raiment, wearing a simple and mean dress and besprinkled with ashes, prostrated themselves before the doors of the judgment hall and thus won over the judges; and if in the case of these earthly courts of justice, the golden ornaments and the pearls and the variegated dress would have been a snare and a betrayal, but forbearance and meekness and ashes and tears and mean garments persuaded the judge, much more would this take place in the case of that impartial and dread tribunal. For what reason will you be able to state, what defense, when the Master lays these pearls to your charge, and brings the poor who have perished with hunger into the midst? On this account Paul said, *"not with braided hair, or gold, or pearls, or costly raiment"* (1 Timothy 2:9). For therein would be a snare. And if we were to enjoy them continually, yet we shall lay them aside with death. But arising out of virtue there is all security, and no vicissitude and changeableness, but here it makes us more secure, and also accompanies us there. Do you wish to possess pearls, and never to lay aside this wealth? Take off all ornament and place it in the hands of Christ through the poor. He will keep all your wealth for you, when He shall raise up your body with much radiancy. Then He shall invest you with better wealth and greater ornament, since this present is mean and absurd. Consider then whom you wish to please, and for whose sake you put on this ornament, not in order that the ropemaker and the coppersmith and the huckster may admire. Then are you not ashamed, nor do you blush when you show yourself to them? Doing all on their account whom you do not consider worthy of accosting.

How then will you laugh this fancy to scorn? If you will remember that word, which you sent forth when thou were initiate, I renounce you, Satan, and your pomp and your service. For the frenzy about pearls is a pomp of Satan. For you received gold not in order that you might bind it on to your body, but in order that you might release and nourish the poor. Say therefore constantly, I renounce you, Satan. Nothing is more safe than this word if we shall prove it by our deeds.

5. This I think it right that you who are about to be initiated should learn. For this word is a covenant with the Master. And just as we, when we buy slaves, first ask those who are being sold if they are

willing to be our servants, so also does Christ. When He is about to receive you into service, He first asks if you wish to leave that cruel and relentless tyrant, and He receives covenants from you. For His service is not forced upon you. And see the lovingkindness of God. For we, before we put down the price, ask those who are being sold, and when we have learned that they are willing, then we put down the price. But Christ not so, but He even put own the price for us all: His precious blood. For, He says, you were bought with a price (1 Corinthians 7:25). Notwithstanding, not even then does He compel those who are unwilling,to serve Him; but except you have grace, He says, and of your own accord and will determinest to enroll yourself under My rule, I do not compel, nor force you. And we should not have chosen to buy wicked slaves. But if we should at any time have so chosen, we buy them with a perverted choice, and put down a corresponding price for them. But Christ, buying ungrateful and lawless slaves, put down the price of a servant of first quality, nay rather much more, and so much greater that neither speech nor thought can set forth its greatness. For neither giving heaven, nor earth, nor sea, but giving up that which is more valuable than all these, His own blood, thus He bought us. And after all these things, He does not require of us witnesses, or registration, but is content with a single word, if you say it from the heart. *"I renounce you, Satan, and your pomp,"* has included all. Let us then say this, *"I renounce you, Satan,"* as men who are about in that world at that day to have that word demanded of them, and let us keep it in order that we may then return this deposit safe. But Satan's pomps are theatres, and the circus, and all sin, and observance of days, and incantations and omens.

"And what are omens?" says one. Often when going forth from his own house he has seen a one-eyed or lame man, and has shunned him as an omen. This is a pomp of Satan. For meeting the man does not make the day turn out ill, but to live in sin. When you go forth, then, beware of one thing—that sin does not meet you. For this it is which trips us up. And without this the devil will be able to do us no harm. What do you say? You see a man, and shunnest him as an omen, and dost not see the snare of the devil, how he sets you at war with him who has done you no wrong, how he makes you the enemy of your brother on no just pretext; but God has bidden us

love our enemies; but you are turned away from him who did you no wrong, having nothing to charge him with, and do you not consider how great is the absurdity, how great the shame, rather how great the danger? Can I speak of anything more absurd? I am shamed, indeed, and I blush. But for your salvation's sake, I am compelled to speak of it. If a virgin meet him he says the day becomes unsuccessful; but if a harlot meet him, it is propitious and profitable and full of much business; are you ashamed? And do you smite your foreheads, and bend to the ground? But do not this on account of the words which I have spoken, but of the deeds which have been done. See then, in this case, how the devil hid his snare, in order that we might turn away from the modest, but salute and be friendly to the unchaste. For since he has heard Christ saying that *"He who looks on a woman to desire her, has already committed adultery with her"* (Matthew 5:28), and has seen many get the better of unchastity, wishing by another wrong to cast them again into sin, by this superstitious observance he gladly persuades them to pay attention to whorish women.

And what is one to say about them who use charms and amulets, and encircle their heads and feet with golden coins of Alexander of Macedon. Are these our hopes, tell me, that after the cross and death of out Master, we should place our hopes of salvation on an image of a Greek king? Do you not know what great result the cross has achieved? It has abolished death, has extinguished sin, has made Hades useless, has undone the power of the devil, and is it not worth trusting for the health of the body? It has raised up the whole world, and do you not take courage in it? And what would you be worthy to suffer, tell me? Thou dost not only have amulets always with you, but incantations bringing drunken and half-witted old women into your house, and are you not ashamed, and do you not blush, after so great philosophy, to be terrified at such things? And there is a graver thing than this error. For when we deliver these exhortations, and lead them away, thinking that they defend themselves, they say that the woman is a Christian who makes these incantations, and utters nothing else than the name of God. On this account I especially hate and turn away from her, because she makes use of the name of God with a view to ribaldry. For even the demons uttered the name of God, but still they were demons, and thus they used to say to Christ

"We know You Who You are, the Holy One of God" (Mark 1:24), and notwithstanding, He rebuked them, and drove them away. On this account, then, I beseech you to cleanse yourselves from this error, and to keep hold of this word as a staff; and just as without sandals and cloak no one of you would choose to go down to the marketplace, so without this word never enter the marketplace; but when you are about to pass over the threshold of the gateway, say this word first: *I leave your ranks, Satan, and your pomp and your service, and I join the ranks of Christ.* And never go forth without this word. This shall be a staff to you, this your armor, this an impregnable fortress; and accompany this word with the sign of the cross on your forehead. For thus not only a man who meets you, but even the devil himself, will be unable to hurt you at all when he sees you everywhere appearing with these weapons; and discipline yourself by these means henceforth, in order that when you receive the seal you may be a well-equipped soldier; and planting your trophy against the devil, may receive the crown of righteousness, which may it be the lot of us all to obtain through the grace and lovingkindess of our Lord Jesus Christ, with Whom be glory to the Father and to the Holy Spirit for ever and ever. Amen.

BASIL THE GREAT

On the Holy Spirit

Basil the Great

Translated by Rev. Blomfield Jackson

Chapter I: *Prefatory remarks on the need of exact investigation of the most minute portions of theology.*

1. Your desire for information, my right well-beloved and most deeply respected brother Amphilochius, I highly commend, and not less your industrious energy. I have been exceedingly delighted at the care and watchfulness shewn in the expression of your opinion that of all the terms concerning God in every mode of speech, not one ought to be left without exact investigation. You have turned to good account your reading of the exhortation of the Lord, "Every one that asketh receiveth, and he that seeketh findeth," and by your diligence in asking might, I ween, stir even the most reluctant to give you a share of what they possess. And this in you yet further moves my admiration, that you do not, according to the manners of the most part of the men of our time, propose your questions by way of mere test, but with the honest desire to arrive at the actual truth. There is no lack in these days of captious listeners and questioners; but to find a character desirous of information, and seeking the truth as a remedy for ignorance, is very difficult. Just as in the hunter's snare, or in the soldier's ambush, the trick is generally ingeniously concealed, so it is with the inquiries of the majority of the questioners who advance arguments, not so much with the view of getting any good out of them, as in order that, in the event of their failing to elicit answers

which chime in with their own desires, they may seem to have fair ground for controversy.

2. If "To the fool on his asking for wisdom, wisdom shall be reckoned," at how high a price shall we value "the wise hearer" who is quoted by the Prophet in the same verse with "the admirable counselor"? It is right, I ween, to hold him worthy of all approbation, and to urge him on to further progress, sharing his enthusiasm, and in all things toiling at his side as he presses onwards to perfection. To count the terms used in theology as of primary importance, and to endeavour to trace out the hidden meaning in every phrase and in every syllable, is a characteristic wanting in those who are idle in the pursuit of true religion, but distinguishing all who get knowledge of "the mark" "of our calling;" for what is set before us is, so far as is possible with human nature, to be made like unto God. Now without knowledge there can be no making like; and knowledge is not got without lessons. The beginning of teaching is speech, and syllables and words are parts of speech. It follows then that to investigate syllables is not to shoot wide of the mark, nor, because the questions raised are what might seem to some insignificant, are they on that account to be held unworthy of heed. Truth is always a quarry hard to hunt, and therefore we must look everywhere for its tracks. The acquisition of true religion is just like that of crafts; both grow bit by bit; apprentices must despise nothing. If a man despise the first elements as small and insignificant, he will never reach the perfection of wisdom. Yea and Nay are but two syllables, yet there is often involved in these little words at once the best of all good things, Truth, and that beyond which wickedness cannot go, a Lie. But why mention Yea and Nay? Before now, a martyr bearing witness for Christ has been judged to have paid in full the claim of true religion by merely nodding his head. If, then, this be so, what term in theology is so small but that the effect of its weight in the scales according as it be rightly or wrongly used is not great? Of the law we are told "not one jot nor one tittle shall pass away;" how then could it be safe for us to leave even the least unnoticed? The very points which you yourself have sought to have thoroughly sifted by us are at the same time both small and great. Their use is the matter of a moment, and peradventure they are therefore made of small account; but, when we reckon

the force of their meaning, they are great. They may be likened to the mustard plant which, though it be the least of shrubseeds, yet when properly cultivated and the forces latent in its germs unfolded, rises to its own sufficient height. If any one laughs when he sees our subtlety, to use the Psalmist's words, about syllables, let him know that he reaps laughter's fruitless fruit; and let us, neither giving in to men's reproaches, nor yet vanquished by their disparagement, continue our investigation. So far, indeed, am I from feeling ashamed of these things because they are small, that, even if I could attain to ever so minute a fraction of their dignity, I should both congratulate myself on having won high honour, and should tell my brother and fellow investigator that no small gain had accrued to him there from. While, then, I am aware that the controversy contained in little words is a very great one, in hope of the prize I do not shrink from toil, with the conviction that the discussion will both prove profitable to myself, and that my hearers will be rewarded with no small benefit. Wherefore now with the help, if I may so say, of the Holy Spirit Himself, I will approach the exposition of the subject, and, if you will, that I may be put in the way of the discussion, I will for a moment revert to the origin of the question before us.

3. Lately when praying with the people, and using the full doxology to God the Father in both forms, at one time "with the Son together with the Holy Ghost," and at another "through the Son in the Holy Ghost," I was attacked by some of those present on the ground that I was introducing novel and at the same time mutually contradictory terms. You, however, chiefly with the view of benefiting them, or, if they are wholly incurable, for the security of such as may fall in with them, have expressed the opinion that some clear instruction ought to be published concerning the force underlying the syllables employed. I will therefore write as concisely as possible, in the endeavour to lay down some admitted principle for the discussion.

Chapter II: *The origin of the heretics' close observation of syllables.*

4. The petty exactitude of these men about syllables and words is not, as might be supposed, simple and straightforward; nor is the

mischief to which it tends a small one. There is involved a deep and covert design against true religion. Their pertinacious contention is to show that the mention of Father, Son, and Holy Ghost is unlike, as though they will thence find it easy to demonstrate that there is a variation in nature. They have an old sophism, invented by Aetius, the champion of this heresy, in one of whose Letters there is a passage to the effect that things naturally unlike are expressed in unlike terms, and, conversely, that things expressed in unlike terms are naturally unlike. In proof of this statement he drags in the words of the Apostle, "One God and Father of whom are all things…and one Lord Jesus Christ by whom are all things." "Whatever, then," he goes on, "is the relation of these terms to one another, such will be the relation of the natures indicated by them; and as the term 'of whom' is unlike the term 'by whom,' so is the Father unlike the Son." On this heresy depends the idle subtlety of these men about the phrases in question. They accordingly assign to God the Father, as though it were His distinctive portion and lot, the phrase "of Whom;" to God the Son they confine the phrase "by Whom;" to the Holy Spirit that of "in Whom," and say that this use of the syllables is never interchanged, in order that, as I have already said, the variation of language may indicate the variation of nature. Verily it is sufficiently obvious that in their quibbling about the words they are endeavouring to maintain the force of their impious argument. By the term "of whom" they wish to indicate the Creator; by the term "through whom," the subordinate agent or instrument; by the term "in whom," or "in which," they mean to shew the time or place. The object of all this is that the Creator of the universe may be regarded as of no higher dignity than an instrument, and that the Holy Spirit may appear to be adding to existing things nothing more than the contribution derived from place or time.

Chapter III: *The systematic discussion of syllables is derived from heathen philosophy.*

5. They have, however, been led into this error by their close study of heathen writers, who have respectively applied the terms "of whom" and "through whom" to things which are by nature dis-

tinct. These writers suppose that by the term "of whom" or "of which" the matter is indicated, while the term "through whom" or "through which" represents the instrument, or, generally speaking, subordinate agency. Or rather—for there seems no reason why we should not take up their whole argument, and briefly expose at once its incompatibility with the truth and its inconsistency with their own teaching—the students of vain philosophy, while expounding the manifold nature of cause and distinguishing its peculiar significations, define some causes as principal, some as cooperative or con-causal, while others are of the character of "sine qua non," or indispensable. For every one of these they have a distinct and peculiar use of terms, so that the maker is indicated in a different way from the instrument. For the maker they think the proper expression is "by whom," maintaining that the bench is produced "by" the carpenter; and for the instrument "through which," in that it is produced "through" or by means of adze and gimlet and the rest. Similarly they appropriate "of which" to the material, in that the thing made is "of" wood, while "according to which" shews the design, or pattern put before the craftsman. For he either first makes a mental sketch, and so brings his fancy to bear upon what he is about, or else he looks at a pattern previously put before him, and arranges his work accordingly. The phrase "on account of which" they wish to be confined to the end or purpose, the bench, as they say, being produced for, or on account of, the use of man. "In which" is supposed to indicate time and place. When was it produced? In this time. And where? In this place. And though place and time contribute nothing to what is being produced, yet without these the production of anything is impossible, for efficient agents must have both place and time. It is these careful distinctions, derived from unpractical philosophy and vain delusion, which our opponents have first studied and admired, and then transferred to the simple and unsophisticated doctrine of the Spirit, to the belittling of God the Word, and the setting at naught of the Divine Spirit. Even the phrase set apart by non-Christian writers for the case of lifeless instruments or of manual service of the meanest kind, I mean the expression "through or by means of which," they do not shrink from transferring to the Lord of all, and Christians feel no shame in applying to the Creator of the universe language belonging to a hammer or a saw.

Chapter IV: *That there is no distinction in the scriptural use of these syllables.*

6. We acknowledge that the word of truth has in many places made use of these expressions; yet we absolutely deny that the freedom of the Spirit is in bondage to the pettiness of Paganism. On the contrary, we maintain that Scripture varies its expressions as occasion requires, according to the circumstances of the case. For instance, suppose, indicate the material, but it is more in accordance with the usage of Scripture to apply this term in the case of the Supreme Cause, as in the words "One God, of whom are all things," and again, "All things of God." The word of truth has, however, frequently used this term in the case of the material, as when it says "Thou shalt make an ark of incorruptible wood;" and "Thou shalt make the candlestick of pure gold;" and "The first man is of the earth, earthy;" and "Thou art formed out of clay as I am." But these men, to the end, as we have already remarked, that they may establish the difference of nature, have laid down the law that this phrase befits the Father alone. This distinction they have originally derived from heathen authorities, but here they have shewn no faithful accuracy of limitation. To the Son they have in conformity with the teaching of their masters given the title of instrument, and to the Spirit that of place, for they say in the Spirit, and through the Son. But when they apply "of whom" to God they no longer follow heathen example, but "go over, as they say, to apostolic usage, as it is said, "But of him are ye in Christ Jesus," and "All things of God." What, then, is the result of this systematic discussion? There is one nature of Cause; another of Instrument; another of Place. So the Son is by nature distinct from the Father, as the tool from the craftsman; and the Spirit is distinct in so far as place or time is distinguished from the nature of tools or from that of them that handle them.

Chapter V: *That "through whom" is said also in the case of the Father, and "of whom" in the case of the Son and of the Spirit.*

7. After thus describing the outcome of our adversaries' arguments, we shall now proceed to shew, as we have proposed, that the

Father does not first take "of whom" and then abandon "through whom" to the Son; and that there is no truth in these men's ruling that the Son refuses to admit the Holy Spirit to a share in "of whom" or in "through whom," according to the limitation of their new-fangled allotment of phrases. "There is one God and Father of whom are all things, and one Lord Jesus Christ through whom are all things." Yes; but these are the words of a writer not laying down a rule, but carefully distinguishing the hypostases. The object of the apostle in thus writing was not to introduce the diversity of nature, but to exhibit the notion of Father and of Son as unconfounded. That the phrases are not opposed to one another and do not, like squadrons in war marshaled one against another, bring the natures to which they are applied into mutual conflict, is perfectly plain from the passage in question. The blessed Paul brings both phrases to bear upon one and the same subject, in the words "of him and through him and to him are all things." That this plainly refers to the Lord will be admitted even by a reader paying but small attention to the meaning of the words. The apostle has just quoted from the prophecy of Isaiah, "Who hath known the mind of the Lord, or who hath been his counselor," and then goes on, "For of him and from him and to him are all things." That the prophet is speaking about God the Word, the Maker of all creation, may be learnt from what immediately precedes: "Who hath measured the waters in the hollow of his hand, and meted out heaven with the span, and comprehended the dust of the earth in a measure, and weighed the mountains in scales, and the hills in a balance? Who hath directed the Spirit of the Lord, or being his counselor hath taught him?" Now the word "who" in this passage does not mean absolute impossibility, but rarity, as in the passage "Who will rise up for me against the evil doers?" and "What man is he that desireth life?" and "Who shall ascend into the hill of the Lord?" So is it in the passage in question, "Who hath directed [lxx., known] the Spirit of the Lord, or being his counselor hath known him?" "For the Father loveth the Son and sheweth him all things." This is He who holds the earth, and hath grasped it with His hand, who brought all things to order and adornment, who poised the hills in their places, and measured the waters, and gave to all things in the universe their proper rank, who encompasseth the whole of heaven with but a small portion of His power, which, in a figure, the prophet calls a span. Well then did the apostle add "Of him and through him and to him are all things." For of Him, to all things that are, comes the cause of their being, according to the will of God the Father. Through Him all things have their continuance and constitution, for He created all things, and metes out to each severally what is necessary for its health and preservation. Wherefore to Him all things are turned, looking with irresistible longing and unspeakable affection to "the author" and maintainer "of" their "life," as it is written "The eyes of all wait upon thee," and again, "These wait all upon thee," and "Thou openest thine hand, and satisfiest the desire of every living thing."

8. But if our adversaries oppose this our interpretation, what argument will save them from being caught in their own trap? For if they will not grant that the three expressions "of him" and "through him" and "to him" are spoken of the Lord, they cannot but be applied to God the Father. Then without question their rule will fall through, for we find not only "of whom," but also "through whom" applied to the Father. And if this latter phrase indicates nothing derogatory, why in the world should it be confined, as though conveying the sense of inferiority, to the Son? If it always and everywhere implies ministry, let them tell us to what superior the God of glory and Father of the Christ is subordinate. They are thus overthrown by their own selves, while our position will be on both sides made sure. Suppose it proved that the passage refers to the Son, "of whom" will be found applicable to the Son. Suppose on the other hand it be insisted that the prophet's words relate to God, then it will be granted that "through whom" is properly used of God, and both phrases have equal value, in that both are used with equal force of God. Under either alternative both terms, being employed of one and the same Person, will be shewn to be equivalent. But let us revert to our subject.

9. In his Epistle to the Ephesians the apostle says, "But speaking the truth in love, may grow up into him in all things, which is the head, even Christ; from whom the whole body fitly joined together and compacted by that which every joint supplieth, according to the effectual working in the measure of every part, maketh increase of the body."

And again in the Epistle to the Colossians, to them that have not the knowledge of the Only Begotten, there is mention of him that holdeth "the head," that is, Christ, "from which all the body by joints and bands having nourishment ministered increaseth with the increase of God." And that Christ is the head of the Church we have learned in another passage, when the apostle says "gave him to be the head over all things to the Church," and "of his fullness have all we received." And the Lord Himself says "He shall take of mine, and shall shew it unto you." In a word, the diligent reader will perceive that "of whom" is used in diverse manners. For instance, the Lord says, "I perceive that virtue is gone out of me." Similarly we have frequently observed "of whom" used of the Spirit. "He that soweth to the spirit," it is said, "shall of the spirit reap life everlasting." John too writes, "Hereby we know that he abideth in us by (ἐκ) the spirit which he hath given us." "That which is conceived in her," says the angel, "is of the Holy Ghost," and the Lord says "that which is born of the spirit is spirit." Such then is the case so far.

10. It must now be pointed out that the phrase "through whom" is admitted by Scripture in the case of the Father and of the Son and of the Holy Ghost alike. It would indeed be tedious to bring forward evidence of this in the case of the Son, not only because it is perfectly well known, but because this very point is made by our opponents. We now show that "through whom" is used also in the case of the Father. "God is faithful," it is said, "by whom (δι' οὗ) ye were called unto the fellowship of his Son," and "Paul an apostle of Jesus Christ by (διά) the will of God;" and again, "Wherefore thou art no more a servant, but a son; and if a son, then an heir through God." And "like as Christ was raised up from the dead by (διά) the glory of God the Father." Isaiah, moreover, says, "Woe unto them that make deep counsel and not through the Lord;" and many proofs of the use of this phrase in the case of the Spirit might be adduced. "God hath revealed him to us," it is said, "by (διά) the spirit;" and in another place, "That good thing which was committed unto thee keep by (διά) the Holy Ghost;" and again, "To one is given by (διά) the spirit the word of wisdom."

11. In the same manner it may also be said of the word "in,"

that Scripture admits its use in the case of God the Father. In the Old Testament it is said through (ἐν) God we shall do valiantly, and, "My praise shall be continually of (ἐν) thee;" and again, "In thy name will I rejoice." In Paul we read, "In God who created all things," and, "Paul and Silvanus and Timotheus unto the church of the Thessalonians in God our Father;" and "if now at length I might have a prosperous journey by (ἐν) the will of God to come to you;" and, "Thou makest thy boast of God." Instances are indeed too numerous to reckon; but what we want is not so much to exhibit an abundance of evidence as to prove that the conclusions of our opponents are unsound. I shall, therefore, omit any proof of this usage in the case of our Lord and of the Holy Ghost, in that it is notorious. But I cannot forbear to remark that "the wise hearer" will find sufficient proof of the proposition before him by following the method of contraries. For if the difference of language indicates, as we are told, that the nature has been changed, then let identity of language compel our adversaries to confess with shame that the essence is unchanged.

12. And it is not only in the case of the theology that the use of the terms varies, but whenever one of the terms takes the meaning of the other we find them frequently transferred from the one subject to the other. As, for instance, Adam says, "I have gotten a man through God," meaning to say the same as from God; and in another passage "Moses commanded…Israel through the word of the Lord," and, again, "Is not the interpretation through God?" Joseph, discoursing about dreams to the prisoners, instead of saying "from God" says plainly "through God." Inversely Paul uses the term "from whom" instead of "through whom," when he says "made from a woman" (A.V., "of" instead of "through a woman"). And this he has plainly distinguished in another passage, where he says that it is proper to a woman to be made of the man, and to a man to be made through the woman, in the words "For as the woman is from [A.V., of] the man, even so is the man also through [A.V., by] the woman." Nevertheless in the passage in question the apostle, while illustrating the variety of usage, at the same time corrects obiter the error of those who supposed that the body of the Lord was a spiritual body, and, to shew that the God-bearing flesh was formed out of the common lump of human nature, gave precedence to the more emphatic preposition.

The phrase "through a woman" would be likely to give rise to the suspicion of mere transit in the generation, while the phrase "of the woman" would satisfactorily indicate that the nature was shared by the mother and the offspring. The apostle was in no wise contradicting himself, but he shewed that the words can without difficulty be interchanged. Since, therefore, the term "from whom" is transferred to the identical subjects in the case of which "through whom" is decided to be properly used, with what consistency can these phrases be invariably distinguished one from the other, in order that fault may be falsely found with true religion?

Chapter VI: *Issue joined with those who assert that the Son is not with the Father, but after the Father. Also concerning the equal glory.*

13. Our opponents, while they thus artfully and perversely encounter our argument, cannot even have recourse to the plea of ignorance. It is obvious that they are annoyed with us for completing the doxology to the Only Begotten together with the Father, and for not separating the Holy Spirit from the Son. On this account they style us innovators, revolutionizers, phrase-coiners, and every other possible name of insult. But so far am I from being irritated at their abuse, that, were it not for the fact that their loss causes me "heaviness and continual sorrow," I could almost have said that I was grateful to them for the blasphemy, as though they were agents for providing me with blessing. For "blessed are ye," it is said, "when men shall revile you for my sake." The grounds of their indignation are these: The Son, according to them, is not together with the Father, but after the Father. Hence it follows that glory should be ascribed to the Father "through him," but not "with him;" inasmuch as "with him" expresses equality of dignity, while "through him" denotes subordination. They further assert that the Spirit is not to be ranked along with the Father and the Son, but under the Son and the Father; not coordinated, but subordinated; not connumerated, but subnumerated.

With technical terminology of this kind they pervert the simplicity and artlessness of the faith, and thus by their ingenuity, suffering no one else to remain in ignorance, they cut off from themselves the plea that ignorance might demand.

14. Let us first ask them this question: In what sense do they say that the Son is "after the Father;" later in time, or in order, or in dignity? But in time no one is so devoid of sense as to assert that the Maker of the ages holds a second place, when no interval intervenes in the natural conjunction of the Father with the Son. And indeed so far as our conception of human relations goes, it is impossible to think of the Son as being later than the Father, not only from the fact that Father and Son are mutually conceived of in accordance with the relationship subsisting between them, but because posteriority in time is predicated of subjects separated by a less interval from the present, and priority of subjects farther off. For instance, what happened in Noah's time is prior to what happened to the men of Sodom, inasmuch as Noah is more remote from our own day; and, again, the events of the history of the men of Sodom are posterior, because they seem in a sense to approach nearer to our own day. But, in addition to its being a breach of true religion, is it not really the extremest folly to measure the existence of the life which transcends all time and all the ages by its distance from the present? Is it not as though God the Father could be compared with, and be made superior to, God the Son, who exists before the ages, precisely in the same way in which things liable to beginning and corruption are described as prior to one another?

The superior remoteness of the Father is really inconceivable, in that thought and intelligence are wholly impotent to go beyond the generation of the Lord; and St. John has admirably confined the conception within circumscribed boundaries by two words, "In the beginning was the Word." For thought cannot travel outside "was," nor imagination beyond "beginning." Let your thought travel ever so far backward you cannot get beyond the "was," and however you may strain and strive to see what is beyond the Son, you will find it impossible to get further than the "beginning." True religion, therefore, thus teaches us to think of the Son together with the Father.

15. If they really conceive of a kind of degradation of the Son in relation to the Father, as though He were in a lower place, so that

the Father sits above, and the Son is thrust off to the next seat below, let them confess what they mean. We shall have no more to say. A plain statement of the view will at once expose its absurdity. They who refuse to allow that the Father pervades all things do not so much as maintain the logical sequence of thought in their argument. The faith of the sound is that God fills all things; but they who divide their up and down between the Father and the Son do not remember even the word of the Prophet: "If I climb up into heaven thou art there; if I go down to hell thou art there also." Now, to omit all proof of the ignorance of those who predicate place of incorporeal things, what excuse can be found for their attack upon Scripture, shameless as their antagonism is, in the passages "Sit thou on my right hand" and "Sat down on the right hand of the majesty of God"? The expression "right hand" does not, as they contend, indicate the lower place, but equality of relation; it is not understood physically, in which case there might be something sinister about God, but Scripture puts before us the magnificence of the dignity of the Son by the use of dignified language indicating the seat of honour. It is left then for our opponents to allege that this expression signifies inferiority of rank. Let them learn that "Christ is the power of God and wisdom of God," and that "He is the image of the invisible God" and "brightness of his glory," and that "Him hath God the Father sealed," by engraving Himself on Him.

Now are we to call these passages, and others like them, throughout the whole of Holy Scripture, proofs of humiliation, or rather public proclamations of the majesty of the Only Begotten, and of the equality of His glory with the Father? We ask them to listen to the Lord Himself, distinctly setting forth the equal dignity of His glory with the Father, in His words, "He that hath seen me hath seen the Father;" and again, "When the Son cometh in the glory of his Father;" that they "should honour the Son even as they honour the Father;" and, "We beheld his glory, the glory as of the only begotten of the Father;" and "the only begotten God which is in the bosom of the Father." Of all these passages they take no account, and then assign to the Son the place set apart for His foes. A father's bosom is a fit and becoming seat for a son, but the place of the footstool is for them that have to be forced to fall.

We have only touched cursorily on these proofs, because our object is to pass on to other points. You at your leisure can put together the items of the evidence, and then contemplate the height of the glory and the preeminence of the power of the Only Begotten. However, to the well-disposed hearer, even these are not insignificant, unless the terms "right hand" and "bosom" be accepted in a physical and derogatory sense, so as at once to circumscribe God in local limits, and invent form, mould, and bodily position, all of which are totally distinct from the idea of the absolute, the infinite, and the incorporeal. There is moreover the fact that what is derogatory in the idea of it is the same in the case both of the Father and the Son; so that whoever repeats these arguments does not take away the dignity of the Son, but does incur the charge of blaspheming the Father; for whatever audacity a man be guilty of against the Son he cannot but transfer to the Father. If he assigns to the Father the upper place by way of precedence, and asserts that the only begotten Son sits below, he will find that to the creature of his imagination attach all the consequent conditions of body. And if these are the imaginations of drunken delusion and phrensied insanity, can it be consistent with true religion for men taught by the Lord himself that "He that honoureth not the Son honoureth not the Father" to refuse to worship and glorify with the Father him who in nature, in glory, and in dignity is conjoined with him? What shall we say? What just defense shall we have in the day of the awful universal judgment of all-creation, if, when the Lord clearly announces that He will come "in the glory of his Father;" when Stephen beheld Jesus standing at the right hand of God; when Paul testified in the spirit concerning Christ "that he is at the right hand of God;" when the Father says, "Sit thou on my right hand;" when the Holy Spirit bears witness that he has sat down on "the right hand of the majesty" of God; we attempt to degrade him who shares the honour and the throne, from his condition of equality, to a lower state? Standing and sitting, I apprehend, indicate the fixity and entire stability of the nature, as Baruch, when he wishes to exhibit the immutability and immobility of the Divine mode of existence, says, "For thou sittest for ever and we perish utterly." Moreover, the place on the right hand indicates in my judgment equality of honour. Rash, then, is the attempt to deprive the Son of participation in the doxology, as though worthy only to be ranked in a lower place of honour.

Chapter VII: *Against those who assert that it is not proper for "with whom" to be said of the Son, and that the proper phrase is "through whom."*

16. But their contention is that to use the phrase "with him" is altogether strange and unusual, while "through him" is at once most familiar in Holy Scripture, and very common in the language of the brotherhood. What is our answer to this? We say, Blessed are the ears that have not heard you and the hearts that have been kept from the wounds of your words. To you, on the other hand, who are lovers of Christ, I say that the Church recognizes both uses, and deprecates neither as subversive of the other. For whenever we are contemplating the majesty of the nature of the Only Begotten, and the excellence of His dignity, we bear witness that the glory is with the Father; while on the other hand, whenever we bethink us of His bestowal on us of good gifts, and of our access to, and admission into, the household of God, we confess that this grace is effected for us through Him and by Him.

It follows that the one phrase "with whom" is the proper one to be used in the ascription of glory, while the other, "through whom," is specially appropriate in giving of thanks. It is also quite untrue to allege that the phrase "with whom" is unfamiliar in the usage of the devout. All those whose soundness of character leads them to hold the dignity of antiquity to be more honourable than mere newfangled novelty, and who have preserved the tradition of their fathers unadulterated, alike in town and in country, have employed this phrase. It is, on the contrary, they who are surfeited with the familiar and the customary, and arrogantly assail the old as stale, who welcome innovation, just as in dress your lovers of display always prefer some utter novelty to what is generally worn. So you may even still see that the language of country folk preserves the ancient fashion, while of these, our cunning experts in logomachy, the language bears the brand of the new philosophy. What our fathers said, the same say we, that the glory of the Father and of the Son is common; wherefore we offer the doxology to the Father with the Son. But we do not rest only on the fact that such is the tradition of the Fathers; for they too followed the sense of Scripture, and started from the evidence which, a few sentences back, I deduced from Scripture and laid before you. For "the brightness" is always thought of with "the glory," "the image" with the archetype, and the Son always and everywhere together with the Father; nor does even the close connexion of the names, much less the nature of the things, admit of separation.

Chapter XXVII: *Of the origin of the word "with," and what force it has. Also concerning the unwritten laws of the church.*

65. The word "in," say our opponents, "is exactly appropriate to the Spirit, and sufficient for every thought concerning Him. Why then, they ask, have we introduced this new phrase, saying, "with the Spirit" instead of "in the Holy Spirit," thus employing an expression which is quite unnecessary, and sanctioned by no usage in the churches? Now it has been asserted in the previous portion of this treatise that the word "in" has not been specially allotted to the Holy Spirit, but is common to the Father and the Son. It has also been, in my opinion, sufficiently demonstrated that, so far from detracting anything from the dignity of the Spirit, it leads all, but those whose thoughts are wholly perverted, to the sublimest height. It remains for me to trace the origin of the word "with;" to explain what force it has, and to shew that it is in harmony with Scripture.

66. Of the beliefs and practices whether generally accepted or publicly enjoined which are preserved in the Church some we possess derived from written teaching; others we have received delivered to us "in a mystery" by the tradition of the apostles; and both of these in relation to true religion have the same force. And these no one will gainsay; no one, at all events, who is even moderately versed in the institutions of the Church. For were we to attempt to reject such customs as have no written authority, on the ground that the importance they possess is small, we should unintentionally injure the Gospel in its very vitals; or, rather, should make our public definition a mere phrase and nothing more. For instance, to take the first and most general example, who is thence who has taught us in writing to

sign with the sign of the cross those who have trusted in the name of our Lord Jesus Christ? What writing has taught us to turn to the East at the prayer? Which of the saints has left us in writing the words of the invocation at the displaying of the bread of the Eucharist and the cup of blessing? For we are not, as is well known, content with what the apostle or the Gospel has recorded, but both in preface and conclusion we add other words as being of great importance to the validity of the ministry, and these we derive from unwritten teaching. Moreover we bless the water of baptism and the oil of the chrism, and besides this the catechumen who is being baptized. On what written authority do we do this? Is not our authority silent and mystical tradition? Nay, by what written word is the anointing of oil itself taught? And whence comes the custom of baptizing thrice? And as to the other customs of baptism from what Scripture do we derive the renunciation of Satan and his angels? Does not this come from that unpublished and secret teaching which our fathers guarded in a silence out of the reach of curious meddling and inquisitive investigation? Well had they learnt the lesson that the awful dignity of the mysteries is best preserved by silence. What the uninitiated are not even allowed to look at was hardly likely to be publicly paraded about in written documents. What was the meaning of the mighty Moses in not making all the parts of the tabernacle open to everyone? The profane he stationed without the sacred barriers; the first courts he conceded to the purer; the Levites alone he judged worthy of being servants of the Deity; sacrifices and burnt offerings and the rest of the priestly functions he allotted to the priests; one chosen out of all he admitted to the shrine, and even this one not always but on only one day in the year, and of this one day a time was fixed for his entry so that he might gaze on the Holy of Holies amazed at the strangeness and novelty of the sight. Moses was wise enough to know that contempt stretches to the trite and to the obvious, while a keen interest is naturally associated with the unusual and the unfamiliar. In the same manner the Apostles and Fathers who laid down laws for the Church from the beginning thus guarded the awful dignity of the mysteries in secrecy and silence, for what is bruited abroad random among the common folk is no mystery at all. This is the reason for our tradition of unwritten precepts and practices, that the knowledge of our dogmas may not become neglected and contemned by the multitude through familiarity. "Dogma" and "Kerugma" are two distinct things; the former is observed in silence; the latter is proclaimed to all the world. One form of this silence is the obscurity employed in Scripture, which makes the meaning of "dogmas" difficult to be understood for the very advantage of the reader: Thus we all look to the East at our prayers, but few of us know that we are seeking our own old country, Paradise, which God planted in Eden in the East. We pray standing, on the first day of the week, but we do not all know the reason. On the day of the resurrection (or "standing again" Grk. ἀνάστασις) we remind ourselves of the grace given to us by standing at prayer, not only because we rose with Christ, and are bound to "seek those things which are above," but because the day seems to us to be in some sense an image of the age which we expect, wherefore, though it is the beginning of days, it is not called by Moses first, but one. For he says "There was evening, and there was morning, one day," as though the same day often recurred. Now "one" and "eighth" are the same, in itself distinctly indicating that really "one" and "eighth" of which the Psalmist makes mention in certain titles of the Psalms, the state which follows after this present time, the day which knows no waning or eventide, and no successor, that age which endeth not or groweth old. Of necessity, then, the church teaches her own foster children to offer their prayers on that day standing, to the end that through continual reminder of the endless life we may not neglect to make provision for our removal thither. Moreover all Pentecost is a reminder of the resurrection expected in the age to come. For that one and first day, if seven times multiplied by seven, completes the seven weeks of the holy Pentecost; for, beginning at the first, Pentecost ends with the same, making fifty revolutions through the like intervening days. And so it is a likeness of eternity, beginning as it does and ending, as in a circling course, at the same point. On this day the rules of the church have educated us to prefer the upright attitude of prayer, for by their plain reminder they, as it were, make our mind to dwell no longer in the present but in the future. Moreover every time we fall upon our knees and rise from off them we shew by the very deed that by our sin we fell down to earth, and by the loving kindness of our Creator were called back to heaven.

67. Time will fail me if I attempt to recount the unwritten

mysteries of the Church. Of the rest I say nothing; but of the very confession of our faith in Father, Son, and Holy Ghost, what is the written source? If it be granted that, as we are baptized, so also under the obligation to believe, we make our confession in like terms as our baptism, in accordance with the tradition of our baptism and in conformity with the principles of true religion, let our opponents grant us too the right to be as consistent in our ascription of glory as in our confession of faith. If they deprecate our doxology on the ground that it lacks written authority, let them give us the written evidence for the confession of our faith and the other matters which we have enumerated. While the unwritten traditions are so many, and their bearing on "the mystery of godliness" is so important, can they refuse to allow us a single word which has come down to us from the Fathers—which we found, derived from untutored custom, abiding in unperverted churches—a word for which the arguments are strong, and which contributes in no small degree to the completeness of the force of the mystery?

68. The force of both expressions has now been explained. I will proceed to state once more wherein they agree and wherein they differ from one another; not that they are opposed in mutual antagonism, but that each contributes its own meaning to true religion. The preposition "in" states the truth rather relatively to ourselves; while "with" proclaims the fellowship of the Spirit with God. Wherefore we use both words, by the one expressing the dignity of the Spirit; by the other announcing the grace that is with us. Thus we ascribe glory to God both "in" the Spirit, and "with" the Spirit; and herein it is not our word that we use, but we follow the teaching of the Lord as we might a fixed rule, and transfer His word to things connected and closely related, and of which the conjunction in the mysteries is necessary. We have deemed ourselves under a necessary obligation to combine in our confession of the faith Him who is numbered with Them at Baptism, and we have treated the confession of the faith as the origin and parent of the doxology. What, then, is to be done? They must now instruct us either not to baptize as we have received, or not to believe as we were baptized, or not to ascribe glory as we have believed. Let any man prove if he can that the relation of sequence in these acts is not necessary and unbroken; or let any

man deny if he can that innovation here must mean ruin everywhere. Yet they never stop dinning in our ears that the ascription of glory "with" the Holy Spirit is unauthorized and unscriptural and the like. We have stated that so far as the sense goes it is the same to say "glory be to the Father and to the Son and to the Holy Ghost," and "glory be to the Father and to the Son with the Holy Ghost." It is impossible for any one to reject or cancel the syllable "and," which is derived from the very words of our Lord, and there is nothing to hinder the acceptance of its equivalent. What amount of difference and similarity there is between the two we have already shewn. And our argument is confirmed by the fact that the Apostle uses either word indifferently, saying at one time "in the name of the Lord Jesus and by the Spirit of our God;" at another "when ye are gathered together, and my Spirit, with the power of our Lord Jesus," with no idea that it makes any difference to the connexion of the names whether he use the conjunction or the preposition.

Chapter XXVIII: *That our opponents refuse to concede in the case of the Spirit the terms which Scripture uses in the case of men, as reigning together with Christ.*

69. But let us see if we can bethink us of any defense of this usage of our fathers; for they who first originated the expression are more open to blame than we ourselves. Paul in his Letter to the Colossians says, "And you, being dead in your sins and the uncircumcision…hath He quickened together with" Christ. Did then God give to a whole people and to the Church the boon of the life with Christ, and yet the life with Christ does not belong to the Holy Spirit? But if this is impious even to think of, is it not rightly reverent so to make our confession, as They are by nature in close conjunction? Furthermore what boundless lack of sensibility does it not shew in these men to confess that the Saints are with Christ, (if, as we know is the case, Paul, on becoming absent from the body, is present with the Lord, and, after departing, is with Christ) and, so far as lies in their power, to refuse to allow to the Spirit to be with Christ even to the same extent as men? And Paul calls himself a "labourer together with God" in the dispensation of the Gospel; will they bring an in-

dictment for impiety against us, if we apply the term "fellow labourer" to the Holy Spirit, through whom in every creature under heaven the Gospel bringeth forth fruit? The life of them that have trusted in the Lord "is hidden," it would seem, "with Christ in God, and when Christ, who is our life, shall appear, then shall" they themselves also "appear with Him in glory;" and is the Spirit of life Himself, "Who made us free from the law of sin," not with Christ, both in the secret and hidden life with Him, and in the manifestation of the glory which we expect to be manifested in the saints? We are "heirs of God and joint heirs with Christ," and is the Spirit without part or lot in the fellowship of God and of His Christ? "The Spirit itself beareth witness with our spirit that we are the children of God;" and are we not to allow to the Spirit even that testimony of His fellowship with God which we have learnt from the Lord? For the height of folly is reached if we through the faith in Christ which is in the Spirit hope that we shall be raised together with Him and sit together in heavenly places, whenever He shall change our vile body from the natural to the spiritual, and yet refuse to assign to the Spirit any share in the sitting together, or in the glory, or anything else which we have received from Him. Of all the boons of which, in accordance with the indefeasible grant of Him who has promised them, we have believed ourselves worthy, are we to allow none to the Holy Spirit, as though they were all above His dignity? It is yours according to your merit to be "ever with the Lord," and you expect to be caught up "in the clouds to meet the Lord in the air and to be ever with the Lord." You declare the man who numbers and ranks the Spirit with the Father and the Son to be guilty of intolerable impiety. Can you really now deny that the Spirit is with Christ?

70. I am ashamed to add the rest. You expect to be glorified together with Christ; ("if so be that we suffer with him that we may be also glorified together;") but you do not glorify the "Spirit of holiness" together with Christ, as though He were not worthy to receive equal honour even with you. You hope to "reign with" Christ; but you "do despite unto the Spirit of grace" by assigning Him the rank of a slave and a subordinate. And I say this not to demonstrate that so much is due to the Spirit in the ascription of glory, but to prove the unfairness of those who will not ever give so much as this,

and shrink from the fellowship of the Spirit with Son and Father as from impiety. Who could touch on these things without a sigh? Is it not so plain as to be within the perception even of a child that this present state of things preludes the threatened eclipse of the faith? The undeniable has become the uncertain. We profess belief in the Spirit, and then we quarrel with our own confessions. We are baptized, and begin to fight again. We call upon Him as the Prince of Life, and then despise Him as a slave like ourselves. We received Him with the Father and the Son, and we dishonour Him as a part of creation. Those who "know not what they ought to pray for," even though they be induced to utter a word of the Spirit with awe, as though coming near His dignity, yet prune down all that exceeds the exact proportion of their speech. They ought rather to bewail their weakness, in that we are powerless to express in words our gratitude for the benefits which we are actually receiving; for He "passes all understanding," and convicts speech of its natural inability even to approach His dignity in the least degree; as it is written in the Book of Wisdom, "Exalt Him as much as you can, for even yet will He far exceed; and when you exalt Him put forth all your strength, and be not weary, for you can never go far enough." Verily terrible is the account to be given for words of this kind by you who have heard from God who cannot lie that for blasphemy against the Holy Ghost there is no forgiveness.

Chapter XXIX: *Enumeration of the illustrious men in the Church who in their writings have used the word "with."*

71. In answer to the objection that the doxology in the form "with the Spirit" has no written authority, we maintain that if there is no other instance of that which is unwritten, then this must not be received. But if the greater number of our mysteries are admitted into our constitution without written authority, then, in company with the many others, let us receive this one. For I hold it apostolic to abide also by the unwritten traditions. "I praise you," it is said, "that ye remember me in all things, and keep the ordinances as I delivered them to you;" and "Hold fast the traditions which ye have been taught whether by word, or our Epistle." One of these tradi-

tions is the practice which is now before us, which they who ordained from the beginning, rooted firmly in the churches, delivering it to their successors, and its use through long custom advances pace by pace with time. If, as in a Court of Law, we were at a loss for documentary evidence, but were able to bring before you a large number of witnesses, would you not give your vote for our acquittal? I think so; for "at the mouth of two or three witnesses shall the matter be established." And if we could prove clearly to you that a long period of time was in our favour, should we not have seemed to you to urge with reason that this suit ought not to be brought into court against us? For ancient dogmas inspire a certain sense of awe, venerable as they are with a hoary antiquity. I will therefore give you a list of the supporters of the word (and the time too must be taken into account in relation to what passes unquestioned). For it did not originate with us. How could it? We, in comparison with the time during which this word has been in vogue, are, to use the words of Job, "but of yesterday." I myself, if I must speak of what concerns me individually, cherish this phrase as a legacy left me by my fathers. It was delivered to me by one who spent a long life in the service of God, and by him I was both baptized, and admitted to the ministry of the church. While examining, so far as I could, if any of the blessed men of old used the words to which objection is now made, I found many worthy of credit both on account of their early date, and also a characteristic in which they are unlike the men of to-day—because of the exactness of their knowledge. Of these some coupled the word in the doxology by the preposition, others by the conjunction, but were in no case supposed to be acting divergently—at least so far as the right sense of true religion is concerned.

72. There is the famous Irenæus, and Clement of Rome; Dionysius of Rome, and, strange to say, Dionysius of Alexandria, in his second Letter to his namesake, on "Conviction and Defense," so concludes. I will give you his very words. "Following all these, we, too, since we have received from the presbyters who were before us a form and rule, offering thanksgiving in the same terms with them, thus conclude our Letter to you. To God the Father and the Son our Lord Jesus Christ, with the Holy Ghost, glory and might for ever and ever; amen." And no one can say that this passage has been altered.

He would not have so persistently stated that he had received a form and rule if he had said "in the Spirit." For of this phrase the use is abundant: it was the use of "with" which required defense. Dionysius moreover in the middle of his treatise thus writes in opposition to the Sabellians, "If by the hypostases being three they say that they are divided, there are three, though they like it not. Else let them destroy the divine Trinity altogether." And again: "most divine on this account after the Unity is the Trinity." Clement, in more primitive fashion, writes, "God lives, and the Lord Jesus Christ, and the Holy Ghost." And now let us hear how Irenæus, who lived near the times of the Apostles, mentions the Spirit in his work "Against the Heresies." "The Apostle rightly calls carnal them that are unbridled and carried away to their own desires, having no desire for the Holy Spirit," and in another passage Irenæus says, "The Apostle exclaimed that flesh and blood cannot inherit the kingdom of the heavens lest we, being without share in the divine Spirit, fall short of the kingdom of the heavens." If any one thinks Eusebius of Palestine worthy of credit on account of his wide experience, I point further to the very words he uses in discussing questions concerning the polygamy of the ancients. Stirring up himself to his work, he writes "invoking the holy God of the Prophets, the Author of light, through our Saviour Jesus Christ, with the Holy Spirit."

73. Origen, too, in many of his expositions of the Psalms, we find using the form of doxology "with the Holy Ghost." The opinions which he held concerning the Spirit were not always and everywhere sound; nevertheless in many passages even he himself reverently recognises the force of established usage, and expresses himself concerning the Spirit in terms consistent with true religion. It is, if I am not mistaken, in the Sixth Book of his Commentary on the Gospel of St. John that he distinctly makes the Spirit an object of worship. His words are: "The washing or water is a symbol of the cleaning of the soul which is washed clean of all filth that comes of wickedness; but none the less is it also by itself, to him who yields himself to the God-head of the adorable Trinity, through the power of the invocations, the origin and source of blessings." And again, in his Exposition of the Epistle to the Romans "the holy powers," he says "are able to receive the Only-begotten, and the Godhead of the

Holy Spirit." Thus I apprehend, the powerful influence of tradition frequently impels men to express themselves in terms contradictory to their own opinions. Moreover this form of the doxology was not unknown even to Africanus the historian. In the Fifth Book of his Epitome of the Times he says "we who know the weight of those terms, and are not ignorant of the grace of faith, render thanks to the Father, who bestowed on us His own creatures, Jesus Christ, the Saviour of the world and our Lord, to whom be glory and majesty with the Holy Ghost, for ever." The rest of the passages may peradventure be viewed with suspicion; or may really have been altered, and the fact of their having been tampered with will be difficult to detect because the difference consists in a single syllable. Those however which I have quoted at length are out of the reach of any dishonest manipulation, and can easily be verified from the actual works.

I will now adduce another piece of evidence which might perhaps seem insignificant, but because of its antiquity must in nowise be omitted by a defendant who is indicted on a charge of innovation. It seemed fitting to our fathers not to receive the gift of the light at eventide in silence, but, on its appearing, immediately to give thanks. Who was the author of these words of thanksgiving at the lighting of the lamps, we are not able to say. The people, however, utter the ancient form, and no one has ever reckoned guilty of impiety those who say "We praise Father, Son, and God's Holy Spirit." And if any one knows the Hymn of Athenogenes, which, as he was hurrying on to his perfecting by fire, he left as a kind of farewell gift to his friends, he knows the mind of the martyrs as to the Spirit. On this head I shall say no more.

74. But where shall I rank the great Gregory, and the words uttered by him? Shall we not place among Apostles and Prophets a man who walked by the same Spirit as they; who never through all his days diverged from the footprints of the saints; who maintained, as long as he lived, the exact principles of evangelical citizenship? I am sure that we shall do the truth a wrong if we refuse to number that soul with the people of God, shining as it did like a beacon in the Church of God; for by the fellow-working of the Spirit the power which he had over demons was tremendous, and so gifted was

he with the grace of the word "for obedience to the faith among… the nations," that, although only seventeen Christians were handed over to him, he brought the whole people alike in town and country through knowledge to God. He too by Christ's mighty name commanded even rivers to change their course, and caused a lake, which afforded a ground of quarrel to some covetous brethren, to dry up. Moreover his predictions of things to come were such as in no wise to fall short of those of the great prophets. To recount all his wonderful works in detail would be too long a task. By the superabundance of gifts, wrought in him by the Spirit in all power and in signs and in marvels, he was styled a second Moses by the very enemies of the Church. Thus in all that he through grace accomplished, alike by word and deed, a light seemed ever to be shining, token of the heavenly power from the unseen which followed him. To this day he is a great object of admiration to the people of his own neighbourhood, and his memory, established in the churches ever fresh and green, is not dulled by length of time. Thus not a practice, not a word, not a mystic rite has been added to the Church besides what he bequeathed to it. Hence truly on account of the antiquity of their institution many of their ceremonies appear to be defective. For his successors in the administration of the Churches could not endure to accept any subsequent discovery in addition to what had had his sanction. Now one of the institutions of Gregory is the very form of the doxology to which objection is now made, preserved by the Church on the authority of his tradition; a statement which may be verified without much trouble by any one who likes to make a short journey. That our Firmilian held this belief is testified by the writings which he has left. The contemporaries also of the illustrious Meletius say that he was of this opinion. But why quote ancient authorities? Now in the East are not the maintainers of true religion known chiefly by this one term, and separated from their adversaries as by a watchword? I have heard from a certain Mesopotamian, a man at once well skilled in the language and of unperverted opinions, that by the usage of his country it is impossible for any one, even though he may wish to do so, to express himself in any other way, and that they are compelled by the idiom of their mother tongue to offer the doxology by the syllable "and," or, I should more accurately say, by their equivalent expressions. We Cappadocians, too, so speak in the dialect of our country, the Spirit having so early as the division of tongues foreseen the utility of the phrase. And what of the whole West, almost from Illyricum to the boundaries of our world? Does it not support this word?

75. How then can I be an innovator and creator of new terms, when I adduce as originators and champions of the word whole nations, cities, custom going back beyond the memory of man, men who were pillars of the church and conspicuous for all knowledge and spiritual power? For this cause this banded array of foes is set in motion against me, and town and village and remotest regions are full of my calumniators. Sad and painful are these things to them that seek for peace, but great is the reward of patience for sufferings endured for the Faith's sake. So besides these let sword flash, let axe be whetted, let fire burn fiercer than that of Babylon, let every instrument of torture be set in motion against me. To me nothing is more fearful than failure to fear the threats which the Lord has directed against them that blaspheme the Spirit. Kindly readers will find a satisfactory defense in what I have said, that I accept a phrase so dear and so familiar to the saints, and confirmed by usage so long, inasmuch as, from the day when the Gospel was first preached up to our own time, it is shewn to have been admitted to all full rights within the churches, and, what is of greatest moment, to have been accepted as bearing a sense in accordance with holiness and true religion. But before the great tribunal what have I prepared to say in my defense? This; that I was in the first place led to the glory of the Spirit by the honour conferred by the Lord in associating Him with Himself and with His Father at baptism; and secondly by the introduction of each of us to the knowledge of God by such an initiation; and above all by the fear of the threatened punishment shutting out the thought of all indignity and unworthy conception. But our opponents, what will they say? After shewing neither reverence for the Lord's honour nor fear of His threats, what kind of defense will they have for their blasphemy? It is for them to make up their mind about their own action or even now to change it. For my own part I would pray most earnestly that the good God will make His peace rule in the hearts of all, so that these men who are swollen with pride and set in battle array against us may be calmed by the Spirit of meekness and of love; and that if they have become utterly savage, and are

in an untamable state, He will grant to us at least to bear with long suffering all that we have to bear at their hands. In short "to them that have in themselves the sentence of death," it is not suffering for the sake of the Faith which is painful; what is hard to bear is to fail to fight its battle. The athlete does not so much complain of being wounded in the struggle as of not being able even to secure admission into the stadium. Or perhaps this was the time for silence spoken of by Solomon the wise. For, when life is buffeted by so fierce a storm that all the intelligence of those who are instructed in the word is filled with the deceit of false reasoning and confounded, like an eye filled with dust, when men are stunned by strange and awful noises, when all the world is shaken and everything tottering to its fall, what profits it to cry, as I am really crying, to the wind?

Chapter XXX: *Exposition of the present state of the Churches.*

76. To what then shall I liken our present condition? It may be compared, I think, to some naval battle which has arisen out of time old quarrels, and is fought by men who cherish a deadly hate against one another, of long experience in naval warfare, and eager for the fight. Look, I beg you, at the picture thus raised before your eyes. See the rival fleets rushing in dread array to the attack. With a burst of uncontrollable fury they engage and fight it out. Fancy, if you like, the ships driven to and fro by a raging tempest, while thick darkness falls from the clouds and blackens all the scenes so that watchwords are indistinguishable in the confusion, and all distinction between friend and foe is lost. To fill up the details of the imaginary picture, suppose the sea swollen with billows and whirled up from the deep, while a vehement torrent of rain pours down from the clouds and the terrible waves rise high. From every quarter of heaven the winds beat upon one point, where both the fleets are dashed one against the other. Of the combatants some are turning traitors; some are deserting in the very thick of the fight; some have at one and the same moment to urge on their boats, all beaten by the gale, and to advance against their assailants. Jealousy of authority and the lust of individual mastery splits the sailors into parties which deal mutual death to one another. Think, besides all this, of the confused and

unmeaning roar sounding over all the sea, from howling winds, from crashing vessels, from boiling surf, from the yells of the combatants as they express their varying emotions in every kind of noise, so that not a word from admiral or pilot can be heard. The disorder and confusion is tremendous, for the extremity of misfortune, when life is despaired of, gives men license for every kind of wickedness. Suppose, too, that the men are all smitten with the incurable plague of mad love of glory, so that they do not cease from their struggle each to get the better of the other, while their ship is actually settling down into the deep.

77. Turn now I beg you from this figurative description to the unhappy reality. Did it not at one time appear that the Arian schism, after its separation into a sect opposed to the Church of God, stood itself alone in hostile array? But when the attitude of our foes against us was changed from one of long standing and bitter strife to one of open warfare, then, as is well known, the war was split up in more ways than I can tell into many subdivisions, so that all men were stirred to a state of inveterate hatred alike by common party spirit and individual suspicion. But what storm at sea was ever so fierce and wild as this tempest of the Churches? In it every landmark of the Fathers has been moved; every foundation, every bulwark of opinion has been shaken: everything buoyed up on the unsound is dashed about and shaken down. We attack one another. We are overthrown by one another. If our enemy is not the first to strike us, we are wounded by the comrade at our side. If a foeman is stricken and falls, his fellow soldier tramples him down. There is at least this bond of union between us that we hate our common foes, but no sooner have the enemy gone by than we find enemies in one another. And who could make a complete list of all the wrecks? Some have gone to the bottom on the attack of the enemy, some through the unsuspected treachery of their allies, some from the blundering of their own officers. We see, as it were, whole churches, crews and all, dashed and shattered upon the sunken reefs of disingenuous heresy, while others of the enemies of the Spirit of Salvation have seized the helm and made shipwreck of the faith. And then the disturbances wrought by the princes of the world have caused the downfall of the people with a violence unmatched by that of hurricane or whirlwind. The

luminaries of the world, which God set to give light to the souls of the people, have been driven from their homes, and a darkness verily gloomy and disheartening has settled on the Churches. The terror of universal ruin is already imminent, and yet their mutual rivalry is so unbounded as to blunt all sense of danger. Individual hatred is of more importance than the general and common warfare, for men by whom the immediate gratification of ambition is esteemed more highly than the rewards that await us in a time to come, prefer the glory of getting the better of their opponents to securing the common welfare of mankind. So all men alike, each as best he can, lift the hand of murder against one another. Harsh rises the cry of the combatants encountering one another in dispute; already all the Church is almost full of the inarticulate screams, the unintelligible noises, rising from the ceaseless agitations that divert the right rule of the doctrine of true religion, now in the direction of excess, now in that of defect. On the one hand are they who confound the Persons and are carried away into Judaism; on the other hand are they that, through the opposition of the natures, pass into heathenism. Between these opposite parties inspired Scripture is powerless to mediate; the traditions of the apostles cannot suggest terms of arbitration. Plain speaking is fatal to friendship, and disagreement in opinion all the ground that is wanted for a quarrel. No oaths of confederacy are so efficacious in keeping men true to sedition as their likeness in error. Every one is a theologue though he have his soul branded with more spots than can be counted. The result is that innovators find a plentiful supply of men ripe for faction, while self-appointed scions of the house of place-hunters reject the government of the Holy Spirit and divide the chief dignities of the Churches. The institutions of the Gospel have now everywhere been thrown into confusion by want of discipline; there is an indescribable pushing for the chief places while every self-advertiser tries to force himself into high office. The result of this lust for ordering is that our people are in a state of wild confusion for lack of being ordered; the exhortations of those in authority are rendered wholly purposeless and void, because there is not a man but, out of his ignorant impudence, thinks that it is just as much his duty to give orders to other people, as it is to obey anyone else.

78. So, since no human voice is strong enough to be heard in

such a disturbance, I reckon silence more profitable than speech, for if there is any truth in the words of the Preacher, "The words of wise men are heard in quiet," in the present condition of things any discussion of them must be anything but becoming. I am moreover restrained by the Prophet's saying, "Therefore the prudent shall keep silence in that time, for it is an evil time," a time when some trip up their neighbours' heels, some stamp on a man when he is down, and others clap their hands with joy, but there is not one to feel for the fallen and hold out a helping hand, although according to the ancient law he is not uncondemned, who passes by even his enemy's beast of burden fallen under his load. This is not the state of things now. Why not? The love of many has waxed cold; brotherly concord is destroyed, the very name of unity is ignored, brotherly admonitions are heard no more, nowhere is there Christian pity, nowhere falls the tear of sympathy. Now there is no one to receive "the weak in faith," but mutual hatred has blazed so high among fellow clansmen that they are more delighted at a neighbour's fall than at their own success. Just as in a plague, men of the most regular lives suffer from the same sickness as the rest, because they catch the disease by communication with the infected, so nowadays by the evil rivalry which possesses our souls we are carried away to an emulation in wickedness, and are all of us each as bad as the others. Hence merciless and sour sit the judges of the erring; unfeeling and hostile are the critics of the well disposed. And to such a depth is this evil rooted among us that we have become more brutish than the brutes; they do at least herd with their fellows, but our most savage warfare is with our own people.

79. For all these reasons I ought to have kept silence, but I was drawn in the other direction by love, which "seeketh not her own," and desires to overcome every difficulty put in her way by time and circumstance. I was taught too by the children at Babylon, that, when there is no one to support the cause of true religion, we ought alone and all unaided to do our duty. They from out of the midst of the flame lifted up their voices in hymns and praise to God, reeking not of the host that set the truth at naught, but sufficient, three only that they were, with one another. Wherefore we too are undismayed at the cloud of our enemies, and, resting our hope on the aid of the Spirit, have, with all boldness, proclaimed the truth. Had I not so done, it

would truly have been terrible that the blasphemers of the Spirit should so easily be emboldened in their attack upon true religion, and that we, with so mighty an ally and supporter at our side, should shrink from the service of that doctrine, which by the tradition of the Fathers has been preserved by an unbroken sequence of memory to our own day. A further powerful incentive to my undertaking was the warm fervour of your "love unfeigned," and the seriousness and taciturnity of your disposition; a guarantee that you would not publish what I was about to say to all the world—not because it would not be worth making known, but to avoid casting pearls before swine. My task is now done. If you find what I have said satisfactory, let this make an end to our discussion of these matters. If you think any point requires further elucidation, pray do not hesitate to pursue the investigation with all diligence, and to add to your information by putting any uncontroversial question. Either through me or through others the Lord will grant full explanation on matters which have yet to be made clear, according to the knowledge supplied to the worthy by the Holy Spirit. Amen.

FUNERAL ORATION ON THE GREAT ST. BASIL

GREGORY NAZIENZEN

Translated by Philip Schaff

1. It has then been ordained that the great Basil, who used so constantly to furnish me with subjects for my discourses, of which he was quite as proud as any other man of his own, should himself now furnish me with the grandest subject which has ever fallen to the lot of an orator. For I think that if anyone desired, in making trial of his powers of eloquence, to test them by the standard of that one of all his subjects which he preferred (as painters do with epochmaking pictures), he would choose that which stood first of all others, but would set aside this as beyond the powers of human eloquence. So great a task is the praise of such a man, not only to me, who have long ago laid aside all thought of emulation, but even to those who live for eloquence, and whose sole object is the gaining of glory by subjects like this. Such is my opinion, and, as I persuade myself, with perfect justice. But I know not what subject I can treat with eloquence, if not this; or what greater favour I can do to myself, to the admirers of virtue, or to eloquence itself, than express our admiration for this man. To me it is the discharge of a most sacred debt. And our speech is a debt beyond all others due to those who have been gifted, in particular, with powers of speech. To the admirers of virtue a discourse is at once a pleasure and an incentive to virtue. For when I have learned the praises of men, I have a distinct idea of their

progress: now, there is none of us all, within whose power it is not to attain to any point whatsoever in that progress. As for eloquence itself, in either case, all must go well with it. For, if the discourse be almost worthy of its subject—eloquence will have given an exhibition of its power: if it fall far short of it, as must be the case when the praises of Basil are being set forth, by an actual demonstration of its incapacity, it will have declared the superiority of the excellences of its subject to all expression in words.

2. These are the reasons which have urged me to speak, and to address myself to this contest. And at my late appearance, long after his praises have been set forth by so many, who have publicly and privately done him honour, let no one be surprised. Yea, may I be pardoned by that divine soul, the object of my constant reverence! And as, when he was amongst us, he constantly corrected me in many points, according to the rights of a friend and the still higher law; for I am not ashamed to say this, for he was a standard of virtue to us all; so now, looking down upon me from above, he will treat me with indulgence. I ask pardon too of any here who are among his warmest admirers, if indeed anyone can be warmer than another, and we are not all abreast in our zeal for his good fame. For it is not contempt which has caused me to fall short of what might have been expected of me: nor have I been so regardless of the claims of virtue or of friendship; nor have I thought that to praise him befitted any other more than me. No! my first reason was, that I shrunk from this task, for I will say the truth, as priests do, who approach their sacred duties before being cleansed both in voice and mind. In the second place, I remind you, though you know it well, of the task in which I was engaged on behalf of the true doctrine, which had been properly forced upon me, and had carried me from home, according, as I suppose, to the will of God, and certainly according to the judgment of our noble champion of the truth, the breath of whose life was pious doctrine alone, such as promotes the salvation of the whole world. As for my bodily health, I ought not, perhaps, to dare to mention it, when my subject is a man so doughty in his conquest of the body, even before his removal hence, and who maintained that no powers of the soul should suffer hindrance from this our fetter. So much for my defense. I do not think I need labour it further, in speaking of

him to you who know so clearly my affairs. I must now proceed with my eulogy, commending myself to his God, in order that my commendations may not prove an insult to the man, and that I may not lag far behind all others; even though we all equally fall as far short of his due, as those who look upon the heavens or the rays of the Sun.

3. Had I seen him to be proud of his birth, and the rights of birth, or any of those infinitely little objects of those whose eyes are on the ground, we should have had to inspect a new catalogue of the Heroes. What details as to his ancestors might I not have laid under contribution! Nor would even history have had any advantage over me, since I claim this advantage, that his celebrity depends, not upon fiction or legend, but upon actual facts attested by many witnesses. On his father's side Pontus offers to me many details, in no wise inferior to its wonders of old time, of which all history and poesy are full; there are many others concerned with this my native land, of illustrious men of Cappadocia, renowned for its youthful progeny, no less than for its horses. Accordingly we match with his father's family that of his mother. What family owns more numerous, or more illustrious generals and governors, or court officials, or again, men of wealth, and lofty thrones, and public honours, and oratorical renown? If it were permitted me to wish to mention them, I would make nothing of the Pelopidæ and Cecropidæ, the Alcmæonids, the Æacidæ, and Heracleidæ, and other most noble families: inasmuch as they, in default of public merit in their house, betake themselves to the region of uncertainty, claiming demigods and divinities, merely mythical personages, as the glory of their ancestors, whose most vaunted details are incredible, and those which we can believe are an infamy.

4. But since our subject is a man who has maintained that each man's nobility is to be judged of according to his own worth, and that, as forms and colours, and likewise our most celebrated and most infamous horses, are tested by their own properties, so we too ought not to be depicted in borrowed plumes; after mentioning one or two traits, which, though inherited from his ancestors, he made his own by his life, and which are specially likely to give pleasure to my hearers, I will then proceed to deal with the man himself. Different families and individuals have different points of distinction and

interest, great or small, which, like a patrimony of longer or shorter descent, come down to posterity: the distinction of his family on either side was piety, which I now proceed to display.

5. There was a persecution, the most frightful and severe of all; I mean, as you know, the persecution of Maximinus, which, following closely upon those which immediately preceded it, made them all seem gentle, by its excessive audacity, and by its eagerness to win the crown of violence in impiety. It was overcome by many of our champions, who wrestled with it to the death, or well-nigh to the death, with only life enough left in them to survive their victory, and not pass away in the midst of the struggle; remaining to be trainers in virtue, living witnesses, breathing trophies, silent exhortations, among whose numerous ranks were found Basil's paternal ancestors, upon whom, in their practice of every form of piety, that period bestowed many a fair garland. So prepared and determined were they to bear readily all those things on account of which Christ crowns those who have imitated His struggle on our behalf.

6. But since their strife must needs be lawful, and the law of martyrdom alike forbids us voluntarily to go to meet it (in consideration for the persecutors, and for the weak) or to shrink from it if it comes upon us; for the former shows foolhardiness, the latter cowardice; in this respect they paid due honour to the Lawgiver; but what was their device, or rather, to what were they led by the Providence which guided them in all things? They betook themselves to a thicket on the mountains of Pontus, of which there are many deep ones of considerable extent, with very few comrades of their flight, or attendants upon their needs. Let others marvel at the length of time, for their flight was exceedingly prolonged, to about seven years, or a little more, and their mode of life, delicately nurtured as they were, was straitened and unusual, as may be imagined, with the discomfort of its exposure to frost and heat and rain: and the wilderness allowed no fellowship or converse with friends: a great trial to men accustomed to the attendance and honour of a numerous retinue. But I will proceed to speak of what is still greater and more extraordinary: nor will anyone fail to credit it, save those who, in their feeble and dangerous judgment, think little of persecutions and dangers for Christ's sake.

7. These noble men, suffering from the lapse of time, and feeling a distaste for ordinary food, felt a longing for something more appetising. They did not indeed speak as Israel did, for they were not murmurers like them, in their afflictions in the desert, after the escape from Egypt—that Egypt would have been better for them than the wilderness, in the bountiful supply of its flesh-pots, and other dainties which they had left behind them there, for the brick-making and the clay seemed nothing to them then in their folly—but in a more pious and faithful manner. For why, said they, is it incredible that the God of wonders, who bountifully fed in the wilderness his homeless and fugitive people, raining bread upon them, and abounding in quails, nourishing them not only with necessaries, but even with luxuries: that He, Who divided the sea, and stayed the sun, and parted the river, with all the other things that He has done; for under such circumstances the mind is wont to recur to history, and sing the praises of God's many wonders: that He, they went on, should feed us champions of piety with dainties to-day? Many animals which have escaped the tables of the rich, have their lairs in these mountains, and many eatable birds fly over our longing heads, any of which can surely be caught at the mere fiat of Thy will! At these words, their quarry lay before them, with food come of its own accord, a complete banquet prepared without effort, stags appearing all at once from some place in the hills. How splendid they were! how fat! how ready for the slaughter! It might almost be imagined that they were annoyed at not having been summoned earlier. Some of them made signs to draw others after them, the rest followed their lead. Who pursued and drove them? No one. What riders? What kind of dogs, what barking, or cry, or young men who had occupied the exits according to the rules of the chase? They were the prisoners of prayer and righteous petition. Who has known such a hunt among men of this, or any day?

AUGUSTINE

Confessions

Saint Augustine

Translated by E. B. Pusey

Book One

Great art Thou, O Lord, and greatly to be praised; great is Thy power, and Thy wisdom infinite. And Thee would man praise; man, but a particle of Thy creation; man, that bears about him his mortality, the witness of his sin, the witness that Thou resistest the proud: yet would man praise Thee; he, but a particle of Thy creation. Thou awakest us to delight in Thy praise; for Thou madest us for Thyself, and our heart is restless, until it repose in Thee. Grant me, Lord, to know and understand which is first, to call on Thee or to praise Thee? and, again, to know Thee or to call on Thee? for who can call on Thee, not knowing Thee? for he that knoweth Thee not, may call on Thee as other than Thou art. Or, is it rather, that we call on Thee that we may know Thee? but how shall they call on Him in whom they have not believed? or how shall they believe without a preacher? and they that seek the Lord shall praise Him: for they that seek shall find Him, and they that find shall praise Him. I will seek Thee, Lord, by calling on Thee; and will call on Thee, believing in Thee; for to us hast Thou been preached. My faith, Lord, shall call on Thee, which Thou hast given me, wherewith Thou hast inspired me, through the Incarnation of Thy Son, through the ministry of the Preacher.

And how shall I call upon my God, my God and Lord, since,

when I call for Him, I shall be calling Him to myself? and what room is there within me, whither my God can come into me? whither can God come into me, God who made heaven and earth? is there, indeed, O Lord my God, aught in me that can contain Thee? do then heaven and earth, which Thou hast made, and wherein Thou hast made me, contain Thee? or, because nothing which exists could exist without Thee, doth therefore whatever exists contain Thee? Since, then, I too exist, why do I seek that Thou shouldest enter into me, who were not, wert Thou not in me? Why? because I am not gone down in hell, and yet Thou art there also. For if I go down into hell, Thou art there. I could not be then, O my God, could not be at all, wert Thou not in me; or, rather, unless I were in Thee, of whom are all things, by whom are all things, in whom are all things? Even so, Lord, even so. Whither do I call Thee, since I am in Thee? or whence canst Thou enter into me? for whither can I go beyond heaven and earth, that thence my God should come into me, who hath said, I fill the heaven and the earth.

Do the heaven and earth then contain Thee, since Thou fillest them? or dost Thou fill them and yet overflow, since they do not contain Thee? And whither, when the heaven and the earth are filled, pourest Thou forth the remainder of Thyself? or hast Thou no need that aught contain Thee, who containest all things, since what Thou fillest Thou fillest by containing it? for the vessels which Thou fillest uphold Thee not, since, though they were broken, Thou wert not poured out. And when Thou art poured out on us, Thou art not cast down, but Thou upliftest us; Thou art not dissipated, but Thou gatherest us. But Thou who fillest all things, fillest Thou them with Thy whole self? or, since all things cannot contain Thee wholly, do they contain part of Thee? and all at once the same part? or each its own part, the greater more, the smaller less? And is, then one part of Thee greater, another less? or, art Thou wholly every where, while nothing contains Thee wholly?

What art Thou then, my God? what, but the Lord God? For who is Lord but the Lord? or who is God save our God? Most highest, most good, most potent, most omnipotent; most merciful, yet most just; most hidden, yet most present; most beautiful, yet most strong, stable, yet incomprehensible; unchangeable, yet all-changing; never new, never old; all-renewing, and bringing age upon the proud, and they know it not; ever working, ever at rest; still gathering, yet nothing lacking; supporting, filling, and overspreading; creating, nourishing, and maturing; seeking, yet having all things. Thou lovest, without passion; art jealous, without anxiety; repentest, yet grievest not; art angry, yet serene; changest Thy works, Thy purpose unchanged; receivest again what Thou findest, yet didst never lose; never in need, yet rejoicing in gains; never covetous, yet exacting usury. Thou receivest over and above, that Thou mayest owe; and who hath aught that is not Thine? Thou payest debts, owing nothing; remittest debts, losing nothing. And what had I now said, my God, my life, my holy joy? or what saith any man when he speaks of Thee? Yet woe to him that speaketh not, since mute are even the most eloquent.

Oh! that I might repose on Thee! Oh! that Thou wouldest enter into my heart, and inebriate it, that I may forget my ills, and embrace Thee, my sole good! What art Thou to me? In Thy pity, teach me to utter it. Or what am I to Thee that Thou demandest my love, and, if I give it not, art wroth with me, and threatenest me with grievous woes? Is it then a slight woe to love Thee not? Oh! for Thy mercies' sake, tell me, O Lord my God, what Thou art unto me. Say unto my soul, I am thy salvation. So speak, that I may hear. Behold, Lord, my heart is before Thee; open Thou the ears thereof, and say unto my soul, I am thy salvation. After this voice let me haste, and take hold on Thee. Hide not Thy face from me. Let me die—lest I die—only let me see Thy face.

Narrow is the mansion of my soul; enlarge Thou it, that Thou mayest enter in. It is ruinous; repair Thou it. It has that within which must offend Thine eyes; I confess and know it. But who shall cleanse it? or to whom should I cry, save Thee? Lord, cleanse me from my secret faults, and spare Thy servant from the power of the enemy. I believe, and therefore do I speak. Lord, Thou knowest. Have I not confessed against myself my transgressions unto Thee, and Thou, my God, hast forgiven the iniquity of my heart? I contend not in judgment with Thee, who art the truth; I fear to deceive myself; lest mine iniquity lie unto itself. Therefore I contend not in judgment with Thee; for if Thou, Lord, shouldest mark iniquities, O Lord, who shall abide it?

Yet suffer me to speak unto Thy mercy, me, dust and ashes. Yet suffer me to speak, since I speak to Thy mercy, and not to scornful man. Thou too, perhaps, despisest me, yet wilt Thou return and have compassion upon me. For what would I say, O Lord my God, but that I know not whence I came into this dying life (shall I call it?) or living death. Then immediately did the comforts of Thy compassion take me up, as I heard (for I remember it not) from the parents of my flesh, out of whose substance Thou didst sometime fashion me. Thus there received me the comforts of woman's milk. For neither my mother nor my nurses stored their own breasts for me; but Thou didst bestow the food of my infancy through them, according to Thine ordinance, whereby Thou distributest Thy riches through the hidden springs of all things. Thou also gavest me to desire no more than Thou gavest; and to my nurses willingly to give me what Thou gavest them. For they, with a heaven-taught affection, willingly gave me what they abounded with from Thee. For this my good from them, was good for them. Nor, indeed, from them was it, but through them; for from Thee, O God, are all good things, and from my God is all my health. This I since learned, Thou, through these Thy gifts, within me and without, proclaiming Thyself unto me. For then I knew but to suck; to repose in what pleased, and cry at what offended my flesh; nothing more.

Afterwards I began to smile; first in sleep, then waking: for so it was told me of myself, and I believed it; for we see the like in other infants, though of myself I remember it not. Thus, little by little, I became conscious where I was; and to have a wish to express my wishes to those who could content them, and I could not; for the wishes were within me, and they without; nor could they by any sense of theirs enter within my spirit. So I flung about at random limbs and voice, making the few signs I could, and such as I could, like, though in truth very little like, what I wished. And when I was not presently obeyed (my wishes being hurtful or unintelligible), then I was indignant with my elders for not submitting to me, with those owing me no service, for not serving me; and avenged myself on them by tears.

Such have I learnt infants to be from observing them; and that I was myself such, they, all unconscious, have shown me better than my nurses who knew it.

And, lo! my infancy died long since, and I live. But Thou, Lord, who for ever livest, and in whom nothing dies: for before the foundation of the worlds, and before all that can be called "before," Thou art, and art God and Lord of all which Thou hast created: in Thee abide, fixed for ever, the first causes of all things unabiding; and of all things changeable, the springs abide in Thee unchangeable: and in Thee live the eternal reasons of all things unreasoning and temporal. Say, Lord, to me, Thy suppliant; say, all-pitying, to me, Thy pitiable one; say, did my infancy succeed another age of mine that died before it? was it that which I spent within my mother's womb? for of that I have heard somewhat, and have myself seen women with child? and what before that life again, O God my joy, was I any where or any body? For this have I none to tell me, neither father nor mother, nor experience of others, nor mine own memory. Dost Thou mock me for asking this, and bid me praise Thee and acknowledge Thee, for that I do know?

I acknowledge Thee, Lord of heaven and earth, and praise Thee for my first rudiments of being, and my infancy, whereof I remember nothing; for Thou hast appointed that man should from others guess much as to himself; and believe much on the strength of weak females. Even then I had being and life, and (at my infancy's close) I could seek for signs whereby to make known to others my sensations. Whence could such a being be, save from Thee, Lord? Shall any be his own artificer? or can there elsewhere be derived any vein, which may stream essence and life into us, save from thee, O Lord, in whom essence and life are one? for Thou Thyself art supremely Essence and Life. For Thou art most high, and art not changed, neither in Thee doth to-day come to a close; yet in Thee doth it come to a close; because all such things also are in Thee. For they had no way to pass away, unless Thou upheldest them. And since Thy years fail not, Thy years are one to-day. How many of ours and our fathers' years have flowed away through Thy "to-day," and from it received the measure and the mould of such being as they had; and still others shall flow away, and so receive the mould of their degree of being. But Thou art still the same, and all things of to-morrow, and all beyond, and all of yesterday, and all behind it, Thou hast done to-day. What is it to me, though any comprehend not this? Let him also rejoice and say, What thing is this? Let him rejoice even thus! and be content rather by not discovering to discover Thee, than by discovering not to discover Thee.

Hear, O God. Alas, for man's sin! So saith man, and Thou pitiest him; for Thou madest him, but sin in him Thou madest not. Who remindeth me of the sins of my infancy? for in Thy sight none is pure from sin, not even the infant whose life is but a day upon the earth. Who remindeth me? doth not each little infant, in whom I see what of myself I remember not? What then was my sin? was it that I hung upon the breast and cried? for should I now so do for food suitable to my age, justly should I be laughed at and reproved. What I then did was worthy reproof; but since I could not understand reproof, custom and reason forbade me to be reproved. For those habits, when grown, we root out and cast away. Now no man, though he prunes, wittingly casts away what is good. Or was it then good, even for a while, to cry for what, if given, would hurt? bitterly to resent, that persons free, and its own elders, yea, the very authors of its birth, served it not? that many besides, wiser than it, obeyed not the nod of its good pleasure? to do its best to strike and hurt, because commands were not obeyed, which had been obeyed to its hurt? The weakness then of infant limbs, not its will, is its innocence. Myself have seen and known even a baby envious; it could not speak, yet it turned pale and looked bitterly on its foster-brother. Who knows not this? Mothers and nurses tell you that they allay these things by I know not what remedies. Is that too innocence, when the fountain of milk is flowing in rich abundance, not to endure one to share it, though in extremest need, and whose very life as yet depends thereon? We bear gently with all this, not as being no or slight evils, but because they will disappear as years increase; for, though tolerated now, the very same tempers are utterly intolerable when found in riper years.

Thou, then, O Lord my God, who gavest life to this my infancy, furnishing thus with senses (as we see) the frame Thou gavest, compacting its limbs, ornamenting its proportions, and, for its general good and safety, implanting in it all vital functions, Thou commandest me to praise Thee in these things, to confess unto Thee, and sing unto Thy name, Thou most Highest. For Thou art God, Almighty and Good, even hadst Thou done naught but only this, which none could do but Thou: whose Unity is the mould of all things; who out of Thy own fairness makest all things fair; and orderest all things by Thy law. This age then, Lord, whereof I have no remembrance, which I take on others' word, and guess from other infants that I have passed, true though the guess be, I am yet loth to count in this life of mine which I live in this world. For no less than that which I spent in my mother's womb, is it hid from me in the shadows of forgetfulness. But if I was shapen in iniquity, and in sin did my mother conceive me, where, I beseech Thee, O my God, where, Lord, or when, was I Thy servant guiltless? But, lo! that period I pass by; and what have I now to do with that, of which I can recall no vestige?

Passing hence from infancy, I came to boyhood, or rather it came to me, displacing infancy. Nor did that depart—(for whither went it?)—and yet it was no more. For I was no longer a speechless infant, but a speaking boy. This I remember; and have since observed how I learned to speak. It was not that my elders taught me words (as, soon after, other learning) in any set method; but I, longing by cries and broken accents and various motions of my limbs to express my thoughts, that so I might have my will, and yet unable to express all I willed, or to whom I willed, did myself, by the understanding which Thou, my God, gavest me, practice the sounds in my memory. When they named any thing, and as they spoke turned towards it, I saw and remembered that they called what they would point out by the name they uttered. And that they meant this thing and no other was plain from the motion of their body, the natural language, as it were, of all nations, expressed by the countenance, glances of the eye, gestures of the limbs, and tones of the voice, indicating the affections of the mind, as it pursues, possesses, rejects, or shuns. And thus by constantly hearing words, as they occurred in various sentences, I collected gradually for what they stood; and having broken in my mouth to these signs, I thereby gave utterance to my will. Thus I exchanged with those about me these current signs of our wills, and so launched deeper into the stormy intercourse of human life, yet depending on parental authority and the beck of elders.

O God my God, what miseries and mockeries did I now experience, when obedience to my teachers was proposed to me, as proper in a boy, in order that in this world I might prosper, and excel in tongue-science, which should serve to the "praise of men," and to deceitful riches. Next I was put to school to get learning, in which I (poor wretch) knew not what use there was; and yet, if idle in learning, I was beaten. For this was judged right by our forefathers; and many, passing the same course before us, framed for us weary paths, through which we were fain to pass; multiplying toil and grief upon the sons of Adam. But, Lord, we found that men called upon Thee, and we learnt from them to think of Thee (according to our powers) as of some great One, who, though hidden from our senses, couldest hear and help us. For so I began, as a boy, to pray to Thee, my aid and refuge; and broke the fetters of my tongue to call on Thee, praying Thee, though small, yet with no small earnestness, that I might not be beaten at school. And when Thou heardest me not (not thereby giving me over to folly), my elders, yea my very parents, who yet wished me no ill, mocked my stripes, my then great and grievous ill.

Is there, Lord, any of soul so great, and cleaving to Thee with so intense affection (for a sort of stupidity will in a way do it); but is there any one who, from cleaving devoutly to Thee, is endued with so great a spirit, that he can think as lightly of the racks and hooks and other torments (against which, throughout all lands, men call on Thee with extreme dread), mocking at those by whom they are feared most bitterly, as our parents mocked the torments which we suffered in boyhood from our masters? For we feared not our torments less; nor prayed we less to Thee to escape them. And yet we sinned, in writing or reading or studying less than was exacted of us. For we wanted not, O Lord, memory or capacity, whereof Thy will gave enough for our age; but our sole delight was play; and for this we were punished by those who yet themselves were doing the like. But elder folks' idleness is called "business"; that of boys, being really the same, is punished by those elders; and none commiserates either boys or men. For will any of sound discretion approve of my being beaten as a boy, because, by playing a ball, I made less progress in studies which I was to learn, only that, as a man, I might play more unbeseemingly? and what else did he who beat me? who, if worsted in some trifling discussion with his fellow-tutor, was more embittered and jealous than I when beaten at ball by a play-fellow?

And yet, I sinned herein, O Lord God, the Creator and Disposer of all things in nature, of sin the Disposer only, O Lord my God, I sinned in transgressing the commands of my parents and those of my masters. For what they, with whatever motive, would have me learn, I might afterwards have put to good use. For I disobeyed, not from a better choice, but from love of play, loving the pride of victory in my contests, and to have my ears tickled with lying fables, that they might itch the more; the same curiosity flashing from my eyes more and more, for the shows and games of my elders. Yet those who give these shows are in such esteem, that almost all wish the same for their children, and yet are very willing that they should be beaten, if those very games detain them from the studies, whereby they would have them attain to be the givers of them. Look with pity, Lord, on these things, and deliver us who call upon Thee now; deliver those too who call not on Thee yet, that they may call on Thee, and Thou mayest deliver them.

As a boy, then, I had already heard of an eternal life, promised us through the humility of the Lord our God stooping to our pride; and even from the womb of my mother, who greatly hoped in Thee, I was sealed with the mark of His cross and salted with His salt. Thou sawest, Lord, how while yet a boy, being seized on a time with sudden oppression of the stomach, and like near to death—Thou sawest, my God (for Thou wert my keeper), with what eagerness and what faith I sought, from the pious care of my mother and Thy Church, the mother of us all, the baptism of Thy Christ, my God and Lord. Whereupon the mother of my flesh, being much troubled (since, with a heart pure in Thy faith, she even more lovingly travailed in birth of my salvation), would in eager haste have provided for my consecration and cleansing by the health-giving sacraments, confessing Thee, Lord Jesus, for the remission of sins, unless I had suddenly recovered. And so, as if I must needs be again polluted should I live, my cleansing was deferred, because the defilements of sin would, after that washing, bring greater and more perilous guilt. I then already believed: and my mother, and the whole household, except my father: yet did not he prevail over the power of my mother's piety in me, that as he did not yet believe, so neither should I. For it was her earnest care that Thou my God, rather than he, shouldest be my father; and in this Thou didst aid her to prevail over her husband, whom she, the better, obeyed, therein also obeying Thee, who hast so commanded.

I beseech Thee, my God, I would fain know, if so Thou willest, for what purpose my baptism was then deferred? was it for my good that the rein was laid loose, as it were, upon me, for me to sin? or was it not laid loose? If not, why does it still echo in our ears on all sides, "Let him alone, let him do as he will, for he is not yet baptised?" but as to bodily health, no one says, "Let him be worse wounded, for he is not yet healed." How much better then, had I been at once healed; and then, by my friends' and my own, my soul's recovered health had been kept safe in Thy keeping who gavest it. Better truly. But how many and great waves of temptation seemed to hang over me after my boyhood! These my mother foresaw; and preferred to expose to them the clay whence I might afterwards be moulded, than the very cast, when made.

In boyhood itself, however (so much less dreaded for me than youth), I loved not study, and hated to be forced to it. Yet I was forced; and this was well done towards me, but I did not well; for, unless forced, I had not learnt. But no one doth well against his will, even though what he doth, be well. Yet neither did they well who forced me, but what was well came to me from Thee, my God. For they were regardless how I should employ what they forced me to learn, except to satiate the insatiate desires of a wealthy beggary, and a shameful glory. But Thou, by whom the very hairs of our head are numbered, didst use for my good the error of all who urged me to learn; and my own, who would not learn, Thou didst use for my punishment—a fit penalty for one, so small a boy and so great a sinner. So by those who did not well, Thou didst well for me; and by my own sin Thou didst justly punish me. For Thou hast commanded, and so it is, that every inordinate affection should be its own punishment.

But why did I so much hate the Greek, which I studied as a boy? I do not yet fully know. For the Latin I loved; not what my first masters, but what the so-called grammarians taught me. For those first lessons, reading, writing and arithmetic, I thought as great a burden and penalty as any Greek. And yet whence was this too, but from the sin and vanity of this life, because I was flesh, and a breath that passeth away and cometh not again? For those first lessons were better certainly, because more certain; by them I obtained, and still retain, the power of reading what I find written, and myself writing what I will; whereas in the others, I was forced to learn the wanderings of one Aeneas, forgetful of my own, and to weep for dead Dido, because she killed herself for love; the while, with dry eyes, I endured my miserable self dying among these things, far from Thee, O God my life.

For what more miserable than a miserable being who commiserates not himself; weeping the death of Dido for love to Aeneas, but weeping not his own death for want of love to Thee, O God. Thou light of my heart, Thou bread of my inmost soul, Thou Power who givest vigour to my mind, who quickenest my thoughts, I loved Thee not. I committed fornication against Thee, and all around me thus fornicating there echoed "Well done! well done!" for the friendship of this world is fornication against Thee; and "Well done! well done!" echoes on till one is ashamed not to be thus a man. And for all this I wept not, I who wept for Dido slain, and "seeking by the sword a stroke and wound extreme," myself seeking the while a worse extreme, the extremest and lowest of Thy creatures, having forsaken Thee, earth passing into the earth. And if forbid to read all this, I was grieved that I might not read what grieved me. Madness like this is thought a higher and a richer learning, than that by which I learned to read and write.

But now, my God, cry Thou aloud in my soul; and let Thy truth tell me, "Not so, not so. Far better was that first study." For, lo, I would readily forget the wanderings of Aeneas and all the rest, rather than how to read and write. But over the entrance of the Grammar School is a veil drawn! true; yet is this not so much an emblem of aught recondite, as a cloak of error. Let not those, whom I no longer fear, cry out against me, while I confess to Thee, my God, whatever my soul will, and acquiesce in the condemnation of my evil ways, that I may love Thy good ways. Let not either buyers or sellers of grammar-learning cry out against me. For if I question them whether it be true that Aeneas came on a time to Carthage, as the poet tells, the less learned will reply that they know not, the more learned that he never did. But should I ask with what letters the name "Aeneas" is written, every one who has learnt this will answer me aright, as to the signs which men have conventionally settled. If, again, I should ask which might be forgotten with least detriment to the concerns of life, reading and writing or these poetic fictions? who does not foresee what all must answer who have not wholly forgotten themselves? I sinned, then, when as a boy I preferred those empty to those more profitable studies, or rather loved the one and hated the other. "One and one, two"; "two and two, four"; this was to me a hateful singsong: "the wooden horse lined with armed men," and "the burning of Troy," and "Creusa's shade and sad similitude," were the choice spectacle of my vanity.

Why then did I hate the Greek classics, which have the like tales? For Homer also curiously wove the like fictions, and is most sweetly vain, yet was he bitter to my boyish taste. And so I suppose would Virgil be to Grecian children, when forced to learn him as I was Homer. Difficulty, in truth, the difficulty of a foreign tongue, dashed, as it were, with gall all the sweetness of Grecian fable. For not one word of it did I understand, and to make me understand I was urged vehemently with cruel threats and punishments. Time was also (as an infant) I knew no Latin; but this I learned without fear or suffering, by mere observation, amid the caresses of my nursery and jests of friends, smiling and sportively encouraging me. This I learned without any pressure of punishment to urge me on, for my heart urged me to give birth to its conceptions, which I could only do by learning words not of those who taught, but of those who talked with me; in whose ears also I gave birth to the thoughts, whatever I conceived. No doubt, then, that a free curiosity has more force in our learning these things, than a frightful enforcement. Only this enforcement restrains the rovings of that freedom, through Thy laws, O my God, Thy laws, from the master's cane to the martyr's trials, being able to temper for us a wholesome bitter, recalling us to Thyself from that deadly pleasure which lures us from Thee.

Hear, Lord, my prayer; let not my soul faint under Thy discipline, nor let me faint in confessing unto Thee all Thy mercies, whereby Thou hast drawn me out of all my most evil ways, that Thou mightest become a delight to me above all the allurements which I once pursued; that I may most entirely love Thee, and clasp Thy hand with all my affections, and Thou mayest yet rescue me from every temptation, even unto the end. For lo, O Lord, my King and my God, for Thy service be whatever useful thing my childhood learned; for Thy service, that I speak, write, read, reckon. For Thou didst grant me Thy discipline, while I was learning vanities; and my sin of delighting in those vanities Thou hast forgiven. In them, indeed, I learnt many a useful word, but these may as well be learned in things not vain; and that is the safe path for the steps of youth.

But woe is thee, thou torrent of human custom! Who shall stand against thee? how long shalt thou not be dried up? how long roll the sons of Eve into that huge and hideous ocean, which even they scarcely overpass who climb the cross? Did not I read in thee of Jove the thunderer and the adulterer? both, doubtless, he could not be; but so the feigned thunder might countenance and pander to real adultery. And now which of our gowned masters lends a sober ear to one who from their own school cries out, "These were Homer's fictions, transferring things human to the gods; would he had brought down things divine to us!" Yet more truly had he said, "These are indeed his fictions; but attributing a divine nature to wicked men, that crimes might be no longer crimes, and whoso commits them might seem to imitate not abandoned men, but the celestial gods."

And yet, thou hellish torrent, into thee are cast the sons of men with rich rewards, for compassing such learning; and a great solemnity is made of it, when this is going on in the forum, within sight of laws appointing a salary beside the scholar's payments; and thou lashest thy rocks and roarest, "Hence words are learnt; hence eloquence; most necessary to gain your ends, or maintain opinions." As if we should have never known such words as "golden shower," "lap," "beguile," "temples of the heavens," or others in that passage, unless Terence had brought a lewd youth upon the stage, setting up Jupiter as his example of seduction.

> "Viewing a picture, where the tale was drawn,
> Of Jove's descending in a golden shower
> To Danae's lap a woman to beguile."

And then mark how he excites himself to lust as by celestial authority:

> "And what God? Great Jove,
> Who shakes heaven's highest temples with his thunder,
> And I, poor mortal man, not do the same!
> I did it, and with all my heart I did it."

Not one whit more easily are the words learnt for all this vileness; but by their means the vileness is committed with less shame. Not that I blame the words, being, as it were, choice and precious vessels; but that wine of error which is drunk to us in them by intoxicated teachers; and if we, too, drink not, we are beaten, and have no sober judge to whom we may appeal. Yet, O my God (in whose presence I now without hurt may remember this), all this unhappily I learnt willingly with great delight, and for this was pronounced a hopeful boy.

Bear with me, my God, while I say somewhat of my wit, Thy gift, and on what dotages I wasted it. For a task was set me, troublesome enough to my soul, upon terms of praise or shame, and fear of stripes, to speak the words of Juno, as she raged and mourned that she could not

> "This Trojan prince from Latinum turn."

Which words I had heard that Juno never uttered; but we were forced to go astray in the footsteps of these poetic fictions, and to say in prose much what he expressed in verse. And his speaking was most applauded, in whom the passions of rage and grief were most preeminent, and clothed in the most fitting language, maintaining the dignity of the character. What is it to me, O my true life, my God, that my declamation was applauded above so many of my own age and class? is not all this smoke and wind? and was there nothing elsewhere-on to exercise my wit and tongue? Thy praises, Lord, Thy praises might have stayed the yet tender shoot of my heart by the prop of Thy Scriptures; so had it not trailed away amid these empty trifles, a defiled prey for the fowls of the air. For in more ways than one do men sacrifice to the rebellious angels.

But what marvel that I was thus carried away to vanities, and went out from Thy presence, O my God, when men were set before me as models, who, if in relating some action of theirs, in itself not ill, they committed some barbarism or solecism, being censured, were abashed; but when in rich and adorned and well-ordered discourse they related their own disordered life, being be-praised, they gloried? These things Thou seest, Lord, and holdest Thy peace; longsuffering, and plenteous in mercy and truth. Wilt Thou hold Thy peace for ever? and even now Thou drawest out of this horrible gulf the soul that seeketh Thee, that thirsteth for Thy pleasures, whose heart saith unto Thee, I have sought Thy face; Thy face, Lord, will I seek. For darkened affections is removal from Thee. For it is not by our feet, or change of place, that men leave Thee, or return unto Thee. Or did that Thy younger son look out for horses or chariots, or ships, fly with visible wings, or journey by the motion of his limbs, that he might in a far country waste in riotous living all Thou gavest at his departure? a loving Father, when Thou gavest, and more loving unto him, when he returned empty. So then in lustful, that is, in darkened affections, is the true distance from Thy face.

Behold, O Lord God, yea, behold patiently as Thou art wont how carefully the sons of men observe the covenanted rules of letters and syllables received from those who spake before them, neglecting the eternal covenant of everlasting salvation received from Thee. Insomuch, that a teacher or learner of the hereditary laws of pronunciation will more offend men by speaking without the aspirate, of a "uman being," in despite of the laws of grammar, than if he, a "human being," hate a "human being" in despite of Thine. As if any enemy could be more hurtful than the hatred with which he is incensed against him; or could wound more deeply him whom he persecutes, than he wounds his own soul by his enmity. Assuredly no science of letters can be so innate as the record of conscience, "that he is doing to another what from another he would be loth to suffer." How deep are Thy ways, O God, Thou only great, that sittest silent on high and by an unwearied law dispensing penal blindness to lawless desires. In quest of the fame of eloquence, a man standing before a human judge, surrounded by a human throng, declaiming against his enemy with fiercest hatred, will take heed most watchfully, lest, by an error of the tongue, he murder the word "human being"; but takes no heed, lest, through the fury of his spirit, he murder the real human being.

This was the world at whose gate unhappy I lay in my boyhood; this the stage where I had feared more to commit a barbarism, than having committed one, to envy those who had not. These things I speak and confess to Thee, my God; for which I had praise from them, whom I then thought it all virtue to please. For I saw not the abyss of vileness, wherein I was cast away from Thine eyes. Before them what more foul than I was already, displeasing even such as myself? with innumerable lies deceiving my tutor, my masters, my parents, from love of play, eagerness to see vain shows and restlessness to imitate them! Thefts also I committed, from my parents' cellar and table, enslaved by greediness, or that I might have to give to boys, who sold me their play, which all the while they liked no less than I. In this play, too, I often sought unfair conquests, conquered myself meanwhile by vain desire of preeminence. And what could I so ill endure, or, when I detected it, upbraided I so fiercely, as that I was doing to others? and for which if, detected, I was upbraided, I chose rather to quarrel than to yield. And is this the innocence of boyhood? Not so, Lord, not so; I cry Thy mercy, my God. For these very sins, as riper years succeed, these very sins are transferred from tutors and masters, from nuts and balls and sparrows, to magistrates and kings, to gold and manors and slaves, just as severer punishments displace the cane. It was the low stature then of childhood which Thou our King didst commend as an emblem of lowliness, when Thou saidst, Of such is the kingdom of heaven.

Yet, Lord, to Thee, the Creator and Governor of the universe, most excellent and most good, thanks were due to Thee our God, even hadst Thou destined for me boyhood only. For even then I was,

I lived, and felt; and had an implanted providence over my wellbeing—a trace of that mysterious Unity whence I was derived; I guarded by the inward sense the entireness of my senses, and in these minute pursuits, and in my thoughts on things minute, I learnt to delight in truth, I hated to be deceived, had a vigorous memory, was gifted with speech, was soothed by friendship, avoided pain, baseness, ignorance. In so small a creature, what was not wonderful, not admirable? But all are gifts of my God: it was not I who gave them me; and good these are, and these together are myself. Good, then, is He that made me, and He is my good; and before Him will I exult for every good which of a boy I had. For it was my sin, that not in Him, but in His creatures-myself and others—I sought for pleasures, sublimities, truths, and so fell headlong into sorrows, confusions, errors. Thanks be to Thee, my joy and my glory and my confidence, my God, thanks be to Thee for Thy gifts; but do Thou preserve them to me. For so wilt Thou preserve me, and those things shall be enlarged and perfected which Thou hast given me, and I myself shall be with Thee, since even to be Thou hast given me.

Book Two

I will now call to mind my past foulness, and the carnal corruptions of my soul; not because I love them, but that I may love Thee, O my God. For love of Thy love I do it; reviewing my most wicked ways in the very bitterness of my remembrance, that Thou mayest grow sweet unto me (Thou sweetness never failing, Thou blissful and assured sweetness); and gathering me again out of that my dissipation, wherein I was torn piecemeal, while turned from Thee, the One Good, I lost myself among a multiplicity of things. For I even burnt in my youth heretofore, to be satiated in things below; and I dared to grow wild again, with these various and shadowy loves: my beauty consumed away, and I stank in Thine eyes; pleasing myself, and desirous to please in the eyes of men.

And what was it that I delighted in, but to love, and be loved? but I kept not the measure of love, of mind to mind, friendship's bright boundary: but out of the muddy concupiscence of the flesh, and the bubblings of youth, mists fumed up which beclouded and overcast my heart, that I could not discern the clear brightness of love from the fog of lustfulness. Both did confusedly boil in me, and hurried my unstayed youth over the precipice of unholy desires, and sunk me in a gulf of flagitiousnesses. Thy wrath had gathered over me, and I knew it not. I was grown deaf by the clanking of the chain of my mortality, the punishment of the pride of my soul, and I strayed further from Thee, and Thou lettest me alone, and I was tossed about, and wasted, and dissipated, and I boiled over in my fornications, and Thou heldest Thy peace, O Thou my tardy joy! Thou then heldest Thy peace, and I wandered further and further from Thee, into more and more fruitless seed-plots of sorrows, with a proud dejectedness, and a restless weariness.

Oh! that some one had then attempered my disorder, and turned to account the fleeting beauties of these, the extreme points of Thy creation! had put a bound to their pleasureableness, that so the tides of my youth might have cast themselves upon the marriage shore, if they could not be calmed, and kept within the object of a family, as Thy law prescribes, O Lord: who this way formest the offspring of this our death, being able with a gentle hand to blunt the thorns which were excluded from Thy paradise? For Thy omnipotency is not far from us, even when we be far from Thee. Else ought I more watchfully to have heeded the voice from the clouds: Nevertheless such shall have trouble in the flesh, but I spare you. And it is good for a man not to touch a woman. And, he that is unmarried thinketh of the things of the Lord, how he may please the Lord; but he that is married careth for the things of this world, how he may please his wife.

To these words I should have listened more attentively, and being severed for the kingdom of heaven's sake, had more happily awaited Thy embraces; but I, poor wretch, foamed like a troubled sea, following the rushing of my own tide, forsaking Thee, and exceeded all Thy limits; yet I escaped not Thy scourges. For what mortal can? For Thou wert ever with me mercifully rigorous, and besprinkling with most bitter alloy all my unlawful pleasures: that I might seek pleasures without alloy. But where to find such, I could not discover, save in Thee, O Lord, who teachest by sorrow, and woundest us, to heal; and killest us, lest we die from Thee. Where was I, and how far was I exiled from the delights of Thy house, in that sixteenth year of the age of my flesh, when the madness of lust (to which human shamelessness giveth free license, though unlicensed by Thy laws) took the rule over me, and I resigned myself wholly to it? My friends meanwhile took no care by marriage to save my fall; their only care was that I should learn to speak excellently, and be a persuasive orator.

For that year were my studies intermitted: whilst after my return from Madaura (a neighbour city, whither I had journeyed to learn grammar and rhetoric), the expenses for a further journey to Carthage were being provided for me; and that rather by the resolution than the means of my father, who was but a poor freeman of Thagaste. To whom tell I this? not to Thee, my God; but before Thee to mine own kind, even to that small portion of mankind as may light upon these writings of mine. And to what purpose? that whosoever reads this, may think out of what depths we are to cry unto Thee. For what is nearer to Thine ears than a confessing heart, and a life of faith? Who did not extol my father, for that beyond the ability of his means, he would furnish his son with all necessaries for a far journey for his studies' sake? For many far abler citizens did no such thing for their children. But yet this same father had no concern how I grew towards Thee, or how chaste I were; so that I were but copious in speech, however barren I were to Thy culture, O God, who art the only true and good Lord of Thy field, my heart.

But while in that my sixteenth year I lived with my parents, leaving all school for a while (a season of idleness being interposed through the narrowness of my parents' fortunes), the briers of unclean desires grew rank over my head, and there was no hand to root them out. When that my father saw me at the baths, now growing towards manhood, and endued with a restless youthfulness, he, as already hence anticipating his descendants, gladly told it to my mother; rejoicing in that tumult of the senses wherein the world forgetteth Thee its Creator, and becometh enamoured of Thy creature, instead of Thyself, through the fumes of that invisible wine of its self-will, turning aside and bowing down to the very basest things. But in my mother's breast Thou hadst already begun Thy temple, and the foundation of Thy holy habitation, whereas my father was as yet but a Catechumen, and that but recently. She then was startled with a holy fear and trembling; and though I was not as yet baptised, feared for me those crooked ways in which they walk who turn their back to Thee, and not their face.

Woe is me! and dare I say that Thou heldest Thy peace, O my God, while I wandered further from Thee? Didst Thou then indeed hold Thy peace to me? And whose but Thine were these words which by my mother, Thy faithful one, Thou sangest in my ears? Nothing whereof sunk into my heart, so as to do it. For she wished, and I remember in private with great anxiety warned me, "not to commit fornication; but especially never to defile another man's wife." These seemed to me womanish advices, which I should blush to obey. But they were Thine, and I knew it not: and I thought Thou wert silent and that it was she who spake; by whom Thou wert not silent unto me; and in her wast despised by me, her son, the son of Thy handmaid, Thy servant. But I knew it not; and ran headlong with such blindness, that amongst my equals I was ashamed of a less shamelessness, when I heard them boast of their flagitiousness, yea, and the more boasting, the more they were degraded: and I took pleasure, not only in the pleasure of the deed, but in the praise. What is worthy of dispraise but vice? But I made myself worse than I was, that I might not be dispraised; and when in any thing I had not sinned as the abandoned ones, I would say that I had done what I had not done, that I might not seem contemptible in proportion as I was innocent; or of less account, the more chaste.

Behold with what companions I walked the streets of Babylon, and wallowed in the mire thereof, as if in a bed of spices and precious ointments. And that I might cleave the faster to its very centre, the invisible enemy trod me down, and seduced me, for that I was easy to be seduced. Neither did the mother of my flesh (who had now fled out of the centre of Babylon, yet went more slowly in the skirts thereof as she advised me to chastity, so heed what she had heard of me from her husband, as to restrain within the bounds of conjugal affection, if it could not be pared away to the quick) what she felt to be pestilent at present and for the future dangerous. She heeded not this, for she feared lest a wife should prove a clog and hindrance to my hopes. Not those hopes of the world to come, which my mother reposed in Thee; but the hope of learning, which both my parents were too desirous I should attain; my father, because he had next to no thought of Thee, and of me but vain conceits; my mother, because she accounted that those usual courses of learning would not only be no hindrance, but even some furtherance towards attaining Thee. For thus I conjecture, recalling, as well as I may, the disposition of my parents. The reins, meantime, were slackened to me, beyond all temper of due severity, to spend my time in sport, yea, even unto dissoluteness in whatsoever I affected. And in all was a mist, intercepting from me, O my God, the brightness of Thy truth; and mine iniquity burst out as from very fatness.

Theft is punished by Thy law, O Lord, and the law written in the hearts of men, which iniquity itself effaces not. For what thief will abide a thief? not even a rich thief, one stealing through want. Yet I lusted to thieve, and did it, compelled by no hunger, nor poverty, but through a cloyedness of well-doing, and a pamperedness of iniquity. For I stole that, of which I had enough, and much better. Nor cared I to enjoy what I stole, but joyed in the theft and sin itself. A pear tree there was near our vineyard, laden with fruit, tempting neither for colour nor taste. To shake and rob this, some lewd young fellows of us went, late one night (having according to our pestilent custom prolonged our sports in the streets till then), and took huge loads, not for our eating, but to fling to the very hogs, having only tasted them. And this, but to do what we liked only, because it was misliked. Behold my heart, O God, behold my heart, which Thou hadst pity upon in the bottom of the bottomless pit. Now, behold, let my heart tell Thee what it sought there, that I should be gratuitously evil, having no temptation to ill, but the ill itself. It was foul, and I loved it; I loved to perish, I loved mine own fault, not that for which I was faulty, but my fault itself. Foul soul, falling from Thy firmament to utter destruction; not seeking aught through the shame, but the shame itself!

For there is an attractiveness in beautiful bodies, in gold and silver, and all things; and in bodily touch, sympathy hath much influence, and each other sense hath his proper object answerably tempered. Worldly honour hath also its grace, and the power of overcoming, and of mastery; whence springs also the thirst of revenge. But yet, to obtain all these, we may not depart from Thee, O Lord, nor decline from Thy law. The life also which here we live hath its own enchantment, through a certain proportion of its own, and a correspondence with all things beautiful here below. Human friendship also is endeared with a sweet tie, by reason of the unity formed of many souls. Upon occasion of all these, and the like, is sin committed, while through an immoderate inclination towards these goods of the lowest order, the better and higher are forsaken—Thou, our Lord God, Thy truth, and Thy law. For these lower things have their delights, but not like my God, who made all things; for in Him doth the righteous delight, and He is the joy of the upright in heart.

When, then, we ask why a crime was done, we believe it not, unless it appear that there might have been some desire of obtaining some of those which we called lower goods, or a fear of losing them. For they are beautiful and comely; although compared with those higher and beatific goods, they be abject and low. A man hath murdered another; why? he loved his wife or his estate; or would rob for his own livelihood; or feared to lose some such things by him; or,wronged, was on fire to be revenged. Would any commit murder upon no cause, delighted simply in murdering? who would believe it? for as for that furious and savage man, of whom it is said that he was gratuitously evil and cruel, yet is the cause assigned; "lest" (saith he) "through idleness hand or heart should grow inactive." And to what end? that, through that practice of guilt, he might, having taken the city, attain to honours, empire, riches, and be freed from fear of the laws, and his embarrassments from domestic needs, and consciousness of villainies. So then, not even Catiline himself loved his own villainies, but something else, for whose sake he did them.

What then did wretched I so love in thee, thou theft of mine, thou deed of darkness, in that sixteenth year of my age? Lovely thou wert not, because thou wert theft. But art thou any thing, that thus

I speak to thee? Fair were the pears we stole, because they were Thy creation, Thou fairest of all, Creator of all, Thou good God; God, the sovereign good and my true good. Fair were those pears, but not them did my wretched soul desire; for I had store of better, and those I gathered, only that I might steal. For, when gathered, I flung them away, my only feast therein being my own sin, which I was pleased to enjoy. For if aught of those pears came within my mouth, what sweetened it was the sin. And now, O Lord my God, I inquire what in that theft delighted me; and behold it hath no loveliness; I mean not such loveliness as in justice and wisdom; nor such as is in the mind and memory, and senses, and animal life of man; nor yet as the stars are glorious and beautiful in their orbs; or the earth, or sea, full of embryo-life, replacing by its birth that which decayeth; nay, nor even that false and shadowy beauty which belongeth to deceiving vices.

For so doth pride imitate exaltedness; whereas Thou alone art God exalted over all. Ambition, what seeks it, but honours and glory? whereas Thou alone art to be honoured above all, and glorious for evermore. The cruelty of the great would fain be feared; but who is to be feared but God alone, out of whose power what can be wrested or withdrawn? when, or where, or whither, or by whom? The tendernesses of the wanton would fain be counted love: yet is nothing more tender than Thy charity; nor is aught loved more healthfully than that Thy truth, bright and beautiful above all. Curiosity makes semblance of a desire of knowledge; whereas Thou supremely knowest all. Yea, ignorance and foolishness itself is cloaked under the name of simplicity and uninjuriousness; because nothing is found more single than Thee: and what less injurious, since they are his own works which injure the sinner? Yea, sloth would fain be at rest; but what stable rest besides the Lord? Luxury affects to be called plenty and abundance; but Thou art the fullness and never-failing plenteousness of incorruptible pleasures. Prodigality presents a shadow of liberality: but Thou art the most overflowing Giver of all good. Covetousness would possess many things; and Thou possessest all things. Envy disputes for excellency: what more excellent than Thou? Anger seeks revenge: who revenges more justly than Thou? Fear startles at things unwonted and sudden, which endangers things beloved, and takes forethought for their safety; but to Thee what unwonted or sudden, or who separateth from Thee what Thou lovest? Or where but with Thee is unshaken safety? Grief pines away for things lost, the delight of its desires; because it would have nothing taken from it, as nothing can from Thee.

Thus doth the soul commit fornication, when she turns from Thee, seeking without Thee, what she findeth not pure and untainted, till she returns to Thee. Thus all pervertedly imitate Thee, who remove far from Thee, and lift themselves up against Thee. But even by thus imitating Thee, they imply Thee to be the Creator of all nature; whence there is no place whither altogether to retire from Thee. What then did I love in that theft? and wherein did I even corruptly and pervertedly imitate my Lord? Did I wish even by stealth to do contrary to Thy law, because by power I could not, so that being a prisoner, I might mimic a maimed liberty by doing with impunity things unpermitted me, a darkened likeness of Thy Omnipotency? Behold, Thy servant, fleeing from his Lord, and obtaining a shadow. O rottenness, O monstrousness of life, and depth of death! could I like what I might not, only because I might not?

What shall I render unto the Lord, that, whilst my memory recalls these things, my soul is not affrighted at them? I will love Thee, O Lord, and thank Thee, and confess unto Thy name; because Thou hast forgiven me these so great and heinous deeds of mine. To Thy grace I ascribe it, and to Thy mercy, that Thou hast melted away my sins as it were ice. To Thy grace I ascribe also whatsoever I have not done of evil; for what might I not have done, who even loved a sin for its own sake? Yea, all I confess to have been forgiven me; both what evils I committed by my own willfulness, and what by Thy guidance I committed not. What man is he, who, weighing his own infirmity, dares to ascribe his purity and innocency to his own strength; that so he should love Thee the less, as if he had less needed Thy mercy, whereby Thou remittest sins to those that turn to Thee? For whosoever, called by Thee, followed Thy voice, and avoided those things which he reads me recalling and confessing of myself, let him not scorn me, who being sick, was cured by that Physician, through whose aid it was that he was not, or rather was less, sick: and for this let him love Thee as much, yea and more; since by whom he sees me to have been recovered from such deep consumption of sin, by Him he sees himself to have been from the like consumption of sin preserved.

What fruit had I then (wretched man!) in those things, of the remembrance whereof I am now ashamed? Especially, in that theft which I loved for the theft's sake; and it too was nothing, and therefore the more miserable I, who loved it. Yet alone I had not done it: such was I then, I remember, alone I had never done it. I loved then in it also the company of the accomplices, with whom I did it? I did not then love nothing else but the theft, yea rather I did love nothing else; for that circumstance of the company was also nothing. What is, in truth? who can teach me, save He that enlighteneth my heart, and discovereth its dark corners? What is it which hath come into my mind to inquire, and discuss, and consider? For had I then loved the pears I stole, and wished to enjoy them, I might have done it alone, had the bare commission of the theft sufficed to attain my pleasure; nor needed I have inflamed the itching of my desires by the excitement of accomplices. But since my pleasure was not in those pears, it was in the offence itself, which the company of fellow-sinners occasioned.

What then was this feeling? For of a truth it was too foul: and woe was me, who had it. But yet what was it? Who can understand his errors? It was the sport, which as it were tickled our hearts, that we beguiled those who little thought what we were doing, and much disliked it. Why then was my delight of such sort that I did it not alone? Because none doth ordinarily laugh alone? ordinarily no one; yet laughter sometimes masters men alone and singly when no one whatever is with them, if anything very ludicrous presents itself to their senses or mind. Yet I had not done this alone; alone I had never done it. Behold my God, before Thee, the vivid remembrance of my soul; alone, I had never committed that theft wherein what I stole pleased me not, but that I stole; nor had it alone liked me to do it, nor had I done it. O friendship too unfriendly! thou incomprehensible inveigler of the soul, thou greediness to do mischief out of mirth and wantonness, thou thirst of others' loss, without lust of my own gain or revenge: but when it is said, "Let's go, let's do it," we are ashamed not to be shameless.

Who can disentangle that twisted and intricate knottiness? Foul is it: I hate to think on it, to look on it. But Thee I long for, O Righteousness and Innocency, beautiful and comely to all pure eyes, and of a satisfaction unsating. With Thee is rest entire, and life imperturbable. Whoso enters into Thee, enters into the joy of his Lord: and shall not fear, and shall do excellently in the All-Excellent. I sank away from Thee, and I wandered, O my God, too much astray from Thee my stay, in these days of my youth, and I became to myself a barren land.

Book Three

To Carthage I came, where there sang all around me in my ears a cauldron of unholy loves. I loved not yet, yet I loved to love, and out of a deep-seated want, I hated myself for wanting not. I sought what I might love, in love with loving, and safety I hated, and a way without snares. For within me was a famine of that inward food, Thyself, my God; yet, through that famine I was not hungered; but was without all longing for incorruptible sustenance, not because filled therewith, but the more empty, the more I loathed it. For this cause my soul was sickly and full of sores, it miserably cast itself forth, desiring to be scraped by the touch of objects of sense. Yet if these had not a soul, they would not be objects of love. To love then, and to be beloved, was sweet to me; but more, when I obtained to enjoy the person I loved, I defiled, therefore, the spring of friendship with the filth of concupiscence, and I beclouded its brightness with the hell of lustfulness; and thus foul and unseemly, I would fain, through exceeding vanity, be fine and courtly. I fell headlong then into the love wherein I longed to be ensnared. My God, my Mercy, with how much gall didst Thou out of Thy great goodness besprinkle for me that sweetness? For I was both beloved, and secretly arrived at the bond of enjoying; and was with joy fettered with sorrow-bringing bonds, that I might be scourged with the iron burning rods of jealousy, and suspicions, and fears, and angers, and quarrels.

Stage-plays also carried me away, full of images of my miseries, and of fuel to my fire. Why is it, that man desires to be made sad, beholding doleful and tragical things, which yet himself would no means suffer? yet he desires as a spectator to feel sorrow at them, and this very sorrow is his pleasure. What is this but a miserable madness? for a man is the more affected with these actions, the less free he is from such affections. Howsoever, when he suffers in his own person, it uses to be styled misery: when he compassionates others, then it is mercy. But what sort of compassion is this for feigned and scenical passions? for the auditor is not called on to relieve, but only to grieve: and he applauds the actor of these fictions the more, the more he grieves. And if the calamities of those persons (whether of old times, or mere fiction) be so acted, that the spectator is not moved to tears, he goes away disgusted and criticising; but if he be moved to passion, he stays intent, and weeps for joy.

Are griefs then too loved? Verily all desire joy. Or whereas no man likes to be miserable, is he yet pleased to be merciful? which because it cannot be without passion, for this reason alone are passions loved?

This also springs from that vein of friendship. But whither goes that vein? whither flows it? wherefore runs it into that torrent of pitch bubbling forth those monstrous tides of foul lustfulness, into which it is willfully changed and transformed, being of its own will precipitated and corrupted from its heavenly clearness? Shall compassion then be put away? by no means. Be griefs then sometimes loved. But beware of uncleanness, O my soul, under the guardianship of my God, the God of our fathers, who is to be praised and exalted above all for ever, beware of uncleanness. For I have not now ceased to pity; but then in the theatres I rejoiced with lovers when they wickedly enjoyed one another, although this was imaginary only in the play. And when they lost one another, as if very compassionate, I sorrowed with them, yet had my delight in both. But now I much more pity him that rejoiceth in his wickedness, than him who is thought to suffer hardship, by missing some pernicious pleasure, and the loss of some miserable felicity. This certainly is the truer mercy, but in it grief delights not. For though he that grieves for the miserable, be commended for his office of charity; yet had he, who is genuinely compassionate, rather there were nothing for him to grieve for. For if good will be ill willed (which can never be), then may he, who truly and sincerely commiserates, wish there might be some miserable, that he might commiserate. Some sorrow may then be allowed, none loved. For thus dost Thou, O Lord God, who lovest souls far more purely than we, and hast more incorruptibly pity on them, yet are wounded with no sorrowfulness. And who is sufficient for these things?

But I, miserable, then loved to grieve, and sought out what to grieve at, when in another's and that feigned and personated misery, that acting best pleased me, and attracted me the most vehemently, which drew tears from me. What marvel that an unhappy sheep, straying from Thy flock, and impatient of Thy keeping, I became infected with a foul disease? And hence the love of griefs; not such as should sink deep into me; for I loved not to suffer, what I loved to look on; but such as upon hearing their fictions should lightly scratch the surface; upon which, as on envenomed nails, followed inflamed swelling, impostumes, and a putrefied sore. My life being such, was it life, O my God?

And Thy faithful mercy hovered over me afar. Upon how grievous iniquities consumed I myself, pursuing a sacrilegious curiosity, that having forsaken Thee, it might bring me to the treacherous abyss, and the beguiling service of devils, to whom I sacrificed my evil actions, and in all these things Thou didst scourge me! I dared even, while Thy solemnities were celebrated within the walls of Thy Church, to desire, and to compass a business deserving death for its fruits, for which Thou scourgedst me with grievous punishments, though nothing to my fault, O Thou my exceeding mercy, my God, my refuge from those terrible destroyers, among whom I wandered with a stiff neck, withdrawing further from Thee, loving mine own ways, and not Thine; loving a vagrant liberty.

Those studies also, which were accounted commendable, had a view to excelling in the courts of litigation; the more bepraised, the craftier. Such is men's blindness, glorying even in their blindness. And now I was chief in the rhetoric school, whereat I joyed proudly, and I swelled with arrogancy, though (Lord, Thou knowest) far quieter and altogether removed from the subvertings of those "Subverters" (for this ill-omened and devilish name was the very badge of gallantry) among whom I lived, with a shameless shame that I was not even as they. With them I lived, and was sometimes delighted with their friendship, whose doings I ever did abhor—i.e., their "subvertings," wherewith they wantonly persecuted the modesty of strangers, which they disturbed by a gratuitous jeering, feeding thereon their malicious birth. Nothing can be liker the very actions of devils than these. What then could they be more truly called than "Subverters"? themselves subverted and altogether perverted first, the deceiving spirits secretly deriding and seducing them, wherein themselves delight to jeer at and deceive others.

Among such as these, in that unsettled age of mine, learned I books of eloquence, wherein I desired to be eminent, out of a damnable and vainglorious end, a joy in human vanity. In the ordinary course of study, I fell upon a certain book of Cicero, whose speech almost all admire, not so his heart. This book of his contains an exhortation to philosophy, and is called "Hortensius." But this book altered my affections, and turned my prayers to Thyself O Lord; and made me have other purposes and desires. Every vain hope at once became worthless to me; and I longed with an incredibly burning desire for an immortality of wisdom, and began now to arise, that I might return to Thee. For not to sharpen my tongue (which thing I seemed to be purchasing with my mother's allowances, in that my nineteenth year, my father being dead two years before), not to sharpen my tongue did I employ that book; nor did it infuse into me its style, but its matter.

How did I burn then, my God, how did I burn to re-mount from earthly things to Thee, nor knew I what Thou wouldest do with me? For with Thee is wisdom. But the love of wisdom is in Greek called "philosophy," with which that book inflamed me. Some there be that seduce through philosophy, under a great, and smooth, and honourable name colouring and disguising their own errors: and almost all who in that and former ages were such, are in that book censured and set forth: there also is made plain that wholesome advice of Thy Spirit, by Thy good and devout servant: Beware lest any man spoil you through philosophy and vain deceit, after the tradition of men, after the rudiments of the world, and not after Christ. For in Him dwelleth all the fullness of the Godhead bodily. And since at that time (Thou, O light of my heart, knowest) Apostolic Scripture was not known to me, I was delighted with that exhortation, so far only, that I was thereby strongly roused, and kindled, and inflamed to love, and seek, and obtain, and hold, and embrace not this or that sect, but wisdom itself whatever it were; and this alone checked me thus unkindled, that the name of Christ was not in it. For this name, according to Thy mercy, O Lord, this name of my Saviour Thy Son, had my tender heart, even with my mother's milk, devoutly drunk in and deeply treasured; and whatsoever was without that name, though never so learned, polished, or true, took not entire hold of me.

I resolved then to bend my mind to the holy Scriptures, that I might see what they were. But behold, I see a thing not understood by the proud, nor laid open to children, lowly in access, in its recesses lofty, and veiled with mysteries; and I was not such as could enter into it, or stoop my neck to follow its steps. For not as I now speak, did I feel when I turned to those Scriptures; but they seemed to me unworthy to be compared to the stateliness of Tully: for my swelling pride shrunk from their lowliness, nor could my sharp wit pierce the interior thereof. Yet were they such as would grow up in a little one. But I disdained to be a little one; and, swollen with pride, took myself to be a great one.

Therefore I fell among men proudly doting, exceeding carnal and prating, in whose mouths were the snares of the Devil, limed with the mixture of the syllables of Thy name, and of our Lord Jesus Christ, and of the Holy Ghost, the Paraclete, our Comforter. These names departed not out of their mouth, but so far forth as the sound only and the noise of the tongue, for the heart was void of truth. Yet they cried out "Truth, Truth," and spake much thereof to me, yet it was not in them: but they spake falsehood, not of Thee only (who truly art Truth), but even of those elements of this world, Thy creatures. And I indeed ought to have passed by even philosophers who spake truth concerning them, for love of Thee, my Father, supremely good, Beauty of all things beautiful. O Truth, Truth, how inwardly did even then the marrow of my soul pant after Thee, when they often and diversely, and in many and huge books, echoed of Thee to me, though it was but an echo? And these were the dishes wherein to me, hungering after Thee, they, instead of Thee, served up the Sun and Moon, beautiful works of Thine, but yet Thy works, not Thyself, no nor Thy first works. For Thy spiritual works are before these corporeal works, celestial though they be, and shining. But I hungered and thirsted not even after those first works of Thine, but after Thee Thyself, the Truth, in whom is no variableness, neither shadow of turning: yet they still set before me in those dishes, glittering fantasies, than which better were it to love this very sun (which is real to our sight at least), than those fantasies which by our eyes deceive our mind. Yet because I thought them to be Thee, I fed thereon; not eagerly, for Thou didst not in them taste to me as Thou art; for Thou wast not these emptinesses, nor was I nourished by them, but exhausted rather. Food in sleep shows very like our food awake; yet are not those asleep nourished by it, for they are asleep. But those were not even any way like to Thee, as Thou hast now spoken to me; for those were corporeal fantasies, false bodies, than which these true bodies, celestial or terrestrial, which with our fleshly sight we behold, are far more certain: these things the beasts and birds discern as well as we, and they are more certain than when we fancy them. And again, we do with more certainty fancy them, than by them conjecture other vaster and infinite bodies which have no being. Such empty husks was I then fed on; and was not fed. But Thou, my soul's Love, in looking for whom I fail, that I may become strong, art neither those bodies which we see, though in heaven; nor those which we see not there; for Thou hast created them, nor dost Thou account them among the chiefest of Thy works. How far then art Thou from those fantasies of mine, fantasies of bodies which altogether are not, than which the images of those bodies, which are, are far more certain, and more certain still the bodies themselves, which yet Thou art not; no, nor yet the soul, which is the life of the bodies. So then, better and more certain is the life of the bodies than the bodies. But Thou art the life of souls, the life of lives, having life in Thyself; and changest not, life of my soul.

Where then wert Thou then to me, and how far from me? Far verily was I straying from Thee, barred from the very husks of the swine, whom with husks I fed. For how much better are the fables of poets and grammarians than these snares? For verses, and poems, and "Medea flying," are more profitable truly than these men's five elements, variously disguised, answering to five dens of darkness, which have no being, yet slay the believer. For verses and poems I can turn to true food, and "Medea flying," though I did sing, I maintained not; though I heard it sung, I believed not: but those things I did believe. Woe, woe, by what steps was I brought down to the depths of hell! toiling and turmoiling through want of Truth, since I sought after Thee, my God (to Thee I confess it, who hadst mercy on me, not as yet confessing), not according to the understanding of the mind, wherein Thou willedst that I should excel the beasts, but according to the sense of the flesh. But Thou wert more inward to me than my most inward part; and higher than my highest. I lighted upon that bold woman, simple and knoweth nothing, shadowed out in Solomon, sitting at the door, and saying, Eat ye bread of secrecies willingly, and drink ye stolen waters which are sweet: she seduced me, because she found my soul dwelling abroad in the eye of my flesh, and ruminating on such food as through it I had devoured.

For other than this, that which really is I knew not; and was, as it were through sharpness of wit, persuaded to assent to foolish deceivers, when they asked me, "whence is evil?" "is God bounded by a bodily shape, and has hairs and nails?" "are they to be esteemed righteous who had many wives at once, and did kill men, and sacrifice living creatures?" At which I, in my ignorance, was much troubled, and departing from the truth, seemed to myself to be making towards it; because as yet I knew not that evil was nothing but a privation of good, until at last a thing ceases altogether to be; which how should I see, the sight of whose eyes reached only to bodies, and of my mind to a phantasm? And I knew not God to be a Spirit, not one who hath parts extended in length and breadth, or whose being was bulk; forevery bulk is less in a part than in the whole: and if it be infinite, it must be less in such part as is defined by a certain space, than in its infinitude; and so is not wholly every where, as Spirit, as God. And what that should be in us, by which we were like to God, and might be rightly said to be after the image of God, I was altogether ignorant.

Nor knew I that true inward righteousness which judgeth not

according to custom, but out of the most rightful law of God Almighty, whereby the ways of places and times were disposed according to those times and places; itself meantime being the same always and every where, not one thing in one place, and another in another; according to which Abraham, and Isaac, and Jacob, and Moses, and David, were righteous, and all those commended by the mouth of God; but were judged unrighteous by silly men, judging out of man's judgment, and measuring by their own petty habits, the moral habits of the whole human race. As if in an armory, one ignorant what were adapted to each part should cover his head with greaves, or seek to be shod with a helmet, and complain that they fitted not: or as if on a day when business is publicly stopped in the afternoon, one were angered at not being allowed to keep open shop, because he had been in the forenoon; or when in one house he observeth some servant take a thing in his hand, which the butler is not suffered to meddle with; or something permitted out of doors, which is forbidden in the dining-room; and should be angry, that in one house, and one family, the same thing is not allotted every where, and to all. Even such are they who are fretted to hear something to have been lawful for righteous men formerly, which now is not; or that God, for certain temporal respects, commanded them one thing, and these another, obeying both the same righteousness: whereas they see, in one man, and one day, and one house, different things to be fit for different members, and a thing formerly lawful, after a certain time not so; in one corner permitted or commanded, but in another rightly forbidden and punished. Is justice therefore various or mutable? No, but the times, over which it presides, flow not evenly, because they are times. But men whose days are few upon the earth, for that by their senses they cannot harmonise the causes of things in former ages and other nations, which they had not experience of, with these which they have experience of, whereas in one and the same body, day, or family, they easily see what is fitting for each member, and season, part, and person; to the one they take exceptions, to the other they submit.

These things I then knew not, nor observed; they struck my sight on all sides, and I saw them not. I indited verses, in which I might not place every foot every where, but differently in different metres; nor even in any one metre the self-same foot in all places.

Yet the art itself, by which I indited, had not different principles for these different cases, but comprised all in one. Still I saw not how that righteousness, which good and holy men obeyed, did far more excellently and sublimely contain in one all those things which God commanded, and in no part varied; although in varying times it prescribed not every thing at once, but apportioned and enjoined what was fit for each. And I in my blindness, censured the holy Fathers, not only wherein they made use of things present as God commanded and inspired them, but also wherein they were foretelling things to come, as God was revealing in them.

Can it at any time or place be unjust to love God with all his heart, with all his soul, and with all his mind; and his neighbour as himself? Therefore are those foul offenses which be against nature, to be every where and at all times detested and punished; such as were those of the men of Sodom: which should all nations commit, they should all stand guilty of the same crime, by the law of God, which hath not so made men that they should so abuse one another. For even that intercourse which should be between God and us is violated, when that same nature, of which He is Author, is polluted by perversity of lust. But those actions which are offenses against the customs of men, are to be avoided according to the customs severally prevailing; so that a thing agreed upon, and confirmed, by custom or law of any city or nation, may not be violated at the lawless pleasure of any, whether native or foreigner. For any part which harmoniseth not with its whole, is offensive. But when God commands a thing to be done, against the customs or compact of any people, though it were never by them done heretofore, it is to be done; and if intermitted, it is to be restored; and if never ordained, is now to be ordained. For lawful if it be for a king, in the state which he reigns over, to command that which no one before him, nor he himself heretofore, had commanded, and to obey him cannot be against the common weal of the state (nay, it were against it if he were not obeyed, for to obey princes is a general compact of human society); how much more unhesitatingly ought we to obey God, in all which He commands, the Ruler of all His creatures! For as among the powers in man's society, the greater authority is obeyed in preference to the lesser, so must God above all.

So in acts of violence, where there is a wish to hurt, whether by reproach or injury; and these either for revenge, as one enemy against another; or for some profit belonging to another, as the robber to the traveler; or to avoid some evil, as towards one who is feared; or through envy, as one less fortunate to one more so, or one well thriven in any thing, to him whose being on a par with himself he fears, or grieves at, or for the mere pleasure at another's pain, as spectators of gladiators, or deriders and mockers of others. These be the heads of iniquity which spring from the lust of the flesh, of the eye, or of rule, either singly, or two combined, or all together; and so do men live ill against the three, and seven, that psaltery of of ten strings, Thy Ten Commandments, O God, most high, and most sweet. But what foul offenses can there be against Thee, who canst not be defiled? or what acts of violence against Thee, who canst not be harmed? But Thou avengest what men commit against themselves, seeing also when they sin against Thee, they do wickedly against their own souls, and iniquity gives itself the lie, by corrupting and perverting their nature, which Thou hast created and ordained, or by an immoderate use of things allowed, or in burning in things unallowed, to that use which is against nature; or are found guilty, raging with heart and tongue against Thee, kicking against the pricks; or when, bursting the pale of human society, they boldly joy in self-willed combinations or divisions, according as they have any object to gain or subject of offence. And these things are done when Thou art forsaken, O Fountain of Life, who art the only and true Creator and Governor of the Universe, and by a self-willed pride, any one false thing is selected therefrom and loved. So then by a humble devoutness we return to Thee; and Thou cleansest us from our evil habits, and art merciful to their sins who confess, and hearest the groaning of the prisoner, and loosest us from the chains which we made for ourselves, if we lift not up against Thee the horns of an unreal liberty, suffering the loss of all, through covetousness of more, by loving more our own private good than Thee, the Good of all.

Amidst these offenses of foulness and violence, and so many iniquities, are sins of men, who are on the whole making proficiency; which by those that judge rightly, are, after the rule of perfection, discommended, yet the persons commended, upon hope of future fruit, as in the green blade of growing corn. And there are some, resembling offenses of foulness or violence, which yet are no sins; because they offend neither Thee, our Lord God, nor human society; when, namely, things fitting for a given period are obtained for the service of life, and we know not whether out of a lust of having; or when things are, for the sake of correction, by constituted authority punished, and we know not whether out of a lust of hurting. Many an action then which in men's sight is disapproved, is by Thy testimony approved; and many, by men praised, are (Thou being witness) condemned: because the show of the action, and the mind of the doer, and the unknown exigency of the period, severally vary. But when Thou on a sudden commandest an unwonted and unthought of thing, yea, although Thou hast sometime forbidden it, and still for the time hidest the reason of Thy command, and it be against the ordinance of some society of men, who doubts but it is to be done, seeing that society of men is just which serves Thee? But blessed are they who know Thy commands! For all things were done by Thy servants; either to show forth something needful for the present, or to foreshow things to come.

These things I being ignorant of, scoffed at those Thy holy servants and prophets. And what gained I by scoffing at them, but to be scoffed at by Thee, being insensibly and step by step drawn on to those follies, as to believe that a fig-tree wept when it was plucked, and the tree, its mother, shed milky tears? Which fig notwithstanding (plucked by some other's, not his own, guilt) had some Manichaean saint eaten, and mingled with his bowels, he should breathe out of it angels, yea, there shall burst forth particles of divinity, at every moan or groan in his prayer, which particles of the most high and true God had remained bound in that fig, unless they had been set at liberty by the teeth or belly of some "Elect" saint! And I, miserable, believed that more mercy was to be shown to the fruits of the earth than men, for whom they were created. For if any one an hungered, not a Manichaean, should ask for any, that morsel would seem as it were condemned to capital punishment, which should be given him.

And Thou sentest Thine hand from above, and drewest my soul out of that profound darkness, my mother, Thy faithful one, weeping to Thee for me, more than mothers weep the bodily deaths of their children. For she, by that faith and spirit which she had from Thee, discerned the death wherein I lay, and Thou heardest her, O Lord; Thou heardest her, and despisedst not her tears, when streaming down, they watered the ground under her eyes in every place where she prayed; yea Thou heardest her. For whence was that dream whereby Thou comfortedst her; so that she allowed me to live with her, and to eat at the same table in the house, which she had begun to shrink from, abhorring and detesting the blasphemies of my error? For she saw herself standing on a certain wooden rule, and a shining youth coming towards her, cheerful and smiling upon her, herself grieving, and overwhelmed with grief. But he having (in order to instruct, as is their wont not to be instructed) inquired of her the causes of her grief and daily tears, and she answering that she was bewailing my perdition, he bade her rest contented, and told her to look and observe, "That where she was, there was I also." And when she looked, she saw me standing by her in the same rule. Whence was this, but that Thine ears were towards her heart? O Thou Good omnipotent, who so carest for every one of us, as if Thou caredst for him only; and so for all, as if they were but one!

Whence was this also, that when she had told me this vision, and I would fain bend it to mean, "That she rather should not despair of being one day what I was"; she presently, without any hesitation, replies: "No; for it was not told me that, 'where he, there thou also'; but 'where thou, there he also'?" I confess to Thee, O Lord, that to the best of my remembrance (and I have oft spoken of this), that Thy answer, through my waking mother—that she was not perplexed by the plausibility of my false interpretation, and so quickly saw what was to be seen, and which I certainly had not perceived before she spake—even then moved me more than the dream itself, by which a joy to the holy woman, to be fulfilled so long after, was, for the consolation of her present anguish, so long before foresignified. For almost nine years passed, in which I wallowed in the mire of that deep pit, and the darkness of falsehood, often assaying to rise, but dashed down the more grievously. All which time that chaste, godly, and sober widow (such as Thou lovest), now more cheered with hope, yet no whit relaxing in her weeping and mourning, ceased not at all hours of her devotions to bewail my case unto Thee. And her prayers entered into Thy presence; and yet Thou sufferedst me to be yet involved and reinvolved in that darkness.

Thou gavest her meantime another answer, which I call to mind; for much I pass by, hasting to those things which more press me to confess unto Thee, and much I do not remember. Thou gavest her then another answer, by a Priest of Thine, a certain Bishop brought up in Thy Church, and well studied in Thy books. Whom when this woman had entreated to vouchsafe to converse with me, refute my errors, unteach me ill things, and teach me good things (for this he was wont to do, when he found persons fitted to receive it), he refused, wisely, as I afterwards perceived. For he answered, that I was yet unteachable, being puffed up with the novelty of that heresy, and had already perplexed divers unskilful persons with captious questions, as she had told him: "but let him alone a while" (saith he), "only pray God for him, he will of himself by reading find what that error is, and how great its impiety." At the same time he told her, how himself, when a little one, had by his seduced mother been consigned over to the Manichees, and had not only read, but frequently copied out almost all, their books, and had (without any argument or proof from any one) seen how much that sect was to be avoided; and had avoided it. Which when he had said, and she would not be satisfied, but urged him more, with entreaties and many tears, that he would see me and discourse with me; he, a little displeased at her importunity, saith, "Go thy ways and God bless thee, for it is not possible that the son of these tears should perish." Which answer she took (as she often mentioned in her conversations with me) as if it had sounded from heaven.

Book Four

For this space of nine years (from my nineteenth year to my eight and twentieth) we lived seduced and seducing, deceived and deceiving, in divers lusts; openly, by sciences which they call liberal; secretly, with a false-named religion; here proud, there superstitious, every where vain. Here, hunting after the emptiness of popular praise, down even to theatrical applauses, and poetic prizes, and strifes for grassy garlands, and the follies of shows, and the intemperance of desires. There, desiring to be cleansed from these defilements, by carrying food to those who were called "elect" and "holy," out of which, in the workhouse of their stomachs, they should forge for us Angels and Gods, by whom we might be cleansed. These things did I follow, and practise with my friends, deceived by me, and with me. Let the arrogant mock me, and such as have not been, to their soul's health, stricken and cast down by Thee, O my God; but I would still confess to Thee mine own shame in Thy praise. Suffer me, I beseech Thee, and give me grace to go over in my present remembrance the wanderings of my forepassed time, and to offer unto Thee the sacrifice of thanksgiving. For what am I to myself without Thee, but a guide to mine own downfall? or what am I even at the best, but an infant sucking the milk Thou givest, and feeding upon Thee, the food that perisheth not? But what sort of man is any man, seeing he is but a man? Let now the strong and the mighty laugh at us, but let us poor and needy confess unto Thee.

In those years I taught rhetoric, and, overcome by cupidity, made sale of a loquacity to overcome by. Yet I preferred (Lord, Thou knowest) honest scholars (as they are accounted), and these I, without artifice, taught artifices, not to be practised against the life of the guiltless, though sometimes for the life of the guilty. And Thou, O God, from afar perceivedst me stumbling in that slippery course, and amid much smoke sending out some sparks of faithfulness, which I showed in that my guidance of such as loved vanity, and sought after leasing, myself their companion. In those years I had one—not in that which is called lawful marriage, but whom I had found out in a wayward passion, void of understanding; yet but one, remaining faithful even to her; in whom I in my own case experienced what difference there is betwixt the self-restraint of the marriage-covenant, for the sake of issue, and the bargain of a lustful love, where children are born against their parents' will, although, once born, they constrain love.

I remember also, that when I had settled to enter the lists for a theatrical prize, some wizard asked me what I would give him to win; but I, detesting and abhorring such foul mysteries, answered, "Though the garland were of imperishable gold, I would not suffer a fly to be killed to gain me it." For he was to kill some living creatures in his sacrifices, and by those honours to invite the devils to favour me. But this ill also I rejected, not out of a pure love for Thee, O God of my heart; for I knew not how to love Thee, who knew not how to conceive aught beyond a material brightness. And doth not a soul, sighing after such fictions, commit fornication against Thee, trust in things unreal, and feed the wind? Still I would not forsooth have sacrifices offered to devils for me, to whom I was sacrificing myself by that superstition. For what else is it to feed the wind, but to feed them, that is by going astray to become their pleasure and derision?

Those impostors then, whom they style Mathematicians, I consulted without scruple; because they seemed to use no sacrifice, nor to pray to any spirit for their divinations: which art, however, Christian and true piety consistently rejects and condemns. For, it is a good thing to confess unto Thee, and to say, Have mercy upon me, heal my soul, for I have sinned against Thee; and not to abuse Thy mercy for a license to sin, but to remember the Lord's words, Behold, thou art made whole, sin no more, lest a worse thing come unto thee. All which wholesome advice they labour to destroy, saying, "The cause of thy sin is inevitably determined in heaven"; and "This did Venus, or Saturn, or Mars": that man, forsooth, flesh and blood, and proud corruption, might be blameless; while the Creator and Ordainer of heaven and the stars is to bear the blame. And who is He but our God? the very sweetness and well-spring of righteousness, who renderest to every man according to his works: and a broken and contrite heart wilt Thou not despise.

There was in those days a wise man, very skillful in physic, and renowned therein, who had with his own proconsular hand put the Agonistic garland upon my distempered head, but not as a physician: for this disease Thou only curest, who resistest the proud, and givest grace to the humble. But didst Thou fail me even by that old man, or forbear to heal my soul? For having become more acquainted with him, and hanging assiduously and fixedly on his speech (for though in simple terms, it was vivid, lively, and earnest), when he had gathered by my discourse that I was given to the books of nativitycasters, he kindly and fatherly advised me to cast them away, and not fruitlessly bestow a care and diligence, necessary for useful things, upon these vanities; saying, that he had in his earliest years studied that art, so as to make it the profession whereby he should live, and that, understanding Hippocrates, he could soon have understood such a study as this; and yet he had given it over, and taken to physic, for no other reason but that he found it utterly false; and he, a grave man, would not get his living by deluding people. "But thou," saith he, "hast rhetoric to maintain thyself by, so that thou followest this of free choice, not of necessity: the more then oughtest thou to give me credit herein, who laboured to acquire it so perfectly as to get my living by it alone." Of whom when I had demanded, how then could many true things be foretold by it, he answered me (as he could) "that the force of chance, diffused throughout the whole order of things, brought this about. For if when a man by haphazard opens the pages of some poet, who sang and thought of something wholly different, a verse oftentimes fell out, wondrously agreeable to the present business: it were not to be wondered at, if out of the soul of man, unconscious what takes place in it, by some higher instinct an answer should be given, by hap, not by art, corresponding to the business and actions of the demander."

And thus much, either from or through him, Thou conveyedst to me, and tracedst in my memory, what I might hereafter examine for myself. But at that time neither he, nor my dearest Nebridius, a youth singularly good and of a holy fear, who derided the whole body of divination, could persuade me to cast it aside, the authority of the authors swaying me yet more, and as yet I had found no certain proof (such as I sought) whereby it might without all doubt appear, that what had been truly foretold by those consulted was the result of haphazard, not of the art of the star-gazers.

In those years when I first began to teach rhetoric in my native town, I had made one my friend, but too dear to me, from a community of pursuits, of mine own age, and, as myself, in the first opening flower of youth. He had grown up of a child with me, and we had been both school-fellows and play-fellows. But he was not yet my friend as afterwards, nor even then, as true friendship is; for true it cannot be, unless in such as Thou cementest together, cleaving unto Thee, by that love which is shed abroad in our hearts by the Holy Ghost, which is given unto us. Yet was it but too sweet, ripened by the warmth of kindred studies: for, from the true faith (which he as a youth had not soundly and thoroughly imbibed), I had warped him also to those superstitious and pernicious fables, for which my mother bewailed me. With me he now erred in mind, nor could my soul be without him. But behold Thou wert close on the steps of Thy fugitives, at once God of vengeance, and Fountain of mercies, turning us to Thyself by wonderful means; Thou tookest that man out of this life, when he had scarce filled up one whole year of my friendship, sweet to me above all sweetness of that my life.

Who can recount all Thy praises, which he hath felt in his one self? What didest Thou then, my God, and how unsearchable is the abyss of Thy judgments? For long, sore sick of a fever, he lay senseless in a death-sweat; and his recovery being despaired of, he was baptised, unknowing; myself meanwhile little regarding, and presuming that his soul would retain rather what it had received of me, not what was wrought on his unconscious body. But it proved far otherwise: for he was refreshed, and restored. Forthwith, as soon as I could speak with him (and I could, so soon as he was able, for I never left him, and we hung but too much upon each other), I essayed to jest with him, as though he would jest with me at that baptism which he had received, when utterly absent in mind and feeling, but had now understood that he had received. But he so shrunk from me, as from an enemy; and with a wonderful and sudden freedom bade me, as I would continue his friend, forbear such language to him. I, all astonished and amazed, suppressed all my emotions till he should grow well, and his health were strong enough for me to deal with him as I would. But he was taken away from my frenzy, that with Thee he might be preserved for my comfort; a few days after in my absence, he was attacked again by the fever, and so departed.

At this grief my heart was utterly darkened; and whatever I beheld was death. My native country was a torment to me, and my father's house a strange unhappiness; and whatever I had shared with him, wanting him, became a distracting torture. Mine eyes sought him every where, but he was not granted them; and I hated all places, for that they had not him; nor could they now tell me, "he is coming," as when he was alive and absent. I became a great riddle to myself, and I asked my soul, why she was so sad, and why she disquieted me sorely: but she knew not what to answer me. And if I said, Trust in God, she very rightly obeyed me not; because that most dear friend, whom she had lost, was, being man, both truer and better than that phantasm she was bid to trust in. Only tears were sweet to me, for they succeeded my friend, in the dearest of my affections.

And now, Lord, these things are passed by, and time hath assuaged my wound. May I learn from Thee, who art Truth, and approach the ear of my heart unto Thy mouth, that Thou mayest tell me why weeping is sweet to the miserable? Hast Thou, although present every where, cast away our misery far from Thee? And Thou abidest in Thyself, but we are tossed about in divers trials. And yet unless we mourned in Thine ears, we should have no hope left. Whence then is sweet fruit gathered from the bitterness of life, from groaning, tears, sighs, and complaints? Doth this sweeten it, that we hope Thou hearest? This is true of prayer, for therein is a longing to approach unto Thee. But is it also in grief for a thing lost, and the sorrow wherewith I was then overwhelmed? For I neither hoped he should return to life nor did I desire this with my tears; but I wept only and grieved. For I was miserable, and had lost my joy. Or is weeping indeed a bitter thing, and for very loathing of the things which we before enjoyed, does it then, when we shrink from them, please us?

But what speak I of these things? for now is no time to question, but to confess unto Thee. Wretched I was; and wretched is every soul bound by the friendship of perishable things; he is torn asunder when he loses them, and then he feels the wretchedness which he had ere yet he lost them. So was it then with me; I wept most bitterly, and found my repose in bitterness. Thus was I wretched, and that wretched life I held dearer than my friend. For though I would willingly have changed it, yet was I more unwilling to part with it than with him; yea, I know not whether I would have parted with it even for him, as is related (if not feigned) of Pylades and Orestes, that they would gladly have died for each other or together, not to live together being to them worse than death. But in me there had arisen some unexplained feeling, too contrary to this, for at once I loathed exceedingly to live and feared to die. I suppose, the more I loved him, the more did I hate, and fear (as a most cruel enemy) death, which had bereaved me of him: and I imagined it would speedily make an end of all men, since it had power over him. Thus was it with me, I remember. Behold my heart, O my God, behold and see into me; for well I remember it, O my Hope, who cleansest me from the impurity of such affections, directing mine eyes towards Thee, and plucking my feet out of the snare. For I wondered that others, subject to death, did live, since he whom I loved, as if he should never die, was dead; and I wondered yet more that myself, who was to him a second self, could live, he being dead. Well said one of his friend, "Thou half of my soul"; for I felt that my soul and his soul were "one soul in two bodies": and therefore was my life a horror to me, because I would not live halved. And therefore perchance I feared to die, lest he whom I had much loved should die wholly.

O madness, which knowest not how to love men, like men! O foolish man that I then was, enduring impatiently the lot of man! I fretted then, sighed, wept, was distracted; had neither rest nor counsel. For I bore about a shattered and bleeding soul, impatient of being borne by me, yet where to repose it, I found not. Not in calm groves, not in games and music, nor in fragrant spots, nor in curious banquetings, nor in the pleasures of the bed and the couch; nor (finally) in books or poesy, found it repose. All things looked ghastly, yea, the very light; whatsoever was not what he was, was revolting and hateful, except groaning and tears. For in those alone found I a little refreshment. But when my soul was withdrawn from them a huge load of misery weighed me down. To Thee, O Lord, it ought to have been raised, for Thee to lighten; I knew it; but neither could nor would; the more, since, when I thought of Thee, Thou wert not to me any solid or substantial thing. For Thou wert not Thyself, but a mere phantom, and my error was my God. If I offered to discharge my load thereon, that it might rest, it glided through the void, and came rushing down again on me; and I had remained to myself a hapless spot, where I could neither be, nor be from thence. For whither should my heart flee from my heart? Whither should I flee from myself? Whither not follow myself? And yet I fled out of my country; for so should mine eyes less look for him, where they were not wont to see him. And thus from Thagaste, I came to Carthage.

Times lose no time; nor do they roll idly by; through our senses they work strange operations on the mind. Behold, they went and came day by day, and by coming and going, introduced into my mind other imaginations and other remembrances; and little by little patched me up again with my old kind of delights, unto which that my sorrow gave way. And yet there succeeded, not indeed other griefs, yet the causes of other griefs. For whence had that former grief so easily reached my very inmost soul, but that I had poured out my soul upon the dust, in loving one that must die, as if he would never die? For what restored and refreshed me chiefly was the solaces of other friends, with whom I did love, what instead of Thee I loved; and this was a great fable, and protracted lie, by whose adulterous stimulus, our soul, which lay itching in our ears, was being defiled. But that fable would not die to me, so oft as any of my friends died. There were other things which in them did more take my mind; to talk and jest together, to do kind offices by turns; to read together honied books; to play the fool or be earnest together; to dissent at times without discontent, as a man might with his own self; and even with the seldomness of these dissentings, to season our more frequent consentings; sometimes to teach, and sometimes learn; long for the absent with impatience; and welcome the coming with joy. These and the like expressions, proceeding out of the hearts of those that loved and were loved again, by the countenance, the tongue, the eyes, and a thousand pleasing gestures, were so much fuel to melt our souls together, and out of many make but one.

This is it that is loved in friends; and so loved, that a man's conscience condemns itself, if he love not him that loves him again, or love not again him that loves him, looking for nothing from his person but indications of his love. Hence that mourning, if one die, and darkenings of sorrows, that steeping of the heart in tears, all sweetness turned to bitterness; and upon the loss of life of the dying, the death of the living. Blessed whoso loveth Thee, and his friend in

Thee, and his enemy for Thee. For he alone loses none dear to him, to whom all are dear in Him who cannot be lost. And who is this but our God, the God that made heaven and earth, and filleth them, because by filling them He created them? Thee none loseth, but who leaveth. And who leaveth Thee, whither goeth or whither fleeth he, but from Thee well-pleased, to Thee displeased? For where doth he not find Thy law in his own punishment? And Thy law is truth, and truth Thou.

Turn us, O God of Hosts, show us Thy countenance, and we shall be whole. For whithersoever the soul of man turns itself, unless toward Thee, it is riveted upon sorrows, yea though it is riveted on things beautiful. And yet they, out of Thee, and out of the soul, were not, unless they were from Thee. They rise, and set; and by rising, they begin as it were to be; they grow, that they may be perfected; and perfected, they wax old and wither; and all grow not old, but all wither. So then when they rise and tend to be, the more quickly they grow that they may be, so much the more they haste not to be. This is the law of them. Thus much has Thou allotted them, because they are portions of things, which exist not all at once, but by passing away and succeeding, they together complete that universe, whereof they are portions. And even thus is our speech completed by signs giving forth a sound: but this again is not perfected unless one word pass away when it hath sounded its part, that another may succeed. Out of all these things let my soul praise Thee, O God, Creator of all; yet let not my soul be riveted unto these things with the glue of love, through the senses of the body. For they go whither they were to go, that they might not be; and they rend her with pestilent longings, because she longs to be, yet loves to repose in what she loves. But in these things is no place of repose; they abide not, they flee; and who can follow them with the senses of the flesh? yea, who can grasp them, when they are hard by? For the sense of the flesh is slow, because it is the sense of the flesh; and thereby is it bounded. It sufficeth for that it was made for; but it sufficeth not to stay things running their course from their appointed starting-place to the end appointed. For in Thy Word, by which they are created, they hear their decree, "hence and hitherto."

Be not foolish, O my soul, nor become deaf in the ear of thine heart with the tumult of thy folly. Hearken thou too.

The Word itself calleth thee to return: and there is the place of rest imperturbable, where love is not forsaken, if itself forsaketh not. Behold, these things pass away, that others may replace them, and so this lower universe be completed by all his parts. But do I depart any whither? saith the Word of God. There fix thy dwelling, trust there whatsoever thou hast thence, O my soul, at least now thou art tired out with vanities. Entrust Truth, whatsoever thou hast from the Truth, and thou shalt lose nothing; and thy decay shall bloom again, and all thy diseases be healed, and thy mortal parts be reformed and renewed, and bound around thee: nor shall they lay thee whither themselves descend; but they shall stand fast with thee, and abide for ever before God, Who abideth and standeth fast for ever.

Why then be perverted and follow thy flesh? Be it converted and follow thee. Whatever by her thou hast sense of, is in part; and the whole, whereof these are parts, thou knowest not; and yet they delight thee. But had the sense of thy flesh a capacity for comprehending the whole, and not itself also, for thy punishment, been justly restricted to a part of the whole, thou wouldest, that whatsoever existeth at this present, should pass away, that so the whole might better please thee. For what we speak also, by the same sense of the flesh thou hearest; yet wouldest not thou have the syllables stay, but fly away, that others may come, and thou hear the whole. And so ever, when any one thing is made up of many, all of which do not exist together, all collectively would please more than they do severally, could all be perceived collectively. But far better than these is He who made all; and He is our God, nor doth He pass away, for neither doth aught succeed Him.

If bodies please thee, praise God on occasion of them, and turn back thy love upon their Maker; lest in these things which please thee, thou displease. If souls please thee, be they loved in God: for they too are mutable, but in Him are they firmly stablished; else would they pass, and pass away. In Him then be they beloved; and carry unto Him along with thee what souls thou canst, and say to them, "Him let us love, Him let us love: He made these, nor is He far off. For He did not make them, and so depart, but they are of Him, and in Him. See there He is, where truth is loved. He is within the very heart, yet hath the heart strayed from Him. Go back into your heart, ye transgressors, and cleave fast to Him that made you. Stand with Him, and ye shall stand fast. Rest in Him, and ye shall be at rest. Whither go ye in rough ways? Whither go ye? The good that you love is from Him; but it is good and pleasant through reference to Him, and justly shall it be embittered, because unjustly is any thing loved which is from Him, if He be forsaken for it. To what end then would ye still and still walk these difficult and toilsome ways? There is no rest, where ye seek it. Seek what ye seek; but it is not there where ye seek. Ye seek a blessed life in the land of death; it is not there. For how should there be a blessed life where life itself is not?

"But our true Life came down hither, and bore our death, and slew him, out of the abundance of His own life: and He thundered, calling aloud to us to return hence to Him into that secret place, whence He came forth to us, first into the Virgin's womb, wherein He espoused the human creation, our mortal flesh, that it might not be for ever mortal, and thence like a bridegroom coming out of his chamber, rejoicing as a giant to run his course. For He lingered not, but ran, calling aloud by words, deeds, death, life, descent, ascension; crying aloud to us to return unto Him. And He departed from our eyes, that we might return into our heart, and there find Him. For He departed, and lo, He is here. He would not be long with us, yet left us not; for He departed thither, whence He never parted, because the world was made by Him. And in this world He was, and into this world He came to save sinners, unto whom my soul confesseth, and He healeth it, for it hath sinned against Him. O ye sons of men, how long so slow of heart? Even now, after the descent of Life to you, will ye not ascend and live? But whither ascend ye, when ye are on high, and set your mouth against the heavens? Descend, that ye may ascend, and ascend to God. For ye have fallen, by ascending against Him." Tell them this, that they may weep in the valley of tears, and so carry them up with thee unto God; because out of His spirit thou speakest thus unto them, if thou speakest, burning with the fire of charity.

These things I then knew not, and I loved these lower beauties, and I was sinking to the very depths, and to my friends I said, "Do we love any thing but the beautiful? What then is the beautiful? and what is beauty? What is it that attracts and wins us to the things we love? for unless there were in them a grace and beauty, they could by no means draw us unto them." And I marked and perceived that in bodies themselves, there was a beauty, from their forming a sort of whole, and again, another from apt and mutual correspondence, as of a part of the body with its whole, or a shoe with a foot, and the like. And this consideration sprang up in my mind, out of my inmost heart, and I wrote "on the fair and fit," I think, two or three books. Thou knowest, O Lord, for it is gone from me; for I have them not, but they are strayed from me, I know not how.

But what moved me, O Lord my God, to dedicate these books unto Hierius, an orator of Rome, whom I knew not by face, but loved for the fame of his learning which was eminent in him, and some words of his I had heard, which pleased me? But more did he please me, for that he pleased others, who highly extolled him, amazed that out of a Syrian, first instructed in Greek eloquence, should afterwards be formed a wonderful Latin orator, and one most learned in things pertaining unto philosophy. One is commended, and, unseen, he is loved: doth this love enter the heart of the hearer from the mouth of the commender? Not so. But by one who loveth is another kindled. For hence he is loved who is commended, when the commender is believed to extol him with an unfeigned heart; that is, when one that loves him, praises him.

For so did I then love men, upon the judgment of men, not Thine, O my God, in Whom no man is deceived. But yet why not for qualities, like those of a famous charioteer, or fighter with beasts in the theatre, known far and wide by a vulgar popularity, but far otherwise, and earnestly, and so as I would be myself commended? For I would not be commended or loved, as actors are (though I myself did commend and love them), but had rather be unknown, than so known; and even hated, than so loved. Where now are the impulses to such various and divers kinds of loves laid up in one soul? Why, since we are equally men, do I love in another what, if I did not hate,

I should not spurn and cast from myself? For it holds not, that as a good horse is loved by him, who would not, though he might, be that horse, therefore the same may be said of an actor, who shares our nature. Do I then love in a man, what I hate to be, who am a man? Man himself is a great deep, whose very hairs Thou numberest, O Lord, and they fall not to the ground without Thee. And yet are the hairs of his head easier to be numbered than his feelings, and the beatings of his heart.

But that orator was of that sort whom I loved, as wishing to be myself such; and I erred through a swelling pride, and was tossed about with every wind, but yet was steered by Thee, though very secretly. And whence do I know, and whence do I confidently confess unto Thee, that I had loved him more for the love of his commenders, than for the very things for which he was commended? Because, had he been unpraised, and these self-same men had dispraised him, and with dispraise and contempt told the very same things of him, I had never been so kindled and excited to love him. And yet the things had not been other, nor he himself other; but only the feelings of the relators. See where the impotent soul lies along, that is not yet stayed up by the solidity of truth! Just as the gales of tongues blow from the breast of the opinionative, so is it carried this way and that, driven forward and backward, and the light is overclouded to it, and the truth unseen. And lo, it is before us. And it was to me a great matter, that my discourse and labours should be known to that man: which should he approve, I were the more kindled; but if he disapproved, my empty heart, void of Thy solidity, had been wounded. And yet the "fair and fit," whereon I wrote to him, I dwelt on with pleasure, and surveyed it, and admired it, though none joined therein.

But I saw not yet, whereon this weighty matter turned in Thy wisdom, O Thou Omnipotent, who only doest wonders; and my mind ranged through corporeal forms; and "fair," I defined and distinguished what is so in itself, and "fit," whose beauty is in correspondence to some other thing: and this I supported by corporeal examples. And I turned to the nature of the mind, but the false notion which I had of spiritual things, let me not see the truth. Yet the force of truth did of itself flash into mine eyes, and I turned away my panting soul from incorporeal substance to lineaments, and colours, and bulky magnitudes. And not being able to see these in the mind, I thought I could not see my mind. And whereas in virtue I loved peace, and in viciousness I abhorred discord; in the first I observed a unity, but in the other, a sort of division. And in that unity I conceived the rational soul, and the nature of truth and of the chief good to consist; but in this division I miserably imagined there to be some unknown substance of irrational life, and the nature of the chief evil, which should not only be a substance, but real life also, and yet not derived from Thee, O my God, of whom are all things. And yet that first I called a Monad, as it had been a soul without sex; but the latter a Duad—anger, in deeds of violence, and in flagitiousness, lust—not knowing whereof I spake. For I had not known or learned that neither was evil a substance, nor our soul that chief and unchangeable good.

For as deeds of violence arise, if that emotion of the soul be corrupted, whence vehement action springs, stirring itself insolently and unrulily; and lusts, when that affection of the soul is ungoverned, whereby carnal pleasures are drunk in, so do errors and false opinions defile the conversation, if the reasonable soul itself be corrupted; as it was then in me, who knew not that it must be enlightened by another light, that it may be partaker of truth, seeing itself is not that nature of truth. For Thou shalt light my candle, O Lord my God, Thou shalt enlighten my darkness: and of Thy fullness have we all received, for Thou art the true light that lighteth every man that cometh into the world; for in Thee there is no variableness, neither shadow of change.

But I pressed towards Thee, and was thrust from Thee, that I might taste of death: for thou resistest the proud. But what prouder, than for me with a strange madness to maintain myself to be that by nature which Thou art? For whereas I was subject to change (so much being manifest to me, my very desire to become wise, being the wish, of worse to become better), yet chose I rather to imagine Thee subject to change, and myself not to be that which Thou art. Therefore I was repelled by Thee, and Thou resistedst my vain stiffneckedness, and I imagined corporeal forms, and, myself flesh, I accused flesh; and, a wind that passeth away, I returned not to Thee, but I passed on and on to things which have no being, neither in Thee, nor in me, nor in the body. Neither were they created for me by Thy truth, but by my vanity devised out of things corporeal. And I was wont to ask Thy faithful little ones, my fellow-citizens (from whom, unknown to myself, I stood exiled), I was wont, prating and foolishly, to ask them, "Why then doth the soul err which God created?" But I would not be asked, "Why then doth God err?" And I maintained that Thy unchangeable substance did err upon constraint, rather than confess that my changeable substance had gone astray voluntarily, and now, in punishment, lay in error.

I was then some six or seven and twenty years old when I wrote those volumes; revolving within me corporeal fictions, buzzing in the ears of my heart, which I turned, O sweet truth, to thy inward melody, meditating on the "fair and fit," and longing to stand and hearken to Thee, and to rejoice greatly at the Bridegroom's voice, but could not; for by the voices of mine own errors, I was hurried abroad, and through the weight of my own pride, I was sinking into the lowest pit. For Thou didst not make me to hear joy and gladness, nor did the bones exult which were not yet humbled.

And what did it profit me, that scarce twenty years old, a book of Aristotle, which they call the ten Predicaments, falling into my hands (on whose very name I hung, as on something great and divine, so often as my rhetoric master of Carthage, and others, accounted learned, mouthed it with cheeks bursting with pride), I read and understood it unaided? And on my conferring with others, who said that they scarcely understood it with very able tutors, not only orally explaining it, but drawing many things in sand, they could tell me no more of it than I had learned, reading it by myself. And the book appeared to me to speak very clearly of substances, such as "man," and of their qualities, as the figure of a man, of what sort it is; and stature, how many feet high; and his relationship, whose brother he is; or where placed; or when born; or whether he stands or sits; or be shod or armed; or does, or suffers anything; and all the innumerable things which might be ranged under these nine Predicaments, of which I have given some specimens, or under that chief Predicament of Substance.

What did all this further me, seeing it even hindered me? when, imagining whatever was, was comprehended under those ten Predicaments, I essayed in such wise to understand, O my God, Thy wonderful and unchangeable Unity also, as if Thou also hadst been subjected to Thine own greatness or beauty; so that (as in bodies) they should exist in Thee, as their subject: whereas Thou Thyself art Thy greatness and beauty; but a body is not great or fair in that it is a body, seeing that, though it were less great or fair, it should notwithstanding be a body. But it was falsehood which of Thee I conceived, not truth, fictions of my misery, not the realities of Thy blessedness. For Thou hadst commanded, and it was done in me, that the earth should bring forth briars and thorns to me, and that in the sweat of my brows I should eat my bread.

And what did it profit me, that all the books I could procure of the so-called liberal arts, I, the vile slave of vile affections, read by myself, and understood? And I delighted in them, but knew not whence came all, that therein was true or certain. For I had my back to the light, and my face to the things enlightened; whence my face, with which I discerned the things enlightened, itself was not enlightened. Whatever was written, either on rhetoric, or logic, geometry, music, and arithmetic, by myself without much difficulty or any instructor, I understood, Thou knowest, O Lord my God; because both quickness of understanding, and acuteness in discerning, is Thy gift: yet did I not thence sacrifice to Thee. So then it served not to my use, but rather to my perdition, since I went about to get so good a portion of my substance into my own keeping; and I kept not my strength for Thee, but wandered from Thee into a far country, to spend it upon harlotries. For what profited me good abilities, not employed to good uses? For I felt not that those arts were attained with great difficulty, even by the studious and talented, until I attempted to explain them to such; when he most excelled in them who followed me not altogether slowly.

But what did this further me, imagining that Thou, O Lord God, the Truth, wert a vast and bright body, and I a fragment of that body? Perverseness too great! But such was I. Nor do I blush, O my God, to confess to Thee Thy mercies towards me, and to call upon Thee, who blushed not then to profess to men my blasphemies, and to bark against Thee. What profited me then my nimble wit in those sciences and all those most knotty volumes, unraveled by me, without aid from human instruction; seeing I erred so foully, and with such sacrilegious shamefulness, in the doctrine of piety? Or what hindrance was a far slower wit to Thy little ones, since they departed not far from Thee, that in the nest of Thy Church they might securely be fledged, and nourish the wings of charity, by the food of a sound faith. O Lord our God, under the shadow of Thy wings let us hope; protect us, and carry us. Thou wilt carry us both when little, and even to hoar hairs wilt Thou carry us; for our firmness, when it is Thou, then is it firmness; but when our own, it is infirmity. Our good ever lives with Thee; from which when we turn away, we are turned aside. Let us now, O Lord, return, that we may not be overturned, because with Thee our good lives without any decay, which good art Thou; nor need we fear, lest there be no place whither to return, because we fell from it: for through our absence, our mansion fell not—Thy eternity.

Book Five

Accept the sacrifice of my confessions from the ministry of my tongue, which Thou hast formed and stirred up to confess unto Thy name. Heal Thou all my bones, and let them say, O Lord, who is like unto Thee? For he who confesses to Thee doth not teach Thee what takes place within him; seeing a closed heart closes not out Thy eye, nor can man's hardheartedness thrust back Thy hand: for Thou dissolvest it at Thy will in pity or in vengeance, and nothing can hide itself from Thy heat. But let my soul praise Thee, that it may love Thee; and let it confess Thy own mercies to Thee, that it may praise Thee. Thy whole creation ceaseth not, nor is silent in Thy praises; neither the spirit of man with voice directed unto Thee, nor creation animate or inanimate, by the voice of those who meditate thereon: that so our souls may from their weariness arise towards Thee, leaning on those things which Thou hast created, and passing on to Thyself, who madest them wonderfully; and there is refreshment and true strength.

Let the restless, the godless, depart and flee from Thee; yet Thou seest them, and dividest the darkness. And behold, the universe with them is fair, though they are foul. And how have they injured Thee? or how have they disgraced Thy government, which, from the heaven to this lowest earth, is just and perfect? For whither fled they, when they fled from Thy presence? or where dost not Thou find them? But they fled, that they might not see Thee seeing them, and, blinded, might stumble against Thee (because Thou forsakest nothing Thou hast made); that the unjust, I say, might stumble upon Thee, and justly be hurt; withdrawing themselves from thy gentleness, and stumbling at Thy uprightness, and falling upon their own ruggedness. Ignorant, in truth, that Thou art every where, Whom no place encompasseth! and Thou alone art near, even to those that remove far from Thee. Let them then be turned, and seek Thee; because not as they have forsaken their Creator, hast Thou forsaken Thy creation.

Let them be turned and seek Thee; and behold, Thou art there in their heart, in the heart of those that confess to Thee, and cast themselves upon Thee, and weep in Thy bosom, after all their rugged ways. Then dost Thou gently wipe away their tears, and they weep the more, and joy in weeping; even for that Thou, Lord—not man of flesh and blood, but—Thou, Lord, who madest them, re-makest and comfortest them. But where was I, when I was seeking Thee? And Thou wert before me, but I had gone away from Thee; nor did I find myself, how much less Thee!

I would lay open before my God that nine-and-twentieth year of mine age. There had then come to Carthage a certain Bishop of the Manichees, Faustus by name, a great snare of the Devil, and many were entangled by him through that lure of his smooth language: which though I did commend, yet could I separate from the truth of the things which I was earnest to learn: nor did I so much regard the service of oratory as the science which this Faustus, so praised among them, set before me to feed upon. Fame had before bespoken him most knowing in all valuable learning, and exquisitely skilled in the liberal sciences. And since I had read and well remembered much of the philosophers, I compared some things of theirs with those long fables of the Manichees, and found the former the more probable; even although they could only prevail so far as to make judgment of this lower world, the Lord of it they could by no means find out. For Thou art great, O Lord, and hast respect unto the humble, but the proud Thou beholdest afar off. Nor dost Thou draw near, but to the contrite in heart, nor art found by the proud, no, not though by curious skill they could number the stars and the sand, and measure the starry heavens, and track the courses of the planets.

For with their understanding and wit, which Thou bestowedst on them, they search out these things; and much have they found out; and foretold, many years before, eclipses of those luminaries, the sun and moon—what day and hour, and how many digits—nor did their calculation fail; and it came to pass as they foretold; and they wrote down the rules they had found out, and these are read at this day, and out of them do others foretell in what year and month of the year, and what day of the month, and what hour of the day, and what part of its light, moon or sun is to be eclipsed, and so it shall be, as it is foreshowed. At these things men, that know not this art, marvel and are astonished, and they that know it, exult, and are puffed up; and by an ungodly pride departing from Thee, and failing of Thy light, they foresee a failure of the sun's light, which shall be, so long before, but see not their own, which is. For they search not religiously whence they have the wit, wherewith they search out this. And finding that Thou madest them, they give not themselves up to Thee, to preserve what Thou madest, nor sacrifice to Thee what they have made themselves; nor slay their own soaring imaginations, as fowls of the air, nor their own diving curiosities (wherewith, like the fishes of the sea, they wander over the unknown paths of the abyss), nor their own luxuriousness, as beasts of the field, that Thou, Lord, a consuming fire, mayest burn up those dead cares of theirs, and recreate themselves immortally.

But they knew not the way, Thy Word, by Whom Thou madest these things which they number, and themselves who number, and the sense whereby they perceive what they number, and the understanding, out of which they number; or that of Thy wisdom there is no number. But the Only Begotten is Himself made unto us wisdom, and righteousness, and sanctification, and was numbered among us, and paid tribute unto Caesar. They knew not this way whereby to descend to Him from themselves, and by Him ascend unto Him. They knew not this way, and deemed themselves exalted amongst the stars and shining; and behold, they fell upon the earth, and their foolish heart was darkened. They discourse many things truly concerning the creature; but Truth, Artificer of the creature, they seek not piously, and therefore find Him not; or if they find Him, knowing Him to be God, they glorify Him not as God, neither are thankful, but become vain in their imaginations, and profess themselves to be wise, attributing to themselves what is Thine; and thereby with most perverse blindness, study to impute to Thee what is their own, forging lies of Thee who art the Truth, and changing the glory of uncorruptible God into an image made like corruptible man, and to birds, and four-footed beasts, and creeping things, changing Thy truth into a lie, and worshiping and serving the creature more than the Creator.

Yet many truths concerning the creature retained I from these men, and saw the reason thereof from calculations, the succession of times, and the visible testimonies of the stars; and compared them with the saying of Manichaeus, which in his frenzy he had written most largely on these subjects; but discovered not any account of the solstices, or equinoxes, or the eclipses of the greater lights, nor whatever of this sort I had learned in the books of secular philosophy. But I was commanded to believe; and yet it corresponded not with what had been established by calculations and my own sight, but was quite contrary.

Doth then, O Lord God of truth, whoso knoweth these things, therefore please Thee? Surely unhappy is he who knoweth all these, and knoweth not Thee: but happy whoso knoweth Thee, though he know not these. And whoso knoweth both Thee and them is not the happier for them, but for Thee only, if, knowing Thee, he glorifies Thee as God, and is thankful, and becomes not vain in his imaginations. For as he is better off who knows how to possess a tree, and return thanks to Thee for the use thereof, although he know not how many cubits high it is, or how wide it spreads, than he that can measure it, and count all its boughs, and neither owns it, nor knows or loves its Creator: so a believer, whose all this world of wealth is, and who having nothing, yet possesseth all things, by cleaving unto Thee, whom all things serve, though he know not even the circles of the Great Bear, yet is it folly to doubt but he is in a better state than one who can measure the heavens, and number the stars, and poise the elements, yet neglecteth Thee who hast made all things in number, weight, and measure.

But yet who bade that Manichaeus write on these things also, skill in which was no element of piety? For Thou hast said to man, Behold piety and wisdom; of which he might be ignorant, though he had perfect knowledge of these things; but these things, since, knowing not, he most impudently dared to teach, he plainly could have no knowledge of piety. For it is vanity to make profession of these worldly things even when known; but confession to Thee is piety.

Wherefore this wanderer to this end spake much of these things, that convicted by those who had truly learned them, it might be manifest what understanding he had in the other abstruser things. For he would not have himself meanly thought of, but went about to persuade men, "That the Holy Ghost, the Comforter and Enricher of Thy faithful ones, was with plenary authority personally within him." When then he was found out to have taught falsely of the heaven and stars, and of the motions of the sun and moon (although these things pertain not to the doctrine of religion), yet his sacrilegious presumption would become evident enough, seeing he delivered things which not only he knew not, but which were falsified, with so mad a vanity of pride, that he sought to ascribe them to himself, as to a divine person.

For when I hear any Christian brother ignorant of these things, and mistaken on them, I can patiently behold such a man holding his opinion; nor do I see that any ignorance as to the position or character of the corporeal creation can injure him, so long as he doth not believe any thing unworthy of Thee, O Lord, the Creator of all. But it doth injure him, if he imagine it to pertain to the form of the doctrine of piety, and will yet affirm that too stiffly whereof he is ignorant. And yet is even such an infirmity, in the infancy of faith, borne by our mother Charity, till the new-born may grow up unto a perfect man, so as not to be carried about with every wind of doctrine. But in him who in such wise presumed to be the teacher, source, guide, chief of all whom he could so persuade, that whoso followed him thought that he followed, not a mere man, but Thy Holy Spirit; who would not judge that so great madness, when once convicted of having taught any thing false, were to be detested and utterly rejected? But I had not as yet clearly ascertained whether the vicissitudes of longer and shorter days and nights, and of day and night itself, with the eclipses of the greater lights, and whatever else of the kind I had read of in other books, might be explained consistently with his sayings; so that, if they by any means might, it should still remain a question to me whether it were so or no; but I might, on account of his reputed sanctity, rest my credence upon his authority.

And for almost all those nine years, wherein with unsettled mind I had been their disciple, I had longed but too intensely for the coming of this Faustus. For the rest of the sect, whom by chance I had lighted upon, when unable to solve my objections about these things, still held out to me the coming of this Faustus, by conference with whom these and greater difficulties, if I had them, were to be most readily and abundantly cleared. When then he came, I found him a man of pleasing discourse, and who could speak fluently and in better terms, yet still but the self-same things which they were wont to say. But what availed the utmost neatness of the cup-bearer to my thirst for a more precious draught? Mine ears were already cloyed with the like, nor did they seem to me therefore better, because better said; nor therefore true, because eloquent; nor the soul therefore wise, because the face was comely, and the language graceful. But they who held him out to me were no good judges of things; and therefore to them he appeared understanding and wise, because in words pleasing. I felt however that another sort of people were suspicious even of truth, and refused to assent to it, if delivered in a smooth and copious discourse. But Thou, O my God, hadst already taught me by wonderful and secret ways, and therefore I believe that Thou taughtest me, because it is truth, nor is there besides Thee any teacher of truth, where or whencesoever it may shine upon us. Of Thyself therefore had I now learned, that neither ought any thing to seem to be spoken truly, because eloquently; nor therefore falsely, because the utterance of the lips is inharmonious; nor, again, therefore true, because rudely delivered; nor therefore false, because the language is rich; but that wisdom and folly are as wholesome and unwholesome food; and adorned or unadorned phrases as courtly or country vessels; either kind of meats may be served up in either kind of dishes.

That greediness then, wherewith I had of so long time expected that man, was delighted verily with his action and feeling when disputing, and his choice and readiness of words to clothe his ideas. I was then delighted, and, with many others and more than they, did I praise and extol him. It troubled me, however, that in the assembly of his auditors, I was not allowed to put in and communicate those questions that troubled me, in familiar converse with him. Which when I might, and with my friends began to engage his ears at such times as it was not unbecoming for him to discuss with me, and had brought forward such things as moved me; I found him first utterly ignorant of liberal sciences, save grammar, and that but in an ordinary way. But because he had read some of Tully's Orations, a very few books of Seneca, some things of the poets, and such few volumes of his own sect as were written in Latin and neatly, and was daily practised in speaking, he acquired a certain eloquence, which proved the more pleasing and seductive because under the guidance of a good wit, and with a kind of natural gracefulness. Is it not thus, as I recall it, O Lord my God, Thou judge of my conscience? before Thee is my heart, and my remembrance, Who didst at that time direct me by the hidden mystery of Thy providence, and didst set those shameful errors of mine before my face, that I might see and hate them.

For after it was clear that he was ignorant of those arts in which I thought he excelled, I began to despair of his opening and solving the difficulties which perplexed me (of which indeed however ignorant, he might have held the truths of piety, had he not been a Manichee). For their books are fraught with prolix fables, of the heaven, and stars, sun, and moon, and I now no longer thought him able satisfactorily to decide what I much desired, whether, on comparison of these things with the calculations I had elsewhere read, the account given in the books of Manichaeus were preferable, or at least as good. Which when I proposed to be considered and discussed, he, so far modestly, shrunk from the burthen. For he knew that he knew not these things, and was not ashamed to confess it. For he was not one of those talking persons, many of whom I had endured, who undertook to teach me these things, and said nothing. But this man had a heart, though not right towards Thee, yet neither altogether treacherous to himself. For he was not altogether ignorant of his own ignorance, nor would he rashly be entangled in a dispute, whence he could neither retreat nor extricate himself fairly. Even for this I liked him the better. For fairer is the modesty of a candid mind, than the knowledge of those things which I desired; and such I found him, in all the more difficult and subtle questions.

My zeal for the writings of Manichaeus being thus blunted, and despairing yet more of their other teachers, seeing that in divers things which perplexed me, he, so renowned among them, had so turned out; I began to engage with him in the study of that literature, on which he also was much set (and which as rhetoric-reader I was at that time teaching young students at Carthage), and to read with him, either what himself desired to hear, or such as I judged fit for his genius. But all my efforts whereby I had purposed to advance in that sect, upon knowledge of that man, came utterly to an end; not that I detached myself from them altogether, but as one finding nothing better, I had settled to be content meanwhile with what I had in whatever way fallen upon, unless by chance something more eligible should dawn upon me. Thus, that Faustus, to so many a snare of death, had now neither willing nor witting it, begun to loosen that wherein I was taken. For Thy hands, O my God, in the secret purpose of Thy providence, did not forsake my soul; and out of my mother's heart's blood, through her tears night and day poured out, was a sacrifice offered for me unto Thee; and Thou didst deal with me by wondrous ways. Thou didst it, O my God: for the steps of a man are ordered by the Lord, and He shall dispose his way. Or how shall we obtain salvation, but from Thy hand, re-making what it made?

Thou didst deal with me, that I should be persuaded to go to Rome, and to teach there rather, what I was teaching at Carthage. And how I was persuaded to this, I will not neglect to confess to

Thee; because herein also the deepest recesses of Thy wisdom, and Thy most present mercy to us, must be considered and confessed. I did not wish therefore to go to Rome, because higher gains and higher dignities were warranted me by my friends who persuaded me to this (though even these things had at that time an influence over my mind), but my chief and almost only reason was, that I heard that young men studied there more peacefully, and were kept quiet under a restraint of more regular discipline; so that they did not, at their pleasures, petulantly rush into the school of one whose pupils they were not, nor were even admitted without his permission. Whereas at Carthage there reigns among the scholars a most disgraceful and unruly license. They burst in audaciously, and with gestures almost frantic, disturb all order which any one hath established for the good of his scholars. Divers outrages they commit, with a wonderful stolidity, punishable by law, did not custom uphold them; that custom evincing them to be the more miserable, in that they now do as lawful what by Thy eternal law shall never be lawful; and they think they do it unpunished, whereas they are punished with the very blindness whereby they do it, and suffer incomparably worse than what they do. The manners then which, when a student, I would not make my own, I was fain as a teacher to endure in others: and so I was well pleased to go where, all that knew it, assured me that the like was not done. But Thou, my refuge and my portion in the land of the living; that I might change my earthly dwelling for the salvation of my soul, at Carthage didst goad me, that I might thereby be torn from it; and at Rome didst proffer me allurements, whereby I might be drawn thither, by men in love with a dying life, the one doing frantic, the other promising vain, things; and, to correct my steps, didst secretly use their and my own perverseness. For both they who disturbed my quiet were blinded with a disgraceful frenzy, and they who invited me elsewhere savoured of earth. And I, who here detested real misery, was there seeking unreal happiness.

But why I went hence, and went thither, Thou knewest, O God, yet showedst it neither to me, nor to my mother, who grievously bewailed my journey, and followed me as far as the sea. But I deceived her, holding me by force, that either she might keep me back or go with me, and I feigned that I had a friend whom I could not leave, till he had a fair wind to sail. And I lied to my mother, and such a mother, and escaped: for this also hast Thou mercifully forgiven me, preserving me, thus full of execrable defilements, from the waters of the sea, for the water of Thy Grace; whereby when I was cleansed, the streams of my mother's eyes should be dried, with which for me she daily watered the ground under her face. And yet refusing to return without me, I scarcely persuaded her to stay that night in a place hard by our ship, where was an Oratory in memory of the blessed Cyprian. That night I privily departed, but she was not behind in weeping and prayer. And what, O Lord, was she with so many tears asking of Thee, but that Thou wouldest not suffer me to sail? But Thou, in the depth of Thy counsels and hearing the main point of her desire, regardest not what she then asked, that Thou mightest make me what she ever asked. The wind blew and swelled our sails, and withdrew the shore from our sight; and she on the morrow was there, frantic with sorrow, and with complaints and groans filled Thine ears, Who didst then disregard them; whilst through my desires, Thou wert hurrying me to end all desire, and the earthly part of her affection to me was chastened by the allotted scourge of sorrows. For she loved my being with her, as mothers do, but much more than many; and she knew not how great joy Thou wert about to work for her out of my absence. She knew not; therefore did she weep and wail, and by this agony there appeared in her the inheritance of Eve, with sorrow seeking what in sorrow she had brought forth. And yet, after accusing my treachery and hardheartedness, she betook herself again to intercede to Thee for me, went to her wonted place, and I to Rome.

And lo, there was I received by the scourge of bodily sickness, and I was going down to hell, carrying all the sins which I had committed, both against Thee, and myself, and others, many and grievous, over and above that bond of original sin, whereby we all die in Adam. For Thou hadst not forgiven me any of these things in Christ, nor had He abolished by His Cross the enmity which by my sins I had incurred with Thee. For how should He, by the crucifixion of a phantasm, which I believed Him to be? So true, then, was the death of my soul, as that of His flesh seemed to me false; and how true the death of His body, so false was the life of my soul, which did not believe it. And now the fever heightening, I was parting and departing for ever. For had I then parted hence, whither had I departed, but into fire and torments, such as my misdeeds deserved in the truth of Thy appointment? And this she knew not, yet in absence prayed for me. But Thou, everywhere present, heardest her where she was, and, where I was, hadst compassion upon me; that I should recover the health of my body, though frenzied as yet in my sacrilegious heart. For I did not in all that danger desire Thy baptism; and I was better as a boy, when I begged it of my mother's piety, as I have before recited and confessed. But I had grown up to my own shame, and I madly scoffed at the prescripts of Thy medicine, who wouldest not suffer me, being such, to die a double death. With which wound had my mother's heart been pierced, it could never be healed. For I cannot express the affection she bore to me, and with how much more vehement anguish she was now in labour of me in the spirit, than at her childbearing in the flesh.

I see not then how she should have been healed, had such a death of mine stricken through the bowels of her love. And where would have been those her so strong and unceasing prayers, unintermitting to Thee alone? But wouldest Thou, God of mercies, despise the contrite and humbled heart of that chaste and sober widow, so frequent in almsdeeds, so full of duty and service to Thy saints, no day intermitting the oblation at Thine altar, twice a day, morning and evening, without any intermission, coming to Thy church, not for idle tattlings and old wives' fables; but that she might hear Thee in Thy discourses, and Thou her in her prayers. Couldest Thou despise and reject from Thy aid the tears of such an one, wherewith she begged of Thee not gold or silver, nor any mutable or passing good, but the salvation of her son's soul? Thou, by whose gift she was such? Never, Lord. Yea, Thou wert at hand, and wert hearing and doing, in that order wherein Thou hadst determined before that it should be done. Far be it that Thou shouldest deceive her in Thy visions and answers, some whereof I have, some I have not mentioned, which she laid up in her faithful heart, and ever praying, urged upon Thee, as Thine own handwriting. For Thou, because Thy mercy endureth for ever, vouchsafest to those to whom Thou forgivest all of their debts, to become also a debtor by Thy promises.

Thou recoveredst me then of that sickness, and healedst the son of Thy handmaid, for the time in body, that he might live, for Thee to bestow upon him a better and more abiding health. And even then, at Rome, I joined myself to those deceiving and deceived "holy ones"; not with their disciples only (of which number was he, in whose house I had fallen sick and recovered); but also with those whom they call "The Elect." For I still thought "that it was not we that sin, but that I know not what other nature sinned in us"; and it delighted my pride, to be free from blame; and when I had done any evil, not to confess I had done any, that Thou mightest heal my soul because it had sinned against Thee: but I loved to excuse it, and to accuse I know not what other thing, which was with me, but which I was not. But in truth it was wholly I, and mine impiety had divided me against myself: and that sin was the more incurable, whereby I did not judge myself a sinner; and execrable iniquity it was, that I had rather have Thee, Thee, O God Almighty, to be overcome in me to my destruction, than myself of Thee to salvation. Not as yet then hadst Thou set a watch before my mouth, and a door of safe keeping around my lips, that my heart might not turn aside to wicked speeches, to make excuses of sins, with men that work iniquity; and, therefore, was I still united with their Elect.

But now despairing to make proficiency in that false doctrine, even those things (with which if I should find no better, I had resolved to rest contented) I now held more laxly and carelessly. For there half arose a thought in me that those philosophers, whom they call Academics, were wiser than the rest, for that they held men ought to doubt everything, and laid down that no truth can be comprehended by man: for so, not then understanding even their meaning, I also was clearly convinced that they thought, as they are commonly reported. Yet did I freely and openly discourage that host of mine from that over-confidence which I perceived him to have in those fables, which the books of Manichaeus are full of. Yet I lived in more familiar friendship with them, than with others who were not of this heresy. Nor did I maintain it with my ancient eagerness; still my intimacy with that sect (Rome secretly harbouring many of them) made me slower to seek any other way: especially since I despaired of finding the truth, from which they had turned me aside, in Thy

Church, O Lord of heaven and earth, Creator of all things visible and invisible: and it seemed to me very unseemly to believe Thee to have the shape of human flesh, and to be bounded by the bodily lineaments of our members. And because, when I wished to think on my God, I knew not what to think of, but a mass of bodies (for what was not such did not seem to me to be anything), this was the greatest, and almost only cause of my inevitable error.

For hence I believed Evil also to be some such kind of substance, and to have its own foul and hideous bulk; whether gross, which they called earth, or thin and subtle (like the body of the air), which they imagine to be some malignant mind, creeping through that earth. And because a piety, such as it was, constrained me to believe that the good God never created any evil nature, I conceived two masses, contrary to one another, both unbounded, but the evil narrower, the good more expansive. And from this pestilent beginning, the other sacrilegious conceits followed on me. For when my mind endeavoured to recur to the Catholic faith, I was driven back, since that was not the Catholic faith which I thought to be so. And I seemed to myself more reverential, if I believed of Thee, my God (to whom Thy mercies confess out of my mouth), as unbounded, at least on other sides, although on that one where the mass of evil was opposed to Thee, I was constrained to confess Thee bounded; than if on all sides I should imagine Thee to be bounded by the form of a human body. And it seemed to me better to believe Thee to have created no evil (which to me ignorant seemed not some only, but a bodily substance, because I could not conceive of mind unless as a subtle body, and that diffused in definite spaces), than to believe the nature of evil, such as I conceived it, could come from Thee. Yea, and our Saviour Himself, Thy Only Begotten, I believed to have been reached forth (as it were) for our salvation, out of the mass of Thy most lucid substance, so as to believe nothing of Him, but what I could imagine in my vanity. His Nature then, being such, I thought could not be born of the Virgin Mary, without being mingled with the flesh: and how that which I had so figured to myself could be mingled, and not defiled, I saw not. I feared therefore to believe Him born in the flesh, lest I should be forced to believe Him defiled by the flesh. Now will Thy spiritual ones mildly and lovingly smile upon me, if they shall read these my confessions. Yet such was I.

Furthermore, what the Manichees had criticised in Thy Scriptures, I thought could not be defended; yet at times verily I had a wish to confer upon these several points with some one very well skilled in those books, and to make trial what he thought thereon; for the words of one Helpidius, as he spoke and disputed face to face against the said Manichees, had begun to stir me even at Carthage: in that he had produced things out of the Scriptures, not easily withstood, the Manichees' answer whereto seemed to me weak. And this answer they liked not to give publicly, but only to us in private. It was, that the Scriptures of the New Testament had been corrupted by I know not whom, who wished to engraff the law of the Jews upon the Christian faith: yet themselves produced not any uncorrupted copies. But I, conceiving of things corporeal only, was mainly held down, vehemently oppressed and in a manner suffocated by those "masses"; panting under which after the breath of Thy truth, I could not breathe it pure and untainted.

I began then diligently to practise that for which I came to Rome, to teach rhetoric; and first, to gather some to my house, to whom, and through whom, I had begun to be known; when lo, I found other offenses committed in Rome, to which I was not exposed in Africa. True, those "subvertings" by profligate young men were not here practised, as was told me: but on a sudden, said they, to avoid paying their master's stipend, a number of youths plot together, and remove to another—breakers of faith, who for love of money hold justice cheap. These also my heart hated, though not with a perfect hatred: for perchance I hated them more because I was to suffer by them, than because they did things utterly unlawful. Of a truth such are base persons, and they go a whoring from Thee, loving these fleeting mockeries of things temporal, and filthy lucre, which fouls the hand that grasps it; hugging the fleeting world, and despising Thee, Who abidest, and recallest, and forgivest the adulteress soul of man, when she returns to Thee. And now I hate such depraved and crooked persons, though I love them if corrigible, so as to prefer to money the learning which they acquire, and to learning, Thee, O God, the truth and fullness of assured good, and most pure peace. But then I rather for my own sake misliked them evil, than liked and wished them good for Thine.

When therefore they of Milan had sent to Rome to the prefect of the city, to furnish them with a rhetoric reader for their city, and sent him at the public expense, I made application (through those very persons, intoxicated with Manichaean vanities, to be freed wherefrom I was to go, neither of us however knowing it) that Symmachus, then prefect of the city, would try me by setting me some subject, and so send me. To Milan I came, to Ambrose the Bishop, known to the whole world as among the best of men, Thy devout servant; whose eloquent discourse did then plentifully dispense unto Thy people the flour of Thy wheat, the gladness of Thy oil, and the sober inebriation of Thy wine. To him was I unknowing led by Thee, that by him I might knowingly be led to Thee. That man of God received me as a father, and showed me an Episcopal kindness on my coming. Thenceforth I began to love him, at first indeed not as a teacher of the truth (which I utterly despaired of in Thy Church), but as a person kind towards myself. And I listened diligently to him preaching to the people, not with that intent I ought, but, as it were, trying his eloquence, whether it answered the fame thereof, or flowed fuller or lower than was reported; and I hung on his words attentively; but of the matter I was as a careless and scornful looker-on; and I was delighted with the sweetness of his discourse, more recondite, yet in manner less winning and harmonious, than that of Faustus. Of the matter, however, there was no comparison; for the one was wandering amid Manichaean delusions, the other teaching salvation most soundly. But salvation is far from sinners, such as I then stood before him; and yet was I drawing nearer by little and little, and unconsciously.

For though I took no pains to learn what he spake, but only to hear how he spake (for that empty care alone was left me, despairing of a way, open for man, to Thee), yet together with the words which I would choose, came also into my mind the things which I would refuse; for I could not separate them. And while I opened my heart to admit "how eloquently he spake," there also entered "how truly he spake"; but this by degrees. For first, these things also had now begun to appear to me capable of defense; and the Catholic faith, for which I had thought nothing could be said against the Manichees' objections, I now thought might be maintained without shamelessness; especially after I had heard one or two places of the Old Testament resolved, and ofttimes "in a figure," which when I understood literally, I was slain spiritually. Very many places then of those books having been explained, I now blamed my despair, in believing that no answer could be given to such as hated and scoffed at the Law and the Prophets. Yet did I not therefore then see that the Catholic way was to be held, because it also could find learned maintainers, who could at large and with some show of reason answer objections; nor that what I held was therefore to be condemned, because both sides could be maintained. For the Catholic cause seemed to me in such sort not vanquished, as still not as yet to be victorious.

Hereupon I earnestly bent my mind, to see if in any way I could by any certain proof convict the Manichees of falsehood. Could I once have conceived a spiritual substance, all their strongholds had been beaten down, and cast utterly out of my mind; but I could not.

Notwithstanding, concerning the frame of this world, and the whole of nature, which the senses of the flesh can reach to, as I more and more considered and compared things, I judged the tenets of most of the philosophers to have been much more probable. So then after the manner of the Academics (as they are supposed) doubting of every thing, and wavering between all, I settled so far, that the Manichees were to be abandoned; judging that, even while doubting, I might not continue in that sect, to which I already preferred some of the philosophers; to which philosophers notwithstanding, for that they were without the saving Name of Christ, I utterly refused to commit the cure of my sick soul. I determined therefore so long to be a Catechumen in the Catholic Church, to which I had been commended by my parents, till something certain should dawn upon me, whither I might steer my course.

Book Six

O Thou, my hope from my youth, where wert Thou to me, and whither wert Thou gone? Hadst not Thou created me, and separated me from the beasts of the field, and fowls of the air? Thou hadst made me wiser, yet did I walk in darkness, and in slippery places, and sought Thee abroad out of myself, and found not the God of my heart; and had come into the depths of the sea, and distrusted and despaired of ever finding truth. My mother had now come to me, resolute through piety, following me over sea and land, in all perils confiding in Thee. For in perils of the sea, she comforted the very mariners (by whom passengers unacquainted with the deep, use rather to be comforted when troubled), assuring them of a safe arrival, because Thou hadst by a vision assured her thereof. She found me in grievous peril, through despair of ever finding truth. But when I had discovered to her that I was now no longer a Manichee, though not yet a Catholic Christian, she was not overjoyed, as at something unexpected; although she was now assured concerning that part of my misery, for which she bewailed me as one dead, though to be reawakened by Thee, carrying me forth upon the bier of her thoughts, that Thou mightest say to the son of the widow, Young man, I say unto thee, Arise; and he should revive, and begin to speak, and Thou shouldest deliver him to his mother. Her heart then was shaken with no tumultuous exultation, when she heard that what she daily with tears desired of Thee was already in so great part realised; in that, though I had not yet attained the truth, I was rescued from falsehood; but, as being assured, that Thou, Who hadst promised the whole, wouldest one day give the rest, most calmly, and with a heart full of confidence, she replied to me, "She believed in Christ, that before she departed this life, she should see me a Catholic believer." Thus much to me. But to Thee, Fountain of mercies, poured she forth more copious prayers and tears, that Thou wouldest hasten Thy help, and enlighten my darkness; and she hastened the more eagerly to the Church, and hung upon the lips of Ambrose, praying for the fountain of that water, which springeth up unto life everlasting. But that man she loved as an angel of God, because she knew that by him I had been brought for the present to that doubtful state of faith I now was in, through which she anticipated most confidently that I should pass from sickness unto health, after the access, as it were, of a sharper fit, which physicians call "the crisis."

When then my mother had once, as she was wont in Afric, brought to the Churches built in memory of the Saints, certain cakes, and bread and wine, and was forbidden by the door-keeper; so soon as she knew that the Bishop had forbidden this, she so piously and obediently embraced his wishes, that I myself wondered how readily she censured her own practice, rather than discuss his prohibition. For wine-bibbing did not lay siege to her spirit, nor did love of wine provoke her to hatred of the truth, as it doth too many (both men and women), who revolt at a lesson of sobriety, as men well-drunk at a draught mingled with water. But she, when she had brought her basket with the accustomed festival-food, to be but tasted by herself, and then given away, never joined therewith more than one small cup of wine, diluted according to her own abstemious habits, which for courtesy she would taste. And if there were many churches of the departed saints that were to be honoured in that manner, she still carried round that same one cup, to be used every where; and this, though not only made very watery, but unpleasantly heated with carrying about, she would distribute to those about her by small sips; for she sought there devotion, not pleasure. So soon, then, as she found this custom to be forbidden by that famous preacher and most pious prelate, even to those that would use it soberly, lest so an occasion of excess might be given to the drunken; and for these, as it were, anniversary funeral solemnities did much resemble the superstition of the Gentiles, she most willingly forbare it: and for a basket filled with fruits of the earth, she had learned to bring to the Churches of the martyrs a breast filled with more purified petitions, and to give what she could to the poor; that so the communication of the Lord's Body might be there rightly celebrated, where, after the example of His Passion, the martyrs had been sacrificed and crowned. But yet it seems to me, O Lord my God, and thus thinks my heart of it in Thy sight, that perhaps she would not so readily have yielded to the cutting off of this custom, had it been forbidden by another, whom she loved not as Ambrose, whom, for my salvation, she loved most entirely; and he her again, for her most religious conversation, whereby in good works, so fervent in spirit, she was constant at church; so that, when he saw me, he often burst forth into her praises; congratulating me that I had such a mother; not knowing what a son she had in me, who doubted of all these things, and imagined the way to life could not be found out.

Nor did I yet groan in my prayers, that Thou wouldest help me; but my spirit was wholly intent on learning, and restless to dispute. And Ambrose himself, as the world counts happy, I esteemed a happy man, whom personages so great held in such honour; only his celibacy seemed to me a painful course. But what hope he bore within him, what struggles he had against the temptations which beset his very excellencies, or what comfort in adversities, and what sweet joys Thy Bread had for the hidden mouth of his spirit, when chewing the cud thereof, I neither could conjecture, nor had experienced. Nor did he know the tides of my feelings, or the abyss of my danger. For I could not ask of him, what I would as I would, being shut out both from his ear and speech by multitudes of busy people, whose weaknesses he served. With whom when he was not taken up (which was but a little time), he was either refreshing his body with the sustenance absolutely necessary, or his mind with reading. But when he was reading, his eye glided over the pages, and his heart searched out the sense, but his voice and tongue were at rest. Ofttimes when we had come (for no man was forbidden to enter, nor was it his wont that any who came should be announced to him), we saw him thus reading to himself, and never otherwise; and having long sat silent (for who durst intrude on one so intent?) we were fain to depart, conjecturing that in the small interval which he obtained, free from the din of others' business, for the recruiting of his mind, he was loth to be taken off; and perchance he dreaded lest if the author he read should deliver any thing obscurely, some attentive or perplexed hearer should desire him to expound it, or to discuss some of the harder questions; so that his time being thus spent, he could not turn over so many volumes as he desired; although the preserving of his voice (which a very little speaking would weaken) might be the truer reason for his reading to himself. But with what intent soever he did it, certainly in such a man it was good.

I however certainly had no opportunity of inquiring what I

wished of that so holy oracle of Thine, his breast, unless the thing might be answered briefly. But those tides in me, to be poured out to him, required his full leisure, and never found it. I heard him indeed every Lord's day, rightly expounding the Word of truth among the people; and I was more and more convinced that all the knots of those crafty calumnies, which those our deceivers had knit against the Divine Books, could be unraveled. But when I understood withal, that "man created by Thee, after Thine own image," was not so understood by Thy spiritual sons, whom of the Catholic Mother Thou hast born again through grace, as though they believed and conceived of Thee as bounded by human shape (although what a spiritual substance should be I had not even a faint or shadowy notion); yet, with joy I blushed at having so many years barked not against the Catholic faith, but against the fictions of carnal imaginations. For so rash and impious had I been, that what I ought by inquiring to have learned, I had pronounced on, condemning. For Thou, Most High, and most near; most secret, and most present; Who hast not limbs some larger, some smaller, but art wholly every where, and no where in space, art not of such corporeal shape, yet hast Thou made man after Thine own image; and behold, from head to foot is he contained in space.

Ignorant then how this Thy image should subsist, I should have knocked and proposed the doubt, how it was to be believed, not insultingly opposed it, as if believed. Doubt, then, what to hold for certain, the more sharply gnawed my heart, the more ashamed I was, that so long deluded and deceived by the promise of certainties, I had with childish error and vehemence, prated of so many uncertainties. For that they were falsehoods became clear to me later. However I was certain that they were uncertain, and that I had formerly accounted them certain, when with a blind contentiousness, I accused Thy Catholic Church, whom I now discovered, not indeed as yet to teach truly, but at least not to teach that for which I had grievously censured her. So I was confounded, and converted: and I joyed, O my God, that the One Only Church, the body of Thine Only Son (wherein the name of Christ had been put upon me as an infant), had no taste for infantine conceits; nor in her sound doctrine maintained any tenet which should confine Thee, the Creator of all, in space, however great and large, yet bounded every where by the limits of a human form.

I joyed also that the old Scriptures of the law and the Prophets were laid before me, not now to be perused with that eye to which before they seemed absurd, when I reviled Thy holy ones for so thinking, whereas indeed they thought not so: and with joy I heard Ambrose in his sermons to the people, oftentimes most diligently recommend this text for a rule, The letter killeth, but the Spirit giveth life; whilst he drew aside the mystic veil, laying open spiritually what, according to the letter, seemed to teach something unsound; teaching herein nothing that offended me, though he taught what I knew not as yet, whether it were true. For I kept my heart from assenting to any thing, fearing to fall headlong; but by hanging in suspense I was the worse killed. For I wished to be as assured of the things I saw not, as I was that seven and three are ten. For I was not so mad as to think that even this could not be comprehended; but I desired to have other things as clear as this, whether things corporeal, which were not present to my senses, or spiritual, whereof I knew not how to conceive, except corporeally. And by believing might I have been cured, that so the eyesight of my soul being cleared, might in some way be directed to Thy truth, which abideth always, and in no part faileth. But as it happens that one who has tried a bad physician, fears to trust himself with a good one, so was it with the health of my soul, which could not be healed but by believing, and lest it should believe falsehoods, refused to be cured; resisting Thy hands, Who hast prepared the medicines of faith, and hast applied them to the diseases of the whole world, and given unto them so great authority.

Being led, however, from this to prefer the Catholic doctrine, I felt that her proceeding was more unassuming and honest, in that she required to be believed things not demonstrated (whether it was that they could in themselves be demonstrated but not to certain persons, or could not at all be), whereas among the Manichees our credulity was mocked by a promise of certain knowledge, and then so many most fabulous and absurd things were imposed to be believed, because they could not be demonstrated. Then Thou, O Lord, little by little with most tender and most merciful hand, touching and composing my heart, didst persuade me—considering what innumerable things I believed, which I saw not, nor was present while they were done, as so many things in secular history, so many reports of places and of cities, which I had not seen; so many of friends, so many of physicians, so many continually of other men, which unless we should believe, we should do nothing at all in this life; lastly, with how unshaken an assurance I believed of what parents I was born, which I could not know, had I not believed upon hearsay—considering all this, Thou didst persuade me, that not they who believed Thy Books (which Thou hast established in so great authority among almost all nations), but they who believed them not, were to be blamed; and that they were not to be heard, who should say to me, "How knowest thou those Scriptures to have been imparted unto mankind by the Spirit of the one true and most true God?" For this very thing was of all most to be believed, since no contentiousness of blasphemous questionings, of all that multitude which I had read in the self-contradicting philosophers, could wring this belief from me, "That Thou art" whatsoever Thou wert (what I knew not), and "That the government of human things belongs to Thee."

This I believed, sometimes more strongly, more weakly otherwhiles; yet I ever believed both that Thou wert, and hadst a care of us; though I was ignorant, both what was to be thought of Thy substance, and what way led or led back to Thee. Since then we were too weak by abstract reasonings to find out truth: and for this very cause needed the authority of Holy Writ; I had now begun to believe that Thou wouldest never have given such excellency of authority to that Writ in all lands, hadst Thou not willed thereby to be believed in, thereby sought. For now what things, sounding strangely in the Scripture, were wont to offend me, having heard divers of them expounded satisfactorily, I referred to the depth of the mysteries, and its authority appeared to me the more venerable, and more worthy of religious credence, in that, while it lay open to all to read, it reserved the majesty of its mysteries within its profounder meaning, stooping to all in the great plainness of its words and lowliness of its style, yet calling forth the intensest application of such as are not light of heart; that so it might receive all in its open bosom, and through narrow passages waft over towards Thee some few, yet many more than if it stood not aloft on such a height of authority, nor drew multitudes within its bosom by its holy lowliness. These things I thought on, and Thou wert with me; I sighed, and Thou heardest me; I wavered, and Thou didst guide me; I wandered through the broad way of the world, and Thou didst not forsake me.

I panted after honours, gains, marriage; and thou deridedst me. In these desires I underwent most bitter crosses, Thou being the more gracious, the less Thou sufferedst aught to grow sweet to me, which was not Thou. Behold my heart, O Lord, who wouldest I should remember all this, and confess to Thee. Let my soul cleave unto Thee, now that Thou hast freed it from that fast-holding birdlime of death. How wretched was it! and Thou didst irritate the feeling of its wound, that forsaking all else, it might be converted unto Thee, who art above all, and without whom all things would be nothing; be converted, and be healed. How miserable was I then, and how didst Thou deal with me, to make me feel my misery on that day, when I was preparing to recite a panegyric of the Emperor, wherein I was to utter many a lie, and lying, was to be applauded by those who knew I lied, and my heart was panting with these anxieties, and boiling with the feverishness of consuming thoughts. For, passing through one of the streets of Milan, I observed a poor beggar, then, I suppose, with a full belly, joking and joyous: and I sighed, and spoke to the friends around me, of the many sorrows of our frenzies; for that by all such efforts of ours, as those wherein I then toiled dragging along, under the goading of desire, the burthen of my own wretchedness, and, by dragging, augmenting it, we yet looked to arrive only at that very joyousness whither that beggar-man had arrived before us, who should never perchance attain it. For what he had obtained by means of a few begged pence, the same was I plotting for by many a toilsome turning and winding; the joy of a temporary felicity. For he verily had not the true joy; but yet I with those my ambitious designs was seeking one much less true. And certainly he was joyous, I anxious; he void of care, I full of fears. But should any ask me, had I rather be merry or fearful? I would answer merry. Again, if he asked had I rather be such as he was, or what I then was? I should choose to be myself, though worn with cares and fears; but out of wrong judgment; for, was it the truth? For I ought not to prefer myself to him, because more learned than he, seeing I had no joy therein, but sought to please men by it; and that not to instruct, but simply to please. Wherefore also Thou didst break my bones with the staff of Thy correction.

Away with those then from my soul who say to her, "It makes a difference whence a man's joy is. That beggar-man joyed in drunkenness; Thou desiredst to joy in glory." What glory, Lord? That which is not in Thee. For even as his was no true joy, so was that no true glory: and it overthrew my soul more. He that very night should digest his drunkenness; but I had slept and risen again with mine, and was to sleep again, and again to rise with it, how many days, Thou, God, knowest. But "it doth make a difference whence a man's joy is." I know it, and the joy of a faithful hope lieth incomparably beyond such vanity. Yea, and so was he then beyond me: for he verily was the happier; not only for that he was thoroughly drenched in mirth, I disemboweled with cares: but he, by fair wishes, had gotten wine; I, by lying, was seeking for empty, swelling praise. Much to this purpose said I then to my friends: and I often marked in them how it fared with me; and I found it went ill with me, and grieved, and doubled that very ill; and if any prosperity smiled on me, I was loth to catch at it, for almost before I could grasp it, it flew away.

These things we, who were living as friends together, bemoaned together, but chiefly and most familiarly did I speak thereof with Alypius and Nebridius, of whom Alypius was born in the same town with me, of persons of chief rank there, but younger than I. For he had studied under me, both when I first lectured in our town, and afterwards at Carthage, and he loved me much, because I seemed to him kind, and learned; and I him, for his great towardliness to virtue, which was eminent enough in one of no greater years. Yet the whirlpool of Carthaginian habits (amongst whom those idle spectacles are hotly followed) had drawn him into the madness of the Circus. But while he was miserably tossed therein, and I, professing rhetoric there, had a public school, as yet he used not my teaching, by reason of some unkindness risen betwixt his father and me. I had found then how deadly he doted upon the Circus, and was deeply grieved that he seemed likely, nay, or had thrown away so great promise: yet had I no means of advising or with a sort of constraint reclaiming him, either by the kindness of a friend, or the authority of a master. For I supposed that he thought of me as did his father; but he was not such; laying aside then his father's mind in that matter, he began to greet me, come sometimes into my lecture room, hear a little, and be gone.

I however had forgotten to deal with him, that he should not, through a blind and headlong desire of vain pastimes, undo so good a wit. But Thou, O Lord, who guidest the course of all Thou hast created, hadst not forgotten him, who was one day to be among Thy children, Priest and Dispenser of Thy Sacrament; and that his amendment might plainly be attributed to Thyself, Thou effectedst it through me, unknowingly. For as one day I sat in my accustomed place, with my scholars before me, he entered, greeted me, sat down, and applied his mind to what I then handled. I had by chance a passage in hand, which while I was explaining, a likeness from the Circensian races occurred to me, as likely to make what I would convey pleasanter and plainer, seasoned with biting mockery of those whom that madness had enthralled; God, Thou knowest that I then thought not of curing Alypius of that infection. But he took it wholly to himself, and thought that I said it simply for his sake. And whence another would have taken occasion of offence with me, that right-minded youth took as a ground of being offended at himself, and loving me more fervently. For Thou hadst said it long ago, and put it into Thy book, Rebuke a wise man and he will love Thee. But I had not rebuked him, but Thou, who employest all, knowing or not knowing, in that order which Thyself knowest (and that order is just), didst of my heart and tongue make burning coals, by which to set on fire the hopeful mind, thus languishing, and so cure it. Let him be silent in Thy praises, who considers not Thy mercies, which confess unto Thee out of my inmost soul. For he upon that speech burst out of that pit so deep, wherein he was willfully plunged, and was blinded with its wretched pastimes; and he shook his mind with a strong self-command; whereupon all the filths of the Circensian pastimes flew off from him, nor came he again thither. Upon this, he prevailed with his unwilling father that he might be my scholar. He gave way, and gave in. And Alypius beginning to be my hearer again, was involved in the same superstition with me, loving in the Manichees that show of continency which he supposed true and unfeigned. Whereas it was a senseless and seducing continency, ensnaring precious souls, unable as yet to reach the depth of virtue, yet readily beguiled with the surface of what was but a shadowy and counterfeit virtue.

He, not forsaking that secular course which his parents had

charmed him to pursue, had gone before me to Rome, to study law, and there he was carried away incredibly with an incredible eagerness after the shows of gladiators. For being utterly averse to and detesting spectacles, he was one day by chance met by divers of his acquaintance and fellow-students coming from dinner, and they with a familiar violence haled him, vehemently refusing and resisting, into the Amphitheatre, during these cruel and deadly shows, he thus protesting: "Though you hale my body to that place, and there set me, can you force me also to turn my mind or my eyes to those shows? I shall then be absent while present, and so shall overcome both you and them." They, hearing this, led him on nevertheless, desirous perchance to try that very thing, whether he could do as he said. When they were come thither, and had taken their places as they could, the whole place kindled with that savage pastime. But he, closing the passage of his eyes, forbade his mind to range abroad after such evil; and would he had stopped his ears also! For in the fight, when one fell, a mighty cry of the whole people striking him strongly, overcome by curiosity, and as if prepared to despise and be superior to it whatsoever it were, even when seen, he opened his eyes, and was stricken with a deeper wound in his soul than the other, whom he desired to behold, was in his body; and he fell more miserably than he upon whose fall that mighty noise was raised, which entered through his ears, and unlocked his eyes, to make way for the striking and beating down of a soul, bold rather than resolute, and the weaker, in that it had presumed on itself, which ought to have relied on Thee. For so soon as he saw that blood, he therewith drunk down savageness; nor turned away, but fixed his eye, drinking in frenzy, unawares, and was delighted with that guilty fight, and intoxicated with the bloody pastime. Nor was he now the man he came, but one of the throng he came unto, yea, a true associate of theirs that brought him thither. Why say more? He beheld, shouted, kindled, carried thence with him the madness which should goad him to return not only with them who first drew him thither, but also before them, yea and to draw in others. Yet thence didst Thou with a most strong and most merciful hand pluck him, and taughtest him to have confidence not in himself, but in Thee. But this was after.

But this was already being laid up in his memory to be a medicine hereafter. So was that also, that when he was yet studying under me at Carthage, and was thinking over at mid-day in the market-place what he was to say by heart (as scholars use to practise), Thou sufferedst him to be apprehended by the officers of the market-place for a thief. For no other cause, I deem, didst Thou, our God, suffer it, but that he who was hereafter to prove so great a man, should already begin to learn that in judging of causes, man was not readily to be condemned by man out of a rash credulity. For as he was walking up and down by himself before the judgment-seat, with his note-book and pen, lo, a young man, a lawyer, the real thief, privily bringing a hatchet, got in, unperceived by Alypius, as far as the leaden gratings which fence in the silversmiths' shops, and began to cut away the lead. But the noise of the hatchet being heard, the silversmiths beneath began to make a stir, and sent to apprehend whomever they should find. But he, hearing their voices, ran away, leaving his hatchet, fearing to be taken with it. Alypius now, who had not seen him enter, was aware of his going, and saw with what speed he made away. And being desirous to know the matter, entered the place; where finding the hatchet, he was standing, wondering and considering it, when behold, those that had been sent, find him alone with the hatchet in his hand, the noise whereof had startled and brought them thither. They seize him, hale him away, and gathering the dwellers in the market-place together, boast of having taken a notorious thief, and so he was being led away to be taken before the judge.

But thus far was Alypius to be instructed. For forthwith, O Lord, Thou succouredst his innocency, whereof Thou alone wert witness. For as he was being led either to prison or to punishment, a certain architect met them, who had the chief charge of the public buildings. Glad they were to meet him especially, by whom they were wont to be suspected of stealing the goods lost out of the marketplace, as though to show him at last by whom these thefts were committed. He, however, had divers times seen Alypius at a certain senator's house, to whom he often went to pay his respects; and recognising him immediately, took him aside by the hand, and inquiring the occasion of so great a calamity, heard the whole matter, and bade all present, amid much uproar and threats, to go with him. So they came to the house of the young man who had done the deed. There, before the door, was a boy so young as to be likely, not apprehending any harm to his master, to disclose the whole. For he had attended his master to the market-place. Whom so soon as Alypius remembered, he told the architect: and he showing the hatchet to the boy, asked him "Whose that was?" "Ours," quoth he presently: and being further questioned, he discovered every thing. Thus the crime being transferred to that house, and the multitude ashamed, which had begun to insult over Alypius, he who was to be a dispenser of Thy Word, and an examiner of many causes in Thy Church, went away better experienced and instructed.

Him then I had found at Rome, and he clave to me by a most strong tie, and went with me to Milan, both that he might not leave me, and might practise something of the law he had studied, more to please his parents than himself. There he had thrice sat as Assessor, with an uncorruptness much wondered at by others, he wondering at others rather who could prefer gold to honesty. His character was tried besides, not only with the bait of covetousness, but with the goad of fear. At Rome he was Assessor to the count of the Italian Treasury. There was at that time a very powerful senator, to whose favours many stood indebted, many much feared. He would needs, by his usual power, have a thing allowed him which by the laws was unallowed. Alypius resisted it: a bribe was promised; with all his heart he scorned it: threats were held out; he trampled upon them: all wondering at so unwonted a spirit, which neither desired the friendship, nor feared the enmity of one so great and so mightily renowned for innumerable means of doing good or evil. And the very judge, whose councilor Alypius was, although also unwilling it should be, yet did not openly refuse, but put the matter off upon Alypius, alleging that he would not allow him to do it: for in truth had the judge done it, Alypius would have decided otherwise. With this one thing in the way of learning was he well-nigh seduced, that he might have books copied for him at Praetorian prices, but consulting justice, he altered his deliberation for the better; esteeming equity whereby he was hindered more gainful than the power whereby he were allowed. These are slight things, but he that is faithful in little, is faithful also in much. Nor can that any how be void, which proceeded out of the mouth of Thy Truth: If ye have not been faithful in the unrighteous

Mammon, who will commit to your trust true riches? And if ye have not been faithful in that which is another man's, who shall give you that which is your own? He being such, did at that time cleave to me, and with me wavered in purpose, what course of life was to be taken.

Nebridius also, who having left his native country near Carthage, yea and Carthage itself, where he had much lived, leaving his excellent family-estate and house, and a mother behind, who was not to follow him, had come to Milan, for no other reason but that with me he might live in a most ardent search after truth and wisdom. Like me he sighed, like me he wavered, an ardent searcher after true life, and a most acute examiner of the most difficult questions. Thus were there the mouths of three indigent persons, sighing out their wants one to another, and waiting upon Thee that Thou mightest give them their meat in due season. And in all the bitterness which by Thy mercy followed our worldly affairs, as we looked towards the end, why we should suffer all this, darkness met us; and we turned away groaning, and saying, How long shall these things be? This too we often said; and so saying forsook them not, for as yet there dawned nothing certain, which these forsaken, we might embrace.

And I, viewing and reviewing things, most wondered at the length of time from that my nineteenth year, wherein I had begun to kindle with the desire of wisdom, settling when I had found her, to abandon all the empty hopes and lying frenzies of vain desires. And lo, I was now in my thirtieth year, sticking in the same mire, greedy of enjoying things present, which passed away and wasted my soul; while I said to myself, "Tomorrow I shall find it; it will appear manifestly and I shall grasp it; lo, Faustus the Manichee will come, and clear every thing! O you great men, ye Academicians, it is true then, that no certainty can be attained for the ordering of life! Nay, let us search the more diligently, and despair not. Lo, things in the ecclesiastical books are not absurd to us now, which sometimes seemed absurd, and may be otherwise taken, and in a good sense. I will take my stand, where, as a child, my parents placed me, until the clear truth be found out. But where shall it be sought or when? Ambrose has no leisure; we have no leisure to read; where shall we find even the books? Whence, or when procure them? from whom borrow them? Let set times be appointed, and certain hours be ordered for the health of our soul. Great hope has dawned; the Catholic Faith teaches not what we thought, and vainly accused it of; her instructed members hold it profane to believe God to be bounded by the figure of a human body: and do we doubt to 'knock,' that the rest 'may be opened'? The forenoons our scholars take up; what do we during the rest? Why not this? But when then pay we court to our great friends, whose favour we need? When compose what we may sell to scholars? When refresh ourselves, unbending our minds from this intenseness of care?

"Perish every thing, dismiss we these empty vanities, and betake ourselves to the one search for truth! Life is vain, death uncertain; if it steals upon us on a sudden, in what state shall we depart hence? and where shall we learn what here we have neglected? and shall we not rather suffer the punishment of this negligence? What, if death itself cut off and end all care and feeling? Then must this be ascertained. But God forbid this! It is no vain and empty thing, that the excellent dignity of the authority of the Christian Faith hath overspread the whole world. Never would such and so great things be by God wrought for us, if with the death of the body the life of the soul came to an end. Wherefore delay then to abandon worldly hopes, and give ourselves wholly to seek after God and the blessed life? But wait! Even those things are pleasant; they have some, and no small sweetness. We must not lightly abandon them, for it were a shame to return again to them. See, it is no great matter now to obtain some station, and then what should we more wish for? We have store of powerful friends; if nothing else offer, and we be in much haste, at least a presidentship may be given us: and a wife with some money, that she increase not our charges: and this shall be the bound of desire. Many great men, and most worthy of imitation, have given themselves to the study of wisdom in the state of marriage."

While I went over these things, and these winds shifted and drove my heart this way and that, time passed on, but I delayed to turn to the Lord; and from day to day deferred to live in Thee, and deferred not daily to die in myself. Loving a happy life, I feared it in its own abode, and sought it, by fleeing from it. I thought I should be too miserable, unless folded in female arms; and of the medicine of Thy mercy to cure that infirmity I thought not, not having tried it. As for continency, I supposed it to be in our own power (though in myself I did not find that power), being so foolish as not to know what is written, None can be continent unless Thou give it; and that Thou wouldest give it, if with inward groanings I did knock at Thine ears, and with a settled faith did cast my care on Thee.

Alypius indeed kept me from marrying; alleging that so could we by no means with undistracted leisure live together in the love of wisdom, as we had long desired. For himself was even then most pure in this point, so that it was wonderful; and that the more, since in the outset of his youth he had entered into that course, but had not stuck fast therein; rather had he felt remorse and revolting at it, living thenceforth until now most continently. But I opposed him with the examples of those who as married men had cherished wisdom, and served God acceptably, and retained their friends, and loved them faithfully. Of whose greatness of spirit I was far short; and bound with the disease of the flesh, and its deadly sweetness, drew along my chain, dreading to be loosed, and as if my wound had been fretted, put back his good persuasions, as it were the hand of one that would unchain me. Moreover, by me did the serpent speak unto Alypius himself, by my tongue weaving and laying in his path pleasurable snares, wherein his virtuous and free feet might be entangled.

For when he wondered that I, whom he esteemed not slightly, should stick so fast in the birdlime of that pleasure, as to protest (so oft as we discussed it) that I could never lead a single life; and urged in my defense when I saw him wonder, that there was great difference between his momentary and scarce-remembered knowledge of that life, which so he might easily despise, and my continued acquaintance whereto if the honourable name of marriage were added, he ought not to wonder why I could not contemn that course; he began also to desire to be married; not as overcome with desire of such pleasure, but out of curiosity. For he would fain know, he said, what that should be, without which my life, to him so pleasing, would to me seem not life but a punishment. For his mind, free from that chain, was amazed at my thraldom; and through that amazement was going on to a desire of trying it, thence to the trial itself, and thence perhaps to sink into that bondage whereat he wondered, seeing he was willing to make a covenant with death; and he that loves danger, shall fall into it. For whatever honour there be in the office of well-ordering a married life, and a family, moved us but slightly. But me for the most part the habit of satisfying an insatiable appetite tormented, while it held me captive; him, an admiring wonder was leading captive. So were we, until Thou, O Most High, not forsaking our dust, commiserating us miserable, didst come to our help, by wondrous and secret ways.

Continual effort was made to have me married. I wooed, I was promised, chiefly through my mother's pains, that so once married, the health-giving baptism might cleanse me, towards which she rejoiced that I was being daily fitted, and observed that her prayers, and Thy promises, were being fulfilled in my faith. At which time verily, both at my request and her own longing, with strong cries of heart she daily begged of Thee, that Thou wouldest by a vision discover unto her something concerning my future marriage; Thou never wouldest. She saw indeed certain vain and fantastic things, such as the energy of the human spirit, busied thereon, brought together; and these she told me of, not with that confidence she was wont, when Thou showedst her any thing, but slighting them. For she could, she said, through a certain feeling, which in words she could not express, discern betwixt Thy revelations, and the dreams of her own soul. Yet the matter was pressed on, and a maiden asked in marriage, two years under the fit age; and, as pleasing, was waited for.

And many of us friends conferring about, and detesting the turbulent turmoils of human life, had debated and now almost resolved on living apart from business and the bustle of men; and this was to be thus obtained; we were to bring whatever we might severally procure, and make one household of all; so that through the truth of our friendship nothing should belong especially to any; but the whole thus derived from all, should as a whole belong to each, and all to all. We thought there might be some often persons in this society; some of whom were very rich, especially Romanianus our townsman, from childhood a very familiar friend of mine, whom the grievous perplexities of his affairs had brought up to court; who was the most earnest for this project; and therein was his voice of great weight, because his ample estate far exceeded any of the rest. We had settled also that two annual officers, as it were, should provide all things necessary, the rest being undisturbed. But when we began to consider whether the wives, which some of us already had, others hoped to have, would allow this, all that plan, which was being so well moulded, fell to pieces in our hands, was utterly dashed and cast aside. Thence we betook us to sighs, and groans, and our steps to follow the broad and beaten ways of the world; for many thoughts were in our heart, but Thy counsel standeth for ever. Out of which counsel Thou didst deride ours, and preparedst Thine own; purposing to give us meat in due season, and to fill our souls with blessing.

Meanwhile my sins were being multiplied, and my concubine being torn from my side as a hindrance to my marriage, my heart which clave unto her was torn and wounded and bleeding. And she returned to Afric, vowing unto Thee never to know any other man, leaving with me my son by her. But unhappy I, who could not imitate a very woman, impatient of delay, inasmuch as not till after two years was I to obtain her I sought not being so much a lover of marriage as a slave to lust, procured another, though no wife, that so by the servitude of an enduring custom, the disease of my soul might be kept up and carried on in its vigour, or even augmented, into the dominion of marriage. Nor was that my wound cured, which had been made by the cutting away of the former, but after inflammation and most acute pain, it mortified, and my pains became less acute, but more desperate.

To Thee be praise, glory to Thee, Fountain of mercies. I was becoming more miserable, and Thou nearer. Thy right hand was continually ready to pluck me out of the mire, and to wash me thoroughly, and I knew it not; nor did anything call me back from a yet deeper gulf of carnal pleasures, but the fear of death, and of Thy judgment to come; which amid all my changes, never departed from my breast. And in my disputes with my friends Alypius and Nebridius of the nature of good and evil, I held that Epicurus had in my mind won the palm, had I not believed that after death there remained a life for the soul, and places of requital according to men's deserts, which

Epicurus would not believe. And I asked, "were we immortal, and to live in perpetual bodily pleasure, without fear of losing it, why should we not be happy, or what else should we seek?" not knowing that great misery was involved in this very thing, that, being thus sunk and blinded, I could not discern that light of excellence and beauty, to be embraced for its own sake, which the eye of flesh cannot see, and is seen by the inner man. Nor did I, unhappy, consider from what source it sprung, that even on these things, foul as they were, I with pleasure discoursed with my friends, nor could I, even according to the notions I then had of happiness, be happy without friends, amid what abundance soever of carnal pleasures. And yet these friends I loved for themselves only, and I felt that I was beloved of them again for myself only.

O crooked paths! Woe to the audacious soul, which hoped, by forsaking Thee, to gain some better thing! Turned it hath, and turned again, upon back, sides, and belly, yet all was painful; and Thou alone rest. And behold, Thou art at hand, and deliverest us from our wretched wanderings, and placest us in Thy way, and dost comfort us, and say, "Run; I will carry you; yea I will bring you through; there also will I carry you."

Book Seven

Deceased was now that my evil and abominable youth, and I was passing into early manhood; the more defiled by vain things as I grew in years, who could not imagine any substance, but such as is wont to be seen with these eyes. I thought not of Thee, O God, under the figure of a human body; since I began to hear aught of wisdom, I always avoided this; and rejoiced to have found the same in the faith of our spiritual mother, Thy Catholic Church. But what else to conceive of Thee I knew not. And I, a man, and such a man, sought to conceive of Thee the sovereign, only, true God; and I did in my inmost soul believe that Thou wert incorruptible, and uninjurable, and unchangeable; because though not knowing whence or how, yet I saw plainly, and was sure, that that which may be corrupted must be inferior to that which cannot; what could not be injured I preferred unhesitatingly to what could receive injury; the unchangeable to things subject to change. My heart passionately cried out against all my phantoms, and with this one blow I sought to beat away from the eye of my mind all that unclean troop which buzzed around it. And lo, being scarce put off, in the twinkling of an eye they gathered again thick about me, flew against my face, and beclouded it; so that though not under the form of the human body, yet was I constrained to conceive of Thee (that incorruptible, uninjurable, and unchangeable, which I preferred before the corruptible, and injurable, and changeable) as being in space, whether infused into the world, or diffused infinitely without it. Because whatsoever I conceived, deprived of this space, seemed to me nothing, yea altogether nothing, not even a void, as if a body were taken out of its place, and the place should remain empty of any body at all, of earth and water, air and heaven, yet would it remain a void place, as it were a spacious nothing.

I then being thus gross-hearted, nor clear even to myself, whatsoever was not extended over certain spaces, nor diffused, nor condensed, nor swelled out, or did not or could not receive some of these dimensions, I thought to be altogether nothing. For over such forms as my eyes are wont to range, did my heart then range: nor yet did I see that this same notion of the mind, whereby I formed those very images, was not of this sort, and yet it could not have formed them, had not itself been some great thing. So also did I endeavour to conceive of Thee, Life of my life, as vast, through infinite spaces on every side penetrating the whole mass of the universe, and beyond it, every way, through unmeasurable boundless spaces; so that the earth should have Thee, the heaven have Thee, all things have Thee, and they be bounded in Thee, and Thou bounded nowhere. For that as the body of this air which is above the earth, hindereth not the light of the sun from passing through it, penetrating it, not by bursting or by cutting, but by filling it wholly: so I thought the body not of heaven, air, and sea only, but of the earth too, pervious to Thee, so that in all its parts, the greatest as the smallest, it should admit Thy presence, by a secret inspiration, within and without, directing all things which Thou hast created. So I guessed, only as unable to conceive aught else, for it was false. For thus should a greater part of the earth contain a greater portion of Thee, and a less, a lesser: and all things should in such sort be full of Thee, that the body of an elephant should contain more of Thee, than that of a sparrow, by how much larger it is, and takes up more room; and thus shouldest Thou make the several portions of Thyself present unto the several portions of the world, in fragments, large to the large, petty to the petty. But such art not Thou. But not as yet hadst Thou enlightened my darkness.

It was enough for me, Lord, to oppose to those deceived deceivers, and dumb praters, since Thy word sounded not out of them; that was enough which long ago, while we were yet at Carthage, Nebridius used to propound, at which all we that heard it were staggered: "That said nation of darkness, which the Manichees are wont to set as an opposing mass over against Thee, what could it have done unto Thee, hadst Thou refused to fight with it? For, if they answered, 'it would have done Thee some hurt,' then shouldest Thou be subject to injury and corruption: but it could do Thee no hurt,' then was no reason brought for Thy fighting with it; and fighting in such wise, as that a certain portion or member of Thee, or offspring of Thy very Substance, should be mingled with opposed powers, and natures not created by Thee, and be by them so far corrupted and changed to the worse, as to be turned from happiness into misery, and need assistance, whereby it might be extricated and purified; and that this offspring of Thy Substance was the soul, which being enthralled, defiled, corrupted, Thy Word, free, pure, and whole, might relieve; that Word itself being still corruptible because it was of one and the same Substance. So then, should they affirm Thee, whatsoever Thou art, that is, Thy Substance whereby Thou art, to be incorruptible, then were all these sayings false and execrable; but if corruptible, the very statement showed it to be false and revolting." This argument then of Nebridius sufficed against those who deserved wholly to be vomited out of the overcharged stomach; for they had no escape, without horrible blasphemy of heart and tongue, thus thinking and speaking of Thee.

But I also as yet, although I held and was firmly persuaded that Thou our Lord the true God, who madest not only our souls, but our bodies, and not only our souls and bodies, but all beings, and all things, wert undefilable and unalterable, and in no degree mutable; yet understood I not, clearly and without difficulty, the cause of evil. And yet whatever it were, I perceived it was in such wise to be sought out, as should not constrain me to believe the immutable God to be mutable, lest I should become that evil I was seeking out. I sought it out then, thus far free from anxiety, certain of the untruth of what these held, from whom I shrunk with my whole heart: for I saw, that through inquiring the origin of evil, they were filled with evil, in that they preferred to think that Thy substance did suffer ill than their own did commit it.

And I strained to perceive what I now heard, that free-will was the cause of our doing ill, and Thy just judgment of our suffering ill. But I was not able clearly to discern it. So then endeavouring to draw my soul's vision out of that deep pit, I was again plunged therein, and endeavouring often, I was plunged back as often. But this raised me a little into Thy light, that I knew as well that I had a will, as that I lived: when then I did will or nill any thing, I was most sure that no other than myself did will and nill: and I all but saw that there was the cause of my sin. But what I did against my will, I saw that I suffered rather than did, and I judged not to be my fault, but my punishment; whereby, however, holding Thee to be just, I speedily confessed myself to be not unjustly punished. But again I said, Who made me? Did not my God, Who is not only good, but goodness itself? Whence then came I to will evil and nill good, so that I am thus justly punished? who set this in me, and ingrafted into me this plant of bitterness, seeing I was wholly formed by my most sweet God? If the devil were the author, whence is that same devil? And if he also by his own perverse will, of a good angel became a devil, whence, again, came in him that evil will whereby he became a devil, seeing the whole nature of angels was made by that most good Creator? By these thoughts I was again sunk down and choked; yet not brought down to that hell of error (where no man confesseth unto Thee), to think rather that Thou dost suffer ill, than that man doth it.

For I was in such wise striving to find out the rest, as one who had already found that the incorruptible must needs be better than the corruptible: and Thee therefore, whatsoever Thou wert, I confessed to be incorruptible. For never soul was, nor shall be, able to conceive any thing which may be better than Thou, who art the sovereign and the best good. But since most truly and certainly, the incorruptible is preferable to the corruptible (as I did now prefer it), then, wert Thou not incorruptible, I could in thought have arrived at something better than my God. Where then I saw the incorruptible to be preferable to the corruptible, there ought I to seek for Thee, and there observe "wherein evil itself was"; that is, whence corruption comes, by which Thy substance can by no means be impaired. For corruption does no ways impair our God; by no will, by no necessity, by no unlooked for chance: because He is God, and what He wills is good, and Himself is that good; but to be corrupted is not good. Nor art Thou against Thy will constrained to any thing, since Thy will is not greater than Thy power. But greater should it be, were Thyself greater than Thyself. For the will and power of God is God Himself. And what can be unlooked for by Thee, Who knowest all things? Nor is there any nature in things, but Thou knowest it. And what should we more say, "why that substance which God is should not be corruptible," seeing if it were so, it should not be God?

And I sought "whence is evil," and sought in an evil way; and saw not the evil in my very search. I set now before the sight of my spirit the whole creation, whatsoever we can see therein (as sea, earth, air, stars, trees, mortal creatures); yea, and whatever in it we do not see, as the firmament of heaven, all angels moreover, and all the spiritual inhabitants thereof. But these very beings, as though they were bodies, did my fancy dispose in place, and I made one great mass of Thy creation, distinguished as to the kinds of bodies; some, real bodies, some, what myself had feigned for spirits. And this mass I made huge, not as it was (which I could not know), but as I thought convenient, yet every way finite. But Thee, O Lord, I imagined on every part environing and penetrating it, though every way infinite: as if there were a sea, every where, and on every side, through unmeasured space, one only boundless sea, and it contained within it some sponge, huge, but bounded; that sponge must needs, in all its parts, be filled from that unmeasurable sea: so conceived I Thy creation, itself finite, full of Thee, the Infinite; and I said, Behold God, and behold what God hath created; and God is good, yea, most mightily and incomparably better than all these: but yet He, the Good, created them good; and see how He environeth and fulfills them. Where is evil then, and whence, and how crept it in hither? What is its root, and what its seed? Or hath it no being? Why then fear we and avoid what is not? Or if we fear it idly, then is that very fear evil, whereby the soul is thus idly goaded and racked. Yea, and so much a greater evil, as we have nothing to fear, and yet do fear. Therefore either is that evil which we fear, or else evil is, that we fear. Whence is it then? seeing God, the Good, hath created all these things good. He indeed, the greater and chiefest Good, hath created these lesser goods; still both Creator and created, all are good. Whence is evil? Or, was there some evil matter of which He made, and formed, and ordered it, yet left something in it which He did not convert into good? Why so then? Had He no might to turn and change the whole, so that no evil should remain in it, seeing He is All-mighty? Lastly, why would He make any thing at all of it, and not rather by the same All-mightiness cause it not to be at all? Or, could it then be against His will? Or if it were from eternity, why suffered He it so to be for infinite spaces of times past, and was pleased so long after to make something out of it? Or if He were suddenly pleased now to effect somewhat, this rather should the All-mighty have effected, that this evil matter should not be, and He alone be, the whole, true, sovereign, and infinite Good. Or if it was not good that He who was good should not also frame and create something that were good, then, that evil matter being taken away and brought to nothing, He might form good matter, whereof to create all things. For He should not be All-mighty, if He might not create something good without the aid of that matter which Himself had not created. These thoughts I revolved in my miserable heart, overcharged with most gnawing cares, lest I should die ere I had found the truth; yet was the faith of Thy Christ, our Lord and Saviour, professed in the Church Catholic, firmly fixed in my heart, in many points, indeed, as yet unformed, and fluctuating from the rule of doctrine; yet did not my mind utterly leave it, but rather daily took in more and more of it.

By this time also had I rejected the lying divinations and impious dotages of the astrologers. Let Thine own mercies, out of my very inmost soul, confess unto Thee for this also, O my God. For Thou,

Thou altogether (for who else calls us back from the death of all errors, save the Life which cannot die, and the Wisdom which needing no light enlightens the minds that need it, whereby the universe is directed, down to the whirling leaves of trees?)—Thou madest provision for my obstinacy wherewith I struggled against Vindicianus, an acute old man, and Nebridius, a young man of admirable talents; the first vehemently affirming, and the latter often (though with some doubtfulness) saying, "That there was no such art whereby to foresee things to come, but that men's conjectures were a sort of lottery, and that out of many things which they said should come to pass, some actually did, unawares to them who spake it, who stumbled upon it, through their oft speaking." Thou providedst then a friend for me, no negligent consulter of the astrologers; nor yet well skilled in those arts, but (as I said) a curious consulter with them, and yet knowing something, which he said he had heard of his father, which how far it went to overthrow the estimation of that art, he knew not. This man then, Firminus by name, having had a liberal education, and well taught in Rhetoric, consulted me, as one very dear to him, what, according to his so-called constellations, I thought on certain affairs of his, wherein his worldly hopes had risen, and I, who had herein now begun to incline towards Nebridius' opinion, did not altogether refuse to conjecture, and tell him what came into my unresolved mind; but added, that I was now almost persuaded that these were but empty and ridiculous follies. Thereupon he told me that his father had been very curious in such books, and had a friend as earnest in them as himself, who with joint study and conference fanned the flame of their affections to these toys, so that they would observe the moments whereat the very dumb animals, which bred about their houses, gave birth, and then observed the relative position of the heavens, thereby to make fresh experiments in this so-called art. He said then that he had heard of his father, that what time his mother was about to give birth to him, Firminus, a womanservant of that friend of his father's was also with child, which could not escape her master, who took care with most exact diligence to know the births of his very puppies. And so it was that (the one for his wife, and the other for his servant, with the most careful observation, reckoning days, hours, nay, the lesser divisions of the hours) both were delivered at the same instant; so that both were constrained to allow the same constellations, even to the minutest points, the one for his son, the other for his new-born slave. For so soon as the women began to be in labour, they each gave notice to the other what was fallen out in their houses, and had messengers ready to send to one another so soon as they had notice of the actual birth, of which they had easily provided, each in his own province, to give instant intelligence. Thus then the messengers of the respective parties met, he averred, at such an equal distance from either house that neither of them could make out any difference in the position of the stars, or any other minutest points; and yet Firminus, born in a high estate in his parents' house, ran his course through the gilded paths of life, was increased in riches, raised to honours; whereas that slave continued to serve his masters, without any relaxation of his yoke, as Firminus, who knew him, told me.

Upon hearing and believing these things, told by one of such credibility, all that my resistance gave way; and first I endeavoured to reclaim Firminus himself from that curiosity, by telling him that upon inspecting his constellations, I ought if I were to predict truly, to have seen in them parents eminent among their neighbours, a noble family in its own city, high birth, good education, liberal learning. But if that servant had consulted me upon the same constellations, since they were his also, I ought again (to tell him too truly) to see in them a lineage the most abject, a slavish condition, and every thing else utterly at variance with the former. Whence then, if I spake the truth, I should, from the same constellations, speak diversely, or if I spake the same, speak falsely: thence it followed most certainly that whatever, upon consideration of the constellations, was spoken truly, was spoken not out of art, but chance; and whatever spoken falsely, was not out of ignorance in the art, but the failure of the chance.

An opening thus made, ruminating with myself on the like things, that no one of those dotards (who lived by such a trade, and whom I longed to attack, and with derision to confute) might urge against me that Firminus had informed me falsely, or his father him; I bent my thoughts on those that are born twins, who for the most part come out of the womb so near one to other, that the small interval (how much force soever in the nature of things folk may pretend it to have) cannot be noted by human observation, or be at all expressed in those figures which the astrologer is to inspect, that he may pronounce truly. Yet they cannot be true: for looking into the same figures, he must have predicted the same of Esau and Jacob, whereas the same happened not to them. Therefore he must speak falsely; or if truly, then, looking into the same figures, he must not give the same answer. Not by art, then, but by chance, would he speak truly. For Thou, O Lord, most righteous Ruler of the Universe, while consulters and consulted know it not, dost by Thy hidden inspiration effect that the consulter should hear what, according to the hidden deservings of souls, he ought to hear, out of the unsearchable depth of Thy just judgment, to Whom let no man say, What is this? Why that? Let him not so say, for he is man.

Now then, O my Helper, hadst Thou loosed me from those fetters: and I sought "whence is evil," and found no way. But Thou sufferedst me not by any fluctuations of thought to be carried away from the Faith whereby I believed Thee both to be, and Thy substance to be unchangeable, and that Thou hast a care of, and wouldest judge men, and that in Christ, Thy Son, Our Lord, and the holy Scriptures, which the authority of Thy Catholic Church pressed upon me, Thou hadst set the way of man's salvation, to that life which is to be after this death. These things being safe and immovably settled in my mind, I sought anxiously "whence was evil?" What were the pangs of my teeming heart, what groans, O my God! yet even there were Thine ears open, and I knew it not; and when in silence I vehemently sought, those silent contritions of my soul were strong cries unto Thy mercy. Thou knewest what I suffered, and no man. For, what was that which was thence through my tongue distilled into the ears of my most familiar friends? Did the whole tumult of my soul, for which neither time nor utterance sufficed, reach them? Yet went up the whole to Thy hearing, all which I roared out from the groanings of my heart; and my desire was before Thee, and the light of mine eyes was not with me: for that was within, I without: nor was that confined to place, but I was intent on things contained in place, but there found I no resting-place, nor did they so receive me, that I could say, "It is enough," "it is well": nor did they yet suffer me to turn back, where it might be well enough with me. For to these things was I superior, but inferior to Thee; and Thou art my true joy when subjected to Thee, and Thou hadst subjected to me what Thou createdst below me. And this was the true temperament, and middle region of my safety, to remain in Thy Image, and by serving Thee, rule the body. But when I rose proudly against Thee, and ran against the Lord with my neck, with the thick bosses of my buckler, even these inferior things were set above me, and pressed me down, and no where was there respite or space of breathing. They met my sight on all sides by heaps and troops, and in thought the images thereof presented themselves unsought, as I would return to Thee, as if they would say unto me, "Whither goest thou, unworthy and defiled?" And these things had grown out of my wound; for Thou "humbledst the proud like one that is wounded," and through my own swelling was I separated from Thee; yea, my pride-swollen face closed up mine eyes.

But Thou, Lord, abidest for ever, yet not for ever art Thou angry with us; because Thou pitiest our dust and ashes, and it was pleasing in Thy sight to reform my deformities; and by inward goads didst Thou rouse me, that I should be ill at ease, until Thou wert manifested to my inward sight. Thus, by the secret hand of Thy medicining was my swelling abated, and the troubled and bedimmed eyesight of my mind, by the smarting anointings of healthful sorrows, was from day to day healed.

And Thou, willing first to show me how Thou resistest the proud, but givest grace unto the humble, and by how great an act of Thy mercy Thou hadst traced out to men the way of humility, in that Thy Word was made flesh, and dwelt among men: Thou procuredst for me, by means of one puffed up with most unnatural pride, certain books of the Platonists, translated from Greek into Latin. And therein I read, not indeed in the very words, but to the very same purpose, enforced by many and divers reasons, that In the beginning was the Word, and the Word was with God, and the Word was God: the Same was in the beginning with God: all things were made by Him, and without Him was nothing made: that which was made by Him is life, and the life was the light of men, and the light shineth in the darkness, and the darkness comprehended it not. And that the soul of man, though it bears witness to the light, yet itself is not that light; but the Word of God, being God, is that true light that lighteth every man that cometh into the world. And that He was in the world, and the world was made by Him, and the world knew Him not. But, that He came unto His own, and His own received Him not; but as many as received Him, to them gave He power to become the sons of God, as many as believed in His name; this I read not there.

Again I read there, that God the Word was born not of flesh nor of blood, nor of the will of man, nor of the will of the flesh, but of God. But that the Word was made flesh, and dwelt among us, I read not there. For I traced in those books that it was many and divers ways said, that the Son was in the form of the Father, and thought it not robbery to be equal with God, for that naturally He was the Same Substance. But that He emptied Himself, taking the form of a servant, being made in the likeness of men, and found in fashion as a man, humbled Himself, and became obedient unto death, and that the death of the cross: wherefore God exalted Him from the dead, and gave Him a name above every name, that at the name of Jesus every knee should how, of things in heaven, and things in earth, and things under the earth; and that every tongue should confess that the Lord Jesus Christ is in the glory of God the Father; those books have not. For that before all times and above all times Thy Only-Begotten Son remaineth unchangeable, co-eternal with Thee, and that of His fullness souls receive, that they may be blessed; and that by participation of wisdom abiding in them, they are renewed, so as to be wise, is there. But that in due time He died for the ungodly; and that Thou sparedst not Thine Only Son, but deliveredst Him for us all, is not there. For Thou hiddest these things from the wise, and revealedst them to babes; that they that labour and are heavy laden might come unto Him, and He refresh them, because He is meek and lowly in heart; and the meek He directeth in judgment, and the gentle He teacheth His ways, beholding our lowliness and trouble, and forgiving all our sins. But such as are lifted up in the lofty walk of some would-be sublimer learning, hear not Him, saying, Learn of Me, for I am meek and lowly in heart, and ye shall find rest to your souls. Although they knew God, yet they glorify Him not as God, nor are thankful, but wax vain in their thoughts; and their foolish heart is darkened; professing that they were wise, they became fools.

And therefore did I read there also, that they had changed the glory of Thy incorruptible nature into idols and divers shapes, into the likeness of the image of corruptible man, and birds, and beasts, and creeping things; namely, into that Egyptian food for which Esau lost his birthright, for that Thy first-born people worshiped the head of a four-footed beast instead of Thee; turning in heart back towards Egypt; and bowing Thy image, their own soul, before the image of a calf that eateth hay. These things found I here, but I fed not on them. For it pleased Thee, O Lord, to take away the reproach of diminution from Jacob, that the elder should serve the younger: and Thou calledst the Gentiles into Thine inheritance. And I had come to Thee from among the Gentiles; and I set my mind upon the gold which Thou willedst Thy people to take from Egypt, seeing Thine it was, wheresoever it were. And to the Athenians Thou saidst by Thy Apostle, that in Thee we live, move, and have our being, as one of their own poets had said. And verily these books came from thence. But I set not my mind on the idols of Egypt, whom they served with Thy gold, who changed the truth of God into a lie, and worshiped and served the creature more than the Creator.

And being thence admonished to return to myself, I entered even into my inward self, Thou being my Guide: and able I was, for Thou wert become my Helper. And I entered and beheld with the eye of my soul (such as it was), above the same eye of my soul, above my mind, the Light Unchangeable. Not this ordinary light, which all flesh may look upon, nor as it were a greater of the same kind, as though the brightness of this should be manifold brighter, and with its greatness take up all space. Not such was this light, but other, yea, far other from these. Nor was it above my soul, as oil is above water, nor yet as heaven above earth: but above to my soul, because It made me; and I below It, because I was made by It. He that knows the Truth, knows what that Light is; and he that knows It, knows eternity. Love knoweth it. O Truth Who art Eternity! and Love Who art Truth! and Eternity Who art Love! Thou art my God, to Thee do I sigh night and day. Thee when I first knew, Thou liftedst me up, that I might see there was what I might see, and that I was not yet such as to see. And Thou didst beat back the weakness of my sight, streaming forth Thy beams of light upon me most strongly, and I trembled with love and awe: and I perceived myself to be far off from Thee, in the region of unlikeness, as if I heard this Thy voice from on high: "I am the food of grown men, grow, and thou shalt feed upon Me; nor shalt thou convert Me, like the food of thy flesh into thee, but thou shalt be converted into Me." And I learned, that Thou for iniquity chastenest man, and Thou madest my soul to consume away like a spider. And I said, "Is Truth therefore nothing because it is not diffused through space finite or infinite?" And Thou criedst to me from afar: "Yet verily, I AM that I AM." And I heard, as the heart heareth, nor had I room to doubt, and I should sooner doubt that I live than that Truth is not, which is clearly seen, being understood by those things which are made. And I beheld the other things below Thee, and I perceived that they neither altogether are, nor altogether are not, for they are, since they are from Thee, but are not, because they are not what Thou art. For that truly is which remains unchangeably. It is good then for me to hold fast unto God; for if I remain not in Him, I cannot in myself; but He remaining in Himself, reneweth all things. And Thou art the Lord my God, since Thou standest not in need of my goodness.

And it was manifested unto me, that those things be good which yet are corrupted; which neither were they sovereignly good, nor unless they were good could be corrupted: for if sovereignly good, they were incorruptible, if not good at all, there were nothing in them to be corrupted. For corruption injures, but unless it diminished goodness, it could not injure. Either then corruption injures not, which cannot be; or which is most certain, all which is corrupted is deprived of good. But if they be deprived of all good, they shall cease to be. For if they shall be, and can now no longer be corrupted, they shall be better than before, because they shall abide incorruptibly. And what more monstrous than to affirm things to become better by losing all their good? Therefore, if they shall be deprived of all good, they shall no longer be. So long therefore as they are, they are good: therefore whatsoever is, is good. That evil then which I sought, whence it is, is not any substance: for were it a substance, it should be good. For either it should be an incorruptible substance, and so a chief good: or a corruptible substance; which unless it were good, could not be corrupted. I perceived therefore, and it was manifested to me that Thou madest all things good, nor is there any substance at all, which Thou madest not; and for that Thou madest not all things equal, therefore are all things; because each is good, and altogether very good, because our God made all things very good.

And to Thee is nothing whatsoever evil: yea, not only to Thee, but also to Thy creation as a whole, because there is nothing without, which may break in, and corrupt that order which Thou hast appointed it. But in the parts thereof some things, because unharmonising with other some, are accounted evil: whereas those very things harmonise with others, and are good; and in themselves are good. And all these things which harmonise not together, do yet with the inferior part, which we call Earth, having its own cloudy and windy sky harmonising with it. Far be it then that I should say, "These things should not be": for should I see naught but these, I should indeed long for the better; but still must even for these alone praise Thee; for that Thou art to be praised, do show from the earth, dragons, and all deeps, fire, hail, snow, ice, and stormy wind, which fulfill Thy word; mountains, and all hills, fruitful trees, and all cedars; beasts, and all cattle, creeping things, and flying fowls; kings of the earth, and all people, princes, and all judges of the earth; young men and maidens, old men and young, praise Thy Name. But when, from heaven, these praise Thee, praise Thee, our God, in the heights all Thy angels, all Thy hosts, sun and moon, all the stars and light, the Heaven of heavens, and the waters that be above the heavens, praise Thy Name; I did not now long for things better, because I conceived of all: and with a sounder judgment I apprehended that the things above were better than these below, but altogether better than those above by themselves.

There is no soundness in them, whom aught of Thy creation displeaseth: as neither in me, when much which Thou hast made, displeased me. And because my soul durst not be displeased at my God, it would fain not account that Thine, which displeased it. Hence it had gone into the opinion of two substances, and had no rest, but talked idly. And returning thence, it had made to itself a God, through infinite measures of all space; and thought it to be Thee, and placed it in its heart; and had again become the temple of its own idol, to

Thee abominable. But after Thou hadst soothed my head, unknown to me, and closed mine eyes that they should not behold vanity, I ceased somewhat of my former self, and my frenzy was lulled to sleep; and I awoke in Thee, and saw Thee infinite, but in another way, and this sight was not derived from the flesh.

And I looked back on other things; and I saw that they owed their being to Thee; and were all bounded in Thee: but in a different way; not as being in space; but because Thou containest all things in Thine hand in Thy Truth; and all things are true so far as they nor is there any falsehood, unless when that is thought to be, which is not. And I saw that all things did harmonise, not with their places only, but with their seasons. And that Thou, who only art Eternal, didst not begin to work after innumerable spaces of times spent; for that all spaces of times, both which have passed, and which shall pass, neither go nor come, but through Thee, working and abiding.

And I perceived and found it nothing strange, that bread which is pleasant to a healthy palate is loathsome to one distempered: and to sore eyes light is offensive, which to the sound is delightful. And Thy righteousness displeaseth the wicked; much more the viper and reptiles, which Thou hast created good, fitting in with the inferior portions of Thy Creation, with which the very wicked also fit in; and that the more, by how much they be unlike Thee; but with the superior creatures, by how much they become more like to Thee. And I inquired what iniquity was, and found it to be no substance, but the perversion of the will, turned aside from Thee, O God, the Supreme, towards these lower things, and casting out its bowels, and puffed up outwardly.

And I wondered that I now loved Thee, and no phantasm for Thee. And yet did I not press on to enjoy my God; but was borne up to Thee by Thy beauty, and soon borne down from Thee by mine own weight, sinking with sorrow into these inferior things. This weight was carnal custom. Yet dwelt there with me a remembrance of Thee; nor did I any way doubt that there was One to whom I might cleave, but that I was not yet such as to cleave to Thee: for that the body which is corrupted presseth down the soul, and the earthly tabernacle weigheth down the mind that museth upon many things. And most certain I was, that Thy invisible works from the creation of the world are clearly seen, being understood by the things that are made, even Thy eternal power and Godhead. For examining whence it was that I admired the beauty of bodies celestial or terrestrial; and what aided me in judging soundly on things mutable, and pronouncing, "This ought to be thus, this not"; examining, I say, whence it was that I so judged, seeing I did so judge, I had found the unchangeable and true Eternity of Truth above my changeable mind. And thus by degrees I passed from bodies to the soul, which through the bodily senses perceives; and thence to its inward faculty, to which the bodily senses represent things external, whitherto reach the faculties of beasts; and thence again to the reasoning faculty, to which what is received from the senses of the body, is referred to be judged. Which finding itself also to be in me a thing variable, raised itself up to its own understanding, and drew away my thoughts from the power of habit, withdrawing itself from those troops of contradictory phantasms; that so it might find what that light was whereby it was bedewed, when, without all doubting, it cried out, "That the unchangeable was to be preferred to the changeable"; whence also it knew That Unchangeable, which, unless it had in some way known, it had had no sure ground to prefer it to the changeable. And thus with the flash of one trembling glance it arrived at THAT WHICH IS. And then I saw Thy invisible things understood by the things which are made. But I could not fix my gaze thereon; and my infirmity being struck back, I was thrown again on my wonted habits, carrying along with me only a loving memory thereof, and a longing for what I had, as it were, perceived the odour of, but was not yet able to feed on. Then I sought a way of obtaining strength sufficient to enjoy Thee; and found it not, until I embraced that Mediator betwixt God and men, the Man Christ Jesus, who is over all, God blessed for evermore, calling unto me, and saying, I am the way, the truth, and the life, and mingling that food which I was unable to receive, with our flesh. For, the Word was made flesh, that Thy wisdom, whereby Thou createdst all things, might provide milk for our infant state. For I did not hold to my Lord Jesus Christ, I, humbled, to the Humble; nor knew I yet whereto His infirmity would guide us. For Thy Word, the Eternal Truth, far above the higher parts of Thy Creation, raises up the subdued unto Itself: but in this lower world built for Itself a lowly habitation of our clay, whereby to abase from themselves such as would be subdued, and bring them over to Himself; allaying their swelling, and fomenting their love; to the end they might go on no further in self-confidence, but rather consent to become weak, seeing before their feet the Divinity weak by taking our coats of skin; and wearied, might cast themselves down upon It, and It rising, might lift them up.

But I thought otherwise; conceiving only of my Lord Christ as of a man of excellent wisdom, whom no one could be equaled unto; especially, for that being wonderfully born of a Virgin, He seemed, in conformity therewith, through the Divine care for us, to have attained that great eminence of authority, for an example of despising things temporal for the obtaining of immortality. But what mystery there lay in "The Word was made flesh," I could not even imagine. Only I had learnt out of what is delivered to us in writing of Him that He did eat, and drink, sleep, walk, rejoiced in spirit, was sorrowful, discoursed; that flesh did not cleave by itself unto Thy Word, but with the human soul and mind. All know this who know the unchangeableness of Thy Word, which I now knew, as far as I could, nor did I at all doubt thereof. For, now to move the limbs of the body by will, now not, now to be moved by some affection, now not, now to deliver wise sayings through human signs, now to keep silence, belong to soul and mind subject to variation. And should these things be falsely written of Him, all the rest also would risk the charge, nor would there remain in those books any saving faith for mankind. Since then they were written truly, I acknowledged a perfect man to be in Christ; not the body of a man only, nor, with the body, a sensitive soul without a rational, but very man; whom, not only as being a form of Truth, but for a certain great excellence of human nature and a more perfect participation of wisdom, I judged to be preferred before others. But Alypius imagined the Catholics to believe God to be so clothed with flesh, that besides God and flesh, there was no soul at all in Christ, and did not think that a human mind was ascribed to Him. And because he was well persuaded that the actions recorded of Him could only be performed by a vital and a rational creature, he moved the more slowly towards the Christian Faith. But understanding afterwards that this was the error of the Apollinarian heretics, he joyed in and was conformed to the Catholic Faith. But somewhat later, I confess, did I learn how in that saying, The Word was made flesh, the Catholic truth is distinguished from the falsehood of Photinus. For the rejection of heretics makes the tenets of Thy Church and sound doctrine to stand out more clearly. For there must also be heresies, that the approved may be made manifest among the weak.

But having then read those books of the Platonists, and thence been taught to search for incorporeal truth, I saw Thy invisible things, understood by those things which are made; and though cast back, I perceived what that was which through the darkness of my mind I was hindered from contemplating, being assured "That Thou wert, and wert infinite, and yet not diffused in space, finite or infinite; and that Thou truly art Who art the same ever, in no part nor motion varying; and that all other things are from Thee, on this most sure ground alone, that they are." Of these things I was assured, yet too unsure to enjoy Thee. I prated as one well skilled; but had I not sought Thy way in Christ our Saviour, I had proved to be, not skilled, but killed. For now I had begun to wish to seem wise, being filled with mine own punishment, yet I did not mourn, but rather scorn, puffed up with knowledge. For where was that charity building upon the foundation of humility, which is Christ Jesus? or when should these books teach me it? Upon these, I believe, Thou therefore willedst that I should fall, before I studied Thy Scriptures, that it might be imprinted on my memory how I was affected by them; and that afterwards when my spirits were tamed through Thy books, and my wounds touched by Thy healing fingers, I might discern and distinguish between presumption and confession; between those who saw whither they were to go, yet saw not the way, and the way that leadeth not to behold only but to dwell in the beatific country. For had I first been formed in Thy Holy Scriptures, and hadst Thou in the familiar use of them grown sweet unto me, and had I then fallen upon those other volumes, they might perhaps have withdrawn me from the solid ground of piety, or, had I continued in that healthful frame which I had thence imbibed, I might have thought that it might have been obtained by the study of those books alone.

Most eagerly then did I seize that venerable writing of Thy Spirit; and chiefly the Apostle Paul. Whereupon those difficulties vanished away, wherein he once seemed to me to contradict himself, and the text of his discourse not to agree with the testimonies of the Law and the Prophets. And the face of that pure word appeared to me one and the same; and I learned to rejoice with trembling. So I began; and whatsoever truth I had read in those other books, I found here amid the praise of Thy Grace; that whoso sees, may not so glory as if he had not received, not only what he sees, but also that he sees (for what hath he, which he hath not received?), and that he may be not only admonished to behold Thee, who art ever the same, but also healed, to hold Thee; and that he who cannot see afar off, may yet walk on the way, whereby he may arrive, and behold, and hold Thee. For, though a man be delighted with the law of God after the inner man, what shall he do with that other law in his members which warreth against the law of his mind, and bringeth him into captivity to the law of sin which is in his members? For, Thou art righteous, O Lord, but we have sinned and committed iniquity, and have done wickedly, and Thy hand is grown heavy upon us, and we are justly delivered over unto that ancient sinner, the king of death; because he persuaded our will to be like his will whereby he abode not in Thy truth. What shall wretched man do? who shall deliver him from the body of his death, but only Thy Grace, through Jesus Christ our Lord, whom Thou hast begotten co-eternal, and formedst in the beginning of Thy ways, in whom the prince of this world found nothing worthy of death, yet killed he Him; and the handwriting, which was contrary to us, was blotted out? This those writings contain not. Those pages present not the image of this piety, the tears of confession, Thy sacrifice, a troubled spirit, a broken and a contrite heart, the salvation of the people, the Bridal City, the earnest of the Holy Ghost, the Cup of our Redemption. No man sings there, Shall not my soul be submitted unto God? for of Him cometh my salvation. For He is my God and my salvation, my guardian, I shall no more be moved. No one there hears Him call, Come unto Me, all ye that labour. They scorn to learn of Him, because He is meek and lowly in heart; for these things hast Thou hid from the wise and prudent, and hast revealed them unto babes. For it is one thing, from the mountain's shaggy top to see the land of peace, and to find no way thither; and in vain to essay through ways unpassable, opposed and beset by fugitives and deserters, under their captain the lion and the dragon: and another to keep on the way that leads thither, guarded by the host of the heavenly General; where they spoil not who have deserted the heavenly army; for they avoid it, as very torment. These things did wonderfully sink into my bowels, when I read that least of Thy Apostles, and had meditated upon Thy works, and trembled exceedingly.

Book Eight

O my God, let me, with thanksgiving, remember, and confess unto Thee Thy mercies on me. Let my bones be bedewed with Thy love, and let them say unto Thee, Who is like unto Thee, O Lord? Thou hast broken my bonds in sunder, I will offer unto Thee the sacrifice of thanksgiving. And how Thou hast broken them, I will declare; and all who worship Thee, when they hear this, shall say, "Blessed be the Lord, in heaven and in earth, great and wonderful is his name." Thy words had stuck fast in my heart, and I was hedged round about on all sides by Thee. Of Thy eternal life I was now certain, though I saw it in a figure and as through a glass. Yet I had ceased to doubt that there was an incorruptible substance, whence was all other substance; nor did I now desire to be more certain of Thee, but more steadfast in Thee. But for my temporal life, all was wavering, and my heart had to be purged from the old leaven. The Way, the Saviour Himself, well pleased me, but as yet I shrunk from going through its straitness. And Thou didst put into my mind, and it seemed good in my eyes, to go to Simplicianus, who seemed to me a good servant of Thine; and Thy grace shone in him. I had heard also that from his very youth he had lived most devoted unto Thee. Now he was grown into years; and by reason of so great age spent in such zealous following of Thy ways, he seemed to me likely to have learned much experience; and so he had. Out of which store I wished that he would tell me (setting before him my anxieties) which were the fittest way for one in my case to walk in Thy paths.

For, I saw the church full; and one went this way, and another that way. But I was displeased that I led a secular life; yea now that my desires no longer inflamed me, as of old, with hopes of honour and profit, a very grievous burden it was to undergo so heavy a bondage.

For, in comparison of Thy sweetness, and the beauty of Thy house which I loved, those things delighted me no longer. But still I was enthralled with the love of woman; nor did the Apostle forbid me to marry, although he advised me to something better, chiefly wishing that all men were as himself was. But I being weak, chose the more indulgent place; and because of this alone, was tossed up and down in all beside, faint and wasted with withering cares, because in other matters I was constrained against my will to conform myself to a married life, to which I was given up and enthralled. I had heard from the mouth of the Truth, that there were some eunuchs which had made themselves eunuchs for the kingdom of heaven's sake: but, saith He, let him who can receive it, receive it. Surely vain are all men who are ignorant of God, and could not out of the good things which are seen, find out Him who is good. But I was no longer in that vanity; I had surmounted it; and by the common witness of all Thy creatures had found Thee our Creator, and Thy Word, God with Thee, and together with Thee one God, by whom Thou createdst all things. There is yet another kind of ungodly, who knowing God, glorified Him not as God, neither were thankful. Into this also had I fallen, but Thy right hand upheld me, and took me thence, and Thou placedst me where I might recover. For Thou hast said unto man, Behold, the fear of the Lord is wisdom, and, Desire not to seem wise; because they who affirmed themselves to be wise, became fools. But I had now found the goodly pearl, which, selling all that I had, I ought to have bought, and I hesitated.

To Simplicianus then I went, the father of Ambrose (a Bishop now) in receiving Thy grace, and whom Ambrose truly loved as a father. To him I related the mazes of my wanderings. But when I mentioned that I had read certain books of the Platonists, which Victorinus, sometime Rhetoric Professor of Rome (who had died a Christian, as I had heard), had translated into Latin, he testified his joy that I had not fallen upon the writings of other philosophers, full of fallacies and deceits, after the rudiments of this world, whereas the Platonists many ways led to the belief in God and His Word. Then to exhort me to the humility of Christ, hidden from the wise, and revealed to little ones, he spoke of Victorinus himself, whom while at Rome he had most intimately known: and of him he related what I will not conceal. For it contains great praise of Thy grace, to be confessed unto Thee, how that aged man, most learned and skilled in the liberal sciences, and who had read, and weighed so many works of the philosophers; the instructor of so many noble Senators, who also, as a monument of his excellent discharge of his office, had (which men of this world esteem a high honour) both deserved and obtained a statue in the Roman Forum; he, to that age a worshiper of idols, and a partaker of the sacrilegious rites, to which almost all the nobility of Rome were given up, and had inspired the people with the love of

> Anubis, barking Deity, and all
> The monster Gods of every kind, who fought
> 'Gainst Neptune, Venus, and Minerva:

whom Rome once conquered, now adored, all which the aged Victorinus had with thundering eloquence so many years defended; he now blushed not to be the child of Thy Christ, and the new-born babe of Thy fountain; submitting his neck to the yoke of humility, and subduing his forehead to the reproach of the Cross. O Lord, Lord, Which hast bowed the heavens and come down, touched the mountains and they did smoke, by what means didst Thou convey Thyself into that breast? He used to read (as Simplicianus said) the holy Scripture, most studiously sought and searched into all the Christian writings, and said to Simplicianus (not openly, but privately and as a friend), "Understand that I am already a Christian." Whereto he answered, "I will not believe it, nor will I rank you among Christians, unless I see you in the Church of Christ." The other, in banter, replied, "Do walls then make Christians?" And this he often said, that he was already a Christian; and Simplicianus as often made the same answer, and the conceit of the "walls" was by the other as often renewed. For he feared to offend his friends, proud daemon-worshipers, from the height of whose Babylonian dignity, as from cedars of Libanus, which the Lord had not yet broken down, he supposed the weight of enmity would fall upon him. But after that by reading and earnest thought he had gathered firmness, and feared to be denied by Christ before the holy angels, should he now be afraid to confess Him before men, and appeared to himself guilty of a heavy offence, in being ashamed of the Sacraments of the humility of Thy Word, and not being ashamed of the sacrilegious rites of those proud daemons, whose pride he had imitated and their rites adopted, he became bold-faced against vanity, and shame-faced towards the truth, and suddenly and unexpectedly said to Simplicianus (as himself told me), "Go we to the Church; I wish to be made a Christian." But he, not containing himself for joy, went with him. And having been admitted to the first Sacrament and become a Catechumen, not long after he further gave in his name, that he might be regenerated by baptism, Rome wondering, the Church rejoicing. The proud saw, and were wroth; they gnashed with their teeth, and melted away. But the Lord God was the hope of Thy servant, and he regarded not vanities and lying madness.

To conclude, when the hour was come for making profession of his faith (which at Rome they, who are about to approach to Thy grace, deliver, from an elevated place, in the sight of all the faithful, in a set form of words committed to memory), the presbyters, he said, offered Victorinus (as was done to such as seemed likely through bashfulness to be alarmed) to make his profession more privately: but he chose rather to profess his salvation in the presence of the holy multitude. "For it was not salvation that he taught in rhetoric, and yet that he had publicly professed: how much less then ought he, when pronouncing Thy word, to dread Thy meek flock, who, when delivering his own words, had not feared a mad multitude!" When, then, he went up to make his profession, all, as they knew him, whispered his name one to another with the voice of congratulation. And who there knew him not? and there ran a low murmur through all the mouths of the rejoicing multitude, Victorinus! Victorinus! Sudden was the burst of rapture, that they saw him; suddenly were they hushed that they might hear him. He pronounced the true faith with an excellent boldness, and all wished to draw him into their very heart; yea by their love and joy they drew him thither, such were the hands wherewith they drew him.

Good God! what takes place in man, that he should more rejoice at the salvation of a soul despaired of, and freed from greater peril, than if there had always been hope of him, or the danger had been less? For so Thou also, merciful Father, dost more rejoice over one penitent than over ninety-nine just persons that need no repentance. And with much joyfulness do we hear, so often as we hear with what joy the sheep which had strayed is brought back upon the shepherd's shoulder, and the groat is restored to Thy treasury, the neighbours rejoicing with the woman who found it; and the joy of the solemn service of Thy house forceth to tears, when in Thy house it is read of Thy younger son, that he was dead, and liveth again; had been lost, and is found. For Thou rejoicest in us, and in Thy holy angels, holy through holy charity. For Thou art ever the same; for all things which abide not the same nor for ever, Thou for ever knowest in the same way.

What then takes place in the soul, when it is more delighted at finding or recovering the things it loves, than if it had ever had them? yea, and other things witness hereunto; and all things are full of witnesses, crying out, "So is it." The conquering commander triumpheth; yet had he not conquered unless he had fought; and the more peril there was in the battle, so much the more joy is there in the triumph. The storm tosses the sailors, threatens shipwreck; all wax pale at approaching death; sky and sea are calmed, and they are exceeding joyed, as having been exceeding afraid. A friend is sick, and his pulse threatens danger; all who long for his recovery are sick in mind with him. He is restored, though as yet he walks not with his former strength; yet there is such joy, as was not, when before he walked sound and strong. Yea, the very pleasures of human life men acquire by difficulties, not those only which fall upon us unlooked for, and against our wills, but even by self-chosen, and pleasure-seeking trouble. Eating and drinking have no pleasure, unless there precede the pinching of hunger and thirst. Men, given to drink, eat certain salt meats, to procure a troublesome heat, which the drink allaying, causes pleasure. It is also ordered that the affianced bride should not at once be given, lest as a husband he should hold cheap whom, as betrothed, he sighed not after.

This law holds in foul and accursed joy; this in permitted and lawful joy; this in the very purest perfection of friendship; this, in him who was dead, and lived again; had been lost and was found. Every where the greater joy is ushered in by the greater pain. What means this, O Lord my God, whereas Thou art everlastingly joy to Thyself, and some things around Thee evermore rejoice in Thee? What means this, that this portion of things thus ebbs and flows alternately displeased and reconciled? Is this their allotted measure? Is this all Thou hast assigned to them, whereas from the highest heavens to the lowest earth, from the beginning of the world to the end of ages, from the angel to the worm, from the first motion to the last, Thou settest each in its place, and realisest each in their season, every thing good after its kind? Woe is me! how high art Thou in the highest, and how deep in the deepest! and Thou never departest, and we scarcely return to Thee.

Up, Lord, and do; stir us up, and recall us; kindle and draw us; inflame, grow sweet unto us, let us now love, let us run. Do not many, out of a deeper hell of blindness than Victorinus, return to Thee, approach, and are enlightened, receiving that Light, which they who receive, receive power from Thee to become Thy sons? But if they be less known to the nations, even they that know them, joy less for them. For when many joy together, each also has more exuberant joy for that they are kindled and inflamed one by the other. Again, because those known to many, influence the more towards salvation, and lead the way with many to follow. And therefore do they also who preceded them much rejoice in them, because they rejoice not in them alone. For far be it, that in Thy tabernacle the persons of the rich should be accepted before the poor, or the noble before the ignoble; seeing rather Thou hast chosen the weak things of the world to confound the strong; and the base things of this world, and the things despised hast Thou chosen, and those things which are not, that Thou mightest bring to naught things that are. And yet even that least of Thy apostles, by whose tongue Thou soundedst forth these words, when through his warfare, Paulus the Proconsul, his pride conquered, was made to pass under the easy yoke of Thy Christ, and became a provincial of the great King; he also for his former name Saul, was pleased to be called Paul, in testimony of so great a victory. For the enemy is more overcome in one, of whom he hath more hold; by whom he hath hold of more. But the proud he hath more hold of, through their nobility; and by them, of more through their authority. By how much the more welcome then the heart of Victorinus was esteemed, which the devil had held as an impregnable possession, the tongue of Victorinus, with which mighty and keen weapon he had slain many; so much the more abundantly ought Thy sons to rejoice, for that our King hath bound the strong man, and they saw his vessels taken from him and cleansed, and made meet for Thy honour; and become serviceable for the Lord, unto every good work.

But when that man of Thine, Simplicianus, related to me this of Victorinus, I was on fire to imitate him; for for this very end had he related it. But when he had subjoined also, how in the days of the Emperor Julian a law was made, whereby Christians were forbidden to teach the liberal sciences or oratory; and how he, obeying this law, chose rather to give over the wordy school than Thy Word, by which Thou makest eloquent the tongues of the dumb; he seemed to me not more resolute than blessed, in having thus found opportunity to wait on Thee only. Which thing I was sighing for, bound as I was, not with another's irons, but by my own iron will. My will the enemy held, and thence had made a chain for me, and bound me. For of a forward will, was a lust made; and a lust served, became custom; and custom not resisted, became necessity. By which links, as it were, joined together (whence I called it a chain) a hard bondage held me enthralled. But that new will which had begun to be in me, freely to serve Thee, and to wish to enjoy Thee, O God, the only assured pleasantness, was not yet able to overcome my former willfulness, strengthened by age. Thus did my two wills, one new, and the other old, one carnal, the other spiritual, struggle within me; and by their discord, undid my soul.

Thus, I understood, by my own experience, what I had read, how the flesh lusteth against the spirit and the spirit against the flesh. Myself verily either way; yet more myself, in that which I approved in myself, than in that which in myself I disapproved. For in this last, it was now for the more part not myself, because in much I rather endured against my will, than acted willingly. And yet it was through me that custom had obtained this power of warring against me, because I had come willingly, whither I willed not. And who has any right to speak against it, if just punishment follow the sinner? Nor had I now any longer my former plea, that I therefore as yet hesitated to be above the world and serve Thee, for that the truth was not altogether ascertained to me; for now it too was. But I still under service to the earth, refused to fight under Thy banner, and feared as much to be freed of all encumbrances, as we should fear to be encumbered with it. Thus with the baggage of this present world was I held down pleasantly, as in sleep: and the thoughts wherein I meditated on Thee were like the efforts of such as would awake, who yet overcome with a heavy drowsiness, are again drenched therein. And as no one would sleep for ever, and in all men's sober judgment waking is better, yet a man for the most part, feeling a heavy lethargy in all his limbs, defers to shake off sleep, and though half displeased, yet, even after it is time to rise, with pleasure yields to it, so was I assured that much better were it for me to give myself up to Thy charity, than to give myself over to mine own cupidity; but though the former course satisfied me and gained the mastery, the latter pleased me and held me mastered. Nor had I any thing to answer Thee calling to me, Awake, thou that sleepest, and arise from the dead, and Christ shall give thee light. And when Thou didst on all sides show me that what Thou saidst was true, I, convicted by the truth, had nothing at all to answer, but only those dull and drowsy words, "Anon, anon," "presently," "leave me but a little." But "presently, presently," had no present, and my "little while" went on for a long while; in vain I delighted in Thy law according to the inner man, when another law in my members rebelled against the law of my mind, and led me captive under the law of sin which was in my members. For the law of sin is the violence of custom, whereby the mind is drawn and holden, even against its will; but deservedly, for that it willingly fell into it. Who then should deliver me thus wretched from the body of this death, but Thy grace only, through Jesus Christ our Lord?

And how Thou didst deliver me out of the bonds of desire, wherewith I was bound most straitly to carnal concupiscence, and out of the drudgery of worldly things, I will now declare, and confess unto Thy name, O Lord, my helper and my redeemer. Amid increasing anxiety, I was doing my wonted business, and daily sighing unto Thee. I attended Thy Church, whenever free from the business under the burden of which I groaned. Alypius was with me, now after the third sitting released from his law business, and awaiting to whom to sell his counsel, as I sold the skill of speaking, if indeed teaching can impart it. Nebridius had now, in consideration of our friendship, consented to teach under Verecundus, a citizen and a grammarian of Milan, and a very intimate friend of us all; who urgently desired, and by the right of friendship challenged from our company, such faithful aid as he greatly needed. Nebridius then was not drawn to this by any desire of advantage (for he might have made much more of his learning had he so willed), but as a most kind and gentle friend, he would not be wanting to a good office, and slight our request. But he acted herein very discreetly, shunning to become known to personages great according to this world, avoiding the distraction of mind thence ensuing, and desiring to have it free and at leisure, as many hours as might be, to seek, or read, or hear something concerning wisdom.

Upon a day then, Nebridius being absent (I recollect not why), lo, there came to see me and Alypius, one Pontitianus, our countryman so far as being an African, in high office in the Emperor's court. What he would with us, I know not, but we sat down to converse, and it happened that upon a table for some game, before us, he observed a book, took, opened it, and contrary to his expectation, found it the Apostle Paul; for he thought it some of those books which I was wearing myself in teaching. Whereat smiling, and looking at me, he expressed his joy and wonder that he had on a sudden found this book, and this only before my eyes. For he was a Christian, and baptised, and often bowed himself before Thee our God in the Church, in frequent and continued prayers. When then I had told him that I bestowed very great pains upon those Scriptures, a conversation arose (suggested by his account) on Antony the Egyptian monk: whose name was in high reputation among Thy servants, though to that hour unknown to us. Which when he discovered, he dwelt the more upon that subject, informing and wondering at our ignorance of one so eminent. But we stood amazed, hearing Thy wonderful works most fully attested, in times so recent, and almost in our own, wrought in the true Faith and Church Catholic. We all wondered; we, that they were so great, and he, that they had not reached us.

Thence his discourse turned to the flocks in the monasteries, and their holy ways, a sweet-smelling savour unto Thee, and the fruitful deserts of the wilderness, whereof we knew nothing. And there was a monastery at Milan, full of good brethren, without the city walls, under the fostering care of Ambrose, and we knew it not. He went on with his discourse, and we listened in intent silence. He told us then how one afternoon at Triers, when the Emperor was taken up with the Circensian games, he and three others, his companions, went out to walk in gardens near the city walls, and there as they happened to walk in pairs, one went apart with him, and the other two wandered by themselves; and these, in their wanderings, lighted upon a certain cottage, inhabited by certain of Thy servants, poor in spirit, of whom is the kingdom of heaven, and there they found a little book containing the life of Antony. This one of them began to read, admire, and kindle at it; and as he read, to meditate on taking up such a life, and giving over his secular service to serve Thee. And these two were of those whom they style agents for the public affairs. Then suddenly, filled with a holy love, and a sober shame, in anger with himself cast his eyes upon his friend, saying, "Tell me, I pray thee, what would we attain by all these labours of ours? what aim we at? what serve we for? Can our hopes in court rise higher than to be the Emperor's favourites? and in this, what is there not brittle, and full of perils? and by how many perils arrive we at a greater peril? and when arrive we thither? But a friend of God, if I wish it, I become now at once." So spake he. And in pain with the travail of a new life, he turned his eyes again upon the book, and read on, and was changed inwardly, where Thou sawest, and his mind was stripped of the world, as soon appeared. For as he read, and rolled up and down the waves of his heart, he stormed at himself a while, then discerned, and determined on a better course; and now being Thine, said to his friend, "Now have I broken loose from those our hopes, and am resolved to serve God; and this, from this hour, in this place, I begin upon. If thou likest not to imitate me, oppose not." The other answered, he would cleave to him, to partake so glorious a reward, so glorious a service. Thus both being now Thine, were building the tower at the necessary cost, the forsaking all that they had, and following Thee. Then Pontitianus and the other with him, that had walked in other parts of the garden, came in search of them to the same place; and finding them, reminded them to return, for the day was now far spent. But they relating their resolution and purpose, and how that will was begun and settled in them, begged them, if they would not join, not to molest them. But the others, though nothing altered from their former selves, did yet bewail themselves (as he affirmed), and piously congratulated them, recommending themselves to their prayers; and so, with hearts lingering on the earth, went away to the palace. But the other two, fixing their heart on heaven, remained in the cottage. And both had affianced brides, who when they heard hereof, also dedicated their virginity unto God.

Such was the story of Pontitianus; but Thou, O Lord, while he was speaking, didst turn me round towards myself, taking me from behind my back where I had placed me, unwilling to observe myself; and setting me before my face, that I might see how foul I was, how crooked and defiled, bespotted and ulcerous. And I beheld and stood aghast; and whither to flee from myself I found not. And if I sought to turn mine eye from off myself, he went on with his relation, and Thou again didst set me over against myself, and thrustedst me before my eyes, that I might find out mine iniquity, and hate it. I had known it, but made as though I saw it not, winked at it, and forgot it.

But now, the more ardently I loved those whose healthful affections I heard of, that they had resigned themselves wholly to Thee to be cured, the more did I abhor myself, when compared with them. For many of my years (some twelve) had now run out with me since my nineteenth, when, upon the reading of Cicero's Hortensius, I was stirred to an earnest love of wisdom; and still I was deferring to reject mere earthly felicity, and give myself to search out that, whereof not the finding only, but the very search, was to be preferred to the treasures and kingdoms of the world, though already found, and to the pleasures of the body, though spread around me at my will. But I wretched, most wretched, in the very commencement of my early youth, had begged chastity of Thee, and said, "Give me chastity and continency, only not yet." For I feared lest Thou shouldest hear me soon, and soon cure me of the disease of concupiscence, which I wished to have satisfied, rather than extinguished. And I had wandered through crooked ways in a sacrilegious superstition, not indeed assured thereof, but as preferring it to the others which I did not seek religiously, but opposed maliciously.

And I had thought that I therefore deferred from day to day to reject the hopes of this world, and follow Thee only, because there did not appear aught certain, whither to direct my course. And now was the day come wherein I was to be laid bare to myself, and my conscience was to upbraid me. "Where art thou now, my tongue? Thou saidst that for an uncertain truth thou likedst not to cast off the baggage of vanity; now, it is certain, and yet that burden still oppresseth thee, while they who neither have so worn themselves out with seeking it, nor for often years and more have been thinking thereon, have had their shoulders lightened, and received wings to fly away." Thus was I gnawed within, and exceedingly confounded with a horrible shame, while Pontitianus was so speaking. And he having brought to a close his tale and the business he came for, went his way; and I into myself. What said I not against myself? with what scourges of condemnation lashed I not my soul, that it might follow me, striving to go after Thee! Yet it drew back; refused, but excused not itself. All arguments were spent and confuted; there remained a mute shrinking; and she feared, as she would death, to be restrained from the flux of that custom, whereby she was wasting to death.

Then in this great contention of my inward dwelling, which I had strongly raised against my soul, in the chamber of my heart, troubled in mind and countenance, I turned upon Alypius. "What ails us?" I exclaim: "what is it? what heardest thou? The unlearned start up and take heaven by force, and we with our learning, and without heart, lo, where we wallow in flesh and blood! Are we ashamed to follow, because others are gone before, and not ashamed not even to follow?" Some such words I uttered, and my fever of mind tore me away from him, while he, gazing on me in astonishment, kept silence. For it was not my wonted tone; and my forehead, cheeks, eyes, colour, tone of voice, spake my mind more than the words I uttered. A little garden there was to our lodging, which we had the use of, as of the whole house; for the master of the house, our host, was not living there. Thither had the tumult of my breast hurried me, where no man might hinder the hot contention wherein I had engaged with myself, until it should end as Thou knewest, I knew not. Only I was healthfully distracted and dying, to live; knowing what evil thing I was, and not knowing what good thing I was shortly to become. I retired then into the garden, and Alypius, on my steps. For his presence did not lessen my privacy; or how could he forsake me so disturbed? We sate down as far removed as might be from the house. I was troubled in spirit, most vehemently indignant that I entered not into Thy will and covenant, O my God, which all my bones cried out unto me to enter, and praised it to the skies. And therein we enter not by ships, or chariots, or feet, no, move not so far as I had come from the house to that place where we were sitting. For, not to go only, but to go in thither was nothing else but to will to go, but to will resolutely and thoroughly; not to turn and toss, this way and that, a maimed and half-divided will, struggling, with one part sinking as another rose.

Lastly, in the very fever of my irresoluteness, I made with my body many such motions as men sometimes would, but cannot, if either they have not the limbs, or these be bound with bands, weakened with infirmity, or any other way hindered. Thus, if I tore my hair, beat my forehead, if locking my fingers I clasped my knee; I willed, I did it. But I might have willed, and not done it; if the power of motion in my limbs had not obeyed. So many things then I did, when "to will" was not in itself "to be able"; and I did not what both I longed incomparably more to do, and which soon after, when I should will, I should be able to do; because soon after, when I should will, I should will thoroughly. For in these things the ability was one with the will, and to will was to do; and yet was it not done: and more easily did my body obey the weakest willing of my soul, in moving its limbs at its nod, than the soul obeyed itself to accomplish in the will alone this its momentous will.

Whence is this monstrousness? and to what end? Let Thy mercy gleam that I may ask, if so be the secret penalties of men, and those darkest pangs of the sons of Adam, may perhaps answer me. Whence is this monstrousness? and to what end? The mind commands the body, and it obeys instantly; the mind commands itself, and is resisted. The mind commands the hand to be moved; and such readiness is there, that command is scarce distinct from obedience. Yet the mind is mind, the hand is body. The mind commands the mind, its own self, to will, and yet it doth not. Whence this monstrousness? and to what end? It commands itself, I say, to will, and would not command, unless it willed, and what it commands is not done. But it willeth not entirely: therefore doth it not command entirely. For so far forth it commandeth, as it willeth: and, so far forth is the thing commanded, not done, as it willeth not. For the will commandeth that there be a will; not another, but itself. But it doth not command entirely, therefore what it commandeth, is not. For were the will entire, it would not even command it to be, because it would already be. It is therefore no monstrousness partly to will, partly to nill, but a disease of the mind, that it doth not wholly rise, by truth upborne, borne down by custom. And therefore are there two wills, for that one of them is not entire: and what the one lacketh, the other hath.

Let them perish from Thy presence, O God, as perish vain talkers and seducers of the soul: who observing that in deliberating there were two wills, affirm that there are two minds in us of two kinds, one good, the other evil. Themselves are truly evil, when they hold these evil things; and themselves shall become good when they hold the truth and assent unto the truth, that Thy Apostle may say to them, Ye were sometimes darkness, but now light in the Lord. But they, wishing to be light, not in the Lord, but in themselves, imagining the nature of the soul to be that which God is, are made more gross darkness through a dreadful arrogancy; for that they went back farther from Thee, the true Light that enlightened every man that cometh into the world. Take heed what you say, and blush for shame: draw near unto Him and be enlightened, and your faces shall not be ashamed. Myself when I was deliberating upon serving the Lord my God now, as I had long purposed, it was I who willed, I who nilled, I, I myself. I neither willed entirely, nor nilled entirely. Therefore was I at strife with myself, and rent asunder by myself. And this rent befell me against my will, and yet indicated, not the presence of another mind, but the punishment of my own. Therefore it was no more I that wrought it, but sin that dwelt in me; the punishment of a sin more freely committed, in that I was a son of Adam.

For if there be so many contrary natures as there be conflicting wills, there shall now be not two only, but many. If a man deliberate whether he should go to their conventicle or to the theatre, these Manichees cry out, Behold, here are two natures: one good, draws this way; another bad, draws back that way. For whence else is this hesitation between conflicting wills? But I say that both be bad: that which draws to them, as that which draws back to the theatre. But they believe not that will to be other than good, which draws to them. What then if one of us should deliberate, and amid the strife of his two wills be in a strait, whether he should go to the theatre or to our church? would not these Manichees also be in a strait what to answer? For either they must confess (which they fain would not) that the will which leads to our church is good, as well as theirs, who have received and are held by the mysteries of theirs: or they must suppose two evil natures, and two evil souls conflicting in one man, and it will not be true, which they say, that there is one good and another bad; or they must be converted to the truth, and no more deny that where one deliberates, one soul fluctuates between contrary wills.

Let them no more say then, when they perceive two conflicting wills in one man, that the conflict is between two contrary souls, of two contrary substances, from two contrary principles, one good, and the other bad. For Thou, O true God, dost disprove, check, and convict them; as when, both wills being bad, one deliberates whether he should kill a man by poison or by the sword; whether he should seize this or that estate of another's, when he cannot both; whether he should purchase pleasure by luxury, or keep his money by covetousness; whether he go to the circus or the theatre, if both be open on one day; or thirdly, to rob another's house, if he have the opportunity; or, fourthly, to commit adultery, if at the same time he have the means thereof also; all these meeting together in the same juncture of time, and all being equally desired, which cannot at one time be acted: for they rend the mind amid four, or even (amid the vast variety of things desired) more, conflicting wills, nor do they yet allege that there are so many divers substances. So also in wills which are good. For I ask them, is it good to take pleasure in reading the Apostle? or good to take pleasure in a sober Psalm? or good to discourse on the Gospel? They will answer to each, "it is good." What then if all give equal pleasure, and all at once? Do not divers wills distract the mind, while he deliberates which he should rather choose? yet are they all good, and are at variance till one be chosen, whither the one entire will may be borne, which before was divided into many. Thus also, when, above, eternity delights us, and the pleasure of temporal good holds us down below, it is the same soul which willeth not this or that with an entire will; and therefore is rent asunder with grievous perplexities, while out of truth it sets this first, but out of habit sets not that aside.

Thus soul-sick was I, and tormented, accusing myself much more severely than my wont, rolling and turning me in my chain, till that were wholly broken, whereby I now was but just, but still was, held. And Thou, O Lord, pressedst upon me in my inward parts by a severe mercy, redoubling the lashes of fear and shame, lest I should again give way, and not bursting that same slight remaining tie, it should recover strength, and bind me the faster. For I said with myself, "Be it done now, be it done now." And as I spake, I all but enacted it: I all but did it, and did it not: yet sunk not back to my former state, but kept my stand hard by, and took breath. And I essayed again, and wanted somewhat less of it, and somewhat less, and all but touched, and laid hold of it; and yet came not at it, nor touched nor laid hold of it; hesitating to die to death and to live to life: and the worse whereto I was inured, prevailed more with me than the better whereto I was unused: and the very moment wherein I was to become other than I was, the nearer it approached me, the greater horror did it strike into me; yet did it not strike me back, nor turned me away, but held me in suspense.

The very toys of toys, and vanities of vanities, my ancient mistresses, still held me; they plucked my fleshy garment, and whispered softly, "Dost thou cast us off? and from that moment shall we no more be with thee for ever? and from that moment shall not this or that be lawful for thee for ever?" And what was it which they suggested in that I said, "this or that," what did they suggest, O my God? Let Thy mercy turn it away from the soul of Thy servant. What defilements did they suggest! what shame! And now I much less than half heard them, and not openly showing themselves and contradicting me, but muttering as it were behind my back, and privily plucking me, as I was departing, but to look back on them. Yet they did retard me, so that I hesitated to burst and shake myself free from them, and to spring over whither I was called; a violent habit saying to me, "Thinkest thou, thou canst live without them?"

But now it spake very faintly. For on that side whither I had set my face, and whither I trembled to go, there appeared unto me the chaste dignity of Continency, serene, yet not relaxedly, gay, honestly alluring me to come and doubt not; and stretching forth to receive and embrace me, her holy hands full of multitudes of good examples: there were so many young men and maidens here, a multitude of youth and every age, grave widows and aged virgins; and Continence herself in all, not barren, but a fruitful mother of children of joys, by Thee her Husband, O Lord. And she smiled on me with a persuasive mockery, as would she say, "Canst not thou what these youths, what these maidens can? or can they either in themselves, and not rather in the Lord their God? The Lord their God gave me unto them. Why standest thou in thyself, and so standest not? cast thyself upon Him, fear not He will not withdraw Himself that thou shouldest fall; cast thyself fearlessly upon Him, He will receive, and will heal thee." And I blushed exceedingly, for that I yet heard the muttering of those toys, and hung in suspense. And she again seemed to say, "Stop thine ears against those thy unclean members on the earth, that they may be mortified. They tell thee of delights, but not as doth the law of the Lord thy God." This controversy in my heart was self against self only. But Alypius sitting close by my side, in silence waited the issue of my unwonted emotion.

But when a deep consideration had from the secret bottom of my soul drawn together and heaped up all my misery in the sight of my heart; there arose a mighty storm, bringing a mighty shower of tears. Which that I might pour forth wholly, in its natural expressions, I rose from Alypius: solitude was suggested to me as fitter for the business of weeping; so I retired so far that even his presence could not be a burden to me. Thus was it then with me, and he perceived something of it; for something I suppose I had spoken, wherein the tones of my voice appeared choked with weeping, and so had risen up. He then remained where we were sitting, most extremely astonished. I cast myself down I know not how, under a certain fig tree, giving full vent to my tears; and the floods of mine eyes gushed out an acceptable sacrifice to Thee. And, not indeed in these words, yet to this purpose, spake I much unto Thee: and Thou, O Lord, how long? how long, Lord, wilt Thou be angry for ever? Remember not our former iniquities, for I felt that I was held by them. I sent up these sorrowful words: How long, how long, "to-morrow, and tomorrow?" Why not now? why not is there this hour an end to my uncleanness?

So was I speaking and weeping in the most bitter contrition of my heart, when, lo! I heard from a neighbouring house a voice, as of boy or girl, I know not, chanting, and oft repeating, "Take up and read; Take up and read." Instantly, my countenance altered, I began to think most intently whether children were wont in any kind of play to sing such words: nor could I remember ever to have heard the like. So checking the torrent of my tears, I arose; interpreting it to be no other than a command from God to open the book, and read the first chapter I should find. For I had heard of Antony, that coming in during the reading of the Gospel, he received the admonition, as if what was being read was spoken to him: Go, sell all that thou hast, and give to the poor, and thou shalt have treasure in heaven, and come and follow me: and by such oracle he was forthwith converted unto Thee. Eagerly then I returned to the place where Alypius was sitting; for there had I laid the volume of the Apostle when I arose thence. I seized, opened, and in silence read that section on which my eyes first fell: Not in rioting and drunkenness, not in chambering and wantonness, not in strife and envying; but put ye on the Lord Jesus Christ, and make not provision for the flesh, in concupiscence. No further would I read; nor needed I: for instantly at the end of this sentence, by a light as it were of serenity infused into my heart, all the darkness of doubt vanished away.

Then putting my finger between, or some other mark, I shut the volume, and with a calmed countenance made it known to Alypius. And what was wrought in him, which I knew not, he thus showed me. He asked to see what I had read: I showed him; and he looked even further than I had read, and I knew not what followed. This followed, him that is weak in the faith, receive; which he applied to himself, and disclosed to me. And by this admonition was he strengthened; and by a good resolution and purpose, and most corresponding to his character, wherein he did always very far differ from me, for the better, without any turbulent delay he joined me. Thence we go in to my mother; we tell her; she rejoiceth: we relate in order how it took place; she leaps for joy, and triumpheth, and blesseth Thee, Who are able to do above that which we ask or think; for she perceived that Thou hadst given her more for me, than she was wont to beg by her pitiful and most sorrowful groanings. For thou convertedst me unto Thyself, so that I sought neither wife, nor any hope of this world, standing in that rule of faith, where Thou hadst showed me unto her in a vision, so many years before. And Thou didst convert her mourning into joy, much more plentiful than she had desired, and in a much more precious and purer way than she erst required, by having grandchildren of my body.

Book Nine

O Lord, I am Thy servant; I am Thy servant, and the son of Thy handmaid: Thou hast broken my bonds in sunder. I will offer to Thee the sacrifice of praise. Let my heart and my tongue praise Thee; yea, let all my bones say, O Lord, who is like unto Thee? Let them say, and answer Thou me, and say unto my soul, I am thy salvation. Who am I, and what am I? What evil have not been either my deeds, or if not my deeds, my words, or if not my words, my will? But Thou, O Lord, are good and merciful, and Thy right hand had respect unto the depth of my death, and from the bottom of my heart emptied that abyss of corruption. And this Thy whole gift was, to nill what I willed, and to will what Thou willedst. But where through all those years, and out of what low and deep recess was my free-will called forth in a moment, whereby to submit my neck to Thy easy yoke, and my shoulders unto Thy light burden, O Christ Jesus, my Helper and my Redeemer? How sweet did it at once become to me, to want the sweetnesses of those toys! and what I feared to be parted from, was now a joy to part with. For Thou didst cast them forth from me, Thou true and highest sweetness. Thou castest them forth, and for them enteredst in Thyself, sweeter than all pleasure, though not to flesh and blood; brighter than all light, but more hidden than all depths, higher than all honour, but not to the high in their own conceits. Now was my soul free from the biting cares of canvassing and getting, and weltering in filth, and scratching off the itch of lust. And my infant tongue spake freely to Thee, my brightness, and my riches, and my health, the Lord my God.

And I resolved in Thy sight, not tumultuously to tear, but gently to withdraw, the service of my tongue from the marts of lip-labour: that the young, no students in Thy law, nor in Thy peace, but in lying dotages and law-skirmishes, should no longer buy at my mouth arms for their madness. And very seasonably, it now wanted but very few days unto the Vacation of the Vintage, and I resolved to endure them, then in a regular way to take my leave, and having been purchased by Thee, no more to return for sale. Our purpose then was known to Thee; but to men, other than our own friends, was it not known. For we had agreed among ourselves not to let it out abroad to any: although to us, now ascending from the valley of tears, and singing that song of degrees, Thou hadst given sharp arrows, and destroying coals against the subtle tongue, which as though advising for us, would thwart, and would out of love devour us, as it doth its meat.

Thou hadst pierced our hearts with Thy charity, and we carried Thy words as it were fixed in our entrails: and the examples of Thy servants, whom for black Thou hadst made bright, and for dead, alive, being piled together in the receptacle of our thoughts, kindled and burned up that our heavy torpor, that we should not sink down to the abyss; and they fired us so vehemently, that all the blasts of subtle tongues from gainsayers might only inflame us the more fiercely, not extinguish us. Nevertheless, because for Thy Name's sake which Thou hast hallowed throughout the earth, this our vow and purpose might also find some to commend it, it seemed like ostentation not to wait for the vacation now so near, but to quit beforehand a public profession, which was before the eyes of all; so that all looking on this act of mine, and observing how near was the time of vintage which I wished to anticipate, would talk much of me, as if I had desired to appear some great one. And what end had it served me, that people should repute and dispute upon my purpose, and that our good should be evil spoken of.

Moreover, it had at first troubled me that in this very summer my lungs began to give way, amid too great literary labour, and to breathe deeply with difficulty, and by the pain in my chest to show that they were injured, and to refuse any full or lengthened speaking; this had troubled me, for it almost constrained me of necessity to lay down that burden of teaching, or, if I could be cured and recover, at least to intermit it. But when the full wish for leisure, that I might see how that Thou art the Lord, arose, and was fixed, in me; my God, Thou knowest, I began even to rejoice that I had this secondary, and that no feigned, excuse, which might something moderate the offence taken by those who, for their sons' sake, wished me never to have the freedom of Thy sons. Full then of such joy, I endured till that interval of time were run; it may have been some twenty days, yet they were endured manfully; endured, for the covetousness which aforetime bore a part of this heavy business, had left me, and I remained alone, and had been overwhelmed, had not patience taken its place. Perchance, some of Thy servants, my brethren, may say that I sinned in this, that with a heart fully set on Thy service, I suffered myself to sit even one hour in the chair of lies. Nor would I be contentious. But hast not Thou, O most merciful Lord, pardoned and remitted this sin also, with my other most horrible and deadly sins, in the holy water?

Verecundus was worn down with care about this our blessedness, for that being held back by bonds, whereby he was most straitly bound, he saw that he should be severed from us. For himself was not yet a Christian, his wife one of the faithful; and yet hereby, more rigidly than by any other chain, was he let and hindered from the journey which we had now essayed. For he would not, he said, be a Christian on any other terms than on those he could not. However, he offered us courteously to remain at his country-house so long as we should stay there. Thou, O Lord, shalt reward him in the resurrection of the just, seeing Thou hast already given him the lot of the righteous. For although, in our absence, being now at Rome, he was seized with bodily sickness, and therein being made a Christian, and one of the faithful, he departed this life; yet hadst Thou mercy not on him only, but on us also: lest remembering the exceeding kindness of our friend towards us, yet unable to number him among Thy flock, we should be agonised with intolerable sorrow. Thanks unto Thee, our God, we are Thine: Thy suggestions and consolations tell us, Faithful in promises, Thou now requitest Verecundus for his country-house of Cassiacum, where from the fever of the world we reposed in Thee, with the eternal freshness of Thy Paradise: for that Thou hast forgiven him his sins upon earth, in that rich mountain, that mountain which yieldeth milk, Thine own mountain.

He then had at that time sorrow, but Nebridius joy. For although he also, not being yet a Christian, had fallen into the pit of that most pernicious error, believing the flesh of Thy Son to be a phantom: yet emerging thence, he believed as we did; not as yet endued with any Sacraments of Thy Church, but a most ardent searcher out of truth. Whom, not long after our conversion and regeneration by Thy Baptism, being also a faithful member of the Church Catholic, and serving Thee in perfect chastity and continence amongst his people in Africa, his whole house having through him first been made Christian, didst Thou release from the flesh; and now he lives in Abraham's bosom. Whatever that be, which is signified by that bosom, there lives my Nebridius, my sweet friend, and Thy child, O Lord, adopted of a freed man: there he liveth. For what other place is there for such a soul? There he liveth, whereof he asked much of me, a poor inexperienced man. Now lays he not his ear to my mouth, but his spiritual mouth unto Thy fountain, and drinketh as much as he can receive, wisdom in proportion to his thirst, endlessly happy. Nor do I think that he is so inebriated therewith, as to forget me; seeing Thou, Lord, Whom he drinketh, art mindful of us. So were we then, comforting Verecundus, who sorrowed, as far as friendship permitted, that our conversion was of such sort; and exhorting him to become faithful, according to his measure, namely, of a married estate; and awaiting Nebridius to follow us, which, being so near, he was all but doing: and so, lo! those days rolled by at length; for long and many they seemed, for the love I bare to the easeful liberty, that I might sing to Thee, from my inmost marrow, My heart hath said unto Thee, I have sought Thy face: Thy face, Lord, will I seek.

Now was the day come wherein I was in deed to be freed of my Rhetoric Professorship, whereof in thought I was already freed. And it was done. Thou didst rescue my tongue, whence Thou hadst before rescued my heart. And I blessed Thee, rejoicing; retiring with all mine to the villa. What I there did in writing, which was now enlisted in Thy service, though still, in this breathing-time as it were, panting from the school of pride, my books may witness, as well what I debated with others, as what with myself alone, before Thee: what with Nebridius, who was absent, my Epistles bear witness. And when shall I have time to rehearse all Thy great benefits towards us at that time, especially when hasting on to yet greater mercies? For my remembrance recalls me, and pleasant is it to me, O Lord, to confess to Thee, by what inward goads Thou tamedst me; and how Thou hast evened me, lowering the mountains and hills of my high imaginations, straightening my crookedness, and smoothing my rough ways; and how Thou also subduedst the brother of my heart, Alypius, unto the name of Thy Only Begotten, our Lord and Saviour Jesus Christ, which he would not at first vouchsafe to have inserted in our writings. For rather would he have them savour of the lofty cedars of the Schools, which the Lord hath now broken down, than of the wholesome herbs of the Church, the antidote against serpents.

Oh, in what accents spake I unto Thee, my God, when I read the Psalms of David, those faithful songs, and sounds of devotion, which allow of no swelling spirit, as yet a Catechumen, and a novice in Thy real love, resting in that villa, with Alypius a Catechumen, my mother cleaving to us, in female garb with masculine faith, with the tranquility of age, motherly love, Christian piety! Oh, what accents did I utter unto Thee in those Psalms, and how was I by them kindled towards Thee, and on fire to rehearse them, if possible, through the whole world, against the pride of mankind! And yet they are sung through the whole world, nor can any hide himself from Thy heat. With what vehement and bitter sorrow was I angered at the Manichees! and again I pitied them, for they knew not those Sacraments, those medicines, and were mad against the antidote which might have recovered them of their madness. How I would they had then been somewhere near me, and without my knowing that they were there, could have beheld my countenance, and heard my words, when I read the fourth Psalm in that time of my rest, and how that Psalm wrought upon me: When I called, the God of my righteousness heard me; in tribulation Thou enlargedst me. Have mercy upon me, O Lord, and hear my prayer. Would that what I uttered on these words, they could hear, without my knowing whether they heard, lest they should think I spake it for their sakes! Because in truth neither should I speak the same things, nor in the same way, if I perceived that they heard and saw me; nor if I spake them would they so receive them, as when I spake by and for myself before Thee, out of the natural feelings of my soul.

I trembled for fear, and again kindled with hope, and with rejoicing in Thy mercy, O Father; and all issued forth both by mine eyes and voice, when Thy good Spirit turning unto us, said, O ye sons of men, how long slow of heart? why do ye love vanity, and seek after leasing? For I had loved vanity, and sought after leasing. And Thou, O Lord, hadst already magnified Thy Holy One, raising Him from the dead, and setting Him at Thy right hand, whence from on high He should send His promise, the Comforter, the Spirit of truth. And He had already sent Him, but I knew it not; He had sent Him, because He was now magnified, rising again from the dead, and ascending into heaven. For till then, the Spirit was not yet given, because Jesus was not yet glorified. And the prophet cries out, How long, slow of heart? why do ye love vanity, and seek after leasing? Know this, that the Lord hath magnified His Holy One. He cries out, How long? He cries out, Know this: and I so long, not knowing, loved vanity, and sought after leasing: and therefore I heard and trembled, because it was spoken unto such as I remembered myself to have been. For in those phantoms which I had held for truths, was there vanity and leasing; and I spake aloud many things earnestly and forcibly, in the bitterness of my remembrance. Which would they had heard, who yet love vanity and seek after leasing! They would perchance have been troubled, and have vomited it up; and Thou wouldest hear them when they cried unto Thee; for by a true death in the flesh did He die for us, who now intercedeth unto Thee for us.

I further read, Be angry, and sin not. And how was I moved, O my God, who had now learned to be angry at myself for things past, that I might not sin in time to come! Yea, to be justly angry; for that it was not another nature of a people of darkness which sinned for me, as they say who are not angry at themselves, and treasure up wrath against the day of wrath, and of the revelation of Thy just judgment. Nor were my good things now without, nor sought with the eyes of flesh in that earthly sun; for they that would have joy from without soon become vain, and waste themselves on the things seen and temporal, and in their famished thoughts do lick their very shadows. Oh that they were wearied out with their famine, and said, Who will show us good things? And we would say, and they hear, The light of Thy countenance is sealed upon us. For we are not that light which enlighteneth every man, but we are enlightened by Thee; that having been sometimes darkness, we may be light in Thee. Oh that they could see the eternal Internal, which having tasted, I was grieved that I could not show It them, so long as they brought me their heart in their eyes roving abroad from Thee, while they said, Who will show us good things? For there, where I was angry within myself in my chamber, where I was inwardly pricked, where I had sacrificed, slaying my old man and commencing the purpose of a new life, putting my trust in Thee—there hadst Thou begun to grow sweet unto me, and hadst put gladness in my heart. And I cried out, as I read this outwardly, finding it inwardly. Nor would I be multiplied with worldly goods; wasting away time, and wasted by time; whereas I had in Thy eternal Simple Essence other corn, and wine, and oil.

And with a loud cry of my heart I cried out in the next verse, O in peace, O for The Self-same! O what said he, I will lay me down and sleep, for who shall hinder us, when cometh to pass that saying which is written, Death is swallowed up in victory? And Thou surpassingly art the Self-same, Who art not changed; and in Thee is rest which forgetteth all toil, for there is none other with Thee, nor are we to seek those many other things, which are not what Thou art: but Thou, Lord, alone hast made me dwell in hope. I read, and kindled; nor found I what to do to those deaf and dead, of whom myself had been, a pestilent person, a bitter and a blind bawler against those writings, which are honied with the honey of heaven, and lightsome with Thine own light: and I was consumed with zeal at the enemies of this Scripture.

When shall I recall all which passed in those holy-days? Yet neither have I forgotten, nor will I pass over the severity of Thy scourge, and the wonderful swiftness of Thy mercy. Thou didst then torment me with pain in my teeth; which when it had come to such height that I could not speak, it came into my heart to desire all my friends present to pray for me to Thee, the God of all manner of health. And this I wrote on wax, and gave it them to read. Presently so soon as with humble devotion we had bowed our knees, that pain went away. But what pain? or how went it away? I was affrighted, O my Lord, my God; for from infancy I had never experienced the like. And the power of Thy Nod was deeply conveyed to me, and rejoicing in faith, I praised Thy Name. And that faith suffered me not to be at ease about my past sins, which were not yet forgiven me by Thy baptism.

The vintage-vacation ended, I gave notice to the Milanese to provide their scholars with another master to sell words to them; for that I had both made choice to serve Thee, and through my difficulty of breathing and pain in my chest was not equal to the Professorship. And by letters I signified to Thy Prelate, the holy man Ambrose, my former errors and present desires, begging his advice what of Thy Scriptures I had best read, to become readier and fitter for receiving so great grace. He recommended Isaiah the Prophet: I believe, because he above the rest is a more clear foreshower of the Gospel and of the calling of the Gentiles. But I, not understanding the first lesson in him, and imagining the whole to be like it, laid it by, to be resumed when better practised in our Lord's own words.

Thence, when the time was come wherein I was to give in my name, we left the country and returned to Milan. It pleased Alypius also to be with me born again in Thee, being already clothed with the humility befitting Thy Sacraments; and a most valiant tamer of the body, so as, with unwonted venture, to wear the frozen ground of Italy with his bare feet. We joined with us the boy Adeodatus, born after the flesh, of my sin. Excellently hadst Thou made him. He was not quite fifteen, and in wit surpassed many grave and learned men. I confess unto Thee Thy gifts, O Lord my God, Creator of all, and abundantly able to reform our deformities: for I had no part in that boy, but the sin. For that we brought him up in Thy discipline, it was Thou, none else, had inspired us with it. I confess unto Thee Thy gifts. There is a book of ours entitled The Master; it is a dialogue between him and me. Thou knowest that all there ascribed to the person conversing with me were his ideas, in his sixteenth year. Much besides, and yet more admirable, I found in him. That talent struck awe into me. And who but Thou could be the workmaster of such wonders? Soon didst Thou take his life from the earth: and I now remember him without anxiety, fearing nothing for his childhood or youth, or his whole self. Him we joined with us, our contemporary in grace, to be brought up in Thy discipline: and we were baptised, and anxiety for our past life vanished from us. Nor was I sated in those days with the wondrous sweetness of considering the depth of Thy counsels concerning the salvation of mankind. How did I weep, in Thy Hymns and Canticles, touched to the quick by the voices of Thy sweet-attuned Church! The voices flowed into mine ears, and the Truth distilled into my heart, whence the affections of my devotion overflowed, and tears ran down, and happy was I therein.

Not long had the Church of Milan begun to use this kind of consolation and exhortation, the brethren zealously joining with harmony of voice and hearts. For it was a year, or not much more, that Justina, mother to the Emperor Valentinian, a child, persecuted Thy servant Ambrose, in favour of her heresy, to which she was seduced by the Arians. The devout people kept watch in the Church, ready to die with their Bishop Thy servant. There my mother Thy handmaid, bearing a chief part of those anxieties and watchings, lived for prayer. We, yet unwarmed by the heat of Thy Spirit, still were stirred up by the sight of the amazed and disquieted city. Then it was first instituted that after the manner of the Eastern Churches, Hymns and Psalms should be sung, lest the people should wax faint through the tediousness of sorrow: and from that day to this the custom is retained, divers (yea, almost all) Thy congregations, throughout other parts of the world following herein.

Then didst Thou by a vision discover to Thy forenamed Bishop where the bodies of Gervasius and Protasius the martyrs lay hid (whom Thou hadst in Thy secret treasury stored uncorrupted so many years), whence Thou mightest seasonably produce them to repress the fury of a woman, but an Empress. For when they were discovered and dug up, and with due honour translated to the Ambrosian Basilica, not only they who were vexed with unclean spirits (the devils confessing themselves) were cured, but a certain man who had for many years been blind, a citizen, and well known to the city, asking and hearing the reason of the people's confused joy, sprang forth desiring his guide to lead him thither. Led thither, he begged to be allowed to touch with his handkerchief the bier of Thy saints, whose death is precious in Thy sight. Which when he had done, and put to his eyes, they were forthwith opened. Thence did the fame spread, thence Thy praises glowed, shone; thence the mind of that enemy, though not turned to the soundness of believing, was yet turned back from her fury of persecuting. Thanks to Thee, O my God. Whence and whither hast Thou thus led my remembrance, that I should confess these things also unto Thee? which great though they be, I had passed by in forgetfulness. And yet then, when the odour of Thy ointments was so fragrant, did we not run after Thee. Therefore did I more weep among the singing of Thy Hymns, formerly sighing after Thee, and at length breathing in Thee, as far as the breath may enter into this our house of grass.

Thou that makest men to dwell of one mind in one house, didst join with us Euodius also, a young man of our own city. Who being an officer of Court, was before us converted to Thee and baptised: and quitting his secular warfare, girded himself to Thine. We were together, about to dwell together in our devout purpose. We sought where we might serve Thee most usefully, and were together returning to Africa: whitherward being as far as Ostia, my mother departed this life. Much I omit, as hastening much. Receive my confessions and thanksgivings, O my God, for innumerable things whereof I am silent. But I will not omit whatsoever my soul would bring forth concerning that Thy handmaid, who brought me forth, both in the flesh, that I might be born to this temporal light, and in heart, that I might be born to Light eternal. Not her gifts, but Thine in her, would I speak of; for neither did she make nor educate herself. Thou createdst her; nor did her father and mother know what a one should come from them. And the sceptre of Thy Christ, the discipline of Thine only Son, in a Christian house, a good member of Thy Church, educated her in Thy fear. Yet for her good discipline was she wont to commend not so much her mother's diligence, as that of a certain decrepit maid-servant, who had carried her father when a child, as little ones used to be carried at the backs of elder girls. For which reason, and for her great age, and excellent conversation, was she, in that Christian family, well respected by its heads. Whence also the charge of her master's daughters was entrusted to her, to which she gave diligent heed, restraining them earnestly, when necessary, with a holy severity, and teaching them with a grave discretion. For, except at those hours wherein they were most temporately fed at their parents' table, she would not suffer them, though parched with thirst, to drink even water; preventing an evil custom, and adding this wholesome advice: "Ye drink water now, because you have not wine in your power; but when you come to be married, and be made mistresses of cellars and cupboards, you will scorn water, but the custom of drinking will abide." By this method of instruction, and the authority she had, she refrained the greediness of childhood, and moulded their very thirst to such an excellent moderation that what they should not, that they would not.

And yet (as Thy handmaid told me her son) there had crept upon her a love of wine. For when (as the manner was) she, as though a sober maiden, was bidden by her parents to draw wine out of the hogshed, holding the vessel under the opening, before she poured the wine into the flagon, she sipped a little with the tip of her lips; for more her instinctive feelings refused. For this she did, not out of any desire of drink, but out of the exuberance of youth, whereby it boils over in mirthful freaks, which in youthful spirits are wont to be kept under by the gravity of their elders. And thus by adding to that little, daily littles (for whoso despiseth little things shall fall by little and little), she had fallen into such a habit as greedily to drink off her little cup brim-full almost of wine. Where was then that discreet old woman, and that her earnest countermanding? Would aught avail against a secret disease, if Thy healing hand, O Lord, watched not over us? Father, mother, and governors absent, Thou present, who createdst, who callest, who also by those set over us, workest something towards the salvation of our souls, what didst Thou then, O my God? how didst Thou cure her? how heal her? didst Thou not out of another soul bring forth a hard and a sharp taunt, like a lancet out of Thy secret store, and with one touch remove all that foul stuff? For a maid-servant with whom she used to go to the cellar, falling to words (as it happens) with her little mistress, when alone with her, taunted her with this fault, with most bitter insult, calling her winebibber. With which taunt she, stung to the quick, saw the foulness of her fault, and instantly condemned and forsook it. As flattering friends pervert, so reproachful enemies mostly correct. Yet not what by them Thou doest, but what themselves purposed, dost Thou repay them. For she in her anger sought to vex her young mistress, not to amend her; and did it in private, either for that the time and place of the quarrel so found them; or lest herself also should have anger, for discovering it thus late. But Thou, Lord, Governor of all in heaven and earth, who turnest to Thy purposes the deepest currents, and the ruled turbulence of the tide of times, didst by the very unhealthiness of one soul heal another; lest any, when he observes this, should ascribe it to his own power, even when another, whom he wished to be reformed, is reformed through words of his.

Brought up thus modestly and soberly, and made subject rather by Thee to her parents, than by her parents to Thee, so soon as she was of marriageable age, being bestowed upon a husband, she served him as her lord; and did her diligence to win him unto Thee, preaching Thee unto him by her conversation; by which Thou ornamentedst her, making her reverently amiable, and admirable unto her husband. And she so endured the wronging of her bed as never to have any quarrel with her husband thereon. For she looked for Thy mercy upon him, that believing in Thee, he might be made chaste. But besides this, he was fervid, as in his affections, so in anger: but she had learnt not to resist an angry husband, not in deed only, but not even in word. Only when he was smoothed and tranquil, and in a temper to receive it, she would give an account of her actions, if haply he had overhastily taken offence. In a word, while many matrons, who had milder husbands, yet bore even in their faces marks of shame, would in familiar talk blame their husbands' lives, she would blame their tongues, giving them, as in jest, earnest advice: "That from the time they heard the marriage writings read to them, they should account them as indentures, whereby they were made servants; and so, remembering their condition, ought not to set themselves up against their lords." And when they, knowing what a choleric husband she endured, marveled that it had never been heard, nor by any token perceived, that Patricius had beaten his wife, or that there had been any domestic difference between them, even for one day, and confidentially asking the reason, she taught them her practice above mentioned. Those wives who observed it found the good, and returned thanks; those who observed it not, found no relief, and suffered.

Her mother-in-law also, at first by whisperings of evil servants incensed against her, she so overcame by observance and persevering endurance and meekness, that she of her own accord discovered to her son the meddling tongues whereby the domestic peace betwixt her and her daughter-in-law had been disturbed, asking him to correct them. Then, when in compliance with his mother, and for the well-ordering of the family, he had with stripes corrected those discovered, at her will who had discovered them, she promised the like reward to any who, to please her, should speak ill of her daughter-in-law to her: and none now venturing, they lived together with a remarkable sweetness of mutual kindness.

This great gift also thou bestowedst, O my God, my mercy, upon that good handmaid of Thine, in whose womb Thou createdst me, that between any disagreeing and discordant parties where she was able, she showed herself such a peacemaker, that hearing on both sides most bitter things, such as swelling and indigested choler uses to break out into, when the crudities of enmities are breathed out in sour discourses to a present friend against an absent enemy, she never would disclose aught of the one unto the other, but what might tend to their reconcilement. A small good this might appear to me, did I not to my grief know numberless persons, who through some horrible and wide-spreading contagion of sin, not only disclose to persons mutually angered things said in anger, but add withal things never spoken, whereas to humane humanity, it ought to seem a light thing not to torment or increase ill will by ill words, unless one study withal by good words to quench it. Such was she, Thyself, her most inward Instructor, teaching her in the school of the heart.

Finally, her own husband, towards the very end of his earthly life, did she gain unto Thee; nor had she to complain of that in him as a believer, which before he was a believer she had borne from him. She was also the servant of Thy servants; whosoever of them knew her, did in her much praise and honour and love Thee; for that through the witness of the fruits of a holy conversation they perceived Thy presence in her heart. For she had been the wife of one man, had requited her parents, had governed her house piously, was well reported of for good works, had brought up children, so often travailing in birth of them, as she saw them swerving from Thee.

Lastly, of all of us Thy servants, O Lord (whom on occasion of Thy own gift Thou sufferest to speak), us, who before her sleeping in Thee lived united together, having received the grace of Thy baptism, did she so take care of, as though she had been mother of us all; so served us, as though she had been child to us all.

The day now approaching whereon she was to depart this life (which day Thou well knewest, we knew not), it came to pass, Thyself, as I believe, by Thy secret ways so ordering it, that she and I stood alone, leaning in a certain window, which looked into the garden of the house where we now lay, at Ostia; where removed from the din of men, we were recruiting from the fatigues of a long journey, for the voyage. We were discoursing then together, alone, very sweetly; and forgetting those things which are behind, and reaching forth unto those things which are before, we were inquiring between ourselves in the presence of the Truth, which Thou art, of what sort the eternal life of the saints was to be, which eye hath not seen, nor ear heard, nor hath it entered into the heart of man. But yet we gasped with the mouth of our heart, after those heavenly streams of Thy fountain, the fountain of life, which is with Thee; that being bedewed thence according to our capacity, we might in some sort meditate upon so high a mystery.

And when our discourse was brought to that point, that the very highest delight of the earthly senses, in the very purest material light, was, in respect of the sweetness of that life, not only not worthy of comparison, but not even of mention; we raising up ourselves with a more glowing affection towards the "Self-same," did by degrees pass through all things bodily, even the very heaven whence sun and moon and stars shine upon the earth; yea, we were soaring higher yet, by inward musing, and discourse, and admiring of Thy works; and we came to our own minds, and went beyond them, that we might arrive at that region of never-failing plenty, where Thou feedest Israel for ever with the food of truth, and where life is the Wisdom by whom all these things are made, and what have been, and what shall be, and she is not made, but is, as she hath been, and so shall she be ever; yea rather, to "have been," and "hereafter to be," are not in her, but only "to be," seeing she is eternal. For to "have been," and to "be hereafter," are not eternal. And while we were discoursing and panting after her, we slightly touched on her with the whole effort of our heart; and we sighed, and there we leave bound the first fruits of the Spirit; and returned to vocal expressions of our mouth, where the word spoken has beginning and end. And what is like unto Thy Word, our Lord, who endureth in Himself without becoming old, and maketh all things new?

We were saying then: If to any the tumult of the flesh were hushed, hushed the images of earth, and waters, and air, hushed also the pole of heaven, yea the very soul be hushed to herself, and by not thinking on self surmount self, hushed all dreams and imaginary revelations, every tongue and every sign, and whatsoever exists only in transition, since if any could hear, all these say, We made not ourselves, but He made us that abideth for ever—If then having uttered this, they too should be hushed, having roused only our ears to Him who made them, and He alone speak, not by them but by Himself, that we may hear His Word, not through any tongue of flesh, nor Angel's voice, nor sound of thunder, nor in the dark riddle of a similitude, but might hear Whom in these things we love, might hear His Very Self without these (as we two now strained ourselves, and in swift thought touched on that Eternal Wisdom which abideth over all)—could this be continued on, and other visions of kind far unlike be withdrawn, and this one ravish, and absorb, and wrap up its beholder amid these inward joys, so that life might be for ever like that one moment of understanding which now we sighed after; were not this, Enter into thy Master's joy? And when shall that be? When we shall all rise again, though we shall not all be changed?

Such things was I speaking, and even if not in this very manner, and these same words, yet, Lord, Thou knowest that in that day when we were speaking of these things, and this world with all its delights became, as we spake, contemptible to us, my mother said, "Son, for mine own part I have no further delight in any thing in this life. What I do here any longer, and to what I am here, I know not, now that my hopes in this world are accomplished. One thing there was for which I desired to linger for a while in this life, that I might see thee a Catholic Christian before I died. My God hath done this for me more abundantly, that I should now see thee withal, despising earthly happiness, become His servant: what do I here?"

What answer I made her unto these things, I remember not. For scarce five days after, or not much more, she fell sick of a fever; and in that sickness one day she fell into a swoon, and was for a while withdrawn from these visible things. We hastened round her; but she was soon brought back to her senses; and looking on me and my brother standing by her, said to us enquiringly, "Where was I?" And then looking fixedly on us, with grief amazed: "Here," saith she, "shall you bury your mother." I held my peace and refrained weeping; but my brother spake something, wishing for her, as the happier lot, that she might die, not in a strange place, but in her own land. Whereat, she with anxious look, checking him with her eyes, for that he still savoured such things, and then looking upon me: "Behold," saith she, "what he saith": and soon after to us both, "Lay," she saith, "this body any where; let not the care for that any way disquiet you: this only I request, that you would remember me at the Lord's altar, wherever you be." And having delivered this sentiment in what words she could, she held her peace, being exercised by her growing sickness.

But I, considering Thy gifts, Thou unseen God, which Thou instillest into the hearts of Thy faithful ones, whence wondrous fruits do spring, did rejoice and give thanks to Thee, recalling what I before knew, how careful and anxious she had ever been as to her place of burial, which she had provided and prepared for herself by the body of her husband. For because they had lived in great harmony together, she also wished (so little can the human mind embrace things divine) to have this addition to that happiness, and to have it remembered among men, that after her pilgrimage beyond the seas, what was earthly of this united pair had been permitted to be united beneath the same earth. But when this emptiness had through the fullness of Thy goodness begun to cease in her heart,

I knew not, and rejoiced admiring what she had so disclosed to me; though indeed in that our discourse also in the window, when she said, "What do I here any longer?" there appeared no desire of dying in her own country. I heard afterwards also, that when we were now at Ostia, she with a mother's confidence, when I was absent, one day discoursed with certain of my friends about the contempt of this life, and the blessing of death: and when they were amazed at such courage which Thou hadst given to a woman, and asked, "Whether she were not afraid to leave her body so far from her own city?" she replied, "Nothing is far to God; nor was it to be feared lest at the end of the world, He should not recognise whence He were to raise me up." On the ninth day then of her sickness, and the fifty-sixth year of her age, and the three-and-thirtieth of mine, was that religious and holy soul freed from the body.

I closed her eyes; and there flowed withal a mighty sorrow into my heart, which was overflowing into tears; mine eyes at the same time, by the violent command of my mind, drank up their fountain wholly dry; and woe was me in such a strife! But when she breathed her last, the boy Adeodatus burst out into a loud lament; then, checked by us all, held his peace. In like manner also a childish feeling in me, which was, through my heart's youthful voice, finding its vent in weeping, was checked and silenced. For we thought it not fitting to solemnise that funeral with tearful lament, and groanings; for thereby do they for the most part express grief for the departed, as though unhappy, or altogether dead; whereas she was neither unhappy in her death, nor altogether dead. Of this we were assured on good grounds, the testimony of her good conversation and her faith unfeigned.

What then was it which did grievously pain me within, but a fresh wound wrought through the sudden wrench of that most sweet and dear custom of living together? I joyed indeed in her testimony, when, in that her last sickness, mingling her endearments with my acts of duty, she called me "dutiful," and mentioned, with great affection of love, that she never had heard any harsh or reproachful sound uttered by my mouth against her. But yet, O my God, Who madest us, what comparison is there betwixt that honour that I paid to her, and her slavery for me? Being then forsaken of so great comfort in her, my soul was wounded, and that life rent asunder as it were, which, of hers and mine together, had been made but one.

The boy then being stilled from weeping, Euodius took up the Psalter, and began to sing, our whole house answering him, the Psalm, I will sing of mercy and judgments to Thee, O Lord. But hearing what we were doing, many brethren and religious women came together; and whilst they (whose office it was) made ready for the burial, as the manner is, I, in a part of the house, where I might properly, together with those who thought not fit to leave me, discoursed upon something fitting the time; and by this balm of truth assuaged that torment, known to Thee, they unknowing and listening intently, and conceiving me to be without all sense of sorrow. But in Thy ears, where none of them heard, I blamed the weakness of my feelings, and refrained my flood of grief, which gave way a little unto me; but again came, as with a tide, yet not so as to burst out into tears, nor to change of countenance; still I knew what I was keeping down in my heart. And being very much displeased that these human things had such power over me, which in the due order and appointment of our natural condition must needs come to pass, with a new grief I grieved for my grief, and was thus worn by a double sorrow.

And behold, the corpse was carried to the burial; we went and returned without tears. For neither in those prayers which we poured forth unto Thee, when the Sacrifice of our ransom was offered for her, when now the corpse was by the grave's side, as the manner there is, previous to its being laid therein, did I weep even during those prayers; yet was I the whole day in secret heavily sad, and with troubled mind prayed Thee, as I could, to heal my sorrow, yet Thou didst not; impressing, I believe, upon my memory by this one instance, how strong is the bond of all habit, even upon a soul, which now feeds upon no deceiving Word. It seemed also good to me to go and bathe, having heard that the bath had its name (*balneum*) from the Greek Balaneion for that it drives sadness from the mind. And this also I confess unto Thy mercy, Father of the fatherless, that I bathed, and was the same as before I bathed. For the bitterness of sorrow could not exude out of my heart. Then I slept, and woke up again, and found my grief not a little softened; and as I was alone in my bed,

I remembered those true verses of Thy Ambrose. For Thou art the

> "Maker of all, the Lord, and Ruler of the height,
> Who, robing day in light, hast poured soft slumbers
> o'er the night,
> That to our limbs the power of toil may be renew'd,
> And hearts be rais'd that sink and cower,
> and sorrows be subdu'd."

And then by little and little I recovered my former thoughts of Thy handmaid, her holy conversation towards Thee, her holy tenderness and observance towards us, whereof I was suddenly deprived: and I was minded to weep in Thy sight, for her and for myself, in her behalf and in my own. And I gave way to the tears which I before restrained, to overflow as much as they desired; reposing my heart upon them; and it found rest in them, for it was in Thy ears, not in those of man, who would have scornfully interpreted my weeping. And now, Lord, in writing I confess it unto Thee. Read it, who will, and interpret it, how he will: and if he finds sin therein, that I wept my mother for a small portion of an hour (the mother who for the time was dead to mine eyes, who had for many years wept for me that I might live in Thine eyes), let him not deride me; but rather, if he be one of large charity, let him weep himself for my sins unto Thee, the Father of all the brethren of Thy Christ.

But now, with a heart cured of that wound, wherein it might seem blameworthy for an earthly feeling, I pour out unto Thee, our God, in behalf of that Thy handmaid, a far different kind of tears, flowing from a spirit shaken by the thoughts of the dangers of every soul that dieth in Adam. And although she having been quickened in Christ, even before her release from the flesh, had lived to the praise of Thy name for her faith and conversation; yet dare I not say that from what time Thou regeneratedst her by baptism, no word issued from her mouth against Thy Commandment. Thy Son, the Truth, hath said, Whosoever shall say unto his brother, Thou fool, shall be in danger of hell fire. And woe be even unto the commendable life of men, if, laying aside mercy, Thou shouldest examine it. But because Thou art not extreme in inquiring after sins, we confidently hope to find some place with Thee. But whosoever reckons up his real merits to Thee, what reckons he up to Thee but Thine own gifts? O that men would know themselves to be men; and that he that glorieth would glory in the Lord.

I therefore, O my Praise and my Life, God of my heart, laying aside for a while her good deeds, for which I give thanks to Thee with joy, do now beseech Thee for the sins of my mother. Hearken unto me, I entreat Thee, by the Medicine of our wounds, Who hung upon the tree, and now sitting at Thy right hand maketh intercession to Thee for us. I know that she dealt mercifully, and from her heart forgave her debtors their debts; do Thou also forgive her debts, whatever she may have contracted in so many years, since the water of salvation. Forgive her, Lord, forgive, I beseech Thee; enter not into judgment with her. Let Thy mercy be exalted above Thy justice, since Thy words are true, and Thou hast promised mercy unto the merciful; which Thou gavest them to be, who wilt have mercy on whom Thou wilt have mercy; and wilt have compassion on whom Thou hast had compassion.

And, I believe, Thou hast already done what I ask; but accept, O Lord, the free-will offerings of my mouth. For she, the day of her dissolution now at hand, took no thought to have her body sumptuously wound up, or embalmed with spices; nor desired she a choice monument, or to be buried in her own land. These things she enjoined us not; but desired only to have her name commemorated at Thy Altar, which she had served without intermission of one day: whence she knew the holy Sacrifice to be dispensed, by which the hand-writing that was against us is blotted out; through which the enemy was triumphed over, who summing up our offenses, and seeking what to lay to our charge, found nothing in Him, in Whom we conquer. Who shall restore to Him the innocent blood? Who repay Him the price wherewith He bought us, and so take us from Him? Unto the Sacrament of which our ransom, Thy handmaid bound her soul by the bond of faith. Let none sever her from Thy protection: let neither the lion nor the dragon interpose himself by force or fraud. For she will not answer that she owes nothing, lest she be convicted and seized by the crafty accuser: but she will answer that her sins are forgiven her by Him, to Whom none can repay that price which He,

Who owed nothing, paid for us.

May she rest then in peace with the husband before and after whom she had never any; whom she obeyed, with patience bringing forth fruit unto Thee, that she might win him also unto Thee. And inspire, O Lord my God, inspire Thy servants my brethren, Thy sons my masters, whom with voice, and heart, and pen I serve, that so many as shall read these Confessions, may at Thy Altar remember Monnica Thy handmaid, with Patricius, her sometimes husband, by whose bodies Thou broughtest me into this life, how I know not. May they with devout affection remember my parents in this transitory light, my brethren under Thee our Father in our Catholic Mother, and my fellow-citizens in that eternal Jerusalem which Thy pilgrim people sigheth after from their Exodus, even unto their return thither. That so my mother's last request of me, may through my confessions, more than through my prayers, be, through the prayers of many, more abundantly fulfilled to her.

AUGUSTINE

City of God

Saint Augustine

Translated by Marcus Dods

Book One

Preface

The glorious city of God is my theme in this work, which you, my dearest son Marcellinus, suggested, and which is due to you by my promise. I have undertaken its defense against those who prefer their own gods to the Founder of this city—a city surpassingly glorious, whether we view it as it still lives by faith in this fleeting course of time, and sojourns as a stranger in the midst of the ungodly, or as it shall dwell in the fixed stability of its eternal seat, which it now with patience waits for, expecting until "righteousness shall return unto judgment," and it obtain, by virtue of its excellence, final victory and perfect peace. A great work this, and an arduous; but God is my helper. For I am aware what ability is requisite to persuade the proud how great is the virtue of humility, which raises us, not by a quite human arrogance, but by a divine grace, above all earthly dignities that totter on this shifting scene. For the King and Founder of this city of which we speak, has in Scripture uttered to His people a dictum of the divine law in these words: "God resisteth the proud, but giveth grace unto the humble." But this, which is God's prerogative, the inflated ambition of a proud spirit also affects, and dearly loves that this be numbered among its attributes, to

"Show pity to the humbled soul,
And crush the sons of pride."

And therefore, as the plan of this work we have undertaken requires, and as occasion offers, we must speak also of the earthly city, which, though it be mistress of the nations, is itself ruled by its lust of rule.

Chapter I: *Of the Adversaries of the Name of Christ, Whom the Barbarians for Christ's Sake Spared When They Stormed the City*

For to this earthly city belong the enemies against whom I have to defend the city of God. Many of them, indeed, being reclaimed from their ungodly error, have become sufficiently creditable citizens of this city; but many are so inflamed with hatred against it, and are so ungrateful to its Redeemer for His signal benefits, as to forget that they would now be unable to utter a single word to its prejudice, had they not found in its sacred places, as they fled from the enemy's steel, that life in which they now boast themselves. Are not those very Romans, who were spared by the barbarians through their respect for Christ, become enemies to the name of Christ? The reliquaries of the martyrs and the churches of the apostles bear witness to this; for in the sack of the city they were open sanctuary for all who fled to them, whether Christian or Pagan. To their very threshold the blood-thirsty enemy raged; there his murderous fury owned a limit. Thither did such of the enemy as had any pity convey those to whom they had given quarter, lest any less mercifully disposed might fall upon them. And, indeed, when even those murderers who everywhere else showed themselves pitiless came to those spots where that was forbidden which the license of war permitted in every other place, their furious rage for slaughter was bridled, and their eagerness to take prisoners was quenched. Thus escaped multitudes who now reproach the Christian religion, and impute to Christ the ills that have befallen their city; but the preservation of their own life—a boon which they owe to the respect entertained for Christ by the barbarians—they attribute not to our Christ, but to their own good luck. They ought rather, had they any right perceptions, to attribute the severities and hardships inflicted by their enemies, to that divine providence which is wont to reform the depraved manners of men by chastisement, and which exercises with similar afflictions the righteous and praiseworthy—either translating them, when they have passed through the trial, to a better world, or detaining them still on earth for ulterior purposes. And they ought to attribute it to the spirit of these Christian times, that, contrary to the custom of war, these bloodthirsty barbarians spared them, and spared them for Christ's sake, whether this mercy was actually shown in promiscuous places, or in those places specially dedicated to Christ's name, and of which the very largest were selected as sanctuaries, that full scope might thus be given to the expansive compassion which desired that a large multitude might find shelter there. Therefore ought they to give God thanks, and with sincere confession flee for refuge to His name, that so they may escape the punishment of eternal fire—they who with lying lips took upon them this name, that they might escape the punishment of present destruction. For of those whom you see insolently and shamelessly insulting the servants of Christ, there are numbers who would not have escaped that destruction and slaughter had they not pretended that they themselves were Christ's servants. Yet now, in ungrateful pride and most impious madness, and at the risk of being punished in everlasting darkness, they perversely oppose that name under which they fraudulently protected themselves for the sake of enjoying the light of this brief life.

Chapter II: *That It is Quite Contrary to the Usage of War, that the Victors Should Spare the Vanquished for the Sake of Their Gods.*

There are histories of numberless wars, both before the building of Rome and since its rise and the extension of its dominion; let these be read, and let one instance be cited in which, when a city had been taken by foreigners, the victors spared those who were found to have fled for sanctuary to the temples of their gods; or one instance in which a barbarian general gave orders that none should be put to the sword who had been found in this or that temple. Did not Æneas see

"Dying Priam at the shrine,

Staining the hearth he made divine?"
Did not Diomede and Ulysses
"Drag with red hands, the sentry slain,
Her fateful image from your fane,
Her chaste locks touch, and stain with gore
The virgin coronal she wore?"
Neither is that true which follows, that
"Thenceforth the tide of fortune changed,
And Greece grew weak."

For after this they conquered and destroyed Troy with fire and sword; after this they beheaded Priam as he fled to the altars. Neither did Troy perish because it lost Minerva. For what had Minerva herself first lost, that she should perish? Her guards perhaps? No doubt; just her guards. For as soon as they were slain, she could be stolen. It was not, in fact, the men who were preserved by the image, but the image by the men. How, then, was she invoked to defend the city and the citizens, she who could not defend her own defenders?

Chapter III: *That the Romans Did Not Show Their Usual Sagacity When They Trusted that They Would Be Benefited by the Gods Who Had Been Unable to Defend Troy.*

And these be the gods to whose protecting care the Romans were delighted to entrust their city! O too, too piteous mistake! And they are enraged at us when we speak thus about their gods, though, so far from being enraged at their own writers, they part with money to learn what they say; and, indeed, the very teachers of these authors are reckoned worthy of a salary from the public purse, and of other honors. There is Virgil, who is read by boys, in order that this great poet, this most famous and approved of all poets, may impregnate their virgin minds, and may not readily be forgotten by them, according to that saying of Horace,

"The fresh cask long keeps its first tang."

Well, in this Virgil, I say, Juno is introduced as hostile to the Trojans, and stirring up Æolus, the king of the winds, against them in the words,

"A race I hate now ploughs the sea,
Transporting Troy to Italy,
And home-gods conquered"

And ought prudent men to have entrusted the defense of Rome to these conquered gods? But it will be said, this was only the saying of Juno, who, like an angry woman, did not know what she was saying. What, then, says Æneas himself—Æneas who is so often designated "pious?" Does he not say,

"Lo! Panthus, 'scaped from death by flight,
Priest of Apollo on the height,
His conquered gods with trembling hands
He bears, and shelter swift demands?"

Is it not clear that the gods (whom he does not scruple to call "conquered") were rather entrusted to Æneas than he to them, when it is said to him,

"The gods of her domestic shrines
Your country to your care consigns?"

If, then, Virgil says that the gods were such as these, and were conquered, and that when conquered they could not escape except under the protection of a man, what a madness is it to suppose that Rome had been wisely entrusted to these guardians, and could not have been taken unless it had lost them! Indeed, to worship conquered gods as protectors and champions, what is this but to worship, not good divinities, but evil omens? Would it not be wiser to believe, not that Rome would never have fallen into so great a calamity had not they first perished, but rather that they would have perished long since had not Rome preserved them as long as she could? For who does not see, when he thinks of it, what a foolish assumption it is that they could not be vanquished under vanquished defenders, and that they only perished because they had lost their guardian gods, when, indeed, the only cause of their perishing was that they chose for their protectors gods condemned to perish? The poets, therefore, when they composed and sang these things about the conquered gods, had no intention to invent falsehoods, but uttered, as honest men, what the truth extorted from them. This, however, will be carefully and copiously discussed in another and more fitting place. Meanwhile I will briefly, and to the best of my ability, explain what I meant to say about these ungrateful men who blasphemously impute to Christ the calamities which they deservedly suffer in consequence of their own wicked ways, while that which is for Christ's sake spared them in spite of their wickedness they do not even take the trouble to notice; and in their mad and blasphemous insolence, they use against His name those very lips wherewith they falsely claimed that same name that their lives might be spared. In the places consecrated to Christ, where for His sake no enemy would injure them, they restrained their tongues that they might be safe and protected; but no sooner do they emerge from these sanctuaries, than they unbridle these tongues to hurl against Him curses full of hate.

Chapter IV: *Of the Asylum of Juno in Troy, Which Saved No One from the Greeks; And of the Churches of the Apostles, Which Protected from the Barbarians All Who Fled to Them.*

Troy itself, the mother of the Roman people, was not able, as I have said, to protect its own citizens in the sacred places of their gods from the fire and sword of the Greeks, though the Greeks worshiped the same gods. Not only so, but

> "Phoenix and Ulysses fell In the void courts by Juno's cell
> Were set the spoils to keep;
> Snatched from the burning shrines away,
> There Ilium's mighty treasure lay,
> Rich altars, bowls of massy gold,
> And captive raiment, rudely rolled
> In one promiscuous heap;
> While boys and matrons, wild with fear,
> In long array were standing near."

In other words, the place consecrated to so great a goddess was chosen, not that from it none might be led out a captive, but that in it all the captives might be immured. Compare now this "asylum"—the asylum not of an ordinary god, not of one of the rank and file of gods, but of Jove's own sister and wife, the queen of all the gods—with the churches built in memory of the apostles. Into it were collected the spoils rescued from the blazing temples and snatched from the gods, not that they might be restored to the vanquished, but divided among the victors; while into these was carried back, with the most religious observance and respect, everything which belonged to them, even though found elsewhere. There liberty was lost; here preserved. There bondage was strict; here strictly excluded. Into that temple men were driven to become the chattels of their enemies, now lording it over them; into these churches men were led by their relenting foes, that they might be at liberty. In fine, the gentle Greeks appropriated that temple of Juno to the purposes of their own avarice and pride; while these churches of Christ were chosen even by the savage barbarians as the fit scenes for humility and mercy. But perhaps, after all, the Greeks did in that victory of theirs spare the temples of those gods whom they worshiped in common with the Trojans, and did not dare to put to the sword or make captive the wretched and vanquished Trojans who fled thither; and perhaps Virgil, in the manner of poets, has depicted what never really happened? But there is no question that he depicted the usual custom of an enemy when sacking a city.

Chapter V: *Cæsar's Statement Regarding the Universal Custom of an Enemy When Sacking a City.*

Even Cæsar himself gives us positive testimony regarding this custom; for, in his deliverance in the senate about the conspirators, he says (as Sallust, a historian of distinguished veracity, writes) "that virgins and boys are violated, children torn from the embrace of their parents, matrons subjected to whatever should be the pleasure of the conquerors, temples and houses plundered, slaughter and burning rife; in fine, all things filled with arms, corpses, blood, and wailing." If he had not mentioned temples here, we might suppose that enemies were in the habit of sparing the dwellings of the gods. And the Roman temples were in danger of these disasters, not from foreign foes, but from Catiline and his associates, the most noble senators and citizens of Rome. But these, it may be said, were abandoned men, and the parricides of their fatherland.

Chapter VI: *That Not Even the Romans, When They Took Cities, Spared the Conquered in Their Temples.*

Why, then, need our argument take note of the many nations who have waged wars with one another, and have nowhere spared the conquered in the temples of their gods? Let us look at the practice of the Romans themselves; let us, I say, recall and review the Romans, whose chief praise it has been "to spare the vanquished and subdue the proud," and that they preferred "rather to forgive than to revenge an injury;" and among so many and great cities which they have stormed, taken, and overthrown for the extension of their dominion, let us be told what temples they were accustomed to exempt, so that whoever took refuge in them was free. Or have they really done this, and has the fact been suppressed by the historians of these events? Is it to be believed, that men who sought out with the greatest eagerness points they could praise, would omit those which, in their own estimation, are the most signal proofs of piety? Marcus Marcellus, a distinguished Roman, who took Syracuse, a most splendidly adorned city, is reported to have bewailed its coming ruin, and to have shed his own tears over it before he spilt its blood. He took steps also to preserve the chastity even of his enemy. For before he gave orders for the storming of the city, he issued an edict forbidding the violation of any free person. Yet the city was sacked according to the custom of war; nor do we anywhere read, that even by so chaste and gentle a commander orders were given that no one should be injured who had fled to this or that temple. And this certainly would by no means have been omitted, when neither his weeping nor his edict preservative of chastity could be passed in silence. Fabius, the conqueror of the city of Tarentum, is praised for abstaining from making booty of the images. For when his secretary proposed the question to him, what he wished done with the statues of the gods, which had been taken in large numbers, he veiled his moderation under a joke. For he asked of what sort they were; and when they reported to him that there were not only many large images, but some of them armed, "Oh," says he, "let us leave with the Tarentines their angry gods." Seeing, then, that the writers of Roman history could not pass in silence, neither the weeping of the one general nor the laughing of the other, neither the chaste pity of the one nor the facetious moderation of the other, on what occasion would it be omitted, if, for the honor of any of their enemy's gods, they had shown this particular form of leniency, that in any temple slaughter or captivity was prohibited?

Chapter VII: *: That the Cruelties Which Occurred in the Sack of Rome Were in Accordance with the Custom of War, Whereas the Acts of Clemency Resulted from the Influence of Christ's Name.*

All the spoiling, then, which Rome was exposed to in the recent calamity—all the slaughter, plundering, burning, and misery—was the result of the custom of war. But what was novel, was that savage barbarians showed themselves in so gentle a guise, that the largest churches were chosen and set apart for the purpose of being filled with the people to whom quarter was given, and that in them none were slain, from them none forcibly dragged; that into them many were led by their relenting enemies to be set at liberty, and that from them none were led into slavery by merciless foes. Whoever does not see that this is to be attributed to the name of Christ, and to the Christian temper, is blind; whoever sees this, and gives no praise, is ungrateful; whoever hinders any one from praising it, is mad. Far be it from any prudent man to impute this clemency to the barbarians. Their fierce and bloody minds were awed, and bridled, and marvelously tempered by Him who so long before said by His prophet, "I will visit their transgression with the rod, and their iniquities with stripes; nevertheless my loving-kindness will I not utterly take from them."

Chapter VIII: *: Of the Advantages and Disadvantages Which Often Indiscriminately Accrue to Good and Wicked Men.*

Will some one say, Why, then, was this divine compassion extended even to the ungodly and ungrateful? Why, but because it was the mercy of Him who daily "maketh His sun to rise on the evil and on the good, and sendeth rain on the just and on the unjust." For though some of these men, taking thought of this, repent of their wickedness and reform, some, as the apostle says, "despising the riches of His goodness and long-suffering, after their hardness and impenitent heart, treasure up unto themselves wrath against the day of wrath and revelation of the righteous judgment of God, who will render to every man according to his deeds:" nevertheless does the patience of God still invite the wicked to repentance, even as the scourge of God educates the good to patience. And so, too, does the mercy of God embrace the good that it may cherish them, as the severity of God arrests the wicked to punish them. To the divine providence it has seemed good to prepare in the world to come for the righteous good things, which the unrighteous shall not enjoy; and for the wicked evil things, by which the good shall not be tormented. But as for the good things of this life, and its ills, God has willed that these should be common to both; that we might not too eagerly covet the things which wicked men are seen equally to enjoy, nor shrink with an unseemly fear from the ills which even good men often suffer.

There is, too, a very great difference in the purpose served both by those events which we call adverse and those called prosperous. For the good man is neither uplifted with the good things of time, nor broken by its ills; but the wicked man, because he is corrupted by this world's happiness, feels himself punished by its unhappiness. Yet often, even in the present distribution of temporal things, does God plainly evince His own interference. For if every sin were now visited with manifest punishment, nothing would seem to be reserved for the final judgment; on the other hand, if no sin received now a plainly divine punishment, it would be concluded that there is no divine providence at all. And so of the good things of this life: if God did not by a very visible liberality confer these on some of those persons who ask for them, we should say that these good things were not at His disposal; and if He gave them to all who sought them, we should suppose that such were the only rewards of His service; and such a service would make us not godly, but greedy rather, and covetous. Wherefore, though good and bad men suffer alike, we must not suppose that there is no difference between the men themselves, because there is no difference in what they both suffer. For even in the likeness of the sufferings, there remains an unlikeness in the sufferers; and though exposed to the same anguish, virtue and vice are not the same thing. For as the same fire causes gold to glow brightly, and chaff to smoke; and under the same flail the straw is beaten small, while the grain is cleansed; and as the lees are not mixed with the oil, though squeezed out of the vat by the same pressure, so the same violence of affliction proves, purges, clarifies the good, but damns, ruins, exterminates the wicked. And thus it is that in the same affliction the wicked detest God and blaspheme, while the good pray and praise. So material a difference does it make, not what ills are suffered, but what kind of man suffers them. For, stirred up with the same movement, mud exhales a horrible stench, and ointment emits a fragrant odor.

Chapter IX: *Of the Reasons for Administering Correction to Bad and Good Together.*

What, then, have the Christians suffered in that calamitous period, which would not profit every one who duly and faithfully considered the following circumstances? First of all, they must humbly consider those very sins which have provoked God to fill the world with such terrible disasters; for although they be far from the excesses of wicked, immoral, and ungodly men, yet they do not judge themselves so clean removed from all faults as to be too good to suffer for these even temporal ills. For every man, however laudably he lives, yet yields in some points to the lust of the flesh. Though he do not fall into gross enormity of wickedness, and abandoned viciousness, and abominable profanity, yet he slips into some sins, either rarely or so much the more frequently as the sins seem of less account. But not to mention this, where can we readily find a man who holds in fit and just estimation those persons on account of whose revolting pride, luxury, and avarice, and cursed iniquities and impiety, God now smites the earth as His predictions threatened? Where is the man who lives with them in the style in which it becomes us to live with them? For often we wickedly blind ourselves to the occasions of teaching and admonishing them, sometimes even of reprimanding and chiding them, either because we shrink from the labor or are ashamed to offend them, or because we fear to lose good friendships, lest this should stand in the way of our advancement, or injure us in some worldly matter, which either our covetous disposition desires to obtain, or our weakness shrinks from losing. So that, although the conduct of wicked men is distasteful to the good, and therefore they do not fall with them into that damnation which in the next life awaits such persons, yet, because they spare their damnable sins through fear, therefore, even though their own sins be slight and venial, they are justly scourged with the wicked in this world, though in eternity they quite escape punishment. Justly, when God afflicts them in common with the wicked, do they find this life bitter, through love of whose sweetness they declined to be bitter to these sinners. If any one forbears to reprove and find fault with those who are doing wrong, because he seeks a more seasonable opportunity, or because he fears they may be made worse by his rebuke, or that other weak persons may be disheartened from endeavoring to lead a good and pious life, and may be driven from the faith; this man's omission seems to be occasioned not by covetousness, but by a charitable consideration. But what is blame-worthy is, that they who themselves revolt from the conduct of the wicked, and live in quite another fashion, yet spare those faults in other men which they ought to reprehend and wean them from; and spare them because they fear to give offence, lest they should injure their interests in those things which good men may innocently and legitimately use—though they use them more greedily than becomes persons who are strangers in this world, and profess the hope of a heavenly country. For not only the weaker brethren who enjoy married life, and have children (or desire to have them), and own houses and establishments, whom the apostle addresses in the churches, warning and instructing them how they should live, both the wives with their husbands, and the husbands with their wives, the children with their parents, and parents with their children, and servants with their masters, and masters with their servants—not only do these weaker brethren gladly obtain and grudgingly lose many earthly and temporal things on account of which they dare not offend men whose polluted and wicked life greatly displeases them; but those also who live at a higher level, who are not entangled in the meshes of married life, but use meagre food and raiment, do often take thought of their own safety and good name, and abstain from finding fault with the wicked, because they fear their wiles and violence. And although they do not fear them to such an extent as to be drawn to the commission of like iniquities, nay, not by any threats or violence soever; yet those very deeds which they refuse to share in the commission of they often decline to find fault with, when possibly they might by finding fault prevent their commission. They abstain from interference, because they fear that, if it fail of good effect, their own safety or reputation may be damaged or destroyed; not because they see that their preservation and good name are needful, that they may be able to influence those who need their instruction, but rather because they weakly relish the flattery and respect of men, and fear the judgments of the people, and the pain or death of the body; that is to say, their non-intervention is the result of selfishness, and not of love.

Accordingly this seems to me to be one principal reason why the good are chastised along with the wicked, when God is pleased to visit with temporal punishments the profligate manners of a community. They are punished together, not because they have spent an equally corrupt life, but because the good as well as the wicked, though not equally with them, love this present life; while they ought to hold it cheap, that the wicked, being admonished and reformed by their example, might lay hold of life eternal. And if they will not be the companions of the good in seeking life everlasting, they should be loved as enemies, and be dealt with patiently. For so long as they live, it remains uncertain whether they may not come to a better mind. These selfish persons have more cause to fear than those to whom it was said through the prophet, "He is taken away in his iniquity, but his blood will I require at the watchman's hand." For watchmen or overseers of the people are appointed in churches, that they may unsparingly rebuke sin. Nor is that man guiltless of the sin we speak of, who, though he be not a watchman, yet sees in the conduct of those with whom the relationships of this life bring him into contact, many things that should be blamed, and yet overlooks them, fearing to give offence, and lose such worldly blessings as may legitimately be desired, but which he too eagerly grasps. Then, lastly, there is another reason why the good are afflicted with temporal calamities—the reason which Job's case exemplifies: that the human spirit may be proved, and that it may be manifested with what fortitude of pious trust, and with how unmercenary a love, it cleaves to God.

Chapter X: *That the Saints Lose Nothing in Losing Temporal Goods.*

These are the considerations which one must keep in view, that he may answer the question whether any evil happens to the faithful and godly which cannot be turned to profit. Or shall we say that the question is needless, and that the apostle is vaporing when he says, "We know that all things work together for good to them that love God?"

They lost all they had. Their faith? Their godliness? The possessions of the hidden man of the heart, which in the sight of God are of great price? Did they lose these? For these are the wealth of Christians, to whom the wealthy apostle said, "Godliness with contentment is great gain. For we brought nothing into this world, and it is certain we can carry nothing out. And having food and raiment, let us be therewith content. But they that will be rich fall into temptation and a snare, and into many foolish and hurtful lusts, which drown men in destruction and perdition. For the love of money is the root of all evil; which, while some coveted after, they have erred from the faith, and pierced themselves through with many sorrows."

They, then, who lost their worldly all in the sack of Rome, if they owned their possessions as they had been taught by the apostle, who himself was poor without, but rich within—that is to say, if they used the world as not using it—could say in the words of Job, heavily tried, but not overcome: "Naked came I out of my mother's womb, and naked shall I return thither: the Lord gave, and the Lord hath taken away; as it pleased the Lord, so has it come to pass: blessed be the name of the Lord." Like a good servant, Job counted the will of his Lord his great possession, by obedience to which his soul was enriched; nor did it grieve him to lose, while yet living, those goods which he must shortly leave at his death. But as to those feebler spirits who, though they cannot be said to prefer earthly possessions to Christ, do yet cleave to them with a somewhat immoderate attachment, they have discovered by the pain of losing these things how much they were sinning in loving them. For their grief is of their own making; in the words of the apostle quoted above, "they have pierced themselves through with many sorrows." For it was well that they who had so long despised these verbal admonitions should receive the teaching of experience. For when the apostle says, "They that will be rich fall into temptation," and so on, what he blames in riches is not the possession of them, but the desire of them. For elsewhere he says, "Charge them that are rich in this world, that they be not high-minded, nor trust in uncertain riches, but in the living God, who giveth us richly all things to enjoy; that they do good, that they be rich in good works, ready to distribute, willing to communicate; laying up in store for themselves a good foundation against the time to come, that they may lay hold on eternal life." They who were making such a use of their property have been consoled for light losses by great gains, and have had more pleasure in those possessions which they have securely laid past, by freely giving them away, than grief in those which they entirely lost by an anxious and selfish hoarding of them. For nothing could perish on earth save what they would be ashamed to carry away from earth. Our Lord's injunction runs, "Lay not up for yourselves treasures upon earth, where moth and rust doth corrupt, and where thieves break through and steal; but lay up for yourselves treasures in heaven, where neither moth nor rust doth corrupt, and where thieves do not break through nor steal: for where your treasure is, there will your heart be also." And they who have listened to this injunction have proved in the time of tribulation how well they were advised in not despising this most trustworthy teacher, and most faithful and mighty guardian of their treasure. For if many were glad that their treasure was stored in places which the enemy chanced not to light upon, how much better founded was the joy of those who, by the counsel of their God, had fled with their treasure to a citadel which no enemy can possibly reach! Thus our Paulinus, bishop of Nola, who voluntarily abandoned vast wealth and became quite poor, though abundantly rich in holiness, when the barbarians sacked Nola, and took him prisoner, used silently to pray, as he afterwards told me, "O Lord, let me not be troubled for gold and silver, for where all my treasure is Thou knowest." For all his treasure was where he had been taught to hide and store it by Him who had also foretold that these calamities would happen in the world. Consequently those persons who obeyed their Lord when He warned them where and how to lay up treasure, did not lose even their earthly possessions in the invasion of the barbarians; while those who are now repenting that they did not obey Him have learnt the right use of earthly goods, if not by the wisdom which would have prevented their loss, at least by the experience which follows it.

But some good and Christian men have been put to the torture, that they might be forced to deliver up their goods to the enemy. They could indeed neither deliver nor lose that good which made themselves good. If, however, they preferred torture to the surrender of the mammon of iniquity, then I say they were not good men. Rather they should have been reminded that, if they suffered so severely for the sake of money, they should endure all torment, if need be, for Christ's sake; that they might be taught to love Him rather who enriches with eternal felicity all who suffer for Him, and not silver and gold, for which it was pitiable to suffer, whether they preserved it by telling a lie or lost it by telling the truth. For under these tortures no one lost Christ by confessing Him, no one preserved wealth save by denying its existence. So that possibly the torture which taught them that they should set their affections on a possession they could not lose, was more useful than those possessions which, without any useful fruit at all, disquieted and tormented their anxious owners. But then we are reminded that some were tortured who had no wealth to surrender, but who were not believed when they said so. These too, however, had perhaps some craving for wealth, and were not willingly poor with a holy resignation; and to such it had to be made plain, that not the actual possession alone, but also the desire of wealth, deserved such excruciating pains. And even if they were destitute of any hidden stores of gold and silver, because they were living in hopes of a better life—I know not indeed if any such person was tortured on the supposition that he had wealth; but if so, then certainly in confessing, when put to the question, a holy poverty, he confessed Christ. And though it was scarcely to be expected that the barbarians should believe him, yet no confessor of a holy poverty could be tortured without receiving a heavenly reward.

Again, they say that the long famine laid many a Christian low. But this, too, the faithful turned to good uses by a pious endurance of it. For those whom famine killed outright it rescued from the ills of this life, as a kindly disease would have done; and those who were only hunger-bitten were taught to live more sparingly, and inured to longer fasts.

Chapter XI: *Of the End of This Life, Whether It is Material that It Be Long Delayed.*

But, it is added, many Christians were slaughtered, and were put to death in a hideous variety of cruel ways. Well, if this be hard to bear, it is assuredly the common lot of all who are born into this life. Of this at least I am certain, that no one has ever died who was not destined to die some time. Now the end of life puts the longest life on a par with the shortest. For of two things which have alike ceased to be, the one is not better, the other worse—the one greater, the other less. And of what consequence is it what kind of death puts an end to life, since he who has died once is not forced to go through the same ordeal a second time? And as in the daily casualties of life every man is, as it were, threatened with numberless deaths, so long as it remains uncertain which of them is his fate, I would ask whether it is not better to suffer one and die, than to live in fear of all? I am not unaware of the poor-spirited fear which prompts us to choose rather to live long in fear of so many deaths, than to die once and so escape them all; but the weak and cowardly shrinking of the flesh is one thing, and the well-considered and reasonable persuasion of the soul quite another. That death is not to be judged an evil which is the end of a good life; for death becomes evil only by the retribution which follows it. They, then, who are destined to die, need not be careful to inquire what death they are to die, but into what place death will usher them. And since Christians are well aware that the death of the godly pauper whose sores the dogs licked was far better than of the wicked rich man who lay in purple and fine linen, what harm could these terrific deaths do to the dead who had lived well?

Chapter XII: *Of the Burial of the Dead: that the Denial of It to Christians Does Them No Injury.*

Further still, we are reminded that in such a carnage as then occurred, the bodies could not even be buried. But godly confidence is not appalled by so ill-omened a circumstance; for the faithful bear in mind that assurance has been given that not a hair of their head shall perish, and that, therefore, though they even be devoured by beasts, their blessed resurrection will not hereby be hindered. The Truth would nowise have said, "Fear not them which kill the body, but are not able to kill the soul," if anything whatever that an enemy could do to the body of the slain could be detrimental to the future life. Or will some one perhaps take so absurd a position as to contend that those who kill the body are not to be feared before death, and lest they kill the body, but after death, lest they deprive it of burial? If this be so, then that is false which Christ says, "Be not afraid of them that kill the body, and after that have no more that they can do;" for it seems they can do great injury to the dead body. Far be it from us to suppose that the Truth can be thus false. They who kill the body are said "to do something," because the deathblow is felt, the body still having sensation; but after that, they have no more that they can do, for in the slain body there is no sensation. And so there are indeed many bodies of Christians lying unburied; but no one has separated them from heaven, nor from that earth which is all filled with the presence of Him who knows whence He will raise again what He created. It is said, indeed, in the Psalm: "The dead bodies of Thy servants have they given to be meat unto the fowls of the heaven, the flesh of Thy saints unto the beasts of the earth. Their blood have they shed like water round about Jerusalem; and there was none to bury them." But this was said rather to exhibit the cruelty of those who did these things, than the misery of those who suffered them. To the eyes of men this appears a harsh and doleful lot, yet "precious in the sight of the Lord is the death of His saints." Wherefore all these last offices and ceremonies that concern the dead, the careful funeral arrangements, and the equipment of the tomb, and the pomp of obsequies, are rather the solace of the living than the comfort of the dead. If a costly burial does any good to a wicked man, a squalid burial, or none at all, may harm the godly. His crowd of domestics furnished the purple-clad Dives with a funeral gorgeous in the eye of man; but in the sight of God that was a more sumptuous funeral which the ulcerous pauper received at the hands of the angels, who did not carry him out to a marble tomb, but bore him aloft to Abraham's bosom.

The men against whom I have undertaken to defend the city of God laugh at all this. But even their own philosophers have despised a careful burial; and often whole armies have fought and fallen for their earthly country without caring to inquire whether they [10] would be left exposed on the field of battle, or become the food of wild beasts. Of this noble disregard of sepulture poetry has well said: "He who has no tomb has the sky for his vault." How much less ought they to insult over the unburied bodies of Christians, to whom it has been promised that the flesh itself shall be restored, and the body formed anew, all the members of it being gathered not only from the earth, but from the most secret recesses of any other of the elements in which the dead bodies of men have lain hid!

Chapter XIII: *Reasons for Burying the Bodies of the Saints.*

Nevertheless the bodies of the dead are not on this account to be despised and left unburied; least of all the bodies of the righteous and faithful, which have been used by the Holy Spirit as His organs and instruments for all good works. For if the dress of a father, or his ring, or anything he wore, be precious to his children, in proportion to the love they bore him, with how much more reason ought we to care for the bodies of those we love, which they wore far more closely and intimately than any clothing! For the body is not an extraneous ornament or aid, but a part of man's very nature. And therefore to the righteous of ancient times the last offices were piously rendered, and sepulchres provided for them, and obsequies celebrated; and they themselves, while yet alive, gave commandment to their sons about the burial, and, on occasion, even about the removal of their bodies to some favorite place. And Tobit, according to the angel's testimony, is commended, and is said to have pleased God by burying the dead. Our Lord Himself, too, though He was to rise again the third day, applauds, and commends to our applause, the good work of the religious woman who poured precious ointment over His limbs, and did it against His burial. And the Gospel speaks with commendation of those who were careful to take down His body from the cross, and wrap it lovingly in costly cerements, and see to its burial. These instances certainly do not prove that corpses have any feeling; but they show that God's providence extends even to the bodies of the dead, and that such pious offices are pleasing to Him, as cherishing faith in the resurrection. And we may also draw from them this wholesome lesson, that if God does not forget even any kind office which loving care pays to the unconscious dead, much more does He reward the charity we exercise towards the living. Other things, indeed, which the holy patriarchs said of the burial and removal of their bodies, they meant to be taken in a prophetic sense; but of these we need not here speak at large, what we have already said being sufficient. But if the want of those things which are necessary for the support of the living, as food and clothing, though painful and trying, does not break down the fortitude and virtuous endurance of good men, nor eradicate piety from their souls, but rather renders it more fruitful, how much less can the absence of the funeral, and of the other customary attentions paid to the dead, render those wretched who are already reposing in the hidden abodes of the blessed! Consequently, though in the sack of Rome and of other towns the dead bodies of the Christians were deprived of these last offices, this is neither the fault of the living, for they could not render them; nor an infliction to the dead, for they cannot feel the loss.

Chapter XIV: *Of the Captivity of the Saints, and that Divine Consolation Never Failed Them Therein.*

But, say they, many Christians were even led away captive. This indeed were a most pitiable fate, if they could be led away to any place where they could not find their God. But for this calamity also sacred Scripture affords great consolation. The three youths were captives; Daniel was a captive; so were other prophets: and God, the comforter, did not fail them. And in like manner He has not failed His own people in the power of a nation which, though barbarous, is yet human—He who did not abandon the prophet in the belly of a monster. These things, indeed, are turned to ridicule rather than credited by those with whom we are debating; though they believe what they read in their own books, that Arion of Methymna, the famous lyrist, when he was thrown overboard, was received on a dolphin's back and carried to land. But that story of ours about the prophet Jonah is far more incredible—more incredible because more marvelous, and more marvelous because a greater exhibition of power.

Chapter XV: *Of Regulus, in Whom We Have an Example of the Voluntary Endurance of Captivity for the Sake of Religion; Which Yet Did Not Profit Him, Though He Was a Worshiper of the Gods.*

But among their own famous men they have a very noble example of the voluntary endurance of captivity in obedience to a religious scruple. Marcus Attilius Regulus, a Roman general, was a prisoner in the hands of the Carthaginians. But they, being more anxious to exchange their prisoners with the Romans than to keep them, sent Regulus as a special envoy with their own ambassadors to negotiate this exchange, but bound him first with an oath, that if he failed to accomplish their wish, he would return to Carthage. He went and persuaded the senate to the opposite course, because he believed it was not for the advantage of the Roman republic to make an exchange of prisoners. After he had thus exerted his influence, the Romans did not compel him to return to the enemy; but what he had sworn he voluntarily performed. But the Carthaginians put him to death with refined, elaborate, and horrible tortures. They shut him up in a narrow box, in which he was compelled to stand, and in which finely sharpened nails were fixed all round about him, so that he could not lean upon any part of it without intense pain; and so they killed him by depriving him of sleep. With justice, indeed, do they applaud the virtue which rose superior to so frightful a fate. However, the gods he swore by were those who are now supposed to avenge the prohibition of their worship, by inflicting these present calamities on the human race. But if these gods, who were worshiped specially in this behalf, that they might confer happiness in this life, either willed or permitted these punishments to be inflicted on one who kept his oath to them, what more cruel punishment could they in their anger have inflicted on a perjured person? But why may I not draw from my reasoning a double inference? Regulus certainly had such reverence for the gods, that for his oath's sake he would neither remain in his own land nor go elsewhere, but without hesitation returned to his bitterest enemies. If he thought that this course would be advantageous with respect to this present life, he was certainly much deceived, for it brought his life to a frightful termination. By his own example, in fact, he taught that the gods do not secure the temporal happiness of their worshipers; since he himself, who was devoted to their worship, as both conquered in battle and taken prisoner, and then, because he refused to act in violation of the oath he had sworn by them, was tortured and put to death by a new, and hitherto unheard of, and all too horrible kind of punishment. And on the supposition that the worshipers of the gods are rewarded by felicity in the life to come, why, then, do they calumniate the influence of Christianity? Why do they assert that this disaster has overtaken the city because it has ceased to worship its gods, since, worship them as assiduously as it may, it may yet be as unfortunate as Regulus was? Or will someone carry so wonderful a blindness to the extent of wildly attempting, in the face of the evident truth, to contend that though one man might be unfortunate, though a worshiper of the gods, yet a whole city could not be so? That is to say, the power of their gods is better adapted to preserve multitudes than individuals—as if a multitude were not composed of individuals.

But if they say that M. Regulus, even while a prisoner and enduring these bodily torments, might yet enjoy the blessedness of a virtuous soul, then let them recognize that true virtue by which a city also may be blessed. For the blessedness of a community and of an individual flow from the same source; for a community is nothing else than a harmonious collection of individuals. So that I am not concerned meantime to discuss what kind of virtue Regulus possessed; enough, that by his very noble example they are forced to own that the gods are to be worshiped not for the sake of bodily comforts or external advantages; for he preferred to lose all such things rather than offend the gods by whom he had sworn. But what can we make of men who glory in having such a citizen, but dread having a city like him? If they do not dread this, then let them acknowledge that some such calamity as befell Regulus may also befall a community, though they be worshiping their gods as diligently as he; and let them no longer throw the blame of their misfortunes on Christianity. But as our present concern is with those Christians who were taken prisoners, let those who take occasion from this calamity to revile our most wholesome religion in a fashion not less imprudent than impudent, consider this and hold their peace; for if it was no reproach to their gods that a most punctilious worshiper of theirs should, for the sake of keeping his oath to them, be deprived of his native land without hope of finding another, and fall into the hands of his enemies, and be put to death by a long-drawn and exquisite torture, much less ought the Christian name to be charged with the captivity of those who believe in its power, since they, in confident expectation of a heavenly country, know that they are pilgrims even in their own homes.

Book Five

Preface

Since, then, it is established that the complete attainment of all we desire is that which constitutes felicity, which is no goddess, but a gift of God, and that therefore men can worship no god save Him who is able to make them happy—and were Felicity herself a goddess, she would with reason be the only object of worship—since, I say, this is established, let us now go on to consider why God, who is able to give with all other things those good gifts which can be possessed by men who are not good, and consequently not happy, has seen fit to grant such extended and long-continued dominion to the Roman empire; for that this was not effected by that multitude of false gods which they worshiped, we have both already adduced, and shall, as occasion offers, yet adduce considerable proof.

Chapter I: *That the Cause of the Roman Empire, and of All Kingdoms, is Neither Fortuitous Nor Consists in the Position of the Stars.*

The cause, then, of the greatness of the Roman empire is neither fortuitous nor fatal, according to the judgment or opinion of those who call those things fortuitous which either have no causes, or such causes as do not proceed from some intelligible order, and those things fatal which happen independently of the will of God and man, by the necessity of a certain order. In a word, human kingdoms are established by divine providence. And if any one attributes their existence to fate, because he calls the will or the power of God itself by the name of fate, let him keep his opinion, but correct his language. For why does he not say at first what he will say afterwards, when some one shall put the question to him, What he means by fate? For when men hear that word, according to the ordinary use of the language, they simply understand by it the virtue of that particular position of the stars which may exist at the time when any one is born or conceived, which some separate altogether from the will of God, whilst others affirm that this also is dependent on that will. But those who are of opinion that, apart from the will of God, the stars determine what we shall do, or what good things we shall possess, or what evils we shall suffer, must be refused a hearing by all, not only by those who hold the true religion, but by those who wish to be the worshipers of any gods whatsoever, even false gods. For what does this opinion really amount to but this, that no god whatever is to be worshiped or prayed to? Against these, however, our present disputation is not intended to be directed, but against those who, in defense of those whom they think to be gods, oppose the Christian religion. They, however, who make the position of the stars depend on the divine will, and in a manner decree what character each man shall have, and what good or evil shall happen to him, if they think that these same stars have that power conferred upon them by the supreme power of God, in order that they may determine these things according to their will, do a great injury to the celestial sphere, in whose most brilliant senate, and most splendid senate-house, as it were, they suppose that wicked deeds are decreed to be done,—such deeds as that, if any terrestrial state should decree them, it would be condemned to overthrow by the decree of the whole human race. What judgment, then, is left to God concerning the deeds of men, who is Lord both of the stars and of men, when to these deeds a celestial necessity is attributed? Or, if they do not say that the stars, though they have indeed received a certain power from God, who is supreme, determine those things according to their own discretion, but simply that His commands are fulfilled by them instrumentally in the application and enforcing of such necessities, are we thus to think concerning God even what it seemed unworthy that we should think concerning the will of the stars? But, if the stars are said rather to signify these things than to effect them, so that that position of the stars is, as it were, a kind of speech predicting, not causing future things—for this has been the opinion of men of no ordinary learning—certainly the mathematicians are not wont so to speak saying, for example, Mars in such or such a position signifies a homicide, but makes a homicide. But, nevertheless, though we grant that they do not speak as they ought, and that we ought to accept as the proper form of speech that employed by the philosophers in predicting those things which they think they discover in the position of the stars, how comes it that they have never been able to assign any cause why, in the life of twins, in their actions, in the events which befall them, in their professions, arts, honors, and other things pertaining to human life, also in their very death, there is often so great a difference, that, as far as these things are concerned, many entire strangers are more like them than they are like each other, though separated at birth by the smallest interval of time, but at conception generated by the same act of copulation, and at the same moment?

Chapter II: *On the Difference in the Health of Twins.*

Cicero says that the famous physician Hippocrates has left in writing that he had suspected that a certain pair of brothers were twins, from the fact that they both took ill at once, and their disease advanced to its crisis and subsided in the same time in each of them. Posidonius the Stoic, who was much given to astrology, used to explain the fact by supposing that they had been born and conceived under the same constellation. In this question the conjecture of the physician is by far more worthy to be accepted, and approaches much nearer to credibility, since, according as the parents were affected in body at the time of copulation, so might the first elements of the fœtuses have been affected, so that all that was necessary for their growth and development up till birth having been supplied from the body of the same mother, they might be born with like constitutions. Thereafter, nourished in the same house, on the same kinds of food, where they would have also the same kinds of air, the same locality, the same quality of water—which, according to the testimony of medical science, have a very great influence, good or bad, on the condition of bodily health—and where they would also be accustomed to the same kinds of exercise, they would have bodily constitutions so similar that they would be similarly affected with sickness at the same time and by the same causes. But, to wish to adduce that particular position of the stars which existed at the time when they were born or conceived as the cause of their being simultaneously affected with sickness, manifests the greatest arrogance, when so many beings of most diverse kinds, in the most diverse conditions, and subject to the most diverse events, may have been conceived and born at the same time, and in the same district, lying under the same sky. But we know that twins do not only act differently, and travel to very different places, but that they also suffer from different kinds of sickness; for which Hippocrates would give what is in my opinion the simplest reason, namely, that, through diversity of food and exercise, which arises not from the constitution of the body, but from the inclination of the mind, they may have come to be different from each other in respect of health. Moreover, Posidonius, or any other asserter of the fatal influence of the stars, will have enough to do to find anything to say to this, if he be unwilling to impose upon the minds of the uninstructed in things of which they are ignorant. But, as to what they attempt to make out from that very small interval of time elapsing between the births of twins, on account of that point in the heavens where the mark of the natal hour is placed, and which they call the "horoscope," it is either disproportionately small to the diversity which is found in the dispositions, actions, habits, and fortunes of twins, or it is disproportionately great when compared with the estate of twins, whether low or high, which is the same for both of them, the cause for whose greatest difference they place, in every case, in the hour on which one is born; and, for this reason, if the one is born so immediately after the other that there is no change in the horoscope, I demand an entire similarity in all that respects them both, which can never be found in the case of any twins. But if the slowness of the birth of the second give time for a change in the horoscope, I demand different parents, which twins can never have.

Chapter III: *Concerning the Arguments Which Nigidius the Mathematician Drew from the Potter's Wheel, in the Question About the Birth of Twins.*

It is to no purpose, therefore, that that famous fiction about the potter's wheel is brought forward, which tells of the answer which Nigidius is said to have given when he was perplexed with this question, and on account of which he was called Figulus. For, having whirled round the potter's wheel with all his strength he marked it with ink, striking it twice with the utmost rapidity, so that the strokes seemed to fall on the very same part of it. Then, when the rotation had ceased, the marks which he had made were found upon the rim of the wheel at no small distance apart. Thus, said he, considering the great rapidity with which the celestial sphere revolves, even though twins were born with as short an interval between their births as there was between the strokes which I gave this wheel, that brief interval of time is equivalent to a very great distance in the celestial sphere. Hence, said he, come whatever dissimilitudes may be remarked in the habits and fortunes of twins. This argument is more fragile than the vessels which are fashioned by the rotation of that wheel. For if there is so much significance in the heavens which cannot be comprehended by observation of the constellations, that, in the case of twins, an inheritance may fall to the one and not to the other, why, in the case of others who are not twins, do they dare, having examined their constellations, to declare such things as pertain to that secret which no one can comprehend, and to attribute them to the precise moment of the birth of each individual? Now, if such predictions in connection with the natal hours of others who are not twins are to be vindicated on the ground that they are founded on the observation of more extended spaces in the heavens, whilst those very small moments of time which separated the births of twins, and correspond to minute portions of celestial space, are to be connected with trifling things about which the mathematicians are not wont to be consulted—for who would consult them as to when he is to sit, when to walk abroad, when and on what he is to dine?—how can we be justified in so speaking, when we can point out such manifold diversity both in the habits, doings, and destinies of twins?

Chapter IV: *Concerning the Twins Esau and Jacob, Who Were Very Unlike Each Other Both in Their Character and Actions.*

In the time of the ancient fathers, to speak concerning illustrious persons, there were born two twin brothers, the one so immediately after the other, that the first took hold of the heel of the second. So great a difference existed in their lives and manners, so great a dissimilarity in their actions, so great a difference in their parents' love for them respectively, that the very contrast between them produced even a mutual hostile antipathy. Do we mean, when we say that they were so unlike each other, that when the one was walking the other was sitting, when the one was sleeping the other was waking—which differences are such as are attributed to those minute portions of space which cannot be appreciated by those who note down the position of the stars which exists at the moment of one's birth, in order that the mathematicians may be consulted concerning it? One of these twins was for a long time a hired servant; the other never served. One of them was beloved by his mother; the other was not so. One of them lost that honor which was so much valued among their people; the other obtained it. And what shall we say of their wives, their children, and their possessions? How different they were in respect to all these! If, therefore, such things as these are connected with those minute intervals of time which elapse between the births of twins, and are not to be attributed to the constellations, wherefore are they predicted in the case of others from the examination of their constellations? And if, on the other hand, these things are said to be predicted, because they are connected, not with minute and inappreciable moments, but with intervals of time which can be observed and noted down, what purpose is that potter's wheel to serve in this matter, except it be to whirl round men who have hearts of clay, in order that they may be prevented from detecting the emptiness of the talk of the mathematicians?

Chapter V: *In What Manner the Mathematicians are Convicted of Professing a Vain Science.*

Do not those very persons whom the medical sagacity of Hippocrates led him to suspect to be twins, because their disease was observed by him to develop to its crisis and to subside again in the same time in each of them—do not these, I say, serve as a sufficient refutation of those who wish to attribute to the influence of the stars that which was owing to a similarity of bodily constitution? For wherefore were they both sick of the same disease, and at the same time, and not the one after the other in the order of their birth? (for certainly they could not both be born at the same time.) Or, if the fact of their having been born at different times by no means necessarily implies that they must be sick at different times, why do they contend that the difference in the time of their births was the cause of their difference in other things? Why could they travel in foreign parts at different times, marry at different times, beget children at different times, and do many other things at different times, by reason of their having been born at different times, and yet could not, for the same reason, also be sick at different times? For if a difference in the moment of birth changed the horoscope, and occasioned dissimilarity in all other things, why has that simultaneousness which belonged to their conception remained in their attacks of sickness? Or, if the destinies of health are involved in the time of conception, but those of other things be said to be attached to the time of birth, they ought not to predict anything concerning health from examination of the constellations of birth, when the hour of conception is not also given, that its constellations may be inspected. But if they say that they predict attacks of sickness without examining the horoscope of conception, because these are indicated by the moments of birth, how could they inform either of these twins when he would be sick, from the horoscope of his birth, when the other also, who had not the same horoscope of birth, must of necessity fall sick at the same time? Again, I ask, if the distance of time between the births of twins is so great as to occasion a difference of their constellations on account of the difference of their horoscopes, and therefore of all the cardinal points to which so much influence is attributed, that even from such change there comes a difference of destiny, how is it possible that this should be so, since they cannot have been conceived at different times? Or, if two conceived at the same moment of time could have different destinies with respect to their births, why may not also two born at the same moment of time have different destinies for life and for death? For if the one moment in which both were conceived did not hinder that the one should be born before the other, why, if two are born at the same moment, should anything hinder them from dying at the same moment? If a simultaneous conception allows of twins being differently affected in the womb, why should not simultaneousness of birth allow of any two individuals having different fortunes in the world? and thus would all the fictions of this art, or rather delusion, be swept away. What strange circumstance is this, that two children conceived at the same time, nay, at the same moment, under the same position of the stars, have different fates which bring them to different hours of birth, whilst two children, born of two different mothers, at the same moment of time, under one and the same position of the stars, cannot have different fates which shall conduct them by necessity to diverse manners of life and of death? Are they at conception as yet without destinies, because they can only have them if they be born? What, therefore, do they mean when they say that, if the hour of the conception be found, many things can be predicted by these astrologers? from which also arose that story which is reiterated by some, that a certain sage chose an hour in which to lie with his wife, in order to secure his begetting an illustrious son. From this opinion also came that answer of Posidonius, the great astrologer and also philosopher, concerning those twins who were attacked with sickness at the same time, namely, "That this had happened to them because they were conceived at the same time, and born at the same time." For certainly he added "conception," lest it should be said to him that they could not both be born at the same time, knowing that at any rate they must both have been conceived at the same time; wishing thus to show that he did not attribute the fact of their being similarly and simultaneously affected with sickness to the similarity of their bodily constitutions as its proximate cause, but that he held that even in respect of the similarity of their health, they were bound together by a sidereal connection. If, therefore, the time of conception has so much to do with the similarity of destinies, these same destinies ought not to be changed by the circumstances of birth; or, if the destinies of twins be said to be changed because they are born at different times, why should we not rather understand that they had been already changed in order that they might be born at different times? Does not, then, the will of men living in the world change the destinies of birth, when the order of birth can change the destinies they had at conception?

Chapter VI: *Concerning Twins of Different Sexes.*

But even in the very conception of twins, which certainly occurs at the same moment in the case of both, it often happens that the one is conceived a male, and the other a female. I know two of different sexes who are twins. Both of them are alive, and in the flower of their age; and though they resemble each other in body, as far as difference of sex will permit, still they are very different in the whole scope and purpose of their lives (consideration being had of those differences which necessarily exist between the lives of males and females)—the one holding the office of a count, and being almost constantly away from home with the army in foreign service, the other never leaving her country's soil, or her native district. Still more—and this is more incredible, if the destinies of the stars are to be believed in, though it is not wonderful if we consider the wills of men, and the free gifts of God—he is married; she is a sacred virgin: he has begotten a numerous offspring; she has never even married. But is not the virtue of the horoscope very great? I think I have said enough to show the absurdity of that. But, say those astrologers, whatever be the virtue of the horoscope in other respects, it is certainly of significance with respect to birth. But why not also with respect to conception, which takes place undoubtedly with one act of copulation? And, indeed, so great is the force of nature, that after a woman has once conceived, she ceases to be liable to conception. Or were they, perhaps, changed at birth, either he into a male, or she into a female, because of the difference in their horoscopes? But, whilst it is not altogether absurd to say that certain sidereal influences have some power to cause differences in bodies alone—as, for instance, we see that the seasons of the year come round by the approaching and receding of the sun, and that certain kinds of things are increased in size or diminished by the waxings and wanings of the moon, such as sea-urchins, oysters, and the wonderful tides of the ocean—it does not follow that the wills of men are to be made subject to the position of the stars. The astrologers, however, when they wish to bind our actions also to the constellations, only set us on investigating whether, even in these bodies, the changes may not be attributable to some other than a sidereal cause. For what is there which more intimately concerns a body than its sex? And yet, under the same position of the stars, twins of different sexes may be conceived. Wherefore, what greater absurdity can be affirmed or believed than that the position of the stars, which was the same for both of them at the time of conception, could not cause that the one child should not have been of a different sex from her brother, with whom she had a common constellation, whilst the position of the stars which existed at the hour of their birth could cause that she should be separated from him by the great distance between marriage and holy virginity?

Chapter VII: *Concerning the Choosing of a Day for Marriage, or for Planting, or Sowing.*

Now, will any one bring forward this, that in choosing certain particular days for particular actions, men bring about certain new destinies for their actions? That man, for instance, according to this doctrine, was not born to have an illustrious son, but rather a contemptible one, and therefore, being a man of learning, he choose an hour in which to lie with his wife. He made, therefore, a destiny which he did not have before, and from that destiny of his own making something began to be fatal which was not contained in the destiny of his natal hour. Oh, singular stupidity! A day is chosen on which to marry; and for this reason, I believe, that unless a day be chosen, the marriage may fall on an unlucky day, and turn out an unhappy one. What then becomes of what the stars have already decreed at the hour of birth? Can a man be said to change by an act of choice that which has already been determined for him, whilst that which he himself has determined in the choosing of a day cannot be changed by another power? Thus, if men alone, and not all things under heaven, are subject to the influence of the stars, why do they choose some days as suitable for planting vines or trees, or for sowing grain, other days as suitable for taming beasts on, or for putting the males to the females, that the cows and mares may be impregnated, and for such-like things? If it be said that certain chosen days have an influence on these things, because the constellations rule over all terrestrial bodies, animate and inanimate, according to differences in moments of time, let it be considered what innumerable multitudes of beings are born or arise, or take their origin at the very same instant of time, which come to ends so different, that they may persuade any little boy that these observations about days are ridiculous. For who is so mad as to dare affirm that all trees, all herbs, all beasts, serpents, birds, fishes, worms, have each separately their own moments of birth or commencement? Nevertheless, men are wont, in order to try the skill of the mathematicians, to bring before them the constellations of dumb animals, the constellations of whose birth they diligently observe at home with a view to this discovery; and they prefer those mathematicians to all others, who say from the inspection of the constellations that they indicate the birth of a beast and not of a man. They also dare tell what kind of beast it is, whether it is a wool-bearing beast, or a beast suited for carrying burthens, or one fit for the plough, or for watching a house; for the astrologers are also tried with respect to the fates of dogs, and their answers concerning these are followed by shouts of admiration on the part of those who consult them. They so deceive men as to make them think that during the birth of a man the births of all other beings are suspended, so that not even a fly comes to life at the same time that he is being born, under the same region of the heavens. And if this be admitted with respect to the fly, the reasoning cannot stop there, but must ascend from flies till it lead them up to camels and elephants. Nor are they willing to attend to this, that when a day has been chosen whereon to sow a field, so many grains fall into the ground simultaneously, germinate simultaneously, spring up, come to perfection, and ripen simultaneously; and yet, of all the ears which are coeval, and, so to speak, congerminal, some are destroyed by mildew, some are devoured by the birds, and some are pulled by men. How can they say that all these had their different constellations, which they see coming to so different ends? Will they confess that it is folly to choose days for such things, and to affirm that they do not come within the sphere of the celestial decree, whilst they subject men alone to the stars, on whom alone in the world God has bestowed free wills? All these things being considered, we have good reason to believe that, when the astrologers give very many wonderful answers, it is to be attributed to the occult inspiration of spirits not of the best kind, whose care it is to insinuate into the minds of men, and to confirm in them, those false and noxious opinions concerning the fatal influence of the stars, and not to their marking and inspecting of horoscopes, according to some kind of art which in reality has no existence.

Chapter VIII: *Concerning Those Who Call by the Name of Fate, Not the Position of the Stars, But the Connection of Causes Which Depends on the Will of God.*

But, as to those who call by the name of fate, not the disposition of the stars as it may exist when any creature is conceived, or born, or commences its existence, but the whole connection and train of causes which makes everything become what it does become, there is no need that I should labor and strive with them in a merely verbal controversy, since they attribute the so-called order and connection of causes to the will and power of God most high, who is most rightly and most truly believed to know all things before they come to pass, and to leave nothing unordained; from whom are all powers, although the wills of all are not from Him. Now, that it is chiefly the will of God most high, whose power extends itself irresistibly through all things which they call fate, is proved by the following verses, of which, if I mistake not, Annæus Seneca is the author:

> "Father supreme, Thou ruler of the lofty heavens,
> Lead me where'er it is Thy pleasure; I will give
> A prompt obedience, making no delay,
> Lo! here I am. Promptly I come to do Thy sovereign will;
> If thy command shall thwart my inclination, I will still
> Follow Thee groaning, and the work assigned,
> With all the suffering of a mind repugnant,
> Will perform, being evil; which, had I been good,
> I should have undertaken and performed, though hard,
> With virtuous cheerfulness.
> The Fates do lead the man that follows willing;
> But the man that is unwilling, him they drag."

Most evidently, in this last verse, he calls that "fate" which he had before called "the will of the Father supreme," whom, he says, he is ready to obey that he may be led, being willing, not dragged, being unwilling, since "the Fates do lead the man that follows willing, but the man that is unwilling, him they drag."

The following Homeric lines, which Cicero translates into Latin, also favor this opinion:

> "Such are the minds of men, as is the light
> Which Father Jove himself doth pour
> Illustrious o'er the fruitful earth."

Not that Cicero wishes that a poetical sentiment should have any weight in a question like this; for when he says that the Stoics, when asserting the power of fate, were in the habit of using these verses from Homer, he is not treating concerning the opinion of that poet, but concerning that of those philosophers, since by these verses, which they quote in connection with the controversy which they hold about fate, is most distinctly manifested what it is which they reckon fate, since they call by the name of Jupiter him whom they reckon the supreme god, from whom, they say, hangs the whole chain of fates.

Chapter IX: *Concerning the Foreknowledge of God and the Free Will of Man, in Opposition to the Definition of Cicero.*

The manner in which Cicero addresses himself to the task of refuting the Stoics, shows that he did not think he could effect anything against them in argument unless he had first demolished divination. And this he attempts to accomplish by denying that there is any knowledge of future things, and maintains with all his might that there is no such knowledge either in God or man, and that there is no prediction of events. Thus he both denies the foreknowledge of God, and attempts by vain arguments, and by opposing to himself certain oracles very easy to be refuted, to overthrow all prophecy, even such as is clearer than the light (though even these oracles are not refuted by him).

But, in refuting these conjectures of the mathematicians, his argument is triumphant, because truly these are such as destroy and refute themselves. Nevertheless, they are far more tolerable who assert the fatal influence of the stars than they who deny the foreknowledge of future events. For, to confess that God exists, and at the same time to deny that He has foreknowledge of future things, is the most manifest folly. This Cicero himself saw, and therefore attempted to assert the doctrine embodied in the words of Scripture, "The fool hath said in his heart, There is no God." That, however, he did not do in his own person, for he saw how odious and offensive such an opinion would be; and therefore, in his book on the nature of the gods, he makes Cotta dispute concerning this against the Stoics, and preferred to give his own opinion in favor of Lucilius Balbus, to whom he assigned the defense of the Stoical position, rather than in favor of Cotta, who maintained that no divinity exists. However, in his book on divination, he in his own person most openly opposes the doctrine of the prescience of future things. But all this he seems to do in order that he may not grant the doctrine of fate, and by so doing destroy free will. For he thinks that, the knowledge of future things being once conceded, fate follows as so necessary a consequence that it cannot be denied.

But, let these perplexing debatings and disputations of the philosophers go on as they may, we, in order that we may confess the most high and true God Himself, do confess His will, supreme power, and prescience. Neither let us be afraid lest, after all, we do not do by will that which we do by will, because He, whose foreknowledge is infallible, foreknew that we would do it. It was this which Cicero was afraid of, and therefore opposed foreknowledge. The Stoics also maintained that all things do not come to pass by necessity, although they contended that all things happen according to destiny. What is it, then, that Cicero feared in the prescience of future things? Doubtless it was this—that if all future things have been foreknown, they will happen in the order in which they have been foreknown; and if they come to pass in this order, there is a certain order of things foreknown by God; and if a certain order of things, then a certain order of causes, for nothing can happen which is not preceded by some efficient cause. But if there is a certain order of causes according to which everything happens which does happen, then by fate, says he, all things happen which do happen. But if this be so, then is there nothing in our own power, and there is no such thing as freedom of will; and if we grant that, says he, the whole economy of human life is subverted. In vain are laws enacted. In vain are reproaches, praises, chidings, exhortations had recourse to; and there is no justice whatever in the appointment of rewards for the good, and punishments for the wicked. And that consequences so disgraceful, and absurd, and pernicious to humanity may not follow, Cicero chooses to reject the foreknowledge of future things, and shuts up the religious mind to this alternative, to make choice between two things, either that something is in our own power, or that there is foreknowledge—both of which cannot be true; but if the one is affirmed, the other is thereby denied. He therefore, like a truly great and wise man, and one who consulted very much and very skillfully for the good of humanity, of those two chose the freedom of the will, to confirm which he denied the foreknowledge of future things; and thus, wishing to make men free he makes them sacrilegious. But the religious mind chooses both, confesses both, and maintains both by the faith of piety. But how so? says Cicero; for the knowledge of future things being granted, there follows a chain of consequences which ends in this, that there can be nothing depending on our own free wills. And further, if there is anything depending on our wills, we must go backwards by the same steps of reasoning till we arrive at the conclusion that there is no foreknowledge of future things. For we go backwards through all the steps in the following order: If there is free will, all things do not happen according to fate; if all things do not happen according to fate, there is not a certain order of causes; and if there is not a certain order of causes, neither is there a certain order of things foreknown by God—for things cannot come to pass except they are preceded by efficient causes—but, if there is no fixed and certain order of causes foreknown by God, all things cannot be said to happen according as He foreknew that they would happen. And further, if it is not true that all things happen just as they have been foreknown by Him, there is not, says he, in God any foreknowledge of future events.

Now, against the sacrilegious and impious darings of reason, we assert both that God knows all things before they come to pass, and that we do by our free will whatsoever we know and feel to be done by us only because we will it. But that all things come to pass by fate, we do not say; nay we affirm that nothing comes to pass by fate; for we demonstrate that the name of fate, as it is wont to be used by those who speak of fate, meaning thereby the position of the stars at the time of each one's conception or birth, is an unmeaning word, for astrology itself is a delusion. But an order of causes in which the highest efficiency is attributed to the will of God, we neither deny nor do we designate it by the name of fate, unless, perhaps, we may understand fate to mean that which is spoken, deriving it from fari, to speak; for we cannot deny that it is written in the sacred Scriptures, "God hath spoken once; these two things have I heard, that power belongeth unto God. Also unto Thee, O God, belongeth mercy: for Thou wilt render unto every man according to his works." Now the expression, "Once hath He spoken," is to be understood as meaning "immovably," that is, unchangeably hath He spoken, inasmuch as He knows unchangeably all things which shall be, and all things which He will do. We might, then, use the word fate in the sense it bears when derived from fari, to speak, had it not already come to be understood in another sense, into which I am unwilling that the hearts of men should unconsciously slide. But it does not follow that, though there is for God a certain order of all causes, there must therefore be nothing depending on the free exercise of our own wills, for our wills themselves are included in that order of causes which is certain to God, and is embraced by His foreknowledge, for human wills are also causes of human actions; and He who foreknew all the causes of things would certainly among those causes not have been ignorant of our wills. For even that very concession which Cicero himself makes is enough to refute him in this argument. For what does it help him to say that nothing takes place without a cause, but that every cause is not fatal, there being a fortuitous cause, a natural cause, and a voluntary cause? It is sufficient that he confesses that whatever happens must be preceded by a cause. For we say that those causes which are called fortuitous are not a mere name for the absence of causes, but are only latent, and we attribute them either to the will of the true God, or to that of spirits of some kind or other. And as to natural causes, we by no means separate them from the will of Him who is the author and framer of all nature. But now as to voluntary causes. They are referable either to God, or to angels, or to men, or to animals of whatever description, if indeed those instinctive movements of animals devoid of reason, by which, in accordance with their own nature, they seek or shun various things, are to be called wills. And when I speak of the wills of angels, I mean either the wills of good angels, whom we call the angels of God, or of the wicked angels, whom we call the angels of the devil, or demons. Also by the wills of men I mean the wills either of the good or of the wicked. And from this we conclude that there are no efficient causes of all things which come to pass unless voluntary causes, that is, such as belong to that nature which is the spirit of life. For the air or wind is called spirit, but, inasmuch as it is a body, it is not the spirit of life. The spirit of life, therefore, which quickens all things, and is the creator of every body, and of every created spirit, is God Himself, the uncreated spirit. In His supreme will resides the power which acts on the wills of all created spirits, helping the good, judging the evil, controlling all, granting power to some, not granting it to others. For, as He is the creator of all natures, so also is He the bestower of all powers, not of all wills; for wicked wills are not from Him, being contrary to nature, which is from Him. As to bodies, they are more subject to wills: some to our wills, by which I mean the wills of all living mortal creatures, but more to the wills of men than of beasts. But all of them are most of all subject to the will of God, to whom all wills also are subject, since they have no power except what He has bestowed upon them. The cause of things, therefore, which makes but is made, is God; but all other causes both make and are made. Such are all created spirits, and especially the rational. Material causes, therefore, which may rather be said to be made than to make, are not to be reckoned among efficient causes, because they can only do what the wills of spirits do by them. How, then, does an order of causes which is certain to the foreknowledge of God necessitate that there should be nothing which is dependent on our wills, when our wills themselves have a very important place in the order of causes? Cicero, then, contends with those who call this order of causes fatal, or rather designate this order itself by the name of fate; to which we have an abhorrence, especially on account of the word, which men have become accustomed to understand as meaning what is not true. But, whereas he denies that the order of all causes is most certain, and perfectly clear to the prescience of God, we detest his opinion more than the Stoics do. For he either denies that God exists—which, indeed, in an assumed personage, he has labored to do, in his book De Natura Deorum—or if he confesses that He exists, but denies that He is prescient of future things, what is that but just "the fool saying in his heart there is no God?" For one who is not prescient of all future things is not God. Wherefore our wills also have just so much power as God willed and foreknew that they should have; and therefore whatever power they have, they have it within most certain limits; and whatever they are to do, they are most assuredly to do, for He whose foreknowledge is infallible foreknew that they would have the power to do it, and would do it. Wherefore, if I should choose to apply the name of fate to anything at all, I should rather say that fate belongs to the weaker of two parties, will to the stronger, who has the other in his power, than that the freedom of our will is excluded by that order of causes, which, by an unusual application of the word peculiar to themselves, the Stoics call Fate.

Chapter X: *Whether Our Wills are Ruled by Necessity.*

Wherefore, neither is that necessity to be feared, for dread of which the Stoics labored to make such distinctions among the causes of things as should enable them to rescue certain things from the dominion of necessity, and to subject others to it. Among those things which they wished not to be subject to necessity they placed our wills, knowing that they would not be free if subjected to necessity. For if that is to be called our necessity which is not in our power, but even though we be unwilling effects what it can effect—as, for instance, the necessity of death—it is manifest that our wills by which we live up-rightly or wickedly are not under such a necessity; for we do many things which, if we were not willing, we should certainly not do. This is primarily true of the act of willing itself—for if we will, it is; if we will not, it is not—for we should not will if we were unwilling. But if we define necessity to be that according to which we say that it is necessary that anything be of such or such a nature, or be done in such and such a manner, I know not why we should have any dread of that necessity taking away the freedom of our will. For we do not put the life of God or the foreknowledge of God under necessity if we should say that it is necessary that God should live forever, and foreknow all things; as neither is His power diminished when we say that He cannot die or fall into error—for this is in such a way impossible to Him, that if it were possible for Him, He would be of less power. But assuredly He is rightly called omnipotent, though He can neither die nor fall into error. For He is called omnipotent on account of His doing what He wills, not on account of His suffering what He wills not; for if that should befall Him, He would by no means be omnipotent. Wherefore, He cannot do some things for the very reason that He is omnipotent. So also, when we say that it is necessary that, when we will, we will by free choice, in so saying we both affirm what is true beyond doubt, and do not still subject our wills thereby to a necessity which destroys liberty. Our wills, therefore, exist as wills, and do themselves whatever we do by willing, and which would not be done if we were unwilling. But when any one suffers anything, being unwilling by the will of another, even in that case will retains its essential validity—we do not mean the will of the party who inflicts the suffering, for we resolve it into the power of God. For if a will should simply exist, but not be able to do what it wills, it would be overborne by a more powerful will. Nor would this be the case unless there had existed will, and that not the will of the other party, but the will of him who willed, but was not able to accomplish what he willed. Therefore, whatsoever a man suffers contrary to his own will, he ought not to attribute to the will of men, or of angels, or of any created spirit, but rather to His will who gives power to wills. It is not the case, therefore, that because God foreknew what would be in the power of our wills, there is for that reason nothing in the power of our wills. For he who foreknew this did not foreknow nothing. Moreover, if He who foreknew what would be in the power of our wills did not foreknow nothing, but something, assuredly, even though He did foreknow, there is something in the power of our wills. Therefore we are by no means compelled, either, retaining the prescience of God, to take away the freedom of the will, or, retaining the freedom of the will, to deny that He is prescient of future things, which is impious. But we embrace both. We faithfully and sincerely confess both. The former, that we may believe well; the latter, that we may live well. For he lives ill who does not believe well concerning God. Wherefore, be it far from us, in order to maintain our freedom, to deny the prescience of Him by whose help we are or shall be free. Consequently, it is not in vain that laws are enacted, and that reproaches, exhortations, praises, and vituperations are had recourse to; for these also He foreknew, and they are of great avail, even as great as He foreknew that they would be of. Prayers, also, are of avail to procure those things which He foreknew that He would grant to those who offered them; and with justice have rewards been appointed for good deeds, and punishments for sins. For a man does not therefore sin because God foreknew that he would sin. Nay, it cannot be doubted but that it is the man himself who sins when he does sin, because He, whose foreknowledge is infallible, foreknew not that fate, or fortune, or something else would sin, but that the man himself would sin, who, if he wills not, sins not. But if he shall not will to sin, even this did God foreknow.

Book Eight

Chapter XI: *How Plato Has Been Able to Approach So Nearly to Christian Knowledge.*

Certain partakers with us in the grace of Christ, wonder when they hear and read that Plato had conceptions concerning God, in which they recognize considerable agreement with the truth of our religion. Some have concluded from this, that when he went to Egypt he had heard the prophet Jeremiah, or, whilst traveling in the same country, had read the prophetic scriptures, which opinion I myself have expressed in certain of my writings. But a careful calculation of dates, contained in chronological history, shows that Plato was born about a hundred years after the time in which Jeremiah prophesied, and, as he lived eighty-one years, there are found to have been about seventy years from his death to that time when Ptolemy, king of Egypt, requested the prophetic scriptures of the Hebrew people to be sent to him from Judea, and committed them to seventy Hebrews, who also knew the Greek tongue, to be translated and kept. Therefore, on that voyage of his, Plato could neither have seen Jeremiah, who was dead so long before, nor have read those same scriptures which had not yet been translated into the Greek language, of which he was a master, unless, indeed, we say that, as he was most earnest in the pursuit of knowledge, he also studied those writings through an interpreter, as he did those of the Egyptians—not, indeed, writing a translation of them (the facilities for doing which were only gained even by Ptolemy in return for munificent acts of kindness, though fear of his kingly authority might have seemed a sufficient motive), but learning as much as he possibly could concerning their contents by means of conversation. What warrants this supposition are the opening verses of Genesis: "In the beginning God made the heaven and earth. And the earth was invisible, and without order; and darkness was over the abyss: and the Spirit of God moved over the waters." For in the Timæus, when writing on the formation of the world, he says that God first united earth and fire; from which it is evident that he assigns to fire a place in heaven. This opinion bears a certain resemblance to the statement, "In the beginning God made heaven and earth." Plato next speaks of those two intermediary elements, water and air, by which the other two extremes, namely, earth and fire, were mutually united; from which circumstance he is thought to have so understood the words, "The Spirit of God moved over the waters." For, not paying sufficient attention to the designations given by those scriptures to the Spirit of God, he may have thought that the four elements are spoken of in that place, because the air also is called spirit. Then, as to Plato's saying that the philosopher is a lover of God, nothing shines forth more conspicuously in those sacred writings. But the most striking thing in this connection, and that which most of all inclines me almost to assent to the opinion that Plato was not ignorant of those writings, is the answer which was given to the question elicited from the holy Moses when the words of God were conveyed to him by the angel; for, when he asked what was the name of that God who was commanding him to go and deliver the Hebrew people out of Egypt, this answer was given: "I am who am; and thou shalt say to the children of Israel, He who is sent me unto you;" as though compared with Him that truly is, because He is unchangeable, those things which have been created mutable are not—a truth which Plato zealously held, and most diligently commended. And I know not whether this sentiment is anywhere to be found in the books of those who were before Plato, unless in that book where it is said, "I am who am; and thou shalt say to the children of Israel, who is sent me unto you."

Chapter XII: *That Even the Platonists, Though They Say These Things Concerning the One True God, Nevertheless Thought that Sacred Rites Were to Be Performed in Honor of Many Gods.*

But we need not determine from what source he learned these things—whether it was from the books of the ancients who preceded him, or, as is more likely, from the words of the apostle: "Because that which is known of God, has been manifested among them, for God hath manifested it to them. For His invisible things from the creation of the world are clearly seen, being understood by those things which have been made, also His eternal power and Godhead." From whatever source he may have derived this knowledge, then, I think I have made it sufficiently plain that I have not chosen the Platonic philosophers undeservedly as the parties with whom to discuss; because the question we have just taken up concerns the natural theology—the question, namely, whether sacred rites are to be performed to one God, or to many, for the sake of the happiness which is to be after death. I have specially chosen them because their juster thoughts concerning the one God who made heaven and earth, have made them illustrious among philosophers. This has given them such superiority to all others in the judgment of posterity, that, though Aristotle, the disciple of Plato, a man of eminent abilities, inferior in eloquence to Plato, yet far superior to many in that respect, had founded the Peripatetic sect—so called because they were in the habit of walking about during their disputations—and though he had, through the greatness of his fame, gathered very many disciples into his school, even during the life of his master; and though Plato at his death was succeeded in his school, which was called the Academy, by Speusippus, his sister's son, and Xenocrates, his beloved disciple, who, together with their successors, were called from this name of the school, Academics; nevertheless the most illustrious recent philosophers, who have chosen to follow Plato, have been unwilling to be called Peripatetics, or Academics, but have preferred the name of Platonists. Among these were the renowned Plotinus, Iamblichus, and Porphyry, who were Greeks, and the African Apuleius, who was learned both in the Greek and Latin tongues. All these, however, and the rest who were of the same school, and also Plato himself, thought that sacred rites ought to be performed in honor of many gods.

Chapter XIII: *Concerning the Opinion of Plato, According to Which He Defined the Gods as Beings Entirely Good and the Friends of Virtue.*

Therefore, although in many other important respects they differ from us, nevertheless with respect to this particular point of difference, which I have just stated, as it is one of great moment, and the question on hand concerns it, I will first ask them to what gods they think that sacred rites are to be performed—to the good or to the bad, or to both the good and the bad? But we have the opinion of Plato affirming that all the gods are good, and that there is not one of the gods bad. It follows, therefore, that these are to be performed to the good, for then they are performed to gods; for if they are not good, neither are they gods. Now, if this be the case (for what else ought we to believe concerning the gods?), certainly it explodes the opinion that the bad gods are to be propitiated by sacred rites in order that they may not harm us, but the good gods are to be invoked in order that they may assist us. For there are no bad gods, and it is to the good that, as they say, the due honor of such rites is to be paid. Of what character, then, are those gods who love scenic displays, even demanding that a place be given them among divine things, and that they be exhibited in their honor? The power of these gods proves that they exist, but their liking such things proves that they are bad. For it is well-known what Plato's opinion was concerning scenic plays. He thinks that the poets themselves, because they have composed songs so unworthy of the majesty and goodness of the gods, ought to be banished from the state. Of what character, therefore, are those gods who contend with Plato himself about those scenic plays? He does not suffer the gods to be defamed by false crimes; the gods command those same crimes to be celebrated in their own honor.

In fine, when they ordered these plays to be inaugurated, they not only demanded base things, but also did cruel things, taking from Titus Latinius his son, and sending a disease upon him because he had refused to obey them, which they removed when he had fulfilled their commands. Plato, however, bad though they were, did not think they were to be feared; but, holding to his opinion with the utmost firmness and constancy, does not hesitate to remove from a well-ordered state all the sacrilegious follies of the poets, with which these gods are delighted because they themselves are impure. But Labeo places this same Plato (as I have mentioned already in the second book) among the demigods. Now Labeo thinks that the bad deities are to be propitiated with bloody victims, and by fasts accompanied with the same, but the good deities with plays, and all other things which are associated with joyfulness. How comes it, then, that the demigod Plato so persistently dares to take away those pleasures, because he deems them base, not from the demigods but from the gods, and these the good gods? And, moreover, those very gods themselves do certainly refute the opinion of Labeo, for they showed themselves in the case of Latinius to be not only wanton and sportive, but also cruel and terrible. Let the Platonists, therefore, explain these things to us, since, following the opinion of their master, they think that all the gods are good and honorable, and friendly to the virtues of the wise, holding it unlawful to think otherwise concerning any of the gods. We will explain it, say they. Let us then attentively listen to them.

Chapter XIV: *Of the Opinion of Those Who Have Said that Rational Souls are of Three Kinds, to Wit, Those of the Celestial Gods, Those of the Aerial Demons, and Those of Terrestrial Men.*

There is, say they, a threefold division of all animals endowed with a rational soul, namely, into gods, men, and demons. The gods occupy the loftiest region, men the lowest, the demons the middle region. For the abode of the gods is heaven, that of men the earth, that of the demons the air. As the dignity of their regions is diverse, so also is that of their natures; therefore the gods are better than men and demons. Men have been placed below the gods and demons, both in respect of the order of the regions they inhabit, and the difference of their merits. The demons, therefore, who hold the middle place, as they are inferior to the gods, than whom they inhabit a lower region, so they are superior to men, than whom they inhabit a loftier one. For they have immortality of body in common with the gods, but passions of the mind in common with men. On which account, say they, it is not wonderful that they are delighted with the obscenities of the theatre, and the fictions of the poets, since they are also subject to human passions, from which the gods are far removed, and to which they are altogether strangers. Whence we conclude that it was not the gods, who are all good and highly exalted, that Plato deprived of the pleasure of theatric plays, by reprobating and prohibiting the fictions of the poets, but the demons.

Of these things many have written: among others Apuleius, the Platonist of Madaura, who composed a whole work on the subject, entitled, Concerning the God of Socrates. He there discusses and explains of what kind that deity was who attended on Socrates, a sort of familiar, by whom it is said he was admonished to desist from any action which would not turn out to his advantage. He asserts most distinctly, and proves at great length, that it was not a god but a demon; and he discusses with great diligence the opinion of Plato concerning the lofty estate of the gods, the lowly estate of men, and the middle estate of demons. These things being so, how did Plato dare to take away, if not from the gods, whom he removed from all human contagion, certainly from the demons, all the pleasures of the theatre, by expelling the poets from the state? Evidently in this way he wished to admonish the human soul, although still confined in these moribund members, to despise the shameful commands of the demons, and to detest their impurity, and to choose rather the splendor of virtue. But if Plato showed himself virtuous in answering and prohibiting these things, then certainly it was shameful of the demons to command them. Therefore either Apuleius is wrong, and Socrates' familiar did not belong to this class of deities, or Plato held contradictory opinions, now honoring the demons, now removing from the well-regulated state the things in which they delighted, or Socrates is not to be congratulated on the friendship of the demon, of which Apuleius was so ashamed that he entitled his book On the God of Socrates, whilst according to the tenor of his discussion, wherein he so diligently and at such length distinguishes gods from demons, he ought not to have entitled it, Concerning the God, but Concerning the Demon of Socrates. But he preferred to put this into the discussion itself rather than into the title of his book. For, through the sound doctrine which has illuminated human society, all, or almost all men have such a horror at the name of demons, that every one who before reading the dissertation of Apuleius, which sets forth the dignity of demons, should have read the title of the book, On the Demon of Socrates, would certainly have thought that the author was not a sane man. But what did even Apuleius find to praise in the demons, except subtlety and strength of body and a higher place of habitation? For when he spoke generally concerning their manners, he said nothing that was good, but very much that was bad. Finally, no one, when he has read that book, wonders that they desired to have even the obscenity of the stage among divine things, or that, wishing to be thought gods, they should be delighted with the crimes of the gods, or that all those sacred solemnities, whose obscenity occasions laughter, and whose shameful cruelty causes horror, should be in agreement with their passions.

Chapter XV: *That the Demons are Not Better Than Men Because of Their Aerial Bodies, or on Account of Their Superior Place of Abode.*

Wherefore let not the mind truly religious, and submitted to the true God, suppose that demons are better than men, because they have better bodies. Otherwise it must put many beasts before itself which are superior to us both in acuteness of the senses, in ease and quickness of movement, in strength and in long-continued vigor of body. What man can equal the eagle or the vulture in strength of vision? Who can equal the dog in acuteness of smell? Who can equal the hare, the stag, and all the birds in swiftness? Who can equal in strength the lion or the elephant? Who can equal in length of life the serpents, which are affirmed to put off old age along with their skin, and to return to youth again? But as we are better than all these by the possession of reason and understanding, so we ought also to be better than the demons by living good and virtuous lives. For divine providence gave to them bodies of a better quality than ours, that that in which we excel them might in this way be commended to us as deserving to be far more cared for than the body, and that we should learn to despise the bodily excellence of the demons compared with goodness of life, in respect of which we are better than they, knowing that we too shall have immortality of body—not an immortality tortured by eternal punishment, but that which is consequent on purity of soul.

But now, as regards loftiness of place, it is altogether ridiculous to be so influenced by the fact that the demons inhabit the air, and we the earth, as to think that on that account they are to be put before us; for in this way we put all the birds before ourselves. But the birds, when they are weary with flying, or require to repair their bodies with food, come back to the earth to rest or to feed, which the demons, they say, do not. Are they, therefore, inclined to say that the birds are superior to us, and the demons superior to the birds? But if it be madness to think so, there is no reason why we should think that, on account of their inhabiting a loftier element, the demons have a claim to our religious submission. But as it is really the case that the birds of the air are not only not put before us who dwell on the earth; but are even subjected to us on account of the dignity of the rational soul which is in us, so also it is the case that the demons, though they are aerial, are not better than we who are terrestrial because the air is higher than the earth, but, on the contrary, men are to be put before demons because their despair is not to be compared to the hope of pious men. Even that law of Plato's, according to which he mutually orders and arranges the four elements, inserting between the two extreme elements—namely, fire, which is in the highest degree mobile, and the immovable earth—the two middle ones, air and water, that by how much the air is higher up than the water, and the fire than the air, by so much also are the waters higher than the earth—this law, I say, sufficiently admonishes us not to estimate the merits of animated creatures according to the grades of the elements. And Apuleius himself says that man is a terrestrial animal in common with the rest, who is nevertheless to be put far before aquatic animals, though Plato puts the waters themselves before the land. By this he would have us understand that the same order is not to be observed when the question concerns the merits of animals, though it seems to be the true one in the gradation of bodies; for it appears to be possible that a soul of a higher order may inhabit a body of a lower, and a soul of a lower order a body of a higher.

Chapter XVI: *What Apuleius the Platonist Thought Concerning the Manners and Actions of Demons.*

The same Apuleius, when speaking concerning the manners

of demons, said that they are agitated with the same perturbations of mind as men; that they are provoked by injuries, propitiated by services and by gifts, rejoice in honors, are delighted with a variety of sacred rites, and are annoyed if any of them be neglected. Among other things, he also says that on them depend the divinations of augurs, soothsayers, and prophets, and the revelations of dreams, and that from them also are the miracles of the magicians. But, when giving a brief definition of them, he says, "Demons are of an animal nature, passive in soul, rational in mind, aerial in body, eternal in time." "Of which five things, the three first are common to them and us, the fourth peculiar to themselves, and the fifth common to therewith the gods." But I see that they have in common with the gods two of the first things, which they have in common with us. For he says that the gods also are animals; and when he is assigning to every order of beings its own element, he places us among the other terrestrial animals which live and feel upon the earth. Wherefore, if the demons are animals as to genus, this is common to them, not only with men, but also with the gods and with beasts; if they are rational as to their mind, this is common to them with the gods and with men; if they are eternal in time, this is common to them with the gods only; if they are passive as to their soul, this is common to them with men only; if they are aerial in body, in this they are alone. Therefore it is no great thing for them to be of an animal nature, for so also are the beasts; in being rational as to mind, they are not above ourselves, for so are we also; and as to their being eternal as to time, what is the advantage of that if they are not blessed? for better is temporal happiness than eternal misery. Again, as to their being passive in soul, how are they in this respect above us, since we also are so, but would not have been so had we not been miserable? Also, as to their being aerial in body, how much value is to be set on that, since a soul of any kind whatsoever is to be set above every body? and therefore religious worship, which ought to be rendered from the soul, is by no means due to that thing which is inferior to the soul. Moreover, if he had, among those things which he says belong to demons, enumerated virtue, wisdom, happiness, and affirmed that they have those things in common with the gods, and, like them, eternally, he would assuredly have attributed to them something greatly to be desired, and much to be prized. And even in that case it would not have been our duty to worship them like God on account of these things, but rather to worship Him from whom we know they had received them. But how much less are they really worthy of divine honor—those aerial animals who are only rational that they may be capable of misery, passive that they may be actually miserable, and eternal that it may be impossible for them to end their misery!

Chapter XVII: *Whether It is Proper that Men Should Worship Those Spirits from Whose Vices It is Necessary that They Be Freed.*

Wherefore, to omit other things, and confine our attention to that which he says is common to the demons with us, let us ask this question: If all the four elements are full of their own animals, the fire and the air of immortal, and the water and the earth of mortal ones, why are the souls of demons agitated by the whirlwinds and tempests of passions?—for the Greek word παθος means perturbation, whence he chose to call the demons "passive in soul," because the word passion, which is derived from πάθος, signified a commotion of the mind contrary to reason. Why, then, are these things in the minds of demons which are not in beasts? For if anything of this kind appears in beasts, it is not perturbation, because it is not contrary to reason, of which they are devoid. Now it is foolishness or misery which is the cause of these perturbations in the case of men, for we are not yet blessed in the possession of that perfection of wisdom which is promised to us at last, when we shall be set free from our present mortality. But the gods, they say, are free from these perturbations, because they are not only eternal, but also blessed; for they also have the same kind of rational souls, but most pure from all spot and plague. Wherefore, if the gods are free from perturbation because they are blessed, not miserable animals, and the beasts are free from them because they are animals which are capable neither of blessedness nor misery, it remains that the demons, like men, are subject to perturbations because they are not blessed but miserable animals. What folly, therefore, or rather what madness, to submit ourselves through any sentiment of religion to demons, when it belongs to the true religion to deliver us from that depravity which makes us like to them! For Apuleius himself, although he is very sparing toward them, and thinks they are worthy of divine honors, is nevertheless compelled to confess that they are subject to anger; and the true religion commands us not to be moved with anger, but rather to resist it. The demons are won over by gifts; and the true religion commands us to favor no one on account of gifts received. The demons are flattered by honors; but the true religion commands us by no means to be moved by such things. The demons are haters of some men and lovers of others, not in consequence of a prudent and calm judgment, but because of what he calls their "passive soul;" whereas the true religion commands us to love even our enemies. Lastly, the true religion commands us to put away all disquietude of heart and agitation of mind, and also all commotions and tempests of the soul, which Apuleius asserts to be continually swelling and surging in the souls of demons. Why, therefore, except through foolishness and miserable error shouldst thou humble thyself to worship a being to whom thou desirest to be unlike in thy life? And why shouldst thou pay religious homage to him whom thou art unwilling to imitate, when it is the highest duty of religion to imitate Him whom thou worshipest?

Chapter XVIII: *What Kind of Religion that is Which Teaches that Men Ought to Employ the Advocacy of Demons in Order to Be Recommended to the Favor of the Good Gods.*

In vain, therefore, have Apuleius, and they who think with him, conferred on the demons the honor of placing them in the air, between the ethereal heavens and the earth, that they may carry to the gods the prayers of men, to men the answers of the gods: for Plato held, they say, that no god has intercourse with man. They who believe these things have thought it unbecoming that men should have intercourse with the gods, and the gods with men, but a befitting thing that the demons should have intercourse with both gods and men, presenting to the gods the petitions of men, and conveying to men what the gods have granted; so that a chaste man, and one who is a stranger to the crimes of the magic arts, must use as patrons, through whom the gods may be induced to hear him, demons who love these crimes, although the very fact of his not loving them ought to have recommended him to them as one who deserved to be listened to with greater readiness and willingness on their part. They love the abominations of the stage, which chastity does not love. They love, in the sorceries of the magicians, "a thousand arts of inflicting harm," which innocence does not love. Yet both chastity and innocence, if they wish to obtain anything from the gods, will not be able to do so by their own merits, except their enemies act as mediators on their behalf. Apuleius need not attempt to justify the fictions of the poets, and the mockeries of the stage. If human modesty can act so faithlessly towards itself as not only to love shameful things, but even to think that they are pleasing to the divinity, we can cite on the other side their own highest authority and teacher, Plato.

Chapter XIX: *Of the Impiety of the Magic Art, Which is Dependent on the Assistance of Malign Spirits.*

Moreover, against those magic arts, concerning which some men, exceedingly wretched and exceedingly impious, delight to boast, may not public opinion itself be brought forward as a witness? For why are those arts so severely punished by the laws, if they are the works of deities who ought to be worshiped? Shall it be said that the Christians have ordained those laws by which magic arts are punished? With what other meaning, except that these sorceries are without doubt pernicious to the human race, did the most illustrious poet say,

> "By heaven, I swear, and your dear life,
> Unwillingly these arms I wield,
> And take, to meet the coming strife,
> Enchantment's sword and shield."

And that also which he says in another place concerning magic arts, "I've seen him to another place transport the standing corn," has reference to the fact that the fruits of one field are said to be transferred to another by these arts which this pestiferous and accursed doctrine teaches. Does not Cicero inform us that, among the laws of the Twelve Tables, that is, the most ancient laws of the Romans, there was a law written which appointed a punishment to be inflicted on him who should do this? Lastly, was it before Christian judges that Apuleius himself was accused of magic arts? Had he known these arts to be divine and pious, and congruous with the works of divine power, he ought not only to have confessed, but also to have professed them, rather blaming the laws by which these things were prohibited and pronounced worthy of condemnation, while they ought to have been held worthy of admiration and respect. For by so doing, either he would have persuaded the judges to adopt his own opinion, or, if they had shown their partiality for unjust laws, and condemned him to death notwithstanding his praising and commending such things, the demons would have bestowed on his soul such rewards as he deserved, who, in order to proclaim and set forth their divine works, had not feared the loss of his human life. As our martyrs, when that religion was charged on them as a crime, by which they knew they were made safe and most glorious throughout eternity, did not choose, by denying it, to escape temporal punishments, but rather by confessing, professing, and proclaiming it, by enduring all things for it with fidelity and fortitude, and by dying for it with pious calmness, put to shame the law by which that religion was prohibited, and caused its revocation. But there is extant a most copious and eloquent oration of this Platonic philosopher, in which he defends himself against the charge of practising these arts, affirming that he is wholly a stranger to them, and only wishing to show his innocence by denying such things as cannot be innocently committed. But all the miracles of the magicians, who he thinks are justly deserving of condemnation, are performed according to the teaching and by the power of demons. Why, then, does he think that they ought to be honored? For he asserts that they are necessary, in order to present our prayers to the gods, and yet their works are such as we must shun if we wish our prayers to reach the true God. Again, I ask, what kind of prayers of men does he suppose are presented to the good gods by the demons? If magical prayers, they will have none such; if lawful prayers, they will not receive them through such beings. But if a sinner who is penitent pour out prayers, especially if he has committed any crime of sorcery, does he receive pardon through the intercession of those demons by whose instigation and help he has fallen into the sin he mourns? or do the demons themselves, in order that they may merit pardon for the penitent, first become penitents because they have deceived them? This no one ever said concerning the demons; for had this been the case, they would never have dared to seek for themselves divine honors. For how should they do so who desired by penitence to obtain the grace of pardon; seeing that such detestable pride could not exist along with a humility worthy of pardon?

Chapter XX: *Whether We are to Believe that the Good Gods are More Willing to Have Intercourse with Demons Than with Men.*

But does any urgent and most pressing cause compel the demons to mediate between the gods and men, that they may offer the prayers of men, and bring back the answers from the gods? and if so, what, pray, is that cause, what is that so great necessity? Because, say they, no god has intercourse with man. Most admirable holiness of God, which has no intercourse with a supplicating man, and yet has intercourse with an arrogant demon! which has no intercourse with a penitent man, and yet has intercourse with a deceiving demon! which has no intercourse with a man fleeing for refuge to the divine nature, and yet has intercourse with a demon feigning divinity! which has no intercourse with a man seeking pardon, and yet has intercourse with a demon persuading to wickedness! which has no intercourse with a man expelling the poets by means of philosophical writings from a well-regulated state, and yet has intercourse with a demon requesting from the princes and priests of a state the theatrical performance of the mockeries of the poets! which has no intercourse with the man who prohibits the ascribing of crime to the gods, and yet has intercourse with a demon who takes delight in the fictitious representation of their crimes! which has no intercourse with a man punishing the crimes of the magicians by just laws, and yet has intercourse with a demon teaching and practising magical arts! which has no intercourse with a man shunning the imitation of a demon, and yet has intercourse with a demon lying in wait for the deception of a man!

Chapter XXI: *Whether the Gods Use the Demons as Messengers and Interpreters, and Whether They are Deceived by Them Willingly, or Without Their Own Knowledge.*

But herein, no doubt, lies the great necessity for this absurdity, so unworthy of the gods, that the ethereal gods, who are concerned about human affairs, would not know what terrestrial men were doing unless the aerial demons should bring them intelligence, because the ether is suspended far away from the earth and far above it, but the air is contiguous both to the ether and to the earth. O admirable wisdom! what else do these men think concerning the gods who, they say, are all in the highest degree good, but that they are concerned about human affairs, lest they should seem unworthy of worship, whilst, on the other hand, from the distance between the elements, they are ignorant of terrestrial things? It is on this account that they have supposed the demons to be necessary as agents, through whom the gods may inform themselves with respect to human affairs, and through whom, when necessary, they may succor men; and it is on account of this office that the demons themselves have been held as deserving of worship. If this be the case, then a demon is better known by these good gods through nearness of body, than a man is by goodness of mind. O mournful necessity, or shall I not rather say detestable and vain error, that I may not impute vanity to the divine nature! For if the gods can, with their minds free from the hindrance of bodies, see our mind, they do not need the demons as messengers from our mind to them; but if the ethereal gods, by means of their bodies, perceive the corporeal indices of minds, as the countenance, speech, motion, and thence understand what the demons tell them, then it is also possible that they may be deceived by the falsehoods of demons. Moreover, if the divinity of the gods cannot be deceived by the demons, neither can it be ignorant of our actions. But I would they would tell me whether the demons have informed the gods that the fictions of the poets concerning the crimes of the gods displease Plato, concealing the pleasure which they themselves take in them; or whether they have concealed both, and have preferred that the gods should be ignorant with respect to this whole matter, or have told both, as well the pious prudence of Plato with respect to the gods as their own lust, which is injurious to the gods; or whether they have concealed Plato's opinion, according to which he was unwilling that the gods should be defamed with falsely alleged crimes through the impious license of the poets, whilst they have not been ashamed nor afraid to make known their own wickedness, which make them love theatrical plays, in which the infamous deeds of the gods are celebrated. Let them choose which they will of these four alternatives, and let them consider how much evil any one of them would require them to think of the gods. For if they choose the first, they must then confess that it was not possible for the good gods to dwell with the good Plato, though he sought to prohibit things injurious to them, whilst they dwelt with evil demons, who exulted in their injuries; and this because they suppose that the good gods can only know a good man, placed at so great a distance from them, through the mediation of evil demons, whom they could know on account of their nearness to themselves. If they shall choose the second, and shall say that both these things are concealed by the demons, so that the gods are wholly ignorant both of Plato's most religious law and the sacrilegious pleasure of the demons, what, in that case, can the gods know to any profit with respect to human affairs through these mediating demons, when they do not know those things which are decreed, through the piety of good men, for the honor of the good gods against the lust of evil demons? But if they shall choose the third, and reply that these intermediary demons have communicated, not only the opinion of Plato, which prohibited wrongs to be done to the gods, but also their own delight in these wrongs, I would ask if such a communication is not rather an insult? Now the gods, hearing both and knowing both, not only permit the approach of those malign demons, who desire and do things contrary to the dignity of the gods and the religion of Plato, but also, through these wicked demons, who are near to them, send good things to the good Plato, who is far away from them; for they inhabit such a place in the concatenated series of the elements, that they can come into contact with those by whom they are accused, but not with him by whom they are defended—knowing the truth on both sides, but not being able to change the weight of the air and the earth. There remains the fourth supposition; but it is worse than the rest. For who will suffer it to be said that the demons have made known the calumnious fictions of the poets concerning the immortal gods, and also the disgraceful mockeries of the theatres, and their own most ardent lust after, and most sweet pleasure in these things, whilst they have concealed from them that Plato, with the gravity of a philosopher, gave it as his opinion that all these things ought to be removed from a well-regulated republic; so that the good gods are now compelled, through such messengers, to know the evil doings of the most wicked beings, that is to say, of the messengers themselves, and are not allowed to know the good deeds of the philosophers, though the former are for the injury, but these latter for the honor of the gods themselves?

Chapter XXII: *That We Must, Notwithstanding the Opinion of Apuleius, Reject the Worship of Demons.*

None of these four alternatives, then, is to be chosen; for we dare not suppose such unbecoming things concerning the gods as the adoption of any one of them would lead us to think. It remains, therefore, that no credence whatever is to be given to the opinion of Apuleius and the other philosophers of the same school, namely, that the demons act as messengers and interpreters between the gods and men to carry our petitions from us to the gods, and to bring back to us the help of the gods. On the contrary, we must believe them to be spirits most eager to inflict harm, utterly alien from righteousness, swollen with pride, pale with envy, subtle in deceit; who dwell indeed in this air as in a prison, in keeping with their own character, because, cast down from the height of the higher heaven, they have been condemned to dwell in this element as the just reward of irretrievable transgression. But, though the air is situated above the earth and the waters, they are not on that account superior in merit to men, who, though they do not surpass them as far as their earthly bodies are concerned, do nevertheless far excel them through piety of mind—they having made choice of the true God as their helper. Over many, however, who are manifestly unworthy of participation in the true religion, they tyrannize as over captives whom they have subdued—the greatest part of whom they have persuaded of their divinity by wonderful and lying signs, consisting either of deeds or of predictions. Some, nevertheless, who have more attentively and diligently considered their vices, they have not been able to persuade that they are gods, and so have feigned themselves to be messengers between the gods and men. Some, indeed, have thought that not even this latter honor ought to be acknowledged as belonging to them, not believing that they were gods, because they saw that they were wicked, whereas the gods, according to their view, are all good. Nevertheless they dared not say that they were wholly unworthy of all divine honor, for fear of offending the multitude, by whom, through inveterate superstition, the demons were served by the performance of many rites, and the erection of many temples.

Book Ten

Chapter VII: *Of the Love of the Holy Angels, Which Prompts Them to Desire that We Worship the One True God, and Not Themselves.*

It is very right that these blessed and immortal spirits, who inhabit celestial dwellings, and rejoice in the communications of their Creator's fullness, firm in His eternity, assured in His truth, holy by His grace, since they compassionately and tenderly regard us miserable mortals, and wish us to become immortal and happy, do not desire us to sacrifice to themselves, but to Him whose sacrifice they know themselves to be in common with us. For we and they together are the one city of God, to which it is said in the psalm, "Glorious things are spoken of thee, O city of God;" the human part sojourning here below, the angelic aiding from above. For from that heavenly city, in which God's will is the intelligible and unchangeable law, from that heavenly council-chamber—for they sit in counsel regarding us—that holy Scripture, descended to us by the ministry of angels, in which it is written, "He that sacrificeth unto any god, save unto the Lord only, he shall be utterly destroyed"—this Scripture, this law, these precepts, have been confirmed by such miracles, that it is sufficiently evident to whom these immortal and blessed spirits, who desire us to be like themselves, wish us to sacrifice.

Chapter VIII: *Of the Miracles Which God Has Condescended to Adhibit Through the Ministry of Angels, to His Promises for the Confirmation of the Faith of the Godly.*

I should seem tedious were I to recount all the ancient miracles, which were wrought in attestation of God's promises which He made to Abraham thousands of years ago, that in his seed all the nations of the earth should be blessed. For who can but marvel that Abraham's barren wife should have given birth to a son at an age when not even a prolific woman could bear children; or, again, that when Abraham sacrificed, a flame from heaven should have run between the divided parts; or that the angels in human form, whom he had hospitably entertained, and who had renewed God's promise of offspring, should also have predicted the destruction of Sodom by fire from heaven; and that his nephew Lot should have been rescued from Sodom by the angels as the fire was just descending, while his wife, who looked back as she went, and was immediately turned into salt, stood as a sacred beacon warning us that no one who is being saved should long for what he is leaving? How striking also were the wonders done by Moses to rescue God's people from the yoke of slavery in Egypt, when the magi of the Pharaoh, that is, the king of Egypt, who tyrannized over this people, were suffered to do some wonderful things that they might be vanquished all the more signally! They did these things by the magical arts and incantations to which the evil spirits or demons are addicted; while Moses, having as much greater power as he had right on his side, and having the aid of angels, easily conquered them in the name of the Lord who made heaven and earth. And, in fact, the magicians failed at the third plague; whereas Moses, dealing out the miracles delegated to him, brought ten plagues upon the land, so that the hard hearts of Pharaoh and the Egyptians yielded, and the people were let go. But, quickly repenting, and essaying to overtake the departing Hebrews, who had crossed the sea on dry ground, they were covered and overwhelmed in the returning waters. What shall I say of those frequent and stupendous exhibitions of divine power, while the people were conducted through the wilderness?—of the waters which could not be drunk, but lost their bitterness, and quenched the thirsty, when at God's command a piece of wood was cast into them? of the manna that descended from heaven to appease their hunger, and which begat worms and putrefied when any one collected more than the appointed quantity, and yet, though double was gathered on the day before the Sabbath (it not being lawful to gather it on that day), remained fresh? of the birds which filled the camp, and turned appetite into satiety when they longed for flesh, which it seemed impossible to supply to so vast a population? of the enemies who met them, and opposed their passage with arms, and were defeated without the loss of a single Hebrew, when Moses prayed with his hands extended in the form of a cross? of the seditious persons who arose among God's people, and separated themselves from the divinely-ordered community, and were swallowed up alive by the earth, a visible token of an invisible punishment? of the rock struck with the rod, and pouring out waters more than enough for all the host? of the deadly serpents' bites, sent in just punishment of sin, but healed by looking at the lifted brazen serpent, so that not only were the tormented people healed, but a symbol of the crucifixion of death set before them in this destruction of death by death? It was this serpent which was preserved in memory of this event, and was afterwards worshiped by the mistaken people as an idol, and was destroyed by the pious and God-fearing king Hezekiah, much to his credit.

Chapter IX: *Of the Illicit Arts Connected with Demonolatry, and of Which the Platonist Porphyry Adopts Some, and Discards Others.*

These miracles, and many others of the same nature, which it were tedious to mention, were wrought for the purpose of commending the worship of the one true God, and prohibiting the worship of a multitude of false gods. Moreover, they were wrought by simple faith and godly confidence, not by the incantations and charms composed under the influence of a criminal tampering with the unseen world, of an art which they call either magic, or by the more abominable title necromancy, or the more honorable designation theurgy; for they wish to discriminate between those whom the people call magicians, who practise necromancy, and are addicted to illicit arts and condemned, and those others who seem to them to be worthy of praise for their practice of theurgy—the truth, however, being that both classes are the slaves of the deceitful rites of the demons whom they invoke under the names of angels.

For even Porphyry promises some kind of purgation of the soul by the help of theurgy, though he does so with some hesitation and shame, and denies that this art can secure to any one a return to God; so that you can detect his opinion vacillating between the profession of philosophy and an art which he feels to be presumptuous and sacrilegious. For at one time he warns us to avoid it as deceitful, and prohibited by law, and dangerous to those who practise it; then again, as if in deference to its advocates, he declares it useful for cleansing one part of the soul, not, indeed, the intellectual part, by which the truth of things intelligible, which have no sensible images, is recognized, but the spiritual part, which takes cognizance of the images of things material. This part, he says, is prepared and fitted for intercourse with spirits and angels, and for the vision of the gods, by the help of certain theurgic consecrations, or, as they call them, mysteries. He acknowledges, however, that these theurgic mysteries impart to the intellectual soul no such purity as fits it to see its God, and recognize the things that truly exist. And from this acknowledgment we may infer what kind of gods these are, and what kind of vision of them is imparted by theurgic consecrations, if by it one cannot see the things which truly exist. He says, further, that the rational, or, as he prefers calling it, the intellectual soul, can pass into the heavens without the spiritual part being cleansed by theurgic art, and that this art cannot so purify the spiritual part as to give it entrance to immortality and eternity. And therefore, although he distinguishes angels from demons, asserting that the habitation of the latter is in the air, while the former dwell in the ether and empyrean, and although he advises us to cultivate the friendship of some demon, who may be able after our death to assist us, and elevate us at least a little above the earth—for he owns that it is by another way we must reach the heavenly society of the angels—he at the same time distinctly warns us to avoid the society of demons, saying that the soul, expiating its sin after death, execrates the worship of demons by whom it was entangled. And of theurgy itself, though he recommends it as reconciling angels and demons, he cannot deny that it treats with powers which either themselves envy the soul its purity, or serve the arts of those who do envy it. He complains of this through the mouth of some Chaldæan or other: "A good man in Chaldæa complains," he says, "that his most strenuous efforts to cleanse his soul were frustrated, because another man, who had influence in these matters, and who envied him purity, had prayed to the powers, and bound them by his conjuring not to listen to his request. Therefore," adds Porphyry, "what the one man bound, the other could not loose." And from this he concludes that theurgy is a craft which accomplishes not only good but evil among gods and men; and that the gods also have passions, and are perturbed and agitated by the emotions which Apuleius attributed to demons and men, but from which he preserved the gods by that sublimity of residence, which, in common with Plato, he accorded to them.

Chapter X: *Concerning Theurgy, Which Promises a Delusive Purification of the Soul by the Invocation of Demons.*

But here we have another and a much more learned Platonist than Apuleius, Porphyry, to wit, asserting that, by I know not what theurgy, even the gods themselves are subjected to passions and perturbations; for by adjurations they were so bound and terrified that they could not confer purity of soul—were so terrified by him who imposed on them a wicked command, that they could not by the same theurgy be freed from that terror, and fulfill the righteous behest of him who prayed to them, or do the good he sought. Who does not see that all these things are fictions of deceiving demons, unless he be a wretched slave of theirs, and an alien from the grace of the true Liberator? For if the Chaldæan had been dealing with good gods, certainly a well-disposed man, who sought to purify his own soul, would have had more influence with them than an evil-disposed man seeking to hinder him. Or, if the gods were just, and considered the man unworthy of the purification he sought, at all events they should not have been terrified by an envious person, nor hindered, as Porphyry avows, by the fear of a stronger deity, but should have simply denied the boon on their own free judgment. And it is surprising that that well-disposed Chaldæan, who desired to purify his soul by theurgical rites, found no superior deity who could either terrify the frightened gods still more, and force them to confer the boon, or compose their fears, and so enable them to do good without compulsion—even supposing that the good theurgist had no rites by which he himself might purge away the taint of fear from the gods whom he invoked for the purification of his own soul. And why is it that there is a god who has power to terrify the inferior gods, and none who has power to free them from fear? Is there found a god who listens to the envious man, and frightens the gods from doing good? and is there not found a god who listens to the well-disposed man, and removes the fear of the gods that they may do him good? O excellent theurgy! O admirable purification of the soul!—a theurgy in which the violence of an impure envy has more influence than the entreaty of purity and holiness. Rather let us abominate and avoid the deceit of such wicked spirits, and listen to sound doctrine. As to those who perform these filthy cleansings by sacrilegious rites, and see in their initiated state (as he further tells us, though we may question this vision) certain wonderfully lovely appearances of angels or gods, this is what the apostle refers to when he speaks of "Satan transforming himself into an angel of light." For these are the delusive appearances of that spirit who longs to entangle wretched souls in the deceptive worship of many and false gods, and to turn them aside from the true worship of the true God, by whom alone they are cleansed and healed, and who, as was said of Proteus, "turns himself into all shapes," equally hurtful, whether he assaults us as an enemy, or assumes the disguise of a friend.

Chapter XI: *Of Porphyry's Epistle to Anebo, in Which He Asks for Information About the Differences Among Demons.*

It was a better tone which Porphyry adopted in his letter to Anebo the Egyptian, in which, assuming the character of an inquirer consulting him, he unmasks and explodes these sacrilegious arts. In that letter, indeed, he repudiates all demons, whom he maintains to be so foolish as to be attracted by the sacrificial vapors, and therefore residing not in the ether, but in the air beneath the moon, and indeed in the moon itself. Yet he has not the boldness to attribute to all the demons all the deceptions and malicious and foolish practices which justly move his indignation. For, though he acknowledges that as a race demons are foolish, he so far accommodates himself to popular ideas as to call some of them benignant demons. He expresses surprise that sacrifices not only incline the gods, but also compel and force them to do what men wish; and he is at a loss to understand how the sun and moon, and other visible celestial bodies—for bodies he does not doubt that they are—are considered gods, if the gods are distinguished from the demons by their incorporeality; also, if they are gods, how some are called beneficent and others hurtful, and how they, being corporeal, are numbered with the gods, who are incorporeal. He inquires further, and still as one in doubt, whether diviners and wonderworkers are men of unusually powerful souls, or whether the power to do these things is communicated by spirits from without. He inclines to the latter opinion, on the ground that it is by the use of stones and herbs that they lay spells on people, and open closed doors, and do similar wonders. And on this account, he says, some suppose that there is a race of beings whose property it is to listen to men—a race deceitful, full of contrivances, capable of assuming all forms, simulating gods, demons, and dead men—and that it is this race which bring about all these things which have the appearance of good or evil, but that what is really good they never help us in, and are indeed unacquainted with, for they make wickedness easy, but throw obstacles in the path of those who eagerly follow virtue; and that they are filled with pride and rashness, delight in sacrificial odors, are taken with flattery. These and the other characteristics of this race of deceitful and malicious spirits, who come into the souls of men and delude their senses, both in sleep and waking, he describes not as things of which he is himself convinced, but only with so much suspicion and doubt as to cause him to speak of them as commonly received opinions. We should sympathize with this great philosopher in the difficulty he experienced in acquainting himself with and confidently assailing the whole fraternity of devils, which any Christian old woman would unhesitatingly describe and most unreservedly detest. Perhaps, however, he shrank from offending Anebo, to whom he was writing, himself the most eminent patron of these mysteries, or the others who marveled at these magical feats as divine works, and closely allied to the worship of the gods.

However, he pursues this subject, and, still in the character of an inquirer, mentions some things which no sober judgment could attribute to any but malicious and deceitful powers. He asks why, after the better class of spirits have been invoked, the worse should be commanded to perform the wicked desires of men; why they do not hear a man who has just left a woman's embrace, while they themselves make no scruple of tempting men to incest and adultery; why their priests are commanded to abstain from animal food for fear of being polluted by the corporeal exhalations, while they themselves are attracted by the fumes of sacrifices and other exhalations; why the initiated are forbidden to touch a dead body, while their mysteries are celebrated almost entirely by means of dead bodies; why it is that a man addicted to any vice should utter threats, not to a demon or to the soul of a dead man, but to the sun and moon, or some of the heavenly bodies, which he intimidates by imaginary terrors, that he may wring from them a real boon—for he threatens that he will demolish the sky, and such like impossibilities—that those gods, being alarmed, like silly children, with imaginary and absurd threats, may do what they are ordered. Porphyry further relates that a man, Chæremon, profoundly versed in these sacred or rather sacrilegious mysteries, had written that the famous Egyptian mysteries of Isis and her husband Osiris had very great influence with the gods to compel them to do what they were ordered, when he who used the spells threatened to divulge or do away with these mysteries, and cried with a threatening voice that he would scatter the members of Osiris if they neglected his orders. Not without reason is Porphyry surprised that a man should utter such wild and empty threats against the gods—not against gods of no account, but against the heavenly gods, and those that shine with sidereal light—and that these threats should be effectual to constrain them with resistless power, and alarm them so that they fulfill his wishes. Not without reason does he, in the character of an inquirer into the reasons of these surprising things, give it to be understood that they are done by that race of spirits which he previously described as if quoting other people's opinions—spirits who deceive not, as he said, by nature, but by their own corruption, and who simulate gods and dead men, but not, as he said, demons, for demons they really are. As to his idea that by means of herbs, and stones, and animals, and certain incantations and noises, and drawings, sometimes fanciful, and sometimes copied from the motions of the heavenly bodies, men create upon earth powers capable of bringing about various results, all that is only the mystification which these demons practise on those who are subject to them, for the sake of furnishing themselves with merriment at the expense of their dupes. Either, then, Porphyry was sincere in his doubts and inquiries, and mentioned these things to demonstrate and put beyond question that they were the work, not of powers which aid us in obtaining life, but of deceitful demons; or, to take a more favorable view of the philosopher, he adopted this method with the Egyptian who was wedded to these errors, and was proud of them, that he might not offend him by assuming the attitude of a teacher, nor discompose his mind by the altercation of a professed assailant, but, by assuming the character of an inquirer, and the humble attitude of one who was anxious to learn, might turn his attention to these matters, and show how worthy they are to be despised and relinquished. Towards the conclusion of his letter, he requests Anebo to inform him what the Egyptian wisdom indicates as the way to blessedness. But as to those who hold intercourse with the gods, and pester them only for the sake of finding a runaway slave, or acquiring property, or making a bargain of a marriage, or such things, he declares that their pretensions to wisdom are vain. He adds that these same gods, even granting that on other points their utterances were true, were yet so ill-advised and unsatisfactory in their disclosures about blessedness, that they cannot be either gods or good demons, but are either that spirit who is called the deceiver, or mere fictions of the imagination.

Chapter XII: *Of the Miracles Wrought by the True God Through the Ministry of the Holy Angels.*

Since by means of these arts wonders are done which quite surpass human power, what choice have we but to believe that these predictions and operations, which seem to be miraculous and divine, and which at the same time form no part of the worship of the one God, in adherence to whom, as the Platonists themselves abundantly testify, all blessedness consists, are the pastime of wicked spirits, who thus seek to seduce and hinder the truly godly? On the other hand, we cannot but believe that all miracles, whether wrought by angels or by other means, so long as they are so done as to commend the worship and religion of the one God in whom alone is blessedness, are wrought by those who love us in a true and godly sort, or through their means, God Himself working in them. For we cannot listen to those who maintain that the invisible God works no visible miracles; for even they believe that He made the world, which surely they will not deny to be visible. Whatever marvel happens in this world, it is certainly less marvelous than this whole world itself—I mean the sky and earth, and all that is in them—and these God certainly made. But, as the Creator Himself is hidden and incomprehensible to man, so also is the manner of creation. Although, therefore, the standing miracle of this visible world is little thought of, because always before us, yet, when we arouse ourselves to contemplate it, it is a greater miracle than the rarest and most unheard-of marvels. For man himself is a greater miracle than any miracle done through his instrumentality. Therefore God, who made the visible heaven and earth, does not disdain to work visible miracles in heaven or earth, that He may thereby awaken the soul which is immersed in things visible to worship Himself, the Invisible. But the place and time of these miracles are dependent on His unchangeable will, in which things future are ordered as if already they were accomplished. For He moves things temporal without Himself moving in time, He does not in one way know things that are to be, and, in another, things that have been; neither does He listen to those who pray otherwise than as He sees those that will pray. For, even when His angels hear us, it is He Himself who hears us in them, as in His true temple not made with hands, as in those men who are His saints; and His answers, though accomplished in time, have been arranged by His eternal appointment.

Chapter XIII: *Of the Invisible God, Who Has Often Made Himself Visible, Not as He Really Is, But as the Beholders Could Bear the Sight.*

Neither need we be surprised that God, invisible as He is, should often have appeared visibly to the patriarchs. For as the sound which communicates the thought conceived in the silence of the mind is not the thought itself, so the form by which God, invisible in His own nature, became visible, was not God Himself. Nevertheless it is He Himself who was seen under that form, as that thought itself is heard in the sound of the voice; and the patriarchs recognized that, though the bodily form was not God, they saw the invisible God. For, though Moses conversed with God, yet he said, "If I have found grace in Thy sight, show me Thyself, that I may see and know Thee." And as it was fit that the law, which was given, not to one man or a few enlightened men, but to the whole of a populous nation, should be accompanied by awe-inspiring signs, great marvels were wrought, by the ministry of angels, before the people on the mount where the law was being given to them through one man, while the multitude beheld the awful appearances. For the people of Israel believed Moses, not as the Lacedæmonians believed their Lycurgus, because he had received from Jupiter or Apollo the laws he gave them. For when the law which enjoined the worship of one God was given to the people, marvelous signs and earthquakes, such as the divine wisdom judged sufficient, were brought about in the sight of all, that they might know that it was the Creator who could thus use creation to promulgate His law.

Chapter XIV: *That the One God is to Be Worshiped Not Only for the Sake of Eternal Blessings, But Also in Connection with Temporal Prosperity, Because All Things are Regulated by His Providence.*

The education of the human race, represented by the people of God, has advanced, like that of an individual, through certain epochs, or, as it were, ages, so that it might gradually rise from earthly to heavenly things, and from the visible to the invisible. This object was kept so clearly in view, that, even in the period when temporal rewards were promised, the one God was presented as the object of worship, that men might not acknowledge any other than the true Creator and Lord of the spirit, even in connection with the earthly blessings of this transitory life. For he who denies that all things, which either angels or men can give us, are in the hand of the one Almighty, is a madman. The Platonist Plotinus discourses concerning providence, and, from the beauty of flowers and foliage, proves that from the supreme God, whose beauty is unseen and ineffable, providence reaches down even to these earthly things here below; and he argues that all these frail and perishing things could not have so exquisite and elaborate a beauty, were they not fashioned by Him whose unseen and unchangeable beauty continually pervades all things. This is proved also by the Lord Jesus, where He says, "Consider the lilies, how they grow; they toil not, neither do they spin. And yet I say unto you that Solomon in all his glory was not arrayed like one of these. But if God so clothe the grass of the field, which to-day is and tomorrow is cast into the oven, how much more shall He clothe you, O ye of little faith.!" It was best, therefore, that the soul of man, which was still weakly desiring earthly things, should be accustomed to seek from God alone even these petty temporal boons, and the earthly necessaries of this transitory life, which are contemptible in comparison with eternal blessings, in order that the desire even of these things might not draw it aside from the worship of Him, to whom we come by despising and forsaking such things.

Chapter XV: *Of the Ministry of the Holy Angels, by Which They Fulfill the Providence of God.*

And so it has pleased Divine Providence, as I have said, and as we read in the Acts of the Apostles, that the law enjoining the worship of one God should be given by the disposition of angels. But among them the person of God Himself visibly appeared, not, indeed, in His proper substance, which ever remains invisible to mortal eyes, but by the infallible signs furnished by creation in obedience to its Creator. He made use, too, of the words of human speech, uttering them syllable by syllable successively, though in His own nature He speaks not in a bodily but in a spiritual way; not to sense, but to the mind; not in words that occupy time, but, if I may so say, eternally, neither beginning to speak nor coming to an end. And what He says is accurately heard, not by the bodily but by the mental ear of His ministers and messengers, who are immortally blessed in the enjoyment of His unchangeable truth; and the directions which they in some ineffable way receive, they execute without delay or difficulty in the sensible and visible world. And this law was given in conformity with the age of the world, and contained at the first earthly promises, as I have said, which, however, symbolized eternal ones; and these eternal blessings few understood, though many took a part in the celebration of their visible signs. Nevertheless, with one consent both the words and the visible rites of that law enjoin the worship of one God—not one of a crowd of gods, but Him who made heaven and earth, and every soul and every spirit which is other than Himself. He created; all else was created; and, both for being and well-being, all things need Him who created them.

Chapter XVI: *Whether Those Angels Who Demand that We Pay Them Divine Honor, or Those Who Teach Us to Render Holy Service, Not to Themselves, But to God, are to Be Trusted About the Way to Life Eternal.*

What angels, then, are we to believe in this matter of blessed and eternal life?—those who wish to be worshiped with religious rites and observances, and require that men sacrifice to them; or those who say that all this worship is due to one God, the Creator, and teach us to render it with true piety to Him, by the vision of whom they are themselves already blessed, and in whom they promise that we shall be so? For that vision of God is the beauty of a vision so great, and is so infinitely desirable, that Plotinus does not hesitate to say that he who enjoys all other blessings in abundance, and has not this, is supremely miserable. Since, therefore, miracles are wrought by some angels to induce us to worship this God, by others, to induce us to worship themselves; and since the former forbid us to worship these, while the latter dare not forbid us to worship God, which are we to listen to? Let the Platonists reply, or any philosophers, or the theurgists, or rather, periurgists—for this name is good enough for those who practise such arts. In short, let all men answer—if, at least, there survives in them any spark of that natural perception which, as rational beings, they possess when created—let them, I say, tell us whether we should sacrifice to the gods or angels who order us to sacrifice to them, or to that One to whom we are ordered to sacrifice by those who forbid us to worship either themselves or these others. If neither the one party nor the other had wrought miracles, but had merely uttered commands, the one to sacrifice to themselves, the other forbidding that, and ordering us to sacrifice to God, a godly mind would have been at no loss to discern which command proceeded from proud arrogance, and which from true religion. I will say more. If miracles had been wrought only by those who demand sacrifice for themselves, while those who forbade this, and enjoined sacrificing to the one God only, thought fit entirely to forego the use of visible miracles, the authority of the latter was to be preferred by all who would use, not their eyes only, but their reason. But since God, for the sake of commending to us the oracles of His truth, has, by means of these immortal messengers, who proclaim His majesty and not their own pride, wrought miracles of surpassing grandeur, certainty, and distinctness, in order that the weak among the godly might not be drawn away to false religion by those who require us to sacrifice to them and endeavor to convince us by stupendous appeals to our senses, who is so utterly unreasonable as not to choose and follow the truth, when he finds that it is heralded by even more striking evidences than falsehood?

As for those miracles which history ascribes to the gods of the heathen—I do not refer to those prodigies which at intervals happen from some unknown physical causes, and which are arranged and appointed by Divine Providence, such as monstrous births, and unusual meteorological phenomena, whether startling only, or also injurious, and which are said to be brought about and removed by communication with demons, and by their most deceitful craft—but I refer to these prodigies which manifestly enough are wrought by their power and force, as, that the household gods which Æneas carried from Troy in his flight moved from place to place; that Tarquin cut a whetstone with a razor; that the Epidaurian serpent attached himself as a companion to Æsculapius on his voyage to Rome; that the ship in which the image of the Phrygian mother stood, and which could not be moved by a host of men and oxen, was moved by one weak woman, who attached her girdle to the vessel and drew it, as proof of her chastity; that a vestal, whose virginity was questioned, removed the suspicion by carrying from the Tiber a sieve full of water without any of it dropping: these, then, and the like, are by no means to be compared for greatness and virtue to those which, we read, were wrought among God's people. How much less can we compare those marvels, which even the laws of heathen nations prohibit and punish—I mean the magical and theurgic marvels, of which the great part are merely illusions practised upon the senses, as the drawing down of the moon, "that," as Lucan says, "it may shed a stronger influence on the plants?" And if some of these do seem to equal those which are wrought by the godly, the end for which they are wrought distinguishes the two, and shows that ours are incomparably the more excellent. For those miracles commend the worship of a plurality of gods, who deserve worship the less the more they demand it; but these of ours commend the worship of the one God, who, both by the testimony of His own Scriptures, and by the eventual abolition of sacrifices, proves that He needs no such offerings. If, therefore, any angels demand sacrifice for themselves, we must prefer those who demand it, not for themselves, but for God, the Creator of all, whom they serve. For thus they prove how sincerely they love us, since they wish by sacrifice to subject us, not to themselves, but to Him by the contemplation of whom they themselves are blessed, and to bring us to Him from whom they themselves have never strayed. If, on the other hand, any angels wish us to sacrifice, not to one, but to many, not, indeed, to themselves, but to the gods whose angels they are, we must in this case also prefer those who are the angels of the one God of gods, and who so bid us to worship Him as to preclude our worshiping any other. But, further, if it be the case, as their pride and deceitfulness rather indicate, that they are neither good angels nor the angels of good gods, but wicked demons, who wish sacrifice to be paid, not to the one only and supreme God, but to themselves, what better protection against them can we choose than that of the one God whom the good angels serve, the angels who bid us sacrifice, not to themselves, but to Him whose sacrifice we ourselves ought to be?

Chapter XVII: *Concerning the Ark of the Covenant, and the Miraculous Signs Whereby God Authenticated the Law and the Promise.*

On this account it was that the law of God, given by the disposition of angels, and which commanded that the one God of gods alone receive sacred worship, to the exclusion of all others, was deposited in the ark, called the ark of the testimony. By this name it is sufficiently indicated, not that God, who was worshiped by all those rites, was shut up and enclosed in that place, though His responses emanated from it along with signs appreciable by the senses, but that His will was declared from that throne. The law itself, too, was engraven on tables of stone, and, as I have said, deposited in the ark, which the priests carried with due reverence during the sojourn in the wilderness, along with the tabernacle, which was in like manner called the tabernacle of the testimony; and there was then an accompanying sign, which appeared as a cloud by day and as a fire by night; when the cloud moved, the camp was shifted, and where it stood the camp was pitched. Besides these signs, and the voices which proceeded from the place where the ark was, there were other miraculous testimonies to the law. For when the ark was carried across Jordan, on the entrance to the land of promise, the upper part of the river stopped in its course, and the lower part flowed on, so as to present both to the ark and the people dry ground to pass over. Then, when it was carried seven times round the first hostile and polytheistic city they came to, its walls suddenly fell down, though assaulted by no hand, struck by no battering-ram. Afterwards, too, when they were now resident in the land of promise, and the ark had, in punishment of their sin, been taken by their enemies, its captors triumphantly placed it in the temple of their favorite god, and left it shut up there, but, on opening the temple next day, they found the image they used to pray to fallen to the ground and shamefully shattered. Then, being themselves alarmed by portents, and still more shamefully punished, they restored the ark of the testimony to the people from whom they had taken it. And what was the manner of its restoration? They placed it on a wagon, and yoked to it cows from which they had taken the calves, and let them choose their own course, expecting that in this way the divine will would be indicated; and the cows without any man driving or directing them, steadily pursued the way to the Hebrews, without regarding the lowing of their calves, and thus restored the ark to its worshipers. To God these and such like wonders are small, but they are mighty to terrify and give wholesome instruction to men. For if philosophers, and especially the Platonists, are with justice esteemed wiser than other men, as I have just been mentioning, because they taught that even these earthly and insignificant things are ruled by Divine Providence, inferring this from the numberless beauties which are observable not only in the bodies of animals, but even in plants and grasses, how much more plainly do these things attest the presence of divinity which happen at the time predicted, and in which that religion is commended which forbids the offering of sacrifice to any celestial, terrestrial, or infernal being, and commands it to be offered to God only, who alone blesses us by His love for us, and by our love to Him, and who, by arranging the appointed times of those sacrifices, and by predicting that they were to pass into a better sacrifice by a better Priest, testified that He has no appetite for these sacrifices, but through them indicated others of more substantial blessing—and all this not that He Himself may be glorified by these honors, but that we may be stirred up to worship and cleave to Him, being inflamed by His love, which is our advantage rather than His?

Chapter XVIII: *Against Those Who Deny that the Books of the Church are to Be Believed About the Miracles Whereby the People of God Were Educated.*

Will some one say that these miracles are false, that they never happened, and that the records of them are lies? Whoever says so, and asserts that in such matters no records whatever can be credited, may also say that there are no gods who care for human affairs. For they have induced men to worship them only by means of miraculous works, which the heathen histories testify, and by which the gods have made a display of their own power rather than done any real service. This is the reason why we have not undertaken in this work, of which we are now writing the tenth book, to refute those who either deny that there is any divine power, or contend that it does not interfere with human affairs, but those who prefer their own god to our God, the Founder of the holy and most glorious city, not knowing that He is also the invisible and unchangeable Founder of this visible and changing world, and the truest bestower of the blessed life which resides not in things created, but in Himself. For thus speaks His most trustworthy prophet: "It is good for me to be united to God." Among philosophers it is a question, what is that end and good to the attainment of which all our duties are to have a relation? The Psalmist did not say, It is good for me to have great wealth, or to wear imperial insignia, purple, sceptre, and diadem; or, as some even of the philosophers have not blushed to say, It is good for me to enjoy sensual pleasure; or, as the better men among them seemed to say, My good is my spiritual strength; but, "It is good for me to be united to God." This he had learned from Him whom the holy angels, with the accompanying witness of miracles, presented as the sole object of worship. And hence he himself became the sacrifice of God, whose spiritual love inflamed him, and into whose ineffable and incorporeal embrace he yearned to cast himself. Moreover, if the worshipers of many gods (whatever kind of gods they fancy their own to be) believe that the miracles recorded in their civil histories, or in the books of magic, or of the more respectable theurgy, were wrought by these gods, what reason have they for refusing to believe the miracles recorded in those writings, to which we owe a credence as much greater as He is greater to whom alone these writings teach us to sacrifice?

Chapter XIX: *On the Reasonableness of Offering, as the True Religion Teaches, a Visible Sacrifice to the One True and Invisible God.*

As to those who think that these visible sacrifices are suitably offered to other gods, but that invisible sacrifices, the graces of purity of mind and holiness of will, should be offered, as greater and better, to the invisible God, Himself greater and better than all others, they must be oblivious that these visible sacrifices are signs of the invisible, as the words we utter are the signs of things. And therefore, as in prayer or praise we direct intelligible words to Him to whom in our heart we offer the very feelings we are expressing, so we are to understand that in sacrifice we offer visible sacrifice only to Him to whom in our heart we ought to present ourselves an invisible sacrifice. It is then that the angels, and all those superior powers who are mighty by their goodness and piety, regard us with pleasure, and rejoice with us and assist us to the utmost of their power. But if we offer such worship to them, they decline it; and when on any mission to men they become visible to the senses, they positively forbid it. Examples of this occur in holy writ. Some fancied they should, by adoration or sacrifice, pay the same honor to angels as is due to God, and were prevented from doing so by the angels themselves, and ordered to render it to Him to whom alone they know it to be due. And the holy angels have in this been imitated by holy men of God. For Paul and Barnabas, when they had wrought a miracle of healing in Lycaonia, were thought to be gods, and the Lycaonians desired to sacrifice to them, and they humbly and piously declined this honor, and announced to them the God in whom they should believe. And those deceitful and proud spirits, who exact worship, do so simply because they know it to be due to the true God. For that which they take pleasure in is not, as Porphyry says and some fancy, the smell of the victims, but divine honors. They have, in fact, plenty odors on all hands, and if they wished more, they could provide them for themselves. But the spirits who arrogate to themselves divinity are delighted not with the smoke of carcasses but with the suppliant spirit which they deceive and hold in subjection, and hinder from drawing near to God, preventing him from offering himself in sacrifice to God by inducing him to sacrifice to others.

Chapter XX: *Of the Supreme and True Sacrifice Which Was Effected by the Mediator Between God and Men.*

And hence that true Mediator, in so far as, by assuming the form of a servant, He became the Mediator between God and men, the man Christ Jesus, though in the form of God He received sacrifice together with the Father, with whom He is one God, yet in the form of a servant He chose rather to be than to receive a sacrifice, that not even by this instance any one might have occasion to suppose that sacrifice should be rendered to any creature. Thus He is both the Priest who offers and the Sacrifice offered. And He designed that there should be a daily sign of this in the sacrifice of the Church, which, being His body, learns to offer herself through Him. Of this true Sacrifice the ancient sacrifices of the saints were the various and numerous signs; and it was thus variously figured, just as one thing is signified by a variety of words, that there may be less weariness when we speak of it much. To this supreme and true sacrifice all false sacrifices have given place.

Chapter XXI: *Of the Power Delegated to Demons for the Trial and Glorification of the Saints, Who Conquer Not by Propitiating the Spirits of the Air, But by Abiding in God.*

The power delegated to the demons at certain appointed and well-adjusted seasons, that they may give expression to their hostility to the city of God by stirring up against it the men who are under their influence, and may not only receive sacrifice from those who willingly offer it, but may also extort it from the unwilling by violent persecution—this power is found to be not merely harmless, but even useful to the Church, completing as it does the number of martyrs, whom the city of God esteems as all the more illustrious and honored citizens, because they have striven even to blood against the sin of impiety. If the ordinary language of the Church allowed it, we might more elegantly call these men our heroes. For this name is said to be derived from Juno, who in Greek is called Hêrê, and hence, according to the Greek myths, one of her sons was called Heros. And these fables mystically signified that Juno was mistress of the air, which they suppose to be inhabited by the demons and the heroes, understanding by heroes the souls of the well-deserving dead. But for a quite opposite reason would we call our martyrs heroes—supposing, as I said, that the usage of ecclesiastical language would admit of it—not because they lived along with the demons in the air, but because they conquered these demons or powers of the air, and among them Juno herself, be she what she may, not unsuitably represented, as she commonly is by the poets, as hostile to virtue, and jealous of men of mark aspiring to the heavens. Virgil, however, unhappily gives way, and yields to her; for, though he represents her as saying, "I am conquered by Æneas," Helenus gives Æneas himself this religious advice:

> "Pay vows to Juno: overbear
> Her queenly soul with gift and prayer."

In conformity with this opinion, Porphyry—expressing, however, not so much his own views as other people's—says that a good god or genius cannot come to a man unless the evil genius has been first of all propitiated, implying that the evil deities had greater power than the good; for, until they have been appeased and give place, the good can give no assistance; and if the evil deities oppose, the good can give no help; whereas the evil can do injury without the good being able to prevent them. This is not the way of the true and truly holy religion; not thus do our martyrs conquer Juno, that is to say, the powers of the air, who envy the virtues of the pious. Our heroes, if we could so call them, overcome Hêrê, not by suppliant gifts, but by divine virtues. As Scipio, who conquered Africa by his valor, is more suitably styled Africanus than if he had appeased his enemies by gifts, and so won their mercy.

Chapter XXII: *Whence the Saints Derive Power Against Demons and True Purification of Heart.*

It is by true piety that men of God cast out the hostile power of the air which opposes godliness; it is by exorcising it, not by propitiating it; and they overcome all the temptations of the adversary by praying, not to him, but to their own God against him. For the devil cannot conquer or subdue any but those who are in league with sin; and therefore he is conquered in the name of Him who assumed humanity, and that without sin, that Himself being both Priest and Sacrifice, He might bring about the remission of sins, that is to say, might bring it about through the Mediator between God and men, the man Christ Jesus, by whom we are reconciled to God, the cleansing from sin being accomplished. For men are separated from God only by sins, from which we are in this life cleansed not by our own virtue, but by the divine compassion; through His indulgence, not through our own power. For, whatever virtue we call our own is itself bestowed upon us by His goodness. And we might attribute too much to ourselves while in the flesh, unless we lived in the receipt of pardon until we laid it down. This is the reason why there has been vouchsafed to us, through the Mediator, this grace, that we who are polluted by sinful flesh should be cleansed by the likeness of sinful flesh. By this grace of God, wherein He has shown His great compassion toward us, we are both governed by faith in this life, and, after this life, are led onwards to the fullest perfection by the vision of immutable truth.

Chapter XXIII: *Of the Principles Which, According to the Platonists, Regulate the Purification of the Soul.*

Even Porphyry asserts that it was revealed by divine oracles that we are not purified by any sacrifices to sun or moon, meaning it to be inferred that we are not purified by sacrificing to any gods. For what mysteries can purify, if those of the sun and moon, which are esteemed the chief of the celestial gods, do not purify? He says, too, in the same place, that "principles" can purify, lest it should be supposed, from his saying that sacrificing to the sun and moon cannot purify, that sacrificing to some other of the host of gods might do so. And what he as a Platonist means by "principles," we know. For he speaks of God the Father and God the Son, whom he calls (writing in Greek) the intellect or mind of the Father; but of the Holy Spirit he says either nothing, or nothing plainly, for I do not understand what other he speaks of as holding the middle place between these two. For if, like Plotinus in his discussion regarding the three principal substances, he wished us to understand by this third the soul of nature, he would certainly not have given it the middle place between these two, that is, between the Father and the Son. For Plotinus places the soul of nature after the intellect of the Father, while Porphyry, making it the mean, does not place it after, but between the others. No doubt he spoke according to his light, or as he thought expedient; but we assert that the Holy Spirit is the Spirit not of the Father only, nor of the Son only, but of both. For philosophers speak as they have a mind to, and in the most difficult matters do not scruple to offend religious ears; but we are bound to speak according to a certain rule, lest freedom of speech beget impiety of opinion about the matters themselves of which we speak.

Chapter XXIV: *Of the One Only True Principle Which Alone Purifies and Renews Human Nature.*

Accordingly, when we speak of God, we do not affirm two or three principles, no more than we are at liberty to affirm two or three gods; although, speaking of each, of the Father, or of the Son, or of the Holy Ghost, we confess that each is God: and yet we do not say, as the Sabellian heretics say, that the Father is the same as the Son, and the Holy Spirit the same as the Father and the Son; but we say that the Father is the Father of the Son, and the Son the Son of the Father, and that the Holy Spirit of the Father and the Son is neither the Father nor the Son. It was therefore truly said that man is cleansed only by a Principle, although the Platonists erred in speaking in the plural of principles. But Porphyry, being under the dominion of these envious powers, whose influence he was at once ashamed of and afraid to throw off, refused to recognize that Christ is the Principle by whose incarnation we are purified. Indeed he despised Him, because of the flesh itself which He assumed, that He might offer a sacrifice for our purification—a great mystery, unintelligible to Porphyry's pride, which that true and benignant Redeemer brought low by His humility, manifesting Himself to mortals by the mortality which He assumed, and which the malignant and deceitful mediators are proud of wanting, promising, as the boon of immortals, a deceptive assistance to wretched men. Thus the good and true Mediator showed that it is sin which is evil, and not the substance or nature of flesh; for this, together with the human soul, could without sin be both assumed and retained, and laid down in death, and changed to something better by resurrection. He showed also that death itself, although the punishment of sin, was submitted to by Him for our sakes without sin, and must not be evaded by sin on our part, but rather, if opportunity serves, be borne for righteousness' sake. For he was able to expiate sins by dying, because He both died, and not for sin of His own. But He has not been recognized by Porphyry as the Principle, otherwise he would have recognized Him as the Purifier. The Principle is neither the flesh nor the human soul in Christ but the Word by which all things were made. The flesh, therefore, does not by its own virtue purify, but by virtue of the Word by which it was assumed, when "the Word became flesh and dwelt among us." For speaking mystically of eating His flesh, when those who did not understand Him were offended and went away, saying, "This is an hard saying, who can hear it?" He answered to the rest who remained, "It is the Spirit that quickeneth; the flesh profiteth nothing." The Principle, therefore, having assumed a human soul and flesh, cleanses the soul and flesh of believers. Therefore, when the Jews asked Him who He was, He answered that He was the Principle. And this we carnal and feeble men, liable to sin, and involved in the darkness of ignorance, could not possibly understand, unless we were cleansed and healed by Him, both by means of what we were, and of what we were not. For we were men, but we were not righteous; whereas in His incarnation there was a human nature, but it was righteous, and not sinful. This is the mediation whereby a hand is stretched to the lapsed and fallen; this is the seed "ordained by angels," by whose ministry the law also was given enjoining the worship of one God, and promising that this Mediator should come.

Chapter XXV: *That All the Saints, Both Under the Law and Before It, Were Justified by Faith in the Mystery of Christ's Incarnation.*

It was by faith in this mystery, and godliness of life, that purification was attainable even by the saints of old, whether before the law was given to the Hebrews (for God and the angels were even then present as instructors), or in the periods under the law, although the promises of spiritual things, being presented in figure, seemed to be carnal, and hence the name of Old Testament. For it was then the prophets lived, by whom, as by angels, the same promise was announced; and among them was he whose grand and divine sentiment regarding the end and supreme good of man I have just now quoted, "It is good for me to cleave to God." In this psalm the distinction between the Old and New Testaments is distinctly announced. For the Psalmist says, that when he saw that the carnal and earthly promises were abundantly enjoyed by the ungodly, his feet were almost gone, his steps had well-nigh slipped; and that it seemed to him as if he had served God in vain, when he saw that those who despised God increased in that prosperity which he looked for at God's hand. He says, too, that, in investigating this matter with the desire of understanding why it was so, he had labored in vain, until he went into the sanctuary of God, and understood the end of those whom he had erroneously considered happy. Then he understood that they were cast down by that very thing, as he says, which they had made their boast, and that they had been consumed and perished for their inequities; and that that whole fabric of temporal prosperity had become as a dream when one awaketh, and suddenly finds himself destitute of all the joys he had imaged in sleep. And, as in this earth or earthy city they seemed to themselves to be great, he says, "O Lord, in Thy city Thou wilt reduce their image to nothing." He also shows how beneficial it had been for him to seek even earthly blessings only from the one true God, in whose power are all things, for he says, "As a beast was I before Thee, and I am always with Thee." "As a beast," he says, meaning that he was stupid. For I ought to have sought from Thee such things as the ungodly could not enjoy as well as I, and not those things which I saw them enjoying in abundance, and hence concluded I was serving Thee in vain, because they who declined to serve Thee had what I had not. Nevertheless, "I am always with Thee," because even in my desire for such things I did not pray to other gods. And consequently he goes on, "Thou hast holden me by my right hand, and by Thy counsel Thou hast guided me, and with glory hast taken me up;" as if all earthly advantages were left-hand blessings, though, when he saw them enjoyed by the wicked, his feet had almost gone. "For what," he says, "have I in heaven, and what have I desired from Thee upon earth?" He blames himself, and is justly displeased with himself; because, though he had in heaven so vast a possession (as he afterwards understood), he yet sought from his God on earth a transitory and fleeting happiness—a happiness of mire, we may say. "My heart and my flesh," he says, "fail, O God of my heart." Happy failure, from things below to things above! And hence in another psalm He says, "My soul longeth, yea, even faileth, for the courts of the Lord." Yet, though he had said of both his heart and his flesh that they were failing, he did not say, O God of my heart and my flesh, but, O God of my heart; for by the heart the flesh is made clean. Therefore, says the Lord, "Cleanse that which is within, and the outside shall be clean also." He then says that God Himself—not anything received from Him, but Himself—is his portion. "The God of my heart, and my portion for ever." Among the various objects of human choice, God alone satisfied him. "For, lo," he says, "they that are far from Thee shall perish: Thou destroyest all them that go a-whoring from Thee"—that is, who prostitute themselves to many gods. And then follows the verse for which all the rest of the psalm seems to prepare: "It is good for me to cleave to God"—not to go far off; not to go a-whoring with a multitude of gods. And then shall this union with God be perfected, when all that is to be redeemed in us has been redeemed. But for the present we must, as he goes on to say, "place our hope in God." "For that which is seen," says the apostle, "is not hope. For what a man sees, why does he yet hope for? But if we hope for that we see not, then do we with patience wait for it." Being, then, for the present established in this hope, let us do what the Psalmist further indicates, and become in our measure angels or messengers of God, declaring His will, and praising His glory and His grace. For when he had said, "To place my hope in God," he goes on, "that I may declare all Thy praises in the gates of the daughter of Zion." This is the most glorious city of God; this is the city which knows and worships one God: she is celebrated by the holy angels, who invite us to their society, and desire us to become fellow-citizens with them in this city; for they do not wish us to worship them as our gods, but to join them in worshiping their God and ours; nor to sacrifice to them, but, together with them, to become a sacrifice to God. Accordingly, whoever will lay aside malignant obstinacy, and consider these things, shall be assured that all these blessed and immortal spirits, who do not envy us (for if they envied they were not blessed), but rather love us, and desire us to be as blessed as themselves, look on us with greater pleasure, and give us greater assistance, when we join them in worshiping one God, Father, Son, and Holy Ghost, than if we were to offer to themselves sacrifice and worship.

Book Eleven

Chapter I: *Of This Part of the Work, Wherein We Begin to Explain the Origin and End of the Two Cities.*

The city of God we speak of is the same to which testimony is borne by that Scripture, which excels all the writings of all nations by its divine authority, and has brought under its influence all kinds of minds, and this not by a casual intellectual movement, but obviously by an express providential arrangement. For there it is written, "Glorious things are spoken of thee, O city of God." And in another psalm we read, "Great is the Lord, and greatly to be praised in the city of our God, in the mountain of His holiness, increasing the joy of the whole earth." And, a little after, in the same psalm, "As we have heard, so have we seen in the city of the Lord of hosts, in the city of our God. God has established it for ever." And in another, "There is a river the streams whereof shall make glad the city of our God, the holy place of the tabernacles of the Most High. God is in the midst of her, she shall not be moved." From these and similar testimonies, all of which it were tedious to cite, we have learned that there is a city of God, and its Founder has inspired us with a love which makes us covet its citizenship. To this Founder of the holy city the citizens of the earthly city prefer their own gods, not knowing that He is the God of gods, not of false, i.e., of impious and proud gods, who, being deprived of His unchangeable and freely communicated light, and so reduced to a kind of poverty-stricken power, eagerly grasp at their own private privileges, and seek divine honors from their deluded subjects; but of the pious and holy gods, who are better pleased to submit themselves to one, than to subject many to themselves, and who would rather worship God than be worshiped as God. But to the enemies of this city we have replied in the ten preceding books, according to our ability and the help afforded by our Lord and King. Now, recognizing what is expected of me, and not unmindful of my promise, and relying, too, on the same succor, I will endeavor to treat of the origin, and progress, and deserved destinies of the two cities (the earthly and the heavenly, to wit), which, as we said, are in this present world commingled, and as it were entangled together. And, first, I will explain how the foundations of these two cities were originally laid, in the difference that arose among the angels.

Chapter II: *Of the Knowledge of God, to Which No Man Can Attain Save Through the Mediator Between God and Men, the Man Christ Jesus.*

It is a great and very rare thing for a man, after he has contemplated the whole creation, corporeal and incorporeal, and has discerned its mutability, to pass beyond it, and, by the continued soaring of his mind, to attain to the unchangeable substance of God, and, in that height of contemplation, to learn from God Himself that none but He has made all that is not of the divine essence. For God speaks with a man not by means of some audible creature dinning in his ears, so that atmospheric vibrations connect Him that makes with him that hears the sound, nor even by means of a spiritual being with the semblance of a body, such as we see in dreams or similar states; for even in this case He speaks as if to the ears of the body, because it is by means of the semblance of a body He speaks, and with the appearance of a real interval of space—for visions are exact representations of bodily objects. Not by these, then, does God speak, but by the truth itself, if any one is prepared to hear with the mind rather than with the body. For He speaks to that part of man which is better than all else that is in him, and than which God Himself alone is better. For since man is most properly understood (or, if that cannot be, then, at least, believed) to be made in God's image, no doubt it is that part of him by which he rises above those lower parts he has in common with the beasts, which brings him nearer to the Supreme. But since the mind itself, though naturally capable of reason and intelligence is disabled by besotting and inveterate vices not merely from delighting and abiding in, but even from tolerating His unchangeable light, until it has been gradually healed, and renewed, and made capable of such felicity, it had, in the first place, to be impregnated with faith, and so purified. And that in this faith it might advance the more confidently towards the truth, the truth itself, God, God's Son, assuming humanity without destroying His divinity, established and founded this faith, that there might be a way for man to man's God through a God-man. For this is the Mediator between God and men, the man Christ Jesus. For it is as man that He is the Mediator and the Way. Since, if the way lieth between him who goes, and the place whither he goes, there is hope of his reaching it; but if there be no way, or if he know not where it is, what boots it to know whither he should go? Now the only way that is infallibly secured against all mistakes, is when the very same person is at once God and man, God our end, man our way.

Chapter III: *Of the Authority of the Canonical Scriptures Composed by the Divine Spirit.*

This Mediator, having spoken what He judged sufficient first by the prophets, then by His own lips, and afterwards by the apostles, has besides produced the Scripture which is called canonical, which has paramount authority, and to which we yield assent in all matters of which we ought not to be ignorant, and yet cannot know of ourselves. For if we attain the knowledge of present objects by the testimony of our own senses, whether internal or external, then, regarding objects remote from our own senses, we need others to bring their testimony, since we cannot know them by our own, and we credit the persons to whom the objects have been or are sensibly present. Accordingly, as in the case of visible objects which we have not seen, we trust those who have, (and likewise with all sensible objects,) so in the case of things which are perceived by the mind and spirit, i.e., which are remote from our own interior sense, it behooves us to trust those who have seen them set in that incorporeal light, or abidingly contemplate them.

Chapter IV: *That the World is Neither Without Beginning, Nor Yet Created by a New Decree of God, by Which He Afterwards Willed What He Had Not Before Willed.*

Of all visible things, the world is the greatest; of all invisible, the greatest is God. But, that the world is, we see; that God is, we believe. That God made the world, we can believe from no one more safely than from God Himself. But where have we heard Him? Nowhere more distinctly than in the Holy Scriptures, where His prophet said, "In the beginning God created the heavens and the earth." Was the prophet present when God made the heavens and the earth? No; but the wisdom of God, by whom all things were made, was there, and wisdom insinuates itself into holy souls, and makes them the friends of God and His prophets, and noiselessly informs them of His works. They are taught also by the angels of God, who always behold the face of the Father, and announce His will to whom it befits. Of these prophets was he who said and wrote, "In the beginning God created the heavens and the earth." And so fit a witness was he of God, that the same Spirit of God, who revealed these things to him, enabled him also so long before to predict that our faith also would be forthcoming.

But why did God choose then to create the heavens and earth which up to that time He had not made? If they who put this question wish to make out that the world is eternal and without beginning, and that consequently it has not been made by God, they are strangely deceived, and rave in the incurable madness of impiety. For, though the voices of the prophets were silent, the world itself, by its well-ordered changes and movements, and by the fair appearance of all visible things, bears a testimony of its own, both that it has been created, and also that it could not have been created save by God, whose greatness and beauty are unutterable and invisible. As for those who own, indeed, that it was made by God, and yet ascribe to it not a temporal but only a creational beginning, so that in some scarcely intelligible way the world should always have existed a created world they make an assertion which seems to them to defend God from the charge of arbitrary hastiness, or of suddenly conceiving the idea of creating the world as a quite new idea, or of casually changing His will, though He be unchangeable. But I do not see how this supposition of theirs can stand in other respects, and chiefly in respect of the soul; for if they contend that it is co-eternal with God, they will be quite at a loss to explain whence there has accrued to it new misery, which through a previous eternity had not existed. For if they said that its happiness and misery ceaselessly alternate, they must say, further, that this alternation will continue for ever; whence will result this absurdity, that, though the soul is called blessed, it is not so in this, that it foresees its own misery and disgrace. And yet, if it does not foresee it, and supposes that it will be neither disgraced nor wretched, but always blessed, then it is blessed because it is deceived; and a more foolish statement one cannot make. But if their idea is that the soul's misery has alternated with its bliss during the ages of the past eternity, but that now, when once the soul has been set free, it will return henceforth no more to misery, they are nevertheless of opinion that it has never been truly blessed before, but begins at last to enjoy a new and uncertain happiness; that is to say, they must acknowledge that some new thing, and that an important and signal thing, happens to the soul which never in a whole past eternity happened it before. And if they deny that God's eternal purpose included this new experience of the soul, they deny that He is the Author of its blessedness, which is unspeakable impiety. If, on the other hand, they say that the future blessedness of the soul is the result of a new decree of God, how will they show that God is not chargeable with that mutability which displeases them? Further, if they acknowledge that it was created in time, but will never perish in time—that it has, like number, a beginning but no end—and that, therefore, having once made trial of misery, and been delivered from it, it will never again return thereto, they will certainly admit that this takes place without any violation of the immutable counsel of God. Let them, then, in like manner believe regarding the world that it too could be made in time, and yet that God, in making it, did not alter His eternal design.

Chapter V: *That We Ought Not to Seek to Comprehend the Infinite Ages of Time Before the World, Nor the Infinite Realms of Space.*

Next, we must see what reply can be made to those who agree that God is the Creator of the world, but have difficulties about the time of its creation, and what reply, also, they can make to difficulties we might raise about the place of its creation. For, as they demand why the world was created then and no sooner, we may ask why it was created just here where it is, and not elsewhere. For if they imagine infinite spaces of time before the world, during which God could not have been idle, in like manner they may conceive outside the world infinite realms of space, in which, if any one says that the Omnipotent cannot hold His hand from working, will it not follow that they must adopt Epicurus' dream of innumerable worlds? with this difference only, that he asserts that they are formed and destroyed by the fortuitous movements of atoms, while they will hold that they are made by God's hand, if they maintain that, throughout the boundless immensity of space, stretching interminably in every direction round the world, God cannot rest, and that the worlds which they suppose Him to make cannot be destroyed. For here the question is with those who, with ourselves, believe that God is spiritual, and the Creator of all existences but Himself. As for others, it is a condescension to dispute with them on a religious question, for they have acquired a reputation only among men who pay divine honors to a number of gods, and have become conspicuous among the other philosophers for no other reason than that, though they are still far from the truth, they are near it in comparison with the rest. While these, then, neither confine in any place, nor limit, nor distribute the divine substance, but, as is worthy of God, own it to be wholly though spiritually present everywhere, will they perchance say that this substance is absent from such immense spaces outside the world, and is occupied in one only, (and that a very little one compared with the infinity beyond), the one, namely, in which is the world? I think they will not proceed to this absurdity. Since they maintain that there is but one world, of vast material bulk, indeed, yet finite, and in its own determinate position, and that this was made by the working of God, let them give the same account of God's resting in the infinite times before the world as they give of His resting in the infinite spaces outside of it. And as it does not follow that God set the world in the very spot it occupies and no other by accident rather than by divine reason, although no human reason can comprehend why it was so set, and though there was no merit in the spot chosen to give it the precedence of infinite others, so neither does it follow that we should suppose that God was guided by chance when He created the world in that and no earlier time, although previous times had been running by during an infinite past, and though there was no difference by which one time could be chosen in preference to another. But if they say that the thoughts of men are idle when they conceive infinite places, since there is no place beside the world, we reply that, by the same showing, it is vain to conceive of the past times of God's rest, since there is no time before the world.

Chapter VI: *That the World and Time Had Both One Beginning, and the One Did Not Anticipate the Other.*

For if eternity and time are rightly distinguished by this, that time does not exist without some movement and transition, while in eternity there is no change, who does not see that there could have been no time had not some creature been made, which by some motion could give birth to change—the various parts of which motion and change, as they cannot be simultaneous, succeed one another—and thus, in these shorter or longer intervals of duration, time would begin? Since then, God, in whose eternity is no change at all, is the Creator and Ordainer of time, I do not see how He can be said to have created the world after spaces of time had elapsed, unless it be said that prior to the world there was some creature by whose movement time could pass. And if the sacred and infallible Scriptures say that in the beginning God created the heavens and the earth, in order that it may be understood that He had made nothing previously—for if He had made anything before the rest, this thing would rather be said to have been made "in the beginning"—then assuredly the world was made, not in time, but simultaneously with time. For that which is made in time is made both after and before some time—after that which is past, before that which is future. But none could then be past, for there was no creature by whose movements its duration could be measured. But simultaneously with time the world was made, if in the world's creation change and motion were created, as seems evident from the order of the first six or seven days. For in these days the morning and evening are counted, until, on the sixth day, all things which God then made were finished, and on the seventh the rest of God was mysteriously and sublimely signalized. What kind of days these were it is extremely difficult, or perhaps impossible for us to conceive, and how much more to say!

Chapter VII: *Of the Nature of the First Days, Which are Said to Have Had Morning and Evening, Before There Was a Sun.*

We see, indeed, that our ordinary days have no evening but by the setting, and no morning but by the rising, of the sun; but the first three days of all were passed without sun, since it is reported to have been made on the fourth day. And first of all, indeed, light was made by the word of God, and God, we read, separated it from the darkness, and called the light Day, and the darkness Night; but what kind of light that was, and by what periodic movement it made evening and morning, is beyond the reach of our senses; neither can we understand how it was, and yet must unhesitatingly believe it. For either it was some material light, whether proceeding from the upper parts of the world, far removed from our sight, or from the spot where the sun was afterwards kindled; or under the name of light the holy city was signified, composed of holy angels and blessed spirits, the city of which the apostle says, "Jerusalem which is above is our eternal mother in heaven;" and in another place, "For ye are all the children of the light, and the children of the day; we are not of the night, nor of darkness." Yet in some respects we may appropriately speak of a morning and evening of this day also. For the knowledge of the creature is, in comparison of the knowledge of the Creator, but a twilight; and so it dawns and breaks into morning when the creature is drawn to the praise and love of the Creator; and night never falls when the Creator is not forsaken through love of the creature. In fine, Scripture, when it would recount those days in order, never mentions the word night. It never says, "Night was," but "The evening and the morning were the first day." So of the second and the rest. And, indeed, the knowledge of created things contemplated by themselves is, so to speak, more colorless than when they are seen in the wisdom of God, as in the art by which they were made. Therefore evening is a more suitable figure than night; and yet, as I said, morning returns when the creature returns to the praise and love of the Creator. When it does so in the knowledge of itself, that is the first day; when in the knowledge of the firmament, which is the name given to the sky between the waters above and those beneath, that is the second day; when in the knowledge of the earth, and the sea, and all things that grow out of the earth, that is the third day; when in the knowledge of the greater and less luminaries, and all the stars, that is the fourth day; when in the knowledge of all animals that swim in the waters and that fly in the air, that is the fifth day; when in the knowledge of all animals that live on the earth, and of man himself, that is the sixth day.

Chapter VIII: *What We are to Understand of God's Resting on the Seventh Day, After the Six Days' Work.*

When it is said that God rested on the seventh day from all His works, and hallowed it, we are not to conceive of this in a childish fashion, as if work were a toil to God, who "spake and it was done"—spake by the spiritual and eternal, not audible and transitory word. But God's rest signifies the rest of those who rest in God, as the joy of a house means the joy of those in the house who rejoice, though not the house, but something else, causes the joy. How much more intelligible is such phraseology, then, if the house itself, by its own beauty, makes the inhabitants joyful! For in this case we not only call it joyful by that figure of speech in which the thing containing is used for the thing contained (as when we say, "The theatres applaud," "The meadows low," meaning that the men in the one applaud, and the oxen in the other low), but also by that figure in which the cause is spoken of as if it were the effect, as when a letter is said to be joyful, because it makes its readers so. Most appropriately, therefore, the sacred narrative states that God rested, meaning thereby that those rest who are in Him, and whom He makes to rest. And this the prophetic narrative promises also to the men to whom it speaks, and for whom it was written, that they themselves, after those good works which God does in and by them, if they have managed by faith to get near to God in this life, shall enjoy in Him eternal rest. This was prefigured to the ancient people of God by the rest enjoined in their sabbath law, of which, in its own place, I shall speak more at large.

Chapter IX: *What the Scriptures Teach Us to Believe Concerning the Creation of the Angels.*

At present, since I have undertaken to treat of the origin of the holy city, and first of the holy angels, who constitute a large part of this city, and indeed the more blessed part, since they have never been expatriated, I will give myself to the task of explaining, by God's help, and as far as seems suitable, the Scriptures which relate to this point. Where Scripture speaks of the world's creation, it is not plainly said whether or when the angels were created; but if mention of them is made, it is implicitly under the name of "heaven," when it is said, "In the beginning God created the heavens and the earth," or perhaps rather under the name of "light," of which presently. But that they were wholly omitted, I am unable to believe, because it is written that God on the seventh day rested from all His works which He made; and this very book itself begins, "In the beginning God created the heavens and the earth," so that before heaven and earth God seems to have made nothing. Since, therefore, He began with the heavens and the earth—and the earth itself, as Scripture adds, was at first invisible and formless, light not being as yet made, and darkness covering the face of the deep (that is to say, covering an undefined chaos of earth and sea, for where light is not, darkness must needs be)—and then when all things, which are recorded to have been completed in six days, were created and arranged, how should the angels be omitted, as if they were not among the works of God, from which on the seventh day He rested? Yet, though the fact that the angels are the work of God is not omitted here, it is indeed not explicitly mentioned; but elsewhere Holy Scripture asserts it in the clearest manner. For in the Hymn of the Three Children in the Furnace it was said, "O all ye works of the Lord bless ye the Lord;" and among these works mentioned afterwards in detail, the angels are named. And in the psalm it is said, "Praise ye the Lord from the heavens, praise Him in the heights. Praise ye Him, all His angels; praise ye Him, all His hosts. Praise ye Him, sun and moon; praise him, all ye stars of light. Praise Him, ye heaven of heavens; and ye waters that be above the heavens. Let them praise the name of the Lord; for He commanded, and they were created." Here the angels are most expressly and by divine authority said to have been made by God, for of them among the other heavenly things it is said, "He commanded, and they were created." Who, then, will be bold enough to suggest that the angels were made after the six days' creation? If any one is so foolish, his folly is disposed of by a scripture of like authority, where God says, "When the stars were made, the angels praised me with a loud voice." The angels therefore existed before the stars; and the stars were made the fourth day. Shall we then say that they were made the third day? Far from it; for we know what was made that day. The earth was separated from the water, and each element took its own distinct form, and the earth produced all that grows on it. On the second day, then? Not even on this; for on it the firmament was made between the waters above and beneath, and was called "Heaven," in which firmament the stars were made on the fourth day. There is no question, then, that if the angels are included in the works of God during these six days, they are that light which was called "Day," and whose unity Scripture signalizes by calling that day not the "first day," but "one day." For the second day, the third, and the rest are not other days; but the same "one" day is repeated to complete the number six or seven, so that there should be knowledge both of God's works and of His rest. For when God said, "Let there be light, and there was light," if we are justified in understanding in this light the creation of the angels, then certainly they were created partakers of the eternal light which is the unchangeable Wisdom of God, by which all things were made, and whom we call the only-begotten Son of God; so that they, being illumined by the Light that created them, might themselves become light and be called "Day," in participation of that unchangeable Light and Day which is the Word of God, by whom both themselves and all else were made. "The true Light, which lighteth every man that cometh into the world"—this Light lighteth also every pure angel, that he may be light not in himself, but in God; from whom if an angel turn away, he becomes impure, as are all those who are called unclean spirits, and are no longer light in the Lord, but darkness in themselves, being deprived of the participation of Light eternal. For evil has no positive nature; but the loss of good has received the name "evil."

Chapter X: *Of the Simple and Unchangeable Trinity, Father, Son, and Holy Ghost, One God, in Whom Substance and Quality are Identical.*

There is, accordingly, a good which is alone simple, and therefore alone unchangeable, and this is God. By this Good have all others been created, but not simple, and therefore not unchangeable. "Created," I say—that is, made, not begotten. For that which is begotten of the simple Good is simple as itself, and the same as itself. These two we call the Father and the Son; and both together with the Holy Spirit are one God; and to this Spirit the epithet Holy is in Scripture, as it were, appropriated. And He is another than the Father and the Son, for He is neither the Father nor the Son. I say "another," not "another thing," because He is equally with them the simple Good, unchangeable and co-eternal. And this Trinity is one God; and none the less simple because a Trinity. For we do not say that the nature of the good is simple, because the Father alone possesses it, or the Son alone, or the Holy Ghost alone; nor do we say, with the Sabellian heretics, that it is only nominally a Trinity, and has no real distinction of persons; but we say it is simple, because it is what it has, with the exception of the relation of the persons to one another. For, in regard to this relation, it is true that the Father has a Son, and yet is not Himself the Son; and the Son has a Father, and is not

Himself the Father. But, as regards Himself, irrespective of relation to the other, each is what He has; thus, He is in Himself living, for He has life, and is Himself the Life which He has.

It is for this reason, then, that the nature of the Trinity is called simple, because it has not anything which it can lose, and because it is not one thing and its contents another, as a cup and the liquor, or a body and its color, or the air and the light or heat of it, or a mind and its wisdom. For none of these is what it has: the cup is not liquor, nor the body color, nor the air light and heat, nor the mind wisdom. And hence they can be deprived of what they have, and can be turned or changed into other qualities and states, so that the cup may be emptied of the liquid of which it is full, the body be discolored, the air darken, the mind grow silly. The incorruptible body which is promised to the saints in the resurrection cannot, indeed, lose its quality of incorruption, but the bodily substance and the quality of incorruption are not the same thing. For the quality of incorruption resides entire in each several part, not greater in one and less in another; for no part is more incorruptible than another. The body, indeed, is itself greater in whole than in part; and one part of it is larger, another smaller, yet is not the larger more incorruptible than the smaller. The body, then, which is not in each of its parts a whole body, is one thing; incorruptibility, which is throughout complete, is another thing—for every part of the incorruptible body, however unequal to the rest otherwise, is equally incorrupt. For the hand, e.g., is not more incorrupt than the finger because it is larger than the finger; so, though finger and hand are unequal, their incorruptibility is equal. Thus, although incorruptibility is inseparable from an incorruptible body, yet the substance of the body is one thing, the quality of incorruption another. And therefore the body is not what it has. The soul itself, too, though it be always wise (as it will be eternally when it is redeemed), will be so by participating in the unchangeable wisdom, which it is not; for though the air be never robbed of the light that is shed abroad in it, it is not on that account the same thing as the light. I do not mean that the soul is air, as has been supposed by some who could not conceive a spiritual nature; but, with much dissimilarity, the two things have a kind of likeness, which makes it suitable to say that the immaterial soul is illumined with the immaterial light of the simple wisdom of God, as the material air is irradiated with material light, and that, as the air, when deprived of this light, grows dark, (for material darkness is nothing else than air wanting light,) so the soul, deprived of the light of wisdom, grows dark.

According to this, then, those things which are essentially and truly divine are called simple, because in them quality and substance are identical, and because they are divine, or wise, or blessed in themselves, and without extraneous supplement. In Holy Scripture, it is true, the Spirit of wisdom is called "manifold" because it contains many things in it; but what it contains it also is, and it being one is all these things. For neither are there many wisdoms, but one, in which are untold and infinite treasures of things intellectual, wherein are all invisible and unchangeable reasons of things visible and changeable which were created by it. For God made nothing unwittingly; not even a human workman can be said to do so. But if He knew all that He made, He made only those things which He had known. Whence flows a very striking but true conclusion, that this world could not be known to us unless it existed, but could not have existed unless it had been known to God.

Chapter XI: *Whether the Angels that Fell Partook of the Blessedness Which the Holy Angels Have Always Enjoyed from the Time of Their Creation.*

And since these things are so, those spirits whom we call angels were never at any time or in any way darkness, but, as soon as they were made, were made light; yet they were not so created in order that they might exist and live in any way whatever, but were enlightened that they might live wisely and blessedly. Some of them, having turned away from this light, have not won this wise and blessed life, which is certainly eternal, and accompanied with the sure confidence of its eternity; but they have still the life of reason, though darkened with folly, and this they cannot lose even if they would. But who can determine to what extent they were partakers of that wisdom before they fell? And how shall we say that they participated in it equally with those who through it are truly and fully blessed, resting in a true certainty of eternal felicity? For if they had equally participated in this true knowledge, then the evil angels would have remained eternally blessed equally with the good, because they were equally expectant of it. For, though a life be never so long, it cannot be truly called eternal if it is destined to have an end; for it is called life inasmuch as it is lived, but eternal because it has no end. Wherefore, although everything eternal is not therefore blessed (for hell-fire is eternal), yet if no life can be truly and perfectly blessed except it be eternal, the life of these angels was not blessed, for it was doomed to end, and therefore not eternal, whether they knew it or not. In the one case fear, in the other ignorance, prevented them from being blessed. And even if their ignorance was not so great as to breed in them a wholly false expectation, but left them wavering in uncertainty whether their good would be eternal or would some time terminate, this very doubt concerning so grand a destiny was incompatible with the plenitude of blessedness which we believe the holy angels enjoyed. For we do not so narrow and restrict the application of the term "blessedness" as to apply it to God only, though doubtless He is so truly blessed that greater blessedness cannot be; and, in comparison of His blessedness, what is that of the angels, though, according to their capacity, they be perfectly blessed?

Chapter XII: *A Comparison of the Blessedness of the Righteous, Who Have Not Yet Received the Divine Reward, with that of Our First Parents in Paradise.*

And the angels are not the only members of the rational and intellectual creation whom we call blessed. For who will take upon him to deny that those first men in Paradise were blessed previously to sin, although they were uncertain how long their blessedness was to last, and whether it would be eternal (and eternal it would have been had they not sinned)—who, I say, will do so, seeing that even now we not unbecomingly call those blessed whom we see leading a righteous and holy life, in hope of immortality, who have no harrowing remorse of conscience, but obtain readily divine remission of the sins of their present infirmity? These, though they are certain that they shall be rewarded if they persevere, are not certain that they will persevere. For what man can know that he will persevere to the end in the exercise and increase of grace, unless he has been certified by some revelation from Him who, in His just and secret judgment, while He deceives none, informs few regarding this matter? Accordingly, so far as present comfort goes, the first man in Paradise was more blessed than any just man in this insecure state; but as regards the hope of future good, every man who not merely supposes, but certainly knows that he shall eternally enjoy the most high God in the company of angels, and beyond the reach of ill—this man, no matter what bodily torments afflict him, is more blessed than was he who, even in that great felicity of Paradise, was uncertain of his fate.

Chapter XIII: *Whether All the Angels Were So Created in One Common State of Felicity, that Those Who Fell Were Not Aware that They Would Fall, and that Those Who Stood Received Assurance of Their Own Perseverance After the Ruin of the Fallen.*

From all this, it will readily occur to any one that the blessedness which an intelligent being desires as its legitimate object results from a combination of these two things, namely, that it uninterruptedly enjoy the unchangeable good, which is God; and that it be delivered from all dubiety, and know certainly that it shall eternally abide in the same enjoyment. That it is so with the angels of light we piously believe; but that the fallen angels, who by their own default lost that light, did not enjoy this blessedness even before they sinned, reason bids us conclude. Yet if their life was of any duration before they fell, we must allow them a blessedness of some kind, though not that which is accompanied with foresight. Or, if it seems hard to believe that, when the angels were created, some were created in ignorance either of their perseverance or their fall, while others were most certainly assured of the eternity of their felicity,—if it is hard to believe that they were not all from the beginning on an equal footing, until these who are now evil did of their own will fall away from the light of goodness, certainly it is much harder to believe that the holy angels are now uncertain of their eternal blessedness, and do not know regarding themselves as much as we have been able to gather regarding them from the Holy Scriptures. For what catholic

Christian does not know that no new devil will ever arise among the good angels, as he knows that this present devil will never again return into the fellowship of the good? For the truth in the gospel promises to the saints and the faithful that they will be equal to the angels of God; and it is also promised them that they will "go away into life eternal." But if we are certain that we shall never lapse from eternal felicity, while they are not certain, then we shall not be their equals, but their superiors. But as the truth never deceives, and as we shall be their equals, they must be certain of their blessedness. And because the evil angels could not be certain of that, since their blessedness was destined to come to an end, it follows either that the angels were unequal, or that, if equal, the good angels were assured of the eternity of their blessedness after the perdition of the others; unless, possibly, some one may say that the words of the Lord about the devil "He was a murderer from the beginning, and abode not in the truth," are to be understood as if he was not only a murderer from the beginning of the human race, when man, whom he could kill by his deceit, was made, but also that he did not abide in the truth from the time of his own creation, and was accordingly never blessed with the holy angels, but refused to submit to his Creator, and proudly exulted as if in a private lordship of his own, and was thus deceived and deceiving. For the dominion of the Almighty cannot be eluded; and he who will not piously submit himself to things as they are, proudly feigns, and mocks himself with a state of things that does not exist; so that what the blessed Apostle John says thus becomes intelligible: "The devil sinneth from the beginning"—that is, from the time he was created he refused righteousness, which none but a will piously subject to God can enjoy. Whoever adopts this opinion at least disagrees with those heretics the Manichees, and with any other pestilential sect that may suppose that the devil has derived from some adverse evil principle a nature proper to himself. These persons are so befooled by error, that, although they acknowledge with ourselves the authority of the gospels, they do not notice that the Lord did not say, "The devil was naturally a stranger to the truth," but "The devil abode not in the truth," by which He meant us to understand that he had fallen from the truth, in which, if he had abode, he would have become a partaker of it, and have remained in blessedness along with the holy angels.

Chapter XIV: *An Explanation of What is Said of the Devil, that He Did Not Abide in the Truth, Because the Truth Was Not in Him.*

Moreover, as if we had been inquiring why the devil did not abide in the truth, our Lord subjoins the reason, saying, "because the truth is not in him." Now, it would be in him had he abode in it. But the phraseology is unusual. For, as the words stand, "He abode not in the truth, because the truth is not in him," it seems as if the truth's not being in him were the cause of his not abiding in it; whereas his not abiding in the truth is rather the cause of its not being in him. The same form of speech is found in the psalm: "I have called upon Thee, for Thou hast heard me, O God," where we should expect it to be said, Thou hast heard me, O God, for I have called upon Thee. But when he had said, "I have called," then, as if some one were seeking proof of this, he demonstrates the effectual earnestness of his prayer by the effect of God's hearing it; as if he had said, The proof that I have prayed is that Thou hast heard me.

Chapter XV: *How We are to Understand the Words, "The Devil Sinneth from the Beginning."*

As for what John says about the devil, "The devil sinneth from the beginning" they who suppose it is meant hereby that the devil was made with a sinful nature, misunderstand it; for if sin be natural, it is not sin at all. And how do they answer the prophetic proofs—either what Isaiah says when he represents the devil under the person of the king of Babylon, "How art thou fallen, O Lucifer, son of the morning!" or what Ezekiel says, "Thou hast been in Eden, the garden of God; every precious stone was thy covering," where it is meant that he was some time without sin; for a little after it is still more explicitly said, "Thou wast perfect in thy ways?" And if these passages cannot well be otherwise interpreted, we must understand by this one also, "He abode not in the truth," that he was once in the truth, but did not remain in it. And from this passage, "The devil sinneth from the beginning," it is not to be supposed that he sinned from the beginning of his created existence, but from the beginning of his sin, when by his pride he had once commenced to sin. There is a passage, too, in the Book of Job, of which the devil is the subject: "This is the beginning of the creation of God, which He made to be a sport to His angels," which agrees with the psalm, where it is said, "There is that dragon which Thou hast made to be a sport therein." But these passages are not to lead us to suppose that the devil was originally created to be the sport of the angels, but that he was doomed to this punishment after his sin. His beginning, then, is the handiwork of God; for there is no nature, even among the least, and lowest, and last of the beasts, which was not the work of Him from whom has proceeded all measure, all form, all order, without which nothing can be planned or conceived. How much more, then, is this angelic nature, which surpasses in dignity all else that He has made, the handiwork of the Most High!

Chapter XVI: *Of the Ranks and Differences of the Creatures, Estimated by Their Utility, or According to the Natural Gradations of Being.*

For, among those beings which exist, and which are not of God the Creator's essence, those which have life are ranked above those which have none; those that have the power of generation, or even of desiring, above those which want this faculty. And, among things that have life, the sentient are higher than those which have no sensation, as animals are ranked above trees. And, among the sentient, the intelligent are above those that have not intelligence—men, e.g., above cattle. And, among the intelligent, the immortal such as the angels, above the mortal, such as men. These are the gradations according to the order of nature; but according to the utility each man finds in a thing, there are various standards of value, so that it comes to pass that we prefer some things that have no sensation to some sentient beings. And so strong is this preference, that, had we the power, we would abolish the latter from nature altogether, whether in ignorance of the place they hold in nature, or, though we know it, sacrificing them to our own convenience. Who, e.g., would not rather have bread in his house than mice, gold than fleas? But there is little to wonder at in this, seeing that even when valued by men themselves (whose nature is certainly of the highest dignity), more is often given for a horse than for a slave, for a jewel than for a maid. Thus the reason of one contemplating nature prompts very different judgments from those dictated by the necessity of the needy, or the desire of the voluptuous; for the former considers what value a thing in itself has in the scale of creation, while necessity considers how it meets its need; reason looks for what the mental light will judge to be true, while pleasure looks for what pleasantly titilates the bodily sense. But of such consequence in rational natures is the weight, so to speak, of will and of love, that though in the order of nature angels rank above men, yet, by the scale of justice, good men are of greater value than bad angels.

Chapter XVII: *That the Flaw of Wickedness is Not Nature, But Contrary to Nature, and Has Its Origin, Not in the Creator, But in the Will.*

It is with reference to the nature, then, and not to the wickedness of the devil, that we are to understand these words, "This is the beginning of God's handiwork;" for, without doubt, wickedness can be a flaw or vice only where the nature previously was not vitiated. Vice, too, is so contrary to nature, that it cannot but damage it. And therefore departure from God would be no vice, unless in a nature whose property it was to abide with God. So that even the wicked will is a strong proof of the goodness of the nature. But God, as He is the supremely good Creator of good natures, so is He of evil wills the most just Ruler; so that, while they make an ill use of good natures, He makes a good use even of evil wills. Accordingly, He caused the devil (good by God's creation, wicked by his own will) to be cast down from his high position, and to become the mockery of His angels—that is, He caused his temptations to benefit those whom he wishes to injure by them. And because God, when He created him, was certainly not ignorant of his future malignity, and foresaw the good which He Himself would bring out of his evil, therefore says the psalm, "This leviathan whom Thou hast made to be a sport therein," that we may see that, even while God in His goodness created him good, He yet had already foreseen and arranged how He would make use of him when he became wicked.

Chapter XVIII: *Of the Beauty of the Universe, Which Becomes, by God's Ordinance, More Brilliant by the Opposition of Contraries.*

For God would never have created any, I do not say angel, but even man, whose future wickedness He foreknew, unless He had equally known to what uses in behalf of the good He could turn him, thus embellishing, the course of the ages, as it were an exquisite poem set off with antitheses. For what are called antitheses are among the most elegant of the ornaments of speech. They might be called in Latin "oppositions," or, to speak more accurately, "contrapositions;" but this word is not in common use among us, though the Latin, and indeed the languages of all nations, avail themselves of the same ornaments of style. In the Second Epistle to the Corinthians the Apostle Paul also makes a graceful use of antithesis, in that place where he says, "By the armor of righteousness on the right hand and on the left, by honor and dishonor, by evil report and good report: as deceivers, and yet true; as unknown, and yet well known; as dying, and, behold, we live; as chastened, and not killed; as sorrowful, yet always rejoicing; as poor, yet making many rich; as having nothing, and yet possessing all things." As, then, these oppositions of contraries lend beauty to the language, so the beauty of the course of this world is achieved by the opposition of contraries, arranged, as it were, by an eloquence not of words, but of things. This is quite plainly stated in the Book of Ecclesiasticus, in this way: "Good is set against evil, and life against death: so is the sinner against the godly. So look upon all the works of the Most High, and these are two and two, one against another."

Chapter XIX: *What, Seemingly, We are to Understand by the Words, "God Divided the Light from the Darkness."*

Accordingly, though the obscurity of the divine word has certainly this advantage, that it causes many opinions about the truth to be started and discussed, each reader seeing some fresh meaning in it, yet, whatever is said to be meant by an obscure passage should be either confirmed by the testimony of obvious facts, or should be asserted in other and less ambiguous texts. This obscurity is beneficial, whether the sense of the author is at last reached after the discussion of many other interpretations, or whether, though that sense remain concealed, other truths are brought out by the discussion of the obscurity. To me it does not seem incongruous with the working of God, if we understand that the angels were created when that first light was made, and that a separation was made between the holy and the unclean angels, when, as is said, "God divided the light from the darkness; and God called the light Day, and the darkness He called Night." For He alone could make this discrimination, who was able also before they fell, to foreknow that they would fall, and that, being deprived of the light of truth, they would abide in the darkness of pride. For, so far as regards the day and night, with which we are familiar, He commanded those luminaries of heaven that are obvious to our senses to divide between the light and the darkness. "Let there be," He says, "lights in the firmament of the heaven, to divide the day from the night;" and shortly after He says, "And God made two great lights; the greater light to rule the day, and the lesser light to rule the night: the stars also. And God set them in the firmament of the heaven, to give light upon the earth, and to rule over the day and over the night, and to divide the light from the darkness." But between that light, which is the holy company of the angels spiritually radiant with the illumination of the truth, and that opposing darkness, which is the noisome foulness of the spiritual condition of those angels who are turned away from the light of righteousness, only He Himself could divide, from whom their wickedness (not of nature, but of will), while yet it was future, could not be hidden or uncertain.

Chapter XX: *Of the Words Which Follow the Separation of Light and Darkness, "And God Saw the Light that It Was Good."*

Then, we must not pass from this passage of Scripture without noticing that when God said, "Let there be light, and there was light," it was immediately added, "And God saw the light that it was good." No such expression followed the statement that He separated the light from the darkness, and called the light Day and the darkness Night, lest the seal of His approval might seem to be set on such darkness, as well as on the light. For when the darkness was not subject of disapprobation, as when it was divided by the heavenly bodies from this light which our eyes discern, the statement that God saw that it was good is inserted, not before, but after the division is recorded. "And God set them," so runs the passage, "in the firmament of the heaven, to give light upon the earth, and to rule over the day and over the night, and to divide the light from the darkness: and God saw that it was good." For He approved of both, because both were sinless. But where God said, "Let there be light, and there was light; and God saw the light that it was good;" and the narrative goes on, "and God divided the light from the darkness! and God called the light Day, and the darkness He called Night," there was not in this place subjoined the statement, "And God saw that it was good," lest both should be designated good, while one of them was evil, not by nature, but by its own fault. And therefore, in this case, the light alone received the approbation of the Creator, while the angelic darkness, though it had been ordained, was yet not approved.

Chapter XXI: *Of God's Eternal and Unchangeable Knowledge and Will, Whereby All He Has Made Pleased Him in the Eternal Design as Well as in the Actual Result.*

For what else is to be understood by that invariable refrain, "And God saw that it was good," than the approval of the work in its design, which is the wisdom of God? For certainly God did not in the actual achievement of the work first learn that it was good, but, on the contrary, nothing would have been made had it not been first known by Him. While, therefore, He sees that that is good which, had He not seen it before it was made, would never have been made, it is plain that He is not discovering, but teaching that it is good. Plato, indeed, was bold enough to say that, when the universe was completed, God was, as it were, elated with joy. And Plato was not so foolish as to mean by this that God was rendered more blessed by the novelty of His creation; but he wished thus to indicate that the work now completed met with its Maker's approval, as it had while yet in design. It is not as if the knowledge of God were of various kinds, knowing in different ways things which as yet are not, things which are, and things which have been. For not in our fashion does He look forward to what is future, nor at what is present, nor back upon what is past; but in a manner quite different and far and profoundly remote from our way of thinking. For He does not pass from this to that by transition of thought, but beholds all things with absolute unchangeableness; so that of those things which emerge in time, the future, indeed, are not yet, and the present are now, and the past no longer are; but all of these are by Him comprehended in His stable and eternal presence. Neither does He see in one fashion by the eye, in another by the mind, for He is not composed of mind and body; nor does His present knowledge differ from that which it ever was or shall be, for those variations of time, past, present, and future, though they alter our knowledge, do not affect His, "with whom is no variableness, neither shadow of turning." Neither is there any growth from thought to thought in the conceptions of Him in whose spiritual vision all things which He knows are at once embraced. For as without any movement that time can measure, He Himself moves all temporal things, so He knows all times with a knowledge that time cannot measure. And therefore He saw that what He had made was good, when He saw that it was good to make it. And when He saw it made, He had not on that account a twofold nor any way increased knowledge of it; as if He had less knowledge before He made what He saw. For certainly He would not be the perfect worker He is, unless His knowledge were so perfect as to receive no addition from His finished works. Wherefore, if the only object had been to inform us who made the light, it had been enough to say, "God made the light;" and if further information regarding the means by which it was made had been intended, it would have sufficed to say, "And God said, Let there be light, and there was light," that we might know not only that God had made the world, but also that He had made it by the word. But because it was right that three leading truths regarding the creature be intimated to us, viz., who made it, by what means, and why, it is written, "God said, Let there be light, and there was light. And God saw the light that it was good." If, then, we ask who made it, it was "God." If, by what means, He said "Let it be," and it was. If we ask, why He made it, "it was good." Neither is there any author more excellent than God, nor any skill more efficacious than the word of God, nor any cause better than that good might be created by the good God. This also Plato has assigned as the most sufficient reason for the creation of the world, that good works might be made by a good God.

Book Fourteen

Chapter I: *That the Disobedience of the First Man Would Have Plunged All Men into the Endless Misery of the Second Death, Had Not the Grace of God Rescued Many.*

We have already stated in the preceding books that God, desiring not only that the human race might be able by their similarity of nature to associate with one another, but also that they might be bound together in harmony and peace by the ties of relationship, was pleased to derive all men from one individual, and created man with such a nature that the members of the race should not have died, had not the two first (of whom the one was created out of nothing, and the other out of him) merited this by their disobedience; for by them so great a sin was committed, that by it the human nature was altered for the worse, and was transmitted also to their posterity, liable to sin and subject to death. And the kingdom of death so reigned over men, that the deserved penalty of sin would have hurled all headlong even into the second death, of which there is no end, had not the undeserved grace of God saved some therefrom. And thus it has come to pass, that though there are very many and great nations all over the earth, whose rites and customs, speech, arms, and dress, are distinguished by marked differences, yet there are no more than two kinds of human society, which we may justly call two cities, according to the language of our Scriptures. The one consists of those who wish to live after the flesh, the other of those who wish to live after the spirit; and when they severally achieve what they wish, they live in peace, each after their kind.

Chapter II: *Of Carnal Life, Which is to Be Understood Not Only of Living in Bodily Indulgence, But Also of Living in the Vices of the Inner Man.*

First, we must see what it is to live after the flesh, and what to live after the spirit. For any one who either does not recollect, or does not sufficiently weigh, the language of sacred Scripture, may, on first hearing what we have said, suppose that the Epicurean philosophers live after the flesh, because they place man's highest good in bodily pleasure; and that those others do so who have been of opinion that in some form or other bodily good is man's supreme good; and that the mass of men do so who, without dogmatizing or philosophizing on the subject, are so prone to lust that they cannot delight in any pleasure save such as they receive from bodily sensations: and he may suppose that the Stoics, who place the supreme good of men in the soul, live after the spirit; for what is man's soul, if not spirit? But in the sense of the divine Scripture both are proved to live after the flesh. For by flesh it means not only the body of a terrestrial and mortal animal, as when it says, "All flesh is not the same flesh, but there is one kind of flesh of men, another flesh of beasts, another of fishes, another of birds," but it uses this word in many other significations; and among these various usages, a frequent one is to use flesh for man himself, the nature of man taking the part for the whole, as in the words, "By the deeds of the law there shall no flesh be justified;" for what does he mean here by "no flesh" but "no man?" And this, indeed, he shortly after says more plainly: "No man shall be justified by the law;" and in the Epistle to the Galatians, "Knowing that man is not justified by the works of the law." And so we understand the words, "And the Word was made flesh"—that is, man, which some not accepting in its right sense, have supposed that Christ had not a human soul. For as the whole is used for the part in the words of Mary Magdalene in the Gospel, "They have taken away my Lord, and I know not where they have laid Him," by which she meant only the flesh of Christ, which she supposed had been taken from the tomb where it had been buried, so the part is used for the whole, flesh being named, while man is referred to, as in the quotations above cited.

Since, then, Scripture uses the word flesh in many ways, which there is not time to collect and investigate, if we are to ascertain what it is to live after the flesh (which is certainly evil, though the nature of flesh is not itself evil), we must carefully examine that passage of the epistle which the Apostle Paul wrote to the Galatians, in which he says, "Now the works of the flesh are manifest, which are these: adultery, fornication, uncleanness, lasciviousness, idolatry, witchcraft, hatred, variance, emulations, wrath, strife, seditions, heresies, envyings, murders, drunkenness, revelings, and such like: of the which I tell you before, as I have also told you in time past, that they which do such things shall not inherit the kingdom of God." This whole passage of the apostolic epistle being considered, so far as it bears on the matter in hand, will be sufficient to answer the question, what it is to live after the flesh. For among the works of the flesh which he said were manifest, and which he cited for condemnation, we find not only those which concern the pleasure of the flesh, as fornications, uncleanness, lasciviousness, drunkenness, revelings, but also those which, though they be remote from fleshly pleasure, reveal the vices of the soul. For who does not see that idolatries, witchcrafts, hatreds, variance, emulations, wrath, strife, heresies, envyings, are vices rather of the soul than of the flesh? For it is quite possible for a man to abstain from fleshly pleasures for the sake of idolatry or some heretical error; and yet, even when he does so, he is proved by this apostolic authority to be living after the flesh; and in abstaining from fleshly pleasure, he is proved to be practising damnable works of the flesh. Who that has enmity has it not in his soul? or who would say to his enemy, or to the man he thinks his enemy, You have a bad flesh towards me, and not rather, You have a bad spirit towards me? In fine, if any one heard of what I may call "carnalities," he would not fail to attribute them to the carnal part of man; so no one doubts that "animosities" belong to the soul of man. Why then does the doctor of the Gentiles in faith and verity call all these and similar things works of the flesh, unless because, by that mode of speech whereby the part is used for the whole, he means us to understand by the word flesh the man himself?

Chapter III: *That the Sin is Caused Not by the Flesh, But by the Soul, and that the Corruption Contracted from Sin is Not Sin But Sin's Punishment.*

But if any one says that the flesh is the cause of all vices and ill conduct, inasmuch as the soul lives wickedly only because it is moved by the flesh, it is certain he has not carefully considered the whole nature of man. For "the corruptible body, indeed, weigheth down the soul." Whence, too, the apostle, speaking of this corruptible body, of which he had shortly before said, "though our outward man perish," says, "We know that if our earthly house of this tabernacle were dissolved, we have a building of God, an house not made with hands, eternal in the heavens. For in this we groan, earnestly desiring to be clothed upon with our house which is from heaven: if so be that being clothed we shall not be found naked. For we that are in this tabernacle do groan, being burdened: not for that we would be unclothed, but clothed upon, that mortality might be swallowed up in life." We are then burdened with this corruptible body; but knowing that the cause of this burdensomeness is not the nature and substance of the body, but its corruption, we do not desire to be deprived of the body, but to be clothed with its immortality. For then, also, there will be a body, but it shall no longer be a burden, being no longer corruptible. At present, then, "the corruptible body presseth down the soul, and the earthly tabernacle weigheth down the mind that museth upon many things," nevertheless they are in error who suppose that all the evils of the soul proceed from the body.

Virgil, indeed, seems to express the sentiments of Plato in the beautiful lines, where he says—

> "A fiery strength inspires their lives,
> An essence that from heaven derives,
> Though clogged in part by limbs of clay
> And the dull 'vesture of decay;'"

but though he goes on to mention the four most common mental emotions—desire, fear, joy, sorrow—with the intention of showing that the body is the origin of all sins and vices, saying—

> "Hence wild desires and groveling fears,
> And human laughter, human tears,
> Immured in dungeon-seeming nights
> They look abroad, yet see no light,"

yet we believe quite otherwise. For the corruption of the body, which weighs down the soul, is not the cause but the punishment of the first sin; and it was not the corruptible flesh that made the soul sinful, but the sinful soul that made the flesh corruptible. And though from this corruption of the flesh there arise certain incitements to vice, and indeed vicious desires, yet we must not attribute to the flesh all the vices of a wicked life, in case we thereby clear the devil of all these, for he has no flesh. For though we cannot call the devil a fornicator or drunkard, or ascribe to him any sensual indulgence (though he is the secret instigator and prompter of those who sin in these ways), yet he is exceedingly proud and envious. And this viciousness has so possessed him, that on account of it he is reserved in chains of darkness to everlasting punishment. Now these vices, which have dominion over the devil, the apostle attributes to the flesh, which certainly the devil has not. For he says "hatred, variance, emulations, strife, envying" are the works of the flesh; and of all these evils, pride is the origin and head, and it rules in the devil though he has no flesh. For who shows more hatred to the saints? who is more at variance with them? who more envious, bitter, and jealous? And since he exhibits all these works, though he has no flesh, how are they works of the flesh, unless because they are the works of man, who is, as I said, spoken of under the name of flesh? For it is not by having flesh, which the devil has not, but by living according to himself—that is, according to man—that man became like the devil. For the devil too, wished to live according to himself when he did not abide in the truth; so that when he lied, this was not of God, but of himself, who is not only a liar, but the father of lies, he being the first who lied, and the originator of lying as of sin.

Chapter IV: *What It is to Live According to Man, and What to Live According to God.*

When, therefore, man lives according to man, not according to God, he is like the devil. Because not even an angel might live according to an angel, but only according to God, if he was to abide in the truth, and speak God's truth and not his own lie. And of man, too, the same apostle says in another place, "If the truth of God hath more abounded through my lie"—"my lie," he said, and "God's truth." When, then, a man lives according to the truth, he lives not according to himself, but according to God; for He was God who said, "I am the truth." When, therefore, man lives according to himself—that is, according to man, not according to God—assuredly he lives according to a lie; not that man himself is a lie, for God is his author and creator, who is certainly not the author and creator of a lie, but because man was made upright, that he might not live according to himself, but according to Him that made him—in other words, that he might do His will and not his own; and not to live as he was made to live, that is a lie. For he certainly desires to be blessed even by not living so that he may be blessed. And what is a lie if this desire be not? Wherefore it is not without meaning said that all sin is a lie. For no sin is committed save by that desire or will by which we desire that it be well with us, and shrink from it being ill with us. That, therefore, is a lie which we do in order that it may be well with us, but which makes us more miserable than we were. And why is this, but because the source of man's happiness lies only in God, whom he abandons when he sins, and not in himself, by living according to whom he sins?

In enunciating this proposition of ours, then, that because some live according to the flesh and others according to the spirit, there have arisen two diverse and conflicting cities, we might equally well have said, "because some live according to man, others according to God." For Paul says very plainly to the Corinthians, "For whereas there is among you envying and strife, are ye not carnal, and walk according to man?" So that to walk according to man and to be carnal are the same; for by flesh, that is, by a part of man, man is meant. For before he said that those same persons were animal whom afterwards he calls carnal, saying, "For what man knoweth the things of a man, save the spirit of man which is in him? even so the things of God knoweth no man, but the Spirit of God. Now we have received not the spirit of this world, but the Spirit which is of God; that we might know the things which are freely given to us of God. Which things also we speak, not in the words which man's wisdom teacheth, but which the Holy Ghost teacheth; comparing spiritual things with spiritual. But the animal man perceiveth not the things of the Spirit of God; for they are foolishness unto him." It is to men of this kind, then, that is, to animal men, he shortly after says, "And I, brethren, could not speak unto you as unto spiritual, but as unto carnal." And this is to be interpreted by the same usage, a part being taken for the whole. For both the soul and the flesh, the component parts of man, can be used to signify the whole man; and so the animal man and the carnal man are not two different things, but one and the same thing, viz., man living according to man. In the same way it is nothing else than men that are meant either in the words,

"By the deeds of the law there shall no flesh be justified;" or in the words, "Seventy-five souls went down into Egypt with Jacob." In the one passage, "no flesh" signifies "no man;" and in the other, by "seventy-five souls" seventy-five men are meant. And the expression, "not in words which man's wisdom teacheth" might equally be "not in words which fleshly wisdom teacheth;" and the expression, "ye walk according to man," might be "according to the flesh." And this is still more apparent in the words which followed: "For while one saith, I am of Paul, and another, I am of Apollos, are ye not men?" The same thing which he had before expressed by "ye are animal," "ye are carnal, he now expresses by "ye are men;" that is, ye live according to man, not according to God, for if you lived according to Him, you should be gods.

Chapter V: *That the Opinion of the Platonists Regarding the Nature of Body and Soul is Not So Censurable as that of the Manichæans, But that Even It is Objectionable, Because It Ascribes the Origin of Vices to the Nature of The Flesh.*

There is no need, therefore, that in our sins and vices we accuse the nature of the flesh to the injury of the Creator, for in its own kind and degree the flesh is good; but to desert the Creator good, and live according to the created good, is not good, whether a man choose to live according to the flesh, or according to the soul, or according to the whole human nature, which is composed of flesh and soul, and which is therefore spoken of either by the name flesh alone, or by the name soul alone. For he who extols the nature of the soul as the chief good, and condemns the nature of the flesh as if it were evil, assuredly is fleshly both in his love of the soul and hatred of the flesh; for these his feelings arise from human fancy, not from divine truth. The Platonists, indeed, are not so foolish as, with the Manichæans, to detest our present bodies as an evil nature; for they attribute all the elements of which this visible and tangible world is compacted, with all their qualities, to God their Creator. Nevertheless, from the death-infected members and earthly construction of the body they believe the soul is so affected, that there are thus originated in it the diseases of desires, and fears, and joy, and sorrow, under which four perturbations, as Cicero calls them, or passions, as most prefer to name them with the Greeks, is included the whole viciousness of human life. But if this be so, how is it that Æneas in Virgil, when he had heard from his father in Hades that the souls should return to bodies, expresses surprise at this declaration, and exclaims:

> "O father! and can thought conceive
> That happy souls this realm would leave,
> And seek the upper sky,
> With sluggish clay to reunite?
> This direful longing for the light,
> Whence comes it, say, and why?"

This direful longing, then, does it still exist even in that boasted purity of the disembodied spirits, and does it still proceed from the death-infected members and earthly limbs? Does he not assert that, when they begin to long to return to the body, they have already been delivered from all these so-called pestilences of the body? From which we gather that, were this endlessly alternating purification and defilement of departing and returning souls as true as it is most certainly false, yet it could not be averred that all culpable and vicious motions of the soul originate in the earthly body; for, on their own showing, "this direful longing," to use the words of their noble exponent, is so extraneous to the body, that it moves the soul that is purged of all bodily taint, and is existing apart from any body whatever, and moves it, moreover, to be embodied again. So that even they themselves acknowledge that the soul is not only moved to desire, fear, joy, sorrow, by the flesh, but that it can also be agitated with these emotions at its own instance.

Chapter VI: *Of the Character of the Human Will Which Makes the Affections of the Soul Right or Wrong.*

But the character of the human will is of moment; because, if it is wrong, these motions of the soul will be wrong, but if it is right, they will be not merely blameless, but even praiseworthy. For the will is in them all; yea, none of them is anything else than will. For what are desire and joy but a volition of consent to the things we wish?

And what are fear and sadness but a volition of aversion from the things which we do not wish? But when consent takes the form of seeking to possess the things we wish, this is called desire; and when consent takes the form of enjoying the things we wish, this is called joy. In like manner, when we turn with aversion from that which we do not wish to happen, this volition is termed fear; and when we turn away from that which has happened against our will, this act of will is called sorrow. And generally in respect of all that we seek or shun, as a man's will is attracted or repelled, so it is changed and turned into these different affections. Wherefore the man who lives according to God, and not according to man, ought to be a lover of good, and therefore a hater of evil. And since no one is evil by nature, but whoever is evil is evil by vice, he who lives according to God ought to cherish towards evil men a perfect hatred, so that he shall neither hate the man because of his vice, nor love the vice because of the man, but hate the vice and love the man. For the vice being cursed, all that ought to be loved, and nothing that ought to be hated, will remain.

Chapter VII: *That the Words Love and Regard (Amor and Dilectio) are in Scripture Used Indifferently of Good and Evil Affection.*

He who resolves to love God, and to love his neighbor as himself, not according to man but according to God, is on account of this love said to be of a good will; and this is in Scripture more commonly called charity, but it is also, even in the same books, called love. For the apostle says that the man to be elected as a ruler of the people must be a lover of good. And when the Lord Himself had asked Peter, "Hast thou a regard for me (*diligis*) more than these?" Peter replied, "Lord, Thou knowest that I love (*amo*) Thee." And again a second time the Lord asked not whether Peter loved (*amaret*) Him, but whether he had a regard (*diligeret*) for Him, and, he again answered, "Lord, Thou knowest that I love (*amo*) Thee." But on the third interrogation the Lord Himself no longer says, "Hast thou a regard (*diligis*) for me,"but "Lovest thou (*amas*) me?" And then the evangelist adds, "Peter was grieved because He said unto him the third time, "Lovest thou (*amas*) me?" though the Lord had not said three times but only once, "Lovest thou (*amas*) me?" and twice "*Dili-*

gis me?" from which we gather that, even when the Lord said *diligis*, He used an equivalent for *amas*. Peter, too, throughout used one word for the one thing, and the third time also replied, "Lord, Thou knowest all things, Thou knowest that I love (*amo*) Thee."

I have judged it right to mention this, because some are of opinion that charity or regard (*dilectio*) is one thing, love (*amor*) another. They say that *dilectio* is used of a good affection, *amor* of an evil love. But it is very certain that even secular literature knows no such distinction. However, it is for the philosophers to determine whether and how they differ, though their own writings sufficiently testify that they make great account of love (*amor*) placed on good objects, and even on God Himself. But we wished to show that the Scriptures of our religion, whose authority we prefer to all writings whatsoever, make no distinction between *amor*, *dilectio*, and *caritas*; and we have already shown that *amor* is used in a good connection. And if any one fancy that *amor* is no doubt used both of good and bad loves, but that *dilectio* is reserved for the good only, let him remember what the psalm says, "He that loveth (*diligit*) iniquity hateth his own soul;" and the words of the Apostle John, "If any man love (*diligere*) the world, the love (*dilectio*) of the Father is not in him." Here you have in one passage *dilectio* used both in a good and a bad sense. And if any one demands an instance of *amor* being used in a bad sense (for we have already shown its use in a good sense), let him read the words, "For men shall be lovers (*amantes*) of their own selves, lovers (*amatores*) of money."

The right will is, therefore, well-directed love, and the wrong will is ill-directed love. Love, then, yearning to have what is loved, is desire; and having and enjoying it, is joy; fleeing what is opposed to it, it is fear; and feeling what is opposed to it, when it has befallen it, it is sadness. Now these motions are evil if the love is evil; good if the love is good. What we assert let us prove from Scripture. The apostle "desires to depart, and to be with Christ." And, "My soul desired to long for Thy judgments;" or if it is more appropriate to say, "My soul longed to desire Thy judgments." And, "The desire of wisdom bringeth to a kingdom." Yet there has always obtained the usage of understanding desire and concupiscence in a bad sense if the object be not defined. But joy is used in a good sense: "Be glad in the Lord, and rejoice, ye righteous." And, "Thou hast put gladness in my heart." And, "Thou wilt fill me with joy with Thy countenance." Fear is used in a good sense by the apostle when he says, "Work out your salvation with fear and trembling." And, "Be not high-minded, but fear." And, "I fear, lest by any means, as the serpent beguiled Eve through his subtlety, so your minds should be corrupted from the simplicity that is in Christ." But with respect to sadness, which Cicero prefers to call sickness (*ægritudo*), and Virgil pain (*dolor*) (as he says, "*Dolent gaudentque*"), but which I prefer to call sorrow, because sickness and pain are more commonly used to express bodily suffering—with respect to this emotion, I say, the question whether it can be used in a good sense is more difficult.

Chapter VIII: *Of the Three Perturbations, Which the Stoics Admitted in the Soul of the Wise Man to the Exclusion of Grief or Sadness, Which the Manly Mind Ought Not to Experience.*

Those emotions which the Greeks call εὐπαθείαι, and which Cicero calls *constantiæ*, the Stoics would restrict to three; and, instead of three "perturbations" in the soul of the wise man, they substituted severally, in place of desire, will; in place of joy, contentment; and for fear, caution; and as to sickness or pain, which we, to avoid ambiguity, preferred to call sorrow, they denied that it could exist in the mind of a wise man. Will, they say, seeks the good, for this the wise man does. Contentment has its object in good that is possessed, and this the wise man continually possesses. Caution avoids evil, and this the wise man ought to avoid. But sorrow arises from evil that has already happened; and as they suppose that no evil can happen to the wise man, there can be no representative of sorrow in his mind. According to them, therefore, none but the wise man wills, is contented, uses caution; and that the fool can do no more than desire, rejoice, fear, be sad. The former three affections Cicero calls *constantiæ*, the last four *perturbationes*. Many, however, calls these last passions; and, as I have said, the Greeks call the former εὐπαθείαι, and the latter πάθη. And when I made a careful examination of Scripture to find whether this terminology was sanctioned by it, I came upon this saying of the prophet: "There is no contentment to the wicked, saith the

Lord;" as if the wicked might more properly rejoice than be contented regarding evils, for contentment is the property of the good and godly. I found also that verse in the Gospel: "Whatsoever ye would that men should do unto you, do ye even so unto them?" which seems to imply that evil or shameful things may be the object of desire, but not of will. Indeed, some interpreters have added "good things," to make the expression more in conformity with customary usage, and have given this meaning, "Whatsoever good deeds that ye would that men should do unto you." For they thought that this would prevent any one from wishing other men to provide him with unseemly, not to say shameful gratifications—luxurious banquets, for example—on the supposition that if he returned the like to them he would be fulfilling this precept. In the Greek Gospel, however, from which the Latin is translated, "good" does not occur, but only, "All things whatsoever ye would that men should do unto you, do ye even so unto them," and, as I believe, because "good" is already included in the word "would;" for He does not say "desire."

Yet though we may sometimes avail ourselves of these precise proprieties of language, we are not to be always bridled by them; and when we read those writers against whose authority it is unlawful to reclaim, we must accept the meanings above mentioned in passages where a right sense can be educed by no other interpretation, as in those instances we adduced partly from the prophet, partly from the Gospel. For who does not know that the wicked exult with joy? Yet "there is no contentment for the wicked, saith the Lord." And how so, unless because contentment, when the word is used in its proper and distinctive significance, means something different from joy? In like manner, who would deny that it were wrong to enjoin upon men that whatever they desire others to do to them they should themselves do to others, lest they should mutually please one another by shameful and illicit pleasure? And yet the precept, "Whatsoever ye would that men should do unto you, do ye even so to them," is very wholesome and just. And how is this, unless because the will is in this place used strictly, and signifies that will which cannot have evil for its object? But ordinary phraseology would not have allowed the saying, "Be unwilling to make any manner of lie," had there not been also an evil will, whose wickedness separates if from that which the angels celebrated, "Peace on earth, of good will to men." For "good" is superfluous if there is no other kind of will but good will. And why should the apostle have mentioned it among the praises of charity as a great thing, that "it rejoices not in iniquity," unless because wickedness does so rejoice? For even with secular writers these words are used indifferently. For Cicero, that most fertile of orators, says, "I desire, conscript fathers, to be merciful." And who would be so pedantic as to say that he should have said "I will" rather than "I desire," because the word is used in a good connection? Again, in Terence, the profligate youth, burning with wild lust, says, "I will nothing else than Philumena." That this "will" was lust is sufficiently indicated by the answer of his old servant which is there introduced: "How much better were it to try and banish that love from your heart, than to speak so as uselessly to inflame your passion still more!" And that contentment was used by secular writers in a bad sense that verse of Virgil testifies, in which he most succinctly comprehends these four perturbations,

> "Hence they fear and desire, grieve and are content"

The same author had also used the expression, "the evil contentments of the mind." So that good and bad men alike will, are cautious, and contented; or, to say the same thing in other words, good and bad men alike desire, fear, rejoice, but the former in a good, the latter in a bad fashion, according as the will is right or wrong. Sorrow itself, too, which the Stoics would not allow to be represented in the mind of the wise man, is used in a good sense, and especially in our writings. For the apostle praises the Corinthians because they had a godly sorrow. But possibly some one may say that the apostle congratulated them because they were penitently sorry, and that such sorrow can exist only in those who have sinned. For these are his words: "For I perceive that the same epistle hath made you sorry, though it were but for a season. Now I rejoice, not that ye were made sorry, but that ye sorrowed to repentance; for ye were made sorry after a godly manner, that ye might receive damage by us in nothing. For godly sorrow worketh repentance to salvation not to be repented of, but the sorrow of the world worketh death. For, behold, this selfsame thing that ye sorrowed after a godly sort, what carefulness it wrought in you!" Consequently the Stoics may defend themselves by replying, that sorrow is indeed useful for repentance of sin, but that this can have no place in the mind of the wise man, inasmuch as no sin attaches to him of which he could sorrowfully repent, nor any other evil the endurance or experience of which could make him sorrowful. For they say that Alcibiades (if my memory does not deceive me), who believed himself happy, shed tears when Socrates argued with him, and demonstrated that he was miserable because he was foolish. In his case, therefore, folly was the cause of this useful and desirable sorrow, wherewith a man mourns that he is what he ought not to be. But the Stoics maintain not that the fool, but that the wise man, cannot be sorrowful.

Chapter IX: *Of the Perturbations of the Soul Which Appear as Right Affections in the Life of the Righteous.*

But so far as regards this question of mental perturbations, we have answered these philosophers in the ninth book of this work, showing that it is rather a verbal than a real dispute, and that they seek contention rather than truth. Among ourselves, according to the sacred Scriptures and sound doctrine, the citizens of the holy city of God, who live according to God in the pilgrimage of this life, both fear and desire, and grieve and rejoice. And because their love is rightly placed, all these affections of theirs are right. They fear eternal punishment, they desire eternal life; they grieve because they themselves groan within themselves, waiting for the adoption, the redemption of their body; they rejoice in hope, because there "shall be brought to pass the saying that is written, Death is swallowed up in victory." In like manner they fear to sin, they desire to persevere; they grieve in sin, they rejoice in good works. They fear to sin, because they hear that "because iniquity shall abound, the love of many shall wax cold." They desire to persevere, because they hear that it is written, "He that endureth to the end shall be saved." They grieve for sin, hearing that "If we say that we have no sin, we deceive ourselves, and the truth is not in us." They rejoice in good works, because they hear that "the Lord loveth a cheerful giver." In like manner, according as they are strong or weak, they fear or desire to be tempted, grieve or rejoice in temptation. They fear to be tempted, because they hear the injunction, "If a man be overtaken in a fault, ye which are spiritual restore such an one in the spirit of meekness; considering thyself, lest thou also be tempted." They desire to be tempted, because they hear one of the heroes of the city of God saying, "Examine me, O Lord, and tempt me: try my reins and my heart." They grieve in temptations, because they see Peter weeping; they rejoice in temptations, because they hear James saying, "My brethren, count it all joy when ye fall into divers temptations."

And not only on their own account do they experience these emotions, but also on account of those whose deliverance they desire and whose perdition they fear, and whose loss or salvation affects them with grief or with joy. For if we who have come into the Church from among the Gentiles may suitably instance that noble and mighty hero who glories in his infirmities, the teacher (doctor) of the nations in faith and truth, who also labored more than all his fellow-apostles, and instructed the tribes of God's people by his epistles, which edified not only those of his own time, but all those who were to be gathered in—that hero, I say, and athlete of Christ, instructed by Him, anointed of His Spirit, crucified with Him, glorious in Him, lawfully maintaining a great conflict on the theatre of this world, and being made a spectacle to angels and men, and pressing onwards for the prize of his high calling—very joyfully do we with the eyes of faith behold him rejoicing with them that rejoice, and weeping with them that weep; though hampered by fightings without and fears within; desiring to depart and to be with Christ; longing to see the Romans, that he might have some fruit among them as among other Gentiles; being jealous over the Corinthians, and fearing in that jealousy lest their minds should be corrupted from the chastity that is in Christ; having great heaviness and continual sorrow of heart for the Israelites, because they, being ignorant of God's righteousness, and going about to establish their own righteousness, have not submitted themselves unto the righteousness of God; and expressing not only his sorrow, but bitter lamentation over some who had formally sinned and had not repented of their uncleanness and fornications.

If these emotions and affections, arising as they do from the love of what is good and from a holy charity, are to be called vices, then let us allow these emotions which are truly vices to pass under the name of virtues. But since these affections, when they are exercised in a becoming way, follow the guidance of right reason, who will dare to say that they are diseases or vicious passions? Wherefore even the Lord Himself, when He condescended to lead a human life in the form of a slave, had no sin whatever, and yet exercised these emotions where He judged they should be exercised. For as there was in Him a true human body and a true human soul, so was there also a true human emotion. When, therefore, we read in the Gospel that the hardheartedness of the Jews moved Him to sorrowful indignation, that He said, "I am glad for your sakes, to the intent ye may believe," that when about to raise Lazarus He even shed tears, that He earnestly desired to eat the passover with His disciples, that as His passion drew near His soul was sorrowful, these emotions are certainly not falsely ascribed to Him. But as He became man when it pleased Him, so, in the grace of His definite purpose, when it pleased Him He experienced those emotions in His human soul.

But we must further make the admission, that even when these affections are well regulated, and according to God's will, they are peculiar to this life, not to that future life we look for, and that often we yield to them against our will. And thus sometimes we weep in spite of ourselves, being carried beyond ourselves, not indeed by culpable desire; but by praiseworthy charity. In us, therefore, these affections arise from human infirmity; but it was not so with the Lord Jesus, for even His infirmity was the consequence of His power. But so long as we wear the infirmity of this life, we are rather worse men than better if we have none of these emotions at all. For the apostle vituperated and abominated some who, as he said, were "without natural affection." The sacred Psalmist also found fault with those of whom he said, "I looked for some to lament with me, and there was none." For to be quite free from pain while we are in this place of misery is only purchased, as one of this world's literati perceived and remarked, at the price of blunted sensibilities both of mind and body. And therefore that which the Greeks call ἀπαθεια, and what the Latins would call, if their language would allow them, *impassibilitas*, if it be taken to mean an impassibility of spirit and not of body, or, in other words, a freedom from those emotions which are contrary to reason and disturb the mind, then it is obviously a good and most desirable quality, but it is not one which is attainable in this life. For the words of the apostle are the confession, not of the common herd, but of the eminently pious, just, and holy men: "If we say we have no sin, we deceive ourselves, and the truth is not in us." When there shall be no sin in a man, then there shall be this απάθεια. At present it is enough if we live without crime; and he who thinks he lives without sin puts aside not sin, but pardon. And if that is to be called apathy, where the mind is the subject of no emotion, then who would not consider this insensibility to be worse than all vices? It may, indeed, reasonably be maintained that the perfect blessedness we hope for shall be free from all sting of fear or sadness; but who that is not quite lost to truth would say that neither love nor joy shall be experienced there? But if by apathy a condition be meant in which no fear terrifies nor any pain annoys, we must in this life renounce such a state if we would live according to God's will, but may hope to enjoy it in that blessedness which is promised as our eternal condition.

For that fear of which the Apostle John says, "There is no fear in love; but perfect love casteth out fear, because fear hath torment. He that feareth is not made perfect in love"—that fear is not of the same kind as the Apostle Paul felt lest the Corinthians should be seduced by the subtlety of the serpent; for love is susceptible of this fear, yea, love alone is capable of it. But the fear which is not in love is of that kind of which Paul himself says, "For ye have not received the spirit of bondage again to fear." But as for that "clean fear which endureth for ever," if it is to exist in the world to come (and how else can it be said to endure for ever?), it is not a fear deterring us from evil which may happen, but preserving us in the good which cannot be lost. For where the love of acquired good is unchangeable, there certainly the fear that avoids evil is, if I may say so, free from anxiety. For under the name of "clean fear" David signifies that will by which we shall necessarily shrink from sin, and guard against it, not with the anxiety of weakness, which fears that we may strongly sin, but with the tranquility of perfect love. Or if no kind of fear at all shall exist in that most imperturbable security of perpetual and blissful delights, then the expression, "The fear of the Lord is clean, enduring for ever," must be taken in the same sense as that other, "The patience of the poor shall not perish for ever." For patience, which is necessary only where ills are to be borne, shall not be eternal, but that which patience leads us to will be eternal. So perhaps this "clean fear" is said to endure for ever, because that to which fear leads shall endure.

And since this is so—since we must live a good life in order to attain to a blessed life, a good life has all these affections right, a bad life has them wrong. But in the blessed life eternal there will be love and joy, not only right, but also assured; but fear and grief there will be none. Whence it already appears in some sort what manner of persons the citizens of the city of God must be in this their pilgrimage, who live after the spirit, not after the flesh—that is to say, according to God, not according to man—and what manner of persons they shall be also in that immortality whither they are journeying. And the city or society of the wicked, who live not according to God, but according to man, and who accept the doctrines of men or devils in the worship of a false and contempt of the true divinity, is shaken with those wicked emotions as by diseases and disturbances. And if there be some of its citizens who seem to restrain and, as it were, temper those passions, they are so elated with ungodly pride, that their disease is as much greater as their pain is less. And if some, with a vanity monstrous in proportion to its rarity, have become enamored of themselves because they can be stimulated and excited by no emotion, moved or bent by no affection, such persons rather lose all humanity than obtain true tranquility. For a thing is not necessarily right because it is inflexible, nor healthy because it is insensible.

Chapter X: *Whether It is to Be Believed that Our First Parents in Paradise, Before They Sinned, Were Free from All Perturbation.*

But it is a fair question, whether our first parent or first parents (for there was a marriage of two), before they sinned, experienced in their animal body such emotions as we shall not experience in the spiritual body when sin has been purged and finally abolished. For if they did, then how were they blessed in that boasted place of bliss, Paradise? For who that is affected by fear or grief can be called absolutely blessed? And what could those persons fear or suffer in such affluence of blessings, where neither death nor ill-health was feared, and where nothing was wanting which a good will could desire, and nothing present which could interrupt man's mental or bodily enjoyment? Their love to God was unclouded, and their mutual affection was that of faithful and sincere marriage; and from this love flowed a wonderful delight, because they always enjoyed what was loved. Their avoidance of sin was tranquil; and, so long as it was maintained, no other ill at all could invade them and bring sorrow. Or did they perhaps desire to touch and eat the forbidden fruit, yet feared to die; and thus both fear and desire already, even in that blissful place, preyed upon those first of mankind? Away with the thought that such could be the case where there was no sin! And, indeed, this is already sin, to desire those things which the law of God forbids, and to abstain from them through fear of punishment, not through love of righteousness. Away, I say, with the thought, that before there was any sin, there should already have been committed regarding that fruit the very sin which our Lord warns us against regarding a woman: "Whosoever looketh on a woman to lust after her, hath committed adultery with her already in his heart." As happy, then, as were these our first parents, who were agitated by no mental perturbations, and annoyed by no bodily discomforts, so happy should the whole human race have been, had they not introduced that evil which they have transmitted to their posterity, and had none of their descendants committed iniquity worthy of damnation; but this original blessedness continuing until, in virtue of that benediction which said, "Increase and multiply," the number of the predestined saints should have been completed, there would then have been bestowed that higher felicity which is enjoyed by the most blessed angels—a blessedness in which there should have been a secure assurance that no one would sin, and no one die; and so should the saints have lived, after no taste of labor, pain, or death, as now they shall live in the resurrection, after they have endured all these things.

Chapter XI: *Of the Fall of the First Man, in Whom Nature Was Created Good, and Can Be Restored Only by Its Author.*

But because God foresaw all things, and was therefore not ignorant that man also would fall, we ought to consider this holy city in connection with what God foresaw and ordained, and not according to our own ideas, which do not embrace God's ordination. For man, by his sin, could not disturb the divine counsel, nor compel God to change what He had decreed; for God's foreknowledge had anticipated both—that is to say, both how evil the man whom He had created good should become, and what good He Himself should even thus derive from him. For though God is said to change His determinations (so that in a tropical sense the Holy Scripture says even that God repented), this is said with reference to man's expectation, or the order of natural causes, and not with reference to that which the Almighty had foreknown that He would do. Accordingly God, as it is written, made man upright, and consequently with a good will. For if he had not had a good will, he could not have been upright. The good will, then, is the work of God; for God created him with it. But the first evil will, which preceded all man's evil acts, was rather a kind of falling away from the work of God to its own works than any positive work. And therefore the acts resulting were evil, not having God, but the will itself for their end; so that the will or the man himself, so far as his will is bad, was as it were the evil tree bringing forth evil fruit. Moreover, the bad will, though it be not in harmony with, but opposed to nature, inasmuch as it is a vice or blemish, yet it is true of it as of all vice, that it cannot exist except in a nature, and only in a nature created out of nothing, and not in that which the Creator has begotten of Himself, as He begot the Word, by whom all things were made. For though God formed man of the dust of the earth, yet the earth itself, and every earthly material, is absolutely created out of nothing; and man's soul, too, God created out of nothing, and joined to the body, when He made man. But evils are so thoroughly overcome by good, that though they are permitted to exist, for the sake of demonstrating how the most righteous foresight of God can make a good use even of them, yet good can exist without evil, as in the true and supreme God Himself, and as in every invisible and visible celestial creature that exists above this murky atmosphere; but evil cannot exist without good, because the natures in which evil exists, in so far as they are natures, are good. And evil is removed, not by removing any nature, or part of a nature, which had been introduced by the evil, but by healing and correcting that which had been vitiated and depraved. The will, therefore, is then truly free, when it is not the slave of vices and sins. Such was it given us by God; and this being lost by its own fault, can only be restored by Him who was able at first to give it. And therefore the truth says, "If the Son shall make you free, ye shall be free indeed;" which is equivalent to saying, If the Son shall save you, ye shall be saved indeed. For He is our Liberator, inasmuch as He is our Saviour.

Man then lived with God for his rule in a paradise at once physical and spiritual. For neither was it a paradise only physical for the advantage of the body, and not also spiritual for the advantage of the mind; nor was it only spiritual to afford enjoyment to man by his internal sensations, and not also physical to afford him enjoyment through his external senses. But obviously it was both for both ends. But after that proud and therefore envious angel (of whose fall I have said as much as I was able in the eleventh and twelfth books of this work, as well as that of his fellows, who, from being God's angels, became his angels), preferring to rule with a kind of pomp of empire rather than to be another's subject, fell from the spiritual Paradise, and essaying to insinuate his persuasive guile into the mind of man, whose unfallen condition provoked him to envy now that himself was fallen, he chose the serpent as his mouthpiece in that bodily Paradise in which it and all the other earthly animals were living with those two human beings, the man and his wife, subject to them, and harmless; and he chose the serpent because, being slippery, and moving in tortuous windings, it was suitable for his purpose. And this animal being subdued to his wicked ends by the presence and superior force of his angelic nature, he abused as his instrument, and first tried his deceit upon the woman, making his assault upon the weaker part of that human alliance, that he might gradually gain the whole, and not supposing that the man would readily give ear to him, or be deceived, but that he might yield to the error of the woman. For as Aaron was not induced to agree with the people when they blindly wished him to make an idol, and yet yielded to constraint; and as it is not credible that Solomon was so blind as to suppose that idols should be worshiped, but was drawn over to such sacrilege by the blandishments of women; so we cannot believe that Adam was deceived, and supposed the devil's word to be truth, and therefore transgressed God's law, but that he by the drawings of kindred yielded to the woman, the husband to the wife, the one human being to the only other human being. For not without significance did the apostle say, "And Adam was not deceived, but the woman being deceived was in the transgression;" but he speaks thus, because the woman accepted as true what the serpent told her, but the man could not bear to be severed from his only companion, even though this involved a partnership in sin. He was not on this account less culpable, but sinned with his eyes open. And so the apostle does not say, "He did not sin," but "He was not deceived." For he shows that he sinned when he says, "By one man sin entered into the world," and immediately after more distinctly, "In the likeness of Adam's transgression." But he meant that those are deceived who do not judge that which they do to be sin; but he knew. Otherwise how were it true "Adam was not deceived?" But having as yet no experience of the divine severity, he was possibly deceived in so far as he thought his sin venial. And consequently he was not deceived as the woman was deceived, but he was deceived as to the judgment which would be passed on his apology: "The woman whom thou gavest to be with me, she gave me, and I did eat." What need of saying more? Although they were not both deceived by credulity, yet both were entangled in the snares of the devil, and taken by sin.

Chatper XII: *Of the Nature of Man's First Sin.*

If any one finds a difficulty in understanding why other sins do not alter human nature as it was altered by the transgression of those first human beings, so that on account of it this nature is subject to the great corruption we feel and see, and to death, and is distracted and tossed with so many furious and contending emotions, and is certainly far different from what it was before sin, even though it were then lodged in an animal body—if, I say, any one is moved by this, he ought not to think that that sin was a small and light one because it was committed about food, and that not bad nor noxious, except because it was forbidden; for in that spot of singular felicity God could not have created and planted any evil thing. But by the precept He gave, God commended obedience, which is, in a sort, the mother and guardian of all the virtues in the reasonable creature, which was so created that submission is advantageous to it, while the fulfillment of its own will in preference to the Creator's is destruction. And as this commandment enjoining abstinence from one kind of food in the midst of great abundance of other kinds was so easy to keep—so light a burden to the memory—and, above all, found no resistance to its observance in lust, which only afterwards sprung up as the penal consequence of sin, the iniquity of violating it was all the greater in proportion to the ease with which it might have been kept.

Book Fifteen

Chapter X: *Of the Different Computation of the Ages of the Antediluvians, Given by the Hebrew Manuscripts and by Our Own.*

Wherefore, although there is a discrepancy for which I cannot account between our manuscripts and the Hebrew, in the very number of years assigned to the antediluvians, yet the discrepancy is not so great that they do not agree about their longevity. For the very first man, Adam, before he begot his son Seth, is in our manuscripts found to have lived 230 years, but in the Hebrew mss. 130. But after he begot Seth, our copies read that he lived 700 years, while the Hebrew give 800. And thus, when the two periods are taken together, the sum agrees. And so throughout the succeeding generations, the period before the father begets a son is always made shorter by 100 years in the Hebrew, but the period after his son is begotten is longer by 100 years in the Hebrew than in our copies. And thus, taking the two periods together, the result is the same in both. And in the sixth generation there is no discrepancy at all. In the seventh, however, of which Enoch is the representative, who is recorded to have been translated without death because he pleased God, there is the same discrepancy as in the first five generations, 100 years more being ascribed to him by our mss. before he begat a son. But still the result agrees; for according to both documents he lived before he was translated 365 years. In the eighth generation the discrepancy is less than in the others, and of a different kind. For Methuselah, whom Enoch begat, lived, before he begat his successor, not 100 years less, but 100 years more, according to the Hebrew reading; and in our mss. again these years are added to the period after he begat his son; so that in this case also the sum-total is the same. And it is only in the ninth generation, that is, in the age of Lamech, Methuselah's son and Noah's father, that there is a discrepancy in the sum total; and even in this case it is slight. For the Hebrew mss. represent him as living twenty-four years more than ours assign to him. For before he begat his son, who was called Noah, six years fewer are given to him by the Hebrew mss. than by ours; but after he begat this son, they give him thirty years more than ours; so that, deducting the former six, there remains, as we said, a surplus of twenty-four.

Chapter XI: *Of Methuselah's Age, Which Seems to Extend Fourteen Years Beyond the Deluge.*

From this discrepancy between the Hebrew books and our own arises the well-known question as to the age of Methuselah; for it is computed that he lived for fourteen years after the deluge, though Scripture relates that of all who were then upon the earth only the eight souls in the ark escaped destruction by the flood, and of these Methuselah was not one. For, according to our books, Methuselah, before he begat the son whom he called Lamech, lived 167 years; then Lamech himself, before his son Noah was born, lived 188 years, which together make 355 years. Add to these the age of Noah at the date of the deluge, 600 years, and this gives a total of 955 from the birth of Methuselah to the year of the flood. Now all the years of the life of Methuselah are computed to be 969; for when he had lived 167 years, and had begotten his son Lamech, he then lived after this 802 years, which makes a total, as we said, of 969 years. From this, if we deduct 955 years from the birth of Methuselah to the flood, there remains fourteen years, which he is supposed to have lived after the flood. And therefore some suppose that, though he was not on earth (in which it is agreed that every living thing which could not naturally live in water perished), he was for a time with his father, who had been translated, and that he lived there till the flood had passed away. This hypothesis they adopt, that they may not cast a slight on the trustworthiness of versions which the Church has received into a position of high authority, and because they believe that the Jewish mss. rather than our own are in error. For they do not admit that this is a mistake of the translators, but maintain that there is a falsified statement in the original, from which, through the Greek, the Scripture has been translated into our own tongue. They say that it is not credible that the seventy translators, who simultaneously and unanimously produced one rendering, could have erred, or, in a case in which no interest of theirs was involved, could have falsified their translation; but that the Jews, envying us our translation of their Law and Prophets, have made alterations in their texts so as to undermine the authority of ours. This opinion or suspicion let each man adopt according to his own judgment. Certain it is that Methuselah did not survive the flood, but died in the very year it occurred, if the numbers given in the Hebrew mss. are true. My own opinion regarding the seventy translators I will, with God's help, state more carefully in its own place, when I have come down (following the order which this work requires) to that period in which their translation was executed. For the present question, it is enough that, according to our versions, the men of that age had lives so long as to make it quite possible that, during the lifetime of the first-born of the two sole parents then on earth, the human race multiplied sufficiently to form a community.

Chapter XII: *Of the Opinion of Those Who Do Not Believe that in These Primitive Times Men Lived So Long as is Stated.*

For they are by no means to be listened to who suppose that in those times years were differently reckoned, and were so short that one of our years may be supposed to be equal to ten of theirs. So that they say, when we read or hear that some man lived 900 years, we should understand ninety, ten of those years making but one of ours, and ten of ours equaling 100 of theirs. Consequently, as they suppose, Adam was twenty-three years of age when he begat Seth, and Seth himself was twenty years and six months old when his son Enos was born, though the Scripture calls these months 205 years. For, on the hypothesis of those whose opinion we are explaining, it was customary to divide one such year as we have into ten parts, and to call each part a year. And each of these parts was composed of six days squared; because God finished His works in six days, that He might rest the seventh. Of this I disputed according to my ability in the eleventh book. Now six squared, or six times six, gives thirty-six days; and this multiplied by ten amounts to 360 days, or twelve lunar months. As for the five remaining days which are needed to complete the solar year, and for the fourth part of a day, which requires that into every fourth or leap-year a day be added, the ancients added such days as the Romans used to call "intercalary," in order to complete the number of the years. So that Enos, Seth's son, was nineteen years old when his son Cainan was born, though Scripture calls these years 190. And so through all the generations in which the ages of the antediluvians are given, we find in our versions that almost no one begat a son at the age of 100 or under, or even at the age of 120 or thereabouts; but the youngest fathers are recorded to have been 160 years old and upwards. And the reason of this, they say, is that no one can beget children when he is ten years old, the age spoken of by those men as 100, but that sixteen is the age of puberty, and competent now to propagate offspring; and this is the age called by them 160. And that it may not be thought incredible that in these days the year was differently computed from our own, they adduce what is recorded by several writers of history, that the Egyptians had a year of four months, the Acarnanians of six, and the Lavinians of thirteen months. The younger Pliny, after mentioning that some writers reported that one man had lived 152 years, another ten more, others 200, others 300, that some had even reached 500 and 600, and a few 800 years of age, gave it as his opinion that all this must be ascribed to mistaken computation. For some, he says, make summer and winter each a year; others make each season a year, like the Arcadians, whose years, he says, were of three months. He added, too, that the Egyptians, of whose little years of four months we have spoken already, sometimes terminated their year at the wane of each moon; so that with them there are produced lifetimes of 1000 years.

By these plausible arguments certain persons, with no desire to weaken the credit of this sacred history, but rather to facilitate belief in it by removing the difficulty of such incredible longevity, have been themselves persuaded, and think they act wisely in persuading others, that in these days the year was so brief that ten of their years equal but one of ours, while ten of ours equal 100 of theirs. But there is the plainest evidence to show that this is quite false. Before producing this evidence, however, it seems right to mention a conjecture which is yet more plausible. From the Hebrew manuscripts we could at once refute this confident statement; for in them Adam is found to have lived not 230 but 130 years before he begat his third son. If, then, this mean thirteen years by our ordinary computation, then he must have begotten his first son when he was only twelve or thereabouts. Who can at this age beget children according to the ordinary and familiar course of nature? But not to mention him, since it is possible he may have been able to beget his like as soon as he was created—for it is not credible that he was created so little as our infants are—not to mention him, his son was not 205 years old when he begot Enos, as our versions have it, but 105, and consequently, according to this idea, was not eleven years old. But what shall I say of his son Cainan, who, though by our version 170 years old, was by the Hebrew text seventy when he beget Mahalaleel? If seventy years in those times meant only seven of our years, what man of seven years old begets children?

Chapter XIII: *Whether, in Computing Years, We Ought to Follow the Hebrew or the Septuagint.*

But if I say this, I shall presently be answered, It is one of the Jews' lies. This, however, we have disposed of above, showing that it cannot be that men of so just a reputation as the seventy translators should have falsified their version. However, if I ask them which of the two is more credible, that the Jewish nation, scattered far and wide, could have unanimously conspired to forge this lie, and so, through envying others the authority of their Scriptures, have deprived themselves of their verity; or that seventy men, who were also themselves Jews, shut up in one place (for Ptolemy king of Egypt had got them together for this work), should have envied foreign nations that same truth, and by common consent inserted these errors: who does not see which can be more naturally and readily believed?

But far be it from any prudent man to believe either that the Jews, however malicious and wrong-headed, could have tampered with so many and so widely-dispersed manuscripts; or that those renowned seventy individuals had any common purpose to grudge the truth to the nations. One must therefore more plausibly maintain, that when first their labors began to be transcribed from the copy in Ptolemy's library, some such misstatement might find its way into the first copy made, and from it might be disseminated far and wide; and that this might arise from no fraud, but from a mere copyist's error. This is a sufficiently plausible account of the difficulty regarding Methuselah's life, and of that other case in which there is a difference in the total of twenty-four years. But in those cases in which there is a methodical resemblance in the falsification, so that uniformly the one version allots to the period before a son and successor is born 100 years more than the other, and to the period subsequent 100 years less, and vice versa, so that the totals may agree—and this holds true of the first, second, third, fourth, fifth, and seventh generations—in these cases error seems to have, if we may say so, a certain kind of constancy, and savors not of accident, but of design.

Accordingly, that diversity of numbers which distinguishes the Hebrew from the Greek and Latin copies of Scripture, and which consists of a uniform addition and deduction of 100 years in each lifetime for several consecutive generations, is to be attributed neither to the malice of the Jews nor to men so diligent and prudent as the seventy translators, but to the error of the copyist who was first allowed to transcribe the manuscript from the library of the abovementioned king. For even now, in cases where numbers contribute nothing to the easier comprehension or more satisfactory knowledge of anything, they are both carelessly transcribed, and still more carelessly emended. For who will trouble himself to learn how many thousand men the several tribes of Israel contained? He sees no resulting benefit of such knowledge. Or how many men are there who are aware of the vast advantage that lies hid in this knowledge? But in this case, in which during so many consecutive generations 100 years are added in one manuscript where they are not reckoned in the other, and then, after the birth of the son and successor, the years which were wanting are added, it is obvious that the copyist who contrived this arrangement designed to insinuate that the antediluvians lived an excessive number of years only because each year was excessively brief, and that he tried to draw the attention to this fact by his statement of their age of puberty at which they became able to beget children. For, lest the incredulous might stumble at the difficulty of so long a lifetime, he insinuated that 100 of their years equaled but ten of ours; and this insinuation he conveyed by adding 100 years whenever he found the age below 160 years or thereabouts, deducting these years again from the period after the son's birth, that the total might harmonize. By this means he intended to ascribe the generation of offspring to a fit age, without diminishing the total sum of years ascribed to the lifetime of the individuals. And the very fact that in the sixth generation he departed from this uniform practice, inclines us all the rather to believe that when the circumstance we have referred to required his alterations, he made them; seeing that when this circumstance did not exist, he made no alteration. For in the same generation he found in the Hebrew ms., that Jared lived before he begat Enoch 162 years, which, according to the short year computation, is sixteen years and somewhat less than two months, an age capable of procreation; and therefore it was not necessary to add 100 short years, and so make the age twenty-six years of the usual length; and of course it was not necessary to deduct, after the son's birth, years which he had not added before it. And thus it comes to pass that in this instance there is no variation between the two manuscripts.

This is corroborated still further by the fact that in the eighth generation, while the Hebrew books assign 182 years to Methuselah before Lamech's birth, ours assign to him twenty less, though usually 100 years are added to this period; then, after Lamech's birth, the twenty years are restored, so as to equalize the total in the two books. For if his design was that these 170 years be understood as seventeen, so as to suit the age of puberty, as there was no need for him adding anything, so there was none for his subtracting anything; for in this case he found an age fit for the generation of children, for the sake of which he was in the habit of adding those 100 years in cases where he did not find the age already sufficient. This difference of twenty years we might, indeed, have supposed had happened accidentally, had he not taken care to restore them afterwards as he had deducted them from the period before, so that there might be no deficiency in the total. Or are we perhaps to suppose that there was the still more astute design of concealing the deliberate and uniform addition of 100 years to the first period and their deduction from the subsequent period—did he design to conceal this by doing something similar, that is to say, adding and deducting, not indeed a century, but some years, even in a case in which there was no need for his doing so? But whatever may be thought of this, whether it be believed that he did so or not, whether, in fine, it be so or not, I would have no manner of doubt that when any diversity is found in the books, since both cannot be true to fact, we do well to believe in preference that language out of which the translation was made into another by translators. For there are three Greek mss., one Latin, and one Syriac, which agree with one another, and in all of these Methuselah is said to have died six years before the deluge.

Chapter XIV: *That the Years in Those Ancient Times Were of the Same Length as Our Own.*

Let us now see how it can be plainly made out that in the enormously protracted lives of those men the years were not so short that ten of their years were equal to only one of ours, but were of as great length as our own, which are measured by the course of the sun. It is proved by this, that Scripture states that the flood occurred in the six hundredth year of Noah's life. But why in the same place is it also written, "The waters of the flood were upon the earth in the six hundredth year of Noah's life, in the second month, the twenty-seventh day of the month," if that very brief year (of which it took ten to make one of ours) consisted of thirty-six days? For so scant a year, if the ancient usage dignified it with the name of year, either has not months, or this month must be three days, so that it may have twelve of them. How then was it here said, "In the six hundredth year, the second month, the twenty-seventh day of the month," unless the months then were of the same length as the months now? For how else could it be said that the flood began on the twenty-seventh day of the second month? Then afterwards, at the end of the flood, it is thus written: "And the ark rested in the seventh month, on the twenty-seventh day of the month, on the mountains of Ararat. And the waters decreased continually until the eleventh month: on the first day of the month were the tops of the mountains seen." But if the months were such as we have, then so were the years. And certainly months of three days each could not have a twenty-seventh day. Or if every measure of time was diminished in proportion, and a thirtieth part of three days was then called a day, then that great deluge, which is recorded to have lasted forty days and forty nights, was really over in less than four of our days. Who can away with such foolishness and absurdity? Far be this error from us—an error which seeks to build up our faith in the divine Scriptures on false conjecture only to demolish our faith at another point. It is plain that the day then was what it now is, a space of four-and-twenty hours, determined by the lapse of day and night; the month then equal to the month now, which is defined by the rise and completion of one moon; the year then equal to the year now, which is completed by twelve lunar months, with the addition of five days and a fourth to adjust it with the course of the sun. It was a year of this length which was reckoned the six hundredth of Noah's life, and in the second month, the twenty-seventh day of the month, the flood began—a flood which, as is recorded, was caused by heavy rains continuing for forty days, which days had not only two hours and a little more, but four-and-twenty hours, completing a night and a day. And consequently those antediluvians lived more than 900 years, which were years as long as those which afterwards Abraham lived 175 of, and after him his son Isaac 180, and his son Jacob nearly 150, and some time after, Moses 120, and men now seventy or eighty, or not much longer, of which years it is said, "their strength is labor and sorrow."

But that discrepancy of numbers which is found to exist between our own and the Hebrew text does not touch the longevity of the ancients; and if there is any diversity so great that both versions cannot be true, we must take our ideas of the real facts from that text out of which our own version has been translated. However, though any one who pleases has it in his power to correct this version, yet it is not unimportant to observe that no one has presumed to emend the Septuagint from the Hebrew text in the many places where they seem to disagree. For this difference has not been reckoned a falsification; and for my own part I am persuaded it ought not to be reckoned so.

But where the difference is not a mere copyist's error, and where the sense is agreeable to truth and illustrative of truth, we must believe that the divine Spirit prompted them to give a varying version, not in their function of translators, but in the liberty of prophesying. And therefore we find that the apostles justly sanction the Septuagint, by quoting it as well as the Hebrew when they adduce proofs from the Scriptures. But as I have promised to treat this subject more carefully, if God help me, in a more fitting place, I will now go on with the matter in hand. For there can be no doubt that, the lives of men being so long, the first-born of the first man could have built a city—a city, however, which was earthly, and not that which is called the city of God, to describe which we have taken in hand this great work.

Chapter XXII: *Of the Fall of the Sons of God Who Were Captivated by the Daughters of Men, Whereby All, with the Exception of Eight Persons, Deservedly Perished in the Deluge.*

When the human race, in the exercise of this freedom of will, increased and advanced, there arose a mixture and confusion of the two cities by their participation in a common iniquity. And this calamity, as well as the first, was occasioned by woman, though not in the same way; for these women were not themselves betrayed, neither did they persuade the men to sin, but having belonged to the earthly city and society of the earthly, they had been of corrupt manners from the first, and were loved for their bodily beauty by the sons of God, or the citizens of the other city which sojourns in this world. Beauty is indeed a good gift of God; but that the good may not think it a great good, God dispenses it even to the wicked. And thus, when the good that is great and proper to the good was abandoned by the sons of God, they fell to a paltry good which is not peculiar to the good, but common to the good and the evil; and when they were captivated by the daughters of men, they adopted the manners of the earthly to win them as their brides, and forsook the godly ways they had followed in their own holy society. And thus beauty, which is indeed God's handiwork, but only a temporal, carnal, and lower kind of good, is not fitly loved in preference to God, the eternal, spiritual, and unchangeable good. When the miser prefers his gold to justice, it is through no fault of the gold, but of the man; and so with every created thing. For though it be good, it may be loved with an evil as well as with a good love: it is loved rightly when it is loved ordinately; evilly, when inordinately. It is this which some one has briefly said in these verses in praise of the Creator: "These are Thine, they are good, because Thou art good who didst create them. There is in them nothing of ours, unless the sin we commit when we forget the order of things, and instead of Thee love that which Thou hast made."

But if the Creator is truly loved, that is, if He Himself is loved and not another thing in His stead, He cannot be evilly loved; for love itself is to be ordinately loved, because we do well to love that which, when we love it, makes us live well and virtuously. So that it seems to me that it is a brief but true definition of virtue to say, it is the order of love; and on this account, in the Canticles, the bride of Christ, the city of God, sings, "Order love within me." It was the order of this love, then, this charity or attachment, which the sons of God disturbed when they forsook God, and were enamored of the daughters of men. And by these two names (sons of God and daughters of men) the two cities are sufficiently distinguished. For though the former were by nature children of men, they had come into possession of another name by grace. For in the same Scripture in which the sons of God are said to have loved the daughters of men, they are also called angels of God; whence many suppose that they were not men but angels.

Chapter XXIII: *Whether We are to Believe that Angels, Who are of a Spiritual Substance, Fell in Love with the Beauty of Women, and Sought Them in Marriage, and that from This Connection Giants Were Born.*

In the third book of this work (c. 5) we made a passing reference to this question, but did not decide whether angels, inasmuch as they are spirits, could have bodily intercourse with women. For it is written, "Who maketh His angels spirits," that is, He makes those who are by nature spirits His angels by appointing them to the duty of bearing His messages. For the Greek word ἄγγελος, which in Latin appears as *angelus*, means a messenger. But whether the Psalmist speaks of their bodies when he adds, "and His ministers a flaming fire," or means that God's ministers ought to blaze with love as with a spiritual fire, is doubtful. However, the same trustworthy Scripture testifies that angels have appeared to men in such bodies as could not only be seen, but also touched. There is, too, a very general rumor, which many have verified by their own experience, or which trustworthy persons who have heard the experience of others corroborate, that sylvans and fauns, who are commonly called *incubi*, had often made wicked assaults upon women, and satisfied their lust upon them; and that certain devils, called Duses by the Gauls, are constantly attempting and effecting this impurity is so generally affirmed, that it were impudent to deny it. From these assertions, indeed, I dare not determine whether there be some spirits embodied in an aerial substance (for this element, even when agitated by a fan, is sensibly felt by the body), and who are capable of lust and of mingling sensibly with women; but certainly I could by no means believe that God's holy angels could at that time have so fallen, nor can I think that it is of them the Apostle Peter said, "For if God spared not the angels that sinned, but cast them down to hell, and delivered them into chains of darkness, to be reserved unto judgment." I think he rather speaks of these who first apostatized from God, along with their chief the devil, who enviously deceived the first man under the form of a serpent. But the same holy Scripture affords the most ample testimony that even godly men have been called angels; for of John it is written: "Behold, I send my messenger (angel) before Thy face, who shall prepare Thy way." And the prophet Malachi, by a peculiar grace specially communicated to him, was called an angel.

But some are moved by the fact that we have read that the fruit of the connection between those who are called angels of God and the women they loved were not men like our own breed, but giants; just as if there were not born even in our own time (as I have mentioned above) men of much greater size than the ordinary stature. Was there not at Rome a few years ago, when the destruction of the city now accomplished by the Goths was drawing near, a woman, with her father and mother, who by her gigantic size over-topped all others? Surprising crowds from all quarters came to see her, and that which struck them most was the circumstance that neither of her parents were quite up to the tallest ordinary stature. Giants therefore might well be born, even before the sons of God, who are also called angels of God, formed a connection with the daughters of men, or of those living according to men, that is to say, before the sons of Seth formed a connection with the daughters of Cain. For thus speaks even the canonical Scripture itself in the book in which we read of this; its words are: "And it came to pass, when men began to multiply on the face of the earth, and daughters were born unto them, that the sons of God saw the daughters of men that they were fair [good]; and they took them wives of all which they chose. And the Lord God said, My Spirit shall not always strive with man, for that he also is flesh: yet his days shall be an hundred and twenty years. There were giants in the earth in those days; and also after that, when the sons of God came in unto the daughters of men, and they bare children to them, the same became the giants, men of renown." These words of the divine book sufficiently indicate that already there were giants in the earth in those days, in which the sons of God took wives of the children of men, when they loved them because they were good, that is, fair. For it is the custom of this Scripture to call those who are beautiful in appearance "good." But after this connection had been formed, then too were giants born. For the words are: "There were giants in the earth in those days, and also after that, when the sons of God came in unto the daughters of men." Therefore there were giants both before, "in those days," and "also after that." And the words, "they bare children to them," show plainly enough that before the sons of God fell in this fashion they begat children to God, not to themselves—that is to say, not moved by the lust of sexual intercourse, but discharging the duty of propagation, intending to produce not a family to gratify their own pride, but citizens to people the city of God; and to these they as God's angels would bear the message, that they should place their hope in God, like him who was born of Seth, the son of resurrection, and who hoped to call on the name of the Lord God, in which hope they and their offspring would be co-heirs of eternal blessings, and brethren in the family of which God is the Father.

But that those angels were not angels in the sense of not being men, as some suppose, Scripture itself decides, which unambiguously declares that they were men. For when it had first been stated that "the angels of God saw the daughters of men that they were fair, and they took them wives of all which they chose," it was immediately added, "And the Lord God said, My Spirit shall not always strive with these men, for that they also are flesh." For by the Spirit of God they had been made angels of God, and sons of God; but declining towards lower things, they are called men, a name of nature, not of grace; and they are called flesh, as deserters of the Spirit, and by their desertion deserted [by Him]. The Septuagint indeed calls them both angels of God and sons of God, though all the copies do not show this, some having only the name" sons of God." And Aquila, whom the Jews prefer to the other interpreters, has translated neither angels of God nor sons of God, but sons of gods. But both are correct. For they were both sons of God, and thus brothers of their own fathers, who were children of the same God; and they were sons of gods, because begotten by gods, together with whom they themselves also were gods, according to that expression of the psalm: "I have said, Ye are gods, and all of you are children of the Most High." For the Septuagint translators are justly believed to have received the Spirit of prophecy; so that, if they made any alterations under His authority, and did not adhere to a strict translation, we could not doubt that this was divinely dictated. However, the Hebrew word may be said to be ambiguous, and to be susceptible of either translation, "sons of God," or "sons of gods."

Let us omit, then, the fables of those scriptures which are called apocryphal, because their obscure origin was unknown to the fathers from whom the authority of the true Scriptures has been transmitted to us by a most certain and well-ascertained succession. For though there is some truth in these apocryphal writings, yet they contain so many false statements, that they have no canonical authority. We cannot deny that Enoch, the seventh from Adam, left some divine writings, for this is asserted by the Apostle Jude in his canonical epistle. But it is not without reason that these writings have no place in that canon of Scripture which was preserved in the temple of the Hebrew people by the diligence of successive priests; for their antiquity brought them under suspicion, and it was impossible to ascertain whether these were his genuine writings, and they were not brought forward as genuine by the persons who were found to have carefully preserved the canonical books by a successive transmission. So that the writings which are produced under his name, and which contain these fables about the giants, saying that their fathers were not men, are properly judged by prudent men to be not genuine; just as many writings are produced by heretics under the names both of other prophets, and more recently, under the names of the apostles, all of which, after careful examination, have been set apart from canonical authority under the title of Apocrypha. There is therefore no doubt that, according to the Hebrew and Christian canonical Scriptures, there were many giants before the deluge, and that these were citizens of the earthly society of men, and that the sons of God, who were according to the flesh the sons of Seth, sunk into this community when they forsook righteousness. Nor need we wonder that giants should be born even from these. For all of their children were not giants; but there were more then than in the remaining periods since the deluge. And it pleased the Creator to produce them, that it might thus be demonstrated that neither beauty, nor yet size and strength, are of much moment to the wise man, whose blessedness lies in spiritual and immortal blessings, in far better and more enduring gifts, in the good things that are the peculiar property of the good, and are not shared by good and bad alike. It is this which another prophet confirms when he says, "These were the giants, famous from the beginning, that were of so great stature, and so expert in war. Those did not the Lord choose, neither gave He the way of knowledge unto them; but they were destroyed because they had no wisdom, and perished through their own foolishness."

Book Eighteen

Chapter I: *Of Those Things Down to the Times of the Saviour Which Have Been Discussed in the Seventeen Books.*

I promised to write of the rise, progress, and appointed end of the two cities, one of which is God's, the other this world's, in which, so far as mankind is concerned, the former is now a stranger. But first of all I undertook, so far as His grace should enable me, to refute the enemies of the city of God, who prefer their gods to Christ its founder, and fiercely hate Christians with the most deadly malice. And this I have done in the first ten books. Then, as regards my threefold promise which I have just mentioned, I have treated distinctly, in the four books which follow the tenth, of the rise of both cities. After that, I have proceeded from the first man down to the flood in one book, which is the fifteenth of this work; and from that again down to Abraham our work has followed both in chronological order. From the patriarch Abraham down to the time of the Israelite kings, at which we close our sixteenth book, and thence down to the advent of Christ Himself in the flesh, to which period the seventeenth book reaches, the city of God appears from my way of writing to have run its course alone; whereas it did not run its course alone in this age, for both cities, in their course amid mankind, certainly experienced chequered times together just as from the beginning. But I did this in order that, first of all, from the time when the promises of God began to be more clear, down to the virgin birth of Him in whom those things promised from the first were to be fulfilled, the course of that city which is God's might be made more distinctly apparent, without interpolation of foreign matter from the history of the other city, although down to the revelation of the new covenant it ran its course, not in light, but in shadow. Now, therefore, I think fit to do what I passed by, and show, so far as seems necessary, how that other city ran its course from the times of Abraham, so that attentive readers may compare the two.

Chapter II: *Of the Kings and Times of the Earthly City Which Were Synchronous with the Times of the Saints, Reckoning from the Rise of Abraham.*

The society of mortals spread abroad through the earth everywhere, and in the most diverse places, although bound together by a certain fellowship of our common nature, is yet for the most part divided against itself, and the strongest oppress the others, because all follow after their own interests and lusts, while what is longed for either suffices for none, or not for all, because it is not the very thing.

For the vanquished succumb to the victorious, preferring any sort of peace and safety to freedom itself; so that they who chose to die rather than be slaves have been greatly wondered at. For in almost all nations the very voice of nature somehow proclaims, that those who happen to be conquered should choose rather to be subject to their conquerors than to be killed by all kinds of warlike destruction. This does not take place without the providence of God, in whose power it lies that any one either subdues or is subdued in war; that some are endowed with kingdoms, others made subject to kings. Now, among the very many kingdoms of the earth into which, by earthly interest or lust, society is divided (which we call by the general name of the city of this world), we see that two, settled and kept distinct from each other both in time and place, have grown far more famous than the rest, first that of the Assyrians, then that of the Romans. First came the one, then the other. The former arose in the east, and, immediately on its close, the latter in the west. I may speak of other kingdoms and other kings as appendages of these.

Ninus, then, who succeeded his father Belus, the first king of Assyria, was already the second king of that kingdom when Abraham was born in the land of the Chaldees. There was also at that time a very small kingdom of Sicyon, with which, as from an ancient date, that most universally learned man Marcus Varro begins, in writing of the Roman race. For from these kings of Sicyon he passes to the Athenians, from them to the Latins, and from these to the Romans. Yet very little is related about these kingdoms, before the foundation of Rome, in comparison with that of Assyria. For although even Sallust, the Roman historian, admits that the Athenians were very famous in Greece, yet he thinks they were greater in fame than in fact. For in speaking of them he says, "The deeds of the Athenians, as I think, were very great and magnificent, but yet somewhat less than reported by fame. But because writers of great genius arose among them, the deeds of the Athenians were celebrated throughout the world as very great. Thus the virtue of those who did them was held to be as great as men of transcendent genius could represent it to be by the power of laudatory words." This city also derived no small glory from literature and philosophy, the study of which chiefly flourished there. But as regards empire, none in the earliest times was greater than the

Assyrian, or so widely extended. For when Ninus the son of Belus was king, he is reported to have subdued the whole of Asia, even to the boundaries of Libya, which as to number is called the third part, but as to size is found to be the half of the whole world. The Indians in the eastern regions were the only people over whom he did not reign; but after his death Semiramis his wife made war on them. Thus it came to pass that all the people and kings in those countries were subject to the kingdom and authority of the Assyrians, and did whatever they were commanded. Now Abraham was born in that kingdom among the Chaldees, in the time of Ninus. But since Grecian affairs are much better known to us than Assyrian, and those who have diligently investigated the antiquity of the Roman nation's origin have followed the order of time through the Greeks to the Latins, and from them to the Romans, who themselves are Latins, we ought on this account, where it is needful, to mention the Assyrian kings, that it may appear how Babylon, like a first Rome, ran its course along with the city of God, which is a stranger in this world. But the things proper for insertion in this work in comparing the two cities, that is, the earthly and heavenly, ought to be taken mostly from the Greek and Latin kingdoms, where Rome herself is like a second Babylon.

At Abraham's birth, then, the second kings of Assyria and Sicyon respectively were Ninus and Europs, the first having been Belus and Ægialeus. But when God promised Abraham, on his departure from Babylonia, that he should become a great nation, and that in his seed all nations of the earth should be blessed, the Assyrians had their seventh king, the Sicyons their fifth; for the son of Ninus reigned among them after his mother Semiramis, who is said to have been put to death by him for attempting to defile him by incestuously lying with him. Some think that she founded Babylon, and indeed she may have founded it anew. But we have told, in the sixteenth book, when or by whom it was founded. Now the son of Ninus and Semiramis, who succeeded his mother in the kingdom, is also called Ninus by some, but by others Ninias, a patronymic word. Telexion then held the kingdom of the Sicyons. In his reign times were quiet and joyful to such a degree, that after his death they worshiped him as a god by offering sacrifices and by celebrating games, which are said to have been first instituted on this occasion.

Chatper III: *What Kings Reigned in Assyria and Sicyon When, According to the Promise, Isaac Was Born to Abraham in His Hundredth Year, and When the Twins Esau and Jacob Were Born of Rebecca to Isaac in His Sixtieth Year.*

In his times also, by the promise of God, Isaac, the son of Abraham, was born to his father when he was a hundred years old, of Sarah his wife, who, being barren and old, had already lost hope of issue. Aralius was then the fifth king of the Assyrians. To Isaac himself, in his sixtieth year, were born twin-sons, Esau and Jacob, whom Rebecca his wife bore to him, their grandfather Abraham, who died on completing a hundred and seventy years, being still alive, and reckoning his hundred and sixtieth year. At that time there reigned as the seventh kings—among the Assyrians, that more ancient Xerxes, who was also called Balæus; and among the Sicyons, Thuriachus, or, as some write his name, Thurimachus. The kingdom of Argos, in which Inachus reigned first, arose in the time of Abraham's grandchildren. And I must not omit what Varro relates, that the Sicyons were also wont to sacrifice at the tomb of their seventh king Thuriachus. In the reign of Armamitres in Assyria and Leucippus in Sicyon as the eighth kings, and of Inachus as the first in Argos, God spoke to Isaac, and promised the same two things to him as to his father—namely, the land of Canaan to his seed, and the blessing of all nations in his seed. These same things were promised to his son, Abraham's grandson, who was at first called Jacob, afterwards Israel, when Belocus was the ninth king of Assyria, and Phoroneus, the son of Inachus, reigned as the second king of Argos, Leucippus still continuing king of Sicyon. In those times, under the Argive king Phoroneus, Greece was made more famous by the institution of certain laws and judges. On the death of Phoroneus, his younger brother Phegous built a temple at his tomb, in which he was worshiped as God, and oxen were sacrificed to him. I believe they thought him worthy of so great honor, because in his part of the kingdom (for their father had divided his territories between them, in which they reigned during his life) he had founded chapels for the worship of the gods, and had taught them to measure time, by months and years, and to that extent to keep count and reckoning of events. Men still uncultivated, admiring him for these novelties, either fancied he was, or resolved that he should be made, a god after his death. Io also is said to have been the daughter of Inachus, who was afterwards called Isis, when she was worshiped in Egypt as a great goddess; although others write that she came as a queen out of Ethiopia, and because she ruled extensively and justly, and instituted for her subjects letters and many useful things, such divine honor was given her there after she died, that if any one said she had been human, he was charged with a capital crime.

Chapter IV: *Of the Times of Jacob and His Son Joseph.*

In the reign of Balæus, the ninth king of Assyria, and Mesappus, the eighth of Sicyon, who is said by some to have been also called Cephisos (if indeed the same man had both names, and those who put the other name in their writings have not rather confounded him with another man), while Apis was third king of Argos, Isaac died, a hundred and eighty years old, and left his twin-sons a hundred and twenty years old. Jacob, the younger of these, belonged to the city of God about which we write (the elder being wholly rejected), and had twelve sons, one of whom, called Joseph, was sold by his brothers to merchants going down to Egypt, while his grandfather Isaac was still alive. But when he was thirty years of age, Joseph stood before Pharaoh, being exalted out of the humiliation he endured, because, in divinely interpreting the king's dreams, he foretold that there would be seven years of plenty, the very rich abundance of which would be consumed by seven other years of famine that should follow. On this account the king made him ruler over Egypt, liberating him from prison, into which he had been thrown for keeping his chastity intact; for he bravely preserved it from his mistress, who wickedly loved him, and told lies to his weakly credulous master, and did not consent to commit adultery with her, but fled from her, leaving his garment in her hands when she laid hold of him. In the second of the seven years of famine Jacob came down into Egypt to his son with all he had, being a hundred and thirty years old, as he himself said in answer to the king's question. Joseph was then thirty-nine, if we add seven years of plenty and two of famine to the thirty he reckoned when honored by the king.

Chapter V: *Of Apis King of Argos, Whom the Egyptians Called Serapis, and Worshiped with Divine Honors.*

In these times Apis king of Argos crossed over into Egypt in ships, and, on dying there, was made Serapis, the chief god of all the Egyptians. Now Varro gives this very ready reason why, after his death, he was called, not Apis, but Serapis. The ark in which he was placed when dead, which every one now calls a sarcophagus, was then called in Greek σορὸς, and they began to worship him when buried in it before his temple was built; and from Soros and Apis he was called first [Sorosapis, or] Sorapis, and then Serapis, by changing a letter, as easily happens. It was decreed regarding him also, that whoever should say he had been a man should be capitally punished. And since in every temple where Isis and Serapis were worshiped there was also an image which, with finger pressed on the lips, seemed to warn men to keep silence, Varro thinks this signifies that it should be kept secret that they had been human. But that bull which, with wonderful folly, deluded Egypt nourished with abundant delicacies in honor of him, was not called Serapis, but Apis, because they worshiped him alive without a sarcophagus. On the death of that bull, when they sought and found a calf of the same color—that is, similarly marked with certain white spots—they believed it was something miraculous, and divinely provided for them. Yet it was no great thing for the demons, in order to deceive them, to show to a cow when she was conceiving and pregnant the image of such a bull, which she alone could see, and by it attract the breeding passion of the mother, so that it might appear in a bodily shape in her young, just as Jacob so managed with the spotted rods that the sheep and goats were born spotted. For what men can do with real colors and substances, the demons can very easily do by showing unreal forms to breeding animals.

Chapter VI: *Who Were Kings of Argos, and of Assyria, When Jacob Died in Egypt.*

Apis, then, who died in Egypt, was not the king of Egypt, but of Argos. He was succeeded by his son Argus, from whose name the land was called Argos and the people Argives, for under the earlier kings neither the place nor the nation as yet had this name. While he then reigned over Argos, and Eratus over Sicyon, and Balæus still remained king of Assyria, Jacob died in Egypt a hundred and forty-seven years old, after he had, when dying, blessed his sons and his grandsons by Joseph, and prophesied most plainly of Christ, saying in the blessing of Judah, "A prince shall not fail out of Judah, nor a leader from his thighs, until those things come which are laid up for him; and He is the expectation of the nations." In the reign of Argus, Greece began to use fruits, and to have crops of corn in cultivated fields, the seed having been brought from other countries. Argus also began to be accounted a god after his death, and was honored with a temple and sacrifices. This honor was conferred in his reign, before being given to him, on a private individual for being the first to yoke oxen in the plough. This was one Homogyrus, who was struck by lightning.

Chapter VII: *Who Were Kings When Joseph Died in Egypt.*

In the reign of Mamitus, the twelfth king of Assyria, and Plemnæus, the eleventh of Sicyon, while Argus still reigned over the Argives, Joseph died in Egypt a hundred and ten years old. After his death, the people of God, increasing wonderfully, remained in Egypt a hundred and forty-five years, in tranquility at first, until those who knew Joseph were dead. Afterward, through envy of their increase, and the suspicion that they would at length gain their freedom, they were oppressed with persecutions and the labors of intolerable servitude, amid which, however, they still grew, being multiplied with God-given fertility. During this period the same kingdoms continued in Assyria and Greece.

Chapter VIII: *Who Were Kings When Moses Was Born, and What Gods Began to Be Worshiped Then.*

When Saphrus reigned as the fourteenth king of Assyria, and Orthopolis as the twelfth of Sicyon, and Criasus as the fifth of Argos, Moses was born in Egypt, by whom the people of God were liberated from the Egyptian slavery, in which they behooved to be thus tried that they might desire the help of their Creator. Some have thought that Prometheus lived during the reign of the kings now named. He is reported to have formed men out of clay, because he was esteemed the best teacher of wisdom; yet it does not appear what wise men there were in his days. His brother Atlas is said to have been a great astrologer; and this gave occasion for the fable that he held up the sky, although the vulgar opinion about his holding up the sky appears rather to have been suggested by a high mountain named after him. Indeed, from those times many other fabulous things began to be invented in Greece; yet, down to Cecrops king of Athens, in whose reign that city received its name, and in whose reign God brought His people out of Egypt by Moses, only a few dead heroes are reported to have been deified according to the vain superstition of the Greeks. Among these were Melantomice, the wife of king Criasus, and Phorbas their son, who succeeded his father as sixth king of the Argives, and Iasus, son of Triopas, their seventh king, and their ninth king, Sthenelas, or Stheneleus, or Sthenelus—for his name is given differently by different authors. In those times also, Mercury, the grandson of Atlas by his daughter Maia, is said to have lived, according to the common report in books. He was famous for his skill in many arts, and taught them to men, for which they resolved to make him, and even believed that he deserved to be, a god after death. Hercules is said to have been later, yet belonging to the same period; although some, whom I think mistaken, assign him an earlier date than Mercury. But at whatever time they were born, it is agreed among grave historians, who have committed these ancient things to writing, that both were men, and that they merited divine honors from mortals because they conferred on them many benefits to make this life more pleasant to them. Minerva was far more ancient than these; for she is reported to have appeared in virgin age in the times of Ogyges at the lake called Triton, from which she is also styled Tritonia, the inventress truly of many works, and the more readily believed to be a goddess because her origin was so little known. For what is sung about her having sprung from the head of Jupiter belongs to the region of poetry and fable, and not to that of history and real fact. And historical writers are not agreed when Ogyges flourished, in whose time also a great flood occurred—not that greatest one from which no man escaped except those who could get into the ark, for neither Greek nor Latin history knew of it, yet a greater flood than that which happened afterward in Deucalion's time. For Varro begins the book I have already mentioned at this date, and does not propose to himself, as the starting-point from which he may arrive at Roman affairs, anything more ancient than the flood of Ogyges, that is, which happened in the time of Ogyges. Now our writers of chronicles—first Eusebius, and afterwards Jerome, who entirely follow some earlier historians in this opinion—relate that the flood of Ogyges happened more than three hundred years after, during the reign of Phoroneus, the second king of Argos. But whenever he may have lived, Minerva was already worshiped as a goddess when Cecrops reigned in Athens, in whose reign the city itself is reported to have been rebuilt or founded.

Chapter IX: *When the City of Athens Was Founded, and What Reason Varro Assigns for Its Name.*

Athens certainly derived its name from Minerva, who in Greek is called Αθηνη, and Varro points out the following reason why it was so called. When an olive-tree suddenly appeared there, and water burst forth in another place, these prodigies moved the king to send to the Delphic Apollo to inquire what they meant and what he should do. He answered that the olive signified Minerva, the water Neptune, and that the citizens had it in their power to name their city as they chose, after either of these two gods whose signs these were. On receiving this oracle, Cecrops convoked all the citizens of either sex to give their vote, for it was then the custom in those parts for the women also to take part in public deliberations. When the multitude was consulted, the men gave their votes for Neptune, the women for Minerva; and as the women had a majority of one, Minerva conquered. Then Neptune, being enraged, laid waste the lands of the Athenians, by casting up the waves of the sea; for the demons have no difficulty in scattering any waters more widely. The same authority said, that to appease his wrath the women should be visited by the Athenians with the three-fold punishment—that they should no longer have any vote; that none of their children should be named after their mothers; and that no one should call them Athenians. Thus that city, the mother and nurse of liberal doctrines, and of so many and so great philosophers, than whom Greece had nothing more famous and noble, by the mockery of demons about the strife of their gods, a male and female, and from the victory of the female one through the women, received the name of Athens; and, on being damaged by the vanquished god, was compelled to punish the very victory of the victress, fearing the waters of Neptune more than the arms of Minerva. For in the women who were thus punished, Minerva, who had conquered, was conquered too, and could not even help her voters so far that, although the right of voting was henceforth lost, and the mothers could not give their names to the children, they might at least be allowed to be called Athenians, and to merit the name of that goddess whom they had made victorious over a male god by giving her their votes. What and how much could be said about this, if we had not to hasten to other things in our discourse, is obvious.

Chapter X: *What Varro Reports About the Term Areopagus, and About Deucalion's Flood.*

Marcus Varro, however, is not willing to credit lying fables against the gods, lest he should find something dishonoring to their majesty; and therefore he will not admit that the Areopagus, the place where the Apostle Paul disputed with the Athenians, got this name because Mars, who in Greek is called Αρης, when he was charged with the crime of homicide, and was judged by twelve gods in that field, was acquitted by the sentence of six; because it was the custom, when the votes were equal, to acquit rather than condemn. Against this opinion, which is much most widely published, he tries, from the notices of obscure books, to support another reason for this name, lest the Athenians should be thought to have called it Areopagus from the words" Mars" and "field," as if it were the field of Mars, to the dishonor of the gods, forsooth, from whom he thinks lawsuits and judgments far removed. And he asserts that this which is said about Mars is not less false than what is said about the three goddesses, to wit, Juno, Minerva, and Venus, whose contest for the palm of beauty, before Paris as judge, in order to obtain the golden apple, is not only related, but is celebrated in songs and dances amid the applause of the theatres, in plays meant to please the gods who take pleasure in these crimes of their own, whether real or fabled. Varro does not believe these things, because they are incompatible with the nature of the gods and of morality; and yet, in giving not a fabulous but a historic reason for the name of Athens, he inserts in his books the strife between Neptune and Minerva as to whose name should be given to that city, which was so great that, when they contended by the display of prodigies, even Apollo dared not judge between them when consulted; but, in order to end the strife of the gods, just as Jupiter sent the three goddesses we have named to Paris, so he sent them to men, when Minerva won by the vote, and yet was defeated by the punishment of her own voters, for she was unable to confer the title of Athenians on the women who were her friends, although she could impose it on the men who were her opponents.

In these times, when Cranaos reigned at Athens as the successor of Cecrops, as Varro writes, but, according to our Eusebius and Jerome, while Cecrops himself still remained, the flood occurred which is called Deucalion's, because it occurred chiefly in those parts of the earth in which he reigned. But this flood did not at all reach Egypt or its vicinity.

Chapter XI: *When Moses Led the People Out of Egypt; And Who Were Kings When His Successor Joshua the Son of Nun Died.*

Moses led the people out of Egypt in the last time of Cecrops king of Athens, when Ascatades reigned in Assyria, Marathus in Sicyon, Triopas in Argos; and having led forth the people, he gave them at Mount Sinai the law he received from God, which is called the Old Testament, because it has earthly promises, and because, through Jesus Christ, there was to be a New Testament, in which the kingdom of heaven should be promised. For the same order behooved to be observed in this as is observed in each man who prospers in God, according to the saying of the apostle, "That is not first which is spiritual, but that which is natural," since, as he says, and that truly, "The first man of the earth, is earthly; the second man, from heaven, is heavenly." Now Moses ruled the people for forty years in the wilderness, and died a hundred and twenty years old, after he had prophesied of Christ by the types of carnal observances in the tabernacle, priesthood, and sacrifices, and many other mystic ordinances. Joshua the son of Nun succeeded Moses, and settled in the land of promise the people he had brought in, having by divine authority conquered the people by whom it was formerly possessed. He also died, after ruling the people twenty-seven years after the death of Moses, when Amyntas reigned in Assyria as the eighteenth king, Coracos as the sixteenth in Sicyon, Danaos as the tenth in Argos, Ericthonius as the fourth in Athens.

Chapter XII: *Of the Rituals of False Gods Instituted by the Kings of Greece in the Period from Israel's Exodus from Egypt Down to the Death of Joshua the Son of Nun.*

During this period, that is, from Israel's exodus from Egypt down to the death of Joshua the son of Nun, through whom that people received the land of promise, rituals were instituted to the false gods by the kings of Greece, which, by stated celebration, recalled the memory of the flood, and of men's deliverance from it, and of that troublous life they then led in migrating to and fro between the heights and the plains. For even the Luperci, when they ascend and descend the sacred path, are said to represent the men who sought the mountain summits because of the inundation of water, and returned to the lowlands on its subsidence. In those times, Dionysus, who was also called Father Liber, and was esteemed a god after death, is said to have shown the vine to his host in Attica. Then the musical games were instituted for the Delphic Apollo, to appease his anger, through which they thought the regions of Greece were afflicted with barrenness, because they had not defended his temple which Danaos burnt when he invaded those lands; for they were warned by his oracle to institute these games. But king Ericthonius first instituted games to him in Attica, and not to him only, but also to Minerva, in which games the olive was given as the prize to the victors, because they relate that Minerva was the discoverer of that fruit, as Liber was of the grape. In those years Europa is alleged to have been carried off by Xanthus king of Crete (to whom we find some give another name), and to have borne him Rhadamanthus, Sarpedon, and Minos, who are more commonly reported to have been the sons of Jupiter by the same woman. Now those who worship such gods regard what we have said about Xanthus king of Crete as true history; but this about Jupiter, which the poets sing, the theatres applaud, and the people celebrate, as empty fable got up as a reason for games to appease the deities, even with the false ascription of crimes to them. In those times Hercules was held in honor in Tyre, but that was not the same one as he whom we spoke of above. In the more secret history there are said to have been several who were called Father Liber and Hercules. This Hercules, whose great deeds are reckoned as twelve (not including the slaughter of Antæus the African, because that affair pertains to another Hercules), is declared in their books to have burned himself on Mount Œta, because he was not able, by that strength with which he had subdued monsters, to endure the disease under which he languished. At that time the king, or rather tyrant Busiris, who is alleged to have been the son of Neptune by Libya the daughter of Epaphus, is said to have offered up his guests in sacrifice to the gods. Now it must not be believed that Neptune committed this adultery, lest the gods should be criminated; yet such things must be ascribed to them by the poets and in the theatres, that they may be pleased with them. Vulcan and Minerva are said to have been the parents of Ericthonius king of Athens, in whose last years Joshua the son of Nun is found to have died. But since they will have it that Minerva is a virgin, they say that Vulcan, being disturbed in the struggle between them, poured out his seed into the earth, and on that account the man born of it received that name; for in the Greek language ἔρις is "strife," and χθὼν "earth," of which two words Ericthonius is a compound. Yet it must be admitted that the more learned disprove and disown such things concerning their gods, and declare that this fabulous belief originated in the fact that in the temple at Athens, which Vulcan and Minerva had in common, a boy who had been exposed was found wrapped up in the coils of a dragon, which signified that he would become great, and, as his parents were unknown, he was called the son of Vulcan and Minerva, because they had the temple in common. Yet that fable accounts for the origin of his name better than this history. But what does it matter to us? Let the one in books that speak the truth edify religious men, and the other in lying fables delight impure demons. Yet these religious men worship them as gods. Still, while they deny these things concerning them they cannot clear them of all crime, because at their demand they exhibit plays in which the very things they wisely deny are basely done, and the gods are appeased by these false and base things. Now, even although the play celebrates an unreal crime of the gods, yet to delight in the ascription of an unreal crime is a real one.

Chapter XXII: *That Rome Was Founded When the Assyrian Kingdom Perished, at Which Time Hezekiah Reigned in Judah.*

To be brief, the city of Rome was founded, like another Babylon, and as it were the daughter of the former Babylon, by which God was pleased to conquer the whole world, and subdue it far and wide by bringing it into one fellowship of government and laws. For there were already powerful and brave peoples and nations trained to arms, who did not easily yield, and whose subjugation necessarily involved great danger and destruction as well as great and horrible labor. For when the Assyrian kingdom subdued almost all Asia, although this was done by fighting, yet the wars could not be very fierce or difficult, because the nations were as yet untrained to resist, and neither so many nor so great as afterward; forasmuch as, after that greatest and indeed universal flood, when only eight men escaped in Noah's ark, not much more than a thousand years had passed when Ninus subdued all Asia with the exception of India. But Rome did not with the same quickness and facility wholly subdue all those nations of the east and west which we see brought under the Roman empire, because, in its gradual increase, in whatever direction it was extended, it found them strong and warlike. At the time when Rome was founded, then, the people of Israel had been in the land of promise seven hundred and eighteen years. Of these years twenty-seven belong to Joshua the son of Nun, and after that three hundred and twenty-nine to the period of the judges. But from the time when the kings began to reign there, three hundred and sixty-two years had passed. And at that time there was a king in Judah called Ahaz, or, as others compute, Hezekiah his successor, the best and most pious king, who it is admitted reigned in the times of Romulus. And in that part of the Hebrew nation called Israel, Hoshea had begun to reign.

Chapter XLII: *By What Dispensation of God's Providence the Sacred Scriptures of the Old Testament Were Translated Out of Hebrew into Greek, that They Might Be Made Known to All the Nations.*

One of the Ptolemies, kings of Egypt, desired to know and have these sacred books. For after Alexander of Macedon, who is also styled the Great, had by his most wonderful, but by no means enduring power, subdued the whole of Asia, yea, almost the whole world, partly by force of arms, partly by terror, and, among other kingdoms of the East, had entered and obtained Judea also, on his death his generals did not peaceably divide that most ample kingdom among them for a possession, but rather dissipated it, wasting all things by wars. Then Egypt began to have the Ptolemies as her kings. The first of them, the son of Lagus, carried many captive out of Judea into Egypt. But another Ptolemy, called Philadelphus, who succeeded him, permitted all whom he had brought under the yoke to return free; and more than that, sent kingly gifts to the temple of God, and begged Eleazar, who was the high priest, to give him the Scriptures, which he had heard by report were truly divine, and therefore greatly desired to have in that most noble library he had made. When the high priest had sent them to him in Hebrew, he afterwards demanded interpreters of him, and there were given him seventy-two, out of each of the twelve tribes six men, most learned in both languages, to wit, the Hebrew and Greek and their translation is now by custom called the Septuagint. It is reported, indeed, that there was an agreement in their words so wonderful, stupendous, and plainly divine, that when they had sat at this work, each one apart (for so it pleased Ptolemy to test their fidelity), they differed from each other in no word which had the same meaning and force, or, in the order of the words; but, as if the translators had been one, so what all had translated was one, because in very deed the one Spirit had been in them all. And they received so wonderful a gift of God, in order that the authority of these Scriptures might be commended not as human but divine, as indeed it was, for the benefit of the nations who should at some time believe, as we now see them doing.

Chapter XLIII: *Of the Authority of the Septuagint Translation, Which, Saving the Honor of the Hebrew Original, is to Be Preferred to All Translations.*

For while there were other interpreters who translated these sacred oracles out of the Hebrew tongue into Greek, as Aquila, Symmachus, and Theodotion, and also that translation which, as the name of the author is unknown, is quoted as the fifth edition, yet the Church has received this Septuagint translation just as if it were the only one; and it has been used by the Greek Christian people, most of whom are not aware that there is any other. From this translation there has also been made a translation in the Latin tongue, which the Latin churches use. Our times, however, have enjoyed the advantage of the presbyter Jerome, a man most learned, and skilled in all three languages, who translated these same Scriptures into the Latin speech, not from the Greek, but from the Hebrew. But although the Jews acknowledge this very learned labor of his to be faithful, while they contend that the Septuagint translators have erred in many places, still the churches of Christ judge that no one should be preferred to the authority of so many men, chosen for this very great work by Eleazar, who was then high priest; for even if there had not appeared in them one spirit, without doubt divine, and the seventy learned men had, after the manner of men, compared together the words of their translation, that what pleased them all might stand, no single translator ought to be preferred to them; but since so great a sign of divinity has appeared in them, certainly, if any other translator of their Scriptures from the Hebrew into any other tongue is faithful, in that case he agrees with these seventy translators, and if he is not found to agree with them, then we ought to believe that the prophetic gift is with them. For the same Spirit who was in the prophets when they spoke these things was also in the seventy men when they translated them, so that assuredly they could also say something else, just as if the prophet himself had said both, because it would be the same Spirit who said both; and could say the same thing differently, so that, although the words were not the same, yet the same meaning should shine forth to those of good understanding; and could omit or add something, so that even by this it might be shown that there was in that work not human bondage, which the translator owed to the words, but rather divine power, which filled and ruled the mind of the translator. Some, however, have thought that the Greek copies of the Septuagint version should be emended from the Hebrew copies; yet they did not dare to take away what the Hebrew lacked and the Septuagint had, but only added what was found in the Hebrew copies and was lacking in the Septuagint, and noted them by placing at the beginning of the verses certain marks in the form of stars which they call asterisks. And those things which the Hebrew copies have not, but the Septuagint have, they have in like manner marked at the beginning of the verses by horizontal spit-shaped marks like those by which we denote ounces; and many copies having these marks are circulated even in Latin. But we cannot, without inspecting both kinds of copies, find out those things which are neither omitted nor added, but expressed differently, whether they yield another meaning not in itself unsuitable, or can be shown to explain the same meaning in another way. If, then, as it behooves us, we behold nothing else in these Scriptures than what the Spirit of God has spoken through men, if anything is in the Hebrew copies and is not in the version of the Seventy, the Spirit of God did not choose to say it through them, but only through the prophets. But whatever is in the Septuagint and not in the Hebrew copies, the same Spirit chose rather to say through the latter, thus showing that both were prophets. For in that manner He spoke as He chose, some things through Isaiah, some through Jeremiah, some through several prophets, or else the same thing through this prophet and through that. Further, whatever is found in both editions, that one and the same Spirit willed to say through both, but so as that the former preceded in prophesying, and the latter followed in prophetically interpreting them; because, as the one Spirit of peace was in the former when they spoke true and concordant words, so the selfsame one Spirit hath appeared in the latter, when, without mutual conference they yet interpreted all things as if with one mouth.

Chapter XLVI: *Of the Birth of Our Saviour, Whereby the Word Was Made Flesh; And of the Dispersion of the Jews Among All Nations, as Had Been Prophesied.*

While Herod, therefore, reigned in Judea, and Cæsar Augustus was emperor at Rome, the state of the republic being already changed, and the world being set at peace by him, Christ was born in Bethlehem of Judah, man manifest out of a human virgin, God hidden out of God the Father. For so had the prophet foretold: "Behold, a virgin shall conceive in the womb, and bring forth a Son, and they shall call His name Immanuel, which, being interpreted, is, God with us." He did many miracles that He might commend God in Himself, some of which, even as many as seemed sufficient to proclaim Him, are contained in the evangelic Scripture. The first of these is, that He was so wonderfully born, and the last, that with His body raised up again from the dead He ascended into heaven. But the Jews who slew Him, and would not believe in Him, because it behooved Him to die and rise again, were yet more miserably wasted by the Romans, and utterly rooted out from their kingdom, where aliens had already ruled over them, and were dispersed through the lands (so that indeed there is no place where they are not), and are thus by their own Scriptures a testimony to us that we have not forged the prophecies about Christ. And very many of them, considering this, even before His passion, but chiefly after His resurrection, believed on Him, of whom it was predicted, "Though the number of the children of Israel be as the sand of the sea, the remnant shall be saved." But the rest are blinded, of whom it was predicted, "Let their table be made before them a trap, and a retribution, and a stumbling-block. Let their eyes be darkened lest they see, and bow down their back alway." Therefore, when they do not believe our Scriptures, their own, which they blindly read, are fulfilled in them, lest perchance any one should say that the Christians have forged these prophecies about Christ which are quoted under the name of the sibyl, or of others, if such there be, who do not belong to the Jewish people. For us, indeed, those suffice which are quoted from the books of our enemies, to whom we make our acknowledgment, on account of this testimony which, in spite of themselves, they contribute by their possession of these books, while they themselves are dispersed among all nations, wherever the Church of Christ is spread abroad. For a prophecy about this thing was sent before in the Psalms, which they also read, where it is written, "My God, His mercy shall prevent me. My God hath shown me concerning mine enemies, that Thou shalt not slay them, lest they should at last forget Thy law: disperse them in Thy might." Therefore God has shown the Church in her enemies the Jews the grace of His compassion, since, as saith the apostle, "their offence is the salvation of the Gentiles." And therefore He has not slain them, that is, He has not let the knowledge that they are Jews be lost in them, although they have been conquered by the Romans, lest they should forget the law of God, and their testimony should be of no avail in this matter of which we treat. But it was not enough that he should say, "Slay them not, lest they should at last forget Thy law," unless he had also added, "Disperse them;" because if they had only been in their own land with that testimony of the Scriptures, and not every where, certainly the Church which is everywhere could not have had them as witnesses among all nations to the prophecies which were sent before concerning Christ.

Chapter XLVII: *Whether Before Christian Times There Were Any Outside of the Israelite Race Who Belonged to the Fellowship of the Heavenly City.*

Wherefore if we read of any foreigner—that is, one neither born of Israel nor received by that people into the canon of the sacred books—having prophesied something about Christ, if it has come or shall come to our knowledge, we can refer to it over and above; not that this is necessary, even if wanting, but because it is not incongruous to believe that even in other nations there may have been men to whom this mystery was revealed, and who were also impelled to proclaim it, whether they were partakers of the same grace or had no experience of it, but were taught by bad angels, who, as we know, even confessed the present Christ, whom the Jews did not acknowledge. Nor do I think the Jews themselves dare contend that no one has belonged to God except the Israelites, since the increase of Israel began on the rejection of his elder brother. For in very deed there was no other people who were specially called the people of God; but they cannot deny that there have been certain men even of other nations who belonged, not by earthly but heavenly fellowship, to the true Israelites, the citizens of the country that is above. Because, if they deny this, they can be most easily confuted by the case of the holy and wonderful man Job, who was neither a native nor a proselyte, that is, a stranger joining the people of Israel, but, being bred of the Idumean race, arose there and died there too, and who is so praised by the divine oracle, that no man of his times is put on a level with him as regards justice and piety. And although we do not find his date in the chronicles, yet from his book, which for its merit the Israelites have received as of canonical authority, we gather that he was in the third generation after Israel. And I doubt not it was divinely provided, that from this one case we might know that among other nations also there might be men pertaining to the spiritual Jerusalem who have lived according to God and have pleased Him. And it is not to be supposed that this was granted to any one, unless the one Mediator between God and men, the Man Christ Jesus, was divinely revealed to him; who was preannounced to the saints of old as yet to come in the flesh, even as He is announced to us as having come, that the self-same faith through Him may lead all to God who are predestinated to be the city of God, the house of God, and the temple of God. But whatever prophecies concerning the grace of God through Christ Jesus are quoted, they may be thought to have been forged by the Christians. So that there is nothing of more weight for confuting all sorts of aliens, if they contend about this matter, and for supporting our friends, if they are truly wise, than to quote those divine predictions about Christ which are written in the books of the Jews, who have been torn from their native abode and dispersed over the whole world in order to bear this testimony, so that the Church of Christ has everywhere increased.

Chapter XLIX: *Of the Indiscriminate Increase of the Church, Wherein Many Reprobate are in This World Mixed with the Elect.*

In this wicked world, in these evil days, when the Church measures her future loftiness by her present humility, and is exercised by goading fears, tormenting sorrows, disquieting labors, and dangerous temptations, when she soberly rejoices, rejoicing only in hope, there are many reprobate mingled with the good, and both are gathered together by the gospel as in a drag net; and in this world, as in a sea, both swim enclosed without distinction in the net, until it is brought ashore, when the wicked must be separated from the good, that in the good, as in His temple, God may be all in all. We acknowledge, indeed, that His word is now fulfilled who spake in the psalm, and said, "I have announced and spoken; they are multiplied above number." This takes place now, since He has spoken, first by the mouth of his forerunner John, and afterward by His own mouth, saying, "Repent: for the kingdom of heaven is at hand." He chose disciples, whom He also called apostles, of lowly birth, unhonored, and illiterate, so that whatever great thing they might be or do, He might be and do it in them. He had one among them whose wickedness He could use well in order to accomplish His appointed passion, and furnish His Church an example of bearing with the wicked. Having sown the holy gospel as much as that behooved to be done by His bodily presence, He suffered, died, and rose again, showing by His passion what we ought to suffer for the truth, and by His resurrection what we ought to hope for in adversity; saving always the mystery of the sacrament, by which His blood was shed for the remission of sins. He held converse on the earth forty days with His disciples, and in their sight ascended into heaven, and after ten days sent the promised Holy Spirit. It was given as the chief and most necessary sign of His coming on those who had believed, that every one of them spoke in the tongues of all nations; thus signifying that the unity of the catholic Church would embrace all nations, and would in like manner speak in all tongues.

Book Nineteen

Chapter IV: *What the Christians Believe Regarding the Supreme Good and Evil, in Opposition to the Philosophers, Who Have Maintained that the Supreme Good is in Themselves.*

If, then, we be asked what the city of God has to say upon these points, and, in the first place, what its opinion regarding the supreme good and evil is, it will reply that life eternal is the supreme good, death eternal the supreme evil, and that to obtain the one and escape the other we must live rightly. And thus it is written, "The just lives by faith," for we do not as yet see our good, and must therefore live by faith; neither have we in ourselves power to live rightly, but can do so only if He who has given us faith to believe in His help do help us when we believe and pray. As for those who have supposed that the sovereign good and evil are to be found in this life, and have placed it either in the soul or the body, or in both, or, to speak more explicitly, either in pleasure or in virtue, or in both; in repose or in virtue, or in both; in pleasure and repose, or in virtue, or in all combined; in the primary objects of nature, or in virtue, or in both—all these have, with a marvelous shallowness, sought to find their blessedness in this life and in themselves. Contempt has been poured upon such ideas by the Truth, saying by the prophet, "The Lord knoweth the thoughts of men" (or, as the Apostle Paul cites the passage, "The Lord knoweth the thoughts of the wise") "that they are vain."

For what flood of eloquence can suffice to detail the miseries of this life? Cicero, in the Consolation on the death of his daughter, has spent all his ability in lamentation; but how inadequate was even his ability here? For when, where, how, in this life can these primary objects of nature be possessed so that they may not be assailed by unforeseen accidents? Is the body of the wise man exempt from any pain which may dispel pleasure, from any disquietude which may banish repose? The amputation or decay of the members of the body puts an end to its integrity, deformity blights its beauty, weakness its health, lassitude its vigor, sleepiness or sluggishness its activity—and which of these is it that may not assail the flesh of the wise man? Comely and fitting attitudes and movements of the body are numbered among the prime natural blessings; but what if some sickness makes the members tremble? what if a man suffers from curvature of the spine to such an extent that his hands reach the ground, and he goes upon all-fours like a quadruped? Does not this destroy all beauty and grace in the body, whether at rest or in motion? What shall I say of the fundamental blessings of the soul, sense and intellect, of which the one is given for the perception, and the other for the comprehension of truth? But what kind of sense is it that remains when a man becomes deaf and blind? where are reason and intellect when disease makes a man delirious? We can scarcely, or not at all, refrain from tears, when we think of or see the actions and words of such frantic persons, and consider how different from and even opposed to their own sober judgment and ordinary conduct their present demeanor is. And what shall I say of those who suffer from demoniacal possession? Where is their own intelligence hidden and buried while the malignant spirit is using their body and soul according to his own will? And who is quite sure that no such thing can happen to the wise man in this life? Then, as to the perception of truth, what can we hope for even in this way while in the body, as we read in the true book of Wisdom, "The corruptible body weigheth down the soul, and the earthly tabernacle presseth down the mind that museth upon many things?" And eagerness, or desire of action, if this is the right meaning to put upon the Greek ὁρμη, is also reckoned among the primary advantages of nature; and yet is it not this which produces those pitiable movements of the insane, and those actions which we shudder to see, when sense is deceived and reason deranged?

In fine, virtue itself, which is not among the primary objects of nature, but succeeds to them as the result of learning, though it holds the highest place among human good things, what is its occupation save to wage perpetual war with vices—not those that are outside of us, but within; not other men's, but our own—a war which is waged especially by that virtue which the Greeks call σωφροσυνη, and we temperance, and which bridles carnal lusts, and prevents them from winning the consent of the spirit to wicked deeds? For we must not fancy that there is no vice in us, when, as the apostle says, "The flesh lusteth against the spirit;" for to this vice there is a contrary virtue, when, as the same writer says, "The spirit lusteth against the flesh." "For these two," he says, "are contrary one to the other, so that you cannot do the things which you would." But what is it we wish to do when we seek to attain the supreme good, unless that the flesh should cease to lust against the spirit, and that there be no vice in us against which the spirit may lust? And as we cannot attain to this in the present life, however ardently we desire it, let us by God's help accomplish at least this, to preserve the soul from succumbing and yielding to the flesh that lusts against it, and to refuse our consent to the perpetration of sin. Far be it from us, then, to fancy that while we are still engaged in this intestine war, we have already found the happiness which we seek to reach by victory. And who is there so wise that he has no conflict at all to maintain against his vices?

What shall I say of that virtue which is called prudence? Is not all its vigilance spent in the discernment of good from evil things, so that no mistake may be admitted about what we should desire and what avoid? And thus it is itself a proof that we are in the midst of evils, or that evils are in us; for it teaches us that it is an evil to consent to sin, and a good to refuse this consent. And yet this evil, to which prudence teaches and temperance enables us not to consent, is removed from this life neither by prudence nor by temperance. And justice, whose office it is to render to every man his due, whereby there is in man himself a certain just order of nature, so that the soul is subjected to God, and the flesh to the soul, and consequently both soul and flesh to God—does not this virtue demonstrate that it is as yet rather laboring towards its end than resting in its finished work? For the soul is so much the less subjected to God as it is less occupied with the thought of God; and the flesh is so much the less subjected to the spirit as it lusts more vehemently against the spirit. So long, therefore, as we are beset by this weakness, this plague, this disease, how shall we dare to say that we are safe? and if not safe, then how can we be already enjoying our final beatitude? Then that virtue which goes by the name of fortitude is the plainest proof of the ills of life, for it is these ills which it is compelled to bear patiently. And this holds good, no matter though the ripest wisdom co-exists with it. And I am at a loss to understand how the Stoic philosophers can presume to say that these are no ills, though at the same time they allow the wise man to commit suicide and pass out of this life if they become so grievous that he cannot or ought not to endure them. But such is the stupid pride of these men who fancy that the supreme good can be found in this life, and that they can become happy by their own resources, that their wise man, or at least the man whom they fancifully depict as such, is always happy, even though he become blind, deaf, dumb, mutilated, racked with pains, or suffer any conceivable calamity such as may compel him to make away with himself; and they are not ashamed to call the life that is beset with these evils happy. O happy life, which seeks the aid of death to end it? If it is happy, let the wise man remain in it; but if these ills drive him out of it, in what sense is it happy? Or how can they say that these are not evils which conquer the virtue of fortitude, and force it not only to yield, but so to rave that it in one breath calls life happy and recommends it to be given up? For who is so blind as not to see that if it were happy it would not be fled from? And if they say we should flee from it on account of the infirmities that beset it, why then do they not lower their pride and acknowledge that it is miserable? Was it, I would ask, fortitude or weakness which prompted Cato to kill himself? for he would not have done so had he not been too weak to endure Cæsar's victory. Where, then, is his fortitude? It has yielded, it has succumbed, it has been so thoroughly overcome as to abandon, forsake, flee this happy life. Or was it no longer happy? Then it was miserable. How, then, were these not evils which made life miserable, and a thing to be escaped from?

And therefore those who admit that these are evils, as the Peripatetics do, and the Old Academy, the sect which Varro advocates, express a more intelligible doctrine; but theirs also is a surprising mistake, for they contend that this is a happy life which is beset by these evils, even though they be so great that he who endures them should commit suicide to escape them. "Pains and anguish of body," says Varro, "are evils, and so much the worse in proportion to their severity; and to escape them you must quit this life." What life, I pray? This life, he says, which is oppressed by such evils. Then it is happy in the midst of these very evils on account of which you say we must quit it? Or do you call it happy because you are at liberty to escape these evils by death? What, then, if by some secret judgment of God you were held fast and not permitted to die, nor suffered to live without these evils? In that case, at least, you would say that such a life was miserable. It is soon relinquished, no doubt but this does not make it not miserable; for were it eternal, you yourself would pronounce it miserable. Its brevity, therefore, does not clear it of misery; neither ought it to be called happiness because it is a brief misery. Certainly there is a mighty force in these evils which compel a man—according to them even a wise man—to cease to be a man that he may escape them, though they say, and say truly, that it is as it were the first and strongest demand of nature that a man cherish himself, and naturally therefore avoid death, and should so stand his own friend as to wish and vehemently aim at continuing to exist as a living creature, and subsisting in this union of soul and body. There is a mighty force in these evils to overcome this natural instinct by which death is by every means and with all a man's efforts avoided, and to overcome it so completely that what was avoided is desired, sought after, and if it cannot in any other way be obtained, is inflicted by the man on himself. There is a mighty force in these evils which make fortitude a homicide—if, indeed, that is to be called fortitude which is so thoroughly overcome by these evils, that it not only cannot preserve by patience the man whom it undertook to govern and defend, but is itself obliged to kill him. The wise man, I admit, ought to bear death with patience, but when it is inflicted by another. If, then, as these men maintain, he is obliged to inflict it on himself, certainly it must be owned that the ills which compel him to this are not only evils, but intolerable evils. The life, then, which is either subject to accidents, or environed with evils so considerable and grievous, could never have been called happy, if the men who give it this name had condescended to yield to the truth, and to be conquered by valid arguments, when they inquired after the happy life, as they yield to unhappiness, and are overcome by overwhelming evils, when they put themselves to death, and if they had not fancied that the supreme good was to be found in this mortal life; for the very virtues of this life, which are certainly its best and most useful possessions, are all the more telling proofs of its miseries in proportion as they are helpful against the violence of its dangers, toils, and woes. For if these are true virtues—and such cannot exist save in those who have true piety—they do not profess to be able to deliver the men who possess them from all miseries; for true virtues tell no such lies, but they profess that by the hope of the future world this life, which is miserably involved in the many and great evils of this world, is happy as it is also safe. For if not yet safe, how could it be happy? And therefore the Apostle Paul, speaking not of men without prudence, temperance, fortitude, and justice, but of those whose lives were regulated by true piety, and whose virtues were therefore true, says, "For we are saved by hope: now hope which is seen is not hope; for what a man seeth, why doth he yet hope for? But if we hope for that we see not, then do we with patience wait for it." As, therefore, we are saved, so we are made happy by hope. And as we do not as yet possess a present, but look for a future salvation, so is it with our happiness, and this "with patience;" for we are encompassed with evils, which we ought patiently to endure, until we come to the ineffable enjoyment of unmixed good; for there shall be no longer anything to endure. Salvation, such as it shall be in the world to come, shall itself be our final happiness. And this happiness these philosophers refuse to believe in, because they do not see it, and attempt to fabricate for themselves a happiness in this life, based upon a virtue which is as deceitful as it is proud.

Chapter V: *Of the Social Life, Which, Though Most Desirable, is Frequently Disturbed by Many Distresses.*

We give a much more unlimited approval to their idea that the life of the wise man must be social. For how could the city of God (concerning which we are already writing no less than the nineteenth book of this work) either take a beginning or be developed, or attain its proper destiny, if the life of the saints were not a social life? But who can enumerate all the great grievances with which human society abounds in the misery of this mortal state? Who can weigh them? Hear how one of their comic writers makes one of his characters express the common feelings of all men in this matter: "I am married; this is one misery. Children are born to me; they are additional cares." What shall I say of the miseries of love which Terence also recounts—"slights, suspicions, quarrels, war to-day, peace tomorrow?" Is not human life full of such things? Do they not often occur even in honorable friendships? On all hands we experience these slights, suspicions, quarrels, war, all of which are undoubted evils; while, on the other hand, peace is a doubtful good, because we do not know the heart of our friend, and though we did know it today, we should be as ignorant of what it might be to-morrow. Who ought to be, or who are more friendly than those who live in the same family? And yet who can rely even upon this friendship, seeing that secret treachery has often broken it up, and produced enmity as bitter as the amity was sweet, or seemed sweet by the most perfect dissimulation? It is on this account that the words of Cicero so move the heart of every one, and provoke a sigh: "There are no snares more dangerous than those which lurk under the guise of duty or the name of relationship. For the man who is your declared foe you can easily baffle by precaution; but this hidden, intestine, and domestic danger not merely exists, but overwhelms you before you can foresee and examine it." It is also to this that allusion is made by the divine saying, "A man's foes are those of his own household"—words which one cannot hear without pain; for though a man have sufficient fortitude to endure it with equanimity, and sufficient sagacity to baffle the malice of a pretended friend, yet if he himself is a good man, he cannot but be greatly pained at the discovery of the perfidy of wicked men, whether they have always been wicked and merely feigned goodness, or have fallen from a better to a malicious disposition. If, then, home, the natural refuge from the ills of life, is itself not safe, what shall we say of the city, which, as it is larger, is so much the more filled with lawsuits civil and criminal, and is never free from the fear, if sometimes from the actual outbreak, of disturbing and bloody insurrections and civil wars?

Chapter VI: *Of the Error of Human Judgments When the Truth is Hidden.*

What shall I say of these judgments which men pronounce on men, and which are necessary in communities, whatever outward peace they enjoy? Melancholy and lamentable judgments they are, since the judges are men who cannot discern the consciences of those at their bar, and are therefore frequently compelled to put innocent witnesses to the torture to ascertain the truth regarding the crimes of other men. What shall I say of torture applied to the accused himself? He is tortured to discover whether he is guilty, so that, though innocent, he suffers most undoubted punishment for crime that is still doubtful, not because it is proved that he committed it, but because it is not ascertained that he did not commit it. Thus the ignorance of the judge frequently involves an innocent person in suffering. And what is still more unendurable—a thing, indeed, to be bewailed, and, if that were possible, watered with fountains of tears—is this, that when the judge puts the accused to the question, that he may not unwittingly put an innocent man to death, the result of this lamentable ignorance is that this very person, whom he tortured that he might not condemn him if innocent, is condemned to death both tortured and innocent. For if he has chosen, in obedience to the philosophical instructions to the wise man, to quit this life rather than endure any longer such tortures, he declares that he has committed the crime which in fact he has not committed. And when he has been condemned and put to death, the judge is still in ignorance whether he has put to death an innocent or a guilty person, though he put the accused to the torture for the very purpose of saving himself from condemning the innocent; and consequently he has both tortured an innocent man to discover his innocence, and has put him to death without discovering it. If such darkness shrouds social life, will a wise judge take his seat on the bench or no? Beyond question he will. For human society, which he thinks it a wickedness to abandon, constrains him and compels him to this duty. And he thinks it no wickedness that innocent witnesses are tortured regarding the crimes of which other men are accused; or that the accused are put to the torture, so that they are often overcome with anguish, and, though innocent, make false confessions regarding themselves, and are punished; or that, though they be not condemned to die, they often die during, or in consequence of, the torture; or that sometimes the accusers, who perhaps have been prompted by a desire to benefit society by bringing criminals to justice, are themselves condemned through the ignorance of the judge, because they are unable to prove the truth of their accusations though they are true, and because the witnesses lie, and the accused endures the torture without being moved to confession. These numerous and important evils he does not consider sins; for the wise judge does these things, not with any intention of doing harm, but because his ignorance compels him, and because human society claims him as a judge. But though we therefore acquit the judge of malice, we must none the less condemn human life as miserable. And if he is compelled to torture and punish the innocent because his office and his ignorance constrain him, is he a happy as well as a guiltless man? Surely it were proof of more profound considerateness and finer feeling were he to recognize the misery of these necessities, and shrink from his own implication in that misery; and had he any piety about him, he would cry to God "From my necessities deliver Thou me."

Chapter VII: *Of the Diversity of Languages, by Which the Intercourse of Men is Prevented; And of the Misery of Wars, Even of Those Called Just.*

After the state or city comes the world, the third circle of human society—the first being the house, and the second the city. And the world, as it is larger, so it is fuller of dangers, as the greater sea is the more dangerous. And here, in the first place, man is separated from man by the difference of languages. For if two men, each ignorant of the other's language, meet, and are not compelled to pass, but, on the contrary, to remain in company, dumb animals, though of different species, would more easily hold intercourse than they, human beings though they be. For their common nature is no help to friendliness when they are prevented by diversity of language from conveying their sentiments to one another; so that a man would more readily hold intercourse with his dog than with a foreigner. But the imperial city has endeavored to impose on subject nations not only her yoke, but her language, as a bond of peace, so that interpreters, far from being scarce, are numberless. This is true; but how many great wars, how much slaughter and bloodshed, have provided this unity! And though these are past, the end of these miseries has not yet come. For though there have never been wanting, nor are yet wanting, hostile nations beyond the empire, against whom wars have been and are waged, yet, supposing there were no such nations, the very extent of the empire itself has produced wars of a more obnoxious description—social and civil wars—and with these the whole race has been agitated, either by the actual conflict or the fear of a renewed outbreak. If I attempted to give an adequate description of these manifold disasters, these stern and lasting necessities, though I am quite unequal to the task, what limit could I set? But, say they, the wise man will wage just wars. As if he would not all the rather lament the necessity of just wars, if he remembers that he is a man; for if they were not just he would not wage them, and would therefore be delivered from all wars. For it is the wrongdoing of the opposing party which compels the wise man to wage just wars; and this wrongdoing, even though it gave rise to no war, would still be matter of grief to man because it is man's wrong-doing. Let every one, then, who thinks with pain on all these great evils, so horrible, so ruthless, acknowledge that this is misery. And if any one either endures or thinks of them without mental pain, this is a more miserable plight still, for he thinks himself happy because he has lost human feeling.

Chapter VIII: *That the Friendship of Good Men Cannot Be Securely Rested In, So Long as the Dangers of This Life Force Us to Be Anxious.*

In our present wretched condition we frequently mistake a friend for an enemy, and an enemy for a friend. And if we escape this pitiable blindness, is not the unfeigned confidence and mutual love of true and good friends our one solace in human society, filled as it is with misunderstandings and calamities? And yet the more friends we have, and the more widely they are scattered, the more numerous are our fears that some portion of the vast masses of the disasters of life may light upon them. For we are not only anxious lest they suffer from famine, war, disease, captivity, or the inconceivable horrors of slavery, but we are also affected with the much more painful dread that their friendship may be changed into perfidy, malice, and injustice. And when these contingencies actually occur—as they do the more frequently the more friends we have, and the more widely they are scattered—and when they come to our knowledge, who but the man who has experienced it can tell with what pangs the heart is torn? We would, in fact, prefer to hear that they were dead, although we could not without anguish hear of even this. For if their life has solaced us with the charms of friendship, can it be that their death should affect us with no sadness? He who will have none of this sadness must, if possible, have no friendly intercourse. Let him interdict or extinguish friendly affection; let him burst with ruthless insensibility the bonds of every human relationship; or let him contrive so to use them that no sweetness shall distill into his spirit. But if this is utterly impossible, how shall we contrive to feel no bitterness in the death of those whose life has been sweet to us? Hence arises that grief which affects the tender heart like a wound or a bruise, and which is healed by the application of kindly consolation. For though the cure is affected all the more easily and rapidly the better condition the soul is in, we must not on this account suppose that there is nothing at all to heal. Although, then, our present life is afflicted, sometimes in a milder, sometimes in a more painful degree, by the death of those very dear to us, and especially of useful public men, yet we would prefer to hear that such men were dead rather than to hear or perceive that they had fallen from the faith, or from virtue—in other words, that they were spiritually dead. Of this vast material for misery the earth is full, and therefore it is written, "Is not human life upon earth a trial?" And with the same reference the Lord says, "Woe to the world because of offenses!" and again, "Because iniquity abounded, the love of many shall wax cold." And hence we enjoy some gratification when our good friends die; for though their death leaves us in sorrow, we have the consolatory assurance that they are beyond the ills by which in this life even the best of men are broken down or corrupted, or are in danger of both results.

Chapter IX: *Of the Friendship of the Holy Angels, Which Men Cannot Be Sure of in This Life, Owing to the Deceit of the Demons Who Hold in Bondage the Worshipers of a Plurality of Gods.*

The philosophers who wished us to have the gods for our friends rank the friendship of the holy angels in the fourth circle of society, advancing now from the three circles of society on earth to the universe, and embracing heaven itself. And in this friendship we have indeed no fear that the angels will grieve us by their death or deterioration. But as we cannot mingle with them as familiarly as with men (which itself is one of the grievances of this life), and as Satan, as we read, sometimes transforms himself into an angel of light, to tempt those whom it is necessary to discipline, or just to deceive, there is great need of God's mercy to preserve us from making friends of demons in disguise, while we fancy we have good angels for our friends; for the astuteness and deceitfulness of these wicked spirits is equaled by their hurtfulness. And is this not a great misery of human life, that we are involved in such ignorance as, but for God's mercy, makes us a prey to these demons? And it is very certain that the philosophers of the godless city, who have maintained that the gods were their friends, had fallen a prey to the malignant demons who rule that city, and whose eternal punishment is to be shared by it. For the nature of these beings is sufficiently evinced by the sacred or rather sacrilegious observances which form their worship, and by the filthy games in which their crimes are celebrated, and which they themselves originated and exacted from their worshipers as a fit propitiation.

Chapter X: *The Reward Prepared for the Saints After They Have Endured the Trial of This Life.*

But not even the saints and faithful worshipers of the one true and most high God are safe from the manifold temptations and deceits of the demons. For in this abode of weakness, and in these wicked days, this state of anxiety has also its use, stimulating us to seek with keener longing for that security where peace is complete and unassailable. There we shall enjoy the gifts of nature, that is to say, all that God the Creator of all natures has bestowed upon ours—gifts not only good, but eternal—not only of the spirit, healed now by wisdom, but also of the body renewed by the resurrection. There the virtues shall no longer be struggling against any vice or evil, but shall enjoy the reward of victory, the eternal peace which no adversary shall disturb. This is the final blessedness, this the ultimate consummation, the unending end. Here, indeed, we are said to be blessed when we have such peace as can be enjoyed in a good life; but such blessedness is mere misery compared to that final felicity. When we mortals possess such peace as this mortal life can afford, virtue, if we are living rightly, makes a right use of the advantages of this peaceful condition; and when we have it not, virtue makes a good use even of the evils a man suffers. But this is true virtue, when it refers all the advantages it makes a good use of, and all that it does in making good use of good and evil things, and itself also, to that end in which we shall enjoy the best and greatest peace possible.

Chapter XI: *Of the Happiness of the Eternal Peace, Which Constitutes the End or True Perfection of the Saints.*

And thus we may say of peace, as we have said of eternal life, that it is the end of our good; and the rather because the Psalmist says of the city of God, the subject of this laborious work, "Praise the Lord, O Jerusalem; praise thy God, O Zion: for He hath strengthened the bars of thy gates; He hath blessed thy children within thee; who hath made thy borders peace." For when the bars of her gates shall be strengthened, none shall go in or come out from her; consequently we ought to understand the peace of her borders as that final peace we are wishing to declare. For even the mystical name of the city itself, that is, Jerusalem, means, as I have already said, "Vision of Peace." But as the word peace is employed in connection with things in this world in which certainly life eternal has no place, we have preferred to call the end or supreme good of this city life eternal rather than peace. Of this end the apostle says, "But now, being freed from sin, and become servants to God, ye have your fruit unto holiness, and the end life eternal." But, on the other hand, as those who are not familiar with Scripture may suppose that the life of the wicked is eternal life, either because of the immortality of the soul, which some of the philosophers even have recognized, or because of the endless punishment of the wicked, which forms a part of our faith, and which seems impossible unless the wicked live for ever, it may therefore be advisable, in order that every one may readily understand what we mean, to say that the end or supreme good of this city is either peace in eternal life, or eternal life in peace. For peace is a good so great, that even in this earthly and mortal life there is no word we hear with such pleasure, nothing we desire with such zest, or find to be more thoroughly gratifying. So that if we dwell for a little longer on this subject, we shall not, in my opinion, be wearisome to our readers, who will attend both for the sake of understanding what is the end of this city of which we speak, and for the sake of the sweetness of peace which is dear to all.

Chapter XII: *That Even the Fierceness of War and All the Disquietude of Men Make Towards This One End of Peace, Which Every Nature Desires.*

Whoever gives even moderate attention to human affairs and to our common nature, will recognize that if there is no man who does not wish to be joyful, neither is there any one who does not wish to have peace. For even they who make war desire nothing but victory—desire, that is to say, to attain to peace with glory. For what else is victory than the conquest of those who resist us? and when this is done there is peace. It is therefore with the desire for peace that wars are waged, even by those who take pleasure in exercising their warlike nature in command and battle. And hence it is obvious that peace is the end sought for by war. For every man seeks peace by waging war, but no man seeks war by making peace. For even they who intentionally interrupt the peace in which they are living have no hatred of peace, but only wish it changed into a peace that suits them better. They do not, therefore, wish to have no peace, but only one more to their mind. And in the case of sedition, when men have separated themselves from the community, they yet do not effect what they wish, unless they maintain some kind of peace with their fellow-conspirators. And therefore even robbers take care to maintain peace with their comrades, that they may with greater effect and greater safety invade the peace of other men. And if an individual happen to be of such unrivaled strength, and to be so jealous of partnership, that he trusts himself with no comrades, but makes his own plots, and commits depredations and murders on his own account, yet he maintains some shadow of peace with such persons as he is unable to kill, and from whom he wishes to conceal his deeds. In his own home, too, he makes it his aim to be at peace with his wife and children, and any other members of his household; for unquestionably their prompt obedience to his every look is a source of pleasure to him. And if this be not rendered, he is angry, he chides and punishes; and even by this storm he secures the calm peace of his own home, as occasion demands. For he sees that peace cannot be maintained unless all the members of the same domestic circle be subject to one head, such as he himself is in his own house. And therefore if a city or nation offered to submit itself to him, to serve him in the same style as he had made his household serve him, he would no longer lurk in a brigand's hiding-places, but lift his head in open day as a king, though the same coveteousness and wickedness should remain in him. And thus all men desire to have peace with their own circle whom they wish to govern as suits themselves. For even those whom they make war against they wish to make their own, and impose on them the laws of their own peace.

But let us suppose a man such as poetry and mythology speak of—a man so insociable and savage as to be called rather a semi-man than a man. Although, then, his kingdom was the solitude of a dreary cave, and he himself was so singularly bad-hearted that he was named Κακός, which is the Greek word for bad; though he had no wife to soothe him with endearing talk, no children to play with, no sons to do his bidding, no friend to enliven him with intercourse, not even his father Vulcan (though in one respect he was happier than his father, not having begotten a monster like himself); although he gave to no man, but took as he wished whatever he could, from whomsoever he could, when he could yet in that solitary den, the floor of which, as Virgil says, was always reeking with recent slaughter, there was nothing else than peace sought, a peace in which no one should molest him, or disquiet him with any assault or alarm. With his own body he desired to be at peace, and he was satisfied only in proportion as he had this peace. For he ruled his members, and they obeyed him; and for the sake of pacifying his mortal nature, which rebelled when it needed anything, and of allaying the sedition of hunger which threatened to banish the soul from the body, he made forays, slew, and devoured, but used the ferocity and savageness he displayed in these actions only for the preservation of his own life's peace. So that, had he been willing to make with other men the same peace which he made with himself in his own cave, he would neither have been called bad, nor a monster, nor a semi-man. Or if the appearance of his body and his vomiting smoky fires frightened men from having any dealings with him, perhaps his fierce ways arose not from a desire to do mischief, but from the necessity of finding a living. But he may have had no existence, or, at least, he was not such as the poets fancifully describe him, for they had to exalt Hercules, and did so at the expense of Cacus. It is better, then, to believe that such a man or semi-man never existed, and that this, in common with many other fancies of the poets, is mere fiction. For the most savage animals (and he is said to have been almost a wild beast) encompass their own species with a ring of protecting peace. They cohabit, beget, produce, suckle, and bring up their young, though very many of them are not gregarious, but solitary—not like sheep, deer, pigeons, starlings, bees, but such as lions, foxes, eagles, bats. For what tigress does not gently purr over her cubs, and lay aside her ferocity to fondle them? What kite, solitary as he is when circling over his prey, does not seek a mate, build a nest, hatch the eggs, bring up the young birds, and maintain with the mother of his family as peaceful a domestic alliance as he can? How much more powerfully do the laws of man's nature move him to hold fellowship and maintain peace with all men so far as in him lies, since even wicked men wage war to maintain the peace of their own circle, and wish that, if possible, all men belonged to them, that all men and things might serve but one head, and might, either through love or fear, yield themselves to peace with him! It is thus that pride in its perversity apes God. It abhors equality with other men under Him; but, instead of His rule, it seeks to impose a rule of its own upon its equals. It abhors, that is to say, the just peace of God, and loves its own unjust peace; but it cannot help loving peace of one kind or other. For there is no vice so clean contrary to nature that it obliterates even the faintest traces of nature.

He, then, who prefers what is right to what is wrong, and what is well-ordered to what is perverted, sees that the peace of unjust men is not worthy to be called peace in comparison with the peace of the just. And yet even what is perverted must of necessity be in harmony with, and in dependence on, and in some part of the order of things, for otherwise it would have no existence at all. Suppose a man hangs with his head downwards, this is certainly a perverted attitude of body and arrangement of its members; for that which nature requires to be above is beneath, and vice versa. This perversity disturbs the peace of the body, and is therefore painful. Nevertheless the spirit is at peace with its body, and labors for its preservation, and hence the suffering; but if it is banished from the body by its pains, then, so long as the bodily framework holds together, there is in the remains a kind of peace among the members, and hence the body remains suspended. And inasmuch as the earthly body tends towards the earth, and rests on the bond by which it is suspended, it tends thus to its natural peace, and the voice of its own weight demands a place for it to rest; and though now lifeless and without feeling, it does not fall from the peace that is natural to its place in creation, whether it already has it, or is tending towards it. For if you apply embalming preparations to prevent the bodily frame from mouldering and dissolving, a kind of peace still unites part to part, and keeps the whole body in a suitable place on the earth—in other words, in a place that is at peace with the body. If, on the other hand, the body receive no such care, but be left to the natural course, it is disturbed by exhalations that do not harmonize with one another, and that offend our senses; for it is this which is perceived in putrefaction until it is assimilated to the elements of the world, and particle by particle enters into peace with them. Yet throughout this process the laws of the most high Creator and Governor are strictly observed, for it is by Him the peace of the universe is administered. For although minute animals are produced from the carcass of a larger animal, all these little atoms, by the law of the same Creator, serve the animals they belong to in peace. And although the flesh of dead animals be eaten by others, no matter where it be carried, nor what it be brought into contact with, nor what it be converted and changed into, it still is ruled by the same laws which pervade all things for the conservation of every mortal race, and which bring things that fit one another into harmony.

Chapter XIII: *Of the Universal Peace Which the Law of Nature Preserves Through All Disturbances, and by Which Every One Reaches His Desert in a Way Regulated by the Just Judge.*

The peace of the body then consists in the duly proportioned arrangement of its parts. The peace of the irrational soul is the harmonious repose of the appetites, and that of the rational soul the harmony of knowledge and action. The peace of body and soul is the well-ordered and harmonious life and health of the living creature. Peace between man and God is the well-ordered obedience of faith to eternal law. Peace between man and man is well-ordered concord. Domestic peace is the well-ordered concord between those of the family who rule and those who obey. Civil peace is a similar concord among the citizens. The peace of the celestial city is the perfectly ordered and harmonious enjoyment of God, and of one another in God. The peace of all things is the tranquility of order. Order is the distribution which allots things equal and unequal, each to its own place. And hence, though the miserable, in so far as they are such, do certainly not enjoy peace, but are severed from that tranquility of order in which there is no disturbance, nevertheless, inasmuch as they are deservedly and justly miserable, they are by their very misery connected with order. They are not, indeed, conjoined with the blessed, but they are disjoined from them by the law of order. And though they are disquieted, their circumstances are notwithstanding adjusted to them, and consequently they have some tranquility of order, and therefore some peace. But they are wretched because, although not wholly miserable, they are not in that place where any mixture of misery is impossible. They would, however, be more wretched if they had not that peace which arises from being in harmony with the natural order of things. When they suffer, their peace is in so far disturbed; but their peace continues in so far as they do not suffer, and in so far as their nature continues to exist. As, then, there may be life without pain, while there cannot be pain without some kind of life, so there may be peace without war, but there cannot be war without some kind of peace, because war supposes the existence of some natures to wage it, and these natures cannot exist without peace of one kind or other.

And therefore there is a nature in which evil does not or even cannot exist; but there cannot be a nature in which there is no good. Hence not even the nature of the devil himself is evil, in so far as it is nature, but it was made evil by being perverted. Thus he did not abide in the truth, but could not escape the judgment of the Truth; he did not abide in the tranquility of order, but did not therefore escape the power of the Ordainer. The good imparted by God to his nature did not screen him from the justice of God by which order was preserved in his punishment; neither did God punish the good which He had created, but the evil which the devil had committed. God did not take back all He had imparted to his nature, but something He took and something He left, that there might remain enough to be sensible of the loss of what was taken. And this very sensibility to pain is evidence of the good which has been taken away and the good which has been left. For, were nothing good left, there could be no pain on account of the good which had been lost. For he who sins is still worse if he rejoices in his loss of righteousness. But he who is in pain, if he derives no benefit from it, mourns at least the loss of health. And as righteousness and health are both good things, and as the loss of any good thing is matter of grief, not of joy—if, at least, there is no compensation, as spiritual righteousness may compensate for the loss of bodily health—certainly it is more suitable for a wicked man to grieve in punishment than to rejoice in his fault. As, then, the joy of a sinner who has abandoned what is good is evidence of a bad will, so his grief for the good he has lost when he is punished is evidence of a good nature. For he who laments the peace his nature has lost is stirred to do so by some relics of peace which make his nature friendly to itself. And it is very just that in the final punishment the wicked and godless should in anguish bewail the loss of the natural advantages they enjoyed, and should perceive that they were most justly taken from them by that God whose benign liberality they had despised. God, then, the most wise Creator and most just Ordainer of all natures, who placed the human race upon earth as its greatest ornament, imparted to men some good things adapted to this life, to wit, temporal peace, such as we can enjoy in this life from health and safety and human fellowship, and all things needful for the preservation and recovery of this peace, such as the objects which are accommodated to our outward senses, light, night, the air, and waters suitable for us, and everything the body requires to sustain, shelter, heal, or beautify it: and all under this most equitable condition, that every man who made a good use of these advantages suited to the peace of this mortal condition, should receive ampler and better blessings, namely, the peace of immortality, accompanied by glory and honor in an endless life made fit for the enjoyment of God and of one another in God; but that he who used the present blessings badly should both lose them and should not receive the others.

Chapter XIV: *Of the Order and Law Which Obtain in Heaven and Earth, Whereby It Comes to Pass that Human Society Is Served by Those Who Rule It.*

The whole use, then, of things temporal has a reference to this result of earthly peace in the earthly community, while in the city of God it is connected with eternal peace. And therefore, if we were irrational animals, we should desire nothing beyond the proper arrangement of the parts of the body and the satisfaction of the appetites—nothing, therefore, but bodily comfort and abundance of pleasures, that the peace of the body might contribute to the peace of the soul. For if bodily peace be wanting, a bar is put to the peace even of the irrational soul, since it cannot obtain the gratification of its appetites. And these two together help out the mutual peace of soul and body, the peace of harmonious life and health. For as animals, by shunning pain, show that they love bodily peace, and, by pursuing pleasure to gratify their appetites, show that they love peace of soul, so their shrinking from death is a sufficient indication of their intense love of that peace which binds soul and body in close alliance. But, as man has a rational soul, he subordinates all this which he has in common with the beasts to the peace of his rational soul, that his intellect may have free play and may regulate his actions, and that he may thus enjoy the well-ordered harmony of knowledge and action which constitutes, as we have said, the peace of the rational soul. And for this purpose he must desire to be neither molested by pain, nor disturbed by desire, nor extinguished by death, that he may arrive at some useful knowledge by which he may regulate his life and manners. But, owing to the liability of the human mind to fall into mistakes, this very pursuit of knowledge may be a snare to him unless he has a divine Master, whom he may obey without misgiving, and who may at the same time give him such help as to preserve his own freedom. And because, so long as he is in this mortal body, he is a stranger to God, he walks by faith, not by sight; and he therefore refers all peace, bodily or spiritual or both, to that peace which mortal man has with the immortal God, so that he exhibits the well-ordered obedience of faith to eternal law. But as this divine Master inculcates two precepts—the love of God and the love of our neighbor—and as in these precepts a man finds three things he has to love—God, himself, and his neighbor—and that he who loves God loves himself thereby, it follows that he must endeavor to get his neighbor to love God, since he is ordered to love his neighbor as himself. He ought to make this endeavor in behalf of his wife, his children, his household, all within his reach, even as he would wish his neighbor to do the same for him if he needed it; and consequently he will be at peace, or in well-ordered concord, with all men, as far as in him lies. And this is the order of this concord, that a man, in the first place, injure no one, and, in the second, do good to every one he can reach. Primarily, therefore, his own household are his care, for the law of nature and of society gives him readier access to them and greater opportunity of serving them. And hence the apostle says,

"Now, if any provide not for his own, and specially for those of his own house, he hath denied the faith, and is worse than an infidel." This is the origin of domestic peace, or the well-ordered concord of those in the family who rule and those who obey. For they who care for the rest rule—the husband the wife, the parents the children, the masters the servants; and they who are cared for obey—the women their husbands, the children their parents, the servants their masters. But in the family of the just man who lives by faith and is as yet a pilgrim journeying on to the celestial city, even those who rule serve those whom they seem to command; for they rule not from a love of power, but from a sense of the duty they owe to others—not because they are proud of authority, but because they love mercy.

Chapter XV: *Of the Liberty Proper to Man's Nature, and the Servitude Introduced by Sin—A Servitude in Which the Man Whose Will is Wicked is the Slave of His Own Lust, Though He is Free So Far as Regards Other Men.*

This is prescribed by the order of nature: it is thus that God has created man. For "let them," He says, "have dominion over the fish of the sea, and over the fowl of the air, and over every creeping thing which creepeth on the earth." He did not intend that His rational creature, who was made in His image, should have dominion over anything but the irrational creation—not man over man, but man over the beasts. And hence the righteous men in primitive times were made shepherds of cattle rather than kings of men, God intending thus to teach us what the relative position of the creatures is, and what the desert of sin; for it is with justice, we believe, that the condition of slavery is the result of sin. And this is why we do not find the word "slave" in any part of Scripture until righteous Noah branded the sin of his son with this name. It is a name, therefore, introduced by sin and not by nature. The origin of the Latin word for slave is supposed to be found in the circumstance that those who by the law of war were liable to be killed were sometimes preserved by their victors, and were hence called servants. And these circumstances could never have arisen save through sin. For even when we wage a just war, our adversaries must be sinning; and every victory, even though gained by wicked men, is a result of the first judgment of God, who humbles the vanquished either for the sake of removing or of punishing their sins. Witness that man of God, Daniel, who, when he was in captivity, confessed to God his own sins and the sins of his people, and declares with pious grief that these were the cause of the captivity. The prime cause, then, of slavery is sin, which brings man under the dominion of his fellow—that which does not happen save by the judgment of God, with whom is no unrighteousness, and who knows how to award fit punishments to every variety of offence. But our Master in heaven says, "Every one who doeth sin is the servant of sin." And thus there are many wicked masters who have religious men as their slaves, and who are yet themselves in bondage; "for of whom a man is overcome, of the same is he brought in bondage." And beyond question it is a happier thing to be the slave of a man than of a lust; for even this very lust of ruling, to mention no others, lays waste men's hearts with the most ruthless dominion. Moreover, when men are subjected to one another in a peaceful order, the lowly position does as much good to the servant as the proud position does harm to the master. But by nature, as God first created us, no one is the slave either of man or of sin. This servitude is, however, penal, and is appointed by that law which enjoins the preservation of the natural order and forbids its disturbance; for if nothing had been done in violation of that law, there would have been nothing to restrain by penal servitude. And therefore the apostle admonishes slaves to be subject to their masters, and to serve them heartily and with good-will, so that, if they cannot be freed by their masters, they may themselves make their slavery in some sort free, by serving not in crafty fear, but in faithful love, until all unrighteousness pass away, and all principality and every human power be brought to nothing, and God be all in all.

Chapter XVI: *Of Equitable Rule.*

And therefore, although our righteous fathers had slaves, and administered their domestic affairs so as to distinguish between the condition of slaves and the heirship of sons in regard to the blessings of this life, yet in regard to the worship of God, in whom we hope for eternal blessings, they took an equally loving oversight of all the members of their household. And this is so much in accordance with the natural order, that the head of the household was called paterfamilias; and this name has been so generally accepted, that even those whose rule is unrighteous are glad to apply it to themselves. But those who are true fathers of their households desire and endeavor that all the members of their household, equally with their own children, should worship and win God, and should come to that heavenly home in which the duty of ruling men is no longer necessary, because the duty of caring for their everlasting happiness has also ceased; but, until they reach that home, masters ought to feel their position of authority a greater burden than servants their service. And if any member of the family interrupts the domestic peace by disobedience, he is corrected either by word or blow, or some kind of just and legitimate punishment, such as society permits, that he may himself be the better for it, and be readjusted to the family harmony from which he had dislocated himself. For as it is not benevolent to give a man help at the expense of some greater benefit he might receive, so it is not innocent to spare a man at the risk of his falling into graver sin. To be innocent, we must not only do harm to no man, but also restrain him from sin or punish his sin, so that either the man himself who is punished may profit by his experience, or others be warned by his example. Since, then, the house ought to be the beginning or element of the city, and every beginning bears reference to some end of its own kind, and every element to the integrity of the whole of which it is an element, it follows plainly enough that domestic peace has a relation to civic peace—in other words, that the well-ordered concord of domestic obedience and domestic rule has a relation to the well-ordered concord of civic obedience and civic rule. And therefore it follows, further, that the father of the family ought to frame his domestic rule in accordance with the law of the city, so that the household may be in harmony with the civic order.

Chapter XVII: *What Produces Peace, and What Discord, Between the Heavenly and Earthly Cities.*

But the families which do not live by faith seek their peace in the earthly advantages of this life; while the families which live by faith look for those eternal blessings which are promised, and use as pilgrims such advantages of time and of earth as do not fascinate and divert them from God, but rather aid them to endure with greater ease, and to keep down the number of those burdens of the corruptible body which weigh upon the soul. Thus the things necessary for this mortal life are used by both kinds of men and families alike, but each has its own peculiar and widely different aim in using them. The earthly city, which does not live by faith, seeks an earthly peace, and the end it proposes, in the well-ordered concord of civic obedience and rule, is the combination of men's wills to attain the things which are helpful to this life. The heavenly city, or rather the part of it which sojourns on earth and lives by faith, makes use of this peace only because it must, until this mortal condition which necessitates it shall pass away. Consequently, so long as it lives like a captive and a stranger in the earthly city, though it has already received the promise of redemption, and the gift of the Spirit as the earnest of it, it makes no scruple to obey the laws of the earthly city, whereby the things necessary for the maintenance of this mortal life are administered; and thus, as this life is common to both cities, so there is a harmony between them in regard to what belongs to it. But, as the earthly city has had some philosophers whose doctrine is condemned by the divine teaching, and who, being deceived either by their own conjectures or by demons, supposed that many gods must be invited to take an interest in human affairs, and assigned to each a separate function and a separate department—to one the body, to another the soul; and in the body itself, to one the head, to another the neck, and each of the other members to one of the gods; and in like manner, in the soul, to one god the natural capacity was assigned, to another education, to another anger, to another lust; and so the various affairs of life were assigned—cattle to one, corn to another, wine to another, oil to another, the woods to another, money to another, navigation to another, wars and victories to another, marriages to another, births and fecundity to another, and other things to other gods: and as the celestial city, on the other hand, knew that one God only was to be worshiped, and that to Him alone was due that service which the Greeks call λατρεία, and which can be given only to a god, it has come to pass that the two cities could not have common laws of religion, and that the heavenly city has been compelled in this matter to dissent, and to become obnoxious to those who think differently, and to stand the brunt of their anger and hatred and persecutions, except in so far as the minds of their enemies have been alarmed by the multitude of the Christians and quelled by the manifest protection of God accorded to them. This heavenly city, then, while it sojourns on earth, calls citizens out of all nations, and gathers together a society of pilgrims of all languages, not scrupling about diversities in the manners, laws, and institutions whereby earthly peace is secured and maintained, but recognizing that, however various these are, they all tend to one and the same end of earthly peace. It therefore is so far from rescinding and abolishing these diversities, that it even preserves and adopts them, so long only as no hindrance to the worship of the one supreme and true God is thus introduced. Even the heavenly city, therefore, while in its state of pilgrimage, avails itself of the peace of earth, and, so far as it can without injuring faith and godliness, desires and maintains a common agreement among men regarding the acquisition of the necessaries of life, and makes this earthly peace bear upon the peace of heaven; for this alone can be truly called and esteemed the peace of the reasonable creatures, consisting as it does in the perfectly ordered and harmonious enjoyment of God and of one another in God. When we shall have reached that peace, this mortal life shall give place to one that is eternal, and our body shall be no more this animal body which by its corruption weighs down the soul, but a spiritual body feeling no want, and in all its members subjected to the will. In its pilgrim state the heavenly city possesses this peace by faith; and by this faith it lives righteously when it refers to the attainment of that peace every good action towards God and man; for the life of the city is a social life.

Chapter XXV: *That Where There is No True Religion There are No True Virtues.*

For though the soul may seem to rule the body admirably, and the reason the vices, if the soul and reason do not themselves obey God, as God has commanded them to serve Him, they have no proper authority over the body and the vices. For what kind of mistress of the body and the vices can that mind be which is ignorant of the true God, and which, instead of being subject to His authority, is prostituted to the corrupting influences of the most vicious demons? It is for this reason that the virtues which it seems to itself to possess, and by which it restrains the body and the vices that it may obtain and keep what it desires, are rather vices than virtues so long as there is no reference to God in the matter. For although some suppose that virtues which have a reference only to themselves, and are desired only on their own account, are yet true and genuine virtues, the fact is that even then they are inflated with pride, and are therefore to be reckoned vices rather than virtues. For as that which gives life to the flesh is not derived from flesh, but is above it, so that which gives blessed life to man is not derived from man, but is something above him; and what I say of man is true of every celestial power and virtue whatsoever.

Chapter XXVI: *Of the Peace Which is Enjoyed by the People that are Alienated from God, and the Use Made of It by the People of God in the Time of Its Pilgrimage.*

Wherefore, as the life of the flesh is the soul, so the blessed life of man is God, of whom the sacred writings of the Hebrews say, "Blessed is the people whose God is the Lord." Miserable, therefore, is the people which is alienated from God. Yet even this people has a peace of its own which is not to be lightly esteemed, though, indeed, it shall not in the end enjoy it, because it makes no good use of it before the end. But it is our interest that it enjoy this peace meanwhile in this life; for as long as the two cities are commingled, we also enjoy the peace of Babylon. For from Babylon the people of God is so freed that it meanwhile sojourns in its company. And therefore the apostle also admonished the Church to pray for kings and those in authority, assigning as the reason, "that we may live a quiet and tranquil life in all godliness and love." And the prophet Jeremiah, when predicting the captivity that was to befall the ancient people of God, and giving them the divine command to go obediently to Babylonia, and thus serve their God, counseled them also to pray for Babylonia, saying, "In the peace thereof shall ye have peace"—the temporal peace which the good and the wicked together enjoy.

Chapter XXVII: *That the Peace of Those Who Serve God Cannot in This Mortal Life Be Apprehended in Its Perfection.*

But the peace which is peculiar to ourselves we enjoy now with God by faith, and shall hereafter enjoy eternally with Him by sight. But the peace which we enjoy in this life, whether common to all or peculiar to ourselves, is rather the solace of our misery than the positive enjoyment of felicity. Our very righteousness, too, though true in so far as it has respect to the true good, is yet in this life of such a kind that it consists rather in the remission of sins than in the perfecting of virtues. Witness the prayer of the whole city of God in its pilgrim state, for it cries to God by the mouth of all its members, "Forgive us our debts as we forgive our debtors. And this prayer is efficacious not for those whose faith is "without works and dead," but for those whose faith "worketh by love." For as reason, though subjected to God, is yet "pressed down by the corruptible body," so long as it is in this mortal condition, it has not perfect authority over vice, and therefore this prayer is needed by the righteous. For though it exercises authority, the vices do not submit without a struggle. For however well one maintains the conflict, and however thoroughly he has subdued these enemies, there steals in some evil thing, which, if it does not find ready expression in act, slips out by the lips, or insinuates itself into the thought; and therefore his peace is not full so long as he is at war with his vices. For it is a doubtful conflict he wages with those that resist, and his victory over those that are defeated is not secure, but full of anxiety and effort. Amidst these temptations, therefore, of all which it has been summarily said in the divine oracles, "Is not human life upon earth a temptation?" who but a proud man can presume that he so lives that he has no need to say to God, "Forgive us our debts?" And such a man is not great, but swollen and puffed up with vanity, and is justly resisted by Him who abundantly gives grace to the humble. Whence it is said, "God resisteth the proud, but giveth grace to the humble." In this, then, consists the righteousness of a man, that he submit himself to God, his body to his soul, and his vices, even when they rebel, to his reason, which either defeats or at least resists them; and also that he beg from God grace to do his duty, and the pardon of his sins, and that he render to God thanks for all the blessings he receives. But, in that final peace to which all our righteousness has reference, and for the sake of which it is maintained, as our nature shall enjoy a sound immortality and incorruption, and shall have no more vices, and as we shall experience no resistance either from ourselves or from others, it will not be necessary that reason should rule vices which no longer exist, but God shall rule the man, and the soul shall rule the body, with a sweetness and facility suitable to the felicity of a life which is done with bondage. And this condition shall there be eternal, and we shall be assured of its eternity; and thus the peace of this blessedness and the blessedness of this peace shall be the supreme good.

Chapter XXVIII: *The End of the Wicked.*

But, on the other hand, they who do not belong to this city of God shall inherit eternal misery, which is also called the second death, because the soul shall then be separated from God its life, and therefore cannot be said to live, and the body shall be subjected to eternal pains. And consequently this second death shall be the more severe, because no death shall terminate it. But war being contrary to peace, as misery to happiness, and life to death, it is not without reason asked what kind of war can be found in the end of the wicked answering to the peace which is declared to be the end of the righteous? The person who puts this question has only to observe what it is in war that is hurtful and destructive, and he shall see that it is nothing else than the mutual opposition and conflict of things.

And can he conceive a more grievous and bitter war than that in which the will is so opposed to passion, and passion to the will, that their hostility can never be terminated by the victory of either, and in which the violence of pain so conflicts with the nature of the body, that neither yields to the other? For in this life, when this conflict has arisen, either pain conquers and death expels the feeling of it, or nature conquers and health expels the pain. But in the world to come the pain continues that it may torment, and the nature endures that it may be sensible of it; and neither ceases to exist, lest punishment also should cease. Now, as it is through the last judgment that men pass to these ends, the good to the supreme good, the evil to the supreme evil, I will treat of this judgment in the following book.

Book Twenty

Chapter VI: *What is the First Resurrection, and What the Second.*

After that He adds the words, "Verily, verily, I say unto you, The hour is coming, and now is, when the dead shall hear the voice of the Son of God; and they that hear shall live. For as the Father hath life in Himself; so hath He given to the Son to have life in Himself." As yet He does not speak of the second resurrection, that is, the resurrection of the body, which shall be in the end, but of the first, which now is. It is for the sake of making this distinction that He says, "The hour is coming, and now is." Now this resurrection regards not the body, but the soul. For souls, too, have a death of their own in wickedness and sins, whereby they are the dead of whom the same lips say, "Suffer the dead to bury their dead"—that is, let those who are dead in soul bury them that are dead in body. It is of these dead, then—the dead in ungodliness and wickedness—that He says, "The hour is coming, and now is, when the dead shall hear the voice of the Son of God; and they that hear shall live." "They that hear," that is, they who obey, believe, and persevere to the end. Here no difference is made between the good and the bad. For it is good for all men to hear His voice and live, by passing to the life of godliness from the death of ungodliness. Of this death the Apostle Paul says, "Therefore all are dead, and He died for all, that they which live should not henceforth live unto themselves, but unto Him which died for them and rose again." Thus all, without one exception, were dead in sins, whether original or voluntary sins, sins of ignorance, or sins committed against knowledge; and for all the dead there died the one only person who lived, that is, who had no sin whatever, in order that they who live by the remission of their sins should live, not to themselves, but to Him who died for all, for our sins, and rose again for our justification, that we, believing in Him who justifies the ungodly, and being justified from ungodliness or quickened from death, may be able to attain to the first resurrection which now is. For in this first resurrection none have a part save those who shall be eternally blessed; but in the second, of which He goes on to speak, all, as we shall learn, have a part, both the blessed and the wretched. The one is the resurrection of mercy, the other of judgment. And therefore it is written in the psalm, "I will sing of mercy and of judgment: unto Thee, O Lord, will I sing."

And of this judgment He went on to say, "And hath given Him authority to execute judgment also, because He is the Son of man." Here He shows that He will come to judge in that flesh in which He had come to be judged. For it is to show this He says, "because He is the Son of man." And then follow the words for our purpose: "Marvel not at this: for the hour is coming, in the which all that are in the graves shall hear His voice, and shall come forth; they that have done good, unto the resurrection of life; and they that have done evil, unto the resurrection of judgment." This judgment He uses here in the same sense as a little before, when He says, "He that heareth my word, and believeth on Him that sent me, hath everlasting life, and shall not come into judgment, but is passed from death to life;" i.e., by having a part in the first resurrection, by which a transition from death to life is made in this present time, he shall not come into damnation, which He mentions by the name of judgment, as also in the place where He says, "but they that have done evil unto the resurrection of judgment," i.e., of damnation. He, therefore, who would not be damned in the second resurrection, let him rise in the first. For "the hour is coming, and now is, when the dead shall hear the voice of the Son of God; and they that hear shall live," i.e., shall not come into damnation, which is called the second death; into which death, after the second or bodily resurrection, they shall be hurled who do not rise in the first or spiritual resurrection. For "the hour is coming" (but here He does not say, "and now is," because it shall come in the end of the world in the last and greatest judgment of God) "when all that are in the graves shall hear His voice and shall come forth." He does not say, as in the first resurrection, "And they that Hear shall live." For all shall not live, at least with such life as ought alone to be called life because it alone is blessed. For some kind of life they must have in order to hear, and come forth from the graves in their rising bodies. And why all shall not live He teaches in the words that follow: "They that have done good, to the resurrection of life"—these are they who shall live; "but they that have done evil, to the resurrection of judgment"—these are they who shall not live, for they shall die in the second death. They have done evil because their life has been evil; and their life has been evil because it has not been renewed in the first or spiritual resurrection which now is, or because they have not persevered to the end in their renewed life. As, then, there are two regenerations, of which I have already made mention—the one according to faith, and which takes place in the present life by means of baptism; the other according to the flesh, and which shall be accomplished in its incorruption and immortality by means of the great and final judgment—so are there also two resurrections—the one the first and spiritual resurrection, which has place in this life, and preserves us from coming into the second death; the other the second, which does not occur now, but in the end of the world, and which is of the body, not of the soul, and which by the last judgment shall dismiss some into the second death, others into that life which has no death.

Chapter VII: *What is Written in the Revelation of John Regarding the Two Resurrections, and the Thousand Years, and What May Reasonably Be Held on These Points.*

The evangelist John has spoken of these two resurrections in the book which is called the Apocalypse, but in such a way that some Christians do not understand the first of the two, and so construe the passage into ridiculous fancies. For the Apostle John says in the aforesaid book, "And I saw an angel come down from heaven... Blessed and holy is he that hath part in the first resurrection: on such the second death hath no power; but they shall be priests of God and of Christ, and shall reign with Him a thousand years." Those who, on the strength of this passage, have suspected that the first resurrection is future and bodily, have been moved, among other things, specially by the number of a thousand years, as if it were a fit thing that the saints should thus enjoy a kind of Sabbath-rest during that period, a holy leisure after the labors of the six thousand years since man was created, and was on account of his great sin dismissed from the blessedness of paradise into the woes of this mortal life, so that thus, as it is written, "One day is with the Lord as a thousand years, and a thousand years as one day," there should follow on the completion of six thousand years, as of six days, a kind of seventh day Sabbath in the succeeding thousand years; and that it is for this purpose the saints rise, viz., to celebrate this Sabbath. And this opinion would not be objectionable, if it were believed that the joys of the saints in that Sabbath shall be spiritual, and consequent on the presence of God; for I myself, too, once held this opinion. But, as they assert that those who then rise again shall enjoy the leisure of immoderate carnal banquets, furnished with an amount of meat and drink such as not only to shock the feeling of the temperate, but even to surpass the measure of credulity itself, such assertions can be believed only by the carnal. They who do believe them are called by the spiritual Chiliasts, which we may literally reproduce by the name Millenarians. It were a tedious process to refute these opinions point by point: we prefer proceeding to show how that passage of Scripture should be understood.

The Lord Jesus Christ Himself says, "No man can enter into a strong man's house, and spoil his goods, except he first bind the strong man"—meaning by the strong man the devil, because he had power to take captive the human race; and meaning by his goods which he was to take, those who had been held by the devil in divers sins and iniquities, but were to become believers in Himself. It was then for the binding of this strong one that the apostle saw in the Apocalypse "an angel coming down from heaven, having the key of the abyss, and a chain in his hand. And he laid hold," he says, "on the dragon, that old serpent, which is called the devil and Satan, and bound him a thousand years"—that is, bridled and restrained his power so that he could not seduce and gain possession of those who were to be freed. Now the thousand years may be understood in two ways, so far as occurs to me: either because these things happen in the sixth thousand of years or sixth millennium (the latter part of which is now passing), as if during the sixth day, which is to be followed by a Sabbath which has no evening, the endless rest of the saints, so that, speaking of a part under the name of the whole, he calls the last part of the millennium—the part, that is, which had yet to expire before the end of the world—a thousand years; or he used the thousand years as an equivalent for the whole duration of this world, employing the number of perfection to mark the fullness of time. For a thousand is the cube of ten. For ten times ten makes a hundred, that is; the square on a plane superficies. But to give this superficies height, and make it a cube, the hundred is again multiplied by ten, which gives a thousand. Besides, if a hundred is sometimes used for totality, as when the Lord said by way of promise to him that left all and followed Him "He shall receive in this world an hundredfold;" of which the apostle gives, as it were, an explanation when he says, "As having nothing, yet possessing all things"—for even of old it had been said, The whole world is the wealth of a believer—with how much greater reason is a thousand put for totality since it is the cube, while the other is only the square? And for the same reason we cannot better interpret the words of the psalm, "He hath been mindful of His covenant for ever, the word which He commanded to a thousand generations," than by understanding it to mean "to all generations."

"And he cast him into the abyss"—i.e., cast the devil into the abyss. By the abyss is meant the countless multitude of the wicked whose hearts are unfathomably deep in malignity against the Church of God; not that the devil was not there before, but he is said to be cast in thither, because, when prevented from harming believers, he takes more complete possession of the ungodly. For that man is more abundantly possessed by the devil who is not only alienated from God, but also gratuitously hates those who serve God. "And shut him up, and set a seal upon him, that he should deceive the nations no more till the thousand years should be fulfilled." "Shut him up"—i.e., prohibited him from going out, from doing what was forbidden. And the addition of "set a seal upon him" seems to me to mean that it was designed to keep it a secret who belonged to the devil's party and who did not. For in this world this is a secret, for we cannot tell whether even the man who seems to stand shall fall, or whether he who seems to lie shall rise again. But by the chain and prison-house of this interdict the devil is prohibited and restrained from seducing those nations which belong to Christ, but which he formerly seduced or held in subjection. For before the foundation of the world God chose to rescue these from the power of darkness, and to translate them into the kingdom of the Son of His love, as the apostle says. For what Christian is not aware that he seduces nations even now, and draws them with himself to eternal punishment, but not those predestined to eternal life? And let no one be dismayed by the circumstance that the devil often seduces even those who have been regenerated in Christ, and begun to walk in God's way.

For "the Lord knoweth them that are His," and of these the devil seduces none to eternal damnation. For it is as God, from whom nothing is hid even of things future, that the Lord knows them; not as a man, who sees a man at the present time (if he can be said to see one whose heart he does not see), but does not see even himself so far as to be able to know what kind of person he is to be. The devil, then, is bound and shut up in the abyss that he may not seduce the nations from which the Church is gathered, and which he formerly seduced before the Church existed. For it is not said "that he should not seduce any man," but "that he should not seduce the nations"—meaning, no doubt, those among which the Church exists—"till the thousand years should be fulfilled"—i.e., either what remains of the sixth day which consists of a thousand years, or all the years which are to elapse till the end of the world.

The words, "that he should not seduce the nations till the thousand years should be fulfilled," are not to be understood as indicating that afterwards he is to seduce only those nations from which the predestined Church is composed, and from seducing whom he is restrained by that chain and imprisonment; but they are used in conformity with that usage frequently employed in Scripture and exemplified in the psalm, "So our eyes wait upon the Lord our God, until He have mercy upon us"—not as if the eyes of His servants would no longer wait upon the Lord their God when He had mercy upon them. Or the order of the words is unquestionably this, "And he shut him up and set a seal upon him, till the thousand years should be fulfilled;" and the interposed clause, "that he should seduce the nations no more," is not to be understood in the connection in which it stands, but separately, and as if added afterwards, so that the whole sentence might be read, "And He shut him up and set a seal upon him till the thousand years should be fulfilled, that he should seduce the nations no more"—i.e., he is shut up till the thousand years be fulfilled, on this account, that he may no more deceive the nations.

Chapter VIII: *Of the Binding and Loosing of the Devil.*

"After that," says John, "he must be loosed a little season." If the binding and shutting up of the devil means his being made unable to seduce the Church, must his loosing be the recovery of this ability? By no means. For the Church predestined and elected before the foundation of the world, the Church of which it is said, "The Lord knoweth them that are His," shall never be seduced by him. And yet there shall be a Church in this world even when the devil shall be loosed, as there has been since the beginning, and shall be always, the places of the dying being filled by new believers. For a little after John says that the devil, being loosed, shall draw the nations whom he has seduced in the whole world to make war against the Church, and that the number of these enemies shall be as the sand of the sea. "And they went up on the breadth of the earth, and compassed the camp of the saints about, and the beloved city: and fire came down from God out of heaven and devoured them. And the devil who seduced them was cast into the lake of fire and brimstone, where the beast and the false prophet are, and shall be tormented day and night for ever and ever." This relates to the last judgment, but I have thought fit to mention it now, lest any one might suppose that in that short time during which the devil shall be loose there shall be no Church upon earth, whether because the devil finds no Church, or destroys it by manifold persecutions. The devil, then, is not bound during the whole time which this book embraces—that is, from the first coming of Christ to the end of the world, when He shall come the second time—not bound in this sense, that during this interval, which goes by the name of a thousand years, he shall not seduce the Church, for not even when loosed shall he seduce it. For certainly if his being bound means that he is not able or not permitted to seduce the Church, what can the loosing of him mean but his being able or permitted to do so? But God forbid that such should be the case! But the binding of the devil is his being prevented from the exercise of his whole power to seduce men, either by violently forcing or fraudulently deceiving them into taking part with him. If he were during so long a period permitted to assail the weakness of men, very many persons, such as God would not wish to expose to such temptation, would have their faith overthrown, or would be prevented from believing; and that this might not happen, he is bound.

But when the short time comes he shall be loosed. For he shall rage with the whole force of himself and his angels for three years and six months; and those with whom he makes war shall have power to withstand all his violence and stratagems. And if he were never loosed, his malicious power would be less patent, and less proof would be given of the steadfast fortitude of the holy city: it would, in short, be less manifest what good use the Almighty makes of his great evil. For the Almighty does not absolutely seclude the saints from his temptation, but shelters only their inner man, where faith resides, that by outward temptation they may grow in grace. And He binds him that he may not, in the free and eager exercise of his malice, hinder or destroy the faith of those countless weak persons, already believing or yet to believe, from whom the Church must be increased and completed; and he will in the end loose him, that the city of God may see how mighty an adversary it has conquered, to the great glory of its Redeemer, Helper, Deliverer. And what are we in comparison with those believers and saints who shall then exist, seeing that they shall be tested by the loosing of an enemy with whom we make war at the greatest peril even when he is bound? Although it is also certain that even in this intervening period there have been and are some soldiers of Christ so wise and strong, that if they were to be alive in this mortal condition at the time of his loosing, they would both most wisely guard against, and most patiently endure, all his snares and assaults.

Now the devil was thus bound not only when the Church began to be more and more widely extended among the nations beyond Judea, but is now and shall be bound till the end of the world, when he is to be loosed. Because even now men are, and doubtless to the end of the world shall be, converted to the faith from the unbelief in which he held them. And this strong one is bound in each instance in which he is spoiled of one of his goods; and the abyss in which he is shut up is not at an end when those die who were alive when first he was shut up in it, but these have been succeeded, and shall to the end of the world be succeeded, by others born after them with a like hate of the Christians, and in the depth of whose blind hearts he is continually shut up as in an abyss. But it is a question whether, during these three years and six months when he shall be loose, and raging with all his force, any one who has not previously believed shall attach himself to the faith. For how in that case would the words hold good, "Who entereth into the house of a strong one to spoil his goods, unless first he shall have bound the strong one?" Consequently this verse seems to compel us to believe that during that time, short as it is, no one will be added to the Christian community, but that the devil will make war with those who have previously become Christians, and that, though some of these may be conquered and desert to the devil, these do not belong to the predestinated number of the sons of God. For it is not without reason that John, the same apostle as wrote this Apocalypse, says in his epistle regarding certain persons, "They went out from us, but they were not of us; for if they had been of us, they would no doubt have remained with us." But what shall become of the little ones? For it is beyond all belief that in these days there shall not be found some Christian children born, but not yet baptized, and that there shall not also be some born during that very period; and if there be such, we cannot believe that their parents shall not find some way of bringing them to the laver of regeneration. But if this shall be the case, how shall these goods be snatched from the devil when he is loose, since into his house no man enters to spoil his goods unless he has first bound him? On the contrary, we are rather to believe that in these days there shall be no lack either of those who fall away from, or of those who attach themselves to the Church; but there shall be such resoluteness, both in parents to seek baptism for their little ones, and in those who shall then first believe, that they shall conquer that strong one, even though unbound—that is, shall both vigilantly comprehend, and patiently bear up against him, though employing such wiles and putting forth such force as he never before used; and thus they shall be snatched from him even though unbound. And yet the verse of the Gospel will not be untrue, "Who entereth into the house of the strong one to spoil his goods, unless he shall first have bound the strong one?" For in accordance with this true saying that order is observed—the strong one first bound, and then his goods spoiled; for the Church is so increased by the weak and strong from all nations far and near, that by its most robust faith in things divinely predicted and accomplished, it shall be able to spoil the goods of even the unbound devil. For as we must own that, "when iniquity abounds, the love of many waxes cold," and that those who have not been written in the book of life shall in large numbers yield to the severe and unprecedented persecutions and stratagems of the devil now loosed, so we cannot but think that not only those whom that time shall find sound in the faith, but also some who till then shall be without, shall become firm in the faith they have hitherto rejected and mighty to conquer the devil even though unbound, God's grace aiding them to understand the Scriptures, in which, among other things, there is foretold that very end which they themselves see to be arriving. And if this shall be so, his binding is to be spoken of as preceding, that there might follow a spoiling of him both bound and loosed; for it is of this it is said, "Who shall enter into the house of the strong one to spoil his goods, unless he shall first have bound the strong one?"

Chapter IX: *What the Reign of the Saints with Christ for a Thousand Years Is, and How It Differs from the Eternal Kingdom.*

But while the devil is bound, the saints reign with Christ during the same thousand years, understood in the same way, that is, of the time of His first coming. For, leaving out of account that kingdom concerning which He shall say in the end, "Come, ye blessed of my Father, take possession of the kingdom prepared for you," the Church could not now be called His kingdom or the kingdom of heaven unless His saints were even now reigning with Him, though in another and far different way; for to His saints He says, "Lo, I am with you always, even to the end of the world." Certainly it is in this present time that the scribe well instructed in the kingdom of God, and of whom we have already spoken, brings forth from his treasure things new and old. And from the Church those reapers shall gather out the tares which He suffered to grow with the wheat till the harvest, as He explains in the words "The harvest is the end of the world; and the reapers are the angels. As therefore the tares are gathered together and burned with fire, so shall it be in the end of the world. The Son of man shall send His angels, and they shall gather out of His kingdom all offenses." Can He mean out of that kingdom in which are no offenses? Then it must be out of His present kingdom, the Church, that they are gathered. So He says, "He that breaketh one of the least of these commandments, and teacheth men so, shall be called least in the kingdom of heaven: but he that doeth and teacheth thus shall be called great in the kingdom of heaven." He speaks of both as being in the kingdom of heaven, both the man who does not perform the commandments which He teaches—for "to break" means not to keep, not to perform—and the man who does and teaches as He did; but the one He calls least, the other great. And He immediately adds, "For I say unto you, that except your righteousness exceed that of the scribes and Pharisees"—that is, the righteousness of those who break what they teach; for of the scribes and Pharisees He elsewhere says, "For they say and do not"—unless therefore, your righteousness exceed theirs that is, so that you do not break but rather do what you teach, "ye shall not enter the kingdom of heaven." We must understand in one sense the kingdom of heaven in which exist together both he who breaks what he teaches and he who does it, the one being least, the other great, and in another sense the kingdom of heaven into which only he who does what he teaches shall enter. Consequently, where both classes exist, it is the Church as it now is, but where only the one shall exist, it is the Church as it is destined to be when no wicked person shall be in her. Therefore the Church even now is the kingdom of Christ, and the kingdom of heaven. Accordingly, even now His saints reign with Him, though otherwise than as they shall reign hereafter; and yet, though the tares grow in the Church along with the wheat, they do not reign with Him. For they reign with Him who do what the apostle says, "If ye be risen with Christ, mind the things which are above, where Christ sitteth at the right hand of God. Seek those things which are above, not the things which are on the earth." Of such persons he also says that their conversation is in heaven. In fine, they reign with Him who are so in His kingdom that they themselves are His kingdom. But in what sense are those the kingdom of Christ who, to say no more, though they are in it until all offenses are gathered out of it at the end of the world, yet seek their own things in it, and not the things that are Christ's?

It is then of this kingdom militant, in which conflict with the enemy is still maintained, and war carried on with warring lusts, or government laid upon them as they yield, until we come to that most peaceful kingdom in which we shall reign without an enemy, and it is of this first resurrection in the present life, that the Apocalypse speaks in the words just quoted. For, after saying that the devil is bound a thousand years and is afterwards loosed for a short season, it goes on to give a sketch of what the Church does or of what is done in the Church in those days, in the words, "And I saw seats and them that sat upon them, and judgment was given." It is not to be supposed that this refers to the last judgment, but to the seats of the rulers and to the rulers themselves by whom the Church is now governed. And no better interpretation of judgment being given can be produced than that which we have in the words, "What ye bind on earth shall be bound in heaven; and what ye loose on earth shall be loosed in heaven." Whence the apostle says, "What have I to do with judging them that are without? do not ye judge them that are within?" "And the souls," says John, "of those who were slain for the testimony of Jesus and for the word of God"—understanding what he afterwards says, "reigned with Christ a thousand years"—that is, the souls of the martyrs not yet restored to their bodies. For the souls of the pious dead are not separated from the Church, which even now is the kingdom of Christ; otherwise there would be no remembrance made of them at the altar of God in the partaking of the body of Christ, nor would it do any good in danger to run to His baptism, that we might not pass from this life without it; nor to reconciliation, if by penitence or a bad conscience any one may be severed from His body. For why are these things practised, if not because the faithful, even though dead, are His members? Therefore, while these thousand years run on, their souls reign with Him, though not as yet in conjunction with their bodies. And therefore in another part of this same book we read, "Blessed are the dead who die in the Lord from henceforth and now, saith the Spirit, that they may rest from their labors; for their works do follow them." The Church, then, begins its reign with Christ now in the living and in the dead. For, as the apostle says, "Christ died that He might be Lord both of the living and of the dead." But he mentioned the souls of the martyrs only, because they who have contended even to death for the truth, themselves principally reign after death; but, taking the part for the whole, we understand the words of all others who belong to the Church, which is the kingdom of Christ.

As to the words following, "And if any have not worshiped the beast nor his image, nor have received his inscription on their forehead, or on their hand," we must take them of both the living and the dead. And what this beast is, though it requires a more careful investigation, yet it is not inconsistent with the true faith to understand it of the ungodly city itself, and the community of unbelievers set in opposition to the faithful people and the city of God. "His image" seems to me to mean his simulation, to wit, in those men who profess to believe, but live as unbelievers. For they pretend to be what they are not, and are called Christians, not from a true likeness but from a deceitful image. For to this beast belong not only the avowed enemies of the name of Christ and His most glorious city, but also the tares which are to be gathered out of His kingdom, the Church, in the end of the world. And who are they who do not worship the beast and his image, if not those who do what the apostle says, "Be not yoked with unbelievers?" For such do not worship, i.e., do not consent, are not subjected; neither do they receive the inscription, the brand of crime, on their forehead by their profession, on their hand by their practice. They, then, who are free from these pollutions, whether they still live in this mortal flesh, or are dead, reign with Christ even now, through this whole interval which is indicated by the thousand years, in a fashion suited to this time.

"The rest of them," he says, "did not live." For now is the hour when the dead shall hear the voice of the Son of God, and they that hear shall live; and the rest of them shall not live. The words added, "until the thousand years are finished," mean that they did not live in the time in which they ought to have lived by passing from death to life. And therefore, when the day of the bodily resurrection arrives, they shall come out of their graves, not to life, but to judgment, namely, to damnation, which is called the second death. For whosoever has not lived until the thousand years be finished, i.e., during this whole time in which the first resurrection is going on—whosoever has not heard the voice of the Son of God, and passed from death to life—that man shall certainly in the second resurrection, the resurrection of the flesh, pass with his flesh into the second death. For he goes to say "This is the first resurrection. Blessed and holy is he that hath part in the first resurrection," or who experiences it.

Now he experiences it who not only revives from the death of sin, but continues in this renewed life. "In these the second death hath no power." Therefore it has power in the rest, of whom he said above, "The rest of them did not live until the thousand years were finished;" for in this whole intervening time called a thousand years, however lustily they lived in the body, they were not quickened to life out of that death in which their wickedness held them, so that by this revived life they should become partakers of the first resurrection, and so the second death should have no power over them.

Chapter X: *What is to Be Replied to Those Who Think that Resurrection Pertains Only to Bodies and Not to Souls.*

There are some who suppose that resurrection can be predicated only of the body, and therefore they contend that this first resurrection (of the Apocalypse) is a bodily resurrection. For, say they, "to rise again" can only be said of things that fall. Now, bodies fall in death. There cannot, therefore, be a resurrection of souls, but of bodies. But what do they say to the apostle who speaks of a resurrection of souls? For certainly it was in the inner and not the outer man that those had risen again to whom he says, "If ye have risen with Christ, mind the things that are above." The same sense he elsewhere conveyed in other words, saying, "That as Christ has risen from the dead by the glory of the Father, so we also may walk in newness of life." So, too, "Awake thou that sleepest, and arise from the dead, and Christ shall give thee light." As to what they say about nothing being able to rise again but what falls, whence they conclude that resurrection pertains to bodies only, and not to souls, because bodies fall, why do they make nothing of the words, "Ye that fear the Lord, wait for His mercy; and go not aside lest ye fall;" and "To his own Master he stands or falls;" and "He that thinketh he standeth, let him take heed lest he fall?" For I fancy this fall that we are to take heed against is a fall of the soul, not of the body. If, then, rising again belongs to things that fall, and souls fall, it must be owned that souls also rise again. To the words, "In them the second death hath no power," are added the words, "but they shall be priests of God and Christ, and shall reign with Him a thousand years;" and this refers not to the bishops alone, and presbyters, who are now specially called priests in the Church; but as we call all believers Christians on account of the mystical chrism, so we call all priests because they are members of the one Priest. Of them the Apostle Peter says, "A holy people, a royal priesthood." Certainly he implied, though in a passing and incidental way, that Christ is God, saying priests of God and Christ, that is, of the Father and the Son, though it was in His servant-form and as Son of man that Christ was made a Priest for ever after the order of Melchisedec. But this we have already explained more than once.

Chapter XI: *Of Gog and Magog, Who are to Be Roused by the Devil to Persecute the Church, When He is Loosed in the End of the World.*

"And when the thousand years are finished, Satan shall be loosed from his prison, and shall go out to seduce the nations which are in the four corners of the earth, Gog and Magog, and shall draw them to battle, whose number is as the sand of the sea." This then, is his purpose in seducing them, to draw them to this battle. For even before this he was wont to use as many and various seductions as he could continue. And the words "he shall go out" mean, he shall burst forth from lurking hatred into open persecution. For this persecution, occurring while the final judgment is imminent, shall be the last which shall be endured by the holy Church throughout the world, the whole city of Christ being assailed by the whole city of the devil, as each exists on earth. For these nations which he names Gog and Magog are not to be understood of some barbarous nations in some part of the world, whether the Getæ and Massagetæ, as some conclude from the initial letters, or some other foreign nations not under the Roman government. For John marks that they are spread over the whole earth, when he says, "The nations which are in the four corners of the earth," and he added that these are Gog and Magog. The meaning of these names we find to be, Gog, "a roof," Magog, "from a roof"—a house, as it were, and he who comes out of the house. They are therefore the nations in which we found that the devil was shut up as in an abyss, and the devil himself coming out from them and going forth, so that they are the roof, he from the roof. Or if we refer both words to the nations, not one to them and one to the devil, then they are both the roof, because in them the old enemy is at present shut up, and as it were roofed in; and they shall be from the roof when they break forth from concealed to open hatred. The words, "And they went up on the breadth of the earth, and encompassed the camp of the saints and the beloved city," do not mean that they have come, or shall come, to one place, as if the camp of the saints and the beloved city should be in some one place; for this camp is nothing else than the Church of Christ extending over the whole world. And consequently wherever the Church shall be—and it shall be in all nations, as is signified by "the breadth of the earth"—there also shall be the camp of the saints and the beloved city, and there it shall be encompassed by the savage persecution of all its enemies; for they too shall exist along with it in all nations—that is, it shall be straightened, and hard pressed, and shut up in the straits of tribulation, but shall not desert its military duty, which is signified by the word "camp."

Chapter XII: *Whether the Fire that Came Down Out of Heaven and Devoured Them Refers to the Last Punishment of the Wicked.*

The words, "And fire came down out of heaven and devoured them," are not to be understood of the final punishment which shall be inflicted when it is said, "Depart from me, ye cursed, into everlasting fire;" for then they shall be cast into the fire, not fire come down out of heaven upon them. In this place "fire out of heaven" is well understood of the firmness of the saints, wherewith they refuse to yield obedience to those who rage against them. For the firmament is "heaven," by whose firmness these assailants shall be pained with blazing zeal, for they shall be impotent to draw away the saints to the party of Antichrist. This is the fire which shall devour them, and this is "from God;" for it is by God's grace the saints become unconquerable, and so torment their enemies. For as in a good sense it is said, "The zeal of Thine house hath consumed me," so in a bad sense it is said, "Zeal hath possessed the uninstructed people, and now fire shall consume the enemies." "And now," that is to say, not the fire of the last judgment. Or if by this fire coming down out of heaven and consuming them, John meant that blow wherewith Christ in His coming is to strike those persecutors of the Church whom He shall then find alive upon earth, when He shall kill Antichrist with the breath of His mouth, then even this is not the last judgment of the wicked; but the last judgment is that which they shall suffer when the bodily resurrection has taken place.

Chapter XIII: *Whether the Time of the Persecution or Antichrist Should Be Reckoned in the Thousand Years.*

This last persecution by Antichrist shall last for three years and six months, as we have already said, and as is affirmed both in the book of Revelation and by Daniel the prophet. Though this time is brief, yet not without reason is it questioned whether it is comprehended in the thousand years in which the devil is bound and the saints reign with Christ, or whether this little season should be added over and above to these years. For if we say that they are included in the thousand years, then the saints reign with Christ during a more protracted period than the devil is bound. For they shall reign with their King and Conqueror mightily even in that crowning persecution when the devil shall now be unbound and shall rage against them with all his might. How then does Scripture define both the binding of the devil and the reign of the saints by the same thousand years, if the binding of the devil ceases three years and six months before this reign of the saints with Christ? On the other hand, if we say that the brief space of this persecution is not to be reckoned as a part of the thousand years, but rather as an additional period, we shall indeed be able to interpret the words, "The priests of God and of Christ shall reign with Him a thousand years; and when the thousand years shall be finished, Satan shall be loosed out of his prison;" for thus they signify that the reign of the saints and the bondage of the devil shall cease simultaneously, so that the time of the persecution we speak of should be contemporaneous neither with the reign of the saints nor with the imprisonment of Satan, but should be reckoned over and above as a superadded portion of time. But then in this case we are forced to admit that the saints shall not reign with Christ during that persecution. But who can dare to say that His members shall not reign with Him at that very juncture when they shall most of all, and with the greatest fortitude, cleave to Him, and when the glory of resistance and the crown of martyrdom shall be more conspicuous in proportion to the hotness of the battle? Or if it is suggested that they may be said not to reign, because of the tribulations which they shall suffer, it will follow that all the saints who have formerly, during the thousand years, suffered tribulation, shall not be said to have reigned with Christ during the period of their tribulation, and consequently even those whose souls the author of this book says that he saw, and who were slain for the testimony of Jesus and the word of God, did not reign with Christ when they were suffering persecution, and they were not themselves the kingdom of Christ, though Christ was then preeminently possessing them. This is indeed perfectly absurd, and to be scouted. But assuredly the victorious souls of the glorious martyrs having overcome and finished all griefs and toils, and having laid down their mortal members, have reigned and do reign with Christ till the thousand years are finished, that they may afterwards reign with Him when they have received their immortal bodies. And therefore during these three years and a half the souls of those who were slain for His testimony, both those which formerly passed from the body and those which shall pass in that last persecution, shall reign with Him till the mortal world come to an end, and pass into that kingdom in which there shall be no death. And thus the reign of the saints with Christ shall last longer than the bonds and imprisonment of the devil, because they shall reign with their King the Son of God for these three years and a half during which the devil is no longer bound. It remains, therefore, that when we read that "the priests of God and of Christ shall reign with Him a thousand years; and when the thousand years are finished, the devil shall be loosed from his imprisonment," that we understand either that the thousand years of the reign of the saints does not terminate, though the imprisonment of the devil does—so that both parties have their thousand years, that is, their complete time, yet each with a different actual duration appropriate to itself, the kingdom of the saints being longer, the imprisonment of the devil shorter—or at least that, as three years and six months is a very short time, it is not reckoned as either deducted from the whole time of Satan's imprisonment, or as added to the whole duration of the reign of the saints, as we have shown above in the sixteenth book regarding the round number of four hundred years, which were specified as four hundred, though actually somewhat more; and similar expressions are often found in the sacred writings, if one will mark them.

Chapter XIV: *Of the Damnation of the Devil and His Adherents; And a Sketch of the Bodily Resurrection of All the Dead, and of the Final Retributive Judgment.*

After this mention of the closing persecution, he summarily indicates all that the devil, and the city of which he is the prince, shall suffer in the last judgment. For he says, "And the devil who seduced them is cast into the lake of fire and brimstone, in which are the beast and the false prophet, and they shall be tormented day and night for ever and ever." We have already said that by the beast is well understood the wicked city. His false prophet is either Antichrist or that image or figment of which we have spoken in the same place. After this he gives a brief narrative of the last judgment itself, which shall take place at the second or bodily resurrection of the dead, as it had been revealed to him: "I saw a throne great and white, and One sitting on it from whose face the heaven and the earth fled away, and their place was not found." He does not say, "I saw a throne great and white, and One sitting on it, and from His face the heaven and the earth fled away," for it had not happened then, i.e., before the living and the dead were judged; but he says that he saw Him sitting on the throne from whose face heaven and earth fled away, but afterwards. For when the judgment is finished, this heaven and earth shall cease to be, and there will be a new heaven and a new earth. For this world shall pass away by transmutation, not by absolute destruction. And therefore the apostle says, "For the figure of this world passeth away. I would have you be without anxiety." The figure, therefore, passes away, not the nature. After John had said that he had seen One sitting on the throne from whose face heaven and earth fled, though not till afterwards, he said, "And I saw the dead, great and small: and the books were opened; and another book was opened, which is the book of the life of each man: and the dead were judged out of those things which were written in the books, according to their deeds." He said that the books were opened, and a book; but he left us at a loss as to the nature of this book, "which is," he says, "the book of the life of each man." By those books, then, which he first mentioned, we are to understand the sacred books old and new, that out of them it might be shown what commandments God had enjoined; and that book of the life of each man is to show what commandments each man has done or omitted to do. If this book be materially considered, who can reckon its size or length, or the time it would take to read a book in which the whole life of every man is recorded? Shall there be present as many angels as men, and shall each man hear his life recited by the angel assigned to him? In that case there will be not one book containing all the lives, but a separate book for every life. But our passage requires us to think of one only. "And another book was opened," it says. We must therefore understand it of a certain divine power, by which it shall be brought about that every one shall recall to memory all his own works, whether good or evil, and shall mentally survey them with a marvelous rapidity, so that this knowledge will either accuse or excuse conscience, and thus all and each shall be simultaneously judged. And this divine power is called a book, because in it we shall as it were read all that it causes us to remember. That he may show who the dead, small and great, are who are to be judged, he recurs to this which he had omitted or rather deferred, and says, "And the sea presented the dead which were in it; and death and hell gave up the dead which were in them." This of course took place before the dead were judged, yet it is mentioned after. And so, I say, he returns again to what he had omitted. But now he preserves the order of events, and for the sake of exhibiting it repeats in its own proper place what he had already said regarding the dead who were judged. For after he had said, "And the sea presented the dead which were in it, and death and hell gave up the dead which were in them," he immediately subjoined what he had already said, "and they were judged every man according to their works." For this is just what he had said before, "And the dead were judged according to their works."

Chapter XV: *Who the Dead are Who are Given Up to Judgment by the Sea, and by Death and Hell.*

But who are the dead which were in the sea, and which the sea presented? For we cannot suppose that those who die in the sea are not in hell, nor that their bodies are preserved in the sea; nor yet, which is still more absurd, that the sea retained the good, while hell received the bad. Who could believe this? But some very sensibly suppose that in this place the sea is put for this world. When John then wished to signify that those whom Christ should find still alive in the body were to be judged along with those who should rise again, he called them dead, both the good to whom it is said, "For ye are dead, and your life is hid with Christ in God," and the wicked of whom it is said, "Let the dead bury their dead." They may also be called dead, because they wear mortal bodies, as the apostle says, "The body indeed is dead because of sin; but the spirit is life because of righteousness;" proving that in a living man in the body there is both a body which is dead, and a spirit which is life. Yet he did not say that the body was mortal, but dead, although immediately after he speaks in the more usual way of mortal bodies. These, then, are the dead which were in the sea, and which the sea presented, to wit, the men who were in this world, because they had not yet died, and whom the world presented for judgment. "And death and hell," he says, "gave up the dead which were in them." The sea presented them because they had merely to be found in the place where they were; but death and hell gave them up or restored them, because they called them back to life, which they had already quitted. And perhaps it was not without reason that neither death nor hell were judged sufficient alone, and both were mentioned—death to indicate the good, who have suffered only death and not hell; hell to indicate the wicked, who suffer also the punishment of hell. For if it does not seem absurd to believe that the ancient saints who believed in Christ and His then future coming, were kept in places far removed indeed from the torments of the wicked, but yet in hell, until Christ's blood and His descent into these places delivered them, certainly good Christians, redeemed by that precious price already paid, are quite unacquainted with hell while they wait for their restoration to the body, and the reception of their reward. After saying, "They were judged every man according to their works," he briefly added what the judgment was: "Death and hell were cast into the lake of fire;" by these names designating the devil and the whole company of his angels, for he is the author of death and the pains of hell. For this is what he had already, by anticipation, said in clearer language: "The devil who seduced them was cast into a lake of fire and brimstone." The obscure addition he had made in the words, "in which were also the beast and the false prophet," he here explains, "They who were not found written in the book of life were cast into the lake of fire." This book is not for reminding God, as if things might escape Him by forgetfulness, but it symbolizes His predestination of those to whom eternal life shall be given. For it is not that God is ignorant, and reads in the book to inform Himself, but rather His infallible prescience is the book of life in which they are written, that is to say, known beforehand.

Chapter XVI: *Of the New Heaven and the New Earth.*

Having finished the prophecy of judgment, so far as the wicked are concerned, it remains that he speak also of the good. Having briefly explained the Lord's words, "These will go away into everlasting punishment," it remains that he explain the connected words, "but the righteous into life eternal." "And I saw," he says, "a new heaven and a new earth: for the first heaven and the first earth have passed away; and there is no more sea." This will take place in the order which he has by anticipation declared in the words, "I saw One sitting on the throne, from whose face heaven and earth fled." For as soon as those who are not written in the book of life have been judged and cast into eternal fire—the nature of which fire, or its position in the world or universe, I suppose is known to no man, unless perhaps the divine Spirit reveal it to some one—then shall the figure of this world pass away in a conflagration of universal fire, as once before the world was flooded with a deluge of universal water. And by this universal conflagration the qualities of the corruptible elements which suited our corruptible bodies shall utterly perish, and our substance shall receive such qualities as shall, by a wonderful transmutation, harmonize with our immortal bodies, so that, as the world itself is renewed to some better thing, it is fitly accommodated to men, themselves renewed in their flesh to some better thing. As for the statement, "And there shall be no more sea," I would not lightly say whether it is dried up with that excessive heat, or is itself also turned into some better thing. For we read that there shall be a new heaven and a new earth, but I do not remember to have anywhere read anything of a new sea, unless what I find in this same book, "As it were a sea of glass like crystal." But he was not then speaking of this end of the world, neither does he seem to speak of a literal sea, but "as it were a sea." It is possible that, as prophetic diction delights in mingling figurative and real language, and thus in some sort veiling the sense, so the words "And there is no more sea" may be taken in the same sense as the previous phrase, "And the sea presented the dead which were in it." For then there shall be no more of this world, no more of the surgings and restlessness of human life, and it is this which is symbolized by the sea.

Chapter XVII: *Of the Endless Glory of the Church.*

"And I saw," he says, "a great city, new Jerusalem, coming down from God out of heaven, prepared as a bride adorned for her husband. And I heard a great voice from the throne, saying, Behold, the tabernacle of God is with men, and He will dwell with them, and they shall be His people, and God Himself shall be with them. And God shall wipe away all tears from their eyes; and there shall be no more death, neither sorrow, nor crying, but neither shall there be any more pain: because the former things have passed away. And He that sat upon the throne said, Behold, I make all things new." This city is said to come down out of heaven, because the grace with which God formed it is of heaven. Wherefore He says to it by Isaiah, "I am the Lord that formed thee." It is indeed descended from heaven from its commencement, since its citizens during the course of this world grow by the grace of God, which cometh down from above through the laver of regeneration in the Holy Ghost sent down from heaven. But by God's final judgment, which shall be administered by His Son Jesus Christ, there shall by God's grace be manifested a glory so pervading and so new, that no vestige of what is old shall remain; for even our bodies shall pass from their old corruption and mortality to new incorruption and immortality. For to refer this promise to the present time, in which the saints are reigning with their King a thousand years, seems to me excessively barefaced, when it is most distinctly said, "God shall wipe away all tears from their eyes; and there shall be no more death, neither sorrow, nor crying, but there shall be no more pain." And who is so absurd, and blinded by contentious opinionativeness, as to be audacious enough to affirm that in the midst of the calamities of this mortal state, God's people, or even one single saint, does live, or has ever lived, or shall ever live, without tears or pain—the fact being that the holier a man is, and the fuller of holy desire, so much the more abundant is the tearfulness of his supplication? Are not these the utterances of a citizen of the heavenly Jerusalem: "My tears have been my meat day and night;" and "Every night shall I make my bed to swim; with my tears shall I water my couch;" and "My groaning is not hid from Thee;" and "My sorrow was renewed?" Or are not those God's children who groan, being burdened, not that they wish to be unclothed, but clothed upon, that mortality may be swallowed up of life? Do not they even who have the first-fruits of the Spirit groan within themselves, waiting for the adoption, the redemption of their body? Was not the Apostle Paul himself a citizen of the heavenly Jerusalem, and was he not so all the more when he had heaviness and continual sorrow of heart for his Israelitish brethren? But when shall there be no more death in that city, except when it shall be said, "O death, where is thy contention? O death, where is thy sting? The sting of death is sin." Obviously there shall be no sin when it can be said, "Where is"—But as for the present it is not some poor weak citizen of this city, but this same Apostle John himself who says, "If we say that we have no sin, we deceive ourselves, and the truth is not in us." No doubt, though this book is called the Apocalypse, there are in it many obscure passages to exercise the mind of the reader, and there are few passages so plain as to assist us in the interpretation of the others, even though we take pains; and this difficulty is increased by the repetition of the same things, in forms so different, that the things referred to seem to be different, although in fact they are only differently stated. But in the words, "God shall wipe away all tears from their eyes; and there shall be no more death, neither sorrow, nor crying, but there shall be no more pain," there is so manifest a reference to the future world and the immortality and eternity of the saints—for only then and only there shall such a condition be realized—that if we think this obscure, we need not expect to find anything plain in any part of Scripture.

Chapter XVIII: *What the Apostle Peter Predicted Regarding the Last Judgment.*

Let us now see what the Apostle Peter predicted concerning this judgment. "There shall come," he says, "in the last days scoffers... Nevertheless we, according to His promise, look for new heavens and a new earth, wherein dwelleth righteousness." There is nothing said here about the resurrection of the dead, but enough certainly regarding the destruction of this world. And by his reference to the deluge he seems as it were to suggest to us how far we should believe the ruin of the world will extend in the end of the world. For he says that the world which then was perished, and not only the earth itself, but also the heavens, by which we understand the air, the place and room of which was occupied by the water. Therefore the whole, or almost the whole, of the gusty atmosphere (which he calls heaven, or rather the heavens, meaning the earth's atmosphere, and not the upper air in which sun, moon, and stars are set) was turned into moisture, and in this way perished together with the earth, whose former appearance had been destroyed by the deluge. "But the heavens and the earth which are now, by the same word are kept in store, reserved unto fire against the day of judgment and perdition of ungodly men." Therefore the heavens and the earth, or the world which was preserved from the water to stand in place of that world which perished in the flood, is itself reserved to fire at last in the day of the judgment and perdition of ungodly men. He does not hesitate to affirm that in this great change men also shall perish: their nature, however, shall notwithstanding continue, though in eternal punishments. Some one will perhaps put the question, If after judgment is pronounced the world itself is to burn, where shall the saints be during the conflagration, and before it is replaced by a new heavens and a new earth, since somewhere they must be, because they have material bodies? We may reply that they shall be in the upper regions into which the flame of that conflagration shall not ascend, as neither did the water of the flood; for they shall have such bodies that they shall be wherever they wish. Moreover, when they have become immortal and incorruptible, they shall not greatly dread the blaze of that conflagration, as the corruptible and mortal bodies of the three men were able to live unhurt in the blazing furnace.

Chapter XIX: *What the Apostle Paul Wrote to the Thessalonians About the Manifestation of Antichrist Which Shall Precede the Day of the Lord.*

I see that I must omit many of the statements of the gospels and epistles about this last judgment, that this volume may not become unduly long; but I can on no account omit what the Apostle Paul says, in writing to the Thessalonians, "We beseech you, brethren, by the coming of our Lord Jesus Christ," etc.

No one can doubt that he wrote this of Antichrist and of the day of judgment, which he here calls the day of the Lord, nor that he declared that this day should not come unless he first came who is called the apostate—apostate, to wit, from the Lord God. And if this may justly be said of all the ungodly, how much more of him? But it is uncertain in what temple he shall sit, whether in that ruin of the temple which was built by Solomon, or in the Church; for the apostle would not call the temple of any idol or demon the temple of God. And on this account some think that in this passage Antichrist means not the prince himself alone, but his whole body, that is, the mass of men who adhere to him, along with him their prince; and they also think that we should render the Greek more exactly were we to read, not "in the temple of God," but "for" or "as the temple of God," as if he himself were the temple of God, the Church. Then as for the words, "And now ye know what withholdeth," i.e., ye know what hindrance or cause of delay there is, "that he might be revealed in his own time;" they show that he was unwilling to make an explicit statement, because he said that they knew. And thus we who have not their knowledge wish and are not able even with pains to understand what the apostle referred to, especially as his meaning is made still more obscure by what he adds. For what does he mean by "For the mystery of iniquity doth already work: only he who now holdeth, let him hold until he be taken out of the way: and then shall the wicked be revealed?" I frankly confess I do not know what he means. I will nevertheless mention such conjectures as I have heard or read.

Some think that the Apostle Paul referred to the Roman empire, and that he was unwilling to use language more explicit, lest he should incur the calumnious charge of wishing ill to the empire which it was hoped would be eternal; so that in saying, "For the mystery of iniquity doth already work," he alluded to Nero, whose deeds already seemed to be as the deeds of Antichrist. And hence some suppose that he shall rise again and be Antichrist. Others, again, suppose that he is not even dead, but that he was concealed that he might be supposed to have been killed, and that he now lives in concealment in the vigor of that same age which he had reached when he was believed to have perished, and will live until he is revealed in his own time and restored to his kingdom. But I wonder that men can be so audacious in their conjectures. However, it is not absurd to believe that these words of the apostle, "Only he who now holdeth, let him hold until he be taken out of the way," refer to the Roman empire, as if it were said, "Only he who now reigneth, let him reign until he be taken out of the way." "And then shall the wicked be revealed:" no one doubts that this means Antichrist. But others think that the words, "Ye know what withholdeth," and "The mystery of iniquity worketh," refer only to the wicked and the hypocrites who are in the Church, until they reach a number so great as to furnish Antichrist with a great people, and that this is the mystery of iniquity, because it seems hidden; also that the apostle is exhorting the faithful tenaciously to hold the faith they hold when he says, "Only he who now holdeth, let him hold until he be taken out of the way," that is, until the mystery of iniquity which now is hidden departs from the Church. For they suppose that it is to this same mystery John alludes when in his epistle he says, "Little children, it is the last time: and as ye have heard that Antichrist shall come, even now are there many antichrists; whereby we know that it is the last time. They went out from us, but they were not of us; for if they had been of us, they would no doubt have continued with us." As therefore there went out from the Church many heretics, whom John calls "many antichrists," at that time prior to the end, and which John calls "the last time," so in the end they shall go out who do not belong to Christ, but to that last Antichrist, and then he shall be revealed.

Thus various, then, are the conjectural explanations of the obscure words of the apostle. That which there is no doubt he said is this, that Christ will not come to judge quick and dead unless Antichrist, His adversary, first come to seduce those who are dead in soul;

although their seduction is a result of God's secret judgment already passed. For, as it is said "his presence shall be after the working of Satan, with all power, and signs, and lying wonders, and with all seduction of unrighteousness in them that perish." For then shall Satan be loosed, and by means of that Antichrist shall work with all power in a lying though a wonderful manner. It is commonly questioned whether these works are called "signs and lying wonders" because he is to deceive men's senses by false appearances, or because the things he does, though they be true prodigies, shall be a lie to those who shall believe that such things could be done only by God, being ignorant of the devil's power, and especially of such unexampled power as he shall then for the first time put forth. For when he fell from heaven as fire, and at a stroke swept away from the holy Job his numerous household and his vast flocks, and then as a whirlwind rushed upon and smote the house and killed his children, these were not deceitful appearances, and yet they were the works of Satan to whom God had given this power. Why they are called signs and lying wonders, we shall then be more likely to know when the time itself arrives. But whatever be the reason of the name, they shall be such signs and wonders as shall seduce those who shall deserve to be seduced, "because they received not the love of the truth that they might be saved." Neither did the apostle scruple to go on to say, "For this cause God shall send upon them the working of error that they should believe a lie." For God shall send, because God shall permit the devil to do these things, the permission being by His own just judgment, though the doing of them is in pursuance of the devil's unrighteous and malignant purpose, "that they all might be judged who believed not the truth, but had pleasure in unrighteousness." Therefore, being judged, they shall be seduced, and, being seduced, they shall be judged. But, being judged, they shall be seduced by those secretly just and justly secret judgments of God, with which He has never ceased to judge since the first sin of the rational creatures; and, being seduced, they shall be judged in that last and manifest judgment administered by Jesus Christ, who was Himself most unjustly judged and shall most justly judge.

Chapter XX: *What the Same Apostle Taught in the First Epistle to the Thessalonians Regarding the Resurrection of the Dead.*

But the apostle has said nothing here regarding the resurrection of the dead; but in his first Epistle to the Thessalonians he says, "We would not have you to be ignorant brethren, concerning them which are asleep," etc. These words of the apostle most distinctly proclaim the future resurrection of the dead, when the Lord Christ shall come to judge the quick and the dead.

But it is commonly asked whether those whom our Lord shall find alive upon earth, personated in this passage by the apostle and those who were alive with him, shall never die at all, or shall pass with incomprehensible swiftness through death to immortality in the very moment during which they shall be caught up along with those who rise again to meet the Lord in the air? For we cannot say that it is impossible that they should both die and revive again while they are carried aloft through the air. For the words, "And so shall we ever be with the Lord," are not to be understood as if he meant that we shall always remain in the air with the Lord; for He Himself shall not remain there, but shall only pass through it as He comes. For we shall go to meet Him as He comes, not where He remains; but "so shall we be with the Lord," that is, we shall be with Him possessed of immortal bodies wherever we shall be with Him. We seem compelled to take the words in this sense, and to suppose that those whom the Lord shall find alive upon earth shall in that brief space both suffer death and receive immortality: for this same apostle says, "In Christ shall all be made alive;" while, speaking of the same resurrection of the body, he elsewhere says, "That which thou sowest is not quickened, except it die." How, then, shall those whom Christ shall find alive upon earth be made alive to immortality in Him if they die not, since on this very account it is said, "That which thou sowest is not quickened, except it die?" Or if we cannot properly speak of human bodies as sown, unless in so far as by dying they do in some sort return to the earth, as also the sentence pronounced by God against the sinning father of the human race runs, "Earth thou art, and unto earth shalt thou return," we must acknowledge that those whom Christ at His coming shall find still in the body are not included in these words of the apostle nor in those of Genesis; for, being caught up into the clouds, they are certainly not sown, neither going nor returning to the earth, whether they experience no death at all or die for a moment in the air.

But, on the other hand, there meets us the saying of the same apostle when he was speaking to the Corinthians about the resurrection of the body, "We shall all rise," or, as other mss. read, "We shall all sleep." Since, then, there can be no resurrection unless death has preceded, and since we can in this passage understand by sleep nothing else than death, how shall all either sleep or rise again if so many persons whom Christ shall find in the body shall neither sleep nor rise again? If, then, we believe that the saints who shall be found alive at Christ's coming, and shall be caught up to meet Him, shall in that same ascent pass from mortal to immortal bodies, we shall find no difficulty in the words of the apostle, either when he says, "That which thou sowest is not quickened, except it die," or when he says, "We shall all rise," or "all sleep," for not even the saints shall be quickened to immortality unless they first die, however briefly; and consequently they shall not be exempt from resurrection which is preceded by sleep, however brief. And why should it seem to us incredible that that multitude of bodies should be, as it were, sown in the air, and should in the air forthwith revive immortal and incorruptible, when we believe, on the testimony of the same apostle, that the resurrection shall take place in the twinkling of an eye, and that the dust of bodies long dead shall return with incomprehensible facility and swiftness to those members that are now to live endlessly? Neither do we suppose that in the case of these saints the sentence, "Earth thou art, and unto earth shalt thou return," is null, though their bodies do not, on dying, fall to earth, but both die and rise again at once while caught up into the air. For "Thou shalt return to earth" means, Thou shalt at death return to that which thou wert before life began. Thou shalt, when examinate, be that which thou wert before thou wast animate. For it was into a face of earth that God breathed the breath of life when man was made a living soul; as if it were said, Thou art earth with a soul, which thou wast not; thou shalt be earth without a soul, as thou wast. And this is what all bodies of the dead are before they rot; and what the bodies of those saints shall be if they die, no matter where they die, as soon as they shall give up that life which they are immediately to receive back again. In this way, then, they return or go to earth, inasmuch as from being living men they shall be earth, as that which becomes cinder is said to go to cinder; that which decays, to go to decay; and so of six hundred other things. But the manner in which this shall take place we can now only feebly conjecture, and shall understand it only when it comes to pass. For that there shall be a bodily resurrection of the dead when Christ comes to judge quick and dead, we must believe if we would be Christians. But if we are unable perfectly to comprehend the manner in which it shall take place, our faith is not on this account vain. Now, however, we ought, as we formerly promised, to show, as far as seems necessary, what the ancient prophetic books predicted concerning this final judgment of God; and I fancy no great time need be spent in discussing and explaining these predictions, if the reader has been careful to avail himself of the help we have already furnished.

Book Twenty-One

Chapter I: *Of the Order of the Discussion, Which Requires that We First Speak of the Eternal Punishment of the Lost in Company with the Devil, and Then of the Eternal Happiness of the Saints.*

I propose, with such ability as God may grant me, to discuss in this book more thoroughly the nature of the punishment which shall be assigned to the devil and all his retainers, when the two cities, the one of God, the other of the devil, shall have reached their proper ends through Jesus Christ our Lord, the Judge of quick and dead. And I have adopted this order, and preferred to speak, first of the punishment of the devils, and afterwards of the blessedness of the saints, because the body partakes of either destiny; and it seems to be more incredible that bodies endure in everlasting torments than that they continue to exist without any pain in everlasting felicity. Consequently, when I shall have demonstrated that that punishment ought not to be incredible, this will materially aid me in proving that which is much more credible, viz., the immortality of the bodies of the saints which are delivered from all pain. Neither is this order out of harmony with the divine writings, in which sometimes, indeed, the blessedness of the good is placed first, as in the words, "They that have done good, unto the resurrection of life; and they that have done evil, unto the resurrection of judgment;" but sometimes also last, as, "The Son of man shall send forth His angels, and they shall gather out of His kingdom all things which offend, and shall cast them into a furnace of fire: there shall be wailing and gnashing of teeth, Then shall the righteous shine forth as the sun in the kingdom of His Father;" and that, "These shall go away into eternal punishment, but the righteous into life eternal." And though we have not room to cite instances, any one who examines the prophets will find that they adopt now the one arrangement and now the other. My own reason for following the latter order I have given.

Chapter II: *Whether It is Possible for Bodies to Last for Ever in Burning Fire.*

What, then, can I adduce to convince those who refuse to believe that human bodies, animated and living, can not only survive death, but also last in the torments of everlasting fires? They will not allow us to refer this simply to the power of the Almighty, but demand that we persuade them by some example. If, then, we reply to them, that there are animals which certainly are corruptible, because they are mortal, and which yet live in the midst of flames; and likewise, that in springs of water so hot that no one can put his hand in it with impunity a species of worm is found, which not only lives there, but cannot live elsewhere; they either refuse to believe these facts unless we can show them, or, if we are in circumstances to prove them by ocular demonstration or by adequate testimony, they contend, with the same scepticism, that these facts are not examples of what we seek to prove, inasmuch as these animals do not live for ever, and besides, they live in that blaze of heat without pain, the element of fire being congenial to their nature, and causing it to thrive and not to suffer—just as if it were not more incredible that it should thrive than that it should suffer in such circumstances. It is strange that anything should suffer in fire and yet live, but stranger that it should live in fire and not suffer. If, then, the latter be believed, why not also the former?

Chapter III: *Whether Bodily Suffering Necessarily Terminates in the Destruction of the Flesh.*

But, say they, there is no body which can suffer and cannot also die. How do we know this? For who can say with certainty that the devils do not suffer in their bodies, when they own that they are grievously tormented? And if it is replied that there is no earthly body—that is to say, no solid and perceptible body, or, in one word, no flesh—which can suffer and cannot die, is not this to tell us only what men have gathered from experience and their bodily senses? For they indeed have no acquaintance with any flesh but that which is mortal; and this is their whole argument, that what they have had no experience of they judge quite impossible. For we cannot call it reasoning to make pain a presumption of death, while, in fact, it is rather a sign of life. For though it be a question whether that which suffers can continue to live for ever, yet it is certain that everything which suffers pain does live, and that pain can exist only in a living subject. It is necessary, therefore, that he who is pained be living, not necessary that pain kill him; for every pain does not kill even those mortal bodies of ours which are destined to die. And that any pain kills them is caused by the circumstance that the soul is so connected with the body that it succumbs to great pain and withdraws; for the structure of our members and vital parts is so infirm that it cannot bear up against that violence which causes great or extreme agony. But in the life to come this connection of soul and body is of such a kind, that as it is dissolved by no lapse of time, so neither is it burst asunder by any pain. And so, although it be true that in this world there is no flesh which can suffer pain and yet cannot die, yet in the world to come there shall be flesh such as now there is not, as there will also be death such as now there is not. For death will not be abolished, but will be eternal, since the soul will neither be able to enjoy God and live, nor to die and escape the pains of the body. The first death drives the soul from the body against her will: the second death holds the soul in the body against her will. The two have this in common, that the soul suffers against her will what her own body inflicts.

Our opponents, too, make much of this, that in this world there is no flesh which can suffer pain and cannot die; while they make nothing of the fact that there is something which is greater than the body. For the spirit, whose presence animates and rules the body, can both suffer pain and cannot die. Here then is something which, though it can feel pain, is immortal. And this capacity, which we now see in the spirit of all, shall be hereafter in the bodies of the damned. Moreover, if we attend to the matter a little more closely, we see that what is called bodily pain is rather to be referred to the soul. For it is the soul not the body, which is pained, even when the pain originates with the body—the soul feeling pain at the point where the body is hurt. As then we speak of bodies feeling and living, though the feeling and life of the body are from the soul, so also we speak of bodies being pained, though no pain can be suffered by the body apart from the soul. The soul, then, is pained with the body in that part where something occurs to hurt it; and it is pained alone, though it be in the body, when some invisible cause distresses it, while the body is safe and sound. Even when not associated with the body it is pained; for certainly that rich man was suffering in hell when he cried, "I am tormented in this flame." But as for the body, it suffers no pain when it is soulless; and even when animate it can suffer only by the soul's suffering. If, therefore, we might draw a just presumption from the existence of pain to that of death, and conclude that where pain can be felt death can occur, death would rather be the property of the soul, for to it pain more peculiarly belongs. But, seeing that that which suffers most cannot die, what ground is there for supposing that those bodies, because destined to suffer, are therefore, destined to die? The Platonists indeed maintained that these earthly bodies and dying members gave rise to the fears, desires, griefs, and joys of the soul. "Hence," says Virgil (i.e., from these earthly bodies and dying members),

> "Hence wild desires and groveling fears,
> And human laughter, human tears."

But in the fourteenth book of this work we have proved that, according to the Platonists' own theory, souls, even when purged from all pollution of the body, are yet possessed by a monstrous desire to return again into their bodies. But where desire can exist, certainly pain also can exist; for desire frustrated, either by missing what it aims at or losing what it had attained, is turned into pain. And therefore, if the soul, which is either the only or the chief sufferer, has yet a kind of immortality of its own, it is inconsequent to say that because the bodies of the damned shall suffer pain, therefore they shall die. In fine, if the body causes the soul to suffer, why can the body not cause death as well as suffering, unless because it does not follow that what causes pain causes death as well? And why then is it incredible that these fires can cause pain but not death to those bodies we speak of, just as the bodies themselves cause pain, but not therefore death, to the souls? Pain is therefore no necessary presumption of death.

Chapter IX: *Of Hell, and the Nature of Eternal Punishments.*

So then what God by His prophet has said of the everlasting punishment of the damned shall come to pass—shall without fail come to pass—"their worm shall not die, neither shall their fire be quenched." In order to impress this upon us most forcibly, the Lord Jesus Himself, when ordering us to cut off our members, meaning thereby those persons whom a man loves as the most useful members of his body, says, "It is better for thee to enter into life maimed, than having two hands to go into hell, into the fire that never shall be quenched; where their worm dieth not, and their fire is not quenched." Similarly of the foot: "It is better for thee to enter halt into life, than having two feet to be cast into hell, into the fire that never shall be quenched; where their worm dieth not, and the fire is not quenched." So, too, of the eye: "It is better for thee to enter into the kingdom of God with one eye, than having two eyes to be cast into hell fire: where their worm dieth not, and the fire is not quenched." He did not shrink from using the same words three times over in one passage. And who is not terrified by this repetition, and by the threat of that punishment uttered so vehemently by the lips of the Lord Himself?

Now they who would refer both the fire and the worm to the spirit, and not to the body, affirm that the wicked, who are separated from the kingdom of God, shall be burned, as it were, by the anguish of a spirit repenting too late and fruitlessly; and they contend that fire is therefore not inappropriately used to express this burning torment, as when the apostle exclaims "Who is offended, and I burn not?" The worm, too, they think, is to be similarly understood. For it is written they say, "As the moth consumes the garment, and the worm the wood, so does grief consume the heart of a man." But they who make no doubt that in that future punishment both body and soul shall suffer, affirm that the body shall be burned with fire, while the soul shall be, as it were, gnawed by a worm of anguish. Though this view is more reasonable—for it is absurd to suppose that either body or soul will escape pain in the future punishment—yet, for my own part, I find it easier to understand both as referring to the body than to suppose that neither does; and I think that Scripture is silent regarding the spiritual pain of the damned, because, though not expressed, it is necessarily understood that in a body thus tormented the soul also is tortured with a fruitless repentance. For we read in the ancient Scriptures, "The vengeance of the flesh of the ungodly is fire and worms." It might have been more briefly said, "The vengeance of the ungodly." Why, then, was it said, "The flesh of the ungodly," unless because both the fire and the worm are to be the punishment of the flesh? Or if the object of the writer in saying, "The vengeance of the flesh," was to indicate that this shall be the punishment of those who live after the flesh (for this leads to the second death, as the apostle intimated when he said, "For if ye live after the flesh, ye shall die" , let each one make his own choice, either assigning the fire to the body and the worm to the soul—the one figuratively, the other really—or assigning both really to the body. For I have already sufficiently made out that animals can live in the fire, in burning without being consumed, in pain without dying, by a miracle of the most omnipotent Creator, to whom no one can deny that this is possible, if he be not ignorant by whom has been made all that is wonderful in all nature. For it is God Himself who has wrought all these miracles, great and small, in this world which I have mentioned, and incomparably more which I have omitted, and who has enclosed these marvels in this world, itself the greatest miracle of all. Let each man, then, choose which he will, whether he thinks that the worm is real and pertains to the body, or that spiritual things are meant by bodily representations, and that it belongs to the soul. But which of these is true will be more readily discovered by the facts themselves, when there shall be in the saints such knowledge as shall not require that their own experience teach them the nature of these punishments, but as shall, by its own fullness and perfection, suffice to instruct them in this matter. For "now we know in part, until that which is perfect is come;" only, this we believe about those future bodies, that they shall be such as shall certainly be pained by the fire.

Chapter X: *Whether the Fire of Hell, If It Be Material Fire, Can Burn the Wicked Spirits, that is to Say, Devils, Who are Immaterial.*

Here arises the question: If the fire is not to be immaterial, analogous to the pain of the soul, but material, burning by contact, so that bodies may be tormented in it, how can evil spirits be punished in it? For it is undoubtedly the same fire which is to serve for the punishment of men and of devils, according to the words of Christ: "Depart from me, ye cursed, into everlasting fire, prepared for the devil and his angels;" unless, perhaps, as learned men have thought, the devils have a kind of body made of that dense and humid air which we feel strikes us when the wind is blowing. And if this kind of substance could not be affected by fire, it could not burn when heated in the baths. For in order to burn, it is first burned, and affects other things as itself is affected. But if any one maintains that the devils have no bodies, this is not a matter either to be laboriously investigated, or to be debated with keenness. For why may we not assert that even immaterial spirits may, in some extraordinary way, yet really be pained by the punishment of material fire, if the spirits of men, which also are certainly immaterial, are both now contained in material members of the body, and in the world to come shall be indissolubly united to their own bodies? Therefore, though the devils have no bodies, yet their spirits, that is, the devils themselves, shall be brought into thorough contact with the material fires, to be tormented by them; not that the fires themselves with which they are brought into contact shall be animated by their connection with these spirits, and become animals composed of body and spirit, but, as I said, this junction will be effected in a wonderful and ineffable way, so that they shall receive pain from the fires, but give no life to them. And, in truth, this other mode of union, by which bodies and spirits are bound together and become animals, is thoroughly marvelous, and beyond the comprehension of man, though this it is which is man.

I would indeed say that these spirits will burn without any body of their own, as that rich man was burning in hell when he exclaimed, "I am tormented in this flame," were I not aware that it is aptly said in reply, that that flame was of the same nature as the eyes he raised and fixed on Lazarus, as the tongue on which he entreated that a little cooling water might be dropped, or as the finger of Lazarus, with which he asked that this might be done—all of which took place where souls exist without bodies. Thus, therefore, both that flame in which he burned and that drop he begged were immaterial, and resembled the visions of sleepers or persons in an ecstasy, to whom immaterial objects appear in a bodily form. For the man himself who is in such a state, though it be in spirit only, not in body, yet sees himself so like to his own body that he cannot discern any difference whatever. But that hell, which also is called a lake of fire and brimstone, will be material fire, and will torment the bodies of the damned, whether men or devils—the solid bodies of the one, aerial bodies of the others; or if only men have bodies as well as souls, yet the evil spirits, though without bodies, shall be so connected with the bodily fires as to receive pain without imparting life. One fire certainly shall be the lot of both, for thus the truth has declared.

Chapter XI: *Whether It is Just that the Punishments of Sins Last Longer Than the Sins Themselves Lasted.*

Some, however, of those against whom we are defending the city of God, think it unjust that any man be doomed to an eternal punishment for sins which, no matter how great they were, were perpetrated in a brief space of time; as if any law ever regulated the duration of the punishment by the duration of the offence punished! Cicero tells us that the laws recognize eight kinds of penalty—damages, imprisonment, scourging, reparation, disgrace, exile, death, slavery. Is there any one of these which may be compressed into a brevity proportioned to the rapid commission of the offence, so that no longer time may be spent in its punishment than in its perpetration, unless, perhaps, reparation? For this requires that the offender suffer what he did, as that clause of the law says, "Eye for eye, tooth for tooth." For certainly it is possible for an offender to lose his eye by the severity of legal retaliation in as brief a time as he deprived another of his eye by the cruelty of his own lawlessness. But if scourging be a reasonable penalty for kissing another man's wife, is not the fault of an instant visited with long hours of atonement, and the momentary delight punished with lasting pain? What shall we say of imprisonment? Must the criminal be confined only for so long a time as he spent on the offence for which he is committed? or is not a penalty of many years' confinement imposed on the slave who has provoked his master with a word, or has struck him a blow that is quickly over? And as to damages, disgrace, exile, slavery, which are commonly inflicted so as to admit of no relaxation or pardon, do not these resemble eternal punishments in so far as this short life allows a resemblance? For they are not eternal only because the life in which they are endured is not eternal; and yet the crimes which are punished with these most protracted sufferings are perpetrated in a very brief space of time. Nor is there any one who would suppose that the pains of punishment should occupy as short a time as the offense; or that murder, adultery, sacrilege, or any other crime, should be measured, not by the enormity of the injury or wickedness, but by the length of time spent in its perpetration. Then as to the award of death for any great crime, do the laws reckon the punishment to consist in the brief moment in which death is inflicted, or in this, that the offender is eternally banished from the society of the living? And just as the punishment of the first death cuts men off from this present mortal city, so does the punishment of the second death cut men off from that future immortal city. For as the laws of this present city do not provide for the executed criminal's return to it, so neither is he who is condemned to the second death recalled again to life everlasting. But if temporal sin is visited with eternal punishment, how, then, they say, is that true which your Christ says, "With the same measure that ye mete withal it shall be measured to you again?" and they do not observe that "the same measure" refers, not to an equal space of time, but to the retribution of evil or, in other words, to the law by which he who has done evil suffers evil.

Besides, these words could be appropriately understood as referring to the matter of which our Lord was speaking when He used them, viz., judgments and condemnation. Thus, if he who unjustly judges and condemns is himself justly judged and condemned, he receives "with the same measure" though not the same thing as he gave. For judgment he gave, and judgment he receives, though the judgment he gave was unjust, the judgment he receives just.

Chapter XII: *Of the Greatness of the First Transgression, on Account of Which Eternal Punishment is Due to All Who are Not Within the Pale of the Saviour's Grace.*

But eternal punishment seems hard and unjust to human perceptions, because in the weakness of our mortal condition there is wanting that highest and purest wisdom by which it can be perceived how great a wickedness was committed in that first transgression. The more enjoyment man found in God, the greater was his wickedness in abandoning Him; and he who destroyed in himself a good which might have been eternal, became worthy of eternal evil. Hence the whole mass of the human race is condemned; for he who at first gave entrance to sin has been punished with all his posterity who were in him as in a root, so that no one is exempt from this just and due punishment, unless delivered by mercy and undeserved grace; and the human race is so apportioned that in some is displayed the efficacy of merciful grace, in the rest the efficacy of just retribution. For both could not be displayed in all; for if all had remained under the punishment of just condemnation, there would have been seen in no one the mercy of redeeming grace. And, on the other hand, if all had been transferred from darkness to light, the severity of retribution would have been manifested in none. But many more are left under punishment than are delivered from it, in order that it may thus be shown what was due to all. And had it been inflicted on all, no one could justly have found fault with the justice of Him who taketh vengeance; whereas, in the deliverance of so many from that just award, there is cause to render the most cordial thanks to the gratuitous bounty of Him who delivers.

Chapter XIII: *Against the Opinion of Those Who Think that the Punishments of the Wicked After Death are Purgatorial.*

The Platonists, indeed, while they maintain that no sins are unpunished, suppose that all punishment is administered for remedial purposes, be it inflicted by human or divine law, in this life or after death; for a man may be scathless here, or, though punished, may yet not amend. Hence that passage of Virgil, where, when he had said of our earthly bodies and mortal members, that our souls derive—

> "Hence wild desires and groveling fears,
> And human laughter, human tears;
> Immured in dungeon-seeming night,
> They look abroad, yet see no light,"

goes on to say:

> "Nay, when at last the life has fled,
> And left the body cold and dead,
> Ee'n then there passes not away
> The painful heritage of clay;
> Full many a long-contracted stain
> Perforce must linger deep in grain.
> So penal sufferings they endure
> For ancient crime, to make them pure;
> Some hang aloft in open view,
> For winds to pierce them through and through,
> While others purge their guilt deep-dyed
> In burning fire or whelming tide."

They who are of this opinion would have all punishments after death to be purgatorial; and as the elements of air, fire, and water are superior to earth, one or other of these may be the instrument of expiating and purging away the stain contracted by the contagion of earth. So Virgil hints at the air in the words, "Some hang aloft for winds to pierce;" at the water in "whelming tide;" and at fire in the expression "in burning fire." For our part, we recognize that even in this life some punishments are purgatorial—not, indeed, to those whose life is none the better, but rather the worse for them, but to those who are constrained by them to amend their life. All other punishments, whether temporal or eternal, inflicted as they are on every one by divine providence, are sent either on account of past sins, or of sins presently allowed in the life, or to exercise and reveal a man's graces. They may be inflicted by the instrumentality of bad men and angels as well as of the good. For even if any one suffers some hurt through another's wickedness or mistake, the man indeed sins whose ignorance or injustice does the harm; but God, who by His just though hidden judgment permits it to be done, sins not. But temporary punishments are suffered by some in this life only, by others after death, by others both now and then; but all of them before that last and strictest judgment. But of those who suffer temporary punishments after death, all are not doomed to those everlasting pains which are to follow that judgment; for to some, as we have already said, what is not remitted in this world is remitted in the next, that is, they are not punished with the eternal punishment of the world to come.

Chapter XVIII: *Of Those Who Fancy That, on Account of the Saints' Intercession, Man Shall Be Damned in the Last Judgment.*

There are others, again, with whose opinions I have become acquainted in conversation, who, though they seem to reverence the holy Scriptures, are yet of reprehensible life, and who accordingly, in their own interest, attribute to God a still greater compassion towards men. For they acknowledge that it is truly predicted in the divine word that the wicked and unbelieving are worthy of punishment, but they assert that, when the judgment comes, mercy will prevail. For, say they, God, having compassion on them, will give them up to the prayers and intercessions of His saints. For if the saints used to pray for them when they suffered from their cruel hatred, how much more will they do so when they see them prostrate and humble suppliants? For we cannot, they say, believe that the saints shall lose their bowels of compassion when they have attained the most perfect and complete holiness; so that they who, when still sinners, prayed for their enemies, should now, when they are freed from sin, withhold from interceding for their suppliants. Or shall God refuse to listen to so many of His beloved children, when their holiness has purged their prayers of all hindrance to His answering them? And the passage of the psalm which is cited by those who admit that wicked men and infidels shall be punished for a long time, though in the end delivered from all sufferings, is claimed also by the persons we are now speaking of as making much more for them. The verse runs: "Shall God forget to be gracious? Shall He in anger shut up His tender mercies?" His anger, they say, would condemn all that are unworthy of everlasting happiness to endless punishment. But if He suffer them to be punished for a long time, or even at all, must He not shut up His tender mercies, which the Psalmist implies He will not do? For he does not say, Shall He in anger shut up His tender mercies for a long period? but he implies that He will not shut them up at all.

And they deny that thus God's threat of judgment is proved to be false even though He condemn no man, any more than we can say that His threat to overthrow Nineveh was false, though the destruction which was absolutely predicted was not accomplished. For He did not say, "Nineveh shall be overthrown if they do not repent and amend their ways," but without any such condition He foretold that the city should be overthrown. And this prediction, they maintain, was true because God predicted the punishment which they deserved, although He was not to inflict it. For though He spared them on their repentance yet He was certainly aware that they would repent, and, notwithstanding, absolutely and definitely predicted that the city should be overthrown. This was true, they say, in the truth of severity, because they were worthy of it; but in respect of the compassion which checked His anger, so that He spared the suppliants from the punishment with which He had threatened the rebellious, it was not true. If, then, He spared those whom His own holy prophet was provoked at His sparing, how much more shall He spare those more wretched suppliants for whom all His saints shall intercede? And they suppose that this conjecture of theirs is not hinted at in Scripture, for the sake of stimulating many to reformation of life through fear of very protracted or eternal sufferings, and of stimulating others to pray for those who have not reformed. However, they think that the divine oracles are not altogether silent on this point; for they ask to what purpose is it said, "How great is Thy goodness which Thou hast hidden for them that fear Thee," if it be not to teach us that the great and hidden sweetness of God's mercy is concealed in order that men may fear? To the same purpose they think the apostle said, "For God hath concluded all men in unbelief, that He may have mercy upon all," signifying that no one should be condemned by God. And yet they who hold this opinion do not extend it to the acquittal or liberation of the devil and his angels. Their human tenderness is moved only towards men, and they plead chiefly their own cause, holding out false hopes of impunity to their own depraved lives by means of this quasi compassion of God to the whole race. Consequently they who promise this impunity even to the prince of the devils and his satellites make a still fuller exhibition of the mercy of God.

Chapter XIX: *Of Those Who Promise Impunity from All Sins Even to Heretics, Through Virtue of Their Participation of the Body of Christ.*

So, too, there are others who promise this deliverance from eternal punishment, not, indeed, to all men, but only to those who have been washed in Christian baptism, and who become partakers of the body of Christ, no matter how they have lived, or what heresy or impiety they have fallen into. They ground this opinion on the saying of Jesus, "This is the bread which cometh down from heaven, that if any man eat thereof, he shall not die. I am the living bread which came down from heaven. If a man eat of this bread, he shall live for ever." Therefore, say they, it follows that these persons must be delivered from death eternal, and at one time or other be introduced to everlasting life.

Chapter XX: *Of Those Who Promise This Indulgence Not to All, But Only to Those Who Have Been Baptized as Catholics, Though Afterwards They Have Broken Out into Many Crimes and Heresies.*

There are others still who make this promise not even to all who have received the sacraments of the baptism of Christ and of His body, but only to the catholics, however badly they have lived. For these have eaten the body of Christ, not only sacramentally but really, being incorporated in His body, as the apostle says, "We, being many, are one bread, one body;" so that, though they have afterwards lapsed into some heresy, or even into heathenism and idolatry, yet by virtue of this one thing, that they have received the baptism of

Christ, and eaten the body of Christ, in the body of Christ, that is to say, in the catholic Church, they shall not die eternally, but at one time or other obtain eternal life; and all that wickedness of theirs shall not avail to make their punishment eternal, but only proportionately long and severe.

Chapter XXI: *Of Those Who Assert that All Catholics Who Continue in the Faith Even Though by the Depravity of Their Lives They Have Merited Hell Fire, Shall Be Saved on Account of the "Foundation" Of Their Faith.*

There are some, too, who found upon the expression of Scripture, "He that endureth to the end shall be saved," and who promise salvation only to those who continue in the Church catholic; and though such persons have lived badly, yet, say they, they shall be saved as by fire through virtue of the foundation of which the apostle says, "For other foundation hath no man laid than that which is laid, which is Christ Jesus. Now if any man build upon this foundation gold, silver, precious stones, wood, hay, stubble; every man's work shall be made manifest: for the day of the Lord shall declare it, for it shall be revealed by fire; and each man's work shall be proved of what sort it is. If any man's work shall endure which he hath built thereupon, he shall receive a reward. But if any man's work shall be burned, he shall suffer loss: but he himself shall be saved; yet so as through fire." They say, accordingly, that the catholic Christian, no matter what his life be, has Christ as his foundation, while this foundation is not possessed by any heresy which is separated from the unity of His body. And therefore, through virtue of this foundation, even though the catholic Christian by the inconsistency of his life has been as one building up wood, hay, stubble, upon it, they believe that he shall be saved by fire, in other words, that he shall be delivered after tasting the pain of that fire to which the wicked shall be condemned at the last judgment.

Chapter XXII: *Of Those Who Fancy that the Sins Which are Intermingled with Alms-Deeds Shall Not Be Charged at the Day of Judgment.*

I have also met with some who are of opinion that such only as neglect to cover their sins with alms-deeds shall be punished in everlasting fire; and they cite the words of the Apostle James, "He shall have judgment without mercy who hath shown no mercy."

Therefore, say they, he who has not amended his ways, but yet has intermingled his profligate and wicked actions with works of mercy, shall receive mercy in the judgment, so that he shall either quite escape condemnation, or shall be liberated from his doom after some time shorter or longer. They suppose that this was the reason why the Judge Himself of quick and dead declined to mention anything else than works of mercy done or omitted, when awarding to those on His right hand life eternal, and to those on His left everlasting punishment. To the same purpose, they say, is the daily petition we make in the Lord's prayer, "Forgive us our debts, as we forgive our debtors." For, no doubt, whoever pardons the person who has wronged him does a charitable action. And this has been so highly commended by the Lord Himself, that He says, "For if ye forgive men their trespasses, your heavenly Father will also forgive you: but if ye forgive not men their trespasses, neither will your Father forgive your trespasses." And so it is to this kind of alms-deeds that the saying of the Apostle James refers, "He shall have judgment without mercy that hath shown no mercy." And our Lord, they say, made no distinction of great and small sins, but "Your Father will forgive your sins, if ye forgive men theirs." Consequently they conclude that, though a man has led an abandoned life up to the last day of it, yet whatsoever his sins have been, they are all remitted by virtue of this daily prayer, if only he has been mindful to attend to this one thing, that when they who have done him any injury ask his pardon, he forgive them from his heart.

When, by God's help, I have replied to all these errors, I shall conclude this (twenty-first) book.

Chapter XXIII: *Against Those Who are of Opinion that the Punishment Neither of the Devil Nor of Wicked Men Shall Be Eternal.*

First of all, it behooves us to inquire and to recognize why the Church has not been able to tolerate the idea that promises cleansing or indulgence to the devil even after the most severe and protracted punishment. For so many holy men, imbued with the spirit of the Old and New Testament, did not grudge to angels of any rank or character that they should enjoy the blessedness of the heavenly kingdom after being cleansed by suffering, but rather they perceived that they could not invalidate nor evacuate the divine sentence which the Lord predicted that He would pronounce in the judgment, saying, "Depart from me, ye cursed, into everlasting fire, prepared for the devil and his angels." For here it is evident that the devil and his angels shall burn in everlasting fire. And there is also that declaration in the Apocalypse, "The devil their deceiver was cast into the lake of fire and brimstone, where also are the beast and the false prophet. And they shall be tormented day and night for ever." In the former passage "everlasting" is used, in the latter "for ever;" and by these words Scripture is wont to mean nothing else than endless duration. And therefore no other reason, no reason more obvious and just, can be found for holding it as the fixed and immovable belief of the truest piety, that the devil and his angels shall never return to the justice and life of the saints, than that Scripture, which deceives no man, says that God spared them not, and that they were condemned beforehand by Him, and cast into prisons of darkness in hell, being reserved to the judgment of the last day, when eternal fire shall receive them, in which they shall be tormented world without end. And if this be so, how can it be believed that all men, or even some, shall be withdrawn from the endurance of punishment after some time has been spent in it? how can this be believed without enervating our faith in the eternal punishment of the devils? For if all or some of those to whom it shall be said, "Depart from me, ye cursed, into everlasting fire, prepared for the devil and his angels," are not to be always in that fire, then what reason is there for believing that the devil and his angels shall always be there? Or is perhaps the sentence of God, which is to be pronounced on wicked men and angels alike, to be true in the case of the angels, false in that of men? Plainly it will be so if the conjectures of men are to weigh more than the word of God. But because this is absurd, they who desire to be rid of eternal punishment ought to abstain from arguing against God, and rather, while yet there is opportunity, obey the divine commands. Then what a fond fancy is it to suppose that eternal punishment means long continued punishment, while eternal life means life without end, since Christ in the very same passage spoke of both in similar terms in one and the same sentence, "These shall go away into eternal punishment, but the righteous into life eternal!" If both destinies are "eternal," then we must either understand both as long-continued but at last terminating, or both as endless. For they are correlative—on the one hand, punishment eternal, on the other hand, life eternal. And to say in one and the same sense, life eternal shall be endless, punishment eternal shall come to an end, is the height of absurdity. Wherefore, as the eternal life of the saints shall be endless, so too the eternal punishment of those who are doomed to it shall have no end.

Chapter XXIV: *Against Those Who Fancy that in the Judgment of God All the Accused Will Be Spared in Virtue of the Prayers of the Saints.*

And this reasoning is equally conclusive against those who, in their own interest, but under the guise of a greater tenderness of spirit, attempt to invalidate the words of God, and who assert that these words are true, not because men shall suffer those things which are threatened by God, but because they deserve to suffer them. For God, they say, will yield them to the prayers of His saints, who will then the more earnestly pray for their enemies, as they shall be more perfect in holiness, and whose prayers will be the more efficacious and the more worthy of God's ear, because now purged from all sin whatsoever. Why, then, if in that perfected holiness their prayers be so pure and all-availing, will they not use them in behalf of the angels for whom eternal fire is prepared, that God may mitigate His sentence and alter it, and extricate them from that fire? Or will there, perhaps, be some one hardy enough to affirm that even the holy angels will make common cause with holy men (then become the equals of God's angels), and will intercede for the guilty, both men and angels, that mercy may spare them the punishment which truth has pronounced them to deserve? But this has been asserted by no one sound in the faith; nor will be. Otherwise there is no reason why the Church should not even now pray for the devil and his angels, since God her Master has ordered her to pray for her enemies. The reason, then, which prevents the Church from now praying for the wicked angels, whom she knows to be her enemies, is the identical reason which shall prevent her, however perfected in holiness, from praying at the last judgment for those men who are to be punished in eternal fire. At present she prays for her enemies among men, because they have yet opportunity for fruitful repentance. For what does she especially beg for them but that "God would grant them repentance," as the apostle says, "that they may return to soberness out of the snare of the devil, by whom they are held captive according to his will?" But if the Church were certified who those are, who, though they are still abiding in this life, are yet predestinated to go with the devil into eternal fire, then for them she could no more pray than for him. But since she has this certainty regarding no man, she prays for all her enemies who yet live in this world; and yet she is not heard in behalf of all. But she is heard in the case of those only who, though they oppose the Church, are yet predestinated to become her sons through her intercession. But if any retain an impenitent heart until death, and are not converted from enemies into sons, does the Church continue to pray for them, for the spirits, i.e., of such persons deceased? And why does she cease to pray for them, unless because the man who was not translated into Christ's kingdom while he was in the body, is now judged to be of Satan's following?

It is then, I say, the same reason which prevents the Church at any time from praying for the wicked angels, which prevents her from praying hereafter for those men who are to be punished in eternal fire; and this also is the reason why, though she prays even for the wicked so long as they live, she yet does not even in this world pray for the unbelieving and godless who are dead. For some of the dead, indeed, the prayer of the Church or of pious individuals is heard; but it is for those who, having been regenerated in Christ, did not spend their life so wickedly that they can be judged unworthy of such compassion, nor so well that they can be considered to have no need of it. As also, after the resurrection, there will be some of the dead to whom, after they have endured the pains proper to the spirits of the dead, mercy shall be accorded, and acquittal from the punishment of the eternal fire. For were there not some whose sins, though not remitted in this life, shall be remitted in that which is to come, it could not be truly said, "They shall not be forgiven, neither in this world, neither in that which is to come." But when the Judge of quick and dead has said, "Come, ye blessed of my Father, inherit the kingdom prepared for you from the foundation of the world," and to those on the other side, "Depart from me, ye cursed, into the eternal fire, which is prepared for the devil and his angels," and "These shall go away into eternal punishment, but the righteous into eternal life," it were excessively presumptuous to say that the punishment of any of those whom God has said shall go away into eternal punishment shall not be eternal, and so bring either despair or doubt upon the corresponding promise of life eternal.

Let no man then so understand the words of the Psalmist, "Shall God forget to be gracious? shall He shut up in His anger His tender mercies" as if the sentence of God were true of good men, false of bad men, or true of good men and wicked angels, but false of bad men. For the Psalmist's words refer to the vessels of mercy and the children of the promise, of whom the prophet himself was one; for when he had said, "Shall God forget to be gracious? shall He shut up in His anger His tender mercies?" and then immediately subjoins, "And I said, Now I begin: this is the change wrought by the right hand of the Most High," he manifestly explained what he meant by the words, "Shall he shut up in His anger His tender mercies?" For God's anger is this mortal life, in which man is made like to vanity, and his days pass as a shadow. Yet in this anger God does not forget to be gracious, causing His sun to shine and His rain to descend on the just and the unjust; and thus He does not in His anger cut short His tender mercies, and especially in what the Psalmist speaks of in the words, "Now I begin: this change is from the right hand of the Most High;" for He changes for the better the vessels of mercy, even while they are still in this most wretched life, which is God's anger, and even while His anger is manifesting itself in this miserable corruption; for "in His anger He does not shut up His tender mercies." And since the truth of this divine canticle is quite satisfied by this application of it, there is no need to give it a reference to that place in which those who do not belong to the city of God are punished in eternal fire. But if any persist in extending its application to the torments of the wicked, let them at least understand it so that the anger of God, which has threatened the wicked with eternal punishment, shall abide, but shall be mixed with mercy to the extent of alleviating the torments which might justly be inflicted; so that the wicked shall neither wholly escape, nor only for a time endure these threatened pains, but that they shall be less severe and more endurable than they deserve. Thus the anger of God shall continue, and at the same time He will not in this anger shut up His tender mercies. But even this hypothesis I am not to be supposed to affirm because I do not positively oppose it.

As for those who find an empty threat rather than a truth in such passages as these: "Depart from me, ye cursed, into everlasting fire;" and "These shall go away into eternal punishment;" and "They shall be tormented for ever and ever;" and "Their worm shall not die, and their fire shall not be quenched"—such persons, I say, are most emphatically and abundantly refuted, not by me so much as by the divine Scripture itself. For the men of Nineveh repented in this life, and therefore their repentance was fruitful, inasmuch as they sowed in that field which the Lord meant to be sown in tears that it might afterwards be reaped in joy. And yet who will deny that God's prediction was fulfilled in their case, if at least he observes that God destroys sinners not only in anger but also in compassion? For sinners are destroyed in two ways—either, like the Sodomites, the men themselves are punished for their sins, or, like the Ninevites, the men's sins are destroyed by repentance. God's prediction, therefore, was fulfilled—the wicked Nineveh was overthrown, and a good Nineveh built up. For its walls and houses remained standing; the city was overthrown in its depraved manners. And thus, though the prophet was provoked that the destruction which the inhabitants dreaded, because of his prediction, did not take place, yet that which God's foreknowledge had predicted did take place, for He who foretold the destruction knew how it should be fulfilled in a less calamitous sense.

But that these perversely compassionate persons may see what is the purport of these words, "How great is the abundance of Thy sweetness, Lord, which Thou hast hidden for them that fear Thee," let them read what follows: "And Thou hast perfected it for them that hope in Thee." For what means, "Thou hast hidden it for them that fear Thee," "Thou hast perfected it for them that hope in Thee," unless this, that to those who through fear of punishment seek to establish their own righteousness by the law, the righteousness of God is not sweet, because they are ignorant of it? They have not tasted it. For they hope in themselves, not in Him; and therefore God's abundant sweetness is hidden from them. They fear God, indeed, but it is with that servile fear "which is not in love; for perfect love casteth out fear." Therefore to them that hope in Him He perfecteth His sweetness, inspiring them with His own love, so that with a holy fear, which love does not cast out, but which endureth for ever, they may, when they glory, glory in the Lord. For the righteousness of God is Christ, "who is of God made unto us," as the apostle says, "wisdom, and righteousness, and sanctification, and redemption: as it is written, He that glorieth, let him glory in the Lord." This righteousness of God, which is the gift of grace without merits, is not known by those who go about to establish their own righteousness, and are therefore not subject to the righteousness of God, which is Christ. But it is in this righteousness that we find the great abundance of God's sweetness, of which the psalm says, "Taste and see how sweet the Lord is." And this we rather taste than partake of to satiety in this our pilgrimage. We hunger and thirst for it now, that hereafter we may be satisfied with it when we see Him as He is, and that is fulfilled which is written, "I shall be satisfied when Thy glory shall be manifested." It is thus that Christ perfects the great abundance of His sweetness to them that hope in Him. But if God conceals His sweetness from them that fear Him in the sense that these our objectors fancy, so that men's ignorance of His purpose of mercy towards the wicked may lead them to fear Him and live better, and so that there may be prayer made for those who are not living as they ought, how then does He perfect His sweetness to them that hope in Him, since, if their dreams be true, it is this very sweetness which will prevent Him from punishing those who do not hope in Him? Let us then seek that sweetness of His, which He perfects to them that hope in Him, not that which He is supposed to perfect to those who despise and blaspheme Him; for in vain, after this life, does a man seek for what he has neglected to provide while in this life.

Then, as to that saying of the apostle, "For God hath concluded all in unbelief, that He may have mercy upon all," it does not mean that He will condemn no one; but the foregoing context shows what is meant. The apostle composed the epistle for the Gentiles who were already believers; and when he was speaking to them of the Jews who were yet to believe, he says, "For as ye in times past believed not God, yet have now obtained mercy through their unbelief; even so have these also now not believed, that through your mercy they also may obtain mercy." Then he added the words in question with which these persons beguile themselves: "For God concluded all in unbelief, that He might have mercy upon all." All whom, if not all those of whom he was speaking, just as if he had said, "Both you and them?" God then concluded all those in unbelief, both Jews and Gentiles, whom He foreknew and predestinated to be conformed to the image of His Son, in order that they might be confounded by the bitterness of unbelief, and might repent and believingly turn to the sweetness of God's mercy, and might take up that exclamation of the psalm, "How great is the abundance of Thy sweetness, O Lord, which Thou hast hidden for them that fear Thee, but hast perfected to them that hope," not in themselves, but "in Thee." He has mercy, then, on all the vessels of mercy. And what means "all?" Both those of the Gentiles and those of the Jews whom He predestinated, called, justified, glorified: none of these will be condemned by Him; but we cannot say none of all men whatever.

Chapter XXV: *Whether Those Who Received Heretical Baptism, and Have Afterwards Fallen Away to Wickedness of Life; Or Those Who Have Received Catholic Baptism, But Have Afterwards Passed Over to Heresy and Schism; Or Those Who Have Remained in the Catholic Church in Which They Were Baptized, But Have Continued to Live Immorally—May Hope Through the Virtue of the Sacraments for the Remission of Eternal Punishment.*

But let us now reply to those who promise deliverance from eternal fire, not to the devil and his angels (as neither do they of whom we have been speaking), nor even to all men whatever, but only to those who have been washed by the baptism of Christ, and have become partakers of His body and blood, no matter how they have lived, no matter what heresy or impiety they have fallen into. But they are contradicted by the apostle, where he says, "Now the works of the flesh are manifest, which are these; fornication, uncleanness, lasciviousness, idolatry, witchcraft, hatred, variances, emulations, wrath, strife, heresies, envyings, drunkenness, revelings, and the like: of the which I tell you before, as I have also told you in time past, for they which do such things shall not inherit the kingdom of God." Certainly this sentence of the apostle is false, if such persons shall be delivered after any lapse of time, and shall then inherit the kingdom of God. But as it is not false, they shall certainly never inherit the kingdom of God. And if they shall never enter that kingdom, then they shall always be retained in eternal punishment; for there is no middle place where he may live unpunished who has not been admitted into that kingdom.

And therefore we may reasonably inquire how we are to understand these words of the Lord Jesus: "This is the bread which cometh down from heaven, that a man may eat thereof, and not die. I am the living bread which came down from heaven. If any man eat of this bread, he shall live for ever." And those, indeed, whom we are now answering, are refuted in their interpretation of this passage by those whom we are shortly to answer, and who do not promise this deliverance to all who have received the sacraments of baptism and the Lord's body, but only to the catholics, however wickedly they live; for these, say they, have eaten the Lord's body not only sacramentally, but really, being constituted members of His body, of which the apostle says, "We being many are one bread, one body." He then who is in the unity of Christ's body (that is to say, in the Christian membership), of which body the faithful have been wont to receive the sacrament at the altar, that man is truly said to eat the body and drink the blood of Christ. And consequently heretics and schismatics being separate from the unity of this body, are able to receive the same sacrament, but with no profit to themselves—nay, rather to their own hurt, so that they are rather more severely judged than liberated after some time. For they are not in that bond of peace which is symbolized by that sacrament.

But again, even those who sufficiently understand that he who is not in the body of Christ cannot be said to eat the body of Christ, are in error when they promise liberation from the fire of eternal punishment to persons who fall away from the unity of that body into heresy, or even into heathenish superstition. For, in the first place, they ought to consider how intolerable it is, and how discordant with sound doctrine, to suppose that many, indeed, or almost all, who have forsaken the Church catholic, and have originated impious heresies and become heresiarchs, should enjoy a destiny superior to those who never were catholics, but have fallen into the snares of these others; that is to say, if the fact of their catholic baptism and original reception of the sacrament of the body of Christ in the true body of Christ is sufficient to deliver these heresiarchs from eternal punishment. For certainly he who deserts the faith, and from a deserter becomes an assailant, is worse than he who has not deserted the faith he never held. And, in the second place, they are contradicted by the apostle, who, after enumerating the works of the flesh, says with reference to heresies, "They who do such things shall not inherit the kingdom of God."

And therefore neither ought such persons as lead an abandoned and damnable life to be confident of salvation, though they persevere to the end in the communion of the Church catholic, and comfort themselves with the words, "He that endureth to the end shall be saved." By the iniquity of their life they abandon that very righteousness of life which Christ is to them, whether it be by fornication, or by perpetrating in their body the other uncleannesses which the apostle would not so much as mention, or by a dissolute luxury, or by doing any one of those things of which he says, "They who do such things shall not inherit the kingdom of God." Consequently, they who do such things shall not exist anywhere but in eternal punishment, since they cannot be in the kingdom of God. For, while they continue in such things to the very end of life, they cannot be said to abide in Christ to the end; for to abide in Him is to abide in the faith of Christ. And this faith, according to the apostle's definition of it, "worketh by love." And "love," as he elsewhere says, "worketh no evil." Neither can these persons be said to eat the body of Christ, for they cannot even be reckoned among His members. For, not to mention other reasons, they cannot be at once the members of Christ and the members of a harlot. In fine, He Himself, when He says, "He that eateth my flesh and drinketh my blood, dwelleth in me, and I in him," shows what it is in reality, and not sacramentally, to eat His body and drink His blood; for this is to dwell in Christ, that He also may dwell in us. So that it is as if He said, He that dwelleth not in me, and in whom I do not dwell, let him not say or think that he eateth my body or drinketh my blood. Accordingly, they who are not Christ's members do not dwell in Him. And they who make themselves members of a harlot, are not members of Christ unless they have penitently abandoned that evil, and have returned to this good to be reconciled to it.

Chapter XXVI: *What It is to Have Christ for a Foundation, and Who They are to Whom Salvation as by Fire is Promised.*

But, say they, the catholic Christians have Christ for a foundation, and they have not fallen away from union with Him, no matter how depraved a life they have built on this foundation, as wood, hay, stubble; and accordingly the well-directed faith by which Christ is their foundation will suffice to deliver them some time from the continuance of that fire, though it be with loss, since those things they have built on it shall be burned. Let the Apostle James summarily reply to them: "If any man say he has faith, and have not works, can faith save him?" And who then is it, they ask, of whom the Apostle Paul says, "But he himself shall be saved, yet so as by fire?" Let us join them in their inquiry; and one thing is very certain, that it is not he of whom James speaks, else we should make the two apostles contradict one another, if the one says, "Though a man's works be evil, his faith will save him as by fire," while the other says, "If he have not good works, can his faith save him?"

We shall then ascertain who it is who can be saved by fire, if we first discover what it is to have Christ for a foundation. And this we may very readily learn from the image itself. In a building the foundation is first. Whoever, then, has Christ in his heart, so that no earthly or temporal things—not even those that are legitimate and allowed—are preferred to Him, has Christ as a foundation. But if these things be preferred, then even though a man seem to have faith in Christ, yet Christ is not the foundation to that man; and much more if he, in contempt of wholesome precepts, seek forbidden gratifications, is he clearly convicted of putting Christ not first but last, since he has despised Him as his ruler, and has preferred to fulfill his own wicked lusts, in contempt of Christ's commands and allowances. Accordingly, if any Christian man loves a harlot, and, attaching himself to her, becomes one body, he has not now Christ for a foundation. But if any one loves his own wife, and loves her as Christ would have him love her, who can doubt that he has Christ for a foundation? But if he loves her in the world's fashion, carnally, as the disease of lust prompts him, and as the Gentiles love who know not God, even this the apostle, or rather Christ by the apostle, allows as a venial fault. And therefore even such a man may have Christ for a foundation. For so long as he does not prefer such an affection or pleasure to Christ, Christ is his foundation, though on it he builds wood, hay, stubble; and therefore he shall be saved as by fire. For the fire of affliction shall burn such luxurious pleasures and earthly loves, though they be not damnable, because enjoyed in lawful wedlock. And of this fire the fuel is bereavement, and all those calamities which consume these joys. Consequently the superstructure will be loss to him who has built it, for he shall not retain it, but shall be agonized by the loss of those things in the enjoyment of which he found pleasure. But by this fire he shall be saved through virtue of the foundation, because even if a persecutor demanded whether he would retain Christ or these things, he would prefer Christ. Would you hear, in the apostle's own words, who he is who builds on the foundation gold, silver, precious stones? "He that is unmarried," he says, "careth for the things that belong to the Lord, how he may please the Lord." Would you hear who he is that buildeth wood, hay, stubble? "But he that is married careth for the things that are of the world, how he may please his wife. "Every man's work shall be made manifest: for the day shall declare it"—the day, no doubt, of tribulation—"because," says he, "it shall be revealed by fire." He calls tribulation fire, just as it is elsewhere said, "The furnace proves the vessels of the potter, and the trial of affliction righteous men." And "The fire shall try every man's work of what sort it is. If any man's work abide"—for a man's care for the things of the Lord, how he may please the Lord, abides—"which he hath built thereupon, he shall receive a reward"—that is, he shall reap the fruit of his care. "But if any man's work shall be burned, he shall suffer loss"—for what he loved he shall not retain: "but he himself shall be saved"—for no tribulation shall have moved him from that stable foundation—"yet so as by fire;" for that which he possessed with the sweetness of love he does not lose without the sharp sting of pain. Here, then, as seems to me, we have a fire which destroys neither, but enriches the one, brings loss to the other, proves both.

But if this passage [of Corinthians] is to interpret that fire of which the Lord shall say to those on His left hand, "Depart from me, ye cursed, into everlasting fire," so that among these we are to believe there are those who build on the foundation wood, hay, stubble, and that they, through virtue of the good foundation, shall after a time be liberated from the fire that is the award of their evil deserts, what then shall we think of those on the right hand, to whom it shall be said, "Come, ye blessed of my Father, inherit the kingdom prepared for you," unless that they are those who have built on the foundation gold, silver, precious stones? But if the fire of which our Lord speaks is the same as that of which the apostle says, "Yet so as by fire," then both—that is to say, both those on the right as well as those on the left—are to be cast into it. For that fire is to try both, since it is said, "For the day of the Lord shall declare it, because it shall be revealed by fire; and the fire shall try every man's work of what sort it is." If, therefore, the fire shall try both, in order that if any man's work abide—i.e., if the superstructure be not consumed by the fire—he may receive a reward, and that if his work is burned he may suffer loss, certainly that fire is not the eternal fire itself. For into this latter fire only those on the left hand shall be cast, and that with final and everlasting doom; but that former fire proves those on the right hand. But some of them it so proves that it does not burn and consume the structure which is found to have been built by them on Christ as the foundation; while others of them it proves in another fashion, so as to burn what they have built up, and thus cause them to suffer loss, while they themselves are saved because they have retained Christ, who was laid as their sure foundation, and have loved

Him above all. But if they are saved, then certainly they shall stand at the right hand, and shall with the rest hear the sentence, “Come, ye blessed of my Father, inherit the kingdom prepared for you;” and not at the left hand, where those shall be who shall not be saved, and shall therefore hear the doom, “Depart from me, ye cursed, into everlasting fire.” For from that fire no man shall be saved, because they all shall go away into eternal punishment, where their worms shall not die, nor their fire be quenched, in which they shall be tormented day and night for ever.

But if it be said that in the interval of time between the death of this body and that last day of judgment and retribution which shall follow the resurrection, the bodies of the dead shall be exposed to a fire of such a nature that it shall not affect those who have not in this life indulged in such pleasures and pursuits as shall be consumed like wood, hay, stubble, but shall affect those others who have carried with them structures of that kind; if it be said that such worldliness, being venial, shall be consumed in the fire of tribulation either here only, or here and hereafter both, or here that it may not be hereafter—this I do not contradict, because possibly it is true. For perhaps even the death of the body is itself a part of this tribulation, for it results from the first transgression, so that the time which follows death takes its color in each case from the nature of the man’s building. The persecutions, too, which have crowned the martyrs, and which Christians of all kinds suffer, try both buildings like a fire, consuming some, along with the builders themselves, if Christ is not found in them as their foundation, while others they consume without the builders, because Christ is found in them, and they are saved, though with loss; and other buildings still they do not consume, because such materials as abide for ever are found in them. In the end of the world there shall be in the time of Antichrist tribulation such as has never before been. How many edifices there shall then be, of gold or of hay, built on the best foundation, Christ Jesus, which that fire shall prove, bringing joy to some, loss to others, but without destroying either sort, because of this stable foundation! But whosoever prefers, I do not say his wife, with whom he lives for carnal pleasure, but any of those relatives who afford no delight of such a kind, and whom it is right to love—whosoever prefers these to Christ, and loves them after a human and carnal fashion, has not Christ as a foundation, and will therefore not be saved by fire, nor indeed at all; for he shall not possibly dwell with the Saviour, who says very explicitly concerning this very matter, "He that loveth father or mother more than me is not worthy of me; and he that loveth son or daughter more than me is not worthy of me." But he who loves his relations carnally, and yet so that he does not prefer them to Christ, but would rather want them than Christ if he were put to the proof, shall be saved by fire, because it is necessary that by the loss of these relations he suffer pain in proportion to his love. And he who loves father, mother, sons, daughters, according to Christ, so that he aids them in obtaining His kingdom and cleaving to Him, or loves them because they are members of Christ, God forbid that this love should be consumed as wood, hay, stubble, and not rather be reckoned a structure of gold, silver, precious stones. For how can a man love those more than Christ whom he loves only for Christ's sake?

Chapter XXVII: *Against the Belief of Those Who Think that the Sins Which Have Been Accompanied with Alms-giving Will Do Them No Harm.*

It remains to reply to those who maintain that those only shall burn in eternal fire who neglect alms-deeds proportioned to their sins, resting this opinion on the words of the Apostle James, "He shall have judgment without mercy that hath showed no mercy." Therefore, they say, he that hath showed mercy, though he has not reformed his dissolute conduct, but has lived wickedly and iniquitously even while abounding in alms, shall have a merciful judgment, so that he shall either be not condemned at all, or shall be delivered from final judgment after a time. And for the same reason they suppose that Christ will discriminate between those on the right hand and those on the left, and will send the one party into His kingdom, the other into eternal punishment, on the sole ground of their attention to or neglect of works of charity. Moreover, they endeavor to use the prayer which the Lord Himself taught as a proof and bulwark of their opinion, that daily sins which are never abandoned can be expiated through alms-deeds, no matter how offensive or of what sort they be. For, say they, as there is no day on which Christians ought not to use this prayer, so there is no sin of any kind which, though committed every day, is not remitted when we say, "Forgive us our debts," if we take care to fulfill what follows, "as we forgive our debtors." For, they go on to say, the Lord does not say, "If ye forgive men their trespasses, your heavenly Father will forgive you your little daily sins," but "will forgive you your sins." Therefore, be they of any kind or magnitude whatever, be they perpetrated daily and never abandoned or subdued in this life, they can be pardoned, they presume, through alms-deeds.

But they are right to inculcate the giving of aims proportioned to past sins; for if they said that any kind of alms could obtain the divine pardon of great sins committed daily and with habitual enormity, if they said that such sins could thus be daily remitted, they would see that their doctrine was absurd and ridiculous. For they would thus be driven to acknowledge that it were possible for a very wealthy man to buy absolution from murders, adulteries, and all manner of wickedness, by paying a daily alms of ten paltry coins. And if it be most absurd and insane to make such an acknowledgment, and if we still ask what are those fitting alms of which even the forerunner of Christ said, "Bring forth therefore fruits meet for repentance," undoubtedly it will be found that they are not such as are done by men who undermine their life by daily enormities even to the very end. For they suppose that by giving to the poor a small fraction of the wealth they acquire by extortion and spoliation they can propitiate Christ, so that they may with impunity commit the most damnable sins, in the persuasion that they have bought from Him a license to transgress, or rather do buy a daily indulgence. And if they for one crime have distributed all their goods to Christ's needy members, that could profit them nothing unless they desisted from all similar actions, and attained charity which worketh no evil He therefore who does alms-deeds proportioned to his sins must first begin with himself. For it is not reasonable that a man who exercises charity towards his neighbor should not do so towards himself, since he hears the Lord saying, "Thou shalt love thy neighbor as thyself," and again, "Have compassion on thy soul, and please God." He then who has not compassion on his own soul that he may please God, how can he be said to do alms-deeds proportioned to his sins? To the same purpose is that written, "He who is bad to himself, to whom can he be good?" We ought therefore to do alms that we may be heard when we pray that our past sins may be forgiven, not that while we continue in them we may think to provide ourselves with a license for wickedness by alms-deeds.

The reason, therefore, of our predicting that He will impute to those on His right hand the alms-deeds they have done, and charge those on His left with omitting the same, is that He may thus show the efficacy of charity for the deletion of past sins, not for impunity in their perpetual commission. And such persons, indeed, as decline to abandon their evil habits of life for a better course cannot be said to do charitable deeds. For this is the purport of the saying, "Inasmuch as ye did it not to one of the least of these, ye did it not to me." He shows them that they do not perform charitable actions even when they think they are doing so. For if they gave bread to a hungering Christian because he is a Christian, assuredly they would not deny to themselves the bread of righteousness, that is, Christ Himself; for God considers not the person to whom the gift is made, but the spirit in which it is made. He therefore who loves Christ in a Christian extends alms to him in the same spirit in which he draws near to Christ, not in that spirit which would abandon Christ if it could do so with impunity. For in proportion as a man loves what Christ disapproves does he himself abandon Christ. For what does it profit a man that he is baptized, if he is not justified? Did not He who said, "Except a man be born of water and of the Spirit, he shall not enter into the kingdom of God," say also, "Except your righteousness shall exceed the righteousness of the scribes and Pharisees, ye shall not enter into the kingdom of heaven?" Why do many through fear of the first saying run to baptism, while few through fear of the second seek to be justified? As therefore it is not to his brother a man says, "Thou fool," if when he says it he is indignant not at the brotherhood, but at the sin of the offender—for otherwise he were guilty of hell fire—so he who extends charity to a Christian does not extend it to a Christian if he does not love Christ in him. Now he does not love Christ who refuses to be justified in Him. Or, again, if a man has been guilty of this sin of calling his brother Fool, unjustly reviling him without any desire to remove his sin, his alms-deeds go a small way towards expiating this fault, unless he adds to this the remedy of reconciliation which the same passage enjoins. For it is there said, "Therefore, if thou bring thy gift to the altar, and there rememberest that thy brother hath aught against thee; leave there thy gift before the altar, and go thy way; first be reconciled to thy brother, and then come and offer thy gift." Just so it is a small matter to do alms-deeds, no matter how great they be, for any sin, so long as the offender continues in the practice of sin.

Then as to the daily prayer which the Lord Himself taught, and which is therefore called the Lord's prayer, it obliterates indeed the sins of the day, when day by day we say, "Forgive us our debts," and when we not only say but act out that which follows, "as we forgive our debtors;" but we utter this petition because sins have been committed, and not that they may be. For by it our Saviour designed to teach us that, however righteously we live in this life of infirmity and darkness, we still commit sins for the remission of which we ought to pray, while we must pardon those who sin against us that we ourselves also may be pardoned. The Lord then did not utter the words, "If ye forgive men their trespasses, your Father will also forgive you your trespasses," in order that we might contract from this petition such confidence as should enable us to sin securely from day to day, either putting ourselves above the fear of human laws, or craftily deceiving men concerning our conduct, but in order that we might thus learn not to suppose that we are without sins, even though we should be free from crimes; as also God admonished the priests of the old law to this same effect regarding their sacrifices, which He commanded them to offer first for their own sins, and then for the sins of the people. For even the very words of so great a Master and Lord are to be intently considered. For He does not say, If ye forgive men their sins, your Father will also forgive you your sins, no matter of what sort they be, but He says, your sins; for it was a daily prayer He was teaching, and it was certainly to disciples already justified He was speaking. What, then, does He mean by "your sins," but those sins from which not even you who are justified and sanctified can be free? While, then, those who seek occasion from this petition to indulge in habitual sin maintain that the Lord meant to include great sins, because He did not say, He will forgive you your small sins, but "your sins," we, on the other hand, taking into account the character of the persons He was addressing, cannot see our way to interpret the expression "your sins" of anything but small sins, because such persons are no longer guilty of great sins. Nevertheless not even great sins themselves—sins from which we must flee with a total reformation of life—are forgiven to those who pray, unless they observe the appended precept, "as ye also forgive your debtors." For if the very small sins which attach even to the life of the righteous be not remitted without that condition, how much further from obtaining indulgence shall those be who are involved in many great crimes, if, while they cease from perpetrating such enormities, they still inexorably refuse to remit any debt incurred to themselves, since the Lord says, "But if ye forgive not men their trespasses, neither will your Father forgive your trespasses?" For this is the purport of the saying of the Apostle James also, "He shall have judgment without mercy that hath showed no mercy." For we should remember that servant whose debt of ten thousand talents his lord canceled, but afterwards ordered him to pay up, because the servant himself had no pity for his fellow-servant, who owed him an hundred pence. The words which the Apostle James subjoins,"And mercy rejoiceth against judgment," find their application among those who are the children of the promise and vessels of mercy. For even those righteous men, who have lived with such holiness that they receive into the eternal habitations others also who have won their friendship with the mammon of unrighteousness, became such only through the merciful deliverance of Him who justifies the ungodly, imputing to him a reward according to grace, not according to debt. For among this number is the apostle, who says, "I obtained mercy to be faithful."

But it must be admitted, that those who are thus received into the eternal habitations are not of such a character that their own life would suffice to rescue them without the aid of the saints, and consequently in their case especially does mercy rejoice against judgment. And yet we are not on this account to suppose that every abandoned profligate, who has made no amendment of his life, is to be received into the eternal habitations if only he has assisted the saints with the mammon of unrighteousness—that is to say, with money or wealth which has been unjustly acquired, or, if rightfully acquired, is yet not the true riches, but only what iniquity counts riches, because it knows not the true riches in which those persons abound, who even receive others also into eternal habitations. There is then a certain kind of life, which is neither, on the one hand, so bad that those who adopt it are not helped towards the kingdom of heaven by any bountiful alms-giving by which they may relieve the wants of the saints, and make friends who could receive them into eternal habitations, nor, on the other hand, so good that it of itself suffices to win for them that great blessedness, if they do not obtain mercy through the merits of those whom they have made their friends. And I frequently wonder that even Virgil should give expression to this sentence of the Lord, in which He says, "Make to yourselves friends of the mammon of unrighteousness, that they may receive you into everlasting habitations;" and this very similar saying, "He that receiveth a prophet, in the name of a prophet, shall receive a prophet's reward; and he that receiveth a righteous man, in the name of a righteous man, shall receive a righteous man's reward." For when that poet described the Elysian fields, in which they suppose that the souls of the blessed dwell, he placed there not only those who had been able by their own merit to reach that abode, but added—

> "And they who grateful memory won
> By services to others done;"

that is, they who had served others, and thereby merited to be remembered by them. Just as if they used the expression so common in Christian lips, where some humble person commends himself to one of the saints, and says, Remember me, and secures that he do so by deserving well at his hand. But what that kind of life we have been speaking of is, and what those sins are which prevent a man from winning the kingdom of God by himself, but yet permit him to avail himself of the merits of the saints, it is very difficult to ascertain, very perilous to define. For my own part, in spite of all investigation, I have been up to the present hour unable to discover this. And possibly it is hidden from us, lest we should become careless in avoiding such sins, and so cease to make progress. For if it were known what these sins are which, though they continue, and be not abandoned for a higher life, do yet not prevent us from seeking and hoping for the intercession of the saints, human sloth would presumptuously wrap itself in these sins, and would take no steps to be disentangled from such wrappings by the deft energy of any virtue, but would only desire to be rescued by the merits of other people, whose friendship had been won by a bountiful use of the mammon of unrighteousness. But now that we are left in ignorance of the precise nature of that iniquity which is venial, even though it be persevered in, certainly we are both more vigilant in our prayers and efforts for progress, and more careful to secure with the mammon of unrighteousness friends for ourselves among the saints.

But this deliverance, which is effected by one's own prayers, or the intercession of holy men, secures that a man be not cast into eternal fire, but not that, when once he has been cast into it, he should after a time be rescued from it. For even those who fancy that what is said of the good ground bringing forth abundant fruit, some thirty, some sixty, some an hundred fold, is to be referred to the saints, so that in proportion to their merits some of them shall deliver thirty men, some sixty, some an hundred—even those who maintain this are yet commonly inclined to suppose that this deliverance will take place at, and not after the day of judgment. Under this impression, some one who observed the unseemly folly with which men promise themselves impunity on the ground that all will be included in this method of deliverance, is reported to have very happily remarked, that we should rather endeavor to live so well that we shall be all found among the number of those who are to intercede for the liberation of others, lest these should be so few in number, that, after they have delivered one thirty, another sixty, another a hundred, there should still remain many who could not be delivered from punishment by their intercessions, and among them every one who has vainly and rashly promised himself the fruit of another's labor. But enough has been said in reply to those who acknowledge the authority of the same sacred Scriptures as ourselves, but who, by a mistaken interpretation of them, conceive of the future rather as they themselves wish, than as the Scriptures teach. And having given this reply, I now, according to promise, close this book.

Book Twenty-Two

Chapter VIII: *Of Miracles Which Were Wrought that the World Might Believe in Christ, and Which Have Not Ceased Since the World Believed.*

Why, they say, are those miracles, which you affirm were wrought formerly, wrought no longer? I might, indeed, reply that miracles were necessary before the world believed, in order that it might believe. And whoever now-a-days demands to see prodigies that he may believe, is himself a great prodigy, because he does not believe, though the whole world does. But they make these objections for the sole purpose of insinuating that even those former miracles were never wrought. How, then, is it that everywhere Christ is celebrated with such firm belief in His resurrection and ascension? How is it that in enlightened times, in which every impossibility is rejected, the world has, without any miracles, believed things marvelously incredible? Or will they say that these things were credible, and therefore were credited? Why then do they themselves not believe? Our argument, therefore, is a summary one—either incredible things which were not witnessed have caused the world to believe other incredible things which both occurred and were witnessed, or this matter was so credible that it needed no miracles in proof of it, and therefore convicts these unbelievers of unpardonable scepticism. This I might say for the sake of refuting these most frivolous objectors. But we cannot deny that many miracles were wrought to confirm that one grand and health-giving miracle of Christ's ascension to heaven with the flesh in which He rose. For these most trustworthy books of ours contain in one narrative both the miracles that were wrought and the creed which they were wrought to confirm. The miracles were published that they might produce faith, and the faith which they produced brought them into greater prominence. For they are read in congregations that they may be believed, and yet they would not be so read unless they were believed. For even now miracles are wrought in the name of Christ, whether by His sacraments or by the prayers or relics of His saints; but they are not so brilliant and conspicuous as to cause them to be published with such glory as accompanied the former miracles. For the canon of the sacred writings, which behooved to be closed, causes those to be everywhere recited, and to sink into the memory of all the congregations; but these modern miracles are scarcely known even to the whole population in the midst of which they are wrought, and at the best are confined to one spot. For frequently they are known only to a very few persons, while all the rest are ignorant of them, especially if the state is a large one; and when they are reported to other persons in other localities, there is no sufficient authority to give them prompt and unwavering credence, although they are reported to the faithful by the faithful.

The miracle which was wrought at Milan when I was there, and by which a blind man was restored to sight, could come to the knowledge of many; for not only is the city a large one, but also the emperor was there at the time, and the occurrence was witnessed by an immense concourse of people that had gathered to the bodies of the martyrs Protasius and Gervasius, which had long lain concealed and unknown, but were now made known to the bishop Ambrose in a dream, and discovered by him. By virtue of these remains the darkness of that blind man was scattered, and he saw the light of day.

But who but a very small number are aware of the cure which was wrought upon Innocentius, ex-advocate of the deputy prefecture, a cure wrought at Carthage, in my presence, and under my own eyes? For when I and my brother Alypius, who were not yet clergymen, though already servants of God, came from abroad, this man received us, and made us live with him, for he and all his household were devotedly pious. He was being treated by medical men for fistulæ, of which he had a large number intricately seated in the rectum. He had already undergone an operation, and the surgeons were using every means at their command for his relief. In that operation he had suffered long-continued and acute pain; yet, among the many folds of the gut, one had escaped the operators so entirely, that, though they ought to have laid it open with the knife, they never touched it. And thus, though all those that had been opened were cured, this one remained as it was, and frustrated all their labor. The patient, having his suspicions awakened by the delay thus occasioned, and fearing greatly a second operation, which another medical man—one of his own domestics—had told him he must undergo, though this man had not even been allowed to witness the first operation, and had been banished from the house, and with difficulty allowed to come back to his enraged master's presence—the patient, I say, broke out to the surgeons, saying, "Are you going to cut me again? Are you, after all, to fulfill the prediction of that man whom you would not allow even to be present?" The surgeons laughed at the unskillful doctor, and soothed their patient's fears with fair words and promises. So several days passed, and yet nothing they tried did him good. Still they persisted in promising that they would cure that fistula by drugs, without the knife. They called in also another old practitioner of great repute in that department, Ammonius (for he was still alive at that time); and he, after examining the part, promised the same result as themselves from their care and skill. On this great authority, the patient became confident, and, as if already well, vented his good spirits in facetious remarks at the expense of his domestic physician, who had predicted a second operation. To make a long story short, after a number of days had thus uselessly elapsed, the surgeons, wearied and confused, had at last to confess that he could only be cured by the knife. Agitated with excessive fear, he was terrified, and grew pale with dread; and when he collected himself and was able to speak, he ordered them to go away and never to return. Worn out with weeping, and driven by necessity, it occurred to him to call in an Alexandrian, who was at that time esteemed a wonderfully skillful operator, that he might perform the operation his rage would not suffer them to do. But when he had come, and examined with a professional eye the traces of their careful work, he acted the part of a good man, and persuaded his patient to allow those same hands the satisfaction of finishing his cure which had begun it with a skill that excited his admiration, adding that there was no doubt his only hope of a cure was by an operation, but that it was thoroughly inconsistent with his nature to win the credit of the cure by doing the little that remained to be done, and rob of their reward men whose consummate skill, care, and diligence he could not but admire when be saw the traces of their work. They were therefore again received to favor; and it was agreed that, in the presence of the Alexandrian, they should operate on the fistula, which, by the consent of all, could now only be cured by the knife. The operation was deferred till the following day. But when they had left, there arose in the house such a wailing, in sympathy with the excessive despondency of the master, that it seemed to us like the mourning at a funeral, and we could scarcely repress it. Holy men were in the habit of visiting him daily; Saturninus of blessed memory, at that time bishop of Uzali, and the presbyter Gelosus, and the deacons of the church of Carthage; and among these was the bishop Aurelius, who alone of them all survives—a man to be named by us with due reverence—and with him I have often spoken of this affair, as we conversed together about the wonderful works of God, and I have found that he distinctly remembers what I am now relating. When these persons visited him that evening according to their custom, he besought them, with pitiable tears, that they would do him the honor of being present next day at what he judged his funeral rather than his suffering. For such was the terror his former pains had produced, that he made no doubt he would die in the hands of the surgeons. They comforted him, and exhorted him to put his trust in God, and nerve his will like a man. Then we went to prayer; but while we, in the usual way, were kneeling and bending to the ground, he cast himself down, as if some one were hurling him violently to the earth, and began to pray; but in what a manner, with what earnestness and emotion, with what a flood of tears, with what groans and sobs, that shook his whole body, and almost prevented him speaking, who can describe! Whether the others prayed, and had not their attention wholly diverted by this conduct, I do not know. For myself, I could not pray at all. This only I briefly said in my heart: "O Lord, what prayers of Thy people dost Thou hear if Thou hearest not these?" For it seemed to me that nothing could be added to this prayer, unless he expired in praying. We rose from our knees, and, receiving the blessing of the bishop, departed, the patient beseeching his visitors to be present next morning, they exhorting him to keep up his heart. The dreaded day dawned. The servants of God were present, as they had promised to be; the surgeons arrived; all that the circumstances required was ready; the frightful instruments are produced; all look on in wonder and suspense. While those who have most influence with the patient are cheering his fainting spirit, his limbs are arranged on the couch so as to suit the hand of the operator; the knots of the bandages are untied; the part is bared; the surgeon examines it, and, with knife in hand, eagerly looks for the sinus that is to be cut. He searches for it with his eyes; he feels for it with his finger; he applies every kind of scrutiny: he finds a perfectly firm cicatrix! No words of mine can describe the joy, and praise, and thanksgiving to the merciful and almighty God which was poured from the lips of all, with tears of gladness. Let the scene be imagined rather than described!

In the same city of Carthage lived Innocentia, a very devout woman of the highest rank in the state. She had cancer in one of her breasts, a disease which, as physicians say, is incurable. Ordinarily, therefore, they either amputate, and so separate from the body the member on which the disease has seized, or, that the patient's life may be prolonged a little, though death is inevitable even if somewhat delayed, they abandon all remedies, following, as they say, the advice of Hippocrates. This the lady we speak of had been advised to by a skillful physician, who was intimate with her family; and she betook herself to God alone by prayer. On the approach of Easter, she was instructed in a dream to wait for the first woman that came out from the baptistery after being baptized, and to ask her to make the sign of Christ upon her sore. She did so, and was immediately cured. The physician who had advised her to apply no remedy if she wished to live a little longer, when he had examined her after this, and found that she who, on his former examination, was afflicted with that disease was now perfectly cured, eagerly asked her what remedy she had used, anxious, as we may well believe, to discover the drug which should defeat the decision of Hippocrates. But when she told him what had happened, he is said to have replied, with religious politeness, though with a contemptuous tone, and an expression which made her fear he would utter some blasphemy against Christ, "I thought you would make some great discovery to me." She, shuddering at his indifference, quickly replied, "What great thing was it for Christ to heal a cancer, who raised one who had been four days dead?" When, therefore, I had heard this, I was extremely indignant that so great a miracle wrought in that well-known city, and on a person who was certainly not obscure, should not be divulged, and I considered that she should be spoken to, if not reprimanded on this score. And when she replied to me that she had not kept silence on the subject, I asked the women with whom she was best acquainted whether they had ever heard of this before. They told me they knew nothing of it. "See," I said, "what your not keeping silence amounts to, since not even those who are so familiar with you know of it." And as I had only briefly heard the story, I made her tell how the whole thing happened, from beginning to end, while the other women listened in great astonishment, and glorified God.

A gouty doctor of the same city, when he had given in his name for baptism, and had been prohibited the day before his baptism from being baptized that year, by black woolly-haired boys who appeared to him in his dreams, and whom he understood to be devils, and when, though they trod on his feet, and inflicted the acutest pain he had ever yet experienced, he refused to obey them, but overcame them, and would not defer being washed in the laver of regeneration, was relieved in the very act of baptism, not only of the extraordinary pain he was tortured with, but also of the disease itself, so that, though he lived a long time afterwards, he never suffered from gout; and yet who knows of this miracle? We, however, do know it, and so, too, do the small number of brethren who were in the neighborhood, and to whose ears it might come.

An old comedian of Curubis was cured at baptism not only of paralysis, but also of hernia, and, being delivered from both afflictions, came up out of the font of regeneration as if he had had nothing wrong with his body. Who outside of Curubis knows of this, or who but a very few who might hear it elsewhere? But we, when we heard of it, made the man come to Carthage, by order of the holy bishop Aurelius, although we had already ascertained the fact on the information of persons whose word we could not doubt.

Hesperius, of a tribunitian family, and a neighbor of our own, has a farm called Zubedi in the Fussalian district; and, finding that his family, his cattle, and his servants were suffering from the malice of evil spirits, he asked our presbyters, during my absence, that one of them would go with him and banish the spirits by his prayers. One went, offered there the sacrifice of the body of Christ, praying with all his might that that vexation might cease. It did cease forthwith, through God's mercy. Now he had received from a friend of his own some holy earth brought from Jerusalem, where Christ, having been buried, rose again the third day. This earth he had hung up in his bedroom to preserve himself from harm. But when his house was purged of that demoniacal invasion, he began to consider what should be done with the earth; for his reverence for it made him unwilling to have it any longer in his bedroom. It so happened that I and Maximinus bishop of Synita, and then my colleague, were in the neighborhood. Hesperius asked us to visit him, and we did so. When he had related all the circumstances, he begged that the earth might be buried somewhere, and that the spot should be made a place of prayer where Christians might assemble for the worship of God. We made no objection: it was done as he desired. There was in that neighborhood a young countryman who was paralytic, who, when he heard of this, begged his parents to take him without delay to that holy place. When he had been brought there, he prayed, and forthwith went away on his own feet perfectly cured.

There is a country-seat called Victoriana, less than thirty miles from Hippo-regius. At it there is a monument to the Milanese martyrs, Protasius and Gervasius. Thither a young man was carried, who, when he was watering his horse one summer day at noon in a pool of a river, had been taken possession of by a devil. As he lay at the monument, near death, or even quite like a dead person, the lady of the manor, with her maids and religious attendants, entered the place for evening prayer and praise, as her custom was, and they began to sing hymns. At this sound the young man, as if electrified, was thoroughly aroused, and with frightful screaming seized the altar, and held it as if he did not dare or were not able to let it go, and as if he were fixed or tied to it; and the devil in him, with loud lamentation, besought that he might be spared, and confessed where and when and how he took possession of the youth. At last, declaring that he would go out of him, he named one by one the parts of his body which he threatened to mutilate as he went out and with these words he departed from the man. But his eye, falling out on his cheek, hung by a slender vein as by a root, and the whole of the pupil which had been black became white. When this was witnessed by those present (others too had now gathered to his cries, and had all joined in prayer for him), although they were delighted that he had recovered his sanity of mind, yet, on the other hand, they were grieved about his eye, and said he should seek medical advice. But his sister's husband, who had brought him there, said, "God, who has banished the devil, is able to restore his eye at the prayers of His saints." Therewith he replaced the eye that was fallen out and hanging, and bound it in its place with his handkerchief as well as he could, and advised him not to loose the bandage for seven days. When he did so, he found it quite healthy. Others also were cured there, but of them it were tedious to speak.

I know that a young woman of Hippo was immediately dispossessed of a devil, on anointing herself with oil, mixed with the tears of the presbyter who had been praying for her. I know also that a bishop once prayed for a demoniac young man whom he never saw, and that he was cured on the spot.

There was a fellow-townsman of ours at Hippo, Florentius, an old man, religious and poor, who supported himself as a tailor. Having lost his coat, and not having means to buy another, he prayed to the Twenty Martyrs, who have a very celebrated memorial shrine in our town, begging in a distinct voice that he might be clothed. Some scoffing young men, who happened to be present, heard him, and followed him with their sarcasm as he went away, as if he had asked the martyrs for fifty pence to buy a coat. But he, walking on in silence, saw on the shore a great fish, gasping as if just cast up, and having secured it with the good-natured assistance of the youths, he sold it for curing to a cook of the name of Catosus, a good Christian man, telling him how he had come by it, and receiving for it three hundred pence, which he laid out in wool, that his wife might exercise her skill upon, and make into a coat for him. But, on cutting up the fish, the cook found a gold ring in its belly; and forthwith, moved with compassion, and influenced, too, by religious fear, gave it up to the man, saying, "See how the Twenty Martyrs have clothed you."

When the bishop Projectus was bringing the relics of the most glorious martyr Stephen to the waters of Tibilis, a great concourse of people came to meet him at the shrine. There a blind woman entreated that she might be led to the bishop who was carrying the relics. He gave her the flowers he was carrying. She took them, applied them to her eyes, and forthwith saw. Those who were present were astounded, while she, with every expression of joy, preceded them, pursuing her way without further need of a guide.

Lucillus bishop of Sinita, in the neighborhood of the colonial town of Hippo, was carrying in procession some relics of the same martyr, which had been deposited in the castle of Sinita. A fistula under which he had long labored, and which his private physician was watching an opportunity to cut, was suddenly cured by the mere carrying of that sacred fardel—at least, afterwards there was no trace of it in his body.

Eucharius, a Spanish priest, residing at Calama, was for a long time a sufferer from stone. By the relics of the same martyr, which the bishop Possidius brought him, he was cured. Afterwards the same priest, sinking under another disease, was lying dead, and already they were binding his hands. By the succor of the same martyr he was raised to life, the priest's cloak having been brought from the oratory and laid upon the corpse.

There was there an old nobleman named Martial, who had a great aversion to the Christian religion, but whose daughter was a Christian, while her husband had been baptized that same year. When he was ill, they besought him with tears and prayers to become a Christian, but he positively refused, and dismissed them from his presence in a storm of indignation. It occurred to the son-in-law to go to the oratory of St. Stephen, and there pray for him with all earnestness that God might give him a right mind, so that he should not delay believing in Christ. This he did with great groaning and tears, and the burning fervor of sincere piety; then, as he left the place, he took some of the flowers that were lying there, and, as it was already night, laid them by his father's head, who so slept. And lo! before dawn, he cries out for some one to run for the bishop; but he happened at that time to be with me at Hippo. So when he had heard that he was from home, he asked the presbyters to come. They came. To the joy and amazement of all, he declared that he believed, and he was baptized. As long as he remained in life, these words were ever on his lips: "Christ, receive my spirit," though he was not aware that these were the last words of the most blessed Stephen when he was stoned by the Jews. They were his last words also, for not long after he himself also gave up the ghost.

There, too, by the same martyr, two men, one a citizen, the other a stranger, were cured of gout; but while the citizen was absolutely cured, the stranger was only informed what he should apply when the pain returned; and when he followed this advice, the pain was at once relieved.

Audurus is the name of an estate, where there is a church that contains a memorial shrine of the martyr Stephen. It happened that, as a little boy was playing in the court, the oxen drawing a wagon went out of the track and crushed him with the wheel, so that immediately he seemed at his last gasp. His mother snatched him up, and laid him at the shrine, and not only did he revive, but also appeared uninjured.

A religious female, who lived at Caspalium, a neighboring estate, when she was so ill as to be despaired of, had her dress brought to this shrine, but before it was brought back she was gone. However, her parents wrapped her corpse in the dress, and, her breath returning, she became quite well.

At Hippo a Syrian called Bassus was praying at the relics of the same martyr for his daughter, who was dangerously ill. He too had brought her dress with him to the shrine. But as he prayed, behold, his servants ran from the house to tell him she was dead. His friends, however, intercepted them, and forbade them to tell him, lest he should bewail her in public. And when he had returned to his house, which was already ringing with the lamentations of his family, and had thrown on his daughter's body the dress he was carrying, she was restored to life.

There, too, the son of a man, Irenæus, one of our tax-gatherers, took ill and died. And while his body was lying lifeless, and the last rites were being prepared, amidst the weeping and mourning of all, one of the friends who were consoling the father suggested that the body should be anointed with the oil of the same martyr. It was done, and he revived.

Likewise Eleusinus, a man of tribunitian rank among us, laid his infant son, who had died, on the shrine of the martyr, which is in the suburb where he lived, and, after prayer, which he poured out there with many tears, he took up his child alive.

What am I to do? I am so pressed by the promise of finishing this work, that I cannot record all the miracles I know; and doubtless several of our adherents, when they read what I have narrated, will regret that I have omitted so many which they, as well as I, certainly know. Even now I beg these persons to excuse me, and to consider how long it would take me to relate all those miracles, which the necessity of finishing the work I have undertaken forces me to omit. For were I to be silent of all others, and to record exclusively the miracles of healing which were wrought in the district of Calama and of Hippo by means of this martyr—I mean the most glorious Stephen—they would fill many volumes; and yet all even of these could not be collected, but only those of which narratives have been written for public recital. For when I saw, in our own times, frequent signs of the presence of divine powers similar to those which had been given of old, I desired that narratives might be written, judging that the multitude should not remain ignorant of these things. It is not yet two years since these relics were first brought to Hipporegius, and though many of the miracles which have been wrought by it have not, as I have the most certain means of knowing, been recorded, those which have been published amount to almost seventy at the hour at which I write. But at Calama, where these relics have been for a longer time, and where more of the miracles were narrated for public information, there are incomparably more.

At Uzali, too, a colony near Utica, many signal miracles were, to my knowledge, wrought by the same martyr, whose relics had found a place there by direction of the bishop Evodius, long before we had them at Hippo. But there the custom of publishing narratives does not obtain, or, I should say, did not obtain, for possibly it may now have been begun. For, when I was there recently, a woman of rank, Petronia, had been miraculously cured of a serious illness of long standing, in which all medical appliances had failed, and, with the consent of the above-named bishop of the place, I exhorted her to publish an account of it that might be read to the people. She most promptly obeyed, and inserted in her narrative a circumstance which I cannot omit to mention, though I am compelled to hasten on to the subjects which this work requires me to treat. She said that she had been persuaded by a Jew to wear next her skin, under all her clothes, a hair girdle, and on this girdle a ring, which, instead of a gem, had a stone which had been found in the kidneys of an ox. Girt with this charm, she was making her way to the threshold of the holy martyr. But, after leaving Carthage, and when she had been lodging in her own demesne on the river Bagrada, and was now rising to continue her journey, she saw her ring lying before her feet. In great surprise she examined the hair girdle, and when she found it bound, as it had been, quite firmly with knots, she conjectured that the ring had been worn through and dropped off; but when she found that the ring was itself also perfectly whole, she presumed that by this great miracle she had received somehow a pledge of her cure, whereupon she untied the girdle, and cast it into the river, and the ring along with it. This is not credited by those who do not believe either that the Lord Jesus Christ came forth from His mother's womb without destroying her virginity, and entered among His disciples when the doors were shut; but let them make strict inquiry into this miracle, and if they find it true, let them believe those others. The lady is of distinction, nobly born, married to a nobleman. She resides at Carthage. The city is distinguished, the person is distinguished, so that they who make inquiries cannot fail to find satisfaction. Certainly the martyr himself, by whose prayers she was healed, believed on the Son of her who remained a virgin; on Him who came in among the disciples when the doors were shut; in fine—and to this tends all that we have been retailing—on Him who ascended into heaven with the flesh in which He had risen; and it is because he laid down his life for this faith that such miracles were done by his means.

Even now, therefore, many miracles are wrought, the same God who wrought those we read of still performing them, by whom He will and as He will; but they are not as well known, nor are they beaten into the memory, like gravel, by frequent reading, so that they cannot fall out of mind. For even where, as is now done among ourselves, care is taken that the pamphlets of those who receive benefit be read publicly, yet those who are present hear the narrative but once, and many are absent; and so it comes to pass that even those who are present forget in a few days what they heard, and scarcely one of them can be found who will tell what he heard to one who he knows was not present.

One miracle was wrought among ourselves, which, though no greater than those I have mentioned, was yet so signal and conspicuous, that I suppose there is no inhabitant of Hippo who did not either see or hear of it, none who could possibly forget it. There were seven brothers and three sisters of a noble family of the Cappadocian Cæsarea, who were cursed by their mother, a new-made widow, on account of some wrong they had done her, and which she bitterly resented, and who were visited with so severe a punishment from Heaven, that all of them were seized with a hideous shaking in all their limbs. Unable, while presenting this loathsome appearance, to endure the eyes of their fellow-citizens, they wandered over almost the whole Roman world, each following his own direction. Two of them came to Hippo, a brother and a sister, Paulus and Palladia, already known in many other places by the fame of their wretched lot. Now it was about fifteen days before Easter when they came, and they came daily to church, and specially to the relics of the most glorious Stephen, praying that God might now be appeased, and restore their former health. There, and wherever they went, they attracted the attention of every one. Some who had seen them elsewhere, and knew the cause of their trembling, told others as occasion offered. Easter arrived, and on the Lord's day, in the morning, when there was now a large crowd present, and the young man was holding the bars of the holy place where the relics were, and praying, suddenly he fell down, and lay precisely as if asleep, but not trembling as he was wont to do even in sleep. All present were astonished. Some were alarmed, some were moved with pity; and while some were for lifting him up, others prevented them, and said they should rather wait and see what would result. And behold! he rose up, and trembled no more, for he was healed, and stood quite well, scanning those who were scanning him. Who then refrained himself from praising God? The whole church was filled with the voices of those who were shouting and congratulating him. Then they came running to me, where I was sitting ready to come into the church. One after another they throng in, the last comer telling me as news what the first had told me already; and while I rejoiced and inwardly gave God thanks, the young man himself also enters, with a number of others, falls at my knees, is raised up to receive my kiss. We go in to the congregation: the church was full, and ringing with the shouts of joy, "Thanks to God! Praised be God!" every one joining and shouting on all sides, "I have healed the people," and then with still louder voice shouting again. Silence being at last obtained, the customary lessons of the divine Scriptures were read. And when I came to my sermon, I made a few remarks suitable to the occasion and the happy and joyful feeling, not desiring them to listen to me, but rather to consider the eloquence of God in this divine work. The man dined with us, and gave us a careful account of his own, his mother's, and his family's calamity. Accordingly, on the following day, after delivering my sermon, I promised that next day I would read his narrative to the people. And when I did so, the third day after Easter Sunday, I made the brother and sister both stand on the steps of the raised place from which I used to speak; and while they stood there their pamphlet was read. The whole congregation, men and women alike, saw the one standing without any unnatural movement, the other trembling in all her limbs; so that those who had not before seen the man himself saw in his sister what the divine compassion had removed from him. In him they saw matter of congratulation, in her subject for prayer. Meanwhile, their pamphlet being finished, I instructed them to withdraw from the gaze of the people; and I had begun to discuss the whole matter somewhat more carefully, when lo! as I was proceeding, other voices are heard from the tomb of the martyr, shouting new congratulations. My audience turned round, and began to run to the tomb. The young woman, when she had come down from the steps where she had been standing, went to pray at the holy relics, and no sooner had she touched the bars than she, in the same way as her brother, collapsed, as if falling asleep, and rose up cured. While, then, we were asking what had happened, and what occasioned this noise of joy, they came into the basilica where we were, leading her from the martyr's tomb in perfect health. Then, indeed, such a shout of wonder rose from men and women together, that the exclamations and the tears seemed like never to come to an end. She was led to the place where she had a little before stood trembling. They now rejoiced that she was like her brother, as before they had mourned that she remained unlike him; and as they had not yet uttered their prayers in her behalf, they perceived that their intention of doing so had been speedily heard. They shouted God's praises without words, but with such a noise that our ears could scarcely bear it. What was there in the hearts of these exultant people but the faith of Christ, for which Stephen had shed his blood?

Chapter IX: *That All the Miracles Which are Done by Means of the Martyrs in the Name of Christ Testify to that Faith Which the Martyrs Had in Christ.*

To what do these miracles witness, but to this faith which preaches Christ risen in the flesh, and ascended with the same into heaven? For the martyrs themselves were martyrs, that is to say, witnesses of this faith, drawing upon themselves by their testimony the hatred of the world, and conquering the world not by resisting it, but by dying. For this faith they died, and can now ask these benefits from the Lord in whose name they were slain. For this faith their marvelous constancy was exercised, so that in these miracles great power was manifested as the result. For if the resurrection of the flesh to eternal life had not taken place in Christ, and were not to be accomplished in His people, as predicted by Christ, or by the prophets who foretold that Christ was to come, why do the martyrs who were slain for this faith which proclaims the resurrection possess such power? For whether God Himself wrought these miracles by that wonderful manner of working by which, though Himself eternal, He produces effects in time; or whether He wrought them by servants, and if so, whether He made use of the spirits of martyrs as He uses men who are still in the body, or effects all these marvels by means of angels, over whom He exerts an invisible, immutable, incorporeal sway, so that what is said to be done by the martyrs is done not by their operation, but only by their prayer and request; or whether, finally, some things are done in one way, others in another, and so that man cannot at all comprehend them—nevertheless these miracles attest this faith which preaches the resurrection of the flesh to eternal life.

Chapter X: *That the Martyrs Who Obtain Many Miracles in Order that the True God May Be Worshiped, are Worthy of Much Greater Honor Than the Demons, Who Do Some Marvels that They Themselves May Be Supposed to Be God.*

Here perhaps our adversaries will say that their gods also have done some wonderful things, if now they begin to compare their gods to our dead men. Or will they also say that they have gods taken from among dead men, such as Hercules, Romulus, and many others whom they fancy to have been received into the number of the gods? But our martyrs are not our gods; for we know that the martyrs and we have both but one God, and that the same. Nor yet are the miracles which they maintain to have been done by means of their temples at all comparable to those which are done by the tombs of our martyrs. If they seem similar, their gods have been defeated by our martyrs as Pharaoh's magi were by Moses. In reality, the demons wrought these marvels with the same impure pride with which they aspired to be the gods of the nations; but the martyrs do these wonders, or rather God does them while they pray and assist, in order that an impulse may be given to the faith by which we believe that they are not our gods, but have, together with ourselves, one God. In fine, they built temples to these gods of theirs, and set up altars, and ordained priests, and appointed sacrifices; but to our martyrs we build, not temples as if they were gods, but monuments as to dead men whose spirits live with God. Neither do we erect altars at these monuments that we may sacrifice to the martyrs, but to the one God of the martyrs and of ourselves; and in this sacrifice they are named in their own place and rank as men of God who conquered the world by confessing Him, but they are not invoked by the sacrificing priest. For it is to God, not to them, he sacrifices, though he sacrifices at their monument; for he is God's priest, not theirs. The sacrifice itself, too, is the body of Christ, which is not offered to them, because they themselves are this body. Which then can more readily be believed to work miracles? They who wish themselves to be reckoned gods by those on whom they work miracles, or those whose sole object in working any miracle is to induce faith in God, and in Christ also as God? They who wished to turn even their crimes into sacred rites, or those who are unwilling that even their own praises be consecrated, and seek that everything for which they are justly praised be ascribed to the glory of Him in whom they are praised? For in the Lord their souls are praised. Let us therefore believe those who both speak the truth and work wonders. For by speaking the truth they suffered, and so won the power of working wonders. And the leading truth they professed is that Christ rose from the dead, and first showed in His own flesh the immortality of the resurrection which He promised should be ours, either in the beginning of the world to come, or in the end of this world.

Chapter XI: *Against the Platonists, Who Argue from the Physical Weight of the Elements that an Earthly Body Cannot Inhabit Heaven.*

But against this great gift of God, these reasoners, "whose thoughts the Lord knows that they are vain" bring arguments from the weights of the elements; for they have been taught by their master Plato that the two greatest elements of the world, and the furthest removed from one another, are coupled and united by the two intermediate, air and water. And consequently they say, since the earth is the first of the elements, beginning from the base of the series, the second the water above the earth, the third the air above the water, the fourth the heaven above the air, it follows that a body of earth cannot live in the heaven; for each element is poised by its own weight so as to preserve its own place and rank. Behold with what arguments human infirmity, possessed with vanity, contradicts the omnipotence of God! What, then, do so many earthly bodies do in the air, since the air is the third element from the earth? Unless perhaps He who has granted to the earthly bodies of birds that they be carried through the air by the lightness of feathers and wings, has not been able to confer upon the bodies of men made immortal the power to abide in the highest heaven. The earthly animals, too, which cannot fly, among which are men, ought on these terms to live under the earth, as fishes, which are the animals of the water, live under the water. Why, then, can an animal of earth not live in the second element, that is, in water, while it can in the third? Why, though it belongs to the earth, is it forthwith suffocated if it is forced to live in the second element next above earth, while it lives in the third, and cannot live out of it? Is there a mistake here in the order of the elements, or is not the mistake rather in their reasonings, and not in the nature of things? I will not repeat what I said in the thirteenth book, that many earthly bodies, though heavy like lead, receive from the workman's hand a form which enables them to swim in water; and yet it is denied that the omnipotent Worker can confer on the human body a property which shall enable it to pass into heaven and dwell there.

But against what I have formerly said they can find nothing to say, even though they introduce and make the most of this order of the elements in which they confide. For if the order be that the earth is first, the water second, the air third, the heaven fourth, then the soul is above all. For Aristotle said that the soul was a fifth body, while Plato denied that it was a body at all. If it were a fifth body, then certainly it would be above the rest; and if it is not a body at all, so much the more does it rise above all. What, then, does it do in an earthly body? What does this soul, which is finer than all else, do in such a mass of matter as this? What does the lightest of substances do in this ponderosity? this swiftest substance in such sluggishness? Will not the body be raised to heaven by virtue of so excellent a nature as this? and if now earthly bodies can retain the souls below, shall not the souls be one day able to raise the earthly bodies above?

If we pass now to their miracles which they oppose to our martyrs as wrought by their gods, shall not even these be found to make for us, and help out our argument? For if any of the miracles of their gods are great, certainly that is a great one which Varro mentions of a vestal virgin, who, when she was endangered by a false accusation of unchastity, filled a sieve with water from the Tiber, and carried it to her judges without any part of it leaking. Who kept the weight of water in the sieve? Who prevented any drop from falling from it through so many open holes? They will answer, Some god or some demon. If a god, is he greater than the God who made the world? If a demon, is he mightier than an angel who serves the God by whom the world was made? If, then, a lesser god, angel, or demon could so sustain the weight of this liquid element that the water might seem to have changed its nature, shall not Almighty God, who Himself created all the elements, be able to eliminate from the earthly body its heaviness, so that the quickened body shall dwell in whatever element the quickening spirit pleases?

Then, again, since they give the air a middle place between the fire above and the water beneath, how is it that we often find it between water and water, and between the water and the earth? For what do they make of those watery clouds, between which and the seas air is constantly found intervening? I should like to know by what weight and order of the elements it comes to pass that very violent and stormy torrents are suspended in the clouds above the earth before they rush along upon the earth under the air. In fine, why is it that throughout the whole globe the air is between the highest heaven and the earth, if its place is between the sky and the water, as the place of the water is between the sky and the earth?

Finally, if the order of the elements is so disposed that, as Plato thinks, the two extremes, fire and earth, are united by the two means, air and water, and that the fire occupies the highest part of the sky, and the earth the lowest part, or as it were the foundation of the world, and that therefore earth cannot be in the heavens, how is fire in the earth? For, according to this reasoning, these two elements, earth and fire, ought to be so restricted to their own places, the highest and the lowest, that neither the lowest can rise to the place of the highest, nor the highest sink to that of the lowest. Thus, as they think that no particle of earth is or shall ever be in the sky so we ought to see no particle of fire on the earth. But the fact is that it exists to such an extent, not only on but even under the earth, that the tops of mountains vomit it forth; besides that we see it to exist on earth for human uses, and even to be produced from the earth, since it is kindled from wood and stones, which are without doubt earthly bodies. But that [upper] fire, they say, is tranquil, pure, harmless, eternal; but this [earthly] fire is turbid, smoky, corruptible, and corrupting. But it does not corrupt the mountains and caverns of the earth in which it rages continually. But grant that the earthly fire is so unlike the other as to suit its earthly position, why then do they object to our believing that the nature of earthly bodies shall some day be made incorruptible and fit for the sky, even as now fire is corruptible and suited to the earth? They therefore adduce from their weights and order of the elements nothing from which they can prove that it is impossible for Almighty God to make our bodies such that they can dwell in the skies.

Chapter XII: *Against the Calumnies with Which Unbelievers Throw Ridicule Upon the Christian Faith in the Resurrection of the Flesh.*

But their way is to feign a scrupulous anxiety in investigating this question, and to cast ridicule on our faith in the resurrection of the body, by asking, Whether abortions shall rise? And as the Lord says, "Verily I say unto you, not a hair of your head shall perish," shall all bodies have an equal stature and strength, or shall there be differences in size? For if there is to be equality, where shall those abortions, supposing that they rise again, get that bulk which they had not here? Or if they shall not rise because they were not born but cast out, they raise the same question about children who have died in childhood, asking us whence they get the stature which we see they had not here; for we will not say that those who have been not only born, but born again, shall not rise again. Then, further, they ask of what size these equal bodies shall be. For if all shall be as tall and large as were the tallest and largest in this world, they ask us how it is that not only children but many full-grown persons 494 shall receive what they here did not possess, if each one is to receive what he had here. And if the saying of the apostle, that we are all to come to the "measure of the age of the fullness of Christ," or that other saying, "Whom He predestinated to be conformed to the image of His Son," is to be understood to mean that the stature and size of Christ's body shall be the measure of the bodies of all those who shall be in His kingdom, then, say they, the size and height of many must be diminished; and if so much of the bodily frame itself be lost, what becomes of the saying, "Not a hair of your head shall perish?" Besides, it might be asked regarding the hair itself, whether all that the barber has cut off shall be restored? And if it is to be restored, who would not shrink from such deformity? For as the same restoration will be made of what has been pared off the nails, much will be replaced on the body which a regard for its appearance had cut off. And where, then, will be its beauty, which assuredly ought to be much greater in that immortal condition than it could be in this corruptible state? On the other hand, if such things are not restored to the body, they must perish; how, then, they say, shall not a hair of the head perish? In like manner they reason about fatness and leanness; for if all are to be equal, then certainly there shall not be some fat, others lean. Some, therefore, shall gain, others lose something. Consequently there will not be a simple restoration of what formerly existed, but, on the one hand, an addition of what had no existence, and, on the other, a loss of what did before exist.

The difficulties, too, about the corruption and dissolution of dead bodies—that one is turned into dust, while another evaporates into the air; that some are devoured by beasts, some by fire, while some perish by shipwreck or by drowning in one shape or other, so that their bodies decay into liquid, these difficulties give them immoderate alarm, and they believe that all those dissolved elements cannot be gathered again and reconstructed into a body. They also make eager use of all the deformities and blemishes which either accident or birth has produced, and accordingly, with horror and derision, cite monstrous births, and ask if every deformity will be preserved in the resurrection. For if we say that no such thing shall be reproduced in the body of a man, they suppose that they confute us by citing the marks of the wounds which we assert were found in the risen body of the Lord Christ. But of all these, the most difficult question is, into whose body that flesh shall return which has been eaten and assimilated by another man constrained by hunger to use it so; for it has been converted into the flesh of the man who used it as his nutriment, and it filled up those losses of flesh which famine had produced. For the sake, then, of ridiculing the resurrection, they ask, Shall this return to the man whose flesh it first was, or to him whose flesh it afterwards became? And thus, too, they seek to give promise to the human soul of alternations of true misery and false happiness, in accordance with Plato's theory; or, in accordance with Porphyry's, that, after many transmigrations into different bodies, it ends its miseries, and never more returns to them, not, however, by obtaining an immortal body, but by escaping from every kind of body.

Chapter XIII: *Whether Abortions, If They are Numbered Among the Dead, Shall Not Also Have a Part in the Resurrection.*

To these objections, then, of our adversaries which I have thus detailed, I will now reply, trusting that God will mercifully assist my endeavors. That abortions, which, even supposing they were alive in the womb, did also die there, shall rise again, I make bold neither to affirm nor to deny, although I fail to see why, if they are not excluded from the number of the dead, they should not attain to the resurrection of the dead. For either all the dead shall not rise, and there will be to all eternity some souls without bodies though they once had them—only in their mother's womb, indeed; or, if all human souls shall receive again the bodies which they had wherever they lived, and which they left when they died, then I do not see how I can say that even those who died in their mother's womb shall have no resurrection. But whichever of these opinions any one may adopt concerning them, we must at least apply to them, if they rise again, all that we have to say of infants who have been born.

Chapter XIV: *Whether Infants Shall Rise in that Body Which They Would Have Had Had They Grown Up.*

What, then, are we to say of infants, if not that they will not rise in that diminutive body in which they died, but shall receive by the marvelous and rapid operation of God that body which time by a slower process would have given them? For in the Lord's words, where He says, "Not a hair of your head shall perish," it is asserted that nothing which was possessed shall be wanting; but it is not said that nothing which was not possessed shall be given. To the dead infant there was wanting the perfect stature of its body; for even the perfect infant lacks the perfection of bodily size, being capable of further growth. This perfect stature is, in a sense, so possessed by all that they are conceived and born with it—that is, they have it potentially, though not yet in actual bulk; just as all the members of the body are potentially in the seed, though, even after the child is born, some of them, the teeth for example, may be wanting. In this seminal principle of every substance, there seems to be, as it were, the beginning of everything which does not yet exist, or rather does not appear, but which in process of time will come into being, or rather into sight. In this, therefore, the child who is to be tall or short is already tall or short. And in the resurrection of the body, we need, for the same reason, fear no bodily loss; for though all should be of equal size, and reach gigantic proportions, lest the men who were largest here should lose anything of their bulk and it should perish, in contradiction to the words of Christ, who said that not a hair of their head should perish, yet why should there lack the means by which that wonderful Worker should make such additions, seeing that He is the Creator, who Himself created all things out of nothing?

Chapter XV: *Whether the Bodies of All the Dead Shall Rise the Same Size as the Lord's Body.*

It is certain that Christ rose in the same bodily stature in which He died, and that it is wrong to say that, when the general resurrection shall have arrived, His body shall, for the sake of equaling the tallest, assume proportions which it had not when He appeared to the disciples in the figure with which they were familiar. But if we say that even the bodies of taller men are to be reduced to the size of the Lord's body, there will be a great loss in many bodies, though He promised that, not a hair of their head should perish. It remains, therefore, that we conclude that every man shall receive his own size which he had in youth, though he died an old man, or which he would have had, supposing he died before his prime. As for what the apostle said of the measure of the age of the fullness of Christ, we must either understand him to refer to something else, viz., to the fact that the measure of Christ will be completed when all the members among the Christian communities are added to the Head; or if we are to refer it to the resurrection of the body, the meaning is that all shall rise neither beyond nor under youth, but in that vigor and age to which we know that Christ had arrived. For even the world's wisest men have fixed the bloom of youth at about the age of thirty; and when this period has been passed, the man begins to decline towards the defective and duller period of old age. And therefore the apostle did not speak of the measure of the body, nor of the measure of the stature, but of "the measure of the age of the fullness of Christ."

Chapter XVI: *What is Meant by the Conforming of the Saints to the Image of The Son of God.*

Then, again, these words, "Predestinate to be conformed to the image of the Son of God," may be understood of the inner man. So in another place He says to us, "Be not conformed to this world, but be ye transformed in the renewing of your mind." In so far, then, as we are transformed so as not to be conformed to the world, we are conformed to the Son of God. It may also be understood thus, that as He was conformed to us by assuming mortality, we shall be conformed to Him by immortality; and this indeed is connected with the resurrection of the body. But if we are also taught in these words what form our bodies shall rise in, as the measure we spoke of before, so also this conformity is to be understood not of size, but of age. Accordingly all shall rise in the stature they either had attained or would have attained had they lived to their prime, although it will be no great disadvantage even if the form of the body be infantine or aged, while no infirmity shall remain in the mind nor in the body itself. So that even if any one contends that every person will rise again in the same bodily form in which he died, we need not spend much labor in disputing with him.

Chapter XVII: *Whether the Bodies of Women Shall Retain Their Own Sex in the Resurrection.*

From the words, "Till we all come to a perfect man, to the measure of the age of the fullness of Christ," and from the words, "Conformed to the image of the Son of God," some conclude that women shall not rise women, but that all shall be men, because God made man only of earth, and woman of the man. For my part, they seem to be wiser who make no doubt that both sexes shall rise. For there shall be no lust, which is now the cause of confusion. For before they sinned, the man and the woman were naked, and were not ashamed. From those bodies, then, vice shall be withdrawn, while nature shall be preserved. And the sex of woman is not a vice, but nature. It shall then indeed be superior to carnal intercourse and child-bearing; nevertheless the female members shall remain adapted not to the old uses, but to a new beauty, which, so far from provoking lust, now extinct, shall excite praise to the wisdom and clemency of God, who both made what was not and delivered from corruption what He made. For at the beginning of the human race the woman was made of a rib taken from the side of the man while he slept; for it seemed fit that even then Christ and His Church should be foreshadowed in this event. For that sleep of the man was the death of Christ, whose side, as He hung lifeless upon the cross, was pierced with a spear, and there flowed from it blood and water, and these we know to be the sacraments by which the Church is "built up." For Scripture used this very word, not saying "He formed" or "framed," but "built her up into a woman;" whence also the apostle speaks of the edification of the body of Christ, which is the Church. The woman, therefore, is a creature of God even as the man; but by her creation from man unity is commended; and the manner of her creation prefigured, as has been said, Christ and the Church. He, then, who created both sexes will restore both. Jesus Himself also, when asked by the Sadducees, who denied the resurrection, which of the seven brothers should have to wife the woman whom all in succession had taken to raise up seed to their brother, as the law enjoined, says, "Ye do err, not knowing the Scriptures nor the power of God." And though it was a fit opportunity for His saying, She about whom you make inquiries shall herself be a man, and not a woman, He said nothing of the kind; but "In the resurrection they neither marry nor are given in marriage, but are as the angels of God in heaven." They shall be equal to the angels in immortality and happiness, not in flesh, nor in resurrection, which the angels did not need, because they could not die. The Lord then denied that there would be in the resurrection, not women, but marriages; and He uttered this denial in circumstances in which the question mooted would have been more easily and speedily solved by denying that the female sex would exist, if this had in truth been foreknown by Him. But, indeed, He even affirmed that the sex should exist by saying, "They shall not be given in marriage," which can only apply to females; "Neither shall they marry," which applies to males. There shall therefore be those who are in this world accustomed to marry and be given in marriage, only they shall there make no such marriages.

Chapter XVIII: *Of the Perfect Man, that Is, Christ; And of His Body, that Is, The Church, Which is His Fullness.*

To understand what the apostle means when he says that we shall all come to a perfect man, we must consider the connection of the whole passage, which runs thus: "He that descended is the same also that ascended up far above all heavens, that He might fill all things. And He gave some, apostles; and some, prophets; and some, evangelists; and some, pastors and teachers; for the perfecting of the saints, for the work of the ministry, for the edifying of the body of Christ: till we all come to the unity of the faith and knowledge of the Son of God, to a perfect man, to the measure of the age of the fullness of Christ: that we henceforth be no more children, tossed and carried about with every wind of doctrine, by the sleight of men, and cunning craftiness, whereby they lie in wait to deceive; but, speaking the truth in love, may grow up in Him in all things, which is the Head, even Christ: from whom the whole body fitly joined together and compacted by that which every joint supplieth, according to the effectual working in the measure of every part, maketh increase of the body, unto the edifying of itself in love." Behold what the perfect man is—the head and the body, which is made up of all the members, which in their own time shall be perfected. But new additions are daily being made to this body while the Church is being built up, to which it is said, "Ye are the body of Christ and His members;" and again, "For His body's sake," he says, "which is the Church;" and again, "We being many are one head, one body." It is of the edification of this body that it is here, too, said, "For the perfecting of the saints, for the work of the ministry, for the edification of the body of Christ;" and then that passage of which we are now speaking is added, "Till we all come to the unity of the faith and knowledge of the Son of God, to a perfect man, to the measure of the age of the fullness of Christ," and so on. And he shows of what body we are to understand this to be the measure, when he says, "That we may grow up into Him in all things, which is the Head, even Christ: from whom the whole body fitly joined together and compacted by that which every joint supplieth, according to the effectual working in the measure of every part." As, therefore, there is a measure of every part, so there is a measure of the fullness of the whole body which is made up of all its parts, and it is of this measure it is said, "To the measure of the age of the fullness of Christ." This fullness he spoke of also in the place where he says of Christ, "And gave Him to be the Head over all things to the Church, which is His body, the fullness of Him that filleth all in all." But even if this should be referred to the form in which each one shall rise, what should hinder us from applying to the woman what is expressly said of the man, understanding both sexes to be included under the general term "man?" For certainly in the saying, "Blessed is he who feareth the Lord," women also who fear the Lord are included.

Chapter XIX: *That All Bodily Blemishes Which Mar Human Beauty in This Life Shall Be Removed in the Resurrection, the Natural Substance of the Body Remaining, But the Quality and Quantity of It Being Altered So as to Produce Beauty.*

What am I to say now about the hair and nails? Once it is understood that no part of the body shall so perish as to produce deformity in the body, it is at the same time understood that such things as would have produced a deformity by their excessive proportions shall be added to the total bulk of the body, not to parts in which the beauty of the proportion would thus be marred. Just as if, after making a vessel of clay, one wished to make it over again of the same clay, it would not be necessary that the same portion of the clay which had formed the handle should again form the new handle, or that what had formed the bottom should again do so, but only that the whole clay should go to make up the whole new vessel, and that no part of it should be left unused. Wherefore, if the hair that has been cropped and the nails that have been cut would cause a deformity were they to be restored to their places, they shall not be restored; and yet no one will lose these parts at the resurrection, for they shall be changed into the same flesh, their substance being so altered as to preserve the proportion of the various parts of the body. However, what our Lord said, "Not a hair of your head shall perish," might more suitably be interpreted of the number, and not of the length of the hairs, as He elsewhere says, "The hairs of your head are all numbered." Nor would I say this because I suppose that any part naturally belonging to the body can perish, but that whatever deformity was in it, and served to exhibit the penal condition in which we mortals are, should be restored in such a way that, while the substance is entirely preserved, the deformity shall perish. For if even a human workman, who has, for some reason, made a deformed statue, can recast it and make it very beautiful, and this without suffering any part of the substance, but only the deformity to be lost—if he can, for example, remove some unbecoming or disproportionate part, not by cutting off and separating this part from the whole, but by so breaking down and mixing up the whole as to get rid of the blemish without diminishing the quantity of his material—shall we not think as highly of the almighty Worker? Shall He not be able to remove and abolish all deformities of the human body, whether common ones or rare and monstrous, which, though in keeping with this miserable life, are yet not to be thought of in connection with that future blessedness; and shall He not be able so to remove them that, while the natural but unseemly blemishes are put an end to, the natural substance shall suffer no diminution?

And consequently overgrown and emaciated persons need not fear that they shall be in heaven of such a figure as they would not be even in this world if they could help it. For all bodily beauty consists in the proportion of the parts, together with a certain agreeableness of color. Where there is no proportion, the eye is offended, either because there is something awanting, or too small, or too large. And thus there shall be no deformity resulting from want of proportion in that state in which all that is wrong is corrected, and all that is defective supplied from resources the Creator wots of, and all that is excessive removed without destroying the integrity of the substance. And as for the pleasant color, how conspicuous shall it be where "the just shall shine forth as the sun in the kingdom of their Father!" This brightness we must rather believe to have been concealed from the eyes of the disciples when Christ rose, than to have been awanting. For weak human eyesight could not bear it, and it was necessary that they should so look upon Him as to be able to recognize Him. For this purpose also He allowed them to touch the marks of His wounds, and also ate and drank—not because He needed nourishment, but because He could take it if He wished. Now, when an object, though present, is invisible to persons who see other things which are present, as we say that that brightness was present but invisible by those who saw other things, this is called in Greek ἀορασία; and our Latin translators, for want of a better word, have rendered this *cæcitas* (blindness) in the book of Genesis. This blindness the men of Sodom suffered when they sought the just Lot's gate and could not find it. But if it had been blindness, that is to say, if they could see nothing, then they would not have asked for the gate by which they might enter the house, but for guides who might lead them away.

But the love we bear to the blessed martyrs causes us, I know not how, to desire to see in the heavenly kingdom the marks of the wounds which they received for the name of Christ, and possibly we shall see them. For this will not be a deformity, but a mark of honor, and will add lustre to their appearance, and a spiritual, if not a bodily beauty. And yet we need not believe that they to whom it has been said, "Not a hair of your head shall perish," shall, in the resurrection, want such of their members as they have been deprived of in their martyrdom. But if it will be seemly in that new kingdom to have some marks of these wounds still visible in that immortal flesh, the places where they have been wounded or mutilated shall retain the scars without any of the members being lost. While, therefore, it is quite true that no blemishes which the body has sustained shall appear in the resurrection, yet we are not to reckon or name these marks of virtue blemishes.

Chapter XX: *That, in the Resurrection, the Substance of Our Bodies, However Disintegrated, Shall Be Entirely Reunited.*

Far be it from us to fear that the omnipotence of the Creator cannot, for the resuscitation and reanimation of our bodies, recall

all the portions which have been consumed by beasts or fire, or have been dissolved into dust or ashes, or have decomposed into water, or evaporated into the air. Far from us be the thought, that anything which escapes our observation in any most hidden recess of nature either evades the knowledge or transcends the power of the Creator of all things. Cicero, the great authority of our adversaries, wishing to define God as accurately as possible, says, "God is a mind free and independent, without materiality, perceiving and moving all things, and itself endowed with eternal movement." This he found in the systems of the greatest philosophers. Let me ask, then, in their own language, how anything can either lie hid from Him who perceives all things, or irrevocably escape Him who moves all things?

This leads me to reply to that question which seems the most difficult of all—To whom, in the resurrection, will belong the flesh of a dead man which has become the flesh of a living man? For if some one, famishing for want and pressed with hunger, use human flesh as food—an extremity not unknown, as both ancient history and the unhappy experience of our own days have taught us—can it be contended, with any show of reason, that all the flesh eaten has been evacuated, and that none of it has been assimilated to the substance of the eater though the very emaciation which existed before, and has now disappeared, sufficiently indicates what large deficiencies have been filled up with this food? But I have already made some remarks which will suffice for the solution of this difficulty also. For all the flesh which hunger has consumed finds its way into the air by evaporation, whence, as we have said, God Almighty can recall it. That flesh, therefore, shall be restored to the man in whom it first became human flesh. For it must be looked upon as borrowed by the other person, and, like a pecuniary loan, must be returned to the lender. His own flesh, however, which he lost by famine, shall be restored to him by Him who can recover even what has evaporated. And though it had been absolutely annihilated, so that no part of its substance remained in any secret spot of nature, the Almighty could restore it by such means as He saw fit. For this sentence, uttered by the Truth, "Not a hair of your head shall perish," forbids us to suppose that, though no hair of a man's head can perish, yet the large portions of his flesh eaten and consumed by the famishing can perish.

From all that we have thus considered, and discussed with such poor ability as we can command, we gather this conclusion, that in the resurrection of the flesh the body shall be of that size which it either had attained or should have attained in the flower of its youth, and shall enjoy the beauty that arises from preserving symmetry and proportion in all its members. And it is reasonable to suppose that, for the preservation of this beauty, any part of the body's substance, which, if placed in one spot, would produce a deformity, shall be distributed through the whole of it, so that neither any part, nor the symmetry of the whole, may be lost, but only the general stature of the body somewhat increased by the distribution in all the parts of that which, in one place, would have been unsightly. Or if it is contended that each will rise with the same stature as that of the body he died in, we shall not obstinately dispute this, provided only there be no deformity, no infirmity, no languor, no corruption—nothing of any kind which would ill become that kingdom in which the children of the resurrection and of the promise shall be equal to the angels of God, if not in body and age, at least in happiness.

Chapter XXI: *Of the New Spiritual Body into Which the Flesh of the Saints Shall Be Transformed.*

Whatever, therefore, has been taken from the body, either during life or after death shall be restored to it, and, in conjunction with what has remained in the grave, shall rise again, transformed from the oldness of the animal body into the newness of the spiritual body, and clothed in incorruption and immortality. But even though the body has been all quite ground to powder by some severe accident, or by the ruthlessness of enemies, and though it has been so diligently scattered to the winds, or into the water, that there is no trace of it left, yet it shall not be beyond the omnipotence of the Creator—no, not a hair of its head shall perish. The flesh shall then be spiritual, and subject to the spirit, but still flesh, not spirit, as the spirit itself, when subject to the flesh, was fleshly, but still spirit and not flesh. And of this we have experimental proof in the deformity of our penal condition. For those persons were carnal, not in a fleshly, but in a spiritual way, to whom the apostle said, "I could not speak to you as unto spiritual, but as unto carnal." And a man is in this life spiritual in such a way, that he is yet carnal with respect to his body, and sees another law in his members warring against the law of his mind; but even in his body he will be spiritual when the same flesh shall have had that resurrection of which these words speak, "It is sown an animal body, it shall rise a spiritual body." But what this spiritual body shall be and how great its grace, I fear it were but rash to pronounce, seeing that we have as yet no experience of it. Nevertheless, since it is fit that the joyfulness of our hope should utter itself, and so show forth God's praise, and since it was from the profoundest sentiment of ardent and holy love that the Psalmist cried, "O Lord, I have loved the beauty of Thy house," we may, with God's help, speak of the gifts He lavishes on men, good and bad alike, in this most wretched life, and may do our best to conjecture the great glory of that state which we cannot worthily speak of, because we have not yet experienced it. For I say nothing of the time when God made man upright; I say nothing of the happy life of "the man and his wife" in the fruitful garden, since it was so short that none of their children experienced it: I speak only of this life which we know, and in which we now are, from the temptations of which we cannot escape so long as we are in it, no matter what progress we make, for it is all temptation, and I ask, Who can describe the tokens of God's goodness that are extended to the human race even in this life?

Chapter XXII: *Of the Miseries and Ills to Which the Human Race is Justly Exposed Through the First Sin, and from Which None Can Be Delivered Save by Christ's Grace.*

That the whole human race has been condemned in its first origin, this life itself, if life it is to be called, bears witness by the host of cruel ills with which it is filled. Is not this proved by the profound and dreadful ignorance which produces all the errors that enfold the children of Adam, and from which no man can be delivered without toil, pain, and fear? Is it not proved by his love of so many vain and hurtful things, which produces gnawing cares, disquiet, griefs, fears, wild joys, quarrels, lawsuits, wars, treasons, angers, hatreds, deceit, flattery, fraud, theft, robbery, perfidy, pride, ambition, envy, murders, parricides, cruelty, ferocity, wickedness, luxury, insolence, impudence, shamelessness, fornications, adulteries, incests, and the numberless uncleannesses and unnatural acts of both sexes, which it is shameful so much as to mention; sacrileges, heresies, blasphemies, perjuries, oppression of the innocent, calumnies, plots, falsehoods, false witnessings, unrighteous judgments, violent deeds, plunderings, and whatever similar wickedness has found its way into the lives of men, though it cannot find its way into the conception of pure minds? These are indeed the crimes of wicked men, yet they spring from that root of error and misplaced love which is born with every son of Adam. For who is there that has not observed with what profound ignorance, manifesting itself even in infancy, and with what superfluity of foolish desires, beginning to appear in boyhood, man comes into this life, so that, were he left to live as he pleased, and to do whatever he pleased, he would plunge into all, or certainly into many of those crimes and iniquities which I mentioned, and could not mention?

But because God does not wholly desert those whom He condemns, nor shuts up in His anger His tender mercies, the human race is restrained by law and instruction, which keep guard against the ignorance that besets us, and oppose the assaults of vice, but are themselves full of labor and sorrow. For what mean those multifarious threats which are used to restrain the folly of children? What mean pedagogues, masters, the birch, the strap, the cane, the schooling which Scripture says must be given a child, "beating him on the sides lest he wax stubborn," and it be hardly possible or not possible at all to subdue him? Why all these punishments, save to overcome ignorance and bridle evil desires—these evils with which we come into the world? For why is it that we remember with difficulty, and without difficulty forget? learn with difficulty, and without difficulty remain ignorant? are diligent with difficulty, and without difficulty are indolent? Does not this show what vitiated nature inclines and tends to by its own weight, and what succor it needs if it is to be delivered? Inactivity, sloth, laziness, negligence, are vices which shun labor, since labor, though useful, is itself a punishment.

But, besides the punishments of childhood, without which there would be no learning of what the parents wish—and the parents rarely wish anything useful to be taught—who can describe, who can conceive the number and severity of the punishments which afflict the human race—pains which are not only the accompaniment of the wickedness of godless men, but are a part of the human condition and the common misery—what fear and what grief are caused by bereavement and mourning, by losses and condemnations, by fraud and falsehood, by false suspicions, and all the crimes and wicked deeds of other men? For at their hands we suffer robbery, captivity, chains, imprisonment, exile, torture, mutilation, loss of sight, the violation of chastity to satisfy the lust of the oppressor, and many other dreadful evils. What numberless casualties threaten our bodies from without—extremes of heat and cold, storms, floods, inundations, lightning, thunder, hail, earthquakes, houses falling; or from the stumbling, or shying, or vice of horses; from countless poisons in fruits, water, air, animals; from the painful or even deadly bites of wild animals; from the madness which a mad dog communicates, so that even the animal which of all others is most gentle and friendly to its own master, becomes an object of intenser fear than a lion or dragon, and the man whom it has by chance infected with this pestilential contagion becomes so rabid, that his parents, wife, children, dread him more than any wild beast! What disasters are suffered by those who travel by land or sea! What man can go out of his own house without being exposed on all hands to unforeseen accidents? Returning home sound in limb, he slips on his own doorstep, breaks his leg, and never recovers. What can seem safer than a man sitting in his chair? Eli the priest fell from his, and broke his neck. How many accidents do farmers, or rather all men, fear that the crops may suffer from the weather, or the soil, or the ravages of destructive animals? Commonly they feel safe when the crops are gathered and housed. Yet, to my certain knowledge, sudden floods have driven the laborers away, and swept the barns clean of the finest harvest. Is innocence a sufficient protection against the various assaults of demons? That no man might think so, even baptized infants, who are certainly unsurpassed in innocence, are sometimes so tormented, that God, who permits it, teaches us hereby to bewail the calamities of this life, and to desire the felicity of the life to come. As to bodily diseases, they are so numerous that they cannot all be contained even in medical books. And in very many, or almost all of them, the cures and remedies are themselves tortures, so that men are delivered from a pain that destroys by a cure that pains. Has not the madness of thirst driven men to drink human urine, and even their own? Has not hunger driven men to eat human flesh, and that the flesh not of bodies found dead, but of bodies slain for the purpose? Have not the fierce pangs of famine driven mothers to eat their own children, incredibly savage as it seems? In fine, sleep itself, which is justly called repose, how little of repose there sometimes is in it when disturbed with dreams and visions; and with what terror is the wretched mind overwhelmed by the appearances of things which are so presented, and which, as it were so stand out before the senses, that we can not distinguish them from realities! How wretchedly do false appearances distract men in certain diseases! With what astonishing variety of appearances are even healthy men sometimes deceived by evil spirits, who produce these delusions for the sake of perplexing the senses of their victims, if they cannot succeed in seducing them to their side!

From this hell upon earth there is no escape, save through the grace of the Saviour Christ, our God and Lord. The very name Jesus shows this, for it means Saviour; and He saves us especially from passing out of this life into a more wretched and eternal state, which is rather a death than a life. For in this life, though holy men and holy pursuits afford us great consolations, yet the blessings which men crave are not invariably bestowed upon them, lest religion should be cultivated for the sake of these temporal advantages, while it ought rather to be cultivated for the sake of that other life from which all evil is excluded. Therefore, also, does grace aid good men in the midst of present calamities, so that they are enabled to endure them with a constancy proportioned to their faith. The world's sages affirm that philosophy contributes something to this—that philosophy which, according to Cicero, the gods have bestowed in its purity only on a few men. They have never given, he says, nor can ever give, a greater gift to men. So that even those against whom we are disputing have been compelled to acknowledge, in some fashion, that the grace of God is necessary for the acquisition, not, indeed, of any philosophy, but of the true philosophy. And if the true philosophy—this sole support against the miseries of this life—has been given by Heaven only to a few, it sufficiently appears from this that the human race has been condemned to pay this penalty of wretchedness. And as, according to their acknowledgment, no greater gift has been bestowed by God, so it must be believed that it could be given only by that God whom they themselves recognize as greater than all the gods they worship.

Chapter XXIII: *Of the Miseries of This Life Which Attach Peculiarly to the Toil of Good Men, Irrespective of Those Which are Common to the Good and Bad.*

But, irrespective of the miseries which in this life are common to the good and bad, the righteous undergo labors peculiar to themselves, in so far as they make war upon their vices, and are involved in the temptations and perils of such a contest. For though sometimes more violent and at other times slacker, yet without intermission does the flesh lust against the spirit and the spirit against the flesh, so that we cannot do the things we would, and extirpate all lust, but can only refuse consent to it, as God gives us ability, and so keep it under, vigilantly keeping watch lest a semblance of truth deceive us, lest a subtle discourse blind us, lest error involve us in darkness, lest we should take good for evil or evil for good, lest fear should hinder us from doing what we ought, or desire precipitate us into doing what we ought not, lest the sun go down upon our wrath, lest hatred provoke us to render evil for evil, lest unseemly or immoderate grief consume us, lest an ungrateful disposition make us slow to recognize benefits received, lest calumnies fret our conscience, lest rash suspicion on our part deceive us regarding a friend, or false suspicion of us on the part of others give us too much uneasiness, lest sin reign in our mortal body to obey its desires, lest our members be used as the instruments of unrighteousness, lest the eye follow lust, lest thirst for revenge carry us away, lest sight or thought dwell too long on some evil thing which gives us pleasure, lest wicked or indecent language be willingly listened to, lest we do what is pleasant but unlawful, and lest in this warfare, filled so abundantly with toil and peril, we either hope to secure victory by our own strength, or attribute it when secured to our own strength, and not to His grace of whom the apostle says, "Thanks be unto God, who giveth us the victory through our Lord Jesus Christ;" and in another place he says, "In all these things we are more than conquerors through Him that loved us." But yet we are to know this, that however valorously we resist our vices, and however successful we are in overcoming them, yet as long as we are in this body we have always reason to say to God, Forgive us our debts." But in that kingdom where we shall dwell for ever, clothed in immortal bodies, we shall no longer have either conflicts or debts—as indeed we should not have had at any time or in any condition, had our nature continued upright as it was created. Consequently even this our conflict, in which we are exposed to peril, and from which we hope to be delivered by a final victory, belongs to the ills of this life, which is proved by the witness of so many grave evils to be a life under condemnation.

Chapter XXIV: *Of the Blessings with Which the Creator Has Filled This Life, Obnoxious Though It Be to the Curse.*

But we must now contemplate the rich and countless blessings with which the goodness of God, who cares for all He has created, has filled this very misery of the human race, which reflects His retributive justice. That first blessing which He pronounced before the fall, when He said, "Increase, and multiply, and replenish the earth," He did not inhibit after man had sinned, but the fecundity originally bestowed remained in the condemned stock; and the vice of sin, which has involved us in the necessity of dying, has yet not deprived us of that wonderful power of seed, or rather of that still more marvelous power by which seed is produced, and which seems to be as it were inwrought and inwoven in the human body. But in this river, as I may call it, or torrent of the human race, both elements are carried along together—both the evil which is derived from him who begets, and the good which is bestowed by Him who creates us. In the original evil there are two things, sin and punishment; in the original good, there are two other things, propagation and conformation. But of the evils, of which the one, sin, arose from our audacity, and the other, punishment, from God's judgment, we have already said as much as suits our present purpose. I mean now to speak of the blessings which God has conferred or still confers upon our nature, vitiated and condemned as it is. For in condemning it He did not withdraw all that He had given it, else it had been annihilated; neither did He, in penally subjecting it to the devil, remove it beyond His own power; for not even the devil himself is outside of God's government, since the devil's nature subsists only by the supreme Creator who gives being to all that in any form exists.

Of these two blessings, then, which we have said flow from God's goodness, as from a fountain, towards our nature, vitiated by sin and condemned to punishment, the one, propagation, was conferred by God's benediction when He made those first works, from which He rested on the seventh day. But the other, conformation, is conferred in that work of His wherein "He worketh hitherto." For were He to withdraw His efficacious power from things, they should neither be able to go on and complete the periods assigned to their measured movements, nor should they even continue in possession of that nature they were created in. God, then, so created man that He gave him what we may call fertility, whereby he might propagate other men, giving them a congenital capacity to propagate their kind, but not imposing on them any necessity to do so. This capacity God withdraws at pleasure from individuals, making them barren; but from the whole race He has not withdrawn the blessing of propagation once conferred. But though not withdrawn on account of sin, this power of propagation is not what it would have been had there been no sin. For since "man placed in honor fell, he has become like the beasts," and generates as they do, though the little spark of reason, which was the image of God in him, has not been quite quenched. But if conformation were not added to propagation, there would be no reproduction of one's kind. For even though there were no such thing as copulation, and God wished to fill the earth with human inhabitants, He might create all these as He created one without the help of human generation. And, indeed, even as it is, those who copulate can generate nothing save by the creative energy of God. As, therefore, in respect of that spiritual growth whereby a man is formed to piety and righteousness, the apostle says, "Neither is he that planteth anything, neither he that watereth, but God that giveth the increase," so also it must be said that it is not he that generates that is anything, but God that giveth the essential form; that it is not the mother who carries and nurses the fruit of her womb that is anything, but God that giveth the increase. For He alone, by that energy wherewith "He worketh hitherto," causes the seed to develop, and to evolve from certain secret and invisible folds into the visible forms of beauty which we see. He alone, coupling and connecting in some wonderful fashion the spiritual and corporeal natures, the one to command, the other to obey, makes a living being. And this work of His is so great and wonderful, that not only man, who is a rational animal, and consequently more excellent than all other animals of the earth, but even the most diminutive insect, cannot be considered attentively without astonishment and without praising the Creator.

It is He, then, who has given to the human soul a mind, in which reason and understanding lie as it were asleep during infancy, and as if they were not, destined, however, to be awakened and exercised as years increase, so as to become capable of knowledge and of receiving instruction, fit to understand what is true and to love what is good. It is by this capacity the soul drinks in wisdom, and becomes endowed with those virtues by which, in prudence, fortitude, temperance, and righteousness, it makes war upon error and the other inborn vices, and conquers them by fixing its desires upon no other object than the supreme and unchangeable Good. And even though this be not uniformly the result, yet who can competently utter or even conceive the grandeur of this work of the Almighty, and the unspeakable boon He has conferred upon our rational nature, by giving us even the capacity of such attainment? For over and above those arts which are called virtues, and which teach us how we may spend our life well, and attain to endless happiness—arts which are given to the children of the promise and the kingdom by the sole grace of God which is in Christ—has not the genius of man invented and applied countless astonishing arts, partly the result of necessity, partly the result of exuberant invention, so that this vigor of mind, which is so active in the discovery not merely of superfluous but even of dangerous and destructive things, betokens an inexhaustible wealth in the nature which can invent, learn, or employ such arts? What wonderful—one might say stupefying—advances has human industry made in the arts of weaving and building, of agriculture and navigation! With what endless variety are designs in pottery, painting, and sculpture produced, and with what skill executed! What wonderful spectacles are exhibited in the theatres, which those who have not seen them cannot credit! How skillful the contrivances for catching, killing, or taming wild beasts! And for the injury of men, also, how many kinds of poisons, weapons, engines of destruction, have been invented, while for the preservation or restoration of health the appliances and remedies are infinite! To provoke appetite and please the palate, what a variety of seasonings have been concocted! To express and gain entrance for thoughts, what a multitude and variety of signs there are, among which speaking and writing hold the first place! what ornaments has eloquence at command to delight the mind! what wealth of song is there to captivate the ear! how many musical instruments and strains of harmony have been devised! What skill has been attained in measures and numbers! with what sagacity have the movements and connections of the stars been discovered! Who could tell the thought that has been spent upon nature, even though, despairing of recounting it in detail, he endeavored only to give a general view of it? In fine, even the defense of errors and misapprehensions, which has illustrated the genius of heretics and philosophers, cannot be sufficiently declared. For at present it is the nature of the human mind which adorns this mortal life which we are extolling, and not the faith and the way of truth which lead to immortality. And since this great nature has certainly been created by the true and supreme God, who administers all things He has made with absolute power and justice, it could never have fallen into these miseries, nor have gone out of them to miseries eternal—saving only those who are redeemed—had not an exceeding great sin been found in the first man from whom the rest have sprung.

Moreover, even in the body, though it dies like that of the beasts, and is in many ways weaker than theirs, what goodness of God, what providence of the great Creator, is apparent! The organs of sense and the rest of the members, are not they so placed, the appearance, and form, and stature of the body as a whole, is it not so fashioned, as to indicate that it was made for the service of a reasonable soul? Man has not been created stooping towards the earth, like the irrational animals; but his bodily form, erect and looking heavenwards, admonishes him to mind the things that are above. Then the marvelous nimbleness which has been given to the tongue and the hands, fitting them to speak, and write, and execute so many duties, and practise so many arts, does it not prove the excellence of the soul for which such an assistant was provided? And even apart from its adaptation to the work required of it, there is such a symmetry in its various parts, and so beautiful a proportion maintained, that one is at a loss to decide whether, in creating the body, greater regard was paid to utility or to beauty. Assuredly no part of the body has been created for the sake of utility which does not also contribute something to its beauty. And this would be all the more apparent, if we knew more precisely how all its parts are connected and adapted to one another, and were not limited in our observations to what appears on the surface; for as to what is covered up and hidden from our view, the intricate web of veins and nerves, the vital parts of all that lies under the skin, no one can discover it. For although, with a cruel zeal for science, some medical men, who are called anatomists, have dissected the bodies of the dead, and sometimes even of sick persons who died under their knives, and have inhumanly pried into the secrets of the human body to learn the nature of the disease and its exact seat, and how it might be cured, yet those relations of which I speak, and which form the concord, or, as the Greeks call it, "harmony," of the whole body outside and in, as of some instrument, no one has been able to discover, because no one has been audacious enough to seek for them. But if these could be known, then even the inward parts, which seem to have no beauty, would so delight us with their exquisite fitness, as to afford a profounder satisfaction to the mind—and the eyes are but its ministers—than the obvious beauty which gratifies the eye. There are some things, too, which have such a place in the body, that they obviously serve no useful purpose, but are solely for beauty, as e.g. the teats on a man's breast, or the beard on his face; for that this is for ornament, and not for protection, is proved by the bare faces of women, who ought rather, as the weaker sex, to enjoy such a defense. If, therefore, of all those members which are exposed to our view, there is certainly not one in which beauty is sacrificed to utility, while there are some which serve no purpose but only beauty, I think it can readily be concluded that in the creation of the human body comeliness was more regarded than necessity. In truth, necessity is a transitory thing; and the time is coming when we shall enjoy one another's beauty without any lust—a condition which will specially redound to the praise of the Creator, who, as it is said in the psalm, has "put on praise and comeliness."

How can I tell of the rest of creation, with all its beauty and utility, which the divine goodness has given to man to please his eye and serve his purposes, condemned though he is, and hurled into these labors and miseries? Shall I speak of the manifold and various loveliness of sky, and earth, and sea; of the plentiful supply and wonderful qualities of the light; of sun, moon, and stars; of the shade of trees; of the colors and perfume of flowers; of the multitude of birds, all differing in plumage and in song; of the variety of animals, of which the smallest in size are often the most wonderful—the works of ants and bees astonishing us more than the huge bodies of whales? Shall I speak of the sea, which itself is so grand a spectacle, when it arrays itself as it were in vestures of various colors, now running through every shade of green, and again becoming purple or blue? Is it not delightful to look at it in storm, and experience the soothing complacency which it inspires, by suggesting that we ourselves are not tossed and shipwrecked? What shall I say of the numberless kinds of food to alleviate hunger, and the variety of seasonings to stimulate appetite which are scattered everywhere by nature, and for which we are not indebted to the art of cookery? How many natural appliances are there for preserving and restoring health! How grateful is the alternation of day and night! how pleasant the breezes that cool the air! how abundant the supply of clothing furnished us by trees and animals! Who can enumerate all the blessings we enjoy? If I were to attempt to detail and unfold only these few which I have indicated in the mass, such an enumeration would fill a volume. And all these are but the solace of the wretched and condemned, not the rewards of the blessed. What then shall these rewards be, if such be the blessings of a condemned state? What will He give to those whom He has predestined to life, who has given such things even to those whom He has predestined to death? What blessings will He in the blessed life shower upon those for whom, even in this state of misery, He has been willing that His only-begotten Son should endure such sufferings even to death? Thus the apostle reasons concerning those who are predestined to that kingdom: "He that spared not His own Son, but delivered Him up for us all, how shall He not with Him also give us all things?" When this promise is fulfilled, what shall we be? What blessings shall we receive in that kingdom, since already we have received as the pledge of them Christ's dying? In what condition shall the spirit of man be, when it has no longer any vice at all; when it neither yields to any, nor is in bondage to any, nor has to make war against any, but is perfected, and enjoys undisturbed peace with itself? Shall it not then know all things with certainty, and without any labor or error, when unhindered and joyfully it drinks the wisdom of God at the fountainhead? What shall the body be, when it is in every respect subject to the spirit, from which it shall draw a life so sufficient, as to stand in need of no other nutriment? For it shall no longer be animal, but spiritual, having indeed the substance of flesh, but without any fleshly corruption.

Chapter XXV: *Of the Obstinacy of Those Individuals Who Impugn the Resurrection of the Body, Though, as Was Predicted, the Whole World Believes It.*

The foremost of the philosophers agree with us about the spiritual felicity enjoyed by the blessed in the life to come; it is only the resurrection of the flesh they call in question, and with all their might deny. But the mass of men, learned and unlearned, the world's wise men and its fools, have believed, and have left in meagre isolation the unbelievers, and have turned to Christ, who in His own resurrection demonstrated the reality of that which seems to our adversaries absurd. For the world has believed this which God predicted, as it was also predicted that the world would believe—a prediction not due to the sorceries of Peter, since it was uttered so long before. He who has predicted these things, as I have already said, and am not ashamed to repeat, is the God before whom all other divinities tremble, as Porphyry himself owns, and seeks to prove, by testimonies from the oracles of these gods, and goes so far as to call Him God the Father and King. Far be it from us to interpret these predictions as they do who have not believed, along with the whole world, in that which it was predicted the world would believe in. For why should we not rather understand them as the world does, whose belief was predicted, and leave that handful of unbelievers to their idle talk and obstinate and solitary infidelity? For if they maintain that they interpret them differently only to avoid charging Scripture with folly, and so doing an injury to that God to whom they bear so notable a testimony, is it not a much greater injury they do Him when they say that His predictions must be understood otherwise than the world believed them, though He Himself praised, promised, accomplished this belief on the world's part? And why cannot He cause the body to rise again, and live for ever? or is it not to be believed that He will do this, because it is an undesirable thing, and unworthy of God? Of His omnipotence, which effects so many great miracles, we have already said enough. If they wish to know what the Almighty cannot do, I shall tell them He cannot lie. Let us therefore believe what He can do, by refusing to believe what He cannot do. Refusing to believe that He can lie, let them believe that He will do what He has promised to do; and let them believe it as the world has believed it, whose faith He predicted, whose faith He praised, whose faith He promised, whose faith He now points to. But how do they prove that the resurrection is an undesirable thing? There shall then be no corruption, which is the only evil thing about the body. I have already said enough about the order of the elements, and the other fanciful objections men raise; and in the thirteenth book I have, in my own judgment, sufficiently illustrated the facility of movement which the incorruptible body shall enjoy, judging from the ease and vigor we experience even now, when the body is in good health. Those who have either not read the former books, or wish to refresh their memory, may read them for themselves.

Chapter XXVI: *That the Opinion of Porphyry, that the Soul, in Order to Be Blessed, Must Be Separated from Every Kind of Body, is Demolished by Plato, Who Says that the Supreme God Promised the Gods that They Should Never Be Ousted from Their Bodies.*

But, say they, Porphyry tells us that the soul, in order to be blessed, must escape connection with every kind of body. It does not avail, therefore, to say that the future body shall be incorruptible, if the soul cannot be blessed till delivered from every kind of body. But in the book above mentioned I have already sufficiently discussed this. This one thing only will I repeat—let Plato, their master, correct his writings, and say that their gods, in order to be blessed, must quit their bodies, or, in other words, die; for he said that they were shut up in celestial bodies, and that, nevertheless, the God who made them promised them immortality—that is to say, an eternal tenure of these same bodies, such as was not provided for them naturally, but only by the further intervention of His will, that thus they might be assured of felicity. In this he obviously overturns their assertion that the resurrection of the body cannot be believed because it is impossible; for, according to him, when the uncreated God promised immortality to the created gods, He expressly said that He would do what was impossible. For Plato tells us that He said, "As ye have had a beginning, so you cannot be immortal and incorruptible; yet ye shall not decay, nor shall any fate destroy you or prove stronger than my will, which more effectually binds you to immortality than the bond of your nature keeps you from it." If they who hear these words have, we do not say understanding, but ears, they cannot doubt that Plato believed that God promised to the gods He had made that He would effect an impossibility. For He who says, "Ye cannot be immortal, but by my will ye shall be immortal," what else does He say than this, "I shall make you what ye cannot be?" The body, therefore, shall be raised incorruptible, immortal, spiritual, by Him who, according to Plato, has promised to do that which is impossible. Why then do they still exclaim that this which God has promised, which the world has believed on God's promise as was predicted, is an impossibility? For what we say is, that the God who, even according to Plato, does impossible things, will do this. It is not, then, necessary to the blessedness of the soul that it be detached from a body of any kind whatever, but that it receive an incorruptible body. And in what incorruptible body will they more suitably rejoice than in that in which they groaned when it was corruptible? For thus they shall not feel that dire craving which Virgil, in imitation of Plato, has ascribed to them when he says that they wish to return again to their bodies. They shall not, I say, feel this desire to return to their bodies, since they shall have those bodies to which a return was desired, and shall, indeed, be in such thorough possession of them, that they shall never lose them even for the briefest moment, nor ever lay them down in death.

Chapter XXVII: *Of the Apparently Conflicting Opinions of Plato and Porphyry, Which Would Have Conducted Them Both to the Truth If They Could Have Yielded to One Another.*

Statements were made by Plato and Porphyry singly, which if they could have seen their way to hold in common, they might possibly have became Christians. Plato said that souls could not exist eternally without bodies; for it was on this account, he said, that the souls even of wise men must some time or other return to their bodies. Porphyry, again, said that the purified soul, when it has returned to the Father, shall never return to the ills of this world. Consequently, if Plato had communicated to Porphyry that which he saw to be true, that souls, though perfectly purified, and belonging to the wise and righteous, must return to human bodies; and if Porphyry, again, had imparted to Plato the truth which he saw, that holy soul, shall never return to the miseries of a corruptible body, so that they should not have each held only his own opinion, but should both have held both truths, I think they would have seen that it follows that the souls return to their bodies, and also that these bodies shall be such as to afford them a blessed and immortal life. For, according to Plato, even holy souls shall return to the body; according to Porphyry, holy souls shall not return to the ills of this world. Let Porphyry then say with Plato, they shall return to the body; let Plato say with Porphyry, they shall not return to their old misery: and they will agree that they return to bodies in which they shall suffer no more. And this is nothing else than what God has promised—that He will give eternal felicity to souls joined to their own bodies. For this, I presume, both of them would readily concede, that if the souls of the saints are to be reunited to bodies, it shall be to their own bodies, in which they have endured the miseries of this life, and in which, to escape these miseries, they served God with piety and fidelity.

Chapter XXVIII: *What Plato or Labeo, or Even Varro, Might Have Contributed to the True Faith of the Resurrection, If They Had Adopted One Another's Opinions into One Scheme.*

Some Christians, who have a liking for Plato on account of his magnificent style and the truths which he now and then uttered, say that he even held an opinion similar to our own regarding the resurrection of the dead. Cicero, however, alluding to this in his Republic, asserts that Plato meant it rather as a playful fancy than as a reality; for he introduces a man who had come to life again, and gave a narrative of his experience in corroboration of the doctrines of Plato. Labeo, too, says that two men died on one day, and met at a cross-road, and that, being afterwards ordered to return to their bodies, they agreed to be friends for life, and were so till they died again. But the resurrection which these writers instance resembles that of those persons whom we have ourselves known to rise again, and who came back indeed to this life, but not so as never to die again. Marcus Varro, however, in his work On the Origin of the Roman People, records something more remarkable; I think his own words should be given. "Certain astrologers," he says, "have written that men are destined to a new birth, which the Greeks call *palingenesy.* This will take place after four hundred and forty years have elapsed; and then the same soul and the same body, which were formerly united in the person, shall again be reunited." This Varro, indeed, or those nameless astrologers—for he does not give us the names of the men whose statement he cites—have affirmed what is indeed not altogether true; for once the souls have returned to the bodies they wore, they shall never afterwards leave them. Yet what they say upsets and demolishes much of that idle talk of our adversaries about the impossibility of the resurrection. For those who have been or are of this opinion, have not thought it possible that bodies which have dissolved into air, or dust, or ashes, or water, or into the bodies of the beasts or even of the men that fed on them, should be restored again to that which they formerly were. And therefore, if Plato and Porphyry, or rather, if their disciples now living, agree with us that holy souls shall return to the body, as Plato says, and that, nevertheless, they shall not return to misery, as Porphyry maintains—if they accept the consequence of these two propositions which is taught by the Christian faith, that they shall receive bodies in which they may live eternally without suffering any misery—let them also adopt from Varro the opinion that they shall return to the same bodies as they were formerly in, and thus the whole question of the eternal resurrection of the body shall be resolved out of their own mouths.

Chapter XXIX: *Of the Beatific Vision.*

And now let us consider, with such ability as God may vouchsafe, how the saints shall be employed when they are clothed in immortal and spiritual bodies, and when the flesh shall live no longer in a fleshly but a spiritual fashion. And indeed, to tell the truth, I am at a loss to understand the nature of that employment, or, shall I rather say, repose and ease, for it has never come within the range of my bodily senses. And if I should speak of my mind or understanding, what is our understanding in comparison of its excellence? For then shall be that "peace of God which," as the apostle says, "passeth all understanding"—that is to say, all human, and perhaps all angelic understanding, but certainly not the divine. That it passeth ours there is no doubt; but if it passeth that of the angels—and he who says "all understanding" seems to make no exception in their favor—then we must understand him to mean that neither we nor the angels can understand, as God understands, the peace which God Himself enjoys. Doubtless this passeth all understanding but His own. But as we shall one day be made to participate, according to our slender capacity, in His peace, both in ourselves, and with our neighbor, and with God our chief good, in this respect the angels understand the peace of God in their own measure, and men too, though now far behind them, whatever spiritual advance they have made. For we must remember how great a man he was who said, "We know in part, and we prophesy in part, until that which is perfect is come;" and "Now we see through a glass, darkly; but then face to face." Such also is now the vision of the holy angels, who are also called our angels, because we, being rescued out of the power of darkness, and receiving the earnest of the Spirit, are translated into the kingdom of Christ, and already begin to belong to those angels with whom we shall enjoy that holy and most delightful city of God of which we have now written so much. Thus, then, the angels of God are our angels, as Christ is God's and also ours. They are God's, because they have not abandoned Him; they are ours, because we are their fellow citizens. The Lord Jesus also said, "See that ye despise not one of these little ones: for I say unto you, That in heaven their angels do always see the face of my Father which is in heaven." As, then, they see, so shall we also see; but not yet do we thus see. Wherefore the apostle uses the words cited a little ago, "Now we see through a glass, darkly; but then face to face." This vision is reserved as the reward of our faith; and of it the Apostle John also says, "When He shall appear, we shall be like Him, for we shall see Him as He is." By "the face" of God we are to understand His manifestation, and not a part of the body similar to that which in our bodies we call by that name.

And so, when I am asked how the saints shall be employed in that spiritual body, I do not say what I see, but I say what I believe, according to that which I read in the psalm, "I believed, therefore have I spoken." I say, then, they shall in the body see God; but whether they shall see Him by means of the body, as now we see the sun, moon, stars, sea, earth, and all that is in it, that is a difficult question. For it is hard to say that the saints shall then have such bodies that they shall not be able to shut and open their eyes as they please; while it is harder still to say that every one who shuts his eyes shall lose the vision of God. For if the prophet Elisha, though at a distance, saw his servant Gehazi, who thought that his wickedness would escape his master's observation and accepted gifts from Naaman the Syrian, whom the prophet had cleansed from his foul leprosy, how much more shall the saints in the spiritual body see all things, not only though their eyes be shut, but though they themselves be at a great distance? For then shall be "that which is perfect," of which the apostle says, "We know in part, and we prophesy in part; but when that which is perfect is come, then that which is in part shall be done away." Then, that he may illustrate as well as possible, by a simile, how superior the future life is to the life now lived, not only by ordinary men, but even by the foremost of the saints, he says, "When I was a child, I understood as a child, I spake as a child, I thought as a child; but when I became a man, I put away childish things. Now we see through a glass, darkly; but then face to face: now I know in part; but then shall I know even as also I am known." If, then, even in this life, in which the prophetic power of remarkable men is no more worthy to be compared to the vision of the future life than childhood is to manhood, Elisha, though distant from his servant, saw him accepting gifts, shall we say that when that which is perfect is come, and the corruptible body no longer oppresses the soul, but is incorruptible and offers no impediment to it, the saints shall need bodily eyes to see, though Elisha had no need of them to see his servant? For, following the Septuagint version, these are the prophet's words: "Did not my heart go with thee, when the man came out of his chariot to meet thee, and thou tookedst his gifts?" Or, as the presbyter Jerome rendered it from the Hebrew, "Was not my heart present when the man turned from his chariot to meet thee?" The prophet said that he saw this with his heart, miraculously aided by God, as no one can doubt. But how much more abundantly shall the saints enjoy this gift when God shall be all in all? Nevertheless the bodily eyes also shall have their office and their place, and shall be used by the spirit through the spiritual body. For the prophet did not forego the use of his eyes for seeing what was before them, though he did not need them to see his absent servant, and though he could have seen these present objects in spirit, and with his eyes shut, as he saw things far distant in a place where he himself was not. Far be it, then, from us to say that in the life to come the saints shall not see God when their eyes are shut, since they shall always see Him with the spirit.

But the question arises, whether, when their eyes are open, they shall see Him with the bodily eye? If the eyes of the spiritual body have no more power than the eyes which we now possess, manifestly God cannot be seen with them. They must be of a very different power if they can look upon that incorporeal nature which is not contained in any place, but is all in every place. For though we say that God is in heaven and on earth, as He, Himself says by the prophet, "I fill heaven and earth," we do not mean that there is one part of God in heaven and another part on earth; but He is all in heaven and all on earth, not at alternate intervals of time, but both at once, as no bodily nature can be. The eye, then, shall have a vastly superior power—the power not of keen sight, such as is ascribed to serpents or eagles, for however keenly these animals see, they can discern nothing but bodily substances—but the power of seeing things incorporeal. Possibly it was this great power of vision which was temporarily communicated to the eyes of the holy Job while yet in this mortal body, when he says to God, "I have heard of Thee by the hearing of the ear; but now mine eye seeth Thee: wherefore I abhor myself, and melt away, and count myself dust and ashes;" although there is no reason why we should not understand this of the eye of the heart, of which the apostle says, "Having the eyes of your heart illuminated." But that God shall be seen with these eyes no Christian doubts who believingly accepts what our God and Master says, "Blessed are the pure in heart: for they shall see God." But whether in the future life God shall also be seen with the bodily eye, this is now our question.

The expression of Scripture, "And all flesh shall see the salvation of God," may without difficulty be understood as if it were said, "And every man shall see the Christ of God." And He certainly was seen in the body, and shall be seen in the body when He judges quick and dead. And that Christ is the salvation of God, many other passages of Scripture witness, but especially the words of the venerable Simeon, who, when he had received into his hands the infant Christ, said, "Now lettest Thou Thy servant depart in peace, according to Thy word: for mine eyes have seen Thy salvation." As for the words of the above-mentioned Job, as they are found in the Hebrew manuscripts, "And in my flesh I shall see God," no doubt they were a prophecy of the resurrection of the flesh; yet he does not say "by the flesh." And indeed, if he had said this, it would still be possible that Christ was meant by "God;" for Christ shall be seen by the flesh in the flesh. But even understanding it of God, it is only equivalent to saying, I shall be in the flesh when I see God. Then the apostle's expression, "face to face," does not oblige us to believe that we shall see God by the bodily face in which are the eyes of the body, for we shall see Him without intermission in spirit. And if the apostle had not referred to the face of the inner man, he would not have said, "But we, with unveiled face beholding as in a glass the glory of the Lord, are transformed into the same image, from glory to glory, as by the spirit of the Lord." In the same sense we understand what the Psalmist sings, "Draw near unto Him, and be enlightened; and your faces shall not be ashamed." For it is by faith we draw near to God, and faith is an act of the spirit, not of the body. But as we do not know what degree of perfection the spiritual body shall attain—for here we speak of a matter of which we have no experience, and upon which the authority of Scripture does not definitely pronounce—it is necessary that the words of the Book of Wisdom be illustrated in us: "The thoughts of mortal men are timid, and our fore-castings uncertain."

For if that reasoning of the philosophers, by which they attempt to make out that intelligible or mental objects are so seen by the mind, and sensible or bodily objects so seen by the body, that the former cannot be discerned by the mind through the body, nor the latter by the mind itself without the body—if this reasoning were trustworthy, then it would certainly follow that God could not be seen by the eye even of a spiritual body. But this reasoning is exploded both by true reason and by prophetic authority. For who is so little acquainted with the truth as to say that God has no cognisance of sensible objects? Has He therefore a body, the eyes of which give Him this knowledge? Moreover, what we have just been relating of the prophet Elisha, does this not sufficiently show that bodily things can be discerned by the spirit without the help of the body? For when that servant received the gifts, certainly this was a bodily or material transaction, yet the prophet saw it not by the body, but by the spirit. As, therefore, it is agreed that bodies are seen by the spirit, what if the power of the spiritual body shall be so great that spirit also is seen by the body? For God is a spirit. Besides, each man recognizes his own life—that life by which he now lives in the body, and which vivifies these earthly members and causes them to grow—by an interior sense, and not by his bodily eye; but the life of other men, though it is invisible, he sees with the bodily eye. For how do we distinguish between living and dead bodies, except by seeing at once both the body and the life which we cannot see save by the eye? But a life without a body we cannot see thus.

Wherefore it may very well be, and it is thoroughly credible, that we shall in the future world see the material forms of the new heavens and the new earth in such a way that we shall most distinctly recognize God everywhere present and governing all things, material as well as spiritual, and shall see Him, not as now we understand the invisible things of God, by the things which are made, and see Him darkly, as in a mirror, and in part, and rather by faith than by bodily vision of material appearances, but by means of the bodies we shall wear and which we shall see wherever we turn our eyes. As we do not believe, but see that the living men around us who are exercising vital functions are alive, though we cannot see their life without their bodies, but see it most distinctly by means of their bodies, so, wherever we shall look with those spiritual eyes of our future bodies, we shall then, too, by means of bodily substances behold God, though a spirit, ruling all things. Either, therefore, the eyes shall possess some quality similar to that of the mind, by which they may be able to discern spiritual things, and among these God—a supposition for which it is difficult or even impossible to find any support in Scripture—or, which is more easy to comprehend, God will be so known by us, and shall be so much before us, that we shall see Him by the spirit in ourselves, in one another, in Himself, in the new heavens and the new earth, in every created thing which shall then exist; and also by the body we shall see Him in every body which the keen vision of the eye of the spiritual body shall reach. Our thoughts also shall be visible to all, for then shall be fulfilled the words of the apostle, "Judge nothing before the time, until the Lord come, who both will bring to light the hidden things of darkness, and will make manifest the thoughts of the heart, and then shall every one have praise of God."

Chapter XXX: *Of the Eternal Felicity of the City of God, and of the Perpetual Sabbath.*

How great shall be that felicity, which shall be tainted with no evil, which shall lack no good, and which shall afford leisure for the praises of God, who shall be all in all! For I know not what other employment there can be where no lassitude shall slacken activity, nor any want stimulate to labor. I am admonished also by the sacred song, in which I read or hear the words, "Blessed are they that dwell in Thy house, O Lord; they will be still praising Thee." All the members and organs of the incorruptible body, which now we see to be suited to various necessary uses, shall contribute to the praises of God; for in that life necessity shall have no place, but full, certain, secure, everlasting felicity. For all those parts of the bodily harmony, which are distributed through the whole body, within and without, and of which I have just been saying that they at present elude our observation, shall then be discerned; and, along with the other great and marvelous discoveries which shall then kindle rational minds in praise of the great Artificer, there shall be the enjoyment of a beauty which appeals to the reason. What power of movement such bodies shall possess, I have not the audacity rashly to define, as I have not the ability to conceive. Nevertheless I will say that in any case, both in motion and at rest, they shall be, as in their appearance, seemly; for into that state nothing which is unseemly shall be admitted. One thing is certain, the body shall forthwith be wherever the spirit wills, and the spirit shall will nothing which is unbecoming either to the spirit or to the body. True honor shall be there, for it shall be denied to none who is worthy, nor yielded to any unworthy; neither shall any unworthy person so much as sue for it, for none but the worthy shall be there. True peace shall be there, where no one shall suffer opposition either from himself or any other. God Himself, who is the Author of virtue, shall there be its reward; for, as there is nothing greater or better, He has promised Himself. What else was meant by His word through the prophet, "I will be your God, and ye shall be my people," than, I shall be their satisfaction, I shall be all that men honorably desire—life, and health, and nourishment, and plenty, and glory, and honor, and peace, and all good things? This, too, is the right interpretation of the saying of the apostle, "That God may be all in all." He shall be the end of our desires who shall be seen without end, loved without cloy, praised without weariness. This outgoing of affection, this employment, shall certainly be, like eternal life itself, common to all.

But who can conceive, not to say describe, what degrees of honor and glory shall be awarded to the various degrees of merit? Yet it cannot be doubted that there shall be degrees. And in that blessed city there shall be this great blessing, that no inferior shall envy any superior, as now the archangels are not envied by the angels, because in strictest concord with him who has received; as in the body the finger does not seek to be the eye, though both members are harmoniously included in the complete structure of the body. And thus, along with his gift, greater or less, each shall receive this further gift of contentment to desire no more than he has.

Neither are we to suppose that because sin shall have no power to delight them, free will must be withdrawn. It will, on the contrary, be all the more truly free, because set free from delight in sinning to take unfailing delight in not sinning. For the first freedom of will which man received when he was created upright consisted in an ability not to sin, but also in an ability to sin; whereas this last freedom of will shall be superior, inasmuch as it shall not be able to sin. This, indeed, shall not be a natural ability, but the gift of God. For it is one thing to be God, another thing to be a partaker of God. God by nature cannot sin, but the partaker of God receives this inability from God. And in this divine gift there was to be observed this gradation, that man should first receive a free will by which he was able not to sin, and at last a free will by which he was not able to sin—the former being adapted to the acquiring of merit, the latter to the enjoying of the reward. But the nature thus constituted, having sinned when it had the ability to do so, it is by a more abundant grace that it is delivered so as to reach that freedom in which it cannot sin. For as the first immortality which Adam lost by sinning consisted in his being able not to die, while the last shall consist in his not being able to die; so the first free will consisted in his being able not to sin, the last in his not being able to sin. And thus piety and justice shall be as indefeasible as happiness. For certainly by sinning we lost both piety and happiness; but when we lost happiness, we did not lose the love of it. Are we to say that God Himself is not free because He cannot sin? In that city, then, there shall be free will, one in all the citizens, and indivisible in each, delivered from all ill, filled with all good, enjoying indefeasibly the delights of eternal joys, oblivious of sins, oblivious of sufferings, and yet not so oblivious of its deliverance as to be ungrateful to its Deliverer.

The soul, then, shall have an intellectual remembrance of its past ills; but, so far as regards sensible experience, they shall be quite forgotten. For a skillful physician knows, indeed, professionally almost all diseases; but experimentally he is ignorant of a great number which he himself has never suffered from. As, therefore, there are two ways of knowing evil things—one by mental insight, the other by sensible experience, for it is one thing to understand all vices by the wisdom of a cultivated mind, another to understand them by the foolishness of an abandoned life—so also there are two ways of forgetting evils. For a well-instructed and learned man forgets them one way, and he who has experimentally suffered from them forgets them another—the former by neglecting what he has learned, the latter by escaping what he has suffered. And in this latter way the saints shall forget their past ills, for they shall have so thoroughly escaped them all, that they shall be quite blotted out of their experience. But their intellectual knowledge, which shall be great, shall keep them acquainted not only with their own past woes, but with the eternal sufferings of the lost. For if they were not to know that they had been miserable, how could they, as the Psalmist says, for ever sing the mercies of God? Certainly that city shall have no greater joy than the celebration of the grace of Christ, who redeemed us by His blood. There shall be accomplished the words of the psalm, "Be still, and know that I am God." There shall be the great Sabbath which has no evening, which God celebrated among His first works, as it is written, "And God rested on the seventh day from all His works which He had made. And God blessed the seventh day, and sanctified it; because that in it He had rested from all His work which God began to make." For we shall ourselves be the seventh day, when we shall be filled and replenished with God's blessing and sanctification. There shall we be still, and know that He is God; that He is that which we ourselves aspired to be when we fell away from Him, and listened to the voice of the seducer, "Ye shall be as gods," and so abandoned God, who would have made us as gods, not by deserting Him, but by participating in Him. For without Him what have we accomplished, save to perish in His anger? But when we are restored by Him, and perfected with greater grace, we shall have eternal leisure to see that He is God, for we shall be full of Him when He shall be all in all. For even our good works, when they are understood to be rather His than ours, are imputed to us that we may enjoy this Sabbath rest. For if we attribute them to ourselves, they shall be servile; for it is said of the Sabbath, "Ye shall do no servile work in it." Wherefore also it is said by Ezekiel the prophet, "And I gave them my Sabbaths to be a sign between me and them, that they might know that I am the Lord who sanctify them." This knowledge shall be perfected when we shall be perfectly at rest, and shall perfectly know that He is God.

This Sabbath shall appear still more clearly if we count the ages as days, in accordance with the periods of time defined in Scripture, for that period will be found to be the seventh. The first age, as the first day, extends from Adam to the deluge; the second from the deluge to Abraham, equaling the first, not in length of time, but in the number of generations, there being ten in each. From Abraham to the advent of Christ there are, as the evangelist Matthew calculates, three periods, in each of which are fourteen generations—one period from Abraham to David, a second from David to the captivity, a third from the captivity to the birth of Christ in the flesh. There are thus five ages in all. The sixth is now passing, and cannot be measured by any number of generations, as it has been said, "It is not for you to know the times, which the Father hath put in His own power." After this period God shall rest as on the seventh day, when He shall give us (who shall be the seventh day) rest in Himself. But there is not now space to treat of these ages; suffice it to say that the seventh shall be our Sabbath, which shall be brought to a close, not by an evening, but by the Lord's day, as an eighth and eternal day, consecrated by the resurrection of Christ, and prefiguring the eternal repose not only of the spirit, but also of the body. There we shall rest and see, see and love, love and praise. This is what shall be in the end without end. For what other end do we propose to ourselves than to attain to the kingdom of which there is no end?

I think I have now, by God's help, discharged my obligation in writing this large work. Let those who think I have said too little, or those who think I have said too much, forgive me; and let those who think I have said just enough join me in giving thanks to God. Amen.

BOETHIUS

THE CONSOLATION OF PHILOSOPHY

BOETHIUS

Translated by H. R. James

Book One
The Sorrows of Boethius

Song I: Boethius' Complaint.

Who wrought my studious numbers
Smoothly once in happier days,
Now perforce in tears and sadness
Learn a mournful strain to raise.
Lo, the Muses, grief-disheveled,
Guide my pen and voice my woe;
Down their cheeks unfeigned the tear drops
To my sad complainings flow!
These alone in danger's hour
Faithful found, have dared attend
On the footsteps of the exile
To his lonely journey's end.
These that were the pride and pleasure
Of my youth and high estate
Still remain the only solace
Of the old man's mournful fate.

Old? Ah yes; swift, ere I knew it,
By these sorrows on me pressed
Age hath come; lo, Grief hath bid me
Wear the garb that fits her best.
O'er my head untimely sprinkled
These white hairs my woes proclaim,
And the skin hangs loose and shriveled
On this sorrow-shrunken frame.
Blest is death that intervenes not
In the sweet, sweet years of peace,
But unto the broken-hearted,
When they call him, brings release!
Yet Death passes by the wretched,
Shuts his ear and slumbers deep;
Will not heed the cry of anguish,
Will not close the eyes that weep.
For, while yet inconstant Fortune
Poured her gifts and all was bright,
Death's dark hour had all but whelmed me
In the gloom of endless night.
Now, because misfortune's shadow
Hath o'erclouded that false face,
Cruel Life still halts and lingers,
Though I loathe his weary race.
Friends, why did ye once so lightly
Vaunt me happy among men?
Surely he who so hath fallen
Was not firmly founded then.

I

While I was thus mutely pondering within myself, and recording my sorrowful complainings with my pen, it seemed to me that there appeared above my head a woman of a countenance exceeding venerable. Her eyes were bright as fire, and of a more than human keenness; her complexion was lively, her vigour showed no trace of enfeeblement; and yet her years were right full, and she plainly seemed not of our age and time. Her stature was difficult to judge.

At one moment it exceeded not the common height, at another her forehead seemed to strike the sky; and whenever she raised her head higher, she began to pierce within the very heavens, and to baffle the eyes of them that looked upon her. Her garments were of an imperishable fabric, wrought with the finest threads and of the most delicate workmanship; and these, as her own lips afterwards assured me, she had herself woven with her own hands. The beauty of this vesture had been somewhat tarnished by age and neglect, and wore that dingy look which marble contracts from exposure. On the lowermost edge was inwoven the Greek letter Π [Greek: P], on the topmost the letter θ [Greek: Th], and between the two were to be seen steps, like a staircase, from the lower to the upper letter. This robe, moreover, had been torn by the hands of violent persons, who had each snatched away what he could clutch. Her right hand held a notebook; in her left she bore a staff. And when she saw the Muses of Poesie standing by my bedside, dictating the words of my lamentations, she was moved awhile to wrath, and her eyes flashed sternly.

'Who,' said she, 'has allowed yon play-acting wantons to approach this sick man—these who, so far from giving medicine to heal his malady, even feed it with sweet poison? These it is who kill the rich crop of reason with the barren thorns of passion, who accustom men's minds to disease, instead of setting them free. Now, were it some common man whom your allurements were seducing, as is usually your way, I should be less indignant. On such a one I should not have spent my pains for naught. But this is one nurtured in the Eleatic and Academic philosophies. Nay, get ye gone, ye sirens, whose sweetness lasteth not; leave him for my muses to tend and heal!' At these words of upbraiding, the whole band, in deepened sadness, with downcast eyes, and blushes that confessed their shame, dolefully left the chamber.

But I, because my sight was dimmed with much weeping, and I could not tell who was this woman of authority so commanding—I was dumbfounded, and, with my gaze fastened on the earth, continued silently to await what she might do next. Then she drew near me and sat on the edge of my couch, and, looking into my face all heavy with grief and fixed in sadness on the ground, she bewailed in these words the disorder of my mind:

Song II: His Despondency.

Alas! in what abyss his mind
Is plunged, how wildly tossed!
Still, still towards the outer night
She sinks, her true light lost,
As oft as, lashed tumultuously
By earth-born blasts, care's waves rise high.
Yet once he ranged the open heavens,
The sun's bright pathway tracked;
Watched how the cold moon waxed and waned;
Nor rested, till there lacked
To his wide ken no star that steers
Amid the maze of circling spheres.
The causes why the blusterous winds
Vex ocean's tranquil face,
Whose hand doth turn the stable globe,
Or why his even race
From out the ruddy east the sun
Unto the western waves doth run:
What is it tempers cunningly
The placid hours of spring,
So that it blossoms with the rose
For earth's engarlanding:
Who loads the year's maturer prime
With clustered grapes in autumn time:
All this he knew—thus ever strove
Deep Nature's lore to guess.
Now, reft of reason's light, he lies,
And bonds his neck oppress;
While by the heavy load constrained,
His eyes to this dull earth are chained.

II

'But the time,' said she, 'calls rather for healing than for lamentation.' Then, with her eyes bent full upon me, 'Art thou that man,' she cries, 'who, erstwhile fed with the milk and reared upon the nourishment which is mine to give, had grown up to the full vigour of a manly spirit? And yet I had bestowed such armour on thee as would have proved an invincible defense, hadst thou not first cast it away. Dost thou know me? Why art thou silent? Is it shame or amazement that hath struck thee dumb? Would it were shame; but, as I see, a stupor hath seized upon thee.' Then, when she saw me not only answering nothing, but mute and utterly incapable of speech, she gently touched my breast with her hand, and said: 'There is no danger; these are the symptoms of lethargy, the usual sickness of deluded minds. For awhile he has forgotten himself; he will easily recover his memory, if only he first recognises me. And that he may do so, let me now wipe his eyes that are clouded with a mist of mortal things.' Thereat, with a fold of her robe, she dried my eyes all swimming with tears.

Song III: The Mists Dispelled.

Then the gloom of night was scattered,
Sight returned unto mine eyes.
So, when haply rainy Caurus
Rolls the storm-clouds through the skies,
Hidden is the sun; all heaven
Is obscured in starless night.
But if, in wild onset sweeping,
Boreas frees day's prisoned light,
All suddenly the radiant god outstreams,
And strikes our dazzled eyesight with his beams.

III

Even so the clouds of my melancholy were broken up. I saw the clear sky, and regained the power to recognise the face of my physician. Accordingly, when I had lifted my eyes and fixed my gaze upon her, I beheld my nurse, Philosophy, whose halls I had frequented from my youth up.

'Ah! why,' I cried, 'mistress of all excellence, hast thou come down from on high, and entered the solitude of this my exile? Is it that thou, too, even as I, mayst be persecuted with false accusations?'

'Could I desert thee, child,' said she, 'and not lighten the burden which thou hast taken upon thee through the hatred of my name, by sharing this trouble? Even forgetting that it were not lawful for Philosophy to leave companionless the way of the innocent, should I, thinkest thou, fear to incur reproach, or shrink from it, as though some strange new thing had befallen? Thinkest thou that now, for the first time in an evil age, Wisdom hath been assailed by peril? Did I not often in days of old, before my servant Plato lived, wage stern warfare with the rashness of folly? In his lifetime, too, Socrates, his master, won with my aid the victory of an unjust death. And when, one after the other, the Epicurean herd, the Stoic, and the rest, each of them as far as in them lay, went about to seize the heritage he left, and were dragging me off protesting and resisting, as their booty, they tore in pieces the garment which I had woven with my own hands, and, clutching the torn pieces, went off, believing that the whole of me had passed into their possession. And some of them, because some traces of my vesture were seen upon them, were destroyed through the mistake of the lewd multitude, who falsely deemed them to be my disciples. It may be thou knowest not of the banishment of Anaxagoras, of the poison draught of Socrates, nor of Zeno's torturing, because these things happened in a distant country; yet mightest thou have learnt the fate of Arrius, of Seneca, of Soranus, whose stories are neither old nor unknown to fame. These men were brought to destruction for no other reason than that, settled as they were in my principles, their lives were a manifest contrast to the ways of the wicked. So there is nothing thou shouldst wonder at, if on the seas of this life we are tossed by storm-blasts, seeing that we have made it our chiefest aim to refuse compliance with evil-doers. And though, maybe, the host of the wicked is many in number, yet is it contemptible, since it is under no leadership, but is hurried hither and thither at the blind driving of mad error. And if at times and seasons they set in array against us, and fall on in overwhelming strength, our leader draws off her forces into the citadel while they are busy plundering the useless baggage. But we from our vantage ground, safe from all this wild work, laugh to see them making prize of the most valueless of things, protected by a bulwark which aggressive folly may not aspire to reach.'

Song IV: Nothing can subdue Virtue.

Whoso calm, serene, sedate,
Sets his foot on haughty fate;
Firm and steadfast, come what will,
Keeps his mien unconquered still;
Him the rage of furious seas,
Tossing high wild menaces,
Nor the flames from smoky forges
That Vesuvius disgorges,
Nor the bolt that from the sky
Smites the tower, can terrify.
Why, then, shouldst thou feel affright
At the tyrant's weakling might?
Dread him not, nor fear no harm,
And thou shall his rage disarm;
But who to hope or fear gives way—
Lost his bosom's rightful sway—
He hath cast away his shield,
Like a coward fled the field;
He hath forged all unaware
Fetters his own neck must bear!

IV

'Dost thou understand?' she asks. 'Do my words sink into thy mind? Or art thou dull "as the ass to the sound of the lyre"? Why dost thou weep? Why do tears stream from thy eyes? "'Speak out, hide it not in thy heart." If thou lookest for the physician's help, thou must needs disclose thy wound.'

Then I, gathering together what strength I could, began: 'Is there still need of telling? Is not the cruelty of fortune against me plain enough? Doth not the very aspect of this place move thee? Is this the library, the room which thou hadst chosen as thy constant resort in my home, the place where we so often sat together and held discourse of all things in heaven and earth? Was my garb and mien like this when I explored with thee nature's hid secrets, and thou didst trace for me with thy wand the courses of the stars, moulding the while my character and the whole conduct of my life after the pattern of the celestial order? Is this the recompense of my obedience? Yet thou hast enjoined by Plato's mouth the maxim, "that states would be happy, either if philosophers ruled them, or if it should so befall that their rulers would turn philosophers." By his mouth likewise thou didst point out this imperative reason why philosophers should enter public life, to wit, lest, if the reins of government be left to unprincipled and profligate citizens, trouble and destruction should come upon the good. Following these precepts, I have tried to apply in the business of public administration the principles which I learnt from thee in leisured seclusion. Thou art my witness and that divinity who hath implanted thee in the hearts of the wise, that I brought to my duties no aim but zeal for the public good. For this cause I have become involved in bitter and irreconcilable feuds, and, as happens inevitably, if a man holds fast to the independence of conscience, I have had to think nothing of giving offence to the powerful in the cause of justice. How often have I encountered and balked Conigastus in his assaults on the fortunes of the weak? How often have I thwarted Trigguilla, steward of the king's household, even when his villainous schemes were as good as accomplished? How often have I risked my position and influence to protect poor wretches from the false charges innumerable with which they were for ever being harassed by the greed and license of the barbarians? No one has ever drawn me aside from justice to oppression. When ruin was overtaking the fortunes of the provincials through the combined pressure of private rapine and public taxation, I grieved no less than the sufferers. When at a season of grievous scarcity a forced sale, disastrous as it was unjustifiable, was proclaimed, and threatened to overwhelm Campania with starvation, I embarked on a struggle with the prætorian prefect in the public interest, I fought the case at the king's judgment-seat, and succeeded in preventing the enforcement of the sale. I rescued the consular Paulinus from the gaping jaws of the court bloodhounds, who in their covetous hopes had already made short work of his wealth. To save Albinus, who was of the same exalted rank, from the penalties of a prejudged charge, I exposed myself to the hatred of Cyprian, the informer.

'Thinkest thou I had laid up for myself store of enmities enough? Well, with the rest of my countrymen, at any rate, my safety should have been assured, since my love of justice had left me no hope of security at court. Yet who was it brought the charges by which I have been struck down? Why, one of my accusers is Basil, who, after being dismissed from the king's household, was driven by his debts to lodge an information against my name. There is Opilio, there is Gaudentius, men who for many and various offenses the king's sentence had condemned to banishment; and when they declined to obey, and sought to save themselves by taking sanctuary, the king, as soon as he heard of it, decreed that, if they did not depart from the city of Ravenna within a prescribed time, they should be branded on the forehead and expelled. What would exceed the rigour of this severity? And yet on that same day these very men lodged an information against me, and the information was admitted. Just Heaven! had I deserved this by my way of life? Did it make them fit accusers that my condemnation was a foregone conclusion? Has fortune no shame—if not at the accusation of the innocent, at least for the vileness of the accusers? Perhaps thou wonderest what is the sum of the charges laid against me? I wished, they say, to save the senate. But how? I am accused of hindering an informer from producing evidence to prove the senate guilty of treason. Tell me, then, what is thy counsel, O my mistress. Shall I deny the charge, lest I bring shame on thee? But I did wish it, and I shall never cease to wish it. Shall I admit it? Then the work of thwarting the informer will come to an end. Shall I call the wish for the preservation of that illustrious house a crime? Of a truth the senate, by its decrees concerning me, has made it such! But blind folly, though it deceive itself with false names, cannot alter the true merits of things, and, mindful of the precept of Socrates, I do not think it right either to keep the truth concealed or allow falsehood to pass. But this, however it may be, I leave to thy judgment and to the verdict of the discerning. Moreover, lest the course of events and the true facts should be hidden from posterity, I have myself committed to writing an account of the transaction.

'What need to speak of the forged letters by which an attempt is made to prove that I hoped for the freedom of Rome? Their falsity would have been manifest, if I had been allowed to use the confession of the informers themselves, evidence which has in all matters the most convincing force. Why, what hope of freedom is left to us? Would there were any! I should have answered with the epigram of Canius when Caligula declared him to have been cognisant of a conspiracy against him. "If I had known," said he, "thou shouldst never have known." Grief hath not so blunted my perceptions in this matter that I should complain because impious wretches contrive their villainies against the virtuous, but at their achievement of their hopes I do exceedingly marvel. For evil purposes are, perchance, due to the imperfection of human nature; that it should be possible for scoundrels to carry out their worst schemes against the innocent, while God beholdeth, is verily monstrous. For this cause, not without reason, one of thy disciples asked, "If God exists, whence comes evil? Yet whence comes good, if He exists not?" However, it might well be that wretches who seek the blood of all honest men and of the whole senate should wish to destroy me also, whom they saw to be a bulwark of the senate and all honest men. But did I deserve such a fate from the Fathers also? Thou rememberest, methinks—since thou didst ever stand by my side to direct what I should do or say—thou rememberest, I say, how at Verona, when the king, eager for the general destruction, was bent on implicating the whole senatorial order in the charge of treason brought against Albinus, with what indifference to my own peril I maintained the innocence of its members, one and all. Thou knowest that what I say is the truth, and that I have never boasted of my good deeds in a spirit of self-praise. For whenever a man by proclaiming his good deeds receives the recompense of fame, he diminishes in a measure the secret reward of a good conscience. What issues have overtaken my innocency thou seest. Instead of reaping the rewards of true virtue, I undergo the penalties of a guilt falsely laid to my charge—nay, more than this; never did an open confession of guilt cause such unanimous severity among the assessors, but that some consideration, either of the mere frailty of human nature, or of fortune's universal instability, availed to soften the verdict of some few. Had I been accused of a design to fire the temples, to slaughter the priests with impious sword, of plotting the massacre of all honest men, I should yet have been produced in court, and only punished on due confession or conviction. Now for my too great zeal towards the senate I have been condemned to outlawry and death, unheard and undefended, at a distance of near five hundred miles away. Oh, my judges, well do ye deserve that no one should hereafter be convicted of a fault like mine!

'Yet even my very accusers saw how honourable was the charge they brought against me, and, in order to overlay it with some shadow of guilt, they falsely asserted that in the pursuit of my ambition I had stained my conscience with sacrilegious acts. And yet thy spirit, indwelling in me, had driven from the chamber of my soul all lust of earthly success, and with thine eye ever upon me, there could be no place left for sacrilege. For thou didst daily repeat in my ear and instill into my mind the Pythagorean maxim, "Follow after God." It was not likely, then, that I should covet the assistance of the vilest spirits, when thou wert moulding me to such an excellence as should conform me to the likeness of God. Again, the innocency of the inner sanctuary of my home, the company of friends of the highest probity, a father-in-law revered at once for his pure character and his active beneficence, shield me from the very suspicion of sacrilege. Yet—atrocious as it is—they even draw credence for this charge from thee; I am like to be thought implicated in wickedness on this very account, that I am imbued with thy teachings and stablished in thy ways. So it is not enough that my devotion to thee should profit me nothing, but thou also must be assailed by reason of the odium which I have incurred. Verily this is the very crown of my misfortunes, that men's opinions for the most part look not to real merit, but to the event; and only recognise foresight where Fortune has crowned the issue with her approval. Whereby it comes to pass that reputation is the first of all things to abandon the unfortunate. I remember with chagrin how perverse is popular report, how various and discordant men's judgments. This only will I say, that the most crushing of misfortune's burdens is, that as soon as a charge is fastened upon the unhappy, they are believed to have deserved their sufferings. I, for my part, who have been banished from all life's blessings, stripped of my honours, stained in repute, am punished for well-doing.

'And now methinks I see the villainous dens of the wicked surging with joy and gladness, all the most recklessly unscrupulous threatening a new crop of lying informations, the good prostrate with terror at my danger, every ruffian incited by impunity to new daring and to success by the profits of audacity, the guiltless not only robbed of their peace of mind, but even of all means of defense. Wherefore I would fain cry out:

Song V: Boethius' Prayer.

'Builder of yon starry dome,
Thou that whirlest, throned eternal,
Heaven's swift globe, and, as they roam,
Guid'st the stars by laws supernal:
So in full-sphered splendour dight
Cynthia dims the lamps of night,
But unto the orb fraternal
Closer drawn, doth lose her light.
'Who at fall of eventide,
Hesper, his cold radiance showeth,
Lucifer his beams doth hide,
Paling as the sun's light groweth,
Brief, while winter's frost holds sway,
By thy will the space of day;
Swift, when summer's fervour gloweth,
Speed the hours of night away.
'Thou dost rule the changing year:
When rude Boreas oppresses,
Fall the leaves; they reappear,
Wooed by Zephyr's soft caresses.
Fields that Sirius burns deep grown
By Arcturus' watch were sown:
Each the reign of law confesses,
Keeps the place that is his own.
'Sovereign Ruler, Lord of all!
Can it be that Thou disdainest
Only man? 'Gainst him, poor thrall,
Wanton Fortune plays her vainest.
Guilt's deserved punishment
Falleth on the innocent;

High uplifted, the profanest
On the just their malice vent.
'Virtue cowers in dark retreats,
Crime's foul stain the righteous beareth,
Perjury and false deceits
Hurt not him the wrong who dareth;
But whene'er the wicked trust
In ill strength to work their lust,
Kings, whom nations' awe declareth
Mighty, grovel in the dust.
'Look, oh look upon this earth,
Thou who on law's sure foundation
Framedst all! Have we no worth,
We poor men, of all creation?
Sore we toss on fortune's tide;
Master, bid the waves subside!
And earth's ways with consummation
Of Thy heaven's order guide!'

V

When I had poured out my griefs in this long and unbroken strain of lamentation, she, with calm countenance, and in no wise disturbed at my complainings, thus spake:

'When I saw thee sorrowful, in tears, I straightway knew thee wretched and an exile. But how far distant that exile I should not know, had not thine own speech revealed it. Yet how far indeed from thy country hast thou, not been banished, but rather hast strayed; or, if thou wilt have it banishment, hast banished thyself! For no one else could ever lawfully have had this power over thee. Now, if thou wilt call to mind from what country thou art sprung, it is not ruled, as once was the Athenian polity, by the sovereignty of the multitude, but "one is its Ruler, one its King," who takes delight in the number of His citizens, not in their banishment; to submit to whose governance and to obey whose ordinances is perfect freedom. Art thou ignorant of that most ancient law of this thy country, whereby it is decreed that no one whatsoever, who hath chosen to fix there his dwelling, may be sent into exile? For truly there is no fear that one who is encompassed by its ramparts and defenses should deserve to be exiled. But he who has ceased to wish to dwell therein, he likewise ceases to deserve to do so. And so it is not so much the aspect of this place which moves me, as thy aspect; not so much the library walls set off with glass and ivory which I miss, as the chamber of thy mind, wherein I once placed, not books, but that which gives books their value, the doctrines which my books contain. Now, what thou hast said of thy services to the commonweal is true, only too little compared with the greatness of thy deservings. The things laid to thy charge whereof thou hast spoken, whether such as redound to thy credit, or mere false accusations, are publicly known. As for the crimes and deceits of the informers, thou hast rightly deemed it fitting to pass them over lightly, because the popular voice hath better and more fully pronounced upon them. Thou hast bitterly complained of the injustice of the senate. Thou hast grieved over my calumniation, and likewise hast lamented the damage to my good name. Finally, thine indignation blazed forth against fortune; thou hast complained of the unfairness with which thy merits have been recompensed. Last of all thy frantic muse framed a prayer that the peace which reigns in heaven might rule earth also. But since a throng of tumultuous passions hath assailed thy soul, since thou art distraught with anger, pain, and grief, strong remedies are not proper for thee in this thy present mood. And so for a time I will use milder methods, that the tumours which have grown hard through the influx of disturbing passion may be softened by gentle treatment, till they can bear the force of sharper remedies.'

Song VI: All Things have their Needful Order.

He who to th' unwilling furrows
Gives the generous grain,
When the Crab with baleful fervours
Scorches all the plain;
He shall find his garner bare,
Acorns for his scanty fare.
Go not forth to cull sweet violets

From the purpled steep,
While the furious blasts of winter
Through the valleys sweep;
Nor the grape o'erhasty bring
To the press in days of spring.
For to each thing God hath given
Its appointed time;
No perplexing change permits He
In His plan sublime.
So who quits the order due
Shall a luckless issue rue.

VI

'First, then, wilt thou suffer me by a few questions to make some attempt to test the state of thy mind, that I may learn in what way to set about thy cure?'

'Ask what thou wilt,' said I, 'for I will answer whatever questions thou choosest to put.'

Then said she: 'This world of ours—thinkest thou it is governed haphazard and fortuitously, or believest thou that there is in it any rational guidance?'

'Nay,' said I, 'in no wise may I deem that such fixed motions can be determined by random hazard, but I know that God, the Creator, presideth over His work, nor will the day ever come that shall drive me from holding fast the truth of this belief.'

'Yes,' said she; 'thou didst even but now affirm it in song, lamenting that men alone had no portion in the divine care. As to the rest, thou wert unshaken in the belief that they were ruled by reason. Yet I marvel exceedingly how, in spite of thy firm hold on this opinion, thou art fallen into sickness. But let us probe more deeply: something or other is missing, I think. Now, tell me, since thou doubtest not that God governs the world, dost thou perceive by what means He rules it?'

'I scarcely understand what thou meanest,' I said, 'much less can I answer thy question.'

'Did I not say truly that something is missing, whereby, as through a breach in the ramparts, disease hath crept in to disturb thy mind? But, tell me, dost thou remember the universal end towards which the aim of all nature is directed?'

'I once heard,' said I, 'but sorrow hath dulled my recollection.'

'And yet thou knowest whence all things have proceeded.'

'Yes, that I know,' said I, 'and have answered that it is from God.'

'Yet how is it possible that thou knowest not what is the end of existence, when thou dost understand its source and origin? However, these disturbances of mind have force to shake a man's position, but cannot pluck him up and root him altogether out of himself. But answer this also, I pray thee: rememberest thou that thou art a man?'

'How should I not?' said I.

'Then, canst thou say what man is?'

'Is this thy question: Whether I know myself for a being endowed with reason and subject to death? Surely I do acknowledge myself such.'

Then she: 'Dost know nothing else that thou art?'

'Nothing.'

'Now,' said she, 'I know another cause of thy disease, one, too, of grave moment. Thou hast ceased to know thy own nature. So, then, I have made full discovery both of the causes of thy sickness and the means of restoring thy health. It is because forgetfulness of thyself hath bewildered thy mind that thou hast bewailed thee as an exile, as one stripped of the blessings that were his; it is because thou knowest not the end of existence that thou deemest abominable and wicked men to be happy and powerful; while, because thou hast forgotten by what means the earth is governed, thou deemest that fortune's changes ebb and flow without the restraint of a guiding hand. These are serious enough to cause not sickness only, but even death; but, thanks be to the Author of our health, the light of nature hath not yet left thee utterly. In thy true judgment concerning the world's government, in that thou believest it subject, not to the random drift of chance, but to divine reason, we have the divine spark from which thy recovery may be hoped. Have, then, no fear; from these weak embers the vital heat shall once more be kindled within thee. But seeing that it is not yet time for strong remedies, and that the mind is manifestly so constituted that when it casts off true opinions it straightway puts on false, wherefrom arises a cloud of confusion that disturbs its true vision, I will now try and disperse these mists by mild and soothing application, that so the darkness of misleading passion may be scattered, and thou mayst come to discern the splendour of the true light.'

Song VII: The Perturbations of Passion.

Stars shed no light
Through the black night,
When the clouds hide;
And the lashed wave,
If the winds rave
O'er ocean's tide—
Though once serene
As day's fair sheen—
Soon fouled and spoiled
By the storm's spite,
Shows to the sight
Turbid and soiled.
Oft the fair rill,
Down the steep hill
Seaward that strays,
Some tumbled block
Of fallen rock

Hinders and stays.
Then art thou fain
Clear and most plain
Truth to discern,
In the right way
Firmly to stay,
Nor from it turn?
Joy, hope and fear
Suffer not near,
Drive grief away:
Shackled and blind
And lost is the mind
Where these have sway.

Book Two
The Vanity of Fortune's Gifts.

I

Thereafter for awhile she remained silent; and when she had restored my flagging attention by a moderate pause in her discourse, she thus began: 'If I have thoroughly ascertained the character and causes of thy sickness, thou art pining with regretful longing for thy former fortune. It is the change, as thou deemest, of this fortune that hath so wrought upon thy mind. Well do I understand that Siren's manifold wiles, the fatal charm of the friendship she pretends for her victims, so long as she is scheming to entrap them—how she unexpectedly abandons them and leaves them overwhelmed with insupportable grief. Bethink thee of her nature, character, and deserts, and thou wilt soon acknowledge that in her thou hast neither possessed, nor hast thou lost, aught of any worth. Methinks I need not spend much pains in bringing this to thy mind, since, even when she was still with thee, even while she was caressing thee, thou usedst to assail her in manly terms, to rebuke her, with maxims drawn from my holy treasure-house. But all sudden changes of circumstances bring inevitably a certain commotion of spirit. Thus it hath come to pass that thou also for awhile hast been parted from thy mind's tranquility. But it is time for thee to take and drain a draught, soft and pleasant to the taste, which, as it penetrates within, may prepare the way for stronger potions. Wherefore I call to my aid the sweet persuasiveness of Rhetoric, who then only walketh in the right way when she forsakes not my instructions, and Music, my handmaid, I bid to join with her singing, now in lighter, now in graver strain.

'What is it, then, poor mortal, that hath cast thee into lamentation and mourning? Some strange, unwonted sight, methinks, have thine eyes seen. Thou deemest Fortune to have changed towards thee; thou mistakest. Such ever were her ways, ever such her nature. Rather in her very mutability hath she preserved towards thee her true constancy. Such was she when she loaded thee with caresses, when she deluded thee with the allurements of a false happiness. Thou hast found out how changeful is the face of the blind goddess. She who still veils herself from others hath fully discovered to thee her whole character. If thou likest her, take her as she is, and do not complain. If thou abhorrest her perfidy, turn from her in disdain, renounce her, for baneful are her delusions. The very thing which is now the cause of thy great grief ought to have brought thee tranquility. Thou hast been forsaken by one of whom no one can be sure that she will not forsake him. Or dost thou indeed set value on a happiness that is certain to depart? Again I ask, Is Fortune's presence dear to thee if she cannot be trusted to stay, and though she will bring sorrow when she is gone? Why, if she cannot be kept at pleasure, and if her flight overwhelms with calamity, what is this fleeting visitant but a token of coming trouble? Truly it is not enough to look only at what lies before the eyes; wisdom gauges the issues of things, and this same Amutability, with its two aspects, makes the threats of Fortune void of terror, and her caresses little to be desired. Finally, thou oughtest to bear with whatever takes place within the boundaries of Fortune's demesne, when thou hast placed thy head beneath her yoke. But if thou wishest to impose a law of staying and departing on her whom thou hast of thine own accord chosen for thy mistress, art thou not acting wrongfully, art thou not embittering by impatience a lot which thou canst not alter? Didst thou commit thy sails to the winds, thou wouldst voyage not whither thy intention was to go, but whither the winds drave thee; didst thou entrust thy seed to the fields, thou wouldst set off the fruitful years against the barren. Thou hast resigned thyself to the sway of Fortune; thou must submit to thy mistress's caprices. What! art thou verily striving to stay the swing of the revolving wheel? Oh, stupidest of mortals, if it takes to standing still, it ceases to be the wheel of Fortune.'

Song I: Fortune's Malice.

Mad Fortune sweeps along in wanton pride,
Uncertain as Euripus' surging tide;
Now tramples mighty kings beneath her feet;
Now sets the conquered in the victor's seat.
She heedeth not the wail of hapless woe,
But mocks the griefs that from her mischief flow.
Such is her sport; so proveth she her power;
And great the marvel, when in one brief hour
She shows her darling lifted high in bliss,
Then headlong plunged in misery's abyss.

II

'Now I would fain also reason with thee a little in Fortune's own words. Do thou observe whether her contentions be just.

"Man," she might say, "why dost thou pursue me with thy daily complainings? What wrong have I done thee? What goods of thine have I taken from thee? Choose an thou wilt a judge, and let us dispute before him concerning the rightful ownership of wealth and rank. If thou succeedest in showing that any one of these things is the true property of mortal man, I freely grant those things to be thine which thou claimest. When nature brought thee forth out of thy mother's womb, I took thee, naked and destitute as thou wast, I cherished thee with my substance, and, in the partiality of my favour for thee, I brought thee up somewhat too indulgently, and this it is which now makes thee rebellious against me. I surrounded thee with a royal abundance of all those things that are in my power. Now it is my pleasure to draw back my hand. Thou hast reason to thank me for the use of what was not thine own; thou hast no right to complain, as if thou hadst lost what was wholly thine. Why, then, dost bemoan thyself? I have done thee no violence. Wealth, honour, and all such things are placed under my control. My handmaidens know their mistress; with me they come, and at my going they depart. I might boldly affirm that if those things the loss of which thou lamentest had been thine, thou couldst never have lost them. Am I alone to be forbidden to do what I will with my own? Unrebuked, the skies now reveal the brightness of day, now shroud the daylight in the darkness of night; the year may now engarland the face of the earth with flowers and fruits, now disfigure it with storms and cold. The sea is permitted to invite with smooth and tranquil surface today, tomorrow to roughen with wave and storm. Shall man's insatiate greed bind me to a constancy foreign to my character? This is my art, this the game I never cease to play. I turn the wheel that spins. I delight to see the high come down and the low ascend. Mount up, if thou wilt, but only on condition that thou wilt not think it a hardship to come down when the rules of my game require it. Wert thou ignorant of my character? Didst not know how Crœsus, King of the Lydians, erstwhile the dreaded rival of Cyrus, was afterwards pitiably consigned to the flame of the pyre, and only saved by a shower sent from heaven? Has it 'scaped thee how Paullus paid a meed of pious tears to the misfortunes of King Perseus, his prisoner? What else do tragedies make such woeful outcry over save the overthrow of kingdoms by the indiscriminate strokes of Fortune? Didst thou not learn in thy childhood how there stand at the threshold of Zeus 'two jars,' 'the one full of blessings, the other of calamities'? How if thou hast drawn over-liberally from the good jar? What if not even now have I departed wholly from thee? What if this very mutability of mine is a just ground for hoping better things? But listen now, and cease to let thy heart consume away with fretfulness, nor expect to live on thine own terms in a realm that is common to all.'"

Song II: Man's Covetousness.

What though Plenty pour her gifts
With a lavish hand,

Numberless as are the stars,
Countless as the sand,
Will the race of man, content,
Cease to murmur and lament?
Nay, though God, all-bounteous, give
Gold at man's desire—
Honours, rank, and fame—content
Not a whit is nigher;
But an all-devouring greed
Yawns with ever-widening need.
Then what bounds can e'er restrain
This wild lust of having,
When with each new bounty fed
Grows the frantic craving?
He is never rich whose fear
Sees grim Want forever near.

III

'If Fortune should plead thus against thee, assuredly thou wouldst not have one word to offer in reply; or, if thou canst find any justification of thy complainings, thou must show what it is. I will give thee space to speak.'

Then said I: 'Verily, thy pleas are plausible—yea, steeped in the honeyed sweetness of music and rhetoric. But their charm lasts only while they are sounding in the ear; the sense of his misfortunes lies deeper in the heart of the wretched. So, when the sound ceases to vibrate upon the air, the heart's indwelling sorrow is felt with renewed bitterness.'

Then said she: 'It is indeed as thou sayest, for we have not yet come to the curing of thy sickness; as yet these are but lenitives conducing to the treatment of a malady hitherto obstinate. The remedies which go deep I will apply in due season. Nevertheless, to deprecate thy determination to be thought wretched, I ask thee, Hast thou forgotten the extent and bounds of thy felicity? I say nothing of how, when orphaned and desolate, thou wast taken into the care of illustrious men; how thou wast chosen for alliance with the highest in the state—and even before thou wert bound to their house by marriage, wert already dear to their love—which is the most precious of all ties. Did not all pronounce thee most happy in the virtues of thy wife, the splendid honours of her father, and the blessing of male issue? I pass over—for I care not to speak of blessings in which others also have shared—the distinctions often denied to age which thou enjoyedst in thy youth. I choose rather to come to the unparalleled culmination of thy good fortune. If the fruition of any earthly success has weight in the scale of happiness, can the memory of that splendour be swept away by any rising flood of troubles? That day when thou didst see thy two sons ride forth from home joint consuls, followed by a train of senators, and welcomed by the goodwill of the people; when these two sat in curule chairs in the Senatehouse, and thou by thy panegyric on the king didst earn the fame of eloquence and ability; when in the Circus, seated between the two consuls, thou didst glut the multitude thronging around with the triumphal largesses for which they looked—methinks thou didst cozen Fortune while she caressed thee, and made thee her darling. Thou didst bear off a boon which she had never before granted to any private person. Art thou, then, minded to cast up a reckoning with Fortune? Now for the first time she has turned a jealous glance upon thee. If thou compare the extent and bounds of thy blessings and misfortunes, thou canst not deny that thou art still fortunate. Or if thou esteem not thyself favoured by Fortune in that thy then seeming prosperity hath departed, deem not thyself wretched, since what thou now believest to be calamitous passeth also. What! art thou but now come suddenly and a stranger to the scene of this life? Thinkest thou there is any stability in human affairs, when man himself vanishes away in the swift course of time? It is true that there is little trust that the gifts of chance will abide; yet the last day of life is in a manner the death of all remaining Fortune. What difference, then, thinkest thou, is there, whether thou leavest her by dying, or she leave thee by fleeing away?'

Song III: All Passes.

When, in rosy chariot drawn,
Phœbus 'gins to light the dawn,

By his flaming beams assailed,
Every glimmering star is paled.
When the grove, by Zephyrs fed,
With rose-blossom blushes red;—
Doth rude Auster breathe thereon,
Bare it stands, its glory gone.
Smooth and tranquil lies the deep
While the winds are hushed in sleep.
Soon, when angry tempests lash,
Wild and high the billows dash.
Thus if Nature's changing face
Holds not still a moment's space,
Fleeting deem man's fortunes; deem
Bliss as transient as a dream.
One law only standeth fast:
Things created may not last.

IV

Then said I: 'True are thine admonishings, thou nurse of all excellence; nor can I deny the wonder of my fortune's swift career. Yet it is this which chafes me the more cruelly in the recalling. For truly in adverse fortune the worst sting of misery is to have been happy.'

'Well,' said she, 'if thou art paying the penalty of a mistaken belief, thou canst not rightly impute the fault to circumstances. If it is the felicity which Fortune gives that moves thee—mere name though it be—come reckon up with me how rich thou art in the number and weightiness of thy blessings. Then if, by the blessing of Providence, thou hast still preserved unto thee safe and inviolate that which, howsoever thou mightest reckon thy fortune, thou wouldst have thought thy most precious possession, what right hast thou to talk of ill-fortune whilst keeping all Fortune's better gifts? Yet Symmachus, thy wife's father—a man whose splendid character does honour to the human race—is safe and unharmed; and while he bewails thy wrongs, this rare nature, in whom wisdom and virtue are so nobly blended, is himself out of danger—a boon thou wouldst have been quick to purchase at the price of life itself. Thy wife yet lives, with her gentle disposition, her peerless modesty and virtue—this the epitome of all her graces, that she is the true daughter of her sire—she lives, I say, and for thy sake only preserves the breath of life, though she loathes it, and pines away in grief and tears for thy absence, wherein, if in naught else, I would allow some marring of thy felicity. What shall I say of thy sons and their consular dignity—how in them, so far as may be in youths of their age, the example of their father's and grandfather's character shines out? Since, then, the chief care of mortal man is to preserve his life, how happy art thou, couldst thou but recognise thy blessings, who possessest even now what no one doubts to be dearer than life! Wherefore, now dry thy tears. Fortune's hate hath not involved all thy dear ones; the stress of the storm that has assailed thee is not beyond measure intolerable, since there are anchors still holding firm which suffer thee not to lack either consolation in the present or hope for the future.'

'I pray that they still may hold. For while they still remain, however things may go, I shall ride out the storm. Yet thou seest how much is shorn of the splendour of my fortunes.'

'We are gaining a little ground,' said she, 'if there is something in thy lot wherewith thou art not yet altogether discontented. But I cannot stomach thy daintiness when thou complainest with such violence of grief and anxiety because thy happiness falls short of completeness. Why, who enjoys such settled felicity as not to have some quarrel with the circumstances of his lot? A troublous matter are the conditions of human bliss; either they are never realized in full, or never stay permanently. One has abundant riches, but is shamed by his ignoble birth. Another is conspicuous for his nobility, but through the embarrassments of poverty would prefer to be obscure. A third, richly endowed with both, laments the loneliness of an unwedded life. Another, though happily married, is doomed to childlessness, and nurses his wealth for a stranger to inherit. Yet another, blest with children, mournfully bewails the misdeeds of son or daughter. Wherefore, it is not easy for anyone to be at perfect peace with the circumstances of his lot. There lurks in each several portion something which they who experience it not know nothing of, but which makes the sufferer wince. Besides, the more favoured a man is by Fortune, the more fastidiously sensitive is he; and, unless all things answer to his whim, he is overwhelmed by the most trifling misfortunes, because utterly unschooled in adversity. So petty are the trifles which rob the most fortunate of perfect happiness! How many are there, dost thou imagine, who would think themselves nigh heaven, if but a small portion from the wreck of thy fortune should fall to them? This very place which thou callest exile is to them that dwell therein their native land. So true is it that nothing is wretched, but thinking makes it so, and conversely every lot is happy if borne with equanimity. Who is so blest by Fortune as not to wish to change his state, if once he gives rein to a rebellious spirit? With how many bitternesses is the sweetness of human felicity blent! And even if that sweetness seem to him to bring delight in the enjoying, yet he cannot keep it from departing when it will. How manifestly wretched, then, is the bliss of earthly fortune, which lasts not for ever with those whose temper is equable, and can give no perfect satisfaction to the anxious-minded!

'Why, then, ye children of mortality, seek ye from without that happiness whose seat is only within us? Error and ignorance bewilder you. I will show thee, in brief, the hinge on which perfect happiness turns. Is there anything more precious to thee than thyself? Nothing, thou wilt say. If, then, thou art master of thyself, thou wilt possess that which thou wilt never be willing to lose, and which Fortune cannot take from thee. And that thou mayst see that happiness cannot possibly consist in these things which are the sport of chance, reflect that, if happiness is the highest good of a creature living in accordance with reason, and if a thing which can in any wise be reft away is not the highest good, since that which cannot be taken away is better than it, it is plain that Fortune cannot aspire to bestow happiness by reason of its instability. And, besides, a man borne along by this transitory felicity must either know or not know its instability. If he knows not, how poor is a happiness which depends on the blindness of ignorance! If he knows it, he needs must fear to lose a happiness whose loss he believes to be possible. Wherefore, a never-ceasing fear suffers him not to be happy. Or does he count the possibility of this loss a trifling matter? Insignificant, then, must be the good whose loss can be borne so equably. And, further, I know thee to be one settled in the belief that the souls of men certainly die not with them, and convinced thereof by numerous proofs; it is clear also that the felicity which Fortune bestows is brought to an end with the death of the body: therefore, it cannot be doubted but that, if happiness is conferred in this way, the whole human race sinks into misery when death brings the close of all. But if we know that many have sought the joy of happiness not through death only, but also through pain and suffering, how can life make men happy by its presence when it makes them not wretched by its loss?'

Song IV: The Golden Mean.

Who founded firm and sure
Would ever live secure,
In spite of storm and blast
Immovable and fast;
Whoso would fain deride
The ocean's threatening tide;—
His dwelling should not seek
On sands or mountain-peak.
Upon the mountain's height
The storm-winds wreak their spite:
The shifting sands disdain
Their burden to sustain.
Do thou these perils flee,
Fair though the prospect be,
And fix thy resting-place
On some low rock's sure base.
Then, though the tempests roar,
Seas thunder on the shore,
Thou in thy stronghold blest
And undisturbed shalt rest;
Live all thy days serene,
And mock the heavens' spleen.

V

'But since my reasonings begin to work a soothing effect within thy mind, methinks I may resort to remedies somewhat stronger. Come, suppose, now, the gifts of Fortune were not fleeting and transitory, what is there in them capable of ever becoming truly thine, or which does not lose value when looked at steadily and fairly weighed in the balance? Are riches, I pray thee, precious either through thy nature or in their own? What are they but mere gold and heaps of money? Yet these fine things show their quality better in the spending than in the hoarding; for I suppose 'tis plain that greed Alva's makes men hateful, while liberality brings fame. But that which is transferred to another cannot remain in one's own possession; and if that be so, then money is only precious when it is given away, and, by being transferred to others, ceases to be one's own. Again, if all the money in the world were heaped up in one man's possession, all others would be made poor. Sound fills the ears of many at the same time without being broken into parts, but your riches cannot pass to many without being lessened in the process. And when this happens, they must needs impoverish those whom they leave. How poor and cramped a thing, then, is riches, which more than one cannot possess as an unbroken whole, which falls not to any one man's lot without the impoverishment of everyone else! Or is it the glitter of gems that allures the eye? Yet, how rarely excellent soever may be their splendour, remember the flashing light is in the jewels, not in the man. Indeed, I greatly marvel at men's admiration of them; for what can rightly seem beautiful to a being endowed with life and reason, if it lack the movement and structure of life? And although such things do in the end take on them more beauty from their Maker's care and their own brilliancy, still they in no wise merit your admiration since their excellence is set at a lower grade than your own.

'Does the beauty of the fields delight you? Surely, yes; it is a beautiful part of a right beautiful whole. Fitly indeed do we at times enjoy the serene calm of the sea, admire the sky, the stars, the moon, the sun. Yet is any of these thy concern? Dost thou venture to boast thyself of the beauty of any one of them? Art thou decked with spring's flowers? is it thy fertility that swelleth in the fruits of autumn? Why art thou moved with empty transports? why embracest thou an alien excellence as thine own? Never will fortune make thine that which the nature of things has excluded from thy ownership. Doubtless the fruits of the earth are given for the sustenance of living creatures. But if thou art content to supply thy wants so far as suffices nature, there is no need to resort to fortune's bounty. Nature is content with few things, and with a very little of these. If thou art minded to force superfluities upon her when she is satisfied, that which thou addest will prove either unpleasant or harmful. But, now, thou thinkest it fine to shine in raiment of divers colours; yet—if, indeed, there is any pleasure in the sight of such things—it is the texture or the artist's skill which I shall admire.

'Or perhaps it is a long train of servants that makes thee happy? Why, if they behave viciously, they are a ruinous burden to thy house, and exceeding dangerous to their own master; while if they are honest, how canst thou count other men's virtue in the sum of thy possessions? From all which 'tis plainly proved that not one of these things which thou reckonest in the number of thy possessions is really thine. And if there is in them no beauty to be desired, why shouldst thou either grieve for their loss or find joy in their continued possession? While if they are beautiful in their own nature, what is that to thee? They would have been not less pleasing in themselves, though never included among thy possessions. For they derive not their preciousness from being counted in thy riches, but rather thou hast chosen to count them in thy riches because they seemed to thee precious.

'Then, what seek ye by all this noisy outcry about fortune? To chase away poverty, I ween, by means of abundance. And yet ye find the result just contrary. Why, this varied array of precious furniture needs more accessories for its protection; it is a true saying that they want most who possess most, and, conversely, they want very little who measure their abundance by nature's requirements, not by the superfluity of vain display. Have ye no good of your own implanted within you, that ye seek your good in things external and separate? Is the nature of things so reversed that a creature divine by right of reason can in no other way be splendid in his own eyes save by the possession of lifeless chattels? Yet, while other things are content with their own, ye who in your intellect are God-like seek from the lowest of things adornment for a nature of supreme excellence, and perceive not how great a wrong ye do your Maker. His will was that mankind should excel all things on earth. Ye thrust down your worth beneath the lowest of things. For if that in which each thing finds its good is plainly more precious than that whose good it is, by your own estimation ye put yourselves below the vilest of things, when ye deem these vile things to be your good: nor does this fall out undeservedly. Indeed, man is so constituted that he then only excels other things when he knows himself; but he is brought lower than the beasts if he lose this self-knowledge. For that other creatures should be ignorant of themselves is natural; in man it shows as a defect. How extravagant, then, is this error of yours, in thinking that anything can be embellished by adornments not its own. It cannot be. For if such accessories add any lustre, it is the accessories that get the praise, while that which they veil and cover remains in its pristine ugliness. And again I say, That is no good, which injures its possessor. Is this untrue? No, quite true, thou sayest. And yet riches have often hurt those that possessed them, since the worst of men, who are all the more covetous by reason of their wickedness, think none but themselves worthy to possess all the gold and gems the world contains. So thou, who now dreadest pike and sword, mightest have trolled a carol "in the robber's face," hadst thou entered the road of life with empty pockets. Oh, wondrous blessedness of perishable wealth, whose acquisition robs thee of security!'

Song V: The Former Age.

Too blest the former age, their life
Who in the fields contented led,
And still, by luxury unspoiled,
On frugal acorns sparely fed.
No skill was theirs the luscious grape
With honey's sweetness to confuse;
Nor China's soft and sheeny silks
T' empurple with brave Tyrian hues.
The grass their wholesome couch, their drink
The stream, their roof the pine's tall shade;

Not theirs to cleave the deep, nor seek
In strange far lands the spoils of trade.
The trump of war was heard not yet,
Nor soiled the fields by bloodshed's stain;
For why should war's fierce madness arm
When strife brought wound, but brought not gain?
Ah! would our hearts might still return
To following in those ancient ways.
Alas! the greed of getting glows
More fierce than Etna's fiery blaze.
Woe, woe for him, whoe'er it was,
Who first gold's hidden store revealed,
And—perilous treasure-trove—dug out
The gems that fain would be concealed!

VI

'What now shall I say of rank and power, whereby, because ye know not true power and dignity, ye hope to reach the sky? Yet, when rank and power have fallen to the worst of men, did ever an Etna, belching forth flame and fiery deluge, work such mischief? Verily, as I think, thou dost remember how thine ancestors sought to abolish the consular power, which had been the foundation of their liberties, on account of the overweening pride of the consuls, and how for that self-same pride they had already abolished the kingly title! And if, as happens but rarely, these prerogatives are conferred on virtuous men, it is only the virtue of those who exercise them that pleases. So it appears that honour cometh not to virtue from rank, but to rank from virtue. Look, too, at the nature of that power which ye find so attractive and glorious! Do ye never consider, ye creatures of earth, what ye are, and over whom ye exercise your fancied lordship? Suppose, now, that in the mouse tribe there should rise up one claiming rights and powers for himself above the rest, would ye not laugh consumedly? Yet if thou lookest to his body alone, what creature canst thou find more feeble than man, who oftentimes is killed by the bite of a fly, or by some insect creeping into the inner passage of his system! Yet what rights can one exercise over another, save only as regards the body, and that which is lower than the body—I mean fortune? What! wilt thou bind with thy mandates the free spirit? Canst thou force from its due tranquility the mind that is firmly composed by reason? A tyrant thought to drive a man of free birth to reveal his accomplices in a conspiracy, but the prisoner bit off his tongue and threw it into the furious tyrant's face; thus, the tortures which the tyrant thought the instrument of his cruelty the sage made an opportunity for heroism. Moreover, what is there that one man can do to another which he himself may not have to undergo in his turn? We are told that Busiris, who used to kill his guests, was himself slain by his guest, Hercules. Regulus had thrown into bonds many of the Carthaginians whom he had taken in war; soon after he himself submitted his hands to the chains of the vanquished. Then, thinkest thou that man hath any power who cannot prevent another's being able to do to him what he himself can do to others?

'Besides, if there were any element of natural and proper good in rank and power, they would never come to the utterly bad, since opposites are not wont to be associated. Nature brooks not the union of contraries. So, seeing there is no doubt that wicked wretches are oftentimes set in high places, it is also clear that things which suffer association with the worst of men cannot be good in their own nature. Indeed, this judgment may with some reason be passed concerning all the gifts of fortune which fall so plentifully to all the most wicked. This ought also to be considered here, I think: No one doubts a man to be brave in whom he has observed a brave spirit residing. It is plain that one who is endowed with speed is swiftfooted. So also music makes men musical, the healing art physicians, rhetoric public speakers. For each of these has naturally its own proper working; there is no confusion with the effects of contrary things—nay, even of itself it rejects what is incompatible. And yet wealth cannot extinguish insatiable greed, nor has power ever made him master of himself whom vicious lusts kept bound in indissoluble fetters; dignity conferred on the wicked not only fails to make them worthy, but contrarily reveals and displays their unworthiness. Why does it so happen? Because ye take pleasure in calling by false names things whose nature is quite incongruous thereto—by names which are easily proved false by the very effects of the things themselves; even so it is; these riches, that power, this dignity, are none of them rightly so called. Finally, we may draw the same conclusion concerning the whole sphere of Fortune, within which there is plainly nothing to be truly desired, nothing of intrinsic excellence; for she neither always joins herself to the good, nor does she make good men of those to whom she is united.'

Song VI: Nero's Infamy.

We know what mischief dire he wrought—
Rome fired, the Fathers slain—
Whose hand with brother's slaughter wet
A mother's blood did stain.
No pitying tear his cheek bedewed,
As on the corpse he gazed;
That mother's beauty, once so fair,
A critic's voice appraised.
Yet far and wide, from East to West,
His sway the nations own;
And scorching South and icy North
Obey his will alone.
Did, then, high power a curb impose
On Nero's phrenzied will?
Ah, woe when to the evil heart
Is joined the sword to kill!

VII

Then said I: 'Thou knowest thyself that ambition for worldly success hath but little swayed me. Yet I have desired opportunity for action, lest virtue, in default of exercise, should languish away.'

Then she: 'This is that "last infirmity" which is able to allure minds which, though of noble quality, have not yet been moulded to any exquisite refinement by the perfecting of the virtues—I mean, the love of glory—and fame for high services rendered to the commonweal. And yet consider with me how poor and unsubstantial a thing this glory is! The whole of this earth's globe, as thou hast learnt from the demonstration of astronomy, compared with the expanse of heaven, is found no bigger than a point; that is to say, if measured by the vastness of heaven's sphere, it is held to occupy absolutely no space at all. Now, of this so insignificant portion of the universe, it is about a fourth part, as Ptolemy's proofs have taught us, which is inhabited by living creatures known to us. If from this fourth part you take away in thought all that is usurped by seas and marshes, or lies a vast waste of waterless desert, barely is an exceeding narrow area left for human habitation. You, then, who are shut in and prisoned in this merest fraction of a point's space, do ye take thought for the blazoning of your fame, for the spreading abroad of your renown? Why, what amplitude or magnificence has glory when confined to such narrow and petty limits?

'Besides, the straitened bounds of this scant dwelling-place are inhabited by many nations differing widely in speech, in usages, in mode of life; to many of these, from the difficulty of travel, from diversities of speech, from want of commercial intercourse, the fame not only of individual men, but even of cities, is unable to reach. Why, in Cicero's days, as he himself somewhere points out, the fame of the Roman Republic had not yet crossed the Caucasus, and yet by that time her name had grown formidable to the Parthians and other nations of those parts. Seest thou, then, how narrow, how confined, is the glory ye take pains to spread abroad and extend! Can the fame of a single Roman penetrate where the glory of the Roman name fails to pass? Moreover, the customs and institutions of different races agree not together, so that what is deemed praise worthy in one country is thought punishable in another. Wherefore, if any love the applause of fame, it shall not profit him to publish his name among many peoples. Then, each must be content to have the range of his glory limited to his own people; the splendid immortality of fame must be confined within the bounds of a single race.

'Once more, how many of high renown in their own times have been lost in oblivion for want of a record! Indeed, of what avail are written records even, which, with their authors, are overtaken by the dimness of age after a somewhat longer time? But ye, when ye think on future fame, fancy it an immortality that ye are begetting for yourselves. Why, if thou scannest the infinite spaces of eternity, what room hast thou left for rejoicing in the durability of thy name? Verily, if a single moment's space be compared with ten thousand years, it has a certain relative duration, however little, since each period is definite. But this same number of years—ay, and a number many times as great—cannot even be compared with endless duration; for, indeed, finite periods may in a sort be compared one with another, but a finite and an infinite never. So it comes to pass that fame, though it extend to ever so wide a space of years, if it be compared to never-lessening eternity, seems not short-lived merely, but altogether nothing. But as for you, ye know not how to act aright, unless it be to court the popular breeze, and win the empty applause of the multitude—nay, ye abandon the superlative worth of conscience and virtue, and ask a recompense from the poor words of others. Let me tell thee how wittily one did mock the shallowness of this sort of arrogance. A certain man assailed one who had put on the name of philosopher as a cloak to pride and vain-glory, not for the practice of real virtue, and added: "Now shall I know if thou art a philosopher if thou bearest reproaches calmly and patiently." The other for awhile affected to be patient, and, having endured to be abused, cried out derisively: "Now, do you see that I am a philosopher?" The other, with biting sarcasm, retorted: "I should have hadst thou held thy peace." Moreover, what concern have choice spirits—for it is of such men we speak, men who seek glory by virtue—what concern, I say, have these with fame after the dissolution of the body in death's last hour? For if men die wholly—which our reasonings forbid us to believe—there is no such thing as glory at all, since he to whom the glory is said to belong is altogether non-existent. But if the mind, conscious of its own rectitude, is released from its earthly prison, and seeks heaven in free flight, doth it not despise all earthly things when it rejoices in its deliverance from earthly bonds, and enters upon the joys of heaven?'

Song VII: Glory may not last.

Oh, let him, who pants for glory's guerdon,
Deeming glory all in all,
Look and see how wide the heaven expandeth,
Earth's enclosing bounds how small!

Shame it is, if your proud-swelling glory
May not fill this narrow room!
Why, then, strive so vainly, oh, ye proud ones!
To escape your mortal doom?
Though your name, to distant regions bruited,
O'er the earth be widely spread,
Though full many a lofty-sounding title
On your house its lustre shed,
Death at all this pomp and glory spurneth
When his hour draweth nigh,
Shrouds alike th' exalted and the humble,
Levels lowest and most high.
Where are now the bones of stanch Fabricius?
Brutus, Cato—where are they?
Lingering fame, with a few graven letters,
Doth their empty name display.
But to know the great dead is not given
From a gilded name alone;
Nay, ye all alike must lie forgotten,
'Tis not you that fame makes known.
Fondly do ye deem life's little hour
Lengthened by fame's mortal breath;
There but waits you—when this, too, is taken—
At the last a second death.

VIII

'But that thou mayst not think that I wage implacable warfare against Fortune, I own there is a time when the deceitful goddess serves men well—I mean when she reveals herself, uncovers her face, and confesses her true character. Perhaps thou dost not yet grasp my meaning. Strange is the thing I am trying to express, and for this cause I can scarce find words to make clear my thought. For truly I believe that Ill Fortune is of more use to men than Good Fortune. For Good Fortune, when she wears the guise of happiness, and most seems to caress, is always lying; Ill Fortune is always truthful, since, in changing, she shows her inconstancy. The one deceives, the other teaches; the one enchains the minds of those who enjoy her favour by the semblance of delusive good, the other delivers them by the knowledge of the frail nature of happiness. Accordingly, thou mayst see the one fickle, shifting as the breeze, and ever self-deceived; the other sober-minded, alert, and wary, by reason of the very discipline of adversity. Finally, Good Fortune, by her allurements, draws men far from the true good; Ill Fortune ofttimes draws men back to true good with grappling-irons. Again, should it be esteemed a trifling boon, thinkest thou, that this cruel, this odious Fortune hath discovered to thee the hearts of thy faithful friends—that other hid from thee alike the faces of the true friends and of the false, but in departing she hath taken away her friends, and left thee thine? What price wouldst thou not have given for this service in the fullness of thy prosperity when thou seemedst to thyself fortunate? Cease, then, to seek the wealth thou hast lost, since in true friends thou hast found the most precious of all riches.'

Song VIII: Love is Lord of all.

Why are Nature's changes bound
To a fixed and ordered round?
What to leaguèd peace hath bent
Every warring element?
Wherefore doth the rosy morn
Rise on Phœbus' car upborne?
Why should Phœbe rule the night,
Led by Hesper's guiding light?
What the power that doth restrain
In his place the restless main,
That within fixed bounds he keeps,
Nor o'er earth in deluge sweeps?
Love it is that holds the chains,
Love o'er sea and earth that reigns;
Love—whom else but sovereign Love?—
Love, high lord in heaven above!
Yet should he his care remit,
All that now so close is knit
In sweet love and holy peace,

Would no more from conflict cease,
But with strife's rude shock and jar
All the world's fair fabric mar.
Tribes and nations Love unites
By just treaty's sacred rites;
Wedlock's bonds he sanctifies
By affection's softest ties.
Love appointeth, as is due,
Faithful laws to comrades true—
Love, all-sovereign Love!—oh, then,
Ye are blest, ye sons of men,
If the love that rules the sky
In your hearts is throned on high!

Book Three
True Happiness and False

I

She ceased, but I stood fixed by the sweetness of the song in wonderment and eager expectation, my ears still strained to listen. And then after a little I said: 'Thou sovereign solace of the stricken soul, what refreshment hast thou brought me, no less by the sweetness of thy singing than by the weightiness of thy discourse! Verily, I think not that I shall hereafter be unequal to the blows of Fortune. Wherefore, I no longer dread the remedies which thou saidst were something too severe for my strength; nay, rather, I am eager to hear of them and call for them with all vehemence.'

Then said she: 'I marked thee fastening upon my words silently and intently, and I expected, or—to speak more truly—I myself brought about in thee, this state of mind. What now remains is of such sort that to the taste indeed it is biting, but when received within it turns to sweetness. But whereas thou dost profess thyself desirous of hearing, with what ardour wouldst thou not burn didst thou but perceive whither it is my task to lead thee!'

'Whither?' said I.

'To true felicity,' said she, 'which even now thy spirit sees in dreams, but cannot behold in very truth, while thine eyes are engrossed with semblances.'

Then said I: 'I beseech thee, do thou show to me her true shape without a moment's loss.'

'Gladly will I, for thy sake,' said she. 'But first I will try to sketch in words, and describe a cause which is more familiar to thee, that, when thou hast viewed this carefully, thou mayst turn thy eyes the other way, and recognise the beauty of true happiness.'

Song I: The Thorns of Error.

Who fain would sow the fallow field,
And see the growing corn,
Must first remove the useless weeds,
The bramble and the thorn.
After ill savour, honey's taste
Is to the mouth more sweet;
After the storm, the twinkling stars
The eyes more cheerly greet.
When night hath past, the bright dawn comes
In car of rosy hue;
So drive the false bliss from thy mind,
And thou shall see the true.

II

For a little space she remained in a fixed gaze, withdrawn, as it were, into the august chamber of her mind; then she thus began:

'All mortal creatures in those anxious aims which find employment in so many varied pursuits, though they take many paths, yet strive to reach one goal—the goal of happiness. Now, the good is that which, when a man hath got, he can lack nothing further. This it is which is the supreme good of all, containing within itself all particular good; so that if anything is still wanting thereto, this cannot be the supreme good, since something would be left outside which might be desired. 'Tis clear, then, that happiness is a state perfected by the assembling together of all good things. To this state, as we have said, all men try to attain, but by different paths. For the desire of the true good is naturally implanted in the minds of men; only error leads them aside out of the way in pursuit of the false. Some, deeming it the highest good to want for nothing, spare no pains to attain affluence; others, judging the good to be that to which respect is most worthily paid, strive to win the reverence of their fellow-citizens by the attainment of official dignity. Some there are who fix the chief good in supreme power; these either wish themselves to enjoy sovereignty, or try to attach themselves to those who have it. Those, again, who think renown to be something of supreme excellence are in haste to spread abroad the glory of their name either through the arts of war or of peace. A great many measure the attainment of good by joy and gladness of heart; these think it the height of happiness to give themselves over to pleasure. Others there are, again, who interchange the ends and means one with the other in their aims; for instance, some want riches for the sake of pleasure and power, some covet power either for the sake of money or in order to bring renown to their name. So it is on these ends, then, that the aim of human acts and wishes is centred, and on others like to these—for instance, noble birth and popularity, which seem to compass a certain renown; wife and children, which are sought for the sweetness of their possession; while as for friendship, the most sacred kind indeed is counted in the category of virtue, not of fortune; but other kinds are entered upon for the sake of power or of enjoyment. And as for bodily excellences, it is obvious that they are to be ranged with the above. For strength and stature surely manifest power; beauty and fleetness of foot bring celebrity; health brings pleasure. It is plain, then, that the only object sought for in all these ways is happiness. For that which each seeks in preference to all else, that is in his judgment the supreme good. And we have defined the supreme good to be happiness. Therefore, that state which each wishes in preference to all others is in his judgment happy.

'Thou hast, then, set before thine eyes something like a scheme of human happiness—wealth, rank, power, glory, pleasure. Now Epicurus, from a sole regard to these considerations, with some consistency concluded the highest good to be pleasure, because all the other objects seem to bring some delight to the soul. But to return to human pursuits and aims: man's mind seeks to recover its proper good, in spite of the mistiness of its recollection, but, like a drunken man, knows not by what path to return home. Think you they are wrong who strive to escape want? Nay, truly there is nothing which can so well complete happiness as a state abounding in all good things, needing nothing from outside, but wholly self-sufficing. Do they fall into error who deem that which is best to be also best deserving to receive the homage of reverence? Not at all. That cannot possibly be vile and contemptible, to attain which the endeavours of nearly all mankind are directed. Then, is power not to be reckoned in the category of good? Why, can that which is plainly more efficacious than anything else be esteemed a thing feeble and void of strength? Or is renown to be thought of no account? Nay, it cannot be ignored that the highest renown is constantly associated with the highest excellence. And what need is there to say that happiness is not haunted by care and gloom, nor exposed to trouble and vexation, since that is a condition we ask of the very least of things, from the possession and enjoyment of which we expect delight? So, then, these are the blessings men wish to win; they want riches, rank, sovereignty, glory, pleasure, because they believe that by these means they will secure independence, reverence, power, renown, and joy of heart. Therefore, it is the good which men seek by such divers courses; and herein is easily shown the might of Nature's power, since, although opinions are so various and discordant, yet they agree in cherishing good as the end.'

Song II: The Bent of Nature.

How the might of Nature sways
All the world in ordered ways,
How resistless laws control
Each least portion of the whole—

Fain would I in sounding verse
On my pliant strings rehearse.
Lo, the lion captive ta'en
Meekly wears his gilded chain;
Yet though he by hand be fed,
Though a master's whip he dread,
If but once the taste of gore
Whet his cruel lips once more,
Straight his slumbering fierceness wakes,
With one roar his bonds he breaks,
And first wreaks his vengeful force
On his trainer's mangled corpse.
And the woodland songster, pent
In forlorn imprisonment,
Though a mistress' lavish care
Store of honeyed sweets prepare;
Yet, if in his narrow cage,
As he hops from bar to bar,
He should spy the woods afar,
Cool with sheltering foliage,
All these dainties he will spurn,
To the woods his heart will turn;
Only for the woods he longs,
Pipes the woods in all his songs.
To rude force the sapling bends,
While the hand its pressure lends;
If the hand its pressure slack,
Straight the supple wood springs back.
Phœbus in the western main
Sinks; but swift his car again
By a secret path is borne
To the wonted gates of morn.
Thus are all things seen to yearn
In due time for due return;
And no order fixed may stay,
Save which in th' appointed way
Joins the end to the beginning
In a steady cycle spinning.

III

'Ye, too, creatures of earth, have some glimmering of your origin, however faint, and though in a vision dim and clouded, yet in some wise, notwithstanding, ye discern the true end of happiness, and so the aim of nature leads you thither—to that true good—while error in many forms leads you astray therefrom. For reflect whether men are able to win happiness by those means through which they think to reach the proposed end. Truly, if either wealth, rank, or any of the rest, bring with them anything of such sort as seems to have nothing wanting to it that is good, we, too, acknowledge that some are made happy by the acquisition of these things. But if they are not able to fulfill their promises, and, moreover, lack many good things, is not the happiness men seek in them clearly discovered to be a false show? Therefore do I first ask thee thyself, who but lately wert living in affluence, amid all that abundance of wealth, was thy mind never troubled in consequence of some wrong done to thee?'

'Nay,' said I, 'I cannot ever remember a time when my mind was so completely at peace as not to feel the pang of some uneasiness.'

'Was it not because either something was absent which thou wouldst not have absent, or present which thou wouldst have away?'

'Yes,' said I.

'Then, thou didst want the presence of the one, the absence of the other?'

'Admitted.'

'But a man lacks that of which he is in want?'

'He does.'

'And he who lacks something is not in all points self-sufficing?'

'No; certainly not,' said I.

'So wert thou, then, in the plenitude of thy wealth, supporting this insufficiency?'

'I must have been.'

'Wealth, then, cannot make its possessor independent and free from all want, yet this was what it seemed to promise. Moreover, I think this also well deserves to be considered—that there is nothing in the special nature of money to hinder its being taken away from those who possess it against their will.'

'I admit it.'

'Why, of course, when every day the stronger wrests it from the weaker without his consent. Else, whence come lawsuits, except in seeking to recover moneys which have been taken away against their owner's will by force or fraud?'

'True,' said I.

'Then, everyone will need some extraneous means of protection to keep his money safe.'

'Who can venture to deny it?'

'Yet he would not, unless he possessed the money which it is possible to lose.'

'No; he certainly would not.'

'Then, we have worked round to an opposite conclusion: the wealth which was thought to make a man independent rather puts him in need of further protection. How in the world, then, can want be driven away by riches? Cannot the rich feel hunger? Cannot they thirst? Are not the limbs of the wealthy sensitive to the winter's cold? "But," thou wilt say, "the rich have the wherewithal to sate their hunger, the means to get rid of thirst and cold." True enough; want can thus be soothed by riches, wholly removed it cannot be. For if this ever-gaping, ever-craving want is glutted by wealth, it needs must be that the want itself which can be so glutted still remains. I do not speak of how very little suffices for nature, and how for avarice nothing is enough. Wherefore, if wealth cannot get rid of want, and makes new wants of its own, how can ye believe that it bestows independence?'

Song III: The Insatiableness of Avarice.

Though the covetous grown wealthy
See his piles of gold rise high;
Though he gather store of treasure
That can never satisfy;
Though with pearls his gorget blazes,
Rarest that the ocean yields;
Though a hundred head of oxen
Travail in his ample fields;
Ne'er shall carking care forsake him
While he draws this vital breath,
And his riches go not with him,
When his eyes are closed in death.

IV

'Well, but official dignity clothes him to whom it comes with honour and reverence! Have, then, offices of state such power as to plant virtue in the minds of their possessors, and drive out vice? Nay, they are rather wont to signalize iniquity than to chase it away, and hence arises our indignation that honours so often fall to the most iniquitous of men. Accordingly, Catullus calls Nonius an "ulcerspot," though "sitting in the curule chair." Dost not see what infamy high position brings upon the bad? Surely their unworthiness will be less conspicuous if their rank does not draw upon them the public notice! In thy own case, wouldst thou ever have been induced by all these perils to think of sharing office with Decoratus, since thou hast discerned in him the spirit of a rascally parasite and informer? No; we cannot deem men worthy of reverence on account of their office, whom we deem unworthy of the office itself. But didst thou see a man endued with wisdom, couldst thou suppose him not worthy of reverence, nor of that wisdom with which he was endued?'

'No; certainly not.'

'There is in Virtue a dignity of her own which she forthwith passes over to those to whom she is united. And since public honours cannot do this, it is clear that they do not possess the true beauty of dignity. And here this well deserves to be noticed—that if a man is the more scorned in proportion as he is despised by a greater number, high position not only fails to win reverence for the wicked, but even loads them the more with contempt by drawing more attention to them. But not without retribution; for the wicked pay back a return in kind to the dignities they put on by the pollution of their touch. Perhaps, too, another consideration may teach thee to confess that true reverence cannot come through these counterfeit dignities. It is this: If one who had been many times consul chanced to visit barbaric lands, would his office win him the reverence of the barbarians? And yet if reverence were the natural effect of dignities, they would not forego their proper function in any part of the world, even as fire never anywhere fails to give forth heat. But since this effect is not due to their own efficacy, but is attached to them by the mistaken opinion of mankind, they disappear straightway when they are set before those who do not esteem them dignities. Thus the case stands with foreign peoples. But does their repute last for ever, even in the land of their origin? Why, the prefecture, which was once a great power, is now an empty name—a burden merely on the senator's fortune; the commissioner of the public corn supply was once a personage—now what is more contemptible than this office? For, as we said just now, that which hath no true comeliness of its own now receives, now loses, lustre at the caprice of those who have to do with it. So, then, if dignities cannot win men reverence, if they are actually sullied by the contamination of the wicked, if they lose their splendour through time's changes, if they come into contempt merely for lack of public estimation, what precious beauty have they in themselves, much less to give to others?'

Song IV: Disgrace of Honours conferred by a Tyrant.

Though royal purple soothes his pride,
And snowy pearls his neck adorn,

Nero in all his riot lives
The mark of universal scorn.
Yet he on reverend heads conferred
Th' inglorious honours of the state.
Shall we, then, deem them truly blessed
Whom such preferment hath made great?

V

'Well, then, does sovereignty and the intimacy of kings prove able to confer power? Why, surely does not the happiness of kings endure for ever? And yet antiquity is full of examples, and these days also, of kings whose happiness has turned into calamity. How glorious a power, which is not even found effectual for its own preservation! But if happiness has its source in sovereign power, is not happiness diminished, and misery inflicted in its stead, in so far as that power falls short of completeness? Yet, however widely human sovereignty be extended, there must still be more peoples left, over whom each several king holds no sway. Now, at whatever point the power on which happiness depends ceases, here powerlessness steals in and makes wretchedness; so, by this way of reckoning, there must needs be a balance of wretchedness in the lot of the king. The tyrant who had made trial of the perils of his condition figured the fears that haunt a throne under the image of a sword hanging over a man's head. What sort of power, then, is this which cannot drive away the gnawings of anxiety, or shun the stings of terror? Fain would they themselves have lived secure, but they cannot; then they boast about their power! Dost thou count him to possess power whom thou seest to wish what he cannot bring to pass? Dost thou count him to possess power who encompasses himself with a body-guard, who fears those he terrifies more than they fear him, who, to keep up the semblance of power, is himself at the mercy of his slaves? Need I say anything of the friends of kings, when I show royal dominion itself so utterly and miserably weak—why ofttimes the royal power in its plenitude brings them low, ofttimes involves them in its fall? Nero drove his friend and preceptor, Seneca, to the choice of the manner of his death. Antoninus exposed Papinianus, who was long powerful at court, to the swords of the soldiery. Yet each of these was willing to renounce his power. Seneca tried to surrender his wealth also to Nero, and go into retirement; but neither achieved his purpose. When they tottered, their very greatness dragged them down. What manner of thing, then, is this power which keeps men in fear while they possess it—which when thou art fain to keep, thou art not safe, and when thou desirest to lay it aside thou canst not rid thyself of? Are friends any protection who have been attached by fortune, not by virtue? Nay; him whom good fortune has made a friend, ill fortune will make an enemy. And what plague is more effectual to do hurt than a foe of one's own household?'

Song V: Self Mastery.

Who on power sets his aim,
First must his own spirit tame;
He must shun his neck to thrust
'Neath th' unholy yoke of lust.
For, though India's far-off land
Bow before his wide command,
Utmost Thule homage pay—
If he cannot drive away
Haunting care and black distress,
In his power, he's powerless.

VI

'Again, how misleading, how base, a thing ofttimes is glory! Well does the tragic poet exclaim:

> '"Oh, fond Repute, how many a time and oft
> Hast them raised high in pride the base-born churl!"

For many have won a great name through the mistaken beliefs of the multitude—and what can be imagined more shameful than that? Nay, they who are praised falsely must needs themselves blush at their own praises! And even when praise is won by merit, still, how does it add to the good conscience of the wise man who measures his good not by popular repute, but by the truth of inner conviction? And if at all it does seem a fair thing to get this same renown spread abroad, it follows that any failure so to spread it is held foul. But if, as I set forth but now, there must needs be many tribes and peoples whom the fame of any single man cannot reach, it follows that he whom thou esteemest glorious seems all inglorious in a neighbouring quarter of the globe. As to popular favour, I do not think it even worthy of mention in this place, since it never cometh of judgment, and never lasteth steadily.

'Then, again, who does not see how empty, how foolish, is the fame of noble birth? Why, if the nobility is based on renown, the renown is another's! For, truly, nobility seems to be a sort of reputation coming from the merits of ancestors. But if it is the praise which brings renown, of necessity it is they who are praised that are famous. Wherefore, the fame of another clothes thee not with splendour if thou hast none of thine own. So, if there is any excellence in nobility of birth, methinks it is this alone—that it would seem to impose upon the nobly born the obligation not to degenerate from the virtue of their ancestors.'

Song VI: True Nobility.

All men are of one kindred stock,
Though scattered far and wide;
For one is Father of us all—
One doth for all provide.
He gave the sun his golden beams,
The moon her silver horn;
He set mankind upon the earth,
As stars the heavens adorn.
He shut a soul—a heaven-born soul—
Within the body's frame;
The noble origin he gave
Each mortal wight may claim.
Why boast ye, then, so loud
Of race and high ancestral line?
If ye behold your being's source,
And God's supreme design,

None is degenerate, none base,
Unless by taint of sin
And cherished vice he foully stain
His heavenly origin.

VII

'Then, what shall I say of the pleasures of the body? The lust thereof is full of uneasiness; the sating, of repentance. What sicknesses, what intolerable pains, are they wont to bring on the bodies of those who enjoy them—the fruits of iniquity, as it were! Now, what sweetness the stimulus of pleasure may have I do not know. But that the issues of pleasure are painful everyone may understand who chooses to recall the memory of his own fleshly lusts. Nay, if these can make happiness, there is no reason why the beasts also should not be happy, since all their efforts are eagerly set upon satisfying the bodily wants. I know, indeed, that the sweetness of wife and children should be right comely, yet only too true to nature is what was said of one—that he found in his sons his tormentors. And how galling such a contingency would be, I must needs put thee in mind, since thou hast never in any wise suffered such experiences, nor art thou now under any uneasiness. In such a case, I agree with my servant Euripides, who said that a man without children was fortunate in his misfortune.'

Song VII: Pleasure's Sting.

This is the way of Pleasure:
She stings them that despoil her;
And, like the wingéd toiler
Who's lost her honeyed treasure,
She flies, but leaves her smart
Deep-rankling in the heart.

VIII

'It is beyond doubt, then, that these paths do not lead to happiness; they cannot guide anyone to the promised goal. Now, I will very briefly show what serious evils are involved in following them. Just consider. Is it thy endeavour to heap up money? Why, thou must wrest it from its present possessor! Art thou minded to put on the splendour of official dignity? Thou must beg from those who have the giving of it; thou who covetest to outvie others in honour must lower thyself to the humble posture of petition. Dost thou long for power? Thou must face perils, for thou wilt be at the mercy of thy subjects' plots. Is glory thy aim? Thou art lured on through all manner of hardships, and there is an end to thy peace of mind. Art fain to lead a life of pleasure? Yet who does not scorn and contemn one who is the slave of the weakest and vilest of things—the body? Again, on how slight and perishable a possession do they rely who set before themselves bodily excellences! Can ye ever surpass the elephant in bulk or the bull in strength? Can ye excel the tiger in swiftness? Look upon the infinitude, the solidity, the swift motion, of the heavens, and for once cease to admire things mean and worthless. And yet the heavens are not so much to be admired on this account as for the reason which guides them. Then, how transient is the lustre of beauty! how soon gone!—more fleeting than the fading bloom of spring flowers. And yet if, as Aristotle says, men should see with the eyes of Lynceus, so that their sight might pierce through obstructions, would not that body of Alcibiades, so gloriously fair in outward seeming, appear altogether loathsome when all its inward parts lay open to the view? Therefore, it is not thy own nature that makes thee seem beautiful, but the weakness of the eyes that see thee. Yet prize as unduly as ye will that body's excellences; so long as ye know that this that ye admire, whatever its worth, can be dissolved away by the feeble flame of a three days' fever. From all which considerations we may conclude as a whole, that these things which cannot make good the advantages they promise, which are never made perfect by the assemblage of all good things—these neither lead as by-ways to happiness, nor themselves make men completely happy.'

Song VIII: Human Folly.

Alas! how wide astray
Doth Ignorance these wretched mortals lead
From Truth's own way!

For not on leafy stems
Do ye within the green wood look for gold,
Nor strip the vine for gems;
Your nets ye do not spread
Upon the hill-tops, that the groaning board
With fish be furnishèd;
If ye are fain to chase
The bounding goat, ye sweep not in vain search
The ocean's ruffled face.
The sea's far depths they know,
Each hidden nook, wherein the waves o'erwash
The pearl as white as snow;
Where lurks the Tyrian shell,
Where fish and prickly urchins do abound,
All this they know full well.
But not to know or care
Where hidden lies the good all hearts desire—
This blindness they can bear;
With gaze on earth low-bent,
They seek for that which reacheth far beyond
The starry firmament.
What curse shall I call down
On hearts so dull? May they the race still run
For wealth and high renown!
And when with much ado
The false good they have grasped—ah, then too late!—
May they discern the true!

IX

'This much may well suffice to set forth the form of false happiness; if this is now clear to thine eyes, the next step is to show what true happiness is.'

'Indeed,' said I, 'I see clearly enough that neither is independence to be found in wealth, nor power in sovereignty, nor reverence in dignities, nor fame in glory, nor true joy in pleasures.'

'Hast thou discerned also the causes why this is so?'

'I seem to have some inkling, but I should like to learn more at large from thee.'

'Why, truly the reason is hard at hand. That which is simple and indivisible by nature human error separates, and transforms from the true and perfect to the false and imperfect. Dost thou imagine that which lacketh nothing can want power?'

'Certainly not.'

'Right; for if there is any feebleness of strength in anything, in this there must necessarily be need of external protection.'

'That is so.'

'Accordingly, the nature of independence and power is one and the same.'

'It seems so.'

'Well, but dost think that anything of such a nature as this can be looked upon with contempt, or is it rather of all things most worthy of veneration?'

'Nay; there can be no doubt as to that.'

'Let us, then, add reverence to independence and power, and conclude these three to be one.'

'We must if we will acknowledge the truth.'

'Thinkest thou, then, this combination of qualities to be obscure and without distinction, or rather famous in all renown? Just consider: can that want renown which has been agreed to be lacking in nothing, to be supreme in power, and right worthy of honour, for the reason that it cannot bestow this upon itself, and so comes to appear somewhat poor in esteem?'

'I cannot but acknowledge that, being what it is, this union of qualities is also right famous.'

'It follows, then, that we must admit that renown is not different from the other three.'

'It does,' said I.

'That, then, which needs nothing outside itself, which can accomplish all things in its own strength, which enjoys fame and compels reverence, must not this evidently be also fully crowned with joy?'

'In sooth, I cannot conceive,' said I, 'how any sadness can find entrance into such a state; wherefore I must needs acknowledge it full of joy—at least, if our former conclusions are to hold.'

'Then, for the same reasons, this also is necessary—that independence, power, renown, reverence, and sweetness of delight, are different only in name, but in substance differ no wise one from the other.'

'It is,' said I.

'This, then, which is one, and simple by nature, human perversity separates, and, in trying to win a part of that which has no parts, fails to attain not only that portion (since there are no portions), but also the whole, to which it does not dream of aspiring.'

'How so?' said I.

'He who, to escape want, seeks riches, gives himself no concern about power; he prefers a mean and low estate, and also denies himself many pleasures dear to nature to avoid losing the money which he has gained. But at this rate he does not even attain to independence—a weakling void of strength, vexed by distresses, mean and despised, and buried in obscurity. He, again, who thirsts alone for power squanders his wealth, despises pleasure, and thinks fame and rank alike worthless without power. But thou seest in how many ways his state also is defective. Sometimes it happens that he lacks necessaries, that he is gnawed by anxieties, and, since he cannot rid himself of these inconveniences, even ceases to have that power which was his whole end and aim. In like manner may we cast up the reckoning in case of rank, of glory, or of pleasure. For since each one of these severally is identical with the rest, whosoever seeks any one of them without the others does not even lay hold of that one which he makes his aim.'

'Well,' said I, 'what then?'

'Suppose anyone desire to obtain them together, he does indeed wish for happiness as a whole; but will he find it in these things which, as we have proved, are unable to bestow what they promise?'

'Nay; by no means,' said I.

'Then, happiness must certainly not be sought in these things which severally are believed to afford some one of the blessings most to be desired.'

'They must not, I admit. No conclusion could be more true.'

'So, then, the form and the causes of false happiness are set before thine eyes. Now turn thy gaze to the other side; there thou wilt straightway see the true happiness I promised.'

'Yea, indeed, 'tis plain to the blind.' said I. 'Thou didst point it out even now in seeking to unfold the causes of the false. For, unless I am mistaken, that is true and perfect happiness which crowns one with the union of independence, power, reverence, renown, and joy. And to prove to thee with how deep an insight I have listened—since all these are the same—that which can truly bestow one of them I know to be without doubt full and complete happiness.'

'Happy art thou, my scholar, in this thy conviction; only one thing shouldst thou add.'

'What is that?' said I.

'Is there aught, thinkest thou, amid these mortal and perishable things which can produce a state such as this?'

'Nay, surely not; and this thou hast so amply demonstrated that no word more is needed.'

'Well, then, these things seem to give to mortals shadows of the true good, or some kind of imperfect good; but the true and perfect good they cannot bestow.'

'Even so,' said I.

'Since, then, thou hast learnt what that true happiness is, and what men falsely call happiness, it now remains that thou shouldst learn from what source to seek this.'

'Yes; to this I have long been eagerly looking forward.'

'Well, since, as Plato maintains in the "Timæus," we ought even in the most trivial matters to implore the Divine protection, what thinkest thou should we now do in order to deserve to find the seat of that highest good?'

'We must invoke the Father of all things,' said I; 'for without this no enterprise sets out from a right beginning.'

'Thou sayest well,' said she; and forthwith lifted up her voice and sang:

Song IX: Invocation.

Maker of earth and sky, from age to age
Who rul'st the world by reason; at whose word
Time issues from Eternity's abyss:
To all that moves the source of movement, fixed
Thyself and moveless. Thee no cause impelled
Extrinsic this proportioned frame to shape
From shapeless matter; but, deep-set within
Thy inmost being, the form of perfect good,

From envy free; and Thou didst mould the whole
To that supernal pattern. Beauteous
The world in Thee thus imaged, being Thyself
Most beautiful. So Thou the work didst fashion
In that fair likeness, bidding it put on
Perfection through the exquisite perfectness
Of every part's contrivance. Thou dost bind
The elements in balanced harmony,
So that the hot and cold, the moist and dry,
Contend not; nor the pure fire leaping up
Escape, or weight of waters whelm the earth.
Thou joinest and diffusest through the whole,
Linking accordantly its several parts,
A soul of threefold nature, moving all.
This, cleft in twain, and in two circles gathered,
Speeds in a path that on itself returns,
Encompassing mind's limits, and conforms
The heavens to her true semblance. Lesser souls
And lesser lives by a like ordinance
Thou sendest forth, each to its starry car
Affixing, and dost strew them far and wide
O'er earth and heaven. These by a law benign
Thou biddest turn again, and render back
To thee their fires. Oh, grant, almighty Father,
Grant us on reason's wing to soar aloft
To heaven's exalted height; grant us to see
The fount of good; grant us, the true light found,
To fix our steadfast eyes in vision clear
On Thee. Disperse the heavy mists of earth,
And shine in Thine own splendour. For Thou art
The true serenity and perfect rest
Of every pious soul—to see Thy face,
The end and the beginning—One the guide,
The traveler, the pathway, and the goal.

X

'Since now thou hast seen what is the form of the imperfect good, and what the form of the perfect also, methinks I should next show in what manner this perfection of felicity is built up. And here I conceive it proper to inquire, first, whether any excellence, such as thou hast lately defined, can exist in the nature of things, lest we be deceived by an empty fiction of thought to which no true reality answers. But it cannot be denied that such does exist, and is, as it were, the source of all things good. For everything which is called imperfect is spoken of as imperfect by reason of the privation of some perfection; so it comes to pass that, whenever imperfection is found in any particular, there must necessarily be a perfection in respect of that particular also. For were there no such perfection, it is utterly inconceivable how that so-called imperfection should come into existence. Nature does not make a beginning with things mutilated and imperfect; she starts with what is whole and perfect, and falls away later to these feeble and inferior productions. So if there is, as we showed before, a happiness of a frail and imperfect kind, it cannot be doubted but there is also a happiness substantial and perfect.'

'Most true is thy conclusion, and most sure,' said I.

'Next to consider where the dwelling-place of this happiness may be. The common belief of all mankind agrees that God, the supreme of all things, is good. For since nothing can be imagined better than God, how can we doubt Him to be good than whom there is nothing better? Now, reason shows God to be good in such wise as to prove that in Him is perfect good. For were it not so, He would not be supreme of all things; for there would be something else more excellent, possessed of perfect good, which would seem to have the advantage in priority and dignity, since it has clearly appeared that all perfect things are prior to those less complete. Wherefore, lest we fall into an infinite regression, we must acknowledge the supreme God to be full of supreme and perfect good. But we have determined that true happiness is the perfect good; therefore true happiness must dwell in the supreme Deity.'

'I accept thy reasonings,' said I; 'they cannot in any wise be disputed.'

'But, come, see how strictly and incontrovertibly thou mayst prove this our assertion that the supreme Godhead hath fullest possession of the highest good.'

'In what way, pray?' said I.

'Do not rashly suppose that He who is the Father of all things hath received that highest good of which He is said to be possessed either from some external source, or hath it as a natural endowment in such sort that thou mightest consider the essence of the happiness possessed, and of the God who possesses it, distinct and different. For if thou deemest it received from without, thou mayst esteem that which gives more excellent than that which has received. But Him we most worthily acknowledge to be the most supremely excellent of all things. If, however, it is in Him by nature, yet is logically distinct, the thought is inconceivable, since we are speaking of God, who is supreme of all things. Who was there to join these distinct essences? Finally, when one thing is different from another, the things so conceived as distinct cannot be identical. Therefore that which of its own nature is distinct from the highest good is not itself the highest good—an impious thought of Him than whom, 'tis plain, nothing can be more excellent. For universally nothing can be better in nature than the source from which it has come; therefore on most true grounds of reason would I conclude that which is the source of all things to be in its own essence the highest good.'

'And most justly,' said I.

'But the highest good has been admitted to be happiness.'

'Yes.'

'Then,' said she, 'it is necessary to acknowledge that God is very happiness.'

'Yes,' said I; 'I cannot gainsay my former admissions, and I see clearly that this is a necessary inference therefrom.'

'Reflect, also,' said she, 'whether the same conclusion is not further confirmed by considering that there cannot be two supreme goods distinct one from the other. For the goods which are different clearly cannot be severally each what the other is: wherefore neither of the two can be perfect, since to either the other is wanting; but since it is not perfect, it cannot manifestly be the supreme good. By no means, then, can goods which are supreme be different one from the other. But we have concluded that both happiness and God are the supreme good; wherefore that which is highest Divinity must also itself necessarily be supreme happiness.'

'No conclusion,' said I, 'could be truer to fact, nor more soundly reasoned out, nor more worthy of God.'

'Then, further,' said she, 'just as geometricians are wont to draw inferences from their demonstrations to which they give the name "deductions," so will I add here a sort of corollary. For since men become happy by the acquisition of happiness, while happiness is very Godship, it is manifest that they become happy by the acquisition of Godship. But as by the acquisition of justice men become just, and wise by the acquisition of wisdom, so by parity of reasoning by acquiring Godship they must of necessity become gods. So every man who is happy is a god; and though in nature God is One only, yet there is nothing to hinder that very many should be gods by participation in that nature.'

'A fair conclusion, and a precious,' said I, 'deduction or corollary, by whichever name thou wilt call it.'

'And yet,' said she, 'not one whit fairer than this which reason persuades us to add.'

'Why, what?' said I.

'Why, seeing happiness has many particulars included under it, should all these be regarded as forming one body of happiness, as it were, made up of various parts, or is there some one of them which forms the full essence of happiness, while all the rest are relative to this?'

'I would thou wouldst unfold the whole matter to me at large.'

'We judge happiness to be good, do we not?'

'Yea, the supreme good.'

'And this superlative applies to all; for this same happiness is adjudged to be the completest independence, the highest power, reverence, renown, and pleasure.'

'What then?'

'Are all these goods—independence, power, and the rest—to be deemed members of happiness, as it were, or are they all relative to good as to their summit and crown?'

'I understand the problem, but I desire to hear how thou wouldst solve it.'

'Well, then, listen to the determination of the matter. Were all these members composing happiness, they would differ severally one from the other. For this is the nature of parts—that by their difference they compose one body. All these, however, have been proved to be the same; therefore they cannot possibly be members, otherwise happiness will seem to be built up out of one member, which cannot be.'

'There can be no doubt as to that,' said I; 'but I am impatient to hear what remains.'

'Why, it is manifest that all the others are relative to the good. For the very reason why independence is sought is that it is judged good, and so power also, because it is believed to be good. The same, too, may be supposed of reverence, of renown, and of pleasant delight. Good, then, is the sum and source of all desirable things. That which has not in itself any good, either in reality or in semblance, can in no wise be desired. Contrariwise, even things which by nature are not good are desired as if they were truly good, if they seem to be so. Whereby it comes to pass that goodness is rightly believed to be the sum and hinge and cause of all things desirable. Now, that for the sake of which anything is desired itself seems to be most wished for. For instance, if anyone wishes to ride for the sake of health, he does not so much wish for the exercise of riding as the benefit of his health. Since, then, all things are sought for the sake of the good, it is not these so much as good itself that is sought by all. But that on account of which all other things are wished for was, we agreed, happiness; wherefore thus also it appears that it is happiness alone which is sought. From all which it is transparently clear that the essence of absolute good and of happiness is one and the same.'

'I cannot see how anyone can dissent from these conclusions.'

'But we have also proved that God and true happiness are one and the same.'

'Yes,' said I.

'Then we can safely conclude, also, that God's essence is seated in absolute good, and nowhere else.'

Song X: The True Light.

Hither come, all ye whose minds
Lust with rosy fetters binds—
Lust to bondage hard compelling
Th' earthy souls that are his dwelling—
Here shall be your labour's close;
Here your haven of repose.
Come, to your one refuge press;
Wide it stands to all distress!
Not the glint of yellow gold
Down bright Hermus' current rolled;
Not the Tagus' precious sands,
Nor in far-off scorching lands
All the radiant gems that hide

Under Indus' storied tide—
Emerald green and glistering white—
Can illume our feeble sight;
But they rather leave the mind
In its native darkness blind.
For the fairest beams they shed
In earth's lowest depths were fed;
But the splendour that supplies
Strength and vigour to the skies,
And the universe controls,
Shunneth dark and ruined souls.
He who once hath seen this light
Will not call the sunbeam bright.

XI

'I quite agree,' said I, 'truly all thy reasonings hold admirably together.'

Then said she: 'What value wouldst thou put upon the boon shouldst thou come to the knowledge of the absolute good?'

'Oh, an infinite,' said I, 'if only I were so blest as to learn to know God also who is the good.'

'Yet this will I make clear to thee on truest grounds of reason, if only our recent conclusions stand fast.'

'They will.'

'Have we not shown that those things which most men desire are not true and perfect good precisely for this cause—that they differ severally one from another, and, seeing that one is wanting to another, they cannot bestow full and absolute good; but that they become the true good when they are gathered, as it were, into one form and agency, so that that which is independence is likewise power, reverence, renown, and pleasant delight, and unless they are all one and the same, they have no claim to be counted among things desirable?'

'Yes; this was clearly proved, and cannot in any wise be doubted.'

'Now, when things are far from being good while they are different, but become good as soon as they are one, is it not true that these become good by acquiring unity?'

'It seems so,' said I.

'But dost not thou allow that all which is good is good by participation in goodness?'

'It is.'

'Then, thou must on similar grounds admit that unity and goodness are the same; for when the effects of things in their natural working differ not, their essence is one and the same.'

'There is no denying it.'

'Now, dost thou know,' said she, 'that all which is abides and subsists so long as it continues one, but so soon as it ceases to be one it perishes and falls to pieces?'

'In what way?'

'Why, take animals, for example. When soul and body come together, and continue in one, this is, we say, a living creature; but when this unity is broken by the separation of these two, the creature dies, and is clearly no longer living. The body also, while it remains in one form by the joining together of its members, presents a human appearance; but if the separation and dispersal of the parts break up the body's unity, it ceases to be what it was. And if we extend our survey to all other things, without doubt it will manifestly appear that each several thing subsists while it is one, but when it ceases to be one perishes.'

'Yes; when I consider further, I see it to be even as thou sayest.'

'Well, is there aught,' said she, 'which, in so far as it acts conformably to nature, abandons the wish for life, and desires to come to death and corruption?'

'Looking to living creatures, which have some faults of choice, I find none that, without external compulsion, forego the will to live, and of their own accord hasten to destruction. For every creature diligently pursues the end of self-preservation, and shuns death and destruction! As to herbs and trees, and inanimate things generally, I am altogether in doubt what to think.'

'And yet there is no possibility of question about this either, since thou seest how herbs and trees grow in places suitable for them, where, as far as their nature admits, they cannot quickly wither and die. Some spring up in the plains, others in the mountains; some grow in marshes, others cling to rocks; and others, again, find a fertile soil in the barren sands; and if you try to transplant these elsewhere, they wither away. Nature gives to each the soil that suits it, and uses her diligence to prevent any of them dying, so long as it is possible for them to continue alive. Why do they all draw their nourishment from roots as from a mouth dipped into the earth, and distribute the strong bark over the pith? Why are all the softer parts like the pith deeply encased within, while the external parts have the strong texture of wood, and outside of all is the bark to resist the weather's inclemency, like a champion stout in endurance? Again, how great is nature's diligence to secure universal propagation by multiplying seed! Who does not know all these to be contrivances, not only for the present maintenance of a species, but for its lasting continuance, generation after generation, for ever? And do not also the things believed inanimate on like grounds of reason seek each what is proper to itself? Why do the flames shoot lightly upward, while the earth presses downward with its weight, if it is not that these motions and situations are suitable to their respective natures? Moreover, each several thing is preserved by that which is agreeable to its nature, even as it is destroyed by things inimical. Things solid like stones resist disintegration by the close adhesion of their parts. Things fluid like air and water yield easily to what divides them, but swiftly flow back and mingle with those parts from which they have been severed, while fire, again, refuses to be cut at all. And we are not now treating of the voluntary motions of an intelligent soul, but of the drift of nature. Even so is it that we digest our food without thinking about it, and draw our breath unconsciously in sleep; nay, even in living creatures the love of life cometh not of conscious will, but from the principles of nature. For oftentimes in the stress of circumstances will chooses the death which nature shrinks from; and contrarily, in spite of natural appetite, will restrains that work of reproduction by which alone the persistence of perishable creatures is maintained. So entirely does this love of self come from drift of nature, not from animal impulse. Providence has furnished things with this most cogent reason for continuance: they must desire life, so long as it is naturally possible for them to continue living. Wherefore in no way mayst thou doubt but that things naturally aim at continuance of existence, and shun destruction.'

'I confess,' said I, 'that what I lately thought uncertain, I now perceive to be indubitably clear.'

'Now, that which seeks to subsist and continue desires to be one; for if its oneness be gone, its very existence cannot continue.'

'True,' said I.

'All things, then, desire to be one.'

'I agree.'

'But we have proved that one is the very same thing as good.'

'We have.'

'All things, then, seek the good; indeed, you may express the fact by defining good as that which all desire.'

'Nothing could be more truly thought out. Either there is no single end to which all things are relative, or else the end to which all things universally hasten must be the highest good of all.'

Then she: 'Exceedingly do I rejoice, dear pupil; thine eye is now fixed on the very central mark of truth. Moreover, herein is revealed that of which thou didst erstwhile profess thyself ignorant.'

'What is that?' said I.

'The end and aim of the whole universe. Surely it is that which is desired of all; and, since we have concluded the good to be such, we ought to acknowledge the end and aim of the whole universe to be "the good."'

Song XI: Reminiscence.

Who truth pursues, who from false ways
His heedful steps would keep,
By inward light must search within
In meditation deep;
All outward bent he must repress
His soul's true treasure to possess.
Then all that error's mists obscured
Shall shine more clear than light,
This fleshly frame's oblivious weight
Hath quenched not reason quite;
The germs of truth still lie within,
Whence we by learning all may win.
Else how could ye the answer due
Untaught to questions give,
Were't not that deep within the soul
Truth's secret sparks do live?
If Plato's teaching erreth not,
We learn but that we have forgot.

XII

Then said I: 'With all my heart I agree with Plato; indeed, this is now the second time that these things have been brought back to my mind—first I lost them through the clogging contact of the body; then after through the stress of heavy grief.'

Then she continued: 'If thou wilt reflect upon thy former admissions, it will not be long before thou dost also recollect that of which erstwhile thou didst confess thyself ignorant.'

'What is that?' said I.

'The principles of the world's government,' said she.

'Yes; I remember my confession, and, although I now anticipate what thou intendest, I have a desire to hear the argument plainly set forth.'

'Awhile ago thou deemedst it beyond all doubt that God doth govern the world.'

'I do not think it doubtful now, nor shall I ever; and by what reasons I am brought to this assurance I will briefly set forth. This world could never have taken shape as a single system out of parts so diverse and opposite were it not that there is One who joins together these so diverse things. And when it had once come together, the very diversity of natures would have dissevered it and torn it asunder in universal discord were there not One who keeps together what He has joined. Nor would the order of nature proceed so regularly, nor could its course exhibit motions so fixed in respect of position, time, range, efficacy, and character, unless there were One who, Himself abiding, disposed these various vicissitudes of change. This power, whatsoever it be, whereby they remain as they were created, and are kept in motion, I call by the name which all recognise—God.'

Then said she: 'Seeing that such is thy belief, it will cost me little trouble, I think, to enable thee to win happiness, and return in safety to thy own country. But let us give our attention to the task that we have set before ourselves. Have we not counted independence in the category of happiness, and agreed that God is absolute happiness?'

'Truly, we have.'

'Then, He will need no external assistance for the ruling of the world. Otherwise, if He stands in need of aught, He will not possess complete independence.'

'That is necessarily so,' said I.

'Then, by His own power alone He disposes all things.'

'It cannot be denied.'

'Now, God was proved to be absolute good.'

'Yes; I remember.'

'Then, He disposes all things by the agency of good, if it be true that He rules all things by His own power whom we have agreed to be good; and He is, as it were, the rudder and helm by which the world's mechanism is kept steady and in order.'

'Heartily do I agree; and, indeed, I anticipated what thou wouldst say, though it may be in feeble surmise only.'

'I well believe it,' said she; 'for, as I think, thou now bringest to the search eyes quicker in discerning truth; but what I shall say next is no less plain and easy to see.'

'What is it?' said I.

'Why,' said she, 'since God is rightly believed to govern all things with the rudder of goodness, and since all things do likewise, as I have taught, haste towards good by the very aim of nature, can it be doubted that His governance is willingly accepted, and that all submit themselves to the sway of the Disposer as conformed and attempered to His rule?'

'Necessarily so,' said I; 'no rule would seem happy if it were a yoke imposed on reluctant wills, and not the safe-keeping of obedient subjects.'

'There is nothing, then, which, while it follows nature, endeavours to resist good.'

'No; nothing.'

'But if anything should, will it have the least success against Him whom we rightly agreed to be supreme Lord of happiness?'

'It would be utterly impotent.'

'There is nothing, then, which has either the will or the power to oppose this supreme good.'

'No; I think not.'

'So, then,' said she, 'it is the supreme good which rules in strength, and graciously disposes all things.'

Then said I: 'How delighted am I at thy reasonings, and the conclusion to which thou hast brought them, but most of all at these very words which thou usest! I am now at last ashamed of the folly that so sorely vexed me.'

'Thou hast heard the story of the giants assailing heaven; but a beneficent strength disposed of them also, as they deserved. But shall we submit our arguments to the shock of mutual collision?—it may be from the impact some fair spark of truth may be struck out.'

'If it be thy good pleasure,' said I.

'No one can doubt that God is all-powerful.'

'No one at all can question it who thinks consistently.'

'Now, there is nothing which One who is all-powerful cannot do.'

'Nothing.'

'But can God do evil, then?'

'Nay; by no means.'

'Then, evil is nothing,' said she, 'since He to whom nothing is impossible is unable to do evil.'

'Art thou mocking me,' said I, 'weaving a labyrinth of tangled arguments, now seeming to begin where thou didst end, and now to end where thou didst begin, or dost thou build up some wondrous circle of Divine simplicity? For, truly, a little before thou didst begin with happiness, and say it was the supreme good, and didst declare it to be seated in the supreme Godhead. God Himself, too, thou didst affirm to be supreme good and all-complete happiness; and from this thou didst go on to add, as by the way, the proof that no one would be happy unless he were likewise God. Again, thou didst say that the very form of good was the essence both of God and of happiness, and didst teach that the absolute One was the absolute good which was sought by universal nature. Thou didst maintain, also, that God rules the universe by the governance of goodness, that all things obey Him willingly, and that evil has no existence in nature. And all this thou didst unfold without the help of assumptions from without, but by inherent and proper proofs, drawing credence one from the other.'

Then answered she: 'Far is it from me to mock thee; nay, by the blessing of God, whom we lately addressed in prayer, we have achieved the most important of all objects. For such is the form of the Divine essence, that neither can it pass into things external, nor take up anything external into itself; but, as Parmenides says of it, '"In body like to a sphere on all sides perfectly rounded," it rolls the restless orb of the universe, keeping itself motionless the while. And if I have also employed reasonings not drawn from without, but lying within the compass of our subject, there is no cause for thee to marvel, since thou hast learnt on Plato's authority that words ought to be akin to the matter of which they treat.'

Song XII: Orpheus and Eurydice.

Blest he whose feet have stood
Beside the fount of good;
Blest he whose will could break
Earth's chains for wisdom's sake!
The Thracian bard, 'tis said,
Mourned his dear consort dead;
To hear the plaintive strain
The woods moved in his train,
And the stream ceased to flow,
Held by so soft a woe;

The deer without dismay
Beside the lion lay;
The hound, by song subdued,
No more the hare pursued,
But the pang unassuaged
In his own bosom raged.
The music that could calm
All else brought him no balm.
Chiding the powers immortal,
He came unto Hell's portal;
There breathed all tender things
Upon his sounding strings,
Each rhapsody high-wrought
His goddess-mother taught—
All he from grief could borrow
And love redoubling sorrow,
Till, as the echoes waken,
All Tænarus is shaken;
Whilst he to ruth persuades
The monarch of the shades
With dulcet prayer. Spell-bound,
The triple-headed hound
At sounds so strangely sweet
Falls crouching at his feet.
The dread Avengers, too,
That guilty minds pursue
With ever-haunting fears,
Are all dissolved in tears.
Ixion, on his wheel,
A respite brief doth feel;
For, lo! the wheel stands still.
And, while those sad notes thrill,
Thirst-maddened Tantalus
Listens, oblivious
Of the stream's mockery
And his long agony.
The vulture, too, doth spare
Some little while to tear

At Tityus' rent side,
Sated and pacified.
At length the shadowy king,
His sorrows pitying,
'He hath prevailèd!' cried;
'We give him back his bride!
To him she shall belong,
As guerdon of his song.
One sole condition yet
Upon the boon is set:
Let him not turn his eyes
To view his hard-won prize,
Till they securely pass
The gates of Hell.' Alas!
What law can lovers move?
A higher law is love!
For Orpheus—woe is me!—
On his Eurydice—
Day's threshold all but won—
Looked, lost, and was undone!
Ye who the light pursue,
This story is for you,
Who seek to find a way
Unto the clearer day.
If on the darkness past
One backward look ye cast,
Your weak and wandering eyes
Have lost the matchless prize.

Book Four
Good and Ill Fortune

I

Softly and sweetly Philosophy sang these verses to the end without losing aught of the dignity of her expression or the seriousness of her tones; then, forasmuch as I was as yet unable to forget my deeply-seated sorrow, just as she was about to say something further, I broke in and cried: 'O thou guide into the way of true light, all that thy voice hath uttered from the beginning even unto now has manifestly seemed to me at once divine contemplated in itself, and by the force of thy arguments placed beyond the possibility of overthrow. Moreover, these truths have not been altogether unfamiliar to me heretofore, though because of indignation at my wrongs they have for a time been forgotten. But, lo! herein is the very chiefest cause of my grief—that, while there exists a good ruler of the universe, it is possible that evil should be at all, still more that it should go unpunished. Surely thou must see how deservedly this of itself provokes astonishment. But a yet greater marvel follows: While wickedness reigns and flourishes, virtue not only lacks its reward, but is even thrust down and trampled under the feet of the wicked, and suffers punishment in the place of crime. That this should happen under the rule of a God who knows all things and can do all things, but wills only the good, cannot be sufficiently wondered at nor sufficiently lamented.'

Then said she: 'It would indeed be infinitely astounding, and of all monstrous things most horrible, if, as thou esteemest, in the well-ordered home of so great a householder, the base vessels should be held in honour, the precious left to neglect. But it is not so. For if we hold unshaken those conclusions which we lately reached, thou shall learn that, by the will of Him of whose realm we are speaking, the good are always strong, the bad always weak and impotent; that vices never go unpunished, nor virtues unrewarded; that good fortune ever befalls the good, and ill fortune the bad, and much more of the sort, which shall hush thy murmurings, and stablish thee in the strong assurance of conviction. And since by my late instructions thou hast seen the form of happiness, hast learnt, too, the seat where it is to be found, all due preliminaries being discharged, I will now show thee the road which will lead thee home. Wings, also, will I fasten to thy mind wherewith thou mayst soar aloft, that so, all disturbing doubts removed, thou mayst return safe to thy country, under my guidance, in the path I will show thee, and by the means which I furnish.'

Song I: The Soul's Flight.

Wings are mine; above the pole
Far aloft I soar.
Clothed with these, my nimble soul
Scorns earth's hated shore,
Cleaves the skies upon the wind,
Sees the clouds left far behind.
Soon the glowing point she nears,
Where the heavens rotate,
Follows through the starry spheres
Phœbus' course, or straight
Takes for comrade 'mid the stars
Saturn cold or glittering Mars;
Thus each circling orb explores
Through Night's stole that peers;
Then, when all are numbered, soars
Far beyond the spheres,
Mounting heaven's supremest height
To the very Fount of light.
There the Sovereign of the world
His calm sway maintains;
As the globe is onward whirled
Guides the chariot reins,
And in splendour glittering
Reigns the universal King.
Hither if thy wandering feet
Find at last a way,
Here thy long-lost home thou'lt greet:
'Dear lost land,' thou'lt say,
'Though from thee I've wandered wide,
Hence I came, here will abide.'
Yet if ever thou art fain
Visitant to be
Of earth's gloomy night again,
Surely thou wilt see
Tyrants whom the nations fear
Dwell in hapless exile here.

II

Then said I: 'Verily, wondrous great are thy promises; yet I do not doubt but thou canst make them good: only keep me not in suspense after raising such hopes.'

'Learn, then, first,' said she, 'how that power ever waits upon the good, while the bad are left wholly destitute of strength. Of these truths the one proves the other; for since good and evil are contraries, if it is made plain that good is power, the feebleness of evil is clearly seen, and, conversely, if the frail nature of evil is made manifest, the strength of good is thereby known. However, to win ampler credence for my conclusion, I will pursue both paths, and draw confirmation for my statements first in one way and then in the other.

'The carrying out of any human action depends upon two things—to wit, will and power; if either be wanting, nothing can be accomplished. For if the will be lacking, no attempt at all is made to do what is not willed; whereas if there be no power, the will is all in vain. And so, if thou seest any man wishing to attain some end, yet utterly failing to attain it, thou canst not doubt that he lacked the power of getting what he wished for.'

'Why, certainly not; there is no denying it.'

'Canst thou, then, doubt that he whom thou seest to have accomplished what he willed had also the power to accomplish it?'

'Of course not.'

'Then, in respect of what he can accomplish a man is to be reckoned strong, in respect of what he cannot accomplish weak?'

'Granted,' said I.

'Then, dost thou remember that, by our former reasonings, it was concluded that the whole aim of man's will, though the means of pursuit vary, is set intently upon happiness?'

'I do remember that this, too, was proved.'

'Dost thou also call to mind how happiness is absolute good, and therefore that, when happiness is sought, it is good which is in all cases the object of desire?'

'Nay, I do not so much call to mind as keep it fixed in my memory.'

'Then, all men, good and bad alike, with one indistinguishable purpose strive to reach good?'

'Yes, that follows.'

'But it is certain that by the attainment of good men become good?'

'It is.'

'Then, do the good attain their object?'

'It seems so.'

'But if the bad were to attain the good which is their object, they could not be bad?'

'No.'

'Then, since both seek good, but while the one sort attain it, the other attain it not, is there any doubt that the good are endued with power, while they who are bad are weak?'

'If any doubt it, he is incapable of reflecting on the nature of things, or the consequences involved in reasoning.'

'Again, supposing there are two things to which the same function is prescribed in the course of nature, and one of these successfully accomplishes the function by natural action, the other is altogether incapable of that natural action, instead of which, in a way other than is agreeable to its nature, it—I will not say fulfills its function, but feigns to fulfill it: which of these two would in thy view be the stronger?'

'I guess thy meaning, but I pray thee let me hear thee more at large.'

'Walking is man's natural motion, is it not?'

'Certainly.'

'Thou dost not doubt, I suppose, that it is natural for the feet to discharge this function?'

'No; surely I do not.'

'Now, if one man who is able to use his feet walks, and another to whom the natural use of his feet is wanting tries to walk on his hands, which of the two wouldst thou rightly esteem the stronger?'

'Go on,' said I; 'no one can question but that he who has the natural capacity has more strength than he who has it not.'

'Now, the supreme good is set up as the end alike for the bad and for the good; but the good seek it through the natural action of the virtues, whereas the bad try to attain this same good through all manner of concupiscence, which is not the natural way of attaining good. Or dost thou think otherwise?'

'Nay; rather, one further consequence is clear to me: for from my admissions it must needs follow that the good have power, and the bad are impotent.'

'Thou anticipatest rightly, and that as physicians reckon is a sign that nature is set working, and is throwing off the disease. But, since I see thee so ready at understanding, I will heap proof on proof. Look how manifest is the extremity of vicious men's weakness; they cannot even reach that goal to which the aim of nature leads and almost constrains them. What if they were left without this mighty, this well-nigh irresistible help of nature's guidance! Consider also how momentous is the powerlessness which incapacitates the wicked. Not light or trivial are the prizes which they contend for, but which they cannot win or hold; nay, their failure concerns the very sum and crown of things. Poor wretches! they fail to compass even that for which they toil day and night. Herein also the strength of the good conspicuously appears. For just as thou wouldst judge him to be the strongest walker whose legs could carry him to a point beyond which no further advance was possible, so must thou needs account him strong in power who so attains the end of his desires that nothing further to be desired lies beyond. Whence follows the obvious conclusion that they who are wicked are seen likewise to be wholly destitute of strength. For why do they forsake virtue and follow vice? Is it from ignorance of what is good? Well, what is more weak and feeble than the blindness of ignorance? Do they know what they ought to follow, but lust drives them aside out of the way? If it be so, they are still frail by reason of their incontinence, for they cannot fight against vice. Or do they knowingly and willfully forsake the good and turn aside to vice? Why, at this rate, they not only cease to have power, but cease to be at all. For they who forsake the common end of all things that are, they likewise also cease to be at all. Now, to some it may seem strange that we should assert that the bad, who form the greater part of mankind, do not exist. But the fact is so. I do not, indeed, deny that they who are bad are bad, but that they are in an unqualified and absolute sense I deny. Just as we call a corpse a dead man, but cannot call it simply "man," so I would allow the vicious to be bad, but that they are in an absolute sense I cannot allow. That only is which maintains its place and keeps its nature; whatever falls away from this forsakes the existence which is essential to its nature. "But," thou wilt say, "the bad have an ability." Nor do I wish to deny it; only this ability of theirs comes not from strength, but from impotence. For their ability is to do evil, which would have had no efficacy at all if they could have continued in the performance of good. So this ability of theirs proves them still more plainly to have no power. For if, as we concluded just now, evil is nothing, 'tis clear that the wicked can effect nothing, since they are only able to do evil.'

''Tis evident.'

'And that thou mayst understand what is the precise force of this power, we determined, did we not, awhile back, that nothing has more power than supreme good?'

'We did,' said I.

'But that same highest good cannot do evil?'

'Certainly not.'

'Is there anyone, then, who thinks that men are able to do all things?'

'None but a madman.'

'Yet they are able to do evil?'

'Ay; would they could not!'

'Since, then, he who can do only good is omnipotent, while they who can do evil also are not omnipotent, it is manifest that they who can do evil have less power. There is this also: we have shown that all power is to be reckoned among things desirable, and that all desirable things are referred to good as to a kind of consummation of their nature. But the ability to commit crime cannot be referred to the good; therefore it is not a thing to be desired. And yet all power is desirable; it is clear, then, that ability to do evil is not power. From all which considerations appeareth the power of the good, and the indubitable weakness of the bad, and it is clear that Plato's judgment was true; the wise alone are able to do what they would, while the wicked follow their own hearts' lust, but can not accomplish what they would. For they go on in their willfulness fancying they will attain what they wish for in the paths of delight; but they are very far from its attainment, since shameful deeds lead not to happiness.'

Song II: The Bondage of Passion.

When high-enthroned the monarch sits,
Resplendent in the pride
Of purple robes, while flashing steel

Guards him on every side;
When baleful terrors on his brow
With frowning menace lower,
And Passion shakes his labouring breast—
How dreadful seems his power!
But if the vesture of his state
From such a one thou tear,
Thou'lt see what load of secret bonds
This lord of earth doth wear.
Lust's poison rankles; o'er his mind
Rage sweeps in tempest rude;
Sorrow his spirit vexes sore,
And empty hopes delude.
Then thou'lt confess: one hapless wretch,
Whom many lords oppress,
Does never what he would, but lives
In thraldom's helplessness.

III

'Thou seest, then, in what foulness unrighteous deeds are sunk, with what splendour righteousness shines. Whereby it is manifest that goodness never lacks its reward, nor crime its punishment. For, verily, in all manner of transactions that for the sake of which the particular action is done may justly be accounted the reward of that action, even as the wreath for the sake of which the race is run is the reward offered for running. Now, we have shown happiness to be that very good for the sake of which all things are done. Absolute good, then, is offered as the common prize, as it were, of all human actions. But, truly, this is a reward from which it is impossible to separate the good man, for one who is without good cannot properly be called good at all; wherefore righteous dealing never misses its reward. Rage the wicked, then, never so violently, the crown shall not fall from the head of the wise, nor wither. Verily, other men's unrighteousness cannot pluck from righteous souls their proper glory. Were the reward in which the soul of the righteous delighteth received from without, then might it be taken away by him who gave it, or some other; but since it is conferred by his own righteousness, then only will he lose his prize when he has ceased to be righteous. Lastly, since every prize is desired because it is believed to be good, who can account him who possesses good to be without reward? And what a prize, the fairest and grandest of all! For remember the corollary which I chiefly insisted on a little while back, and reason thus: Since absolute good is happiness, 'tis clear that all the good must be happy for the very reason that they are good. But it was agreed that those who are happy are gods. So, then, the prize of the good is one which no time may impair, no man's power lessen, no man's unrighteousness tarnish; 'tis very Godship. And this being so, the wise man cannot doubt that punishment is inseparable from the bad. For since good and bad, and likewise reward and punishment, are contraries, it necessarily follows that, corresponding to all that we see accrue as reward of the good, there is some penalty attached as punishment of evil. As, then, righteousness itself is the reward of the righteous, so wickedness itself is the punishment of the unrighteous.

Now, no one who is visited with punishment doubts that he is visited with evil. Accordingly, if they were but willing to weigh their own case, could they think themselves free from punishment whom wickedness, worst of all evils, has not only touched, but deeply tainted?

'See, also, from the opposite standpoint—the standpoint of the good—what a penalty attends upon the wicked. Thou didst learn a little since that whatever is is one, and that unity itself is good. Accordingly, by this way of reckoning, whatever falls away from goodness ceases to be; whence it comes to pass that the bad cease to be what they were, while only the outward aspect is still left to show they have been men. Wherefore, by their perversion to badness, they have lost their true human nature. Further, since righteousness alone can raise men above the level of humanity, it must needs be that unrighteousness degrades below man's level those whom it has cast out of man's estate. It results, then, that thou canst not consider him human whom thou seest transformed by vice. The violent despoiler of other men's goods, enflamed with covetousness, surely resembles a wolf. A bold and restless spirit, ever wrangling in law-courts, is like some yelping cur. The secret schemer, taking pleasure in fraud and stealth, is own brother to the fox. The passionate man, phrenzied with rage, we might believe to be animated with the soul of a lion. The coward and runaway, afraid where no fear is, may be likened to the timid deer. He who is sunk in ignorance and stupidity lives like a dull ass. He who is light and inconstant, never holding long to one thing, is for all the world like a bird. He who wallows in foul and unclean lusts is sunk in the pleasures of a filthy hog. So it comes to pass that he who by forsaking righteousness ceases to be a man cannot pass into a Godlike condition, but actually turns into a brute beast.'

Song III: Circe's Cup.

Th' Ithacan discreet,
And all his storm-tossed fleet,
Far o'er the ocean wave
The winds of heaven drave—
Drave to the mystic isle,
Where dwelleth in her guile
That fair and faithless one,
The daughter of the Sun.
There for the stranger crew
With cunning spells she knew
To mix th' enchanted cup.
For whoso drinks it up,
Must suffer hideous change
To monstrous shapes and strange.
One like a boar appears;
This his huge form uprears,
Mighty in bulk and limb—
An Afric lion—grim
With claw and fang. Confessed
A wolf, this, sore distressed
When he would weep, doth howl;
And, strangely tame, these prowl
The Indian tiger's mates.
And though in such sore straits,
The pity of the god

Who bears the mystic rod
Had power the chieftain brave
From her fell arts to save;
His comrades, unrestrained,
The fatal goblet drained.
All now with low-bent head,
Like swine, on acorns fed;
Man's speech and form were reft,
No human feature left;
But steadfast still, the mind,
Unaltered, unresigned,
The monstrous change bewailed.
How little, then, availed
The potencies of ill!
These herbs, this baneful skill,
May change each outward part,
But cannot touch the heart.
In its true home, deep-set,
Man's spirit liveth yet.
Those poisons are more fell,
More potent to expel
Man from his high estate,
Which subtly penetrate,
And leave the body whole,
But deep infect the soul.

IV

Then said I: 'This is very true. I see that the vicious, though they keep the outward form of man, are rightly said to be changed into beasts in respect of their spiritual nature; but, inasmuch as their cruel and polluted minds vent their rage in the destruction of the good, I would this license were not permitted to them.'

'Nor is it,' said she, 'as shall be shown in the fitting place. Yet if that license which thou believest to be permitted to them were taken away, the punishment of the wicked would be in great part remitted.

For verily, incredible as it may seem to some, it needs must be that the bad are more unfortunate when they have accomplished their desires than if they are unable to get them fulfilled. If it is wretched to will evil, to have been able to accomplish evil is more wretched; for without the power the wretched will would fail of effect. Accordingly, those whom thou seest to will, to be able to accomplish, and to accomplish crime, must needs be the victims of a threefold wretchedness, since each one of these states has its own measure of wretchedness.'

'Yes,' said I; 'yet I earnestly wish they might speedily be quit of this misfortune by losing the ability to accomplish crime.'

'They will lose it,' said she, 'sooner than perchance thou wishest, or they themselves think likely; since, verily, within the narrow bounds of our brief life there is nothing so late in coming that anyone, least of all an immortal spirit, should deem it long to wait for. Their great expectations, the lofty fabric of their crimes, is oft overthrown by a sudden and unlooked for ending, and this but sets a limit to their misery. For if wickedness makes men wretched, he is necessarily more wretched who is wicked for a longer time; and were it not that death, at all events, puts an end to the evil doings of the wicked, I should account them wretched to the last degree. Indeed, if we have formed true conclusions about the ill fortune of wickedness, that wretchedness is plainly infinite which is doomed to be eternal.'

Then said I: 'A wonderful inference, and difficult to grant; but I see that it agrees entirely with our previous conclusions.'

'Thou art right,' said she; 'but if anyone finds it hard to admit the conclusion, he ought in fairness either to prove some falsity in the premises, or to show that the combination of propositions does not adequately enforce the necessity of the conclusion; otherwise, if the premises be granted, nothing whatever can be said against the inference of the conclusion. And here is another statement which seems not less wonderful, but on the premises assumed is equally necessary.'

'What is that?'

'The wicked are happier in undergoing punishment than if no penalty of justice chasten them. And I am not now meaning what might occur to anyone—that bad character is amended by retribution, and is brought into the right path by the terror of punishment, or that it serves as an example to warn others to avoid transgression; but I believe that in another way the wicked are more unfortunate when they go unpunished, even though no account be taken of amendment, and no regard be paid to example.'

'Why, what other way is there beside these?' said I.

Then said she: 'Have we not agreed that the good are happy, and the evil wretched?'

'Yes,' said I.

'Now, if,' said she, 'to one in affliction there be given along with his misery some good thing, is he not happier than one whose misery is misery pure and simple without admixture of any good?'

'It would seem so.'

'But if to one thus wretched, one destitute of all good, some further evil be added besides those which make him wretched, is he not to be judged far more unhappy than he whose ill fortune is alleviated by some share of good?'

'It could scarcely be otherwise.'

'Surely, then, the wicked, when they are punished, have a good thing added to them—to wit, the punishment which by the law of justice is good; and likewise, when they escape punishment, a new evil attaches to them in that very freedom from punishment which thou hast rightly acknowledged to be an evil in the case of the unrighteous.'

'I cannot deny it.'

'Then, the wicked are far more unhappy when indulged with an unjust freedom from punishment than when punished by a just retribution. Now, it is manifest that it is just for the wicked to be punished, and for them to escape unpunished is unjust.'

'Why, who would venture to deny it?'

'This, too, no one can possibly deny—that all which is just is good, and, conversely, all which is unjust is bad.'

Then I answered: 'These inferences do indeed follow from what we lately concluded; but tell me,' said I, 'dost thou take no account of the punishment of the soul after the death of the body?'

'Nay, truly,' said she, 'great are these penalties, some of them inflicted, I imagine, in the severity of retribution, others in the mercy of purification. But it is not my present purpose to speak of these. So far, my aim hath been to make thee recognise that the power of the bad which shocked thee so exceedingly is no power; to make thee see that those of whose freedom from punishment thou didst complain are never without the proper penalties of their unrighteousness; to teach thee that the license which thou prayedst might soon come to an end is not long-enduring; that it would be more unhappy if it lasted longer, most unhappy of all if it lasted for ever; thereafter that the unrighteous are more wretched if unjustly let go without punishment than if punished by a just retribution—from which point of view it follows that the wicked are afflicted with more severe penalties just when they are supposed to escape punishment.'

Then said I: 'While I follow thy reasonings, I am deeply impressed with their truth; but if I turn to the common convictions of men, I find few who will even listen to such arguments, let alone admit them to be credible.'

'True,' said she; 'they cannot lift eyes accustomed to darkness to the light of clear truth, and are like those birds whose vision night illumines and day blinds; for while they regard, not the order of the universe, but their own dispositions of mind, they think the license to commit crime, and the escape from punishment, to be fortunate. But mark the ordinance of eternal law. Hast thou fashioned thy soul to the likeness of the better, thou hast no need of a judge to award the prize—by thine own act hast thou raised thyself in the scale of excellence; hast thou perverted thy affections to baser things, look not for punishment from one without thee—thine own act hath degraded thee, and thrust thee down. Even so, if alternately thou turn thy gaze upon the vile earth and upon the heavens, though all without thee stand still, by the mere laws of sight thou seemest now sunk in the mire, now soaring among the stars. But the common herd regards not these things. What, then? Shall we go over to those whom we have shown to be like brute beasts? Why, suppose, now, one who had quite lost his sight should likewise forget that he had ever possessed the faculty of vision, and should imagine that nothing was wanting in him to human perfection, should we deem those who saw as well as ever blind? Why, they will not even assent to this, either—that they who do wrong are more wretched than those who suffer wrong, though the proof of this rests on grounds of reason no less strong.'

'Let me hear these same reasons,' said I.

'Wouldst thou deny that every wicked man deserves punishment?'

'I would not, certainly.'

'And that those who are wicked are unhappy is clear in manifold ways?'

'Yes,' I replied.

'Thou dost not doubt, then, that those who deserve punishment are wretched?'

'Agreed,' said I.

'So, then, if thou wert sitting in judgment, on whom wouldst thou decree the infliction of punishment—on him who had done the wrong, or on him who had suffered it?'

'Without doubt, I would compensate the sufferer at the cost of the doer of the wrong.'

'Then, the injurer would seem more wretched than the injured?'

'Yes; it follows. And so for this and other reasons resting on the same ground, inasmuch as baseness of its own nature makes men wretched, it is plain that a wrong involves the misery of the doer, not of the sufferer.'

'And yet,' says she, 'the practice of the law-courts is just the opposite: advocates try to arouse the commiseration of the judges for those who have endured some grievous and cruel wrong; whereas pity is rather due to the criminal, who ought to be brought to the judgment seat by his accusers in a spirit not of anger, but of compassion and kindness, as a sick man to the physician, to have the ulcer of his fault cut away by punishment. Whereby the business of the advocate would either wholly come to a standstill, or, did men prefer to make it serviceable to mankind, would be restricted to the practice of accusation. The wicked themselves also, if through some chink or cranny they were permitted to behold the virtue they have forsaken, and were to see that by the pains of punishment they would rid themselves of the uncleanness of their vices, and win in exchange the recompense of righteousness, they would no longer think these sufferings pains; they would refuse the help of advocates, and would commit themselves wholly into the hands of their accusers and judges. Whence it comes to pass that for the wise no place is left for hatred; only the most foolish would hate the good, and to hate the bad is unreasonable. For if vicious propensity is, as it were, a disease of the soul like bodily sickness, even as we account the sick in body by no means deserving of hate, but rather of pity, so, and much more, should they be pitied whose minds are assailed by wickedness, which is more frightful than any sickness.'

Song IV: The Unreasonableness of Hatred.

Why all this furious strife? Oh, why
With rash and willful hand provoke death's destined day?
If death ye seek—lo! Death is nigh,
Not of their master's will those coursers swift delay!
The wild beasts vent on man their rage,

Yet 'gainst their brothers' lives men point the murderous steel;
Unjust and cruel wars they wage,
And haste with flying darts the death to meet or deal.
No right nor reason can they show;
'Tis but because their lands and laws are not the same.
Wouldst thou give each his due; then know
Thy love the good must have, the bad thy pity claim.

V

On this I said: 'I see how there is a happiness and misery founded on the actual deserts of the righteous and the wicked. Nevertheless, I wonder in myself whether there is not some good and evil in fortune as the vulgar understand it. Surely, no sensible man would rather be exiled, poor and disgraced, than dwell prosperously in his own country, powerful, wealthy, and high in honour. Indeed, the work of wisdom is more clear and manifest in its operation when the happiness of rulers is somehow passed on to the people around them, especially considering that the prison, the law, and the other pains of legal punishment are properly due only to mischievous citizens on whose account they were originally instituted. Accordingly, I do exceedingly marvel why all this is completely reversed—why the good are harassed with the penalties due to crime, and the bad carry off the rewards of virtue; and I long to hear from thee what reason may be found for so unjust a state of disorder. For assuredly I should wonder less if I could believe that all things are the confused result of chance. But now my belief in God's governance doth add amazement to amazement. For, seeing that He sometimes assigns fair fortune to the good and harsh fortune to the bad, and then again deals harshly with the good, and grants to the bad their hearts' desire, how does this differ from chance, unless some reason is discovered for it all?'

'Nay; it is not wonderful,' said she, 'if all should be thought random and confused when the principle of order is not known. And though thou knowest not the causes on which this great system depends, yet forasmuch as a good ruler governs the world, doubt not for thy part that all is rightly done.'

Song V: Wonder and Ignorance.

Who knoweth not how near the pole
Bootes' course doth go,
Must marvel by what heavenly law
He moves his Wain so slow;
Why late he plunges 'neath the main,
And swiftly lights his beams again.
When the full-orbèd moon grows pale
In the mid course of night,
And suddenly the stars shine forth
That languished in her light,
Th' astonied nations stand at gaze,
And beat the air in wild amaze.
None marvels why upon the shore
The storm-lashed breakers beat,
Nor why the frost-bound glaciers melt
At summer's fervent heat;
For here the cause seems plain and clear,
Only what's dark and hid we fear.
Weak-minded folly magnifies
All that is rare and strange,
And the dull herd's o'erwhelmed with awe
At unexpected change.
But wonder leaves enlightened minds,
When ignorance no longer blinds.

VI

'True,' said I; 'but, since it is thy office to unfold the hidden cause of things, and explain principles veiled in darkness, inform me, I pray thee, of thine own conclusions in this matter, since the marvel of it is what more than aught else disturbs my mind.'

A smile played one moment upon her lips as she replied: 'Thou callest me to the greatest of all subjects of inquiry, a task for which the most exhaustive treatment barely suffices. Such is its nature that, as fast as one doubt is cut away, innumerable others spring up like Hydra's heads, nor could we set any limit to their renewal did we not apply the mind's living fire to suppress them. For there come within its scope the questions of the essential simplicity of providence, of the order of fate, of unforeseen chance, of the Divine knowledge and predestination, and of the freedom of the will. How heavy is the weight of all this thou canst judge for thyself. But, inasmuch as to know these things also is part of the treatment of thy malady, we will try to give them some consideration, despite the restrictions of the narrow limits of our time. Moreover, thou must for a time dispense with the pleasures of music and song, if so be that thou findest any delight therein, whilst I weave together the connected train of reasons in proper order.'

'As thou wilt,' said I.

Then, as if making a new beginning, she thus discoursed: 'The coming into being of all things, the whole course of development in things that change, every sort of thing that moves in any wise, receives its due cause, order, and form from the steadfastness of the Divine mind. This mind, calm in the citadel of its own essential simplicity, has decreed that the method of its rule shall be manifold. Viewed in the very purity of the Divine intelligence, this method is called providence; but viewed in regard to those things which it moves and disposes, it is what the ancients called fate. That these two are different will easily be clear to anyone who passes in review their respective efficacies. Providence is the Divine reason itself, seated in the Supreme Being, which disposes all things; fate is the disposition inherent in all things which move, through which providence joins all things in their proper order. Providence embraces all things, however different, however infinite; fate sets in motion separately individual things, and assigns to them severally their position, form, and time.

'So the unfolding of this temporal order unified into the foreview of the Divine mind is providence, while the same unity broken up and unfolded in time is fate. And although these are different, yet is there a dependence between them; for the order of destiny issues from the essential simplicity of providence. For as the artificer, forming in his mind beforehand the idea of the thing to be made, carries out his design, and develops from moment to moment what he had before seen in a single instant as a whole, so God in His providence ordains all things as parts of a single unchanging whole, but carries out these very ordinances by fate in a time of manifold unity. So whether fate is accomplished by Divine spirits as the ministers of providence, or by a soul, or by the service of all nature—whether by the celestial motion of the stars, by the efficacy of angels, or by the many-sided cunning of demons—whether by all or by some of these the destined series is woven, this, at least, is manifest: that providence is the fixed and simple form of destined events, fate their shifting series in order of time, as by the disposal of the Divine simplicity they are to take place. Whereby it is that all things which are under fate are subjected also to providence, on which fate itself is dependent; whereas certain things which are set under providence are above the chain of fate—viz., those things which by their nearness to the primal Divinity are steadfastly fixed, and lie outside the order of fate's movements. For as the innermost of several circles revolving round the same centre approaches the simplicity of the midmost point, and is, as it were, a pivot round which the exterior circles turn, while the outermost, whirled in ampler orbit, takes in a wider and wider sweep of space in proportion to its departure from the indivisible unity of the centre—while, further, whatever joins and allies itself to the centre is narrowed to a like simplicity, and no longer expands vaguely into space—even so whatsoever departs widely from primal mind is involved more deeply in the meshes of fate, and things are free from fate in proportion as they seek to come nearer to that central pivot; while if aught cleaves close to supreme mind in its absolute fixity, this, too, being free from movement, rises above fate's necessity. Therefore, as is reasoning to pure intelligence, as that which is generated to that which is, time to eternity, a circle to its centre, so is the shifting series of fate to the steadfastness and simplicity of providence.

'It is this causal series which moves heaven and the stars, attempers the elements to mutual accord, and again in turn transforms them into new combinations; this which renews the series of all things that are born and die through like successions of germ and birth; it is its operation which binds the destinies of men by an indissoluble nexus of causality, and, since it issues in the beginning from unalterable providence, these destinies also must of necessity be immutable. Accordingly, the world is ruled for the best if this unity abiding in the Divine mind puts forth an inflexible order of causes. And this order, by its intrinsic immutability, restricts things mutable which otherwise would ebb and flow at random. And so it happens that, although to you, who are not altogether capable of understanding this order, all things seem confused and disordered, nevertheless there is everywhere an appointed limit which guides all things to good. Verily, nothing can be done for the sake of evil even by the wicked themselves; for, as we abundantly proved, they seek good, but are drawn out of the way by perverse error; far less can this order which sets out from the supreme centre of good turn aside anywhither from the way in which it began.

'"Yet what confusion," thou wilt say, "can be more unrighteous than that prosperity and adversity should indifferently befall the good, what they like and what they loathe come alternately to the bad!" Yes; but have men in real life such soundness of mind that their judgments of righteousness and wickedness must necessarily correspond with facts? Why, on this very point their verdicts conflict, and those whom some deem worthy of reward, others deem worthy of punishment. Yet granted there were one who could rightly distinguish the good and bad, yet would he be able to look into the soul's inmost constitution, as it were, if we may borrow an expression used of the body? The marvel here is not unlike that which astonishes one who does not know why in health sweet things suit some constitutions, and bitter others, or why some sick men are best alleviated by mild remedies, others by severe. But the physician who distinguishes the precise conditions and characteristics of health and sickness does not marvel. Now, the health of the soul is nothing but righteousness, and vice is its sickness. God, the guide and physician of the mind, it is who preserves the good and banishes the bad. And He looks forth from the lofty watch-tower of His providence, perceives what is suited to each, and assigns what He knows to be suitable.

'This, then, is what that extraordinary mystery of the order of destiny comes to—that something is done by one who knows, whereat the ignorant are astonished. But let us consider a few instances whereby appears what is the competency of human reason to fathom the Divine unsearchableness. Here is one whom thou deemest the perfection of justice and scrupulous integrity; to all-knowing Providence it seems far otherwise. We all know our Lucan's admonition that it was the winning cause that found favour with the gods, the beaten cause with Cato. So, shouldst thou see anything in this world happening differently from thy expectation, doubt not but events are rightly ordered; it is in thy judgment that there is perverse confusion.

'Grant, however, there be somewhere found one of so happy a character that God and man alike agree in their judgments about him; yet is he somewhat infirm in strength of mind. It may be, if he fall into adversity, he will cease to practise that innocency which has failed to secure his fortune. Therefore, God's wise dispensation spares him whom adversity might make worse, will not let him suffer who is ill fitted for endurance. Another there is perfect in all virtue, so holy and nigh to God that providence judges it unlawful that aught untoward should befall him; nay, doth not even permit him to be afflicted with bodily disease. As one more excellent than I hath said:

> "'The very body of the holy saint
> Is built of purest ether."

Often it happens that the governance is given to the good that a restraint may be put upon superfluity of wickedness. To others providence assigns some mixed lot suited to their spiritual nature; some it will plague lest they grow rank through long prosperity; others it will suffer to be vexed with sore afflictions to confirm their virtues by the exercise and practice of patience. Some fear overmuch what they have strength to bear; others despise overmuch that to which their strength is unequal. All these it brings to the test of their true self through misfortune. Some also have bought a name revered to future ages at the price of a glorious death; some by invincible constancy under their sufferings have afforded an example to others that virtue cannot be overcome by calamity—all which things, without doubt, come to pass rightly and in due order, and to the benefit of those to whom they are seen to happen.

'As to the other side of the marvel, that the bad now meet with affliction, now get their hearts' desire, this, too, springs from the same causes. As to the afflictions, of course no one marvels, because all hold the wicked to be ill deserving. The truth is, their punishments both frighten others from crime, and amend those on whom they are inflicted; while their prosperity is a powerful sermon to the good, what judgments they ought to pass on good fortune of this kind, which often attends the wicked so assiduously.

'There is another object which may, I believe, be attained in such cases: there is one, perhaps, whose nature is so reckless and violent that poverty would drive him more desperately into crime. His disorder providence relieves by allowing him to amass money. Such a one, in the uneasiness of a conscience stained with guilt, while he contrasts his character with his fortune, perchance grows alarmed lest he should come to mourn the loss of that whose possession is so pleasant to him. He will, then, reform his ways, and through the fear of losing his fortune he forsakes his iniquity. Some, through a prosperity unworthily borne, have been hurled headlong to ruin; to some the power of the sword has been committed, to the end that the good may be tried by discipline, and the bad punished. For while there can be no peace between the righteous and the wicked, neither can the wicked agree among themselves. How should they, when each is at variance with himself, because his vices rend his conscience, and ofttimes they do things which, when they are done, they judge ought not to have been done. Hence it is that this supreme providence brings to pass this notable marvel—that the bad make the bad good. For some, when they see the injustice which they themselves suffer at the hands of evil-doers, are inflamed with detestation of the offenders, and, in the endeavour to be unlike those whom they hate, return to the ways of virtue. It is the Divine power alone to which things evil are also good, in that, by putting them to suitable use, it bringeth them in the end to some good issue. For order in some way or other embraceth all things, so that even that which has departed from the appointed laws of the order, nevertheless falleth within an order, though another order, that nothing in the realm of providence may be left to haphazard. But "'Hard were the task, as a god, to recount all, nothing omitting."

Nor, truly, is it lawful for man to compass in thought all the mechanism of the Divine work, or set it forth in speech. Let us be content to have apprehended this only—that God, the creator of universal nature, likewise disposeth all things, and guides them to good; and while He studies to preserve in likeness to Himself all that He has created, He banishes all evil from the borders of His commonweal through the links of fatal necessity. Whereby it comes to pass that, if thou look to disposing providence, thou wilt nowhere find the evils which are believed so to abound on earth.

'But I see thou hast long been burdened with the weight of the subject, and fatigued with the prolixity of the argument, and now lookest for some refreshment of sweet poesy. Listen, then, and may the draught so restore thee that thou wilt bend thy mind more resolutely to what remains.'

Song VI: The Universal Aim.

Wouldst thou with unclouded mind
View the laws by God designed,
Lift thy steadfast gaze on high
To the starry canopy;
See in rightful league of love
All the constellations move.
Fiery Sol, in full career,
Ne'er obstructs cold Phoebe's sphere;
When the Bear, at heaven's height,
Wheels his coursers' rapid flight,
Though he sees the starry train
Sinking in the western main,
He repines not, nor desires
In the flood to quench his fires.
In true sequence, as decreed,
Daily morn and eve succeed;
Vesper brings the shades of night,
Lucifer the morning light.
Love, in alternation due,
Still the cycle doth renew,

And discordant strife is driven
From the starry realm of heaven.
Thus, in wondrous amity,
Warring elements agree;
Hot and cold, and moist and dry,
Lay their ancient quarrel by;
High the flickering flame ascends,
Downward earth for ever tends.
So the year in spring's mild hours
Loads the air with scent of flowers;
Summer paints the golden grain;
Then, when autumn comes again,
Bright with fruit the orchards glow;
Winter brings the rain and snow.
Thus the seasons' fixed progression,
Tempered in a due succession,
Nourishes and brings to birth
All that lives and breathes on earth.
Then, soon run life's little day,
All it brought it takes away.
But One sits and guides the reins,
He who made and all sustains;
King and Lord and Fountain-head,
Judge most holy, Law most dread;
Now impels and now keeps back,
Holds each waverer in the track.
Else, were once the power withheld
That the circling spheres compelled
In their orbits to revolve,
This world's order would dissolve,
And th' harmonious whole would all
In one hideous ruin fall.
But through this connected frame
Runs one universal aim;
Towards the Good do all things tend,
Many paths, but one the end.
For naught lasts, unless it turns
Backward in its course, and yearns

To that Source to flow again
Whence its being first was ta'en.

VII

'Dost thou, then, see the consequence of all that we have said?'

'Nay; what consequence?'

'That absolutely every fortune is good fortune.'

'And how can that be?' said I.

'Attend,' said she. 'Since every fortune, welcome and unwelcome alike, has for its object the reward or trial of the good, and the punishing or amending of the bad, every fortune must be good, since it is either just or useful.'

'The reasoning is exceeding true,' said I, 'the conclusion, so long as I reflect upon the providence and fate of which thou hast taught me, based on a strong foundation. Yet, with thy leave, we will count it among those which just now thou didst set down as paradoxical.'

'And why so?' said she.

'Because ordinary speech is apt to assert, and that frequently, that some men's fortune is bad.'

'Shall we, then, for awhile approach more nearly to the language of the vulgar, that we may not seem to have departed too far from the usages of men?'

'At thy good pleasure,' said I.

'That which advantageth thou callest good, dost thou not?'

'Certainly.'

'And that which either tries or amends advantageth?'

'Granted.'

'Is good, then?'

'Of course.'

'Well, this is their case who have attained virtue and wage war with adversity, or turn from vice and lay hold on the path of virtue.'

'I cannot deny it.'

'What of the good fortune which is given as reward of the good—do the vulgar adjudge it bad?'

'Anything but that; they deem it to be the best, as indeed it is.'

'What, then, of that which remains, which, though it is harsh, puts the restraint of just punishment on the bad—does popular opinion deem it good?'

'Nay; of all that can be imagined, it is accounted the most miserable.'

'Observe, then, if, in following popular opinion, we have not ended in a conclusion quite paradoxical.'

'How so?' said I.

'Why, it results from our admissions that of all who have attained, or are advancing in, or are aiming at virtue, the fortune is in every case good, while for those who remain in their wickedness fortune is always utterly bad.'

'It is true,' said I; 'yet no one dare acknowledge it.'

'Wherefore,' said she, 'the wise man ought not to take it ill, if ever he is involved in one of fortune's conflicts, any more than it becomes a brave soldier to be offended when at any time the trumpet sounds for battle. The time of trial is the express opportunity for the one to win glory, for the other to perfect his wisdom. Hence, indeed, virtue gets its name, because, relying on its own efficacy, it yieldeth not to adversity. And ye who have taken your stand on virtue's steep ascent, it is not for you to be dissolved in delights or enfeebled by pleasure; ye close in conflict—yea, in conflict most sharp—with all fortune's vicissitudes, lest ye suffer foul fortune to overwhelm or fair fortune to corrupt you. Hold the mean with all your strength. Whatever falls short of this, or goes beyond, is fraught with scorn of happiness, and misses the reward of toil. It rests with you to make your fortune what you will. Verily, every harsh-seeming fortune, unless it either disciplines or amends, is punishment.'

Song VII: The Hero's Path.

Ten years a tedious warfare raged,
Ere Ilium's smoking ruins paid
For wedlock stained and faith betrayed,
And great Atrides' wrath assuaged.
But when heaven's anger asked a life,
And baffling winds his course withstood,
The king put off his fatherhood,
And slew his child with priestly knife.
When by the cavern's glimmering light
His comrades dear Odysseus saw
In the huge Cyclops' hideous maw
Engulfed, he wept the piteous sight.
But blinded soon, and wild with pain—
In bitter tears and sore annoy—
For that foul feast's unholy joy
Grim Polyphemus paid again.
His labours for Alcides win
A name of glory far and wide;
He tamed the Centaur's haughty pride,
And from the lion reft his skin.
The foul birds with sure darts he slew;
The golden fruit he stole—in vain
The dragon's watch; with triple chain
From hell's depths Cerberus he drew.
With their fierce lord's own flesh he fed

The wild steeds; Hydra overcame
With fire. 'Neath his own waves in shame
Maimed Achelous hid his head.
Huge Cacus for his crimes was slain;
On Libya's sands Antæus hurled;
The shoulders that upheld the world
The great boar's dribbled spume did stain.
Last toil of all—his might sustained
The ball of heaven, nor did he bend
Beneath; this toil, his labour's end,
The prize of heaven's high glory gained.
Brave hearts, press on! Lo, heavenward lead
These bright examples! From the fight
Turn not your backs in coward flight;
Earth's conflict won, the stars your meed!

Book Five
Free Will and God's Foreknowledge

I

She ceased, and was about to pass on in her discourse to the exposition of other matters, when I break in and say: 'Excellent is thine exhortation, and such as well beseemeth thy high authority; but I am even now experiencing one of the many difficulties which, as thou saidst but now, beset the question of providence. I want to know whether thou deemest that there is any such thing as chance at all, and, if so, what it is.'

Then she made answer: 'I am anxious to fulfill my promise completely, and open to thee a way of return to thy native land. As for these matters, though very useful to know, they are yet a little removed from the path of our design, and I fear lest digressions should fatigue thee, and thou shouldst find thyself unequal to completing the direct journey to our goal.'

'Have no fear for that,' said I. 'It is rest to me to learn, where learning brings delight so exquisite, especially when thy argument has been built up on all sides with undoubted conviction, and no place is left for uncertainty in what follows.'

She made answer: 'I will accede to thy request;' and forthwith she thus began: 'If chance be defined as a result produced by random movement without any link of causal connection, I roundly affirm that there is no such thing as chance at all, and consider the word to be altogether without meaning, except as a symbol of the thing designated. What place can be left for random action, when God constraineth all things to order? For *ex nihilo nihil* is sound doctrine which none of the ancients gainsaid, although they used it of material substance, not of the efficient principle; this they laid down as a kind of basis for all their reasonings concerning nature. Now, if a thing arise without causes, it will appear to have arisen from nothing. But if this cannot be, neither is it possible for there to be chance in accordance with the definition just given.'

'Well,' said I, 'is there, then, nothing which can properly be called chance or accident, or is there something to which these names are appropriate, though its nature is dark to the vulgar?'

'Our good Aristotle,' says she, 'has defined it concisely in his "Physics," and closely in accordance with the truth.'

'How, pray?' said I.

'Thus,' says she: 'Whenever something is done for the sake of a particular end, and for certain reasons some other result than that designed ensues, this is called chance; for instance, if a man is digging the earth for tillage, and finds a mass of buried gold. Now, such a find is regarded as accidental; yet it is not *ex nihilo*, for it has its proper causes, the unforeseen and unexpected concurrence of which has brought the chance about. For had not the cultivator been digging, had not the man who hid the money buried it in that precise spot, the gold would not have been found. These, then, are the reasons why the find is a chance one, in that it results from causes which met together and concurred, not from any intention on the part of the discoverer.

Since neither he who buried the gold nor he who worked in the field intended that the money should be found, but, as I said, it happened by coincidence that one dug where the other buried the treasure. We may, then, define chance as being an unexpected result flowing from a concurrence of causes where the several factors had some definite end. But the meeting and concurrence of these causes arises from that inevitable chain of order which, flowing from the fountain-head of Providence, disposes all things in their due time and place.'

Song I: Chance.

In the rugged Persian highlands,
Where the masters of the bow
Skill to feign a flight, and, fleeing,
Hurl their darts and pierce the foe;
There the Tigris and Euphrates
At one source their waters blend,
Soon to draw apart, and plainward
Each its separate way to wend.
When once more their waters mingle
In a channel deep and wide,
All the flotsam comes together
That is borne upon the tide:
Ships, and trunks of trees, uprooted
In the torrent's wild career,
Meet, as 'mid the swirling waters
Chance their random way may steer.
Yet the shelving of the channel
And the flowing water's force
Guides each movement, and determines
Every floating fragment's course.
Thus, where'er the drift of hazard
Seems most unrestrained to flow,
Chance herself is reined and bitted,
And the curb of law doth know.

II

'I am following needfully,' said I, 'and I agree that it is as thou sayest. But in this series of linked causes is there any freedom left to our will, or does the chain of fate bind also the very motions of our souls?'

'There is freedom,' said she; 'nor, indeed, can any creature be rational, unless he be endowed with free will. For that which hath the natural use of reason has the faculty of discriminative judgment, and of itself distinguishes what is to be shunned or desired. Now, everyone seeks what he judges desirable, and avoids what he thinks should be shunned. Wherefore, beings endowed with reason possess also the faculty of free choice and refusal. But I suppose this faculty not equal alike in all. The higher Divine essences possess a clear-sighted judgment, an uncorrupt will, and an effective power of accomplishing their wishes. Human souls must needs be comparatively free while they abide in the contemplation of the Divine mind, less free when they pass into bodily form, and still less, again, when they are enwrapped in earthly members. But when they are given over to vices, and fall from the possession of their proper reason, then indeed their condition is utter slavery. For when they let their gaze fall from the light of highest truth to the lower world where darkness reigns, soon ignorance blinds their vision; they are disturbed by baneful affections, by yielding and assenting to which they help to promote the slavery in which they are involved, and are in a manner led captive by reason of their very liberty. Yet He who seeth all things from eternity beholdeth these things with the eyes of His providence, and assigneth to each what is predestined for it by its merits: '"All things surveying, all things overhearing."'

Song II: The True Sun.

Homer with mellifluous tongue
Phœbus' glorious light hath sung,
Hymning high his praise;
Yet his feeble rays
Ocean's hollows may not brighten,

Nor earth's central gloom enlighten.
But the might of Him, who skilled
This great universe to build,
Is not thus confined;
Not earth's solid rind,
Nor night's blackest canopy,
Baffle His all-seeing eye.
All that is, hath been, shall be,
In one glance's compass, He
Limitless descries;
And, save His, no eyes
All the world survey—no, none!
Him, then, truly name the Sun.

III

Then said I: 'But now I am once more perplexed by a problem yet more difficult.'

'And what is that?' said she; 'yet, in truth, I can guess what it is that troubles you.'

'It seems,' said I, 'too much of a paradox and a contradiction that God should know all things, and yet there should be free will. For if God foresees everything, and can in no wise be deceived, that which providence foresees to be about to happen must necessarily come to pass. Wherefore, if from eternity He foreknows not only what men will do, but also their designs and purposes, there can be no freedom of the will, seeing that nothing can be done, nor can any sort of purpose be entertained, save such as a Divine providence, incapable of being deceived, has perceived beforehand. For if the issues can be turned aside to some other end than that foreseen by providence, there will not then be any sure foreknowledge of the future, but uncertain conjecture instead, and to think this of God I deem impiety.

'Moreover, I do not approve the reasoning by which some think to solve this puzzle. For they say that it is not because God has foreseen the coming of an event that therefore it is sure to come to pass, but, conversely, because something is about to come to pass, it cannot be hidden from Divine providence; and accordingly the necessity passes to the opposite side, and it is not that what is foreseen must necessarily come to pass, but that what is about to come to pass must necessarily be foreseen. But this is just as if the matter in debate were, which is cause and which effect—whether foreknowledge of the future cause of the necessity, or the necessity of the future of the foreknowledge. But we need not be at the pains of demonstrating that, whatsoever be the order of the causal sequence, the occurrence of things foreseen is necessary, even though the foreknowledge of future events does not in itself impose upon them the necessity of their occurrence. For example, if a man be seated, the supposition of his being seated is necessarily true; and, conversely, if the supposition of his being seated is true, because he is really seated, he must necessarily be sitting. So, in either case, there is some necessity involved—in this latter case, the necessity of the fact; in the former, of the truth of the statement. But in both cases the sitter is not therefore seated because the opinion is true, but rather the opinion is true because antecedently he was sitting as a matter of fact. Thus, though the cause of the truth of the opinion comes from the other side, yet there is a necessity on both sides alike. We can obviously reason similarly in the case of providence and the future. Even if future events are foreseen because they are about to happen, and do not come to pass because they are foreseen, still, all the same, there is a necessity, both that they should be foreseen by God as about to come to pass, and that when they are foreseen they should happen, and this is sufficient for the destruction of free will. However, it is preposterous to speak of the occurrence of events in time as the cause of eternal foreknowledge. And yet if we believe that God foresees future events because they are about to come to pass, what is it but to think that the occurrence of events is the cause of His supreme providence? Further, just as when I know that anything is, that thing necessarily is, so when I know that anything will be, it will necessarily be. It follows, then, that things foreknown come to pass inevitably.

'Lastly, to think of a thing as being in any way other than what it is, is not only not knowledge, but it is false opinion widely different from the truth of knowledge. Consequently, if anything is about to be, and yet its occurrence is not certain and necessary, how can anyone foreknow that it will occur? For just as knowledge itself is free from all admixture of falsity, so any conception drawn from knowledge cannot be other than as it is conceived. For this, indeed, is the cause why knowledge is free from falsehood, because of necessity each thing must correspond exactly with the knowledge which grasps its nature. In what way, then, are we to suppose that God foreknows these uncertainties as about to come to pass? For if He thinks of events which possibly may not happen at all as inevitably destined to come to pass, He is deceived; and this it is not only impious to believe, but even so much as to express in words. If, on the other hand, He sees them in the future as they are in such a sense as to know that they may equally come to pass or not, what sort of foreknowledge is this which comprehends nothing certain nor fixed? What better is this than the absurd vaticination of Teiresias?

> "'Whate'er I say
> Shall either come to pass—or not."

In that case, too, in what would Divine providence surpass human opinion if it holds for uncertain things the occurrence of which is uncertain, even as men do? But if at that perfectly sure Fountain-head of all things no shadow of uncertainty can possibly be found, then the occurrence of those things which He has surely foreknown as coming is certain. Wherefore there can be no freedom in human actions and designs; but the Divine mind, which foresees all things without possibility of mistake, ties and binds them down to one only issue. But this admission once made, what an upset of human affairs manifestly ensues! Vainly are rewards and punishments proposed for the good and bad, since no free and voluntary motion of the will has deserved either one or the other; nay, the punishment of the wicked and the reward of the righteous, which is now esteemed the perfection of justice, will seem the most flagrant injustice, since men are determined either way not by their own proper volition, but by the necessity of what must surely be. And therefore neither virtue nor vice is anything, but rather good and ill desert are confounded together without distinction. Moreover, seeing that the whole course of events is deduced from providence, and nothing is left free to human design, it comes to pass that our vices also are referred to the Author of all good—a thought than which none more abominable can possibly be conceived. Again, no ground is left for hope or prayer, since how can we hope for blessings, or pray for mercy, when every object of desire depends upon the links of an unalterable chain of causation? Gone, then, is the one means of intercourse between God and man—the communion of hope and prayer—if it be true that we ever earn the inestimable recompense of the Divine favour at the price of a due humility; for this is the one way whereby men seem able to hold communion with God, and are joined to that unapproachable light by the very act of supplication, even before they obtain their petitions. Then, since these things can scarcely be believed to have any efficacy, if the necessity of future events be admitted, what means will there be whereby we may be brought near and cleave to Him who is the supreme Head of all? Wherefore it needs must be that the human race, even as thou didst erstwhile declare in song, parted and dissevered from its Source, should fall to ruin.'

Song III: Truth's Paradoxes.

Why does a strange discordance break
The ordered scheme's fair harmony?
Hath God decreed 'twixt truth and truth
There may such lasting warfare be,
That truths, each severally plain,
We strive to reconcile in vain?
Or is the discord not in truth,
Since truth is self consistent ever?
But, close in fleshly wrappings held,
The blinded mind of man can never
Discern—so faint her taper shines—
The subtle chain that all combines?
Ah! then why burns man's restless mind
Truth's hidden portals to unclose?
Knows he already what he seeks?
Why toil to seek it, if he knows?
Yet, haply if he knoweth not,
Why blindly seek he knows not what?

Who for a good he knows not sighs?
Who can an unknown end pursue?
How find? How e'en when haply found
Hail that strange form he never knew?
Or is it that man's inmost soul
Once knew each part and knew the whole?
Now, though by fleshly vapours dimmed,
Not all forgot her visions past;
For while the several parts are lost,
To the one whole she cleaveth fast;
Whence he who yearns the truth to find
Is neither sound of sight nor blind.
For neither does he know in full,
Nor is he reft of knowledge quite;
But, holding still to what is left,
He gropes in the uncertain light,
And by the part that still survives
To win back all he bravely strives.

IV

Then said she: 'This debate about providence is an old one, and is vigorously discussed by Cicero in his "Divination"; thou also hast long and earnestly pondered the problem, yet no one has had diligence and perseverance enough to find a solution. And the reason of this obscurity is that the movement of human reasoning cannot cope with the simplicity of the Divine foreknowledge; for if a conception of its nature could in any wise be framed, no shadow of uncertainty would remain. With a view of making this at last clear and plain, I will begin by considering the arguments by which thou art swayed. First, I inquire into the reasons why thou art dissatisfied with the solution proposed, which is to the effect that, seeing the fact of foreknowledge is not thought the cause of the necessity of future events, foreknowledge is not to be deemed any hindrance to the freedom of the will. Now, surely the sole ground on which thou arguest the necessity of the future is that things which are foreknown cannot fail to come to pass. But if, as thou wert ready to acknowledge just now, the fact of foreknowledge imposes no necessity on things future, what reason is there for supposing the results of voluntary action constrained to a fixed issue? Suppose, for the sake of argument, and to see what follows, we assume that there is no foreknowledge. Are willed actions, then, tied down to any necessity in this case?'

'Certainly not.'

'Let us assume foreknowledge again, but without its involving any actual necessity; the freedom of the will, I imagine, will remain in complete integrity. But thou wilt say that, even although the foreknowledge is not the necessity of the future event's occurrence, yet it is a sign that it will necessarily happen. Granted; but in this case it is plain that, even if there had been no foreknowledge, the issues would have been inevitably certain. For a sign only indicates something which is, does not bring to pass that of which it is the sign. We require to show beforehand that all things, without exception, happen of necessity in order that a preconception may be a sign of this necessity. Otherwise, if there is no such universal necessity, neither can any preconception be a sign of a necessity which exists not. Manifestly, too, a proof established on firm grounds of reason must be drawn not from signs and loose general arguments, but from suitable and necessary causes. But how can it be that things foreseen should ever fail to come to pass? Why, this is to suppose us to believe that the events which providence foresees to be coming were not about to happen, instead of our supposing that, although they should come to pass, yet there was no necessity involved in their own nature compelling their occurrence. Take an illustration that will help to convey my meaning. There are many things which we see taking place before our eyes—the movements of charioteers, for instance, in guiding and turning their cars, and so on. Now, is any one of these movements compelled by any necessity?'

'No; certainly not. There would be no efficacy in skill if all motions took place perforce.'

'Then, things which in taking place are free from any necessity as to their being in the present must also, before they take place, be about to happen without necessity. Wherefore there are things which will come to pass, the occurrence of which is perfectly free from necessity. At all events, I imagine that no one will deny that things now taking place were about to come to pass before they were actually happening. Such things, however much foreknown, are in their occurrence free. For even as knowledge of things present imports no necessity into things that are taking place, so foreknowledge of the future imports none into things that are about to come. But this, thou wilt say, is the very point in dispute—whether any foreknowing is possible of things whose occurrence is not necessary. For here there seems to thee a contradiction, and, if they are foreseen, their necessity follows; whereas if there is no necessity, they can by no means be foreknown; and thou thinkest that nothing can be grasped as known unless it is certain, but if things whose occurrence is uncertain are foreknown as certain, this is the very mist of opinion, not the truth of knowledge. For to think of things otherwise than as they are, thou believest to be incompatible with the soundness of knowledge.

'Now, the cause of the mistake is this—that men think that all knowledge is cognized purely by the nature and efficacy of the thing known. Whereas the case is the very reverse: all that is known is grasped not conformably to its own efficacy, but rather conformably to the faculty of the knower. An example will make this clear: the roundness of a body is recognised in one way by sight, in another by touch. Sight looks upon it from a distance as a whole by a simultaneous reflection of rays; touch grasps the roundness piecemeal, by contact and attachment to the surface, and by actual movement round the periphery itself. Man himself, likewise, is viewed in one way by Sense, in another by Imagination, in another way, again, by Thought, in another by pure Intelligence. Sense judges figure clothed in material substance, Imagination figure alone without matter. Thought transcends this again, and by its contemplation of universals considers the type itself which is contained in the individual. The eye of Intelligence is yet more exalted; for overpassing the sphere of the universal, it will behold absolute form itself by the pure force of the mind's vision. Wherein the main point to be considered is this: the higher faculty of comprehension embraces the lower, while the lower cannot rise to the higher. For Sense has no efficacy beyond matter, nor can Imagination behold universal ideas, nor Thought embrace pure form; but Intelligence, looking down, as it were, from its higher standpoint in its intuition of form, discriminates also the several elements which underlie it; but it comprehends them in the same way as it comprehends that form itself, which could be cognized by no other than itself. For it cognizes the universal of Thought, the figure of Imagination, and the matter of Sense, without employing Thought, Imagination, or Sense, but surveying all things, so to speak, under the aspect of pure form by a single flash of intuition. Thought also, in considering the universal, embraces images and sense-impressions without resorting to Imagination or Sense. For it is Thought which has thus defined the universal from its conceptual point of view: "Man is a two-legged animal endowed with reason." This is indeed a universal notion, yet no one is ignorant that the thing is imaginable and presentable to Sense, because Thought considers it not by Imagination or Sense, but by means of rational conception. Imagination, too, though its faculty of viewing and forming representations is founded upon the senses, nevertheless surveys sense-impressions without calling in Sense, not in the way of Sense-perception, but of Imagination. See'st thou, then, how all things in cognizing use rather their own faculty than the faculty of the things which they cognize? Nor is this strange; for since every judgment is the act of the judge, it is necessary that each should accomplish its task by its own, not by another's power.'

Song IV: A Psychological Fallacy.

From the Porch's murky depths
Comes a doctrine sage,
That doth liken living mind
To a written page;
Since all knowledge comes through Sense,
Graven by Experience.
'As,' say they, 'the pen its marks
Curiously doth trace
On the smooth unsullied white
Of the paper's face,
So do outer things impress
Images on consciousness.'

But if verily the mind
Thus all passive lies;
If no living power within
Its own force supplies;
If it but reflect again,
Like a glass, things false and vain—
Whence the wondrous faculty
That perceives and knows,
That in one fair ordered scheme
Doth the world dispose;
Grasps each whole that Sense presents,
Or breaks into elements?
So divides and recombines,
And in changeful wise
Now to low descends, and now
To the height doth rise;
Last in inward swift review
Strictly sifts the false and true?
Of these ample potencies
Fitter cause, I ween,
Were Mind's self than marks impressed
By the outer scene.
Yet the body through the sense
Stirs the soul's intelligence.
When light flashes on the eye,
Or sound strikes the ear,
Mind aroused to due response
Makes the message clear;
And the dumb external signs
With the hidden forms combines.

V

'Now, although in the case of bodies endowed with sentiency the qualities of external objects affect the sense-organs, and the activity of mind is preceded by a bodily affection which calls forth the mind's action upon itself, and stimulates the forms till that moment lying inactive within, yet, I say, if in these bodies endowed with sentiency the mind is not inscribed by mere passive affection, but of its own efficacy discriminates the impressions furnished to the body, how much more do intelligences free from all bodily affections employ in their discrimination their own mental activities instead of conforming to external objects? So on these principles various modes of cognition belong to distinct and different substances. For to creatures void of motive power—shell-fish and other such creatures which cling to rocks and grow there—belongs Sense alone, void of all other modes of gaining knowledge; to beasts endowed with movement, in whom some capacity of seeking and shunning seems to have arisen, Imagination also. Thought pertains only to the human race, as Intelligence to Divinity alone; hence it follows that that form of knowledge exceeds the rest which of its own nature cognizes not only its proper object, but the objects of the other forms of knowledge also. But what if Sense and Imagination were to gainsay Thought, and declare that universal which Thought deems itself to behold to be nothing? For the object of Sense and Imagination cannot be universal; so that either the judgment of Reason is true and there is no sense-object, or, since they know full well that many objects are presented to Sense and Imagination, the conception of Reason, which looks on that which is perceived by Sense and particular as if it were a something "universal," is empty of content. Suppose, further, that Reason maintains in reply that it does indeed contemplate the object of both Sense and Imagination under the form of universality, while Sense and Imagination cannot aspire to the knowledge of the universal, since their cognizance cannot go beyond bodily figures, and that in the cognition of reality we ought rather to trust the stronger and more perfect faculty of judgment. In a dispute of this sort, should not we, in whom is planted the faculty of reasoning as well as of imagining and perceiving, espouse the cause of Reason?

'In like manner is it that human reason thinks that Divine Intelligence cannot see the future except after the fashion in which its own knowledge is obtained. For thy contention is, if events do not appear to involve certain and necessary issues, they cannot be foreseen as certainly about to come to pass. There is, then, no foreknowledge of such events; or, if we can ever bring ourselves to believe that there is, there can be nothing which does not happen of necessity. If, however, we could have some part in the judgment of the Divine mind, even as we participate in Reason, we should think it perfectly just that human Reason should submit itself to the Divine mind, no less than we judged that Imagination and Sense ought to yield to Reason. Wherefore let us soar, if we can, to the heights of that Supreme Intelligence; for there Reason will see what in itself it cannot look upon; and that is in what way things whose occurrence is not certain may yet be seen in a sure and definite foreknowledge; and that this foreknowledge is not conjecture, but rather knowledge in its supreme simplicity, free of all limits and restrictions.'

Song V: The Upward Look.

In what divers shapes and fashions
Do the creatures great and small
Over wide earth's teeming surface skim,
Or scud, or walk, or crawl!
Some with elongated body
Sweep the ground, and, as they move,
Trail perforce with writhing belly
In the dust a sinuous groove;
Some, on light wing upward soaring,
Swiftly do the winds divide,
And through heaven's ample spaces
In free motion smoothly glide;
These earth's solid surface pressing,
With firm paces onward rove,
Ranging through the verdant meadows,
Crouching in the woodland grove.
Great and wondrous is their variance!
Yet in all the head low-bent
Dulls the soul and blunts the senses,
Though their forms be different.
Man alone, erect, aspiring,
Lifts his forehead to the skies,
And in upright posture steadfast

Seems earth's baseness to despise.
If with earth not all besotted,
To this parable give ear,
Thou whose gaze is fixed on heaven,
Who thy face on high dost rear:
Lift thy soul, too, heavenward;
Haply lest it stain its heavenly worth,
And thine eyes alone look upward,
While thy mind cleaves to the earth!

VI

'Since, then, as we lately proved, everything that is known is cognized not in accordance with its own nature, but in accordance with the nature of the faculty that comprehends it, let us now contemplate, as far as lawful, the character of the Divine essence, that we may be able to understand also the nature of its knowledge.

'God is eternal; in this judgment all rational beings agree. Let us, then, consider what eternity is. For this word carries with it a revelation alike of the Divine nature and of the Divine knowledge. Now, eternity is the possession of endless life whole and perfect at a single moment. What this is becomes more clear and manifest from a comparison with things temporal. For whatever lives in time is a present proceeding from the past to the future, and there is nothing set in time which can embrace the whole space of its life together. To-morrow's state it grasps not yet, while it has already lost yesterday's; nay, even in the life of to-day ye live no longer than one brief transitory moment. Whatever, therefore, is subject to the condition of time, although, as Aristotle deemed of the world, it never have either beginning or end, and its life be stretched to the whole extent of time's infinity, it yet is not such as rightly to be thought eternal. For it does not include and embrace the whole space of infinite life at once, but has no present hold on things to come, not yet accomplished. Accordingly, that which includes and possesses the whole fullness of unending life at once, from which nothing future is absent, from which nothing past has escaped, this is rightly called eternal; this must of necessity be ever present to itself in full self-possession, and hold the infinity of movable time in an abiding present. Wherefore they deem not rightly who imagine that on Plato's principles the created world is made co-eternal with the Creator, because they are told that he believed the world to have had no beginning in time, and to be destined never to come to an end. For it is one thing for existence to be endlessly prolonged, which was what Plato ascribed to the world, another for the whole of an endless life to be embraced in the present, which is manifestly a property peculiar to the Divine mind. Nor need God appear earlier in mere duration of time to created things, but only prior in the unique simplicity of His nature. For the infinite progression of things in time copies this immediate existence in the present of the changeless life, and when it cannot succeed in equaling it, declines from movelessness into motion, and falls away from the simplicity of a perpetual present to the infinite duration of the future and the past; and since it cannot possess the whole fullness of its life together, for the very reason that in a manner it never ceases to be, it seems, up to a certain point, to rival that which it cannot complete and express by attaching itself indifferently to any present moment of time, however swift and brief; and since this bears some resemblance to that ever-abiding present, it bestows on everything to which it is assigned the semblance of existence. But since it cannot abide, it hurries along the infinite path of time, and the result has been that it continues by ceaseless movement the life the completeness of which it could not embrace while it stood still. So, if we are minded to give things their right names, we shall follow Plato in saying that God indeed is eternal, but the world everlasting.

'Since, then, every mode of judgment comprehends its objects conformably to its own nature, and since God abides for ever in an eternal present, His knowledge, also transcending all movement of time, dwells in the simplicity of its own changeless present, and, embracing the whole infinite sweep of the past and of the future, contemplates all that falls within its simple cognition as if it were now taking place. And therefore, if thou wilt carefully consider that immediate presentment whereby it discriminates all things, thou wilt more rightly deem it not foreknowledge as of something future, but knowledge of a moment that never passes. For this cause the name chosen to describe it is not prevision, but providence, because, since utterly removed in nature from things mean and trivial, its outlook embraces all things as from some lofty height. Why, then, dost thou insist that the things which are surveyed by the Divine eye are involved in necessity, whereas clearly men impose no necessity on things which they see? Does the act of vision add any necessity to the things which thou seest before thy eyes?'

'Assuredly not.'

'And yet, if we may without unfitness compare God's present and man's, just as ye see certain things in this your temporary present, so does He see all things in His eternal present. Wherefore this Divine anticipation changes not the natures and properties of things, and it beholds things present before it, just as they will hereafter come to pass in time. Nor does it confound things in its judgment, but in the one mental view distinguishes alike what will come necessarily and what without necessity. For even as ye, when at one and the same time ye see a man walking on the earth and the sun rising in the sky, distinguish between the two, though one glance embraces both, and judge the former voluntary, the latter necessary action: so also the Divine vision in its universal range of view does in no wise confuse the characters of the things which are present to its regard, though future in respect of time. Whence it follows that when it perceives that something will come into existence, and yet is perfectly aware that this is unbound by any necessity, its apprehension is not opinion, but rather knowledge based on truth. And if to this thou sayest that what God sees to be about to come to pass cannot fail to come to pass, and that what cannot fail to come to pass happens of necessity, and wilt tie me down to this word necessity, I will acknowledge that thou affirmest a most solid truth, but one which scarcely anyone can approach to who has not made the Divine his special study. For my answer would be that the same future event is necessary from the standpoint of Divine knowledge, but when considered in its own nature it seems absolutely free and unfettered. So, then, there are two necessities—one simple, as that men are necessarily mortal; the other conditioned, as that, if you know that someone is walking, he must necessarily be walking. For that which is known cannot indeed be otherwise than as it is known to be, and yet this fact by no means carries with it that other simple necessity. For the former necessity is not imposed by the thing's own proper nature, but by the addition of a condition. No necessity compels one who is voluntarily walking to go forward, although it is necessary for him to go forward at the moment of walking. In the same way, then, if Providence sees anything as present, that must necessarily be, though it is bound by no necessity of nature. Now, God views as present those coming events which happen of free will. These, accordingly, from the standpoint of the Divine vision are made necessary conditionally on the Divine cognizance; viewed, however, in themselves, they desist not from the absolute freedom naturally theirs. Accordingly, without doubt, all things will come to pass which God foreknows as about to happen, but of these certain proceed of free will; and though these happen, yet by the fact of their existence they do not lose their proper nature, in virtue of which before they happened it was really possible that they might not have come to pass.

'What difference, then, does the denial of necessity make, since, through their being conditioned by Divine knowledge, they come to pass as if they were in all respects under the compulsion of necessity? This difference, surely, which we saw in the case of the instances I formerly took, the sun's rising and the man's walking; which at the moment of their occurrence could not but be taking place, and yet one of them before it took place was necessarily obliged to be, while the other was not so at all. So likewise the things which to God are present without doubt exist, but some of them come from the necessity of things, others from the power of the agent. Quite rightly, then, have we said that these things are necessary if viewed from the standpoint of the Divine knowledge; but if they are considered in themselves, they are free from the bonds of necessity, even as everything which is accessible to sense, regarded from the standpoint of Thought, is universal, but viewed in its own nature particular. "But," thou wilt say, "if it is in my power to change my purpose, I shall make void providence, since I shall perchance change something which comes within its foreknowledge." My answer is: Thou canst indeed turn aside thy purpose; but since the truth of providence is ever at hand to see that thou canst, and whether thou dost, and whither thou turnest thyself, thou canst not avoid the Divine foreknowledge, even as thou canst not escape the sight of a present spectator, although of thy free will thou turn thyself to various actions. Wilt thou, then, say: "Shall the Divine knowledge be changed at my discretion, so that, when I will this or that, providence changes its knowledge correspondingly?"

'Surely not.'

'True, for the Divine vision anticipates all that is coming, and transforms and reduces it to the form of its own present knowledge, and varies not, as thou deemest, in its foreknowledge, alternating to this or that, but in a single flash it forestalls and includes thy mutations without altering. And this ever-present comprehension and survey of all things God has received, not from the issue of future events, but from the simplicity of His own nature. Hereby also is resolved the objection which a little while ago gave thee offence—that our doings in the future were spoken of as if supplying the cause of God's knowledge. For this faculty of knowledge, embracing all things in its immediate cognizance, has itself fixed the bounds of all things, yet itself owes nothing to what comes after.

'And all this being so, the freedom of man's will stands unshaken, and laws are not unrighteous, since their rewards and punishments are held forth to wills unbound by any necessity. God, who foreknoweth all things, still looks down from above, and the ever-present eternity of His vision concurs with the future character of all our acts, and dispenseth to the good rewards, to the bad punishments. Our hopes and prayers also are not fixed on God in vain, and when they are rightly directed cannot fail of effect. Therefore, withstand vice, practise virtue, lift up your souls to right hopes, offer humble prayers to Heaven. Great is the necessity of righteousness laid upon you if ye will not hide it from yourselves, seeing that all your actions are done before the eyes of a Judge who seeth all things.'

www.ingramcontent.com/pod-product-compliance
Lightning Source LLC
Chambersburg PA
CBHW072005180726
48291CB00001BA/15

* 9 7 8 1 9 4 4 4 8 2 0 1 5 *